COMPARATIVE STUDIES IN SPECIAL EDUCATION

Comparative Studies in Special Education

Kas Mazurek
Margret A. Winzer

Editors

GALLAUDET UNIVERSITY PRESS

Washington, D.C.

Gallaudet University Press
Washington, DC 20002

Library of Congress Cataloging-in-Publication Data

Comparative studies in special education / Kasper Mazurek, Margret A.
  Winzer, editors.
    p.   cm.
    Includes bibliogaphical references and index.
    ISBN 1–56368–027–0 : $55.95
    1. Special education—Cross-cultural studies.   I. Mazurek, Kas.
  II. Winzer, M. A. (Margret A.), 1940–
LC3965.C54   1994
371.9—dc20   94–212
                                                 CIP

For Dr. Nick Kach
scholar, mentor, colleague, friend

CONTENTS

Part V: Integrated Special Education

FOREWORD

Comparative Studies in Special Education is an attempt to fill a void in the literature available to students and scholars in both special education and comparative education. That void is the result of the direction scholarship in education has taken recently.

Over the last two decades, academic work in almost all areas has exhibited a trend toward ever-increasing specialization. The consequence is a fragmentation of scholarship and publishing that has witnessed remarkable progress in extending the *depth* of investigation in narrow and precisely defined subfields while, simultaneously, resulting in a pronounced lack of integrative studies and publications that serve to keep both scholars and students abreast of the evolving *scope* of their general fields of study. The results for both special educators and comparative educators have been unfortunate in that there are fewer and fewer sources available offering a general overview and synthesis of developments around the globe.

One consequence of this state of affairs is that educational scholars, students, practitioners, and policy makers have to access a wide variety of books and journals to try to piece together a coherent picture of the ongoing research, social experiments, relevant legislation, in-place structures and processes, accepted professional practices, and educational goals and objectives in nations around the world. The practical reality of this situation is that, all too often, not only individual scholars and teachers but, indeed, entire national educational systems are formulating and pursuing objectives without the benefit of knowing the experiences, successes, and failures of their colleagues around the world.

Comparative Studies in Special Education seeks to remedy this negative consequence of the fragmentation of study and publication by looking at twenty-six case studies which, taken together, examine special education provisions for the majority of children alive in the world today. The text, written by distinguished special educators from around the globe, is a series of reports and analyses that focus on (a) the current state of special education in selected nations, (b) major issues and controversies in the field of special education within those nations, and (c) emerging and future trends in the field of special education.

To facilitate comparisons and to stimulate creative ideas for meeting the special needs of the world's children, each case study addresses the following categories and themes.

- *Prevalence of Exceptional Conditions:* Prevalence of handicapping conditions among the general population and among the school-age population; conditions that have unusually high numbers: etiologies for handicapping conditions that are specific to a particular region.
- *Identification of Exceptionalities:* Medical and psychoeducational identification of handicapping conditions; medical identification of handicaps prenatally, in infancy, in preschool, and in the childhood years; medical use of screening and high risk registers; psychoeducational assessment of students with handicapping conditions; differences in identification procedures for severely as opposed to mildly handicapped individuals; the role of psychological services.
- *Labeling the Handicapped Population:* Provisions for labeling children; use of categorical and noncategorical (generic) approaches to the labeling of students with exceptionalities.
- *The Social Context of Special Education:* The changing nature of views of exceptionality; recent changes in views of disability and perceptions of handicapped people in society; major factors accounting for the preceding changes; political, economic, and other factors influencing educational policy and practice in special education; foreign influences on the theoretical bases, policy formation, and practice of special education.
- *The Legal and Bureaucratic Structure of Special Education:* Mandatory and permissive legislation in place for children with exceptionalities; policies in place for the education of children with exceptionalities.
- *Teachers, Schools, Curriculum, and Pedagogy for Special Education:* The education of special education teachers; settings for the instruction of children with exceptionalities (institutions, segregated classrooms, integrated settings); teaching and instruction for children with various handicapping conditions.
- *Major Controversies and Issues in Special Education:* The controversy over mainstreaming; integrated *versus* segregated educational settings; deinstitutionalization; funding; who should receive services; the rights of parents *versus* children *versus* the state.
- *Emerging and Future Trends in Special Education:* Evolving directions in the theory and practice of special education.

The organization of the text along the above parameters thus makes *Comparative Studies in Special Education* both an encyclopedic resource and an analytical treatise. That is, the contributors first present clear, concrete, and comprehensive data on essential aspects of special education in nations around the globe, and second, they provide an analysis in the form of discussions on major issues, future trends, etc. Thus, within the covers of a single text, are gathered data and analyses that, as a group, provide an overview of special education as it affects the majority of children with special needs in today's world.

However, there are many and profound limitations and potential dangers in attempting to provide a coherent picture of special education around the globe. In the interest of clarifying the nature and thrust of this text, we bring but three of the major problems to the attention of readers.

First, whether implicitly or explicitly, an organizational model must be employed. While facilitating obvious functional and heuristic goals, models also tend to be value-loaded, and they subtly but surely influence the direction of data gathering, analysis, discussion, and conclusions in predetermined directions. Therefore, while this text necessarily has an organizational framework, that framework both is explicit and is formulated on the least intrusive principles the editors could conceive. Accordingly, the sections into which the represented nations are grouped do not in any manner imply a hierarchy of less or more desirable special education principles or practices. All the sections are meant to convey are the structures for providing special education in the represented nations.

Therefore, the reader is cautioned that while *Comparative Studies in Special Education* serves the functions of being an encylopedic resource and analytical treatise, as has been noted earlier, every attempt has been made to avoid being prescriptive. Data are presented, but the editors are not selectively employing them in advocacy of any particular special educational model. Similarly, analyses are offered, solutions proposed, and ideals advocated by each contributor in the context of his or her nation, but the debates remain open-ended. They must ultimately be resolved by, and to the satisfaction of, our readers; the editors avoid imposing any resolutions or advocating specific directions/resolutions. That is why the editors expressly rejected the temptation to write a summative concluding chapter. While the data and analyses for gleaning a coherent picture of special education around the world are to be found within this text, it is up to the individual reader to put together that picture from the case studies presented.

Second, the question of *who* shall speak for the nations represented must be answered. The editors chose to let the nations speak for themselves rather than having someone speak about them. The choice, however, is really a no-win scenario. The argument for having experts from outside a nation report upon and analyze special education is that the contribution can be said to come from someone who is objective because he or she is impervious to any ideological/social/professional/political constraints with which nationals or residents may have to contend. The argument against using outsiders is twofold: first is the question of whether any outsider can have truly intimate knowledge of a social system; second is the charge of cultural bias in the investigator because he or she, by definition, is observing and interpreting from the world-view of another cultural perspective.

The editors chose to solicit contributions only from experts in special education who were themselves residents of and active professionals within the educational systems of the nations they wrote about. Deeming it crucial to allow the inherent perspectives and cultural uniquenesses of contributors and nations to come through to readers, editing was kept to a minimum. The editors therefore consider any unevenness in tone and expression found in the essays to be a strength of the text. Every attempt was made to allow the contributors to speak in their own voices as residents of the nations represented.

Third, changes are occurring so rapidly in today's world that it is difficult for comparative studies texts to be current. Indeed, a glance at the list of nations represented illustrates how profoundly and quickly events can transform nations around the world. Since this text has been compiled, official apartheid has finally been abolished in South Africa, an historic agreement has been forged between Israel and the Palestinian peoples, Russia continues to undergo fundamental political and economic transitions, and Czechoslovakia has peacefully divided into two autonomous nations.

Such changes will always plague any text that attempts to report on and analyze contemporary realities. To minimize this, the contributors have done more than merely use the most recent data available in their nations. Care has been taken to examine the newest developments relevant for special education, and proposals and initiatives still in the embryonic stages of development also are reported. And, most importantly, many of the key elements found in each contribution (i.e., the debate over segregated *versus* integrated special education, appropriate training for special education teachers, etc.) really are timeless in the sense that they are part of an ongoing discussion among special educators.

Therefore, *Comparative Studies in Special Education* is as much a part of the worldwide debate over how educators may best meet the needs of children with exceptionalities, as it is a source of insight into the nature of that debate and a base of information on special education practices around the world. As we emphasize in the following introduction, much can be learned from the varied experiences and approaches of the nations represented. Around the world, starting from differing philosophical bases and employing differing practices in sometimes radically different cultural and social contexts, dedicated and caring professionals are working tirelessly to improve the educational services, vocational opportunities, and social experiences of the many millions of children with exceptionalities in our midst. Some of those dedicated individuals are represented as contributors in the following chapters.

ACKNOWLEDGEMENTS

*T*he editors are indebted to many individuals. First are our contributors, whose timely and insightful manuscripts constitute the essence of this book.

We particularly wish to acknowledge the assistance and hard work of Ms. Barbara Krushel, who typed many drafts of the text. Her competence, attention to detail, positive suggestions, and unfailing good cheer and optimism ensured the successful completion of our task. The contribution of Ms. Joyce Ito to the typing of the manuscript was also a great help. A number of our students also devoted many hours to collecting and typing materials. To this end, the efforts of Ms. Cheryl Colley, Mr. John Russell, and Mr. Mark Swanson were especially helpful. The skills of Ms. Sonya Manes enhanced the final draft.

Gallaudet University Press was a wonderfully efficient, encouraging, and helpful publisher. The assistance of Dr. Elaine Costello, Director, and Ms. Ivey Pittle Wallace, Managing Editor, are most appreciated.

Institutional encouragement of this project, particularly from the Special Education Outreach Centre (SEOC) of the Faculty of Education at the University of Lethbridge, made a great difference. The support services for research provided by the Faculty of Education at the University of Lethbridge were an ongoing help, and the climate for that support was facilitated by the Dean of the Faculty, Dr. Eric Mokosch. Finally, the editors wish to acknowledge an ongoing debt to Mr. Ray McHugh, Director of Research Services, University of Lethbridge, who is unconditionally enthusiastic in his support of research activities at our university and an unfailing source of advice, encouragement, and assistance.

ACKNOWLEDGEMENTS

INTRODUCTION

*I*n the most general terms, special education is education individualized and adjusted to accommodate the unique learning needs of students who are, in some domain of functioning, above or below what is considered normal in their culture and social context. Areas of need include impairments in the physical, intellectual, communication, and social aspects of functioning. The special education population may also include children at risk because of environmental or biological factors. Gifted and talented students may also be counted among those requiring special education, for they too need adapted programs in order to reach their full potential.

While the population encompassed under the general rubric of special education is large and fluid, the activities, tenets, and disciplines that contribute to the enterprise are not restricted to education within a formal setting for school-age pupils. On the contrary. Programs for prevention and early identification of disabling conditions underlie special education, while practices such as early intervention and adult rehabilitation supplement the process. Educators may form the core personnel, but they are surrounded by professionals and paraprofessionals from a range of disciplines—medicine, public health, social work, and psychology, to mention only a few.

It is only recently that the concepts and practices of special education have impinged on the consciousness of educators, researchers, and policy makers in the world arena. Special education services have received considerably increased attention in recent years largely as a result of the International Year of the Disabled in 1981, which sparked interest in both the welfare and the education of people with disabilities around the world. The International Year of the Disabled assisted in bringing about changing social conceptions regarding the rights of disabled persons and their role in the community. It affirmed an emerging major interest in the social and educational welfare of disabled persons that has occurred in all countries in all stages of development (Rampaul, Freeze, and Bock 1992; Ward 1984).

The past two decades have witnessed significant increases in public awareness and understanding of exceptional individuals, and a burgeoning interest in prospects for their care, education, and rehabilitation. Yet although remarkable progress has been made in the prevention and treatment of disabilities, the World Health Organization estimates that among the millions of disabled persons in the world, only 1 to 2 percent have access to any habilitation or restorative services. For many nations, there are other national objectives that compete with education for limited resources. At the same time, the sheer magnitude of needs—from early detection and intervention programs, to educational and teaching materials, to more and better educated teachers and teacher educators—is overwhelming. For other nations, not as intensely preoccupied with social and economic problems, the prospects for persons with disabilities are optimistic, although much remains to be done.

Worldwide, rehabilitation and educational services for persons with disabilities are a focus of increased attention. Hence, we feel that a text of this nature is both timely and relevant. Special educators, wherever they are on the globe, are immersed in similar problems and controversies. Our major goal is not merely to present details of prevalence figures, etiologies, and rehabilitation and special education efforts around the world, important as these in themselves may be. The object is to investigate special education practice within its social context and to assist readers in comparing and examining the threads and themes that arise from this investigation.

The Nature and Utility of Comparative Studies

Comparative studies is not an academic discipline. That is, it does not have its own unique theories, methods of inquiry, or distinct subject matter for investigation. It is, rather, an academic field of study which liberally borrows its theoretical foundations, research methodologies, and phenomena to be studied from other disciplines.

One consequence of this eclecticism is that comparative studies is defined in sometimes fundamentally different ways by its own practitioners (Altbach, Arnove, and Kelly 1982; Altbach and Kelly 1986; Krugly-Smolska 1989; Schriewer and Holmes 1988). The result, as Schriewer and Holmes (1988) note, is that comparative educators continue to exert "considerable . . . intellectual efforts devoted to establishing the purpose and utility of this field of study, to defining its nature and relationships to other disciplines, and to clarifying its methodological principles and specific procedures" (v). In other words, comparative studies is an area of research and scholarship still in the process of inventing itself.

We raise this issue because we do not want to mislead special educators into thinking that this text follows—in method, approach, format, or interpretation—universally agreed upon canons of comparative studies. Quite simply, such agreement does not exist (Mazurek 1990). Comparative studies has come into academic prominence only in the past three decades—although, of course, its roots go back much farther in time. In this respect, its lineage is as youthful as that of special education. Although special education practices and theories date back to the middle of the eighteenth century, major academic interest dates back only to the mid-1960s.

Comparative studies does have much to offer the scholar, student, and practitioner of special education. However, as shall be seen, the undertaking of a comparative study, the utility of such studies, the confidence with which conclusions can be drawn, and the validity of potential lessons which may be learned are complex matters. Special educators are therefore encouraged to read the results of this comparative study from a critical perspective and with care. Indeed, as the reflective reader engages this text, as many questions may be raised as are answered. As a preliminary guide and framework, readers may wish to consider the following six potential benefits of a comparative study in special education, and the inherent limitations of each.

Comparative Education Studies Inform and Improve Regional Practices

Comparative educators rely on the collective wisdom and experiences of other societies, groups of individuals, and institutions in the global community and recognize that there is much to be gained by becoming informed of each other's work, experiences, successes, and failures. The assumption is that we can see the solution to our own problems a lot more clearly if we draw upon the collective wisdom and experiences of others around the world. The greatest hope and ultimate utility of comparative studies is to help groups and institutions reflect upon their own practices, policies, and theories by bringing to bear relevant information and insights from around the world.

Thus, by its very nature, comparative studies is internationalist in outlook and counters xenophobic and parochial cultural and national tendencies. That is one reason why, as Kidd (1974) observes, "some of the national [comparative education] societies are entitled 'society for international and comparative education' " (47). In the same vein, comparative education courses and programs across the globe are increasingly using the title *international education* rather than *comparative education*. The two terms are often used interchangeably.

However, a major caveat must be introduced here. There are real and important sociopolitical-economic idiosyncrasies in the various national milieus in which special education is practiced. It is certain that there are unique elements to each specific context, and unique problems and issues arise which demand tailored solutions. For these reasons those who conduct comparative studies are always cautious about the degree to which global generalizations can be made from case studies.

The greatest potential danger here is the specter of cultural imperialism or hegemony. Conflict theorists have produced a powerful and convincing body of literature arguing that the perceptions and practices of some internationally dominant cultures and nations have become so globally preeminent that they are exported to and imposed upon other nations and cultures. Of course, the process can be and often is subtle; indeed, the importing nations may welcome and encourage such influxes of ideas and practices. Nevertheless the warnings of Carnoy (1974) that education may indeed be a form of "cultural imperialism" continue to be echoed two decades later.

Comparative Studies Provide a Data Base

Before any lessons can be drawn, it is obvious that a body of empirically precise information on education around the world must first be provided. That, indeed, is the task which occupies the majority of comparative studies in education. "Typically," Altbach, Arnove, and Kelly (1982) observe, "texts in the field of comparative education are based on country-by-country descriptions of the organization, content, and functioning of education systems within their national settings" (3). Thus the lion's share of any "typical" comparative study in education will be devoted to enumerating such things as the structural elements of a nation's educational system, financing, legislation, and policies governing schooling, curricula, teacher training, pedagogy, student body characteristics, and enrollment ratios.

Clearly, such information is important. But it is a mistake to conclude that data so gathered are objective or value-free in the positivistic sense. After all, data are collected not randomly but within certain parameters and upon specific subjects. Therefore definitions become crucial and there is a great danger that data will be collected along the preconceived, usually implicit, worldview of the researcher. For example, the very concept of "education" is usually equated in the western industrial societies with "schooling." Thus the very large and extremely important area of "nonformal" education emphasized by writers such as Coombs (1985) has, until recently, not even been reported in comparative studies because it was not thought of as education as it was not part of formal schooling.

Numerous other examples may be provided. In the context of this text, as the reader shall discover, conflicting views exist on a question as basic as What constitutes a disabled population? Accordingly, to report on student populations is not as straightforward a task as one might hope. For some writers and in some nations, physiological conditions such as deafness and blindness share equal epistemological status with conditions of social and economic disadvantage.

This is, in fact, a major problem for all comparative studies. It causes us to question whether even basic data can be compiled with confidence because shared definitions of what constitutes the basic subject matter of our reports are often elusive. Edmund King cautioned precisely this in his classic comparative study *Other Schools and Ours:* "While striving for as much objectivity as possible, we recognize some uncomfortable facts. First, what we 'see' or 'understand' in the phenomena of some alien system of education (or even our own) may not be *recognized* in the same terms which alternative observers or the natives would use" (King 1979, 45; emphasis in original). A decade and a half later, comparative educators have not made any discernible progress on resolving this epistemological and methodological dilemma.

Comparative Studies Allow Us to Understand the Social Context That Gives Rise to Regional Practices

It is tempting to cope with the preceding problem by simply avoiding it altogether. That is, if comparative educators are so worried by the possibility of not understanding what education in another nation and culture is really like because researchers may see it through the filter of their own ethnocentric *weltanschauung,* then why not seek the meaning of educational ideologies, policies, and practices within the parameters of the culture itself? This is what is labeled the *functional* approach to comparative studies. It recognizes that all social enterprises are contextual and their sense and significance can only be comprehended with explicit reference to the social/cultural milieu within which they exist and operate.

This approach has the virtue of consciously striving not to impose the values of the observer upon what are recognized to be culturally contextual ideas and practices. Thus, in the case of special education, one would acknowledge that there are great differences in the philosophies of special educators, in the institutional structures and pedagogical practices which derive from those philosophies, and in the social perceptions and treatment of children with special needs. The diversity within special education around the globe is, in other words, merely a reflection of the diversity of cultures around the world. This perspective is fine—as far as it goes. However, it only provides a satisfactory answer to the question of why things are as they are. It does not allow us to evaluate, to judge, or to make recommendations. It leaves us informed, but it also leaves us impotent to act or even to draw significant conclusions.

To illustrate, we may use an example which is current in comparative studies. We know that the rights, privileges, treatment, and condition of women vary greatly across the spectrum of nations in the world. We can "explain" this variance perfectly well by employing the social context perspective. That is, the treatment and status of women before the law, in the home, in terms of quality of educational and economic opportunity, and so on are determined by such variables as the history of a nation, its customs and traditions, its religious orientations, and its legal foundations. That being discovered and understood, the question then arises: What do we *do* with this knowledge? The question assumes poignant significance if we discover, for example, that in one culture girls and boys are equally valued and consequently have equal access to special education. However, we also discover that in another culture, girls are valued less than boys and are therefore denied such access (or, worse, become the victims of socially sanctioned infanticide). Possessing this knowledge, can comparative and special educators in good conscience simply sit back and say, "things are as they are because the social milieus of these two cultures are different; it is not for us to judge and it is not for us to pass comment"?

If we do, then there seems to be little value to comparative studies in special education (or, indeed, in any other field) beyond the obvious goal of gaining knowledge for the sake of gaining knowledge—worthy as that objective may be. However, to borrow from Marx, the point is not merely to understand the world; it is equally to change it—presumably for the better! Unfortunately, there is nothing in the functionalist logic of the social-context explanatory framework which provides any direction here. Above all, we cannot judge the values of either of the hypothetical cultures in our above illustration because *both* cultures derived their special education ideologies and practices—contrary as they may be—through precisely the same process. The cultural milieu determines attitudes and practices in special education, in turn special education is ideologically and pragmatically supportive of and reinforces the general social milieu.

It is a circular argument—a tautology from which there is no escape. This is the classic dilemma of the functionalist social perspective and the trap of social relativism. It dooms us to remain cultural voyeurs—appreciating why other cultures (and our own) are as they are but having no yardsticks by which to measure against each other the relative values and practices of cultures. If socialization determines all, then on what basis can we have the audacity to claim that some practices, some ideologies, are "better" or "worse" than others? The answer, of course, is that such claims cannot be made. The argument that the conventions of my culture are better than the conventions of your culture leads only to a logical impasse unless external criteria by which better and worse may be measured are invoked. Some comparative studies have dared to propose and employ precisely such external criteria.

Comparative Studies Help Us Make Value Judgments on Cultural Practices

Comparative educators who reject the previously discussed perspective in which socialization explains and justifies anything and everything, would point out that our world is full of explicit standards by which cultural ideas and practices may be judged. To cite but one example, the United Nations' Declaration of Human Rights is a treatise on inalienable, fundamental, universally applicable standards which, it is held, are independent of time, geography, and cultural idiosyncrasy. In other words there are, it can be argued, human and cultural universals that provide the touchstones against which ideas and practices may be measured and evaluated.

In the arena of comparative studies, the most potent and widespread manifestation of this orientation is found in what is known as development theory. Originally formulated as an economic theory, it has become extended into the sociopolitical realm and serves as a macrotheory on what constitutes national "civilization." In this expanded form, the orientation is openly and unashamedly messianic in proclaiming that it is possible to speak of carrying the seeds of progress to every corner of the earth. By implication, it must therefore be obvious that many regions are lacking in such virtue, and the decent and charitable thing for those who possess this holy grail is to share it with the unfortunate who have not yet drunk of its noble and liberating elixir.

Because it is a comparative concept, *development* is inherently hierarchical and evaluative. After all, development is a term which makes sense only in relation to a state of underdevelopment. As one major writer eloquently phrases it, "Development, in its essence, must represent the entire gamut of change by which an entire *social system, . . .* moves away from a condition of life widely perceived as unsatisfactory and toward a situation or condition of life regarded as materially and spiritually 'better' " (Todaro 1981, 70).

Such thinking necessitates that we go well beyond the gathering of data and the appreciation of the social contexts that determine ideologies and practices in any given nation. We can now "judge" the degree to which a nation is "developed." We can, so to speak, place its development on a continuum between, using Todaro's vocabulary, "unsatisfactory" and "materially and spiritually better." Applied to special education, the consequences are clear. Just as some nations' economic systems are more "developed" than others', just as some governments and legal systems are more "humane" than others, so too are some special education philosophies and practices more "advanced" than others.

Predictably, the immediate and practical consequence of applying this line of reasoning has been a reaction of outrage by some nations labeled as underdeveloped. The charge that the definition of development is ethnocentric, culturally biased, intellectually myopic, and colonial in its im-perialistic arrogance has credence. To describe one nation as underdeveloped vis-à-vis another because it has fewer paved roads or a higher infant mortality rate is one thing; to make the same claim in the arena of social customs and practices is quite another! The ensuing scathing criticism of development theory affected all research which was seen even implicitly as measuring the relative merit or virtue of national ideologies and social practices. It made many scholars increasingly reluctant to introduce evaluative elements into their research or to report any conclusions they might draw from their studies. Cultural tolerance, respect for cultural pluralism, refusal to pass judgment on alien social practices—these have become the ethical beacons for many comparative educators. Indeed, in some places they have become national ideologies as well. In the editors' home nation of Canada, cultural tolerance and pluralism are enshrined in and protected by the constitution itself. Other nations hold the same values and recognize them in diverse ways, such as the passage of human rights legislation and developing cultur-ally sensitive mandatory school curricula.

Does this then mean that comparative studies must restrict themselves merely to describing the different social realities of the world's nations? Refusing to accept this conclusion, increasing numbers of comparative edu-cators today are attempting to combine the best elements of all of our preceding discussion. That is, the desirability of building a data base and comprehensively describing the social milieus of nations is acknowledged. Coincidentally, and even more importantly, the desirability of using the data and insights so obtained both to inform and improve regional practices and to make normative judgments and evaluations is also affirmed. The form that this alleged synthesis takes is called the *issues* approach to comparative studies. Today, this approach is the dominant paradigm in the writing of comparative educational studies.

Comparative Studies Help Us Understand the Pressing Issues of Our Times

The most interesting characteristics of the issues approach are first, that reliable data—gathered through both quantitative and qualitative research methodologies—are the foundation for the field of comparative studies. Second, that knowledge base must be put in the service of the cause of ameliorating the major social inequalities of our day. It is an orientation which consciously seeks to put science in the service of humanistic causes. As one of the landmark texts defining this new tradition puts it, the impera-tive is to identify the "salient issues with which education systems around the world are grappling" and to be particularly concerned with the "opportunities for and outcomes of schooling for traditionally disadvantaged and excluded groups—namely women and minority youths." (Altbach, Arnove, and Kelly 1982, 3).

In large measure the social issues approach is a response to a major paradox of the late twentieth century: despite the boom in social scientific knowledge, age-old social problems continue to plague the world. "While research efforts mounted, illiteracy was not being eradicated, social equality was not emerging, and attempts to link education with economic development had been tempered by harsh realities" (Urch 1987, 543). Thus the social issues approach to comparative studies is clearly a call to political action and for social amelioration in the face of a "growing realization that the research carried out so painstakingly throughout the world seldom translated into action" (Urich 1987, 543).

In principle, this may be most laudable; in specific context it becomes problematic. The problem here is identical to the one discussed in the preceding section on using comparative studies to help us make value judgments on cultural practices. That is, the very definition of a social issue is always culturally loaded. Using the very example of our citation from Altbach, Arnove, and Kelly, how does one objectively come to understand how women are disadvantaged in any given culture? What are obvious criteria to some—such as, perhaps, differential income, educational, and occupational levels between men and women—may not be seen as disadvantages at all by the cultural group itself. A society in which tradition, custom, and religion sanction strict role distinctions is a society in which neither the men nor the women perceive themselves to be either subjects or subjugators; both sexes may see themselves as merely living in harmony with the natural/religious order of things.

The obvious consequence is that such a culture will resent the definition of its way of life and its deepest values as an issue to be resolved and a problem to be overcome. Again the charge of cultural imperialism is levied against the comparative educator who is so presumptuous as to define (at least implicitly) social normalcy and to call for social changes in the name of amelioration of injustices. Thus the social issues approach to comparative studies remains vulnerable to the charge that it is ideologically biased.

Comparative Studies Facilitate Theoretical Understanding

Finally, it may be claimed that comparative studies, as does all social science, furthers human understanding at the levels of theory development, theory testing, and model building. This occurs at several levels. At one level, there is the struggle to elaborate a research paradigm for comparative studies itself. As was noted at the beginning of this chapter, comparative studies is not a discipline; it is a field of study. Therefore, because it borrows its theoretical and methodological principles ad hoc from a variety of social sciences, there is a fundamental, ongoing, and heated debate over precisely what comparative studies is and what are its rules of practice. This dilemma described by Carlos Olivera as a "crisis of theory" (1988, 197) is significant, but it is only of marginal interest to special educators and beyond the scope of this text.

What is of significance to special educators in the field of comparative education is the relational context within which special education around the world is portrayed. That is, Is special education examined as an individual phenomenon, in isolation from other social institutions and forces? Is special education conceptualized from a macrotheoretical perspective wherein its ideologies, policies, and attendant practices follow the dynamics of pervasive, structural forces? Is special education explained as a dependent variable—an effect of other, more fundamental, social forces which are its cause? The answers to questions such as these are important because they provide the conceptual framework within which our very understanding of what special education is, how it evolves, and how its future will be shaped are answered. These differing views of special education are further examined in the following section of this chapter and throughout the text.

Comparative Special Education

The paradigms of comparative education allow us to conceptualize, contrast, and compare diverse philosophies of, approaches to, and practices in special education and rehabilitation. On the other hand, comparative studies also looks for commonalities, and many of the themes that arise in the philosophy and process of current special education are worldwide and relate to recurrent questions that plague the enterprise. These include questions about the following issues:

1. How schooling is to be provided, for how long, in what form, to whom, and at what cost.
2. How systems can accommodate what may be described as conflicts in limitations. These revolve around strained resources, providing appropriate education for all children, and embedding mounting numbers of children with special needs into educational programs.
3. How school systems can accommodate all students with special needs without deleteriously affecting the lives of other students and their teachers.
4. How to ameliorate the impact of conditions that result from poverty, malnutrition, and poor living conditions.

5. How public and social attitudes toward persons with disabilities can be altered positively.
6. How the political will, embodied in legislation, can be translated into efficient practice that is acceptable to all stakeholders in the enterprise—students with disabilities, teachers and school administrators, parents of students with disabilities, and parents of non-disabled children.
7. How procedures for early identification and early intervention can be appropriately and economically implemented.
8. How psychoeducational identification procedures can be appropriately employed using measures that are culturally fair, efficient, and cost effective.
9. How links between training and employment can be more closely forged.
10. How schools can involve parents and families more deeply in the education and training enterprises.
11. How alternatives to current models can be conceptualized and practiced.
12. How research can be translated into educational practice.
13. How to adequately train classroom teachers to program for and accommodate special learners.
14. How to provide appropriate services to children with special needs in rural communities.

These common threads, which wind through special education in nearly all the nations we survey in this text, are neither transitory nor superficial; they are at the root of current rehabilitative and special education theory and practice. Their impact, however, is modified or exacerbated by the cultural, social, and economic conditions existing in a particular country.

The urgency of the common themes is starkly illustrated in the increasing need for special services. While prevalence estimates are extremely fluid and uncertain, it can be stated that the need for special services is increasing, the population to be served is growing, and the impact of disabilities on an individual and on his or her society is mounting. The world population is increasing; from 4.6 billion in 1980 it should reach 6 billion in the year 2000. Out of approximately 150 million children in the world today, about 120 million live in the Third World and the majority of them survive in conditions of extreme poverty (Weisinger-Ferris 1989). Girls under the age of fifteen constitute between 35 and 52 percent of the female population in these countries. The majority of these girls grow up in environments of social and cultural discrimination, forced into early marriages and childbearing.

UNESCO estimates that one hundred million children from six to eleven years of age are not attending school at all (Guma 1992). In Africa as a whole, for example, fewer than 50 percent of all children attend primary school. Even at this level, dropout rates are extremely high, quality of education is low, and the relative cost of education is high (Tsang 1988). Hence, enormous numbers of individuals, especially in countries of the Third World, remain illiterate. Rates of illiteracy are far higher among females than among males and far higher in rural than in urban areas. In many countries, girls tend to start school later, study less, and drop out earlier than boys—if they go to school at all. In rural India, for example, only one-third of girls go to school compared to slightly more than half of all boys.

Added to illiteracy and poverty are the staggering proportions of disability. It is estimated that more than five hundred million people in the world today suffer from physical, mental, or sensory impairments. In the Third World, 15 to 20 percent of the total population suffers from some disability; many are children. In 1980 UNICEF estimated that of the 140 million disabled children in the world, 120 million live in developing countries—88 million in Asia, 18 million in Africa, and 13 million in Latin America (UNICEF 1988). A later UNESCO report estimated that there are more than 200 million children in developing countries who are either experiencing learning difficulties in school or who are excluded completely (Hegarty 1990).

In highly industrialized and Third-World countries, the causes of disabilities vary. In the former, there is an increase in disability due to such factors as negative stress situations, chronic and degenerative diseases, industrial and traffic accidents, and psychosocial factors. In countries of the Third World, salient factors include the following:

1. A high proportion of impoverished families living on the margin of survival
2. Widespread illiteracy
3. Little availability of basic services for health, education, and social welfare
4. Insufficient, or a lack of, programs for the prevention of disabling conditions
5. The paucity or absence of services to reduce the impact of disability
6. An absence of information as to the causes of disabilities and measures for their prevention and rehabilitation
7. Negative community attitudes and perceptions

In many nations, the major causes of disabling conditions are those that are largely preventable. About fifteen million of the world's infants and children die each year from preventable causes (WHO 1989), largely the result of poverty, malnutrition, hunger, illiteracy, and poor hygienic conditions. Some three million die from preventable diseases—more than half of these from measles (Tsang 1988).

Waterborne blindness, trachoma, measles, and vitamin A deficiency result in vast numbers of individuals with severe visual impairments and blindness; chronic otitis media is a major etiology in hearing loss. Physical handicaps result from tuberculosis, leprosy, and consanguineous marriages, among a myriad of causes. In Africa, an estimated eight million persons are infected with HIV virus, the primary agent causing AIDS.

According to the United Nation's 1992 Human Development Report, startling social and economic disparities based on race, religion, and color plague both the developed and the developing world (Stackhouse 1992). Hence, factors such as emotional deprivation, poverty, or membership in disadvantaged groups can affect the severity and prevalence of disability.

Paramount in any comprehensive system of special education and rehabilitation is prevention. Of all the approaches that can be taken, prevention is the most likely to be cost effective in the long run. A number of developments, which should be seen as part of a worldwide movement in the direction of greater emphasis on primary health care, rehabilitation, and basic education, are in the making. The UNICEF strategy (1980, par. 65–73) on childhood disabilities stresses the following:

1. The prevention of all impairments that can be prevented
2. When impairment has occurred, the reduction to the maximum degree possible of the consequences through appropriate treatment and early detection
3. Support to the family, strengthening its capacity to assist the disabled child, since the most serious effect of disability may be the disruption of the normal development cycle for the child

Views of Special Education

Special education, as philosophy and as practice, may be viewed and conceptualized in a number of ways. First of all, the functionalist point of view sees special education as inevitably related to the social, political, economic, and even religious structures of a society. In any society, attitudes and values are fashioned by the prevailing culture, government, religion, and economic conditions, and education in general tends to reflect the political and legal foundations on which that society is built.

A more developmental orientation sees the care and training of persons with disabilities as a mirror of social attitudes. The education and care of exceptional individuals and the way in which a society responds to the problems of deviance and disability reflect the general cultural attitudes concerning the obligations of a society to its individual citizens. Hence, a society's treatment of those who are weak and dependent is one critical indicator of its social progress (Winzer 1993). Generally, the training and education of people with exceptionalities follows the care and education of those who are developing normally. Limited resources are first directed toward the greatest number, not to the small minority requiring specialized assistance. The disproportionate amount of time, money, and effort needed for each disabled child is disregarded in the effort to provide universal elementary education.

Another view sees special education as an appropriate mobilization of human capital. The central tenet is that usefulness determines the value of a person to society; this explanation places emphasis on the training and socializing functions of schooling and to the value added to an individual's productive skills and hence to his or her social value. Social benefits are the keystone of rehabilitation and educational systems; with training, persons with disabilities can contribute more fully to the economy of a country.

Humanitarian views permit benevolent and charitable deeds; dependent and disabled persons have a moral, if not a legal, right to charity and education. This was the view that prompted churches, philanthropic organizations, and other nongovernment organizations (NGOs) to initiate special schooling.

Another view holds that the provision of equal access to educational and rehabilitation services for all people, exceptionality notwithstanding, is an integral component of civil rights that disallow discrimination on any grounds. The concept of rights is based directly in law. While this view embodies the humanistic notion of the intrinsic value of individuals, it extends beyond humanism with its insistence that individuals exercise some role in determining decisions that affect them. This final orientation largely underlies the care and education of the eleven million disabled children in Europe and the six million in North America.

These views of special education, and others, are presented in this text which is designed to give a broad overview of special education as it is conceptualized and practiced in the world today. The contributors come from a variety of disciplines—education, psychology, sociology, rehabilitation, and educational administration—and all are involved in some way in special education in their own countries. The nations represented are diverse; each contributor elucidates and explains a type of special education as it is currently presented within certain geographical and cultural boundaries.

Models Used in This Text

There are a number of ways that the diverse nations represented in this text could be organized. We have elected to divide the text into parts, each part devoted to a type or model of special education practice as we perceive it currently existing in specific countries. This does not imply that one model is better or more promising than another; it is more a convenient and appropriate method to group countries that are conceptualizing and practicing special education in various forms bounded by their specific social and economic limitations. Essentially, our models are founded on the political will, public commitment, and the number of children served, not on an ideological commitment to educational integration as it is currently perceived in Western societies. Indeed, the object is not to provide the examples of prosperous Western countries as guides or ideal models of special education. Simply transplanting western models, philosophically and pragmatically founded on the mandates of the American Public Law 94-142 or the United Kingdom's Warnock Report may be inappropriate for many nations. Promoting models of mainstreaming and integration drawn from highly developed systems and trying to fit them to the unique circumstances of varied nations may doom the enterprise of special education to isolation and ultimate failure.

Nor are these models pure in the sense that special education in a number of countries could be categorized in diverse ways. David Donald's paper on South Africa, which opens this text, is a case in point. Donald's cogent discussion of the policies and practices of special education in South Africa stress the racial inequalities present. Special education for white urban children complements practices seen in Australia, Canada, and other developed nations. In contrast, the black majority in South Africa is essentially denied special education provisions. Large numbers of students require assistance, few facilities exist, and integration is described by Donald as "mainstreaming by default." In other nations, disparities in service provision fall along urban-rural lines. Disabled students living in urban centers have ready access to a range of services while geography largely denies such provisions to many others.

Limited special education, the model discussed in part I, applies to countries where rehabilitation services and special education remain relatively remote for a large proportion of the population of persons with disabilities. It may require decades before ideological commitment, political will, training, and knowledge meld to allow a comprehensive network of services.

In the educational sphere, many of these countries are constrained by a matrix of limitations. Newly independent, they are still shaking off the shackles of their former colonial masters. As emerging countries on the world stage, many are in economically straitened circumstances. The provision of universal education to all elementary-age children is the goal, but not yet achieved. In most countries, it has been the government's policy to address educational opportunity first and to face the issues of equality of access later. Special education may be a priority for professionals, theorists, and parents of children with disabilities, but neither the will nor the commitment of a tiny cadre can initiate services within the greater need for general education. For example, few, if any, African or South African countries have either the political will, the skills, or the financial resources to provide more than a cosmetic level of special education (Miles 1989b).

South Africa is probably the only country in the world that has race-based education, with a bureaucracy of sixteen different departments (Guma 1992). In South Africa, politics, economics, and public attitudes have not melded in any positive way to provide facilities for the black majority. The Palestinian minority in Israel works under similar constraints. As Samir Dukmak points out, grand efforts in rehabilitation and education are being initiated in the West Bank and Gaza Strip without the approbation of the Israeli government. Senegal and Papua New Guinea paint a different picture. As new nations recently emerged from colonial jurisdiction, the major priority lies in providing universal compulsory elementary education for all children.

In the nations grouped in part II of the text, the goal of universal special education, supplemented by a complex of preventative, rehabilitative, and early intervention services remains a dream, but one that is pursued with avidity. In these nations, the concepts of special education are accepted and the political will is manifested in legislation or policies designed to ensure more equitable social treatment and educational access for persons with disabilities. Nigeria, India, Pakistan, Indonesia, Brazil, Uruguay, Egypt, and China fall under the model of emerging special education in that legislation, policies, and commitment are apparent, if not yet fully manifested in practice.

Part III encompasses nations where the enterprise is a reality, serving many individuals requiring assistance. Nevertheless, much remains to be done in relation to public and professional attitudes. Special education, while functioning parallel to or inserted within the context of the regular educational system, nevertheless remains relatively isolated. Keep in mind, however, that this may be a conscious conceptualization of how the principles and processes of special education should be implemented. This approach concentrates education and rehabilitation services within highly specialized schools and agencies on the basis that instruction and treatment can be most effectively and efficiently provided in such settings. Russia and Japan provide the purest examples of this model. Nations such as Czechoslovakia, Taiwan, and Hong Kong, while retaining a complex of special schools and settings, are also experimenting with the education of some children with disabilities in regular milieus.

A contrasting approach stresses the importance of integration and inclusive schooling. Advocates of inclusive education argue for the dismantling of segregated establishments as early as possible, with the responsibility for all disadvantaged and vulnerable groups being adopted by the natural units of family and community. This is the approach that characterizes the nations represented in part IV. Within the constraints of local conditions, these nations have adopted the tenets of mainstreaming and seek to provide equal access for all, or nearly all, students with disabilities in the neighborhood school and regular classroom.

Israel and Poland retain specialized schooling but, to various degrees, have adopted principles that draw more students within the orbit of the public schools. Canada and Australia provide cogent case studies of systems attempting to integrate greater numbers of students in normalized environments in the face of major financial restraints and professional controversy. Legislation, litigation, and parental wishes add impetus to the movement for full educational integration but the means by which it can be most efficiently and appropriately accomplished remain contentious.

The community's full acceptance of responsibility for disabled individuals implies a willingness to deploy its resources, both human and financial, in their service. The principles of normalization emerged from Scandinavia; enabling legislation emerged from the United States initially in the form of Public Law 94-142, the Education for All Handicapped Children Act; new ways of describing and handling students with exceptional conditions were illuminated in Britain's Warnock Report. In part V, the case studies represent attempts to implement integrated schooling for the great majority of children with exceptional conditions. But even as full educational integration has become a reality, difficulties and controversies still beset the implementation and, indeed, the philosophies underlying service provision. James Kauffman and Betty Hallenbeck, for example, point to areas of contention surrounding inclusive schooling in the United States. The authors from England and Wales and from New Zealand discuss the subversion of reform promises in the face of straitened economic resources.

Recurring Themes

Earlier in this introduction, we pointed out some general themes that are found in discussions of special education worldwide. To assist readers in comparing and evaluating the themes that emerge from the case studies in this text, two thematic tables have been compiled by the editors. These are designed to provide an overview of the major factors affecting special education—both positive and negative—on which the contributing authors focused. No claim for completeness is made—each author pointed to a range of issues, contributing factors, and movements in special education in his or her own country within the constraints of space that this text allowed. We have merely drawn out those themes that appear with some consistency throughout the case studies. Hence the major themes discussed next are simply to be used as a guide for readers of this text.

The most consistent observation made by the contributing authors is that special education was initially viewed as a humanitarian concern and the reserve of charities and NGOs. In one way, the Western school transplanted to the Third World by missionaries may seem to have been an important source of new attitudes toward disabled persons. On the other hand, the influence of Western models and mandates may not promise the most appropriate system for all nations. Whatever its aims, Western special education embraces certain concepts of the child and development, certain modern theories of learning, and beliefs about the rights of individual children (Miles 1989b). But as Miles (1989b) also observes, these notions are perceived very differently, if at all, in Asian societies. Across India and Pakistan, for example, there are hundreds of centers where activities bear some resemblance to those in Western special schools. But they are all in cities, in the "modern sector" and, with few exceptions, remain culturally and conceptually dependent on the West.

The most consistently mentioned factors that hinder special education are as follows (see also table i.1):

Limited financial resources. For many authors in this text, the worldwide recession and the constraining effect it is having upon education in general and special education in particular are a great concern. Prosperous industrialized nations realize that special education may be dramatically reformulated in light of new economic priorities. At the same time less prosperous nations, even more deeply affected by limited resources, trade imbalances, and deepening recession, may also be affected by rapid political changes, civil unrest, and effects of war.

Disparities in identification. In nearly every case study, the authors point out that prevalence figures are unclear or unknown. In nations with emerging special education services, as well as in those with highly sophisticated systems, this theme emerges. The murky prevalence estimates revolve around lack of consensus on definition and identification, unclear categories, the number of persons affected by extrinsic causes and those at risk for disabling conditions, and the lack of national surveys or epidemiological data.

It is also important to note that while every society recognizes certain forms of human differences as abnormal or exceptional, at some point a social or medical judgment, influenced by a society's norms, is made and an individual comes to be regarded as exceptional, disabled, or different. Sensory impairments and physical disabilities are readily recognized but mental retardation, especially in its milder forms, is largely dependent on cultural expectations. Many countries of the Third World find extremely low preva-

TABLE i.1.   Factors Hindering Special Education

Factors	Numbers of Countries Reporting
Limited financial resources	11
Top-heavy bureaucracy	3
Rapidly changing political structures	7
Lack of access to appropriate health services	9
High rates of sensory impairments	7
Preventable causes as a major etiology	9
Widespread poverty and socioeconomic disadvantage	9
Preventable causes, diseases	5
Preventable causes, extrinsic factors	6
Civil unrest/war as a major cause	4
Consanguineous marriages	4
Increases in multiple and neurological disabilities	5
Reliance on traditional healing	2
General shortage of public schools and classrooms	4
High pupil-teacher ratio	6
High dropout rates	5
High illiteracy	5
Ethnic diversity	4
Gender inequalities	2
Major disparities in special educational services	5
Racial inequalities	4
Major rural-urban inequalities	15
Regional diversity of educational policies	9
Negative social attitudes toward the handicapped	9
Limited special education legislation	6
No special education legislation	5
Economic arguments against special education	1
Lack of appropriate psychoeducational measures	6
Lack of qualified teachers	9
Language of instruction	5
Lack of parental input	4

lence rates of retardation, when compared to the prevalence of sensory, motor, or physical disabilities.

Unmet educational needs. As a process, special education is usually initiated after nations have made significant progress in the provision of universal elementary education. So many of our authors stress the long-range goals in their countries to eradicate illiteracy and provide education for all children.

They also speak to the precarious nature of school systems characterized by high pupil-teacher ratios and high dropout rates. Equal access to schooling is further confounded in some instances by ethnic and gender inequalities.

Regional disparities. Even when special education is provided at some level, we often find regional disparities and the persistence of racial inequalities. The most consistent disparity is major rural-urban inequalities in the provision of and access to educational, rehabilitative, and health services.

Negative social attitudes. The lack of significant public attention to persons with disabilities manifests itself in a lack of educational and rehabilitative services. In nations where there are generally held negative attitudes toward disabled persons, a public will to create services expressed in legislation and policies is not found.

Insufficient assessments. Before children can be identified as exceptional or provided special services, medical and psychoeducational assessment is necessary. A number of authors point out the limitations of psychoeducational measures in such areas as insufficient local norms, reliance on traditional IQ tests, and cultural biases.

Inadequate teacher training. The delivery of special education is hindered by a lack of trained teachers. In some countries, teacher training in special education is sparse or unavailable; in other places, the problems revolve around the most efficient manner in which to train regular classroom teachers to respond to the needs of students with exceptionalities.

Unfamiliar language; lack of family support. Delivery is also hindered if the language of instruction does not match that of the child's home or community. Furthermore, since parents can act as decision makers, advocates for their own children, and volunteers, and so enhance the practice of special education, a number of authors cite the lack of parental input as a hindrance.

The following factors are consistently mentioned by the authors as facilitating special education (see also table i.2):

Universal elementary education. While highly industrialized nations provide universal access to schools, the attainment of universal elementary education is a priority for nations of the Third World. As this goal moves within range, more and more attention becomes directed toward those with special needs.

Disease prevention. With the high numbers of preventable causes in many nations, special education is seen as a melding of education, rehabilitation, and preventative measures. Indeed, preventative measures form the core of many efforts. Massive vaccination programs are being undertaken, or are planned, to eradicate potential causes of disability conditions.

Early identification and intervention. Early identification and its corollary, early intervention, are becoming priorities in nations where basic special education services are in place.

Legislation. Legislation specifically directed toward the disabled population is a manifestation of social and political willingness to move toward the implementation of special education services, regardless of the underlying philosophy guiding special education.

TABLE i.2. Factors Facilitating Special Education

Factors	Number of Countries Reporting
Universal access to schools	16
Universal elementary education a priority	3
High priority on preventative programs	16
Rehabilitation programs a priority	10
Increasing rehabilitation services	7
Early identification	14
Early intervention	15
Economic arguments for special education	4
In-place special education legislation	14
Influence of PL 94-142 and/or Warnock Report	15
Influence of 1981 Year of the Disabled	5
Teacher-training programs in place	21
Special education curricula	7
Provision for gifted students	5
Transition programming	2

Year of the Disabled. The International Year of the Disabled in 1981 may be seen as a benchmark in interest about and commitment to people with disabilities worldwide. Since 1981, many countries, especially in the Third World, have promulgated legislation and policies aimed at eradicating preventable causes of disability, providing basic rehabilitation services and special education, and allowing greater integration of disabled persons into vocational and social experiences.

Teacher training. For special education to be successful, an adequately trained cadre of teachers is necessary. Teacher-training programs correlate positively with the implementation and delivery of special education. Due to a lack of trained teachers and other professionals and paraprofessionals in most developing countries, sufficient skills and knowledge are not available to mount a comprehensive system of special education, even if other crucial factors are in place. Even in countries attempting new mandates in special education delivery, the manner in which regular classroom teachers can be efficiently trained to handle special needs pupils remains controversial.

Emerging interest in gifted children. In general, most programs are directed to students functioning below the norm on some domain. Children with the most visible and serious needs, although generally relatively small in percentage, are easily identified and universally acknowledged. These include children with impairments of physical functioning, mental ability, hearing, and vision. In a few nations, legislation and policies are aimed at the population of gifted students. In addition, the specific problems of disabled adolescents in the workforce are the focus of new initiatives in transition programs.

References

Altbach, P. G., and Kelly, G. P., eds. 1986. *New approaches to comparative education.* Chicago: University of Chicago Press.

Altbach, P. G., Arnove, R. F., and Kelly, G. P., eds. 1982. *Comparative education.* New York: Macmillan.

Carnoy, M. 1974. *Education as cultural imperialism.* New York: David McKay.

Carpenter, R. L. 1987. Special education teacher preparation and service delivery in a developing country: Indonesia. *Teacher Education and Special Education* 10:37–43.

Chen, Y. Y. 1991. Special education in China. Paper presented at the International Conference on Mental Retardation, April, Hong Kong.

Coombs, P. H. 1985. *The world crisis in education: The view from the eighties.* Oxford: Oxford University Press.

Guma, M. D. 1992. Special education for a whole generation of politically constructed learning-disabled in South Africa. *International Journal of Special Education* 7:133–38.

Hegerty, S. 1990. *The education of children and young people with disabilities: Principles and practices.* Paris: UNESCO.

Kidd, R. J. 1974. *Whilst time is burning: A report on education for development.* Ottawa: International Development Research Centre.

King, E. J. 1979. *Other schools and ours: Comparative studies for today.* 5th. ed. London: Holt, Rinehart and Winston.

Krugly-Smolska, E. T. 1989. Theoretical models in comparative education: An attempt at synthesis. *Canadian and International Education* 18:54–64.

Mazurek, K. 1990. Multicultural education and comparative education: Notes on theory and method. *Journal of Learning about Learning* 2:53–58.

Miles, M. 1989a. Disability policies in Pakistan: Is anyone winning? *International Journal of Special Education* 4:1–16.

Miles, M. 1989b. The role of special education in information based rehabilitation. *International Journal of Special Education* 4:111–18.

Olivera, C. W. 1988. Comparative education: What kind of knowledge? In J. Schriewer and B. Holmes, eds. *Theories and models in comparative education.* New York: Peter Lang.

Rampaul, W. E., Freeze, D. R., and Bock, J. 1992. A model for international special education service delivery in developing countries. *International Journal of Special Education* 7:101–8.

Schriewer, J., and Homes, B., eds. 1988. *Theories and methods in comparative education.* New York: Peter Lang.

Stackhouse, J. 1992. Growth of poverty alarming, UN says. *Toronto Globe and Mail,* 18 May, A7.

Todaro, M. P. 1981. *Economic development in the third world.* 2d. ed. New York: Longman.

Tsang, M. C. 1988. Cost analysis for educational policy making; A review of cost studies in education in developing countries. *Review of Educational Research* 58:181–230.

UNICEF. 1980. *Childhood disability: Report of Rehabilitation International to the Executive Board of UNICEF.* New York: UNICEF.

UNICEF. 1991. The disabled child: A new approach to prevention and rehabilitation. *Assignment children, 54.* Geneva: UNICEF.

United Nations. 1979. *World social situation including the elimination of all major social obstacles.* New York: United Nations. Document No. E/cn.5/1989/2.

Urch, G. E. 1987. Review of P. G. Altbach and G. P. Kelly, eds. *New approaches to comparative education. Educational Studies,* 18:538–44.

Wang, H. B., and Rule, S. 1992. Mainstreaming: Increasing services in China to young children with disabilities. *International Journal of Special Education* 7:219–27.

Ward, J. 1984. The rehabilitation of the disabled: A challenge for the 80s. *The Exceptional Child* 3:5–18.

Wiesinger-Ferris, R. 1989. Partnership between the developed and the developing countries to promote special education and disability prevention. *International Journal of Special Education* 4:101–9.

Winzer, M. A. 1993. *The history of special education.* Washington, D.C.: Gallaudet University Press.

World Health Organization. 1989.

COMPARATIVE STUDIES IN SPECIAL EDUCATION

PART 1

LIMITED SPECIAL EDUCATION

Extrinsic structural education factors such as high pupil-teacher ratios and lack of essential teaching materials and resources in South African education both create and exacerbate special educational need. This classroom, which has better facilities than many others, has 55 children ranging in age from 7 to 9 years. PHOTO BY David R. Donald

A blind student using a brailler at Faniufa Commuity School in Papua New Guinea. PHOTO BY Richard Cornish and Andrew Winuan

A group of physically disabled students at the Bethlehem Arab Society Centre of Rehabilitation in the West Bank. PHOTO BY Samir Dukmak

*F*or disabled persons in many countries special education, training, and rehabilitation remain an elusive dream. This is not necessarily to say that commitment is lacking within political and educational sectors, but it does say that economic, social, and political difficulties in some regions of the world are so overwhelming that they relegate special education to the status of a peripheral priority. Looming social concerns such as solving structural economic problems, providing universal elementary education, and establishing basic health services overshadow the pressing needs of a small and by definition politically and socially disadvantaged special needs minority. This point is made saliently by each author in this section and provides the underlying rationale for grouping South Africa, Papua New Guinea, Senegal, and the West Bank and Gaza Strip together. However, within this stress upon the fundamental and causal relationship between pressing problems in the economic and political realms and the provision of special education, each author also focused upon other, attendant, crucial aspects found within the unique context of his own region.

The difficulties and dilemmas of Papua New Guinea in trying to provide special education services in the face of a massive lack of access to universal primary schooling for the general population are illustrative of the situations many countries confront. When at least 30 percent of the elementary school-age population is unable to access schools, then education and rehabilitative services for persons with disabilities necessarily shift to a tiny smattering of schools operated by voluntary agencies and overwhelmingly restricted to urban areas. Similarly, in the comprehensive discussion of the situation in Senegal, the author points to the difficulties of a nation struggling to set its own course in the wake of a disintegrating and dysfunctional colonial structure while caught in the throes of economic hardship.

In light of the above tenets, it may strike some readers as odd that an economically and militarily powerful nation such as South Africa has been included in part I. For a small, privileged, caucasian, and largely urban numerical minority of the South African population, the placing of their nation in this part I of the text is indeed unwarranted. However, writing of the general South African educational system, Mangezi Guma (1992) points out that "[s]ince 1976, the South African education system, especially as it

3

affects Blacks, has been in a state of permanent disruption. The school system for Blacks is collapsing under the sustained assault of students and teachers on the one hand and stress-fatigue on the other, brought about by an [sic] monstrous inefficient bureaucracy" (134). Our first author, addressing special education, speaks in similar tones. His chapter focuses upon the 80 percent of South African children who do not enjoy appropriate access to schooling. This is the black population for whom there are almost no services whatsoever. It is about this huge South African numerical majority population that our first chapter speaks, and of the impoverished socio-economic circumstances that cause that group's vastly increased prevalence of special needs due to extrinsic causes resulting from poverty, malnutrition, and other preventable etiologies—all within the boundaries of a modern, technologically sophisticated, and wealthy state. The author speaks further of the top-heavy bureaucracy of South African education, which has not put in place legislation or policies to ensure the education, training, or rehabilitation of disabled persons in the black South African communities.

Remarkable parallels can be drawn between this latter aspect of South Africa and the situation which is illuminated in the West Bank and the Gaza Strip. Because the West Bank and the Gaza Strip are occupied territories, there has been no allowance for legislation or policies for individuals with special needs. However, in the face of increasing numbers of persons with disabilities brought about by civil unrest, private organizations such as the Arab-Bethlehem Society are making significant contributions to training and educating disabled persons of all ages.

Thus the primary necessity of resolving the overwhelmingly constraining influences of severely limited social and economic resources for populations with special needs—whether they are part of a majority in an economically disadvantaged nation or are a minority within a prosperous nation—is grappled with by each author in these diverse countries. A look at the degree to which additional contributing factors such as racial inequality, civil unrest, and a lack of political will on the part of the political and economic majority can also radically affect the situation provides us with insight into the complexity of the social matrix within which special education must be understood and into the profound and diverse challenges that are faced by special educators around the globe. Nevertheless, despite monumental challenges, some advances are apparent and are documented by the authors.

1

South Africa

DAVID R. DONALD

*I*n most developing countries resource limitations have generally resulted in the demand for basic education taking precedence over provision for special educational needs. The irony in this is that the incidence of disability, and therefore of special educational need, in such contexts is estimated to be considerably higher than in more developed contexts (Wiesinger-Ferris 1989). Thus, social and educational disadvantage are reproduced in an interacting cycle of poverty, associated health risks, inadequate health care, limited access to services, overcrowded and underresourced basic education, and lack of special educational facilities within this system (Donald, in press). South Africa is no exception to this pattern. Indeed, the situation is compounded by the racial inequalities that have been created and perpetuated by the policy of apartheid. Recent political developments, although desirable, have as yet had minimal impact on the real social and educational experience of the majority of South Africans. This chapter will be concerned with describing this reality, the inequities in it, and the challenges that the nature and extent of special educational need pose for the process of educational reconstruction in South Africa.

To date, the delivery of education in South Africa has been the responsibility of a complex and uncoordinated arrangement of eighteen different

About the Author • Dr. David R. Donald is a professor of educational psychology and head of the School of Education at the University of Cape Town. His interest in and concern with special education needs date back to his original professional training and practice as a school psychologist in South Africa in the 1960s.

For the past twenty years, his focus as an academic has been on the development of training programs for psychologists and special educationists appropriate to South African conditions and on a range of research issues related to this broad area of concern.

education departments basically divided across racial and ethnic lines (Donald and Csapo 1989). The inequalities, hegemonic distortions, and bureaucratic wastage that have characterized this system (Nkomo 1990) have been felt even more severely in relation to special education (Gwalla-Ogisi 1990). Not only have there been gross disparities of special educational provision between these departments but there have also been eighteen differing definitions of special educational need, eighteen different policies regarding the provision of education for children with special educational need, and eighteen different and uncoordinated delivery systems. In addition, because of this fragmentation, comparable information from the different departments is almost impossible to access. The presentation of a comprehensible national picture therefore has had to involve a degree of simplification, estimation, and extrapolation.

Most rationally, and not necessarily following the bureaucratic divisions, the total system may be divided between those special educational services that have been reasonably well developed in departments serving whites, coloreds, and Indians—20 percent of the school-going population—and those that have been grossly underdeveloped in departments serving Africans—80 percent of the schoolgoing population.[1] As indicated, this involves an inevitable oversimplification as whites have generally been somewhat better served than coloreds and Indians and there is some degree of interdepartmental and regional variation in services for Africans (Donald and Metcalfe 1992). Nevertheless, the differences are so marked between the two major groupings that the overall system is best understood in these terms.

Both historically and in terms of current educational initiatives emanating from the state, the issue of special educational need in South Africa has been relegated to the periphery of educational concern. In all departments of education, the provision of specialized educational services has lagged behind the estimated need (Donald 1991), and recent cutbacks and retrenchments have followed and exacerbated this pattern. Various reasons for this marginalization could be hypothesized. The most likely is that the relatively high cost of providing specialized educational services has not been seen as justified in relation to the perceived economic return. The almost complete neglect of special educational provision in African education would appear to confirm that this has been the philosophy within a social system where capital has blatantly served the apartheid order.

Another likely and not unrelated reason is the perception that meeting special educational need has little to do with the effectiveness and "productivity" of the mainstream of education. This perception is based on the assumption that children with special educational need are relatively few in number and that ignoring their need will therefore have little overall effect.

Arguments such as these need to be challenged on fundamental moral, social, educational, and economic grounds. In order to do this, however, it is necessary to examine more closely the real nature and extent of special educational need in a country like South Africa.

Prevalence of Exceptionality and Special Educational Need

Exceptionality and special educational need are usually conceptualized as overlapping and therefore as synonymous. Thus, exceptionality refers to children who, because of physical, sensory, cognitive, or other exceptionalities, experience special educational need to the extent that they require some form of specialized educational intervention if they are to be effectively educated (Brennan 1985). Moreover, children with special educational need are commonly understood to constitute a relatively small proportion— approximately 10 percent—of the school-going population. Generally this understanding has evolved in relatively advantaged social and educational contexts typical of most of North America, Western Europe, and indeed of the privileged sector of South African society. In severely disadvantaged contexts such as exist for the majority of the population in South Africa, however, this conceptualization needs to be fundamentally altered.

Basically, the conventional understanding assumes that exceptionality, and therefore special educational need, is created where there is a deficit or disability within or *intrinsic* to the learner. However, in contexts where severe social and educational disadvantage operate, deficits are created that are structural and systemic in nature and are therefore *extrinsic* to the learner. Under these conditions, special educational need, rather than "exceptionality," manifests itself as the need for special educational support in the acquisition of basic educational skills delayed or denied to learners through lack of access to, or inadequacy of, the existing educational system. Following this premise, the notion that special educational need refers to only a relatively small group of children has to be challenged on a number of important counts.

First, in contexts of widespread poverty and disadvantage such as exist in South Africa, intrinsic disability may be created at up to double the rate of incidence than is the case in more privileged contexts (Wiesinger-Ferris 1989). As indicated previously, this relates to cycles of reproduction that interact to produce disproportionately high incidence rates of disability and special educational need. Thus, people who are subjected to poverty are inevitably more prone to the health risks associated with malnutrition, disease and infection than are those who are not (Olver 1984; White 1980). What is important is that many of those health risks associated with poverty commonly result in cognitive or sensory impairments that are likely to create special educational need.

In the South African context, this has been amply verified in a number of studies that, inter alia, have consistently demonstrated the damaging cyclical relationship between malnutrition and cognitive development (Richter and Griesel, in press) and the relationship among diseases that are particularly common under conditions of poverty (for example, tuberculosis, pneumonia, gastroenteritis, and measles), secondary cerebral infection, and resultant disabilities such as cerebral palsy and mental retardation (Arens et al. 1987; Arens and Molteno 1989). The impact of the current AIDS epidemic on vulnerability to diseases such as tuberculosis, pneumonia, and so on, is of further and immediate concern in this reproductive cycle. In addition, lack of access to appropriate health services (Buch 1988; Olver 1984) and the inadequacy of basic health screening in schools (Frets-Van Buuren, Letuma, and Daynes 1990) compound the problem. Under such conditions, it is likely that the number of children with intrinsic disabilities and special educational need may in fact constitute a significant proportion of the school-age population.

Second, the heritage of social and educational disadvantage under the system of apartheid has created a very large group of children with extrinsically generated special educational need. Factors that have contributed to this need are both structural and systemic in nature, and are educational and socioeconomic in origin. Thus, structural educational factors such as the shortage of schools and classrooms, high pupil-teacher ratios, teacher underqualification, and lack of essential teaching materials and resources (Cooper et al. 1990) have been compounded by complex systemic factors such as the language of instruction issue and its relationship to early reading skill (Donald 1992a), and issues around curricular content and a rigidly instrumental process of teaching (Thembela 1986). The effects of these conditions are reflected in very high failure rates in the early grades (Taylor 1989) and widespread underachievement in relation to potential in African education (Donald 1989). More direct socioeconomic factors have contributed to the excessively high dropout rate in education (Donald 1992b), to the widespread breakdown of both nuclear and extended family structure (Berman and Reynolds 1986; Donald 1989), and to the numbers of children "on the street" (Richter 1988; Swart-Kruger, in press) or who economically are forced to seek work before acquiring even the basic educational skills (Gordon 1987).

In almost all cases, the learners who are being considered here have, for one reason or another, not acquired adequate basic educational skills, especially those related most essentially to literacy and numeracy, at a time in their development when this should normally have occurred. Given current thinking on a system of compulsory primary education for South Africa, the dilemma is how to reincorporate these "marginalized" children into the mainstream of education. Most essentially, if they are to be reincorporated at age-appropriate levels, the fundamental relationship of literacy and numeracy skills to all other dimensions of the curriculum—as well as the inability of these learners to progress, or to be motivated to progress, without these skills—creates a compelling need for special educational support in the difficult but crucial bridging process that will be required.

Finally, in disadvantaged social and educational contexts there is a multiplicative *interactive* effect between intrinsic disability and extrinsic factors. Clearly the relative interactive impact of extrinsic factors on a child with, say, a mild intrinsic learning disability will depend on the severity of the extrinsic factors. Where these are severe, the result would almost certainly be a child with special educational need. Where they are not, the child could well cope unassisted in a well-run mainstream. The net effect is that children with even mild intrinsic disabilities or impairments, who also suffer extrinsic social and educational disadvantages, are more likely to manifest with special educational need. The overall extent of special educational need is thus increased. The almost total lack of special educational facilities in African education for children with the more diffuse intrinsic disabilities, such as mild hearing impairment, mild mental handicap, learning disability, speech and language difficulties, or emotional and behavioral problems (Donald and Metcalfe 1992) would indicate that the extent of unmet interactive special educational need is a severe problem within the system.

Despite these indicators of the extent of special educational need in South Africa, the process of arriving at reliable estimates of incidence is problematic on a number of counts. These problems have been elaborated by Donald (1992b), but for the present may be summarized as follows:

1. Because of the unreliability or unavailability of local information most estimates have been based on incidence statistics gathered in First-World, developed contexts. For a variety of reasons, including those mentioned above, such statistics inevitably underestimate the need in underdeveloped and disadvantaged contexts.
2. Although special educational need is relative and not absolute, estimates of the extent of this need tend to be based on available evidence around the incidence of intrinsic disabilities that are clear and medically identifiable (e.g., Hattingh 1987). Such a practice is not only problematic in terms of the actual relativity of special educational need, but it also excludes all children whose need is extrinsic (socio-educational in origin) or where there is an interaction between the more diffuse and ill-defined intrinsic disabilities and extrinsic factors.

3. Because statistics in relation to the most disadvantaged are the least reliable (particularly given a lack of epidemiological data and inconsistent and incomplete statistics among different government departments in South Africa), the very factors that create higher incidence rates of intrinsic, extrinsic, and interactional special educational need are the most difficult to quantify.

Within these constraints, Donald (1992b) has generated two sets of estimates. The first is a conservative set based on available statistics and minimal extrapolation. The second is what is possibly a more "real" set for the African population because it attempts to take the research and arguments around increased incidence into account (see table 1.1).

Although conceptually the line between intrinsic and interactive special educational need is relative and not absolute, the division has been determined by the form of available statistics and is useful in so far as it relates to the general pattern of service provision (Donald and Metcalfe 1992). Thus, the intrinsic grouping includes what are most often the severe and chronic conditions—physical disabilities, sensory loss, neurological disabilities (e.g., cerebral palsy, epilepsy, and so on), and moderate and severe mental handicap. The interactive grouping includes the generally more mild and ill-defined conditions—mild mental handicap, learning disabilities, speech and

TABLE 1.1. Estimated Special Education Need in South Africa, 1990

	African	White	Colored	Indian	Total	% of School Population
Intrinsic						
Conserv.	492,934	60,033	54,186	15,013	622,166	6.44
Real	765,427	60,033	54,186	15,013	894,659	9.26
Interactive						
Conserv.	765,425	93,219	84,140	23,311	966,095	10.00
Real	1,148,140	93,219	84,140	23,311	1,348,810	13.96
Extrinsic						
Conserv.	1,487,936	—	—	—	1,487,936	15.40
Real	1,930,728	—	—	—	1,930,728	19.98
Total						
Conserv.	2,746,295	153,252	138,326	38,324	3,076,197	31.84
Real	3,844,295	153,252	138,326	38,324	4,174,197	43.21

language difficulties, and emotional and behavioral problems. The extrinsic grouping includes a necessarily rough estimate of the numbers of African children who might require special educational support, particularly if compulsory primary education were to come into effect.

For each of the subcategories mentioned, incidence rates (percentage of school population) were derived mainly from two relatively recent government reports (Hattingh 1987; Human Services Research Council 1987). The extent of the extrinsic category has been estimated from the tentative information that is available on dropouts in the first two grades (and the cumulative numbers that would have to be reintegrated and helped with compulsory primary education), numbers of "street children," and the primary school failure rate (Donald 1992b).

The most obvious implication from this summary table is that special educational need is proportionately greatest for those who are the most disadvantaged.[2] For every one hundred children conservatively estimated to have special educational need, eighty-nine are African. On the more real estimate, ninety-two are African. Given the almost total lack of special educational services in departments of education that have thus far served the African community (Donald 1991; Donald and Metcalfe 1992; Gwalla-Ogisi 1990), the inequity, extent, and urgency of this problem cannot be overemphasized.

Identification and Labeling of Exceptionalities

In general, facilities for the identification of exceptionalities in South Africa have followed the pattern of inequality and difference between the developed and underdeveloped sectors. In the developed sector, sophisticated diagnostic services exist through hospitals, private medical services, child, family, and school clinics, and special schools. In these contexts there is characteristically a multidisciplinary team of medical, paramedical, psychological, and special educational consultants who will make a detailed physical, neurological, cognitive, emotional, and scholastic assessment of a child's needs. Although not exclusively, school psychological services play a major role in this process. School psychologists and remedial (special education) teachers are the main diagnosticians, backed up where necessary with referral to other specialists. The relative availability and quality of such services in the "developed" sector vary across the interacting dimensions of urban/rural and affluent/poor: For those who happen to be urban and affluent, availability and the quality of service are high. For those who happen to be rural and poor, services are generally inaccessible, and for those who happen to make up some intermediate combination, services are available but vary in accessibility and quality.

By contrast, in the underdeveloped sector, services for African children, with very few exceptions, are almost totally lacking. School psychological services, generally known as auxiliary services in African education, are minimally staffed (Donald and Csapo 1989). No school clinics have been established and, among all eleven African education departments in 1990, there were only seventy-one special schools providing 9,811 special educational placements for over 7.5 million African children enrolled in school at that stage—a ratio of 1 to 780 (Donald and Metcalfe 1992).

To add to the lack of specialists and settings for identification, there has also been a lack of appropriate tests for psychoeducational assessment. Whereas a wide range of tests have been developed or adapted for local use in the developed sector, it is only relatively recently that some tests in African languages and with local norms have been developed for use in African education (Donald and Csapo 1989). Under these conditions, facilities for the identification of children with special educational needs—let alone their placement and appropriate education—are hopelessly inadequate.

In 1987, one of the eleven departments—the Department of Education and Training—introduced the Panel for Identification, Diagnosis and Assistance (PIDA system) in an attempt to provide a school-based service for special educational needs. These panels are comprised of nominated teachers from the school, the principal and, where possible, they are supposed to operate with the assistance of school psychologists and remedial advisors. However, there exists a general non-availability of remedial advisors; the estimated ratio is approximately 1 to 20,000 students in urban areas (Donald and Metcalfe 1992). There is also a lack of school psychologists—the ratio is approximately 1 per 30,000 students (Donald and Csapo 1989). Moreover, research evidence gathered from teachers themselves suggests that many feel inadequate and resent the imposition of the PIDA system in a situation where overextended and underqualified staff are supposed to solve problems for which they have neither the training nor appropriate backup support, materials, or referral options available (Donald and Hlongwane 1989; Green, Donald, and Macintosh, in press).

Evidence from these two studies indicates that in-service teacher training in the most basic identification procedures is possible, but that this requires a specialist to engage in intensive and extended consultative interaction with a PIDA team. Significantly these and another study (Makosana 1991) also show that a high proportion of problems referred to PIDA teams require basic medical identification and intervention. Taken together with the evidence of Frets-Van Buuren, Letuma, and Daynes (1990) regarding the inadequacy of health screening in schools, these findings would indicate that the identification of basic health problems is as much at issue as the identification of special educational needs.

As regards labeling, the issue of normalizing those with exceptionalities through noncategorical approaches has barely come to the fore. At this stage, the issue of identifying and helping these children at all takes precedence.

The Social Context of Special Education

As already indicated, political and socioeconomic factors in South Africa have been major determinants behind the creation and reproduction of special educational need, as well as behind the gross inequality of service provision between the developed and underdeveloped sectors of the society. The following information and statistics, elaborated in Donald and Metcalfe (1992), give further substance to the inequality of service provision.

Within the overall imbalance of per capita expenditure between the developed and underdeveloped sectors of the education system (Donald and Csapo 1989), the imbalance with regard to special educational provision has been particularly severe. In 1987, a year for which the most recent and reliable financial figures are obtainable for the country as a whole, the combined special education budget across all African education departments constituted only 12 percent of the total national special education budget.

More specifically and recently, 37 percent of all special schools in 1990 were in white education departments (serving 9.6 percent of the 1990 school-going population), while only 29.6 percent were in African education departments (serving 79.2 percent of the 1990 school-going population). The majority of the latter are state-aided schools that have been initiated by churches and other NGOs rather than the state itself. In general, these schools have provided special education for children with severe and chronic disabilities within what has been defined above as the intrinsic grouping.

For children with special educational need in the interactive grouping, the disparities have been even more severe. For the mildly mentally handicapped, for instance, special or adaptation classes within mainstream schools are provided to varying extents in all departments in the developed sector. In 1990, approximately 25,000 children were accommodated in 1,860 such classes in the white education departments alone. By contrast there were only 70 such classes in Department of Education and Training schools (the largest African education department), and it is estimated that no more than 1,300 mildly mentally handicapped African children, in total, received special educational help in 1990. This represents only .7 percent of the conservative estimate of need in this area.

Equally, for children with learning disabilities, speech and language difficulties, and emotional and behavioral problems, specialized extracurricular support has been extensively provided within the mainstream of the developed sector, again particularly for white children. For African children, on the other hand, the only service that has been developed is the PIDA system mentioned earlier. To date this has been so ineffective that it constitutes no real service at all.

Thus, these inequalities in the area of special educational provision underline the fundamental distortion of socioeconomic, and ultimately political, factors in the creation and perpetuation of special educational need in South African society.

Legislation and Policies

As might be expected, legislation for the education of exceptional children has been limited to the advantaged sector. The Education Services Act of 1967 together with its amendments, and the Mentally Retarded Children's Training Act of 1974 both make specific provision for the special schooling of white children with exceptionalities that fall under the intrinsic grouping that includes physical disabilities, sensory loss, neurological disabilities, and moderate and severe mental handicap. Less specifically, general legislation passed for the education of coloreds and Indians has included reference to the needs of exceptional children. No specific legislation has been passed for the education of African children with exceptionalities. Legislation entrenching the rights of all children to an appropriate education of the order of the Public Law 94-142 in the United States has not even been considered. There is hope, however, that the Bill of Rights currently under negotiation as a cornerstone to a new constitution will encompass this entitlement.

Within the diversity of policies across different education departments, two major policy patterns are apparent regarding the delivery of special education. In the developed sector, the pattern has been for self-contained special education, in the form of special schools and classes, to be set up for children with needs in the intrinsic grouping—physical disabilities, sensory loss, neurological disabilities, and moderate and severe mental handicap—as well as for some of those in the interactive grouping—notably mild mental handicap and severe learning disability. In addition, extensive extracurricular remedial and therapeutic services have been available within the mainstream for mainly white children with mild learning disabilities, speech and language difficulties, and emotional and behavioral problems.

By contrast, in the underdeveloped sector the lack of any clear policy has resulted in a system that may be said to be mainstreamed in the sense that very few children are separated into self-contained special schools or classes. However, this is no more than mainstreaming by default as it results from a sheer lack of services. Ironically, despite the battles that have been fought over this issue in other developed countries, African parents and teachers do not see this system of mainstreaming to be an advantage. Quite understand-ably, it is the self-contained services in the developed sector which, having been denied to these parents and teachers, that are generally regarded as desirable.

Major Controversies and Issues in Special Education

It should now be apparent that issues affecting special education in South Africa are particularly closely bound up with the broader political, social, and educational issues that, at this time, confront the society as a whole. Since the processes of transformation are complex and as yet uncertain, the fate of special education is therefore equally uncertain. Within this complex-ity and uncertainty however, there are a number of key issues that can be identified as central to the processes of decision making and policy formula-tion. Unless these issues are faced with honesty and resolve, progress in meeting the challenges of special educational need in South Africa is unlikely to occur.

Governance and Control

Perhaps the most central issue affecting special education in South Africa is the question of governance and control. Historically, the inequalities and inefficiencies that have come to characterize the present education system have been created out of the hegemony, the segregation, and the bureau-cratic wastage of the apartheid order. The control of education through so many racially constituted and unequally resourced education departments has been ethically and functionally unacceptable. The formation of one democratically and nonracially constituted education ministry is a demand, therefore, that must be met as an absolute priority if the inequalities and inefficiencies of the past are to be redressed and coordinated. In special education, more than in any other area of education, the differences in resources, the differences in conceptualization and definition, the differences in models of service provision, and the confusion and wastage generated between departments, has bedeviled the development of a rational and effec-tive special educational service. Given the need for central coordination, there is at the same time a tension around this, and the need for devolution of control on a regional basis. In special education in particular, the need for parents and local communities to have a meaningful say in the nature and form of special educational provision for their children constitutes an essen-tial ingredient in the democratization of the education system in South Africa.

Within the overall issue of governance and control and the needs for rational planning, coordination, and democratization of special education there are a number of equally vexing and basic issues regarding resources and their distribution. The need to establish an effective and universal system of compulsory education, at least at primary level, is now generally accepted as a major goal in the process of transformation and educational reconstruction. Given the extent of this basic educational provision and the degree of redress that will be required within it, it is clear that the costs will be high. Since the provision of special educational resources is particularly costly, there is a very real danger that these resources will be sacrificed in the face of overall fiscal constraints.

On one level such reasoning is understandable. However, if the real nature and extent of special educational need, as outlined in the first section of this chapter, is taken into account, then it should be clear that such needs cannot be divorced from the concerns of even the most basic system of universal primary education. Most particularly, unless the full range of special educational need, from intrinsic through to extrinsic, is taken into account, the system is likely to become even more weighed down than it presently is with student failure, dropout, teacher frustration, and parent dissatisfaction. Ultimately, in economic terms alone, the issue that must be faced is that the crippling effects of unmet special educational need on all dimensions of classroom practice, and the social and economic dependencies that result, would considerably outweigh the short-term economic gains of not providing for special educational need.

Regarding resource distribution, another issue is the tension between the needs for equality and redress. Although this issue affects the whole process of educational reconstruction, it is of particular concern in the area of special education. Because special educational needs have been so totally neglected in African education, a simple equalization in the distribution of resources would not necessarily redress the imbalances of the past. In particular, the extensive existence of what has been defined as extrinsic special educational need and the interaction of extrinsic factors with intrinsic disabilities in African education will demand more resources than will those sectors of the education system that have been more privileged in the past. Although the logic of this is apparent, it will again put particular strains on a limited fiscus and may not be as readily accepted as the logic demands.

Service Delivery

The issue of what model of service delivery should apply in special education in South Africa is complex and is unlikely to be easily resolved. As has already been pointed out, an extensive self-contained model has evolved in the developed sector while the sheer lack of services in the underdeveloped sector has resulted in a system of mainstreaming by default rather than by design.

The international trend toward mainstreaming and the education of all children in the least restrictive educational environment cannot be ignored in this context. The principles that have informed the ethical and educational arguments in favor of mainstreaming in developed contexts are equally powerful and relevant in underdeveloped contexts. Yet ironically, in the process of educational transformation in South Africa, parents and teachers who, on the one hand, have had access to extensive self-contained services are unlikely to perceive mainstreaming as an advantage when, with redress and redistribution of resources, the mainstream overall will at best be thinly equipped and ill-prepared to offer special educational services. On the other hand, parents and teachers who have to this point been denied access to the well-resourced, self-contained services in the developed sector are unlikely to perceive a poorly resourced mainstream service as preferable.

This is further complicated by the economic realities of the situation. To extend to all students in need the well-resourced, self-contained special educational services, such as currently exist in the privileged sector, will be an impossibility within the general financial constraints of educational reconstruction. Yet, to provide a fully resourced and effective mainstream special educational service is even less feasible, not only for financial reasons but because the mainstream itself requires such radical systemic and functional change before an individualized, needs-centered approach could work in it.

A possible alternative would appear to be an evolutionary one in which a process of *progressive mainstreaming* is set in motion. This would require a coordinated sequence of action within both the mainstream and with regard to self-contained facilities. Initially, to meet immediate need, existing special educational services would have to be more equitably distributed. For those sectors and regions of the country that have no services at all (Donald and Metcalfe 1992), there would appear to be no alternative but to provide essential self-contained special schooling for at least those who fall into what has been defined as the severe and chronic intrinsic grouping. Progressively these same facilities, and the specialized personnel serving them, would have to adapt to fulfilling a more supportive function in relation to the mainstream and less of a self-contained role.

At the same time, the capacity of the mainstream to provide for special educational need would have to be developed. As emphasized, the enforcement of compulsory primary education will dramatically increase the numbers of children who will require special educational support for extrinsic reasons. The ability of teachers to cope with this demand as well as with those children in the interactive grouping, let alone children with more severe disabilities, will require a radical transformation of mainstream structures, facilities, and support systems. Most problematically it will require restructuring of systemic factors, including the curriculum, the general pattern of parent-teacher and pupil-teacher interaction, and the actual process of teaching that currently occurs in the majority of classrooms across the country. Thus, despite the ultimate desirability of mainstreaming, anyone who advocates immediate and universal mainstreaming in this context can have no conception of the depth and extent of this challenge. It can be no other than a painfully slow and evolutionary process.

Parameters of Special Education

How the parameters of special education are conceptualized and defined is crucial to the place that will be assigned to it in the overall reconstruction of the education system in South Africa. The central issue here is whether special education should be limited to a narrowly conceived curative service or whether it should be directed more broadly to include systemic and preventative intervention. Ultimately this boils down to the question of who has special educational need and of how the parameters of this need should be delineated.

As has already been argued, any conceptualization of special educational need as related only to intrinsically generated learner deficits is problematic in a context like South Africa where extrinsically generated socioeducational disadvantage is so prevalent. Nevertheless, it would be naive to assume that such a conceptualization would not have practical advantages, particularly to a hard-pressed state. Thus, in pure fiscal terms, the responsibility for providing special educational services could be contained within a relatively unambiguous frame and could be limited to a small minority who manifest with clear deficit-related exceptionality (viz., those with severe and chronic intrinsic disability).

Given current economic realities and the competition for resources within education alone, this conceptualization cannot be dismissed lightly. It may be decided that this is the only financially viable way of providing some special educational service to at least some of the children in need. The problems associated with such a conceptualization, however, need to be clearly articulated and understood within the decision making around this issue. Most fundamentally, such a conceptualization reifies the notion of special educational need as only an intrinsic or learner-deficit related phenomenon. This not only excludes the legitimate needs of those with extrinsically generated—and inevitably most of those with interactively generated—special educational need, but it also ignores the structural and systemic factors that contribute to this need. The mainstream of education and the social structure of society are thus effectively absolved from responsibility.

Further, such a conceptualization tends to "medicalize" special educational need, separating it artificially from broader social, emotional, and educational developmental goals that are the common right of all children. Finally, it perpetuates categorization, labeling, and separation of the children concerned. It is therefore in contradiction to the democratic and human developmental principles of maximum participation and choice embodied in the notion of mainstreaming.

Clearly, from any principled position, special educational need must be conceptualized as encompassing the full intrinsic-extrinsic continuum. This is not only important for reasons that are the converse of those listed above. It also opens the way for a development of the mainstream in ways that would be of benefit to all children. As indicated, and given what is occurring in most South African classrooms at present, a needs-oriented and more facilitative approach to teaching and learning is not a peripheral concern. It is central to the reconstruction of education as a whole. Beyond this, the whole question of prevention becomes centrally situated. Economically—let alone from moral, social, health, and educational grounds—preventative programs that tackle the reproductive cycles mentioned earlier in this chapter are essential in the reconstruction of the society as a whole. If the extent of special educational need is to be reduced—and economically this would seem to be essential, apart from other reasons that may be less persuasive to a fiscally constrained government—then extensive preventative intervention must become a priority.

Research

Ostensibly, the need for research in the field of special education in South Africa would not appear to be as urgent an issue as those that have been mentioned so far. However, if more effective ways of both preventing and meeting special educational needs, as they have been defined, are to be planned *and* executed then it is clear that there are three major areas of research that require concerted attention.

First, there is the need for more extensive and reliable epidemiological data. It should have become apparent from the arguments presented above that current information on the incidence of disability and special educational need is not only unreliable but is likely to reflect a severe underestimation of actual incidence. No matter how cogent the arguments are, however, this is still a hypothesis and needs to be verified. No substantive planning to meet these needs can be undertaken without a clearer indication of the extent and the type of resources required. This, in turn, cannot be realistically determined and advocated, within a context in which competition for resources is severe, unless the epidemiological data are clear and unequivocal.

The second area of research is equally urgent. For economic, social, and cultural reasons, models of service delivery that have been developed in Western, First-World contexts are not necessarily the most appropriate in the South African context. Thus, as has been described, the particular issues and problems associated with mainstreaming in this context will not easily be resolved. If, in the essential process of democratizing education, further inappropriate top-down decision making is to be avoided, then research not only into what is possible within the given resources but also into what models of service delivery work, why they work, and what the recipients, particularly parents and teachers, think of them, becomes essential.

An extension of this is the way the role of the traditional African healer has remained unacknowledged in formal systems of service delivery. Despite this, there is evidence that a significant proportion of parents and teachers, in both rural and urban communities, identify with the beliefs and practices of traditional African healing. Confronted with educational problems, including special educational need, parents in particular regard traditional healing as an important resource to turn to (Madlala 1990). Certainly the situation is complex and for many there is a conflict between a modern, industrialized lifestyle and traditional African belief systems. However, in precisely this context, a collaborative model of service delivery involving both conventional psychological counseling and consultation with traditional African healers has been shown, in some educational case studies, to be effective (Donald and Hlongwane 1989). Nevertheless, the relationship is far from unproblematic. What is needed is further research that probes both the potential and the dimensions of conflict in this relationship so that all sources of help, regarded as legitimate in the community, can be optimized for the benefit of parents and children with disabilities and special educational need.

The third area of research that is required relates to the whole area of prevention. As has been stressed, a major factor in the creation and reproduction of special educational need is the role that poverty, health, and health access play in this cycle. As much as urgent intervention is required in order to break into this cycle, it is clear that, if such intervention is to be focused and effective, then further research is required that prioritizes and specifies more exactly the relationship between poverty and those health risks that create special educational need. With equal urgency, research is needed into how access to appropriate health services can be facilitated if prevention is to become a reality.

Emerging and Future Trends

As has been emphasized throughout this chapter, the future of special education in South Africa is intimately related not only to its history but to the political, economic, social, and educational choices that lie ahead. There are no certainties in this. However, given present economic realities, the extensive demands of general social reconstruction—education reconstruction in particular—and the pattern and shape of policy decisions to date, there is a real danger that special education will continue to be peripheralized in the process of educational reconstruction.

The thrust of this chapter has been to accept this danger as real but not as inevitable. In seeking to substantiate and clarify the extent of special educational need, the disparities and contradictions in current provision, and the special educational issues that must inevitably be faced if educational and social reconstruction are to be real, this chapter has sought to challenge the danger; to pose alternatives; and, above all, to argue that concern with special educational need is a central and not a peripheral issue in the policy decisions that lie ahead. In conclusion, the following points summarize the essence of this argument.

First, on even the conservative estimates of incidence given in this chapter, it should be clear that the numbers of children who are likely to be in need of special educational support are substantial and cannot be regarded as peripheral to the concerns of the education system as a whole. Moreover, if the fundamental principles of redress and equity are to be applied to educational reconstruction in South Africa, then it must be acknowledged that *all* children with special educational need are disadvantaged and 90 percent of these children have been *doubly* disadvantaged. Redressing this double disadvantage is an imperative on the most basic moral and equity principles.

Second, from both the overall extent of the need and the degree to which it is determined by extrinsic factors, it should be clear that special education is as much a social as it is an educational issue. Thus the responsibility for both meeting and preventing special educational need must lie as much in the health and welfare domain as in the educational domain. Within this, the responsibility in the educational domain cannot be limited to the provision of specialist services but must extend into the structural and systemic dimensions of educational reconstruction at all levels.

Finally, the assumption that the neglect of special educational need has little effect on education as a whole and that this neglect is economically justifiable in terms of the relative cost of appropriate provision can now be challenged as fallacious. In relation to both the nature and the extent of special educational need as it has been defined in this chapter, what should be clear is that neglect of this need, particularly under conditions of compulsory primary education, will produce and perpetuate a crippling effect not only on substantial numbers of children but also on general classroom practice, the morale of teachers, and therefore on the output of education as a whole. In addition, the social consequences of such neglect would be to create dependencies that would affect parents, health, and social services as well as, ultimately, the economy. Given even the conservative incidence estimations, it is clear that ignoring special educational need would involve ignoring the educational, social, and economic development of a substantial proportion of South African youth. The short-term economic savings in such a policy will surely not outweigh the long-term losses.

Notes

1. The racial classifications African, white, colored, and Indian are recognized as part of the unacceptable heritage of apartheid and are used in this chapter only in the sense that they reflect existing structures and divisions in the society.

2. As has been consistently emphasized, the higher and possibly more real incidence rates for intrinsic and interactive special educational need as well as the existence of extrinsic special educational need are all related to socioeducational disadvantage. The fact that this has been estimated only in relation to African population statistics does not imply that such socioeducational disadvantage is limited to this group. It is the heritage of apartheid that statistics have been kept in this form and that an alternative analysis reflecting people, as opposed to population groups, who have been socioeducationally disadvantaged is not possible. However, it is also true that under apartheid the African community has suffered the greatest socioeducational disadvantage and, representing 80 percent of the school-age population, the general need is most clearly estimated in this form.

References

Arens, L., Deeny, J., Molteno, C., and Kibel, M. 1987. Tuberculous meningitis in children in the Western Cape: Neurological sequelae. *Pediatric Reviews and Communications* 1:257–75.

Arens, L., and Molteno, C. 1989. A comparative study of postnatally-acquired cerebral palsy in Cape Town. *Developmental Medicine and Child Neurology* 31:246–54.

Berman, S., and Reynolds, P. 1986. *Growing up in a divided society.* Johannesburg: Ravan Press.

Brennan, W. 1985. *Curriculum for special needs.* Milton Keynes: Open University.

Buch, E. 1988. Current facilities and services in the health sector in South Africa. In C. Owen, ed. *Towards a National Health Service.* In proceedings of the 1987 National Medical and Dental Association conference, University of the Western Cape.

Cooper, C., McCaul, C., Hamilton, R., Delvare, I., Moonsamy, J., and Mueller, K. 1990. *Race relations survey, 1989–90.* Johannesburg: South African Institute of Race Relations.

Donald, D. 1989. *Applied child psychology in South African society: Purposes, problems and paradigm shifts.* Pietermaritzburg: University of Natal Press.

———. 1991. Training needs in educational psychology for South African social and educational conditions. *South African Journal of Psychology* 21:38–44.

————. 1992a. Reading as a linguistic process: Language and literacy policy implications. *Southern African Journal of Applied Language Studies* 1:1–15.

————. 1992b. Estimation of the incidence of special educational need in South Africa. Research report of National Education Policy Investigation, Johannesburg.

————. In press. Children with special educational needs: The reproduction of disadvantage in poorly served communities. In A. Dawes and D. Donald, eds. *Childhood and adversity in South Africa*. Cape Town: David Philip.

Donald, D., and Csapo, M. 1989. School psychology in South Africa. In P. Saigh and T. Oakland, eds. *International perspectives on psychology in the schools*. Hillside, N.J.: Lawrence Erlbaum.

Donald, D., and Hlongwane, M. 1989. Consultative psychological service delivery in the context of Black education in South Africa. *International Journal of Special Education* 4:119–28.

Donald, D., and Metcalfe, M. 1992. *Final special education report*. Johannesburg: National Education Policy Investigation.

Frets-Van Buuren, J., Letuma, E., and Daynes, G. 1990. Observations on early school failure in Zulu children. *South African Medical Journal* 77:144–46.

Gordon, A. 1987. *Another mielie in the bag*. Pretoria: Human Sciences Research Council.

Green, L., Donald, D., and Macintosh, I. In press. Indirect service delivery for special educational needs in South Africa: A comparative study of five consultative interventions. *International Journal of Special Education*.

Gwalla-Ogisi, N. 1990. Special education in South Africa. In M. Nkomo, ed. *Pedagogy of domination: Towards a democratic education in South Africa*. Trenton, N.J.: Africa World Press.

Hattingh, J., ed. 1987. *Disability in the Republic of South Africa: Main report*. Pretoria: Department of National Health and Population Development.

Human Sciences Research Council. 1987. *Education for the Black disabled*. Pretoria: Human Sciences Research Council.

Madlala, C. 1990. Traditional and Western approaches to educational problems. M.A. Ed. diss., University of Natal.

Makosana, S. 1991. Consultation at Nomlinganiselo School. In proceedings of the South African Association of Learning Disabilities national conference, pp. 80–86, University of the Witwatersrand.

Nkomo, M., ed. 1990. *Pedagogy of domination: Towards a democratic education in South Africa*. Trenton, N.J.: Africa World Press.

Olver, G. 1984. *Poverty, health and health care in South Africa*. Carnegie conference paper no. 166, Second Carnegie inquiry into poverty and development in South Africa, University of Cape Town.

Richter, L. 1988. Street children: The nature and scope of the problem in South Africa. *The Child Care Worker* 6 (7).

Richter, L., and Griesel, R. In press. Malnutrition, low birth weight and related influences on psychological development. In A. Dawes and D. Donald, eds. *Childhood and adversity in South Africa*. Cape Town: David Philip.

Swart-Kruger, J. In press. Children of the South African street. In A. Dawes and D. Donald, eds. *Childhood and adversity in South Africa*. Cape Town: David Philip.

Taylor, N. 1989. *Falling at the first hurdle*. Research report no. 1., Education Policy Unit, University of the Witwatersrand.

Thembela, A. 1986. Educational obstacles to Black advancement. In R. Smollan, ed. *Black Advancement in the South African economy*, 73–80. Johannesburg: Macmillan.

White, N. 1980. The nutritional status of children in Crossroads and Nqutu. In F. Wilson and G. Westcott, eds. *Hunger, work and health*. Johannesburg: Ravan Press.

Wiesinger-Ferris, R. 1989. Partnership between the developed and developing countries to promote special education and disability prevention. *International Journal of Special Education* 4:101–09.

2

Papua New Guinea

BAREND VLAARDINGERBROEK

AMBROSE TOTTENHAM

GRAEME LEACH

*P*apua New Guinea occupies the eastern half of the island of New Guinea and is north of Australia, from which it gained independence in 1975. Papua New Guinea has a population of about 3.6 million, about 85 percent of whom live in traditional communities. In 1989 there were 11,700 people for every physician. The infant mortality rate was estimated at 68 per 1000 and the life expectancy was estimated at fifty-one years. Illiteracy rates for men and women were estimated at 52 percent and 70 percent respectively (Foresight 1989).

The goal of universal primary education remains to be achieved in Papua New Guinea. Only about 70 percent of children are presently able to enroll

About the Authors • Barend Vlaardingerbroek is a lecturer in science education at the University of Papua New Guinea's Goroka Teachers College. His interests include science education in the context of developing countries, educational cross-cultural psychology, and educational equity for the disabled. • Brothers Ambrose Tottenham, C.F.C., and Graeme Leach, C.F.C., are respectively engaged in education and rehabilitation of the visually and hearing impaired in Papua New Guinea. At the time of writing, they were at the Mt. Sion Center for the Blind and St. Benedict's Teachers College respectively.

The authors gratefully acknowledge the assistance of Maba Lohia, Port Moresby Special Education Centre; Alphonse Pu, Western Highlands Association for the Disabled; Donna Mailil and Richard Vasi, Morobe Handicapped Children's Association; Ruth Sangkol, St. John's Association for the Blind; and Dorothy Lusmore, Creative Self Help Centre in preparing this chapter.

in grade 1. Education is also fiercely competitive at higher levels; only about 32 percent of primary school graduates can enter junior high school, and only about one in every ten grade 10 school graduates can continue on to advanced levels.

Prevalence of Exceptional Conditions

Data on the incidence of handicapping conditions are very difficult to obtain in a country where births and deaths commonly remain unregistered. A pilot survey of the Papuan region carried out in 1979 suggested that about 10 percent of the population suffers from at least one disability, and about 2.5 percent of the population would benefit from rehabilitation services. The leading categories of disability revealed in this study were hearing and visual impairment, followed by limb dysfunction, and speech impairment. The level of intellectual retardation recorded was notably low (Griew and Colodey 1981; Welfare Services Division 1990). More recent estimates support of 2.5 percent as being indicative of the level of handicaps among the school-age population. Up to two-thirds of these students are described as hearing impaired (National Education Board 1991; Pu 1992).

A major former cause of handicaps, especially auditory and intellectual, was endemic cretinism, but this was brought under effective control by iodination programs in the 1970s (Harris and Helai 1981). As is commonly the case for developing countries, most cases of hearing and visual impairment among children continue to be brought about by preventable infectious diseases associated with poor hygiene, particularly otitis media and conjunctivitis and their complications (Biddulph and Stace 1986).

Enumeration of disabling conditions in the population is further complicated by attitudes toward handicapped family members, commonly characterized by hiding such people from the view of outsiders, and denying their existence (Harris and Helai 1981). In some areas, infanticide has been a traditional strategy for dealing with infant disability (McRae 1980). Traditional beliefs regarding the origin of disabilities in children are many and varied, but common themes include the breaking of food taboos during gestation, sorcery or malevolent spirits, and impregnation or fetus exchange by demons.

Moreover, the extent to which an exceptionality is a disability, or whether a disability is mild or severe, involves certain culturally associated value judgments. A mild degree of intellectual impairment, for example, may not be handicapping in a village context.

Identification and Labeling of Exceptionalities

In the absence of either a national register of disability or compulsory primary schooling, the identification of disabled persons is largely a matter of the family's notifying one of the agencies and enlisting its assistance. Mission or rural health workers often act as intermediaries in the notification process. As well as being identified by concerned families who notify the various agencies of the presence of disability, some cases are brought to light by community outreach programs and primary school population screening programs conducted by provincial associations working in liaison with local health departments.

The Social Context of Special Education Legislation and Policies

Until recently, given the nation's inability to provide universal primary education, the view that special education should be of low priority predominated. As in Western societies, services for the disabled began to grow as an awareness that these people have rights was awakened. The National Board for the Disabled was established in 1978, and a rehabilitation officer's position was created within the Department of Home Affairs and Youth in 1987. That same year, a process of deliberation toward a national policy on exceptionality began. This culminated in the National Plan for the Prevention of Disability and the Integration of Disabled Persons in National Development in 1990. The plan has three goals: the protection of disabled persons' rights, the prevention of disability, and provisions for rehabilitation (Welfare Services Division 1990).

The constitutional goals of "Integral Human Development" and "Equality and Participation" were invoked by the 1991 Education Sector Review when it recommended that the proportion of public expenditure on special education should equal that of the prevalence of handicaps (stated as 2.5 percent). Stressing the need to implement integrated schooling for students with exceptionalities wherever possible, the review also recommended that all teachers be trained to cope with the presence of handicapped children and young people in regular classes. While the need for special education centers for people who cannot realistically be integrated into the regular education system will naturally remain, it has also been recommended that such centers be fully recognized and affiliated with the national education system (National Education Board 1991).

Currently, the new government eventuating from the 1992 national elections has pledged to give high priority to special education in Papua

New Guinea. The disabled appear to have a more hopeful future than ever before, and developments are expected to proceed at hitherto unprecedented rates.

General Services for Persons with Exceptionalities

Only about one in every three hundred disabled people in Papua New Guinea gets some assistance (National Education Board 1991), chiefly from the nongovernment organizations listed in table 2.1. Funding comes from a variety of internal and external sources. The National Board for Disabled Persons in Port Moresby is responsible for the allocation of government funds to the various nongovernment organizations. Major external sponsors include such bodies as the Christoffel Blindenmission, the Red Cross Society, Helen Keller International, and organizations such as the Lions' Clubs.

As may be inferred from table 2.1, the location of services for the disabled generally favors those living in or near urban centers. Rural people are furthermore discouraged from accompanying disabled family members to such centers by the withdrawal from the extended family network that such a move entails (Harris and Helai 1981).

TABLE 2.1. Nongovernment Organizations Providing Assistance to Persons with Exceptionalities

Nongovernment Organization	Location[a]	Clients[b]
Port Moresby Special Education Centre	Port Moresby	180
Papua New Guinea Rehabilitation Centre	Port Moresby	53
St. John Association for the Blind	Port Moresby	45
Cheshire Homes	Port Moresby	11
Port Moresby Sheltered Workshop	Port Moresby	11
Morobe Association for the Disabled	Lae	147
Lae Rehabilitation Centre	Lae	12
Lae Sheltered Workshop	Lae	12
Creative Self Help Centre	Madang	90
East New Britain Project for the Disabled	Rabaul	112
Mt. Sion Centre for the Blind	Goroka	26
Western Highlands Association for the Disabled	Mt. Hagen	273
Callan Services for Disabled Persons	Wewak	38

Source: National Education Board. 1991.

[a] Port Moresby (the national capital) and Lae are the two major urban centers of the country, and Madang, Rabaul, Goroka, Mt. Hagen, and Wewak are provincial capitals.

[b] Clients include all persons who receive some assistance through community-based rehabilitation programs (the vast majority of clients are in this category).

Educational Opportunities for Persons with Exceptionalities

Given financial and organizational restraints (Pu 1992), the residential-special school model is usually not a practicable option for developing countries. Virtually all children with exceptionalities who can enter the education system do so as integrated students. Organizational models of integration include individual placement in regular classrooms, the location of special units in regular schools, and students' dual attendance at a regular classroom and a special center (Jenkinson 1987).

The first of these models is the norm in Papua New Guinea, although the Port Moresby Special Education Centre provides center-based primary schooling for about twenty deaf children. The third model—dual attendance in a regular classroom and a special center—applies to children resident at Mt. Sion Centre for the Blind, of which there are about ten at any one time (for details see Vlaardingerbroek 1992). Table 2.2 presents the presence of children and young persons with exceptionalities as they occur throughout the national education system.

To promote educational equity for persons with disabilities, various agencies also conduct home-based early intervention programs and involve disabled children in preschool programs which may be integrated or center based. At present, 134 children are recipients of early intervention, while 87 are attending integrated preschools. The role of the special center preschool as a bridging experience is especially important with reference to disability-specific training.

TABLE 2.2.   Integrated Education of Children and Young People with Exceptionalities

Impairment Category	Education Level		
	Primary	Secondary	Postschool
Hearing	48[a]	1	0
Visual	34	7	4
Physical	18	5	2
Intellectual/emotional	15	0	0
Multiple	3	0	0
Total	118	13	6

Sources:
Port Moresby Special Education Centre
St. John Association for the Blind
Morobe Association for the Disabled
Creative Self Help Centre
Mt. Sion Centre for the Blind
Western Highlands Association for the Disabled
Callan Services for Disabled Persons

[a] Includes ten children at the Demonstration primary school in the St. Benedict's Teacher College campus at Wewak.

The special center remains a vital adjunct to the integrated education process, particularly in the case of sensory impairment. Mt. Sion Centre for the Blind staff transcribe not only teaching materials and tests into braille for its integrated students but also national examinations at the primary and secondary level for the National Department of Education.

Teacher Training for Special Education

In 1991 there were thirty registered teachers included among the staff of seven of the nongovernment organizations listed in table 2.1 (National Education Board 1991). Hitherto, all specialist training of educational personnel in special education has occurred overseas, especially in Britain, Australia, and New Zealand.

The situation is changing rapidly. Staff from the National Board for Disabled Persons, Port Moresby Special Education Centre, and the St. John's Association for the Blind now regularly conduct in-service courses in special education for senior primary teachers. At the teacher-training college level, the pioneer has been St. Benedict's Teachers College, which offers a certificate level course in disability for teachers and nurses in both the full-time in-service and part-time modes. The College also conducts a program on integrated education for children with exceptionalities as part of the professional studies component of its preservice training course. Elective courses in special education will be offered as of 1993.

The National Education Board Committee (1991) recommended that special education units be created within each teachers' college and that a senior lecturer position be created for each. The committee also recommended the creation of a special education unit within the National Institute of Teacher Education to coordinate special education and prepare specialist curriculum materials.

Controversies in Special Education

In Papua New Guinea, public attitudes toward disability are generally prejudicial and resentment may arise from proposals to increase funding to sectors of the population with special needs (Welfare Services Division 1990). That public support for special needs programs is erratic is evidenced by the generally low level of community support for special needs projects (National Education Board 1991). It is not entirely incomprehensible that such feelings should arise in a developing-nation context where services for the majority, nonexceptional population are scarce. It therefore remains to be seen whether there will be a political "price" to pay for the implementation of the various recommendations hitherto noted.

Winkley (1990) has also discussed the problems of overreliance on overseas agencies, especially in terms of human resources, which some see as a problem inherent to many special needs programs in developing countries. He has argued the case that more emphasis needs to be placed on developing indigenous expertise.

References

Biddulph, J., and Stace, J. 1986. *Child health for health extension officers and nurses*. Port Moresby: Papua New Guinea Government Printing Office.

Foresight. 1989. *Prevention of blindness and services for people with visual disabilities in the South Pacific*. Australia: Australian Overseas Aid and Prevention of Blindness Ltd.

Griew, A., and Colodey, D. 1981. A pilot survey for disability in Papua. *Papua New Guinea Journal of Education* 17:156–68.

Harris, P. D. G., and Helai, P. 1981. Handicapped children in Papua New Guinea: The position prior to 1979. *Papua New Guinea Journal of Education* 17:142–55.

Jenkinson, J. C. 1987. *School and disability: Research and practice for integration*. Victoria, Australia: Australian Council for Educational Research.

McRae, H. 1980. Laws relating to fertility control and family planning in Papua New Guinea. *Melanesian Law Journal* 18:5–53.

National Education Board. 1991. *Special Education*. Port Moresby: Department of Education.

Pu, A. 1992. *Special education in Papua New Guinea*. Paper presented at the Extraordinary Education Faculty Meeting, September, University of Papua New Guinea.

Vlaardingerbroek, B. 1992. Integrated primary schooling of blind children in Papua New Guinea. *International Journal of Rehabilitation Research* 15:162–65.

Welfare Services Division. 1990. *Papua New Guinea national plan for the prevention of disability and the integration of disabled persons in national development*. Port Moresby: Department of Home Affairs and Youth.

Winkley, P. 1990. Sustainability: Ensuring localization and minimizing dependence. *Journal of Visual Impairment and Blindness* 84:316–18.

3

Senegal

SABOU SARR

Translated by Brian Titley

Senegal is situated in the extreme west of Africa. It has an area of 201,400 square kilometers and a population of 5,353,266. Approximately 80 percent of Senegalese live in rural areas, practice agriculture, and are of the Islamic faith. The population is made up of diverse ethnic groups ranging from the Sahelian to the black African. This gives the country a rich and varied culture. The Senegalese economy is based mainly on agriculture, although an incipient industry produces some goods for the market.

Senegal, just like other countries in the world, has always had handicapped people. This phenomenon is a social reality. Although not a clearly identifiable or homogeneous social group, the handicapped constitute the most disadvantaged and most marginalized of the Senegalese population.

Traditionally, the blind, the insane, and the paralyzed were looked after by the family. They lived in harmony under their parents' protection. But in contemporary society, the modern family, increasingly nuclear in structure and succumbing to the effects and pressures of underdevelopment, cannot satisfy the needs of its handicapped members. As well, the country's decision makers, who give priority to satisfying the needs of the greatest number of people, tend to neglect the specific needs of the handicapped and

---

About the Author • A native of Saint Louis, Senegal, Sabou Sarr is president of l'ONG Fondation Enfant Développement in Dakar. He holds a doctorat 3é cycle from Université Claude Bernard in Lyon and is a Chevalier de l'Ordre du Mérite, an Officier des Palmes Académiques, and a Chevalier de l'Ordre National du LION. In a diverse educational career, he has taught in elementary and secondary schools, in the Ecole Normale Supérieure in Dakar, and has served as the head of the Division des enseignements spéciaux et de l'enseignement arabe in the Ministère de l'Education Nationale.

thereby relegate them and their families to the most underprivileged levels of society.

Disabilities, in reducing the employability of the handicapped and by the same token their income, accentuate social inequalities. Thus, a large number of handicapped live on public charity and on the fringes of urban life. Many handicapped people—men, women, and children—take up begging. They are seen in the streets, in places of worship, and in public places.

Handicapped women face a particularly difficult situation. First of all, they are women in a society that denies them equal status with men. Thus, they are subjected to all the problems to which women are subjected regularly in Senegalese society in addition to the problems arising from their disabilities.

To counter this phenomenon, the Senegalese state has adopted a social policy aimed at the socioeconomic and professional advancement and integration of the handicapped. The state is interested in the rehabilitation of the handicapped for several reasons. These include social progress; the democratization of education and equality of opportunity for all; scientific and cultural progress in a modern civilization; and the increase in public awareness of the specific needs of the handicapped.

This new social policy began with the dawn of independence in Senegal and the creation of the Ministry of Public Health and Social Affairs. The difficulties of living in the contemporary world, and the appearance of new social realities bringing poverty, malnutrition, and selfishness, spurred the need for a better social policy. In addition, Senegal observed the International Year of the Disabled in 1981 and was a signatory to the International Convention of the United Nations in this matter, further signs of the country's commitment to helping the handicapped.

The Nature and Scope of the Concept

A disability or handicap is a disadvantage resulting from illness or incapacity which prevents someone from fulfilling normal functions relative to age, sex, or sociocultural position. A handicap can be due to a genetic anomaly or an illness or traumatism causing injury, disorder, or deficiency. Deficiencies can be locomotor, intellectual, aesthetic (social/behavioral), or visual. However, this definition of handicap is only partially relevant. Linguistic or medical-legal definitions do not do justice to the handicap, since these definitions do not enable us to imagine the difficult circumstances that beset the handicapped person in everyday life. Also, the social sciences—anthropology, psychology, and sociology— have expanded this notion of disability to include a wide range of social, economic, and cultural factors. According to the Nigerian sociologist, Maiga, racial or ethnic membership can, in this way, constitute in itself a handicap under certain ideological conditions. Membership in the untouchable caste in India or in the black race in South Africa under the apartheid system are cases in point. Underdevelopment is equally a handicap.

Prevalence Rates and Causes of Handicaps

To really understand the situation of handicapped children, one needs to know, at least approximately, their number and their distribution by age, sex, disability category, and social class. It is also evident that for the requirements of schooling, indicators of prevalence are very useful to us. The statistics are useful since they allow for better planning of structures, equipment, and training.

In Senegal, however, one runs up against obstacles of a human, financial, and material nature—an insufficiency of means. In this regard, the establishment of a reliable data base is far from easy. The services responsible for the prevention and early identification of disabilities and the rehabilitation of the handicapped are few in number, are concentrated in urban centers, and are only in reach of a tiny proportion of the handicapped population. Specialized personnel, whether in the area of medical, professional, or social rehabilitation, are insufficient in number for the task, and in some categories are completely nonexistent.

Moreover, the majority of prenatal or perinatal deficiencies, whether due to genetic or environmental factors, are not sufficiently documented at the hospital level. Early detection techniques, psychological, medical, and social surveys, and medical files are not properly used. We also lack the quantity of suitable instruments and specialized personnel, such as medical statisticians and clinical psychologists, found in developed countries.

In Senegal, many disabilities are linked to transmittable diseases and malnutrition. Highway work, domestic accidents, drugs, traumatism, infection, underdevelopment, lack of sanitary services, and cardiovascular diseases are other causes of disability. The clear correlation between disability and poverty on the one hand and between rural life and poverty on the other is also worth noting. The most impoverished echelons of Senegalese society living in the countryside or in the slums of our large towns are the principal targets of crippling diseases.

Many locomotor disabilities are the result of infectious diseases. For example, poliomyelitis has a significant rate among our population. There were twenty-five cases of the disease noted in 1979 in one hospital in Fann (Dakar) and three thousand cases registered in hospitals in 1980. One can believe that this figure represents but a portion of those afflicted by this disease. Leprosy is another cause of disabilities. There were forty-five thousand lepers registered in 1980; 30 to 40 percent of the twenty thousand lepers counted in social rehabilitation villages were mutilated.

Osteomyelitic infections including cancerous or noncancerous ulcers, mycetoma, and rheumatoid arthritis also form a large portion of the diseases that cripple the locomotor system. As well, cerebro-meninginal attacks and diabetes cause locomotor disabilities. Birth defects such as clubfoot or hunchback are among the further causes of locomotor disability.

In Senegal seven thousand traffic accidents a year are recorded. This number will grow, taking into account the average automobile increase rate of 5 percent annually. Similarly, accidents on the job are following an ascending curve due especially to the beginnings of industrialization experienced in the country.

There are more than fifty thousand blind persons. Blindness has three major causes in Senegal—keratoconjunctivis, onchocerciasis (river blindness), and degenerative diseases. Other causes of visual impairment include trachoma and xerophthalmia. Deaf-and-dumbness is often a consequence of childhood infectious fevers that seriously damage the nervous system. Congenital causes also exist.

The number of mentally handicapped persons is considerably lower than that of the physically handicapped. Nonetheless, the number is increasing sharply because of urbanization and maladjustment. Apart from birth defects (trisomy 21), it is well to include accidental injuries to the skull, the results of childhood infectious fevers (encephalitis), tertiary syphilis, emotional disturbances, drug addiction, and social dislocation.

From these examples, it can be seen that there are numerous causes of disability in Senegal. It must be admitted, however, that the principal cause of disability is our state of underdevelopment; myriad limitations do not allow the implementation of a public health policy adequate to our aims. Nonetheless, measures have been taken to reduce certain causes of handicaps.

Classification of Structures

Disabled children and adolescents ought to be entitled to prevention, early detection, care, and education. But this point of view presupposes the putting in place of structures that cater to the needs of handicapped youths and following an active policy of rehabilitation. Senegal, notwithstanding its modest means and its status as a country on the path of development, makes laudable efforts in this domain.

Medical-sanitary measures in Senegal give priority to preventative over curative medicine and priority to medicine for all over individual medicine. The network of medical-sanitary structures includes regional hospitals; centers for maternal and infant health; rural and urban maternity hospitals; health clinics in rural areas; an institute of social hygiene; an institute of pediatrics; centers for maternal and infant care; seven epidemic disease sections; ten leper hospitals; and two regional psychiatric centers. Due to the opening of rural maternity hospitals in 1978, these medical-sanitary structures increased their hospital capacity from 5,836 beds in 1977 to 7,091 beds in 1978.

Institutional structures for the locomotor disabled include the Artificial Limb Center of Dakar. Its purpose is the rehabilitation and the fitting of artificial limbs. The Shelter Center is a private institution designed for the rehabilitation, preschool education, and artificial limb fitting of young polio victims in a residential setting. The Disabled Shoemaking Center provides for the training of the disabled in shoemaking in a six-month apprenticeship. Already three trained apprentices of shoemakers have been placed in three different regions. The Poignée de Mil (Handful of Millet) is an independent organization of disabled craftsmen who make and sell their handicrafts. Apart from these institutions, all the young locomotor disabled of school age can attend public school with their nondisabled comrades, where they can take advantage of grants for orthopedic equipment.

For cured and mutilated lepers there are Care Centers and Villages of Social Rehabilitation. Villages of social rehabilitation doubling as care centers exist also. The majority of these institutions make available to lepers educational structures (schools, social centers), clinics (dispensaries, maternity hospitals), and cultural centers. It is also possible to provide the patients with craft activities. Table 3.1 provides an overview of institutions in Senegal.

TABLE 3.1. Institutions of Special Education and Training

Type of Disability	Public Institutions	Private Institutions	Trustee Organizations for Public Institutions
Visually impaired	Institut national des Jeunes aveugles à Thiès (Senégal) (INJAT)	Centre de l'ABRI à Dakar	Ministère de l'Education Nationale Ministère Développement Social
Locomotor disabled	Centre TALIBOU DABO de Grand-Yoff-Dakar	Centre de Coordonnerie des Infirmes Locomoteurs à Dakar	Ministère Santé Publique Ministère de l'Education Nationale
Auditorily impaired	Centre verbo-tonal de Dakar	La Poitnée de mil à Dakar	Ministère de l'Education Nationale
Mentally impaired	Centre de sauvegarde des enfants déficients mentaux Dakar	Centres de reclassement social des Hanseniens	

Note: This table represents all the public and private institutions concerned with different kinds of disability in Senegal.

The Law and Its Limits

For disabled persons in Senegal, the law is embryonic. Preventative measures and aid to the disabled fall into two categories.

Legal-administrative measures consist of a whole range of laws, degrees, orders, and circulars governing the protection of human rights and public assistance. There is specific legislation applying to lepers and the insane. These are Act 75-80 of 9 July 1975, relative to the treatment of mental illness and the detention of certain categories of the insane; Act 76-03 of 25 March 1976, relative to the treatment of leprosy and the social rehabilitation of cured and mutilated lepers; and Decree 60-245 of 13 July 1960, governing public relief in Senegal.

Apart from these national laws, Senegal adheres to many pieces of international legislation concerning human rights in general and the rights of the handicapped in particular. Nevertheless, in Senegal the disabled encounter various obstacles regarding the use of space, the environment, and social life. They face architectural, legal, and sociocultural barriers.

In our country, where young people form the largest part of the productive population, handicapped children constitute an important proportion of those afflicted with disabilities. This social group deserves special attention in our society because it could become usefully productive if suitably educated and kept from beggary.

A matter of first priority is educational legislation ensuring access to school and training for the disabled. Up through the present, in spite of concerted efforts by the state in medical rehabilitation, there are gaps and inadequacies in the area of social legislation. Also needed are appropriate professional training, the establishment of adequate structures, disabled allowances, social support during special education, employment in reserved positions, the elimination of architectural obstacles, and so on.

The Social Context of Special Education

Education in Senegal is seen as having both an economic and a social role. Development is achieved by human beings who are active agents of change and who can also secure the production of material resources. In addition, education contributes fundamentally to development in providing qualified manpower and technicians so that physical effort is not wasted. Those with disabilities can live, but only with dependence on a group of individuals in society. Education, however, provides an alternative to this relationship—it enables individuals to subsist by themselves and gives them the requisite resources. Education, therefore, aims at autonomy.

In this age, the economic function of education is closely linked to its social function. The first function of education is to socialize. Socialization is the process by which a group transmits its cultural heritage to its members in order to ensure economic and cultural survival. Education can be seen as synonymous with socialization in that it prepares the individual for life and harmonious integration in society.

The emphasis of training is on sociableness, on the creation of a social environment that encourages disabled children to live normally with their handicap. The social and familiar environment of the disabled child, architectural and social barriers, and general negative reactions all act as a brake on full social integration. The special educator therefore must give full attention to interpersonal relations when helping to design an environment that suits the needs of these children.

Schools, Teachers, and Pedagogy

In Senegal, as in all countries, special education requires the intervention of a multidisciplinary pedagogical team: specialized teachers, psychologists, physicians, social workers, and adult educators. The education of the handicapped child is achieved by concerted action on the part of this coordinated team, working together to ensure the harmonious development of the child.

One cannot perceive the development of the Senegalese child except in the context of his or her own culture, social relations, and moral values. It is for this reason that the family setting is an important element in the early education of the handicapped child.

In effect, the range of disabilities presents pedagogical challenges in the case of each student. Every learner is a unique pedagogical project since the IQ varies from one student to the next. Linguistic diversity adds another complication. And the diverse sociocultural milieus also affect the learning process.

Pedagogy

Reeducation, also known as special education in the sense of readapting handicapped children, has as its final aim to provide the child with the means for social adjustment. In this spirit, one speaks of the reeducation of maladjusted delinquents, problem children, the sensory handicapped, the mentally deficient, and so on. Reeducation uses methods taken from physiology and anatomy, adapted to each age level, depending on the interests and needs of the child. One speaks also, to use Claparéde's term, of functional education. From this perspective, handicapped children benefit also from a pedagogy known as *curative*, applied in the English-speaking world to *problem children*.

In effect, special education is a form of enriched general education that seeks to improve the lives of those who suffer from various handicaps. It calls upon specially trained educators using modern pedagogical methods and technical equipment to remedy certain forms of deficiency. It entails the realization of the potential of disabled children in a changing society in which maladjustments multiply for diverse reasons (technological civilization, environment, accidents, and so on). The difference between special and regular education is in methodology, although the ultimate aim of both is the same: helping the student become useful to society.

Our approach to special education takes into account the specific needs of the handicapped child. Special education doesn't employ trick methods or inappropriate textbooks. Every pedagogical procedure relates to the individual's environment. Frequently, considering the importance of the environment, the special educator and his or her students may make, as far as possible, teaching materials adapted to the environmental context. The special pedagogy must focus on the specific handicap at the root of the maladjustment and recognize that certain indispensable functions such as those of perception, expression, and communication, are limited. These limitations demand the development of compensatory activities.

In special education, the systematic approach, which allows for the analysis of an educational strategy suitable to the environment, is best adapted to our realities. For those with physical disabilities, pedagogy must focus on security and efficiency. These children need to feel that they are under the control of educators who understand them and who show that they are aware of their problems without resorting to a poorly adapted psychoanalysis. These educators must know how to give confidence to students as they become aware of their disabilities.

Teacher Training

The training of special educators is difficult. It involves training educators capable of practicing a pedagogy differentiated according to the peculiar circumstances, behavior, and educational challenges of their students, since physical, motor, sensory, and mental disabilities all demand unique adaptations in teaching. Insofar as the special educator must ensure the personal development of the disabled, awareness of moral and social responsibilities, and acquisition of knowledge the teacher must have a general level of education equivalent to a degree.

Providing a balanced personality for the handicapped Senegalese child requires a better psychological approach then that emerging from our cultural reality. To educate a child implies having a global perception of the society in which he or she lives. Nonetheless, one often observes a shortage of information and studies on the psychology of the Senegalese child and on the problems of his or her growth.

Teachers will often encounter psychological problems for which no immediate solutions are available since every handicapped child is a field of investigation demanding individual research. For a new pedagogical approach, the specialized teacher must be familiar with scientific expertise in special education and with basic medical knowledge, especially in genetic biology, genetic psychology, and psychoanalysis as they relate to biomedical data.

Knowledge of the handicapped child is basic to undertaking any educational action. Teachers should not perceive themselves as experts from the beginning. Special education requires a long period of observation because the handicapped, sensing themselves to be different from others, will not participate so freely in the sociocultural context. They may hide their true selves. The education of the handicapped child is therefore impossible without first liberating the personality.

At present, schools for the training of special educators do not exist. Training does take place, but through study grants in foreign countries. We do not have the structures and resources to do it ourselves. However, the reform of our school system envisages having, in the long term, this training, which is the keystone of all systems of special education.

Major Controversies and Issues

In a general sense, the disability problem in underdeveloped countries is intimately linked to a precarious economy arising from the debilitating effects of underdevelopment—crises, permanent poverty, and destruction of the physical environment. The present situation of special education in Senegal and in underdeveloped countries is critical. We are victims of the global economic crisis. Frequently the financial and material means to improve conditions do not exist, even when there is political will. The socioeconomic and political challenges are too great to overcome.

Even if they are suitably trained, the disabled in underdeveloped countries encounter difficulty in getting paid employment because of underemployment and unemployment. Further, urbanization and the rural exodus have serious repercussions as far as employment is concerned.

In order to solve those problems that are beyond the capacity of the state at present, the associations of the disabled in all categories must better organize themselves in order to concentrate their efforts on researching solutions and working with the state in seeking compensatory legislation, assistance, and social security.

In industrialized countries as in the developing countries, it is increasingly realized that placing disabled children in specialized institutions is not the best solution for reasons both of economy and rational organization. In effect, and especially in taking into account the difficult economic situation in developing countries, the modern tendency favors rehabilitation in ordinary educational settings. Educational integration in a normal milieu allows disabled children to develop side by side with the nondisabled, and to learn at an early age to accept their disability. They realize that upon adulthood they will have to share in a common social milieu the same cares and concerns as those different from them.

On the other hand, the specialized school tends to give students a pessimistic view of their abilities, which jeopardizes chances of succeeding insofar as they will be inclined to conform to the negative image. Segregation in specialized structures, then, serves to create psychological barriers.

One cannot stress too much the important aspects of integrated education. This type of teaching tends to limit the high costs of the construction of specialized facilities and the outfitting of highly qualified personnel, important considerations for a country of limited means and lacking the advanced techniques of rich countries. It allows access to schooling to a much greater number of children at a time when we are promoting mass education. However, a model that accomplishes integration but alienates the local population as little as possible is preferred. Here, as elsewhere in Africa, obstructions to rehabilitation are most numerous in the rural milieu where the disabled are more likely to be found. In these areas new education methods must be found—but they must be indigenous and respectful of the social and cultural background of the disabled child.

In bringing about the social and educational integration of disabled children, the family plays a crucial role. While a family's ignorance regarding the problems attendant on their child's disability can pose a major challenge to the child's development, the family is also the child's principal caregiver and can be a powerful pressure group—in Senegal, associations of parents of disabled children have done pioneer work.

The family's attitude can determine the outcomes of the deficiency. The disabled child, even in the context of his or her family, feels different from other children. But the child doesn't have to adopt negative attitudes—feelings of pity or of blame, which limit abilities, aptitudes, and independence. The family must help the child early on to play a constructive role in society and to overcome the disability. It is important, therefore, to reject certain attitudes towards special education, especially the *dependency syndrome* of the models used in the West, which are unsuitable to African realities.

It is important to take legal measures, to anticipate the need for competent specialized personnel, support services, and specially adapted educational structures. This presupposes early identification, evaluation, and medical and social intervention prior to full integration.

In the field of special education, further pedagogical research is a necessity. It implies systematic observation, description, and evaluation of the pedagogical process as applied to disabled students.

The importance of prevention in an underdeveloped country such as Senegal is self-evidently a condition of progress in matters of health. It is all the more important since the means of sanitation are limited. Health costs, too, are becoming a problem because of insufficiency of human and financial resources. Prevention, however, if rationally and efficiently applied, could reduce the financial costs to the state of curative medicine and ensure an increase in productive capacity.

In the domain of health education, priority must also be given to preventative measures, beginning with the pregnant woman and the young child. Attention must also be given to early identification and intervention in maternity centers, dispensaries, hospitals, social centers, preschool institutions, and schools. Preventative medicine ought to occupy the first place in all health systems, and especially in Senegal. To achieve these goals, priority must be given to the training of preventative health workers in sufficient numbers.

The eradication of most contagious diseases, sensory deficiencies, and maladjustments requires mass vaccination. As a matter of primary prevention, increased efforts must go to vaccination in our maternity and infant centers, especially in rural areas where the population rarely has access, or has difficulties in access to health care. The World Health Organization recommends an extended vaccination program and vaccination of breast-feeding babies against parasitical infections which appear early among children in the tropics. But the viability of that program depends on vaccines requiring refrigeration. The legal requirement to vaccinate all the children of civil servants and the military and the withholding of family allowances from those who refuse and from forgers of vaccination certificates are positive moves in the direction of increased vaccination.

Future Trends

Education of the disabled is recognized in the principles of the universal rights of man and ought to be a moral obligation for all societies. "The physically, mentally and socially disadvantaged child must receive the treatment, education and special care which his circumstances recognize" (The Universal Declaration of the Rights of the Child 1959). Associated with this human right is the notion of equal opportunities for all, independent of race, religion, and creed. The term *right of advancement* is sometimes used in this connection. For President Kéba Mbaye, it means the "right of development" which circumscribes the life of every human in the sense of personal improvement, taking into account the options and resources available in each country and sustained by universal solidarity.

Today, far from being a luxury or a waste, education is a developmental necessity in all underdeveloped countries. In this sense, education can be considered an indicator of development or, to quote J. Coleman, "Education is the key that unlocks the door to modernization." Or one can cite Hosteliz who considers education as one of the most important, if not the most important, variable in economic progress.

One of the assumptions of modern pedagogy arising from notions of social and scientific progress is that of the school encouraging in all students a concern for the democratization of national education, and school availability without discrimination to everyone of school age. To better adapt this concept of our educational system to our concerns and realities, the National Commission of Reform issued its Etats Généraux de l'Education et de la Formation (General Conditions of Education and Training) in which it advocated in the context of the *new school* special structures for the education of disabled children.

Some noteworthy aspects of the report mention that special education in the new school involves all the sectors dealing with disabled children or those generally maladjusted. This includes those motor disabled, deaf and dumb, and those psychologically or socially disabled. For each of these categories, two types of teachers will be trained: educators specializing in the age group of three to twelve years and educators specializing in the age group twelve to twenty-five years. These specialists in each category will be under the supervision of special education inspectors.

This social aim requires the eradication of psychological and social barriers, the development of good interpersonal relationships, and the adoption of another perspective on the disabled. In the new school that we are presently developing, special education will have to foster the autonomy and socialization of the young handicapped, and their capacity to understand and fit into their environment. In addition, it will have to point out to them the way to proceed so that they no longer have to carry the full weight of their disabilities. It will have to enable each deficient child to develop and grow while retaining his or her cultural identity in a tolerant, open, and democratic society.

4

West Bank and Gaza Strip

SAMIR J. DUKMAK

*P*alestine is a very small country. In the 1948 war, 75 percent of its land was occupied by Israelis. The West Bank and Gaza Strip, which is even less than the remaining 25 percent, was occupied in the 1967 war. Currently it is estimated that more than one and one-half million Palestinians live under Israeli occupation in the West Bank and Gaza Strip alone. More than two million live outside Palestine, the majority of whom left the country due to the two wars (Dukmak 1991). According to Abu-Gazaleh et al. (1990), an estimated six hundred thousand Palestinians live in the Gaza Strip, three-fourths of whom are refugees. More than half of the Palestinians in the West Bank live in villages and refugee camps. The economy of the West Bank and Gaza is dependent upon income from small shop and factory owners, small farmers, others involved in agriculture, and laborers who work in the Israeli side (Abu-Gazaleh et al. 1990).

The absence of a national government in the area leads to the absence of a national health apparatus, which means that there is no infrastructure to provide people with health services. This is reflected in a neglect of primary health care, a lack of an adequate health insurance plan, insufficient and unequal distribution of health services, an absence of coordination among health institutions, and a lack of long-term planning of solutions for health

About the Author • Samir J. Dukmak is a member of the Central National Committee for Rehabilitation in the West Bank. He is also employed by the British Agency "Action around Bethlehem Children with Disability," working as a children service and community projects coordinator as well as a consultant and representative of the agency at the Bethlehem Arab Society for Rehabilitation (BASR). His work with BASR dates back to 1985. At that time, as a new graduate of the University of Bethlehem, he worked as a social worker before going to London in 1986 for further studies under the sponsorship of Christian Aid.

problems. This also means that there is no integrated system of services for persons with physical and mental handicaps in the West Bank and Gaza such as the social and medical benefits received by Israeli citizens with handicaps (Ballantyne 1988).

The United Nations Relief and Works Agency (UNRWA) does administer the camps and provides all registered refugees with health, education, and welfare services. Those who are not refugees, however, are served either through the Israeli health system at a minimum level or through private health institutions which are relatively good. Many health agencies and institutions in the West Bank and Gaza agree that the quality and quantity of health and educational services provided by the Israeli government have deteriorated since 1980. The UNRWA itself is reported as offering significantly better services, although these are still far from adequate (Benevenisti 1984). According to Ballantyne (1988), Israeli authorities in the last few years have cut health spending by 50 percent and are reducing health staff by 25 percent, while fees paid by patients have increased. Furthermore, patients who are covered by health insurance are no longer permitted to be referred to Israeli hospitals, even in life-threatening circumstances in which necessary care is not available in the West Bank or Gaza Strip hospitals.

The Israeli government hospitals in the occupied territories are maintained at grossly inadequate levels. In addition, the Israeli authorities have imposed new regulations requiring the administration of government hospitals to demand payment from injured patients belonging to the *Intifada* (uprising) before these patients can receive treatment.

Since 1987, the Intifada has stepped up its activity, so health conditions have become worse, and the number of persons with disabilities has impressively increased. This was the reason behind establishing legal committees for the purpose of setting health policy, coordinating health services, and seeking means to improve health and rehabilitation services. The Central National Committee for Rehabilitation, established in 1990, is one of these committees.

Prevalence of Exceptional Conditions

It is very difficult to determine the exact number of people with disabilities in the West Bank and Gaza Strip due to the absence of a national government which would normally be responsible for establishing prevalence and setting up a national health policy in the area. Carrying out a comprehensive study in the whole area also is difficult due to the lack of financial support and initiatives to start such a job. Several studies were carried out by private agencies and individuals on a small scale.

The World Health Organization (WHO) argues that people with disability comprise about 10 percent of the world's population. In the developing countries about a hundred studies have been done that conclude that 7 to 10 percent of the population is disabled (Helender et al. 1989). According to Ingram et al. (1985), 2 to 3 percent of the world's population have some degree of mental handicap, which is identified in the period between birth and fourteen years. Each of these figures represent all types of disabilities including minor ones not requiring rehabilitation or other forms of special services.

In the West Bank of the occupied territories a door-to-door survey was carried out by El-imili (1984) in three cities and three refugee camps in the greater Bethlehem area, a total population of 43,085. It was found that 743 individuals (1.5 percent of the total population) were disabled. It was also found that 22 percent of the disabled suffered from mental retardation, 30 percent from physical disability, 20 percent from hearing and speech impairments, 14 percent from multiple disabilities, 9 percent from visual impairment, 3 percent from seizures, and 1.4 percent from mental disease. Table 4.1 shows the population and the numbers and percentages of persons with disabilities for each of the areas studied.

Another door-to-door survey was carried out in 1986 in the Gaza Strip among a sample of refugees. This survey revealed that 2.4 percent of preschool and school-age children were disabled. It was found that those disabled suffered from the following disabilities: hearing impairment (11 percent); visual impairment (8 percent); physical disability (16 percent); poliomyelitis (5 percent); and seizure disorders (4 percent). The rest of the disabled persons suffered from mixed types of disabilities (Giacaman 1989).

A third study, which used children of all ages and in all camps as a sample (29,476 children), was also carried out in the Gaza Strip in 1987, by Saunders. It was found that 714 (2.4 percent) of children from all ages proved to be suffering from a disability (see table 4.2).

Baker (1988) estimated the number of people with different disabilities in the entire occupied territories to be 37,700 of whom 17,443 have been identified. On the other hand, the Society for the Care of the Handicapped in the Gaza Strip in its project proposal (1988) estimated the number of children and adults with handicaps in the Gaza Strip alone to be 20,000.

TABLE 4.1.   Percentage of Disability According to Population and Area of Residence

Place	Population	Number with Disability	% with Disability
Bethlehem City	15,500	317	2.0
Beit Sahour City	8,233	154	1.9
Beit Jala City	10,209	123	1.2
Dehiesheh Camp	5,143	116	2.3
Aida Camp	2,500	16	0.6
Aza Camp	1,500	17	1.1
Total	43,085	743	

TABLE 4.2. Number and Percentage of Children According
to Type of Disability

Type of Disability	Number of Affected Children	%
Mental handicap	152	21
Physical handicap	42	6
Hearing problem	269	38
Visual problem	51	7
Developmental delay	65	9
Epilepsy	29	4
Multiple handicap	102	14
Unknown	4	1
Total	714	100

Since the Intifada started in 1987, Gaza Strip has experienced the worst
forms of violence in the Occupied Territories. This could be the reason
behind the increased number of children with disabilities.

A recent study has been carried out by this writer (Dukmak 1992). I
studied the files of all children (325) ages three to fourteen who were
admitted to one of the largest institutions in the West Bank, the Bethlehem
Arab Society for Rehabilitation and its branches between 1984 and 1992.
This study found that cerebral palsy is the handicap that affects the highest
percentage of children (53 percent). The second and third most common
disabilities are mental retardation (16 percent) and hearing impairments
(11.7 percent). Table 4.3 shows the type of disability, its frequency, percentage, and cumulative percentage.

The mental retardation category percentage includes all types of problems which cause mental retardation such as Down's syndrome, micro-
cephalus, and hydrocephalus. Down's syndrome alone accounts for 4.2
percent of the total children with mental retardation. The degree of mental

TABLE 4.3. Type of Disability, at Bethlehem Arab Society
for Rehabilitation

Type of Disability	Frequency	%	Cumulative %
Cerebral palsy	149	53.0	53.0
Mental retardation	45	16.0	69.0
Hearing impairments	33	11.7	80.7
Polio	14	5.0	85.6
Developmental delay	13	4.6	90.2
Spina bifida	8	2.8	93.0
Other disabilities	19	6.8	100.0

Note: Missing cases here ($N = 44$) were not considered in the above percentages; the valid cases were 281.

retardation starts from mild and goes to the profound category. The same study also shows that the number of cerebral palsy cases in some areas is higher than in other areas. For example, the percentage of cerebral palsy cases out of the total population with disabilities differs among the following regions: Nablus area (89.9 percent); Hebron (68 percent); Gaza (65.5 percent); Ramallah (60 percent); and Bethlehem area (37.9 percent). Table 4.4 shows the number of children with disabilities in each area in the West Bank and Gaza Strip and its percentage, as well as the number of children with cerebral palsy and its percentage.

The high percentage of children with cerebral palsy in Nablus, Hebron, Gaza Strip, and Ramallah may be due to the fact that intermarriage and early marriage among females are more common in these areas than in any other areas in the country. This practice reflects a strong tradition or belief that emphasizes the property of the family should not go to other families. So when females reach fifteen or sixteen years of age (if not before) they should get married as quickly as possible to their relatives before strangers come and take them. Another attitude which parents might have toward early marriage, especially of their daughters, argues that the sooner the daughters get married the better in order for them to be protected from the wickedness of others.

The Bethlehem area has a smaller percentage of children with cerebral palsy (37.8) compared to the other areas because services for the disabled in greater Bethlehem are more advanced in both quality and quantity. Therefore, people are more aware of the causes of disability and start giving up the related archaic traditions and attitudes. Almost each community in the greater Bethlehem area has a program going on for persons with disabilities in which many activities are carried out to change attitudes toward people with disabilities and the disability itself.

The above studies show that the prevalence of disability in the West Bank and Gaza ranges from 1.5 percent to 3.3 percent. Assuming that the

TABLE 4.4.   Children with Cerebral Palsy, by Area of Residence

Area	Children with Disability	Number with C.P.	% with C.P. (of Disabled)	% with C.P. (of All Children)
Bethlehem	143	54	51.4	37.8
Ramallah	20	12	7.2	60.0
Hebron	50	34	18.0	68.0
Nablus	27	24	9.7	88.9
Gaza	29	19	10.4	65.5
Jerusalem	5	2	1.8	40.0
Jericho	4	1	1.4	25.0
Total	278	146	100.0	

Note: All percentages in this table exclude the 47 missing cases.

population of the Occupied Territories is 1.5 million, the minimum number of persons with disabilities (children and adults) would be 22,500, while the maximum number would be 49,500. Taking the average of this range, then, the number of children and adults with disabilities in the Occupied Territories would be 36,000.

These statistics are based on the assumption that the population of the West Bank and Gaza is 1.5 million. They are also based on old studies that were carried out between 1984 and 1988. It is important to note that the Intifada has played a crucial role in increasing the number of persons with disabilities in the Occupied Territories. According to various private and governmental medical sources (Shehadeh 1990), approximately 45,000 injuries occurred as a result of the Intifada between 1987 and 1990. In 1988 alone, 25,000 injuries occurred (Giacaman 1989).

Causes of Exceptionalities

There are only one or two causes of disability specific to the occupied territories of Palestine. However, one or more of the following can be the direct or indirect cause of disabling conditions: prenatal and postnatal identifications; perinatal complications; accidents or traumas; intermarriage; gene and chromosome abnormalities; and poverty. In the 1992 study carried out by the writer, prenatal, perinatal, and postnatal problems as well as intermarriage and mother's age during pregnancy, were studied as contributing factors to exceptionalities.

In studying the prenatal problems, it was found that 262 mothers out of a 325 sample did not experience any problems during pregnancy, while of the rest 13 mothers had vaginal bleeding, 9 took medicine, 6 were exposed

TABLE 4.5. Types of Prenatal Problems

Type of pre-natal problem	Frequency	%	Cumulative
Vaginal bleeding	13	4.0	4.0
Taking medicines	9	2.8	6.8
Exposure to X ray	6	1.8	8.6
General bad health	4	1.2	9.8
High blood pressure	3	0.9	10.7
Other problems	7	2.1	12.8
No problems	262	80.6	93.4
Unfilled[a]	21	6.5	100.0
Total	325	100.0	

[a] There were 21 files in which the section on prenatal problems was left blank.

to X rays, and 4 were in general bad health during their pregnancy. Ten mothers had different problems such as high blood pressure, diabetes, or smoking. Table 4.5 shows the types and percentages of problems in the prenatal stage.

Perinatal problems were mainly caused by lack of oxygen, difficult delivery, and jaundice. These affected many newborns as follows: 40 children (12.3 percent) out of 325 disabled children experienced lack of oxygen during delivery, and 7 children (2.2 percent) suffered from jaundice. On the other hand, 277 (85.2 percent) of the disabled children were not exposed to any problems during delivery. Postnatal problems might also play a role in causing disabilities in about one-third of the sample. High fever (13.5 percent), jaundice (3.4 percent), meningitis (2.8 percent), traffic accidents (2.8 percent), and poliomyelitis (2.2 percent) are the major problems that children suffered from after delivery. There were 201 files with no mention of any postnatal problems.

The same study also shows that intermarriage has a major effect in causing disabilities. It was concluded that 141 (43.4 percent) of the disabled children had parents who were cousins. The majority of those (22.2 percent) were first cousins. Third cousins were less (5.8 percent) and second cousins the minority (4 percent). A small number of disabled children (11.4 percent) had parents who were relatives but with type of relationship between them not mentioned in the files. In the case of the parents of a large percentage of disabled children (25.5 percent), it was not known whether they were relatives or not because nothing was mentioned in their files.

The mother's age during pregnancy was also identified in the study. It is well known that there is a correlation between the mother's age and disability since many children with disability are born to mothers ages less than twenty and more than thirty-five years. In the study, fifty-six children (23.4 percent) with disability were born to mothers ages twenty years and below. Another twenty-eight (11.7 percent) were born to mothers aged thirty-five years and above. However, about half of the disabled children (64.9 percent) were born to mothers ages twenty-one to thirty-four. Table 4.6 gathers all the previously mentioned causes or problems that might correlate with disability in the 1992 study. Intermarriage, young mothers, older mothers, postnatal high fever, and lack of oxygen during delivery occur at high rates; therefore, they can be considered major factors linked to disabilities for a large number of children in the sample.

The study also shows a considerable correlation between perinatal problems and cerebral palsy. It was found that twenty-five children with cerebral palsy (16.8 percent) suffered from lack of oxygen during delivery, while 3.4 percent of children were born with jaundice. About 8 percent were born without suffering from any perinatal problems. A high correlation was also identified between cerebral palsy and parents of children with cerebral palsy

TABLE 4.6. Causes of Disability

Causes of Disability	Frequency	Percent
Vaginal bleeding during pregnancy	13	4.0
Taking medicines during pregnancy	9	2.8
Exposure to X ray during pregnancy	6	1.8
Lack of Oxygen during delivery	40	12.3
Born with jaundice	7	2.2
Postnatal high fever	44	13.5
Postnatal jaundice	11	3.4
Postnatal meningitis	9	2.8
Traumas and accidents	9	2.8
Poliomyelitis	7	2.2
Intermarriage	141	43.4
Mothers age 20 years or less	56	23.4
Mothers age 35 years or greater	28	11.7

Note: Causes with percentages of less than 1.5 have not been considered in the table. Missing cases ($N = 86$) were not included in these percentages; valid cases were 239.

who were relatives. It was found that sixty-eight children (58 percent) with cerebral palsy in the study have parents who were first cousins (25 percent), second cousins (6 percent), or third cousins (6 percent). Another 11 percent had parents who were related to each other, but the kind of relationship between them was not identified. On the other hand, 41.9 percent of parents of children with cerebral palsy were not relatives. Thirty-two missing cases were excluded from the percentages.

A considerable correlation was identified between cerebral palsy and a mother's age during pregnancy. It was found that 21 percent of children with cerebral palsy were born to mothers aged twenty years and below. Those without cerebral palsy who were born to mothers of thirty-five years and above were only 9.7 percent. Of children with hearing problems, 42.4 percent were born to mothers ages twenty years and below.

As mentioned earlier, the political situation, the Intifada specifically, has increased the causes of disability. The political situation in the occupied West Bank and Gaza Strip has had an impact on our disabled population and will have major significance for those who may be disabled in the future. According to Shehadeh (1990), the 1987–90 confrontation between Palestinians and Israeli soldiers included the use of plastic, rubber, and high-velocity bullets by the Israelis. This has so far caused approximately 45,000 injuries both in the West Bank and Gaza Strip (casualties both recognized and unrecognized by the Israeli government). The number of admitted casualties in the Gaza Strip as of June 1990 is only 2,699.

The violence has led many people to have one or more physical, mental, or emotional problems. Krammer (1990) argues that there are two forms of violence common to confrontations with the Intifada—"beating and gun-shot"—leading to contusions and wounds, fractures, and central nerve lesions (head and spinal cord injuries).

The political situation (mainly the Intifada confrontations) has affected not only individuals' mental and physical functioning but also their emotional and behavioral well-being. A study carried out in Gaza Strip by Sarraj and Abu-Hein (1992) investigated children's psychological and behavioral responses to trauma. The study was carried out on a random sample of 1,564 children aged eight to fifteen. One part of the study examined the experience of trauma, self-esteem, and the degree of anxiety and fear. The results show that 96.3 percent of the children were exposed to night raids in their homes. As well, 49.8 percent were subjected to physical beatings, and 29 percent were shot and wounded. The results also show a significant positive correlation between personal exposure to trauma and heightened self-esteem. On the other hand, there is a statistically significant correlation between witnessing violence and lowered self-esteem.

Another study was carried out in the West Bank by Khamis (1990) to investigate the psychosocial adjustment among persons with Intifada-related injuries. The study was carried out on a sample of 131 persons, 49 of whom lived in refugee camps, 50 in rural areas, and 32 in urban areas. It was found that persons who had invisible deformities [e.g., emotional problems] were more adjusted than those who had visible deformities, which were manifested in negative self-concept and less approval by others, and typified by feelings of stigma.

A third study was carried out on the same sample by Khamis (1993) in order to investigate posttraumatic stress disorder. It was found that 71 percent in the sample had experienced symptoms of post-traumatic stress disorder and that the trauma had a statistically significant effect on self-concept. These persons showed negative self-concept, experienced more dependency on others and disapproval by others, and exhibited high levels of frustration.

Identification of Exceptional Conditions

One great difficulty facing those professionals who work with persons with disabilities concerns medical screening and high-risk registers. On many occasions, for example, inappropriate or improper screening is given by professionals who are not qualified to do so. The lack of clinics with professionals in the appropriate field leads to improper medical use of screening and high-risk registers. Proper screening is carried out currently by a few neurologists and psychiatrists in their private clinics. However, for the psychoeducational assessment of students with handicapping conditions, there are, as far as the writer's knowledge and experience go, apart from the

Wechsler and Stanford-Binet intelligence scales, no national or international standardized psychoeducational assessment tests for students with handicapping conditions. There is nothing to match the American Association on Mental Deficiency Adaptive Behavioral Scales or any learning disability assessment test. Even the Wechsler and Stanford-Binet IQ tests are standardized in Egypt.

Due to the current political situation, psychological services have been started in the occupied West Bank and Gaza Strip through the work of the Gaza Community Mental Health Program (GCMHP) in the Gaza Strip and the Young Men's Christian Association (YMCA) in Jerusalem. The majority of employees in these programs are psychologists, social workers, and vocational rehabilitation professionals. The main work of these professionals is to visit persons who are experiencing traumatic violence as a result of the Intifada confrontations and to help them to get rid of mental disturbance. Due to the mental disturbance that children suffer from as a result of traumatic experiences, the Gaza Community Mental Health Program has initiated an educational campaign. The groups distribute handouts that explain psychological and behavioral disturbances, their symptoms, and the role of the family in prevention and treatment of these disturbances (Saba 1992).

Labeling Exceptional Conditions

In the absence of a national government in the occupied West Bank and Gaza Strip and due to the fact that there is no legislation in the present educational act that emphasizes education for pupils with disabilities, there are no provisions for labeling children. All persons with mental handicaps are labeled as mentally retarded and all those who have any physical problem are labeled as physically disabled. There is no labeling for those who have hearing and speech disorders, conduct disorders, emotional disorders, and the like. The categorical approaches to the labeling of persons with exceptionalities are only used by professionals and those who are working with such groups of people.

The Social Context of Special Education

Palestinian society, like any other society in the world, is built on certain customs, traditions, beliefs, values, and a unique lifestyle. For example, hiding, rejecting, and neglecting a person with a disability are common phenomenons among Palestinians and express the shame and stigma felt at having such a person. Such an attitude reflects a strong belief that having a person with a disability is a punishment from God to the parents for doing bad things or committing a sin in the past. Another belief teaches that the person with a disability is born with evil wickedness, and, therefore, the parents should keep away from him or her.

According to Saunders (1985), whose information is based on a study about community attitude toward handicaps in the Gaza Strip, a team of workers would frequently encounter cases in which parents were rejecting and neglecting their handicapped children. These parents would express shame and seek to shut out their children. Parents were also identified whose knowledge of handicaps was very limited. Sometimes, disability itself was viewed as a contagious disease and therefore it was believed the unaffected should keep away from it and from people who have it. Some of the mothers, who have been given neither hope nor help by doctors and educators, discussed the problems freely and were interested in whatever advice and help could be offered.

At present, the views of disability and persons with disability have changed—there are less cases of rejection, neglect, viewing disability as a contagious disease, and the like. Parents nowadays talk more openly about their disabled children and the problems they face in coping with them. Many parents do not hide their disabled children anymore, and they send them to community centers and other institutions for help. These centers are the places where parents meet each other and talk about their problems. That does not mean that all archaic attitudes people might have toward both disability and persons with disability have disappeared. A lot of work still has to be done to dispel these attitudes. There are a few major factors that account for the recent changes in views of disability and perceptions of people with disability in Palestinian society. These factors are summarized in the following three sections.

Present Political Situation

Since the beginning of the Palestinian Intifada in 1987, the political situation in the West Bank and Gaza Strip has been in turmoil. Violence has reached a peak through confrontation with the Israeli occupation, causing permanent disability to thousands of young adults. However, being disabled or even injured as a result of a patriotic act is an honor for the people, for those around them, and for the society as a whole.

This has led many other parents to raise their hands and shout, asking for help without being shy. They more readily accept their disabled children. In this respect, the Intifada has played a positive and major role in changing many archaic attitudes that people have toward disability and persons with disability.

The Development of Centralized Rehabilitation Services

In the last ten years, centralized rehabilitation services have impressively improved due to the fact that many people have become aware of the need for a larger quantity of advanced rehabilitation services. An increased number of people have visited these institutions either for rehabilitation or for social services. They see what is being done for people with disability in terms of rehabilitation and various activities and this has helped to change many negative attitudes toward disabilities and those who have them.

The Creation of Decentralized Rehabilitation Services

The increased number of people with disabilities made some of the country's decision makers believe in the idea of community-based rehabilitation. We started implementing it in 1985 in the form of outreach programs. Since then, many communities, with the cooperation of the concerned institutions, have initiated community day-care centers and home-based rehabilitation programs. Initiating a community program usually involves many community members. The involvement of these members in the preparation process and later participation in its activities can help in changing their attitudes. Those community members who participate neither in the preparation process nor in the activities can undergo a change in attitude through listening to those who participate in the program's activities or by observing what is being done.

Educational Activities

The recent changes in views of disability and of people with disability in society is encouraging the education of school-age children with disabilities. The current political situation influences not only special education but also the whole educational system in the country. In the absence of a national government, there is no ministry for education, but there is an educational department controlled by the Israeli authorities which implements educational regulations. This department follows the Jordanian Act regulations that came out more than thirty years ago. Since then, the Ministry of Education in Jordan has made several changes in the old act which, for political reasons, have never been implemented in the West Bank. The old Jordanian educational act does not have any regulation related to special education. Moreover, the Israeli authorities reject any policy, new program, or strategy which leads to improvement of the current situation.

In addition to political factors, economic factors are influencing policy and practice in special education. There is no national government in the country to form a policy in special education and provide for those who need it, and the private Palestinian institutions or agencies cannot afford to carry out such a huge task. There is a newly formed body in the country under the name of the Central National Committee for Rehabilitation, whose task is to coordinate, supervise, and finance, if possible, programs related to the rehabilitation of persons with disabilities in the country. This committee does not, however, have the power yet to impose or make decisions at a national level, nor does it have the financial capabilities to sponsor any large project in special education or rehabilitation as a whole.

Special education in the West Bank and Gaza Strip is practiced in a few institutions by qualified special educators. These professionals apply the theoretical bases of the country from which they graduated. For example, those who graduated from the United States apply what they learned there to the place where they now work; this is also the case with those who graduated from England, Germany, or any other place in the world. Yet, no matter how these professionals were influenced by either American legislation, the British Warnock Report, or other decisions, they are not decision makers and cannot influence Israeli decision makers who refuse, for political reasons, to make any changes in the current educational system.

Legislation and Policies

There is not any legislation of any kind in place for children with exceptionalities due to the absence of a national government in the country. For political reasons, the Israeli authorities have not made, and will not make, any modification to the current educational act.

Teachers, Schools, Curriculum, and Pedagogy

Special education services in the West Bank and Gaza are very limited due to the fact that it is a new field still in its early stages of development and, as mentioned earlier, there is no policy in the area that emphasizes education for children with disabilities. Even children with specific learning difficulties in ordinary schools who make inadequate progress are excluded more often than helped (Saunders 1985).

None of the universities or educational institutes in the country gives certification in special education; the few qualified special educators have received their education in the West. There is also a very small number of uncertified special education teachers in the West Bank and Gaza Strip. They receive some teaching skills through their working experience in the field and/or through informal training from those qualified special educators.

The number of institutions which provided educational programs for different types of disability through 1986, regardless of the effectiveness of those programs, was thirty-seven. The number of school-age children with disabilities in these institutions was 2,907. Table 4.7 shows the number of institutions that serve each type of disability and the number of children served in each institution (Abu-Al-Humos 1990).

The number of professionals who work in such institutions is 243. Of these, 44 percent think that there is a lack of professional people such as psychologists, teachers, special educators, vocational training professionals, and others. However, 55 percent of the institutions/centers think that they have enough specialized personnel. Personnel who work at these institutions receive training courses for a period ranging between one week and four months. According to Abu-Al-Humos (1990), 77 percent of the institutions give training courses for their employees and 94 percent of the employees respond positively to these courses. The training courses are given in different fields which may include special education, deaf education, physiotherapy, and the like.

It has been found that 33 percent of the employees have high school qualifications (*Tawjihi*), 38 percent have diplomas in a related or unrelated field, and 29 percent have bachelor's degrees in related or unrelated fields. Fifty percent of the employees have a minimum of one year experience working with persons with disabilities (Abu-Al-Humos 1990).

According to Fasheh (1990), nineteen institutions and centers serve persons with mental handicaps in the West Bank. There are six centers in Jerusalem area, five in the Nablus area, four in the Bethlehem area, two in Ramallah, and two in the Hebron area. Ten of these centers are sponsored by local Palestinian charitable societies, one by a local Palestinian private society, five by foreign private agencies, one by the Israeli department of social welfare, and two by the Ministry of Education and Jerusalem Municipality. Almost all of these institutions or centers have educational programs for their school-age children. Gaza Strip also has a few centers serving persons with disabilities, the majority of whom suffer from mental handicaps. There are no figures that show the number of centers or institutions.

TABLE 4.7. Number of Institutions and Children Served, by Disability Type

Type of Disability	Number of Institutions	Number of Disabled Served	% of Total Disability
Hearing impairment	5	167	5.7
Visual impairment	7	304	10.5
Mental handicap	12	339	11.7
Motor disability	6	1438	49.5
Multiple handicap	7	659	22.7
Total	37	2907	

According to Abu-Ghazaleh et al. (1990), persons who suffer from mental retardation constitute the largest number of those with disabilities. Many of the centers are community day centers, which means that clients in each of these centers mainly come from the same community, and are integrated in their communities. Nevertheless, in these day centers the students are segregated from normal children who attend ordinary schools.

The idea of creating a community special education center for teaching children with mental retardation was initiated by the Bethlehem Arab Society for Rehabilitation in 1986 in El-Khader village in greater Bethlehem. A few years before that, a school for teaching children with hearing impairment had been initiated in Bethlehem city (this school is currently sponsored by Italy). Greater Bethlehem area alone currently has four community day centers which provide special education for children with mental handicaps, hearing impairments, and learning disabilities. In addition to these centers, another four will be completely set up in different Greater Bethlehem communities in 1993. These four centers, like the first four, will be set up by the Bethlehem Arab Society for Rehabilitation.

The effectiveness of special education differs from one place to another and from one center to another in the West Bank and Gaza Strip. Since the time children gain instruction in special education does not exceed a few years (around four years), it is very rare to find an effective special education program in the country. Many teachers think that they are practicing special education, but what they are actually doing is very far from special education. In a few places where qualified special educators who received their education in the West work, many skills in the field of special education are being implemented. These qualified special educators assess children, organize programs, and train and supervise other teachers to implement the programs. Special education programs are implemented using the behavioral approach, which is based on task analysis and behavioral targets.

The special education programs are provided through private institutions because, in the absence of a national government in the country, the Israeli educational system provides no special education for the occupied territories. Therefore, the normal support systems available in Western society do not exist.

Major Controversies and Issues in Special Education

Mainstreaming is a very recent idea in the West Bank and Gaza Strip. Therefore, not much has been done about it. However, mainstreaming here simply means the education of persons with disability in ordinary schools together with normal students.

Recent research was carried out by Dukmak (1991) to study the attitudes of school directors toward integrating children with disabilities in mainstream schools of the greater Bethlehem area in the West Bank. The research included twenty-seven government and private schools in different cities, villages, and refugee camps in the greater Bethlehem area. The results show that 89 percent of the interviewed directors accepted the idea of beginning a class for pupils with disabilities in their schools. Another 11 percent did not accept it. They believed that they were not prepared for integration at the moment and that integration has a negative influence on normal children. In the same study, 78 percent of the directors thought that teachers and pupils would accept integration, and 48 percent thought that the idea would be accepted by parents.

In this study, 96 percent of the directors thought that the lack of financial support and trained teachers would constitute major obstacles to integration. Other problems they mentioned were lack of games and sports facilities, lack of transportation to and from school, and lack of medical or health care units in the school which would be urgently needed for those students with health problems. In respect to the schools' accessibility, it was found that 96 percent of directors thought that the physical environment of their schools had to be made accessible in order to receive pupils with disabilities, especially those who suffer from motor problems (Dukmak 1991).

Recommendations were suggested to implement the integration program. Crucial were the financial support needed for training courses, accessibility of schools, salaries for teachers, and the like. Other suggestions included lectures, study days, and visits to institutions that house people with disabilities for those directors, teachers, pupils, and parents who have negative attitudes toward integration.

This study was initiated before carrying out any integration project in mainstream schools. However, since completing the study and obtaining the results, four pilot projects to integrate pupils with disabilities in mainstream schools have started in the West Bank. The first project has been carried out by the United Nations Relief and Works Agency (UNRWA), following the writer's recommendations. This project took the form of two special education classrooms in two UNRWA schools in Fawar refugee camp in the Hebron area of the West Bank. These two classrooms serve about thirty pupils. Some have learning disabilities and some have mild mental retardation. These pupils have been assessed by the writer together with a psychologist from Catholic Relief Services (CRS), and an educational program for each pupil has been planned accordingly. Programs are implemented individually by teachers who have been trained in special education and, so far, the pupils have made considerable progress. It is worth mentioning here that a pupil's attendance at the special education class depends on the child's difficulties, so some pupils attend once a week, some twice a week, and others most of the week. Nevertheless, all pupils, no matter how profound their degree of disability, should attend classes in their ordinary school.

The second pilot project was carried out by the Bethlehem Arab Society for Rehabilitation under the supervision of the writer. This project took the form of setting up a community special education center in Nahalin village in greater Bethlehem. The center was set up as a result of the Israeli Education Authority's refusal to start special education classes in its schools in Nahalin. There are no private schools in the village. The center serves pupils with mild and moderate mental retardation as well as pupils with learning disabilities. The majority of pupils come daily to the center for a minimum of three hours after they finish schooling in their ordinary school. These pupils have experienced very serious difficulties in their ordinary schools and, as a result, many of them left their schools for a while. They went back to school once the center opened and are currently making satisfactory progress. Hence, as a result of opening the center, pupils with disabilities are kept integrated into their ordinary schools.

The third type of integration program for children with disability in the West Bank and Gaza Strip was initiated by CRS in 1986 as a home-based rehabilitation program. The philosophy behind this program is that institutions, no matter how large they are, cannot receive all persons with disabilities from the region. In addition, institutions segregate persons from their families and can destroy individual-family ties. This does not mean ignoring the role of institutions because there will always be a need for these institutions for difficult cases which cannot be served in the community, and for referral to for more comprehensive services.

This home-based rehabilitation program, which mainly serves children, is found in a few communities in the West Bank and Gaza. Each child in the program is visited at least once a week by a home-based teacher or rehabilitation worker who works with both the child and the family. The teacher prepares lessons for attaining three to five objectives in the areas of self-help, cognition, fine motor, gross motor, and social skills to be taught to the child by the mother. The following week the teacher visits the child again to evaluate the work of the mother and see how much progress the child has made. The teacher/rehabilitation worker also works on changing negative social attitudes that family members might have toward disability and persons with disabilities. The teacher does not leave the family unless he or she is sure that the family, mainly the mother, can cope with and teach her child in an appropriate way. Follow-up with the family once every two or three months afterwards by the teacher is very important.

Teachers or rehabilitation workers who make these visits are usually employed by the institutions in the area regardless of the communities these teachers come from. There is an effort nowadays which emphasizes that these home-based teachers or rehabilitation workers should work in their communities and be paid by their communities too. They know their communities more than anyone else and are well known by people there which can facilitate their work. This is real community-based rehabilitation, different from the outreach approach to community service. There is a plan nowadays to initiate such programs in each community in the West Bank and Gaza Strip.

The fourth type of integration program for persons with disability was initiated by the Bethlehem Arab Society for Rehabilitation in 1986. It took the form of establishing a community-based rehabilitation day center in El-Khader village of the greater Bethlehem area. The idea behind this center is to keep disabled persons in their community rather than taking them to an institution in the city and segregating them from family and community. The clients in the center receive education (within the existing special education services) and other rehabilitation services that are available. This type of center mainly receives clients with the moderate category of disability but sometimes with the severe category too. This depends on the staff and quality of services provided.

The Bethlehem Arab Society strategy in these centers is to set up the center after initiation by the community itself, and with the community's cooperation. After two to three years of training and experience, the local committee takes over the center's administrative and financial responsibility, leaving the professional role to the Bethlehem Arab Society. There are currently four centers in the greater Bethlehem area (there will be eight in a few months) professionally supervised by the Bethlehem Arab Society. These exist along with other centers which are supervised by other institutions in the West Bank.

The majority of funding for all these programs, both centralized and decentralized, came from foreign agencies. Currently, a few-income generating projects have started making some profit which will be used for rehabilitation services. Rehabilitation and social services are mainly given to children with disabilities as well as to poor people. There are no provisions of any kind for children, parents, or the state to receive services or allowances of any kind from the Israeli government.

Emerging and Future Trends

The state of special education in the occupied West Bank and Gaza Strip is evolving in several directions. One step concerns training in special education. A committee of special educators has been established at the University of Bethlehem to plan a diploma course in special education for pupils with disabilities. Bethlehem University is a private agency. If the university obtains the needed financial support and teaching personnel, it can adopt such a training course, but it cannot set up a policy or legislation to implement special education at the national level, which can only be done through a national government mandate.

The study of the attitudes of school directors toward mainstreaming (Dukmak 1991) and the two pilot mainstreaming projects in private schools have led to a plan to begin a classroom for pupils with learning difficulties in each private school in the greater Bethlehem area. Since there is no national government, the Bethlehem Arab Society for Rehabilitation, as a national body, should be very soon carrying a campaign to people, teachers, and school directors to show them the necessity of beginning a classroom in each private school, starting with Bethlehem region. The Bethlehem Arab Society for Rehabilitation can provide full supervision and training to upgrade the skills of the teachers involved.

Spreading the idea of a home-based rehabilitation program in the occupied West Bank and Gaza Strip can help develop the role of special education in the rehabilitation process. A few national bodies, such as Medical Relief Committees and the Bethlehem Arab Society for Rehabilitation, together with a few international bodies, such as Diakonia (a Swedish organization) and Catholic Relief Services, are carrying out a campaign to encourage people and direct them to support such a program. All these organizations have, so far, made good progress.

References

Abu-Al-Humos, N. 1990. *The reality of educational institutions for people with disability in the West Bank and Gaza Strip*. The Association of University Graduates, Educational paper no. 7. Hebron, The West Bank, Research Center.

Abu-Ghazaleh, H., et al. 1990. Primary and secondary prevention services provided to mentally handicapped infants, children, and youth in the Gaza Strip. *International Journal of Special Education* 5 (1):21–27.

Baker, A. 1988. Informal educational program in the occupied West Bank and Gaza Strip. Research paper. Bir Zeit University.

Ballantyne, S. 1988. *Physiotherapy—fact finding visit to the West Bank and Gaza Strip*. Final report, December.

Benevenisti, M. 1984. *U.S.A. governmental funded projects in the West Bank and Gaza (1977–1983) (Palestinian Sector)*. Working paper no. 13. 1984, the West Bank Data Base Project.

Dukmak, S. 1991. The integration in education for school age children with disabilities in the West Bank. A paper presented at the second Biennial Conference on Special Education, May, Milwaukee, Wis.

El-imili, J. 1984. A statistical research on disability in the West Bank. A study carried out under the supervision of four institutions in the area: Bethlehem Arab Society for

Rehabilitation, Mental Health Society, Friends of the Sick Society, and Palestine Counseling Center.

Fasheh, V. 1990. Need assessment for sheltered workshops for mentally handicapped adults in the West Bank. A study supported by AMIDEAST, Jerusalem.

Galloway, D., and Goodwin, C. 1979. *Educating slow learning and maladjusted children: Integration or segregation.* United Kingdom: Group Limited.

Giacaman, R. 1989. *Towards the formulation of a rehabilitation policy: Disability in the West Bank.* West Bank: Bir Zeit University.

Hegarty, S. 1987. *Special needs in ordinary schools: Meeting special needs in ordinary schools.* United Kingdom: Cassel Educational Limited.

Helender, E., et al. 1989. *Training in the community for people with disabilities.* Training manual. Geneva: World Health Organization.

Ingram, M., et al. 1985. *Notes on psychiatry.* 6th ed.. United Kingdom: Churchill Livingstone.

Khamis, V. 1990. Victims of the Intifada: The psychosocial adjustment of the injured. Paper presented at the Annual Conference of the Naim Foundation and Georgetown University on Culture, Conflict and Trauma, October, Washington D.C.

———. 1993. Post-traumatic stress disorder among the injured of the Intifada. *Journal of Traumatic Stress.*

Krammer, U. 1990. Medical study on the Physiotherapy Emergency Programme in Gaza Strip. Study funded by UNICEF and administrated by UNRWA.

Miles, M. 1985. Where there is no rehabilitation plan. Report. Peshawar, Pakistan.

Saba, R. 1992. *Gaza community mental health program newsletter*, no. 3. West Bank: The Benevolent Society Print.

Sarraj, E., and Abu-Hein, F. 1992. Trauma violence and children: The Palestinian experience. *Gaza Community Mental Health Program Newsletter*, no. 3, July. West Bank: The Benevolent Society Print.

Saunders, C. A. 1985. *Prevalence of handicapping conditions affecting children and a case finding intervention in the refugee camp population of Gaza Strip.* Gaza Strip: The Society for the Care of Handicapped Children.

Shehadeh, E. 1989. Rehabilitation under occupation. A paper presented at the International Meeting on Human Resources in the Field of Disability, August 1989, Talliu, Estonian Soviet Socialist Republic, USSR.

———. 1990. The maimed of the Intifida: Meeting the challenge. Paper presented at the Second Annual Conference of the Naim Foundation and Georgetown University on Culture, Conflict, and Trauma, October, Washington, D.C.

The Society for the Care of the Handicapped in the Gaza Strip. 1988. Training and education of rehabilitation personnel in the Gaza Strip: A programme leading to self-sufficient services. Project proposal.

PART 2

EMERGING SPECIAL EDUCATION

Disabled students integrated into a regular classroom in Santa Catarina, Brazil. PHOTO BY Lucia Dellagnelo

Training for visual-perceptual development at the Fatima Jinnah Centre for Mentally Retarded Children in Islamabad, Pakistan. PHOTO BY Mah Nazir Riaz

*F*our striking characteristics of the countries represented in part II are perhaps readily apparent. First, these are populous nations. In combination, they are home to the majority of the world's population. Second, these nations are extremely diverse regions characterized by marked geographic and ethnic differences. Third, some 80 percent of the world's people with disabilities live in these countries. Finally, of the estimated ten million blind persons in the world today, the great majority live in countries of the Third World (see Ahuja 1990). The numbers of persons with disabilities resulting from extrinsic causes may be rising in these regions as well. For example, Africa's population growth is the world's fastest (the average family has six children). Today about one hundred million Africans are malnourished; the World Bank estimates that by the end of the decade the number of Africans living in extreme poverty will have increased by 50 percent.

However, our underlying reasons for grouping these nations together are not those mentioned so far. There are a number of other, and for the purposes of this text, more fundamental common threads linking Nigeria, the Islamic Republic of Iran, Brazil, Indonesia, Egypt, Pakistan, China, India, and Uruguay. The first similarity is actually an extension of one of the organizing principles of part I. That is, many of the nations within this section are also grappling with the huge problem of trying to provide universal access to elementary education for their populations. Nevertheless, great as the obstacles to accomplishing this primary objective are, the countries in this section have already clearly demonstrated their political will to provide basic educational rehabilitation services for their special needs population. However, because the continuing battle to provide for the basic educational needs of the normal population has not yet been won, the realization of these nations' explicit goals for meeting the needs of its citizens with special needs is continually frustrated and progress is painfully slow. Thus, from the standpoint of fulfillment of a common goal, the nations in part II differ from those in part I essentially in degree. Whereas the nations in part I are consumed by the Herculean task of working toward universal access to schools to the point where they have yet to focus their attention on their special needs populations, the nations in part II are also fighting the same uphill battle but are already planning ahead to tackle the next obstacle—that of providing educational services for disabled persons.

Second, each of these countries was, to a greater or lesser extent, influenced by the mandate of the 1981 Year of the Disabled. This served as a reference point and an inspiration for initiatives in special education in each of these countries.

Third, each of these nations has promulgated national legislation directly aimed at special education. However, because internally these nations are economically, demographically, and geographically diverse, there are significant regional discrepancies in the strength, focus, and implementation of polices and practices. Moreover, the breadth and the depth of legislation and policies differ. For example, although the constitution of India refers to the rights of disabled persons and there are national policies dealing with special education, there is no encompassing enabling legislation at the national level. However, India is a decentralized nation, and in some of its states strong policies dealing with special education are in place. In the case of Pakistan, we see that by l986 a stated set of objectives was in place that constituted a coherent policy in regard to special education. Since the People's Republic of China passed the Compulsory Education Act in 1986 and implemented the Five-Year Plan for the Disabled (1991–92), special education has developed dramatically (Chen 1991). Both the act and the plan focus on increasing the number of children with disabilities attending public school. Although these laws focus primarily on school-age children, recent years have witnessed increased attention to the needs of infants and preschoolers with disabilities (Wang and Rule 1992).

The severity of the problems to be solved is well documented in each chapter. For example, the normal Indo-Pakistan education system expects a heavy dropout rate at every level since places are provided for only a fraction of those who want them (Miles 1989b). The chapter on Pakistan speaks to the 84 percent of women in that country who remain illiterate; the chapter on China discusses the 20 percent illiteracy rate of the rural Chinese population. Another author cautions that the "faltering" school system in Brazil is simply unable to keep pace with the demands of the growing population. In such circumstances, in spite of these nations' political and legislative commitments to addressing the needs of their special needs population, it is obvious that the priority of providing for the regular population is frustrating the desire to make significant progress on the special needs front.

Cautious optimism is apparent in some of the case studies. Indonesia provides an excellent illustration. Following the revolution which began in 1945 and the attainment of independence in 1949, Indonesia struggled to unify itself as a country and to organize an infrastructure for the provision of public services and national order. Twenty years ago, universal education was a dream. Even so, the government was able to provide teachers and buildings in sufficient numbers and today claims nearly universal primary education (Carpenter 1987). In Indonesia, the current five-year plan targets providing educational services to 30 percent of the population of children with handicaps by 1990 and service to 100 percent by 1995.

Currently, the eradication of illiteracy and of the preventable causes of disabilities in the general population are the two major fronts on which the nations in this section have taken vigorous action. Consequently, in each of these case studies, the authors discuss the impact of a large illiterate population upon special education. They also focus on the preventable nature of many disabilities. The chapter on Nigeria, for example, details the devastating effects of leprosy, tuberculosis, trachoma, waterborne blindness, and other preventable causes. Because causes such as leprosy, tuberculosis, and trachoma are so prevalent, preventative and vaccination programs form the core of special education and remediation, and the distribution of accurate health information is a central priority. It is upon these foundation blocks that the special education commitments of these nations are being constructed.

References

Ahuja, S. C. 1990. Rehabilitation of visually handicapped Indians: The problem and the numbers. *Journal of Visual Impairment and Blindness.* 270–73.

Carpenter, R. L. 1987. Special education teacher preparation and service delivery in a developing country: Indonesia. *Teacher Education and Special Education* 10:37–43.

Chen, Y. Y. 1991. Special education in China. Paper presented at the International Conference on Mental Retardation, April, Hong Kong.

5

Nigeria

THERESA B. ABANG

Nigeria gained its independence from Britain in October 1960. Since independence, Nigeria has been ruled by eight different governments—six military and two constitutionally elected. The current military government is setting the stage for the third constitutionally elected civilian government. Today, Nigeria has twenty-one states and more than 120 million people with 250 ethnic and language groups (Obiakor 1991).

Special education is a fairly new phenomenon in the Nigerian educational system (Obiakor 1985). Since 1948, Nigeria has seen sporadic attempts to initiate special education programs. The earliest schools owe their beginnings to mission and humanitarian groups (Ojile 1989). In the last decade, despite cultural, socioeconomic, and political constraints, great strides have been taken in special education in Nigeria. Many problems still exist, however, especially in the placement of special education within the general education system and the establishment of a suitable philosophy that will reflect all the basic structures of the system (Obiakor 1985).

About the Author • Theresa Abang is a Nigerian, born in a little town in Bokyi Local Government of Cross River State. She started her teaching profession with normal children and later switched to working with children with special needs. Her early training was in the education of blind children at the College of Teachers of the Blind in Great Britain. She later went to the United States where she obtained bachelor's and master's degrees at the Catholic University of America and a doctorate at the American University.

In 1980, she started the Department of Special Education at the University of Jos, Plateau State, Nigeria, and in 1987 she became the first professor of special education in Nigeria. Her numerous positions in the University of Jos have included head of department and dean. Sr. Theresa is a Catholic Sister in the Congregation of the Handmaids of the Holy Child Jesus. She is the first female religious to achieve such an academic position in Nigeria. She is the author of many books and journal articles including *Handbook of Special Education for Educators in Developing Countries* and *Handbook for Special Education for the Visually Handicapped*.

In September 1976, Nigeria took a giant step for all children with the institution of the Universal Primary Education Program aimed at eradicating illiteracy, ignorance, and superstition. At about the same time, more structured policies concerning the education and training of persons with special needs were initiated. Legal provision and necessary funds were made available within the framework of the Universal Primary Education Program.

Prevalence of Exceptional Conditions

One of the greatest tragedies in human terms is that in developing countries thousands of people of all ages are plagued by preventable diseases that cause death and various forms of disabilities. Disease brought about by bacterial infections is a major cause of disabilities. In Nigeria today tribal wars, ignorance, and poverty are also responsible for various disabilities. In fact, Ojile (1989) argues that at the end of the Nigerian civil war in 1970 there were many young disabled persons. Some were deaf from the impact of explosions, others blind or retarded from illness, malnutrition, and infectious diseases occurring in the war camps. Others were crippled from wounds sustained in the war. The belief that rehabilitation for these individuals rested on educational provisions prompted provisions within the Universal Primary Education Act of 1976.

Mental disabilities, sensory impairments, and physical handicaps are prominent among the disabled population of Nigeria. Some etiologies are restricted to regions of Africa. Some, sadly, are quite preventable.

Visual impairments are common and attributed to diverse etiologies. Onchocerciasis, also known as river blindness, is a disease caused by the nematode worm (*Onchocerca volvulus*) that is transmitted by a form of blackfly (simulium). The victim of this fly suffers intense itching, disfiguring skin changes, and eye problems which eventually lead to loss of vision. It happens that this disease, which generally attacks young children, is accompanied by a high temperature, after which a rash appears on the child's body. Sometimes the rash gets into the eyes of the victim and, if not adequately treated by a medical doctor, can result in blindness. This generally happens when the parents of the child resort to herbal treatment in which the herbalist gets some herbs, rubs them between his palms, and applies some drops into the child's eyes.

In this and other cases, the application of herbs to the eyes can be extremely dangerous. I recall an incident where a lady who went to a farm to collect some wood to make a fire accidentally got a piece of wood in her eye. After she removed the little speck from her eye, she thought it would have a cooling effect to apply some drops extracted from nearby herbs. This she did, but the eye began to swell by the minute. Less than forty-eight hours after she applied the herbs, the pressure in the eye was so intense that the eye exploded, and the eyeball popped out from the socket and was hanging on her chest. Fortunately, her son rushed her to an eye hospital where the eye was removed.

Another method of eye treatment sometimes used in the villages is to apply palm wine to the eyes. It is believed that palm wine has a lot of yeast and that this is good for the eyes. There may be some merits in this argument. But although positive results have been recorded in this method of treatment, it most often results in blindness.

Onchocerciasis occurs in Africa, Central and South America, and the Eastern Mediterranean countries of Yemen and Sudan. Ninety million people are at risk in these regions. There are twenty million infected cases, and 95 percent of these occur in Africa alone. In Africa where it is most predominant, onchocerciasis is found in Senegal, Guinea, Mali, Volta, River Basin, Upper Volta, Ivory Coast, Ghana, Togo, Dahomey, Nigeria, Cameroon, Chad, Zaire, the Central African Republic of Sudan, Uganda, Abyssinia, and Tanzania (Bisley 1981).

A survey in Ghana, Upper Volta, and Mali revealed that in a population of 3,020,000, there were 498,000 persons infected with onchocerciasis. Of these, 21,860, or 4 percent, were blinded by the disease. About 20 to 25 percent of people over thirty were blind. Seven million people in Nigeria are estimated to be infected with the worm; 120,000 Nigerians are estimated to be blinded by the disease.

Measles is another cause of blindness in Nigeria. It remains prevalent although currently being brought under control under the expanded immunization program.

Trachoma is another eye disease that can result in blindness. The cause is chlamydial: microorganisms infect the conjunctiva, the lining of the lid, and cornea. Trachoma thrives mostly in overcrowded areas so it is common in the northern part of Nigeria. Often families are large and room space small. Sometimes there are many people crowded in a single room, sharing beds or sleeping mats. At other times articles of clothing are shared, including towels. When healthy individuals come in contact with these infected items, they also get infected.

Malnutrition is the leading cause of preventable blindness among young children in developing countries. Nutritional blindness is brought about by the lack of vitamin A which leads to dryness of the eye (xerophthalmia), followed by softening of the cornea (keratomalacia). Failure to consume foods such as fish, vegetables, eggs, and others rich in vitamin A may result in this problem. The first two years of life are the most critical years. The first sign of the problem is night blindness and sensitivity to light. As it progresses, a white foamy spot on the white part of the eye appears. The eyes lose their shine and become rough and dry. The cornea becomes scarred, impairing vision, and finally softens and ruptures, leaving the victim totally blind. In the early state, the condition can be reversed with vitamin A therapy. However, once blindness occurs, sight cannot be restored—the child will be blind throughout life.

Blindness is not the only disabling condition in Nigeria. A major cause of physical disabilities is poliomyelitis. This is the crippling disease that has caused many African children, including those in Nigeria, to become physically disabled. Poliomyelitis is an infectious, potentially disabling disease, brought about by one of three types of ultramicroscopic virus. The virus enters the body through the mouth—by way of contaminated food, water, or a utensil—in hand-to-mouth contact. It can also be contracted by inhalation. The virus then grows and multiplies in the throat or cells lining the intestinal tract and may make its way to the bloodstream. When it reaches the nerve cells in the spinal cord, it also multiplies there, feeding on the nerve cells themselves. When a majority of the nerve cells that control motion are affected, paralysis occurs. Nerve cells that are destroyed are lost forever, since they cannot be regenerated by the body.

What is most disheartening is the fact that this disease can be easily prevented and the disability averted. In the past, through carelessness and ignorance, these children were not taken for immunization until the disease struck. At this point it may be too late to save the child. The medical personnel may only succeed in saving the child's life, but the disease leaves the child with one or both legs crippled.

Although there was a high incidence of polio in Nigeria, this is now under control. Still, there are occasional outbreaks of the disease in the north of Nigeria. The reason for the rapid spread may be attributed to the hot weather. The outbreak generally occurs during the hot seasons.

As well as diseases, injections of heavy antibiotics, generally given in an effort to treat fevers, render hundreds of children paralyzed. Some of these fevers could very well be treated with drugs taken orally to minimize the possibilities of paralysis. It is hoped that the treatment with oral drugs will be administered more readily than injections.

Schistosomiasis, commonly known as bilharzia, is another cause of disability in Nigeria. The disease is endemic, not only in Nigeria but in other Third-World countries. It is estimated that about three million people are affected in western Nigeria alone. In one state in the north of Nigeria, 78 percent of the population has been recorded as having urinary schistosomiasis (Ajayi 1992). The disease renders most of its victims disabled and hence reduces productivity.

Dracunculiasis is also known as guinea worm infection. It is more rampant in the tropical regions of the world, notably in Pakistan, India, and East and West Africa. An estimated 130 million people in Africa and Asia are at risk from the infection (Ajayi 1992). Guinea worm infection is prevalent in about nineteen African countries, of which Nigeria is one. In fact, Nigeria has about 60 percent of the world's cases of guinea worm infections. It has an estimate of 2.5 million cases annually and an estimated population at risk of 7 million. Permanent disabilities occur in about 5,000 persons annually (Ajayi 1992).

Olrunyomi (1982) reveals that in the Plateau State of Nigeria, in five local government areas—namely, Awe, Nassarawa, Keffi, Lafia, and Shendam—a total of 11,812 active cases were identified in 1988. One of Nigeria's leading papers, the *Nigerian Concord,* reported that up to 1,000 people were down with guinea worm in about seventy villages of Packero local government of Niger State (30 March 1992). According to the chairman of the local government, Alaji Danjuma Baba, the local government's economy has been grossly affected by the inability of farmers to go to the farm due to sores brought about by guinea worms.

When people are affected by guinea worm infections, the worms form itchy blisters in the affected area. These blisters then break open, causing ulcers. Attempts to extract the worms may lead to some serious consequences. Dracunculiasis can be very disabling; it can sometimes result in amputation of the affected limb. The disease leaves most of its victims unable to engage in any useful work. Their feet are all sores, and they can hardly walk.

In one way, dracunculiasis can be said to be a neglected cause of disabilities in Nigeria and many other developing countries of the world. On the other hand, the number of sufferers in Nigeria has been greatly reduced due to the aggressive measures the state governments have taken to combat the crippling disease. The local government, with the assistance of Peace Corps volunteers from the United States, are also doing their best to fight the disease. Two thousand water filters have been distributed to the people in the affected area to ensure good drinking water. Drugs costing four hundred thousand naira have also been distributed to the affected victims.

One of the tragedies of this century is that forty years after the discovery of a cure for tuberculosis, the disease, which was thought to be retreating, has come back in full swing. Tuberculosis, or TB as it is commonly known, is caused by a tiny rod-shaped bacillus. It is a debilitating disease which leaves many of its victims crippled. It can affect several parts of the body including the lungs, causing wasting of the lung tissue and even resulting in death. It can also attack the glands causing lumps on the neck or the armpits. These lumps may burst and result in sores. Bones and joints can be attacked, causing crippling of hips and knees or painful deformity of the spine. The president of the Lung Association said recently that twenty million people in the world today suffer from the disease.

Meningitis is another disease responsible for disabilities in Nigeria. It is better termed, however, meningoencephalitis. The disease is defined as an inflammation of the meninges. When the Piarachnoid is congested and infiltrated with inflammatory cells, a thin layer of pus forms, which may later result in adhesions. This, in turn, causes obstruction of the flow of cerebrospinal fluid and can lead to hydrocephalus. Damage to the cranial nerves at the base of the brain may then result.

There are often outbreaks of meningitis in the Northern part of Nigeria. When this occurs, it leaves behind deaths and disabilities. If not promptly treated, it may result in permanent neurological sequelae, or death. When victims survive, possible complications include seizures, subdural effusion, minimal brain dysfunction syndrome, mild to severe mental retardation, cerebral palsy, hearing and visual loss, and motor deficits including hemiparesis.

The word *leprosy* originates from the Latin word *lepra* meaning scaly skin. The disease is one of the most dreaded in the world though it is less infectious than tuberculosis. There are over ten million people with the disease. However, because of the taboo associated with it, the true dimension of the problem in any country is generally not disclosed and thus is not reflected in official statistics. The majority of the victims live in the tropical regions of the world. India has about one quarter of all the leprosy victims. There is also a high prevalence of the disease in Southeast Asia and Africa, and it is also found in moderately high rates in Central and South America. Nigeria and Zaire have a high incidence rate. However, due to the introduction of modern drugs, the rate in Nigeria is being greatly reduced.

Leprosy is caused by bacteria known as *Mycobacterium leprae*. There are two types of leprosy: tuberculoid and lepromatous. The first symptom of the tuberculoid type is a reddish patch on the skin. If not treated, the disease spreads, destroying peripheral nerve tissue, and causing a loss of muscle power and lack of sensitivity to temperature and pain. The affected part of the skin can be placed over a flame and no pain is experienced. Consequently, as the victim accidentally burns insensitive areas, they result in ulcers and subsequent infection. In the lepromatous type of leprosy, the bacillus multiplies and causes nerve damage. Nodules form, eyebrows are lost, eye and nose damage occurs. There is a thickening and loosening of facial skin which gives a "lion like" appearance.

The disease leaves most of its victims disabled, often leading to such deformities as loss of fingers, toes, and eyesight. The disease is believed to be spread by contact with open lesions. Transmission is relatively common among parents, and children, husbands, and wives. It is not common between health workers and patients.

Otitis media is a middle ear infection. It is a common cause of hearing impairment among school-age children in Nigeria and in most African countries. When the middle ear is infected, bacteria travels up the Eustachian tube. The mucosa of the middle ear gets inflamed and thickens. When this happens, the space inside it is filled with pus. In most cases, the eardrum swells and perforates, and deafness can result.

Preventive Measures

To prevent such disabilities, immunization against the diseases that cause them are being vigorously pursued. With the launching of the campaign on immunization, the six killer diseases in Nigeria will be reduced or eradicated in the near future. These diseases are meningitis, tuberculosis, whooping cough, diphtheria, poliomyelitis, and measles. The number of children with disabilities will be greatly reduced when all people learn the importance of inoculation against these diseases. There is also immunization against tetanus, and a lot of effort is being made by the federal and state governments to minimize, if not eradicate, guinea worm infection in Nigeria by the year 2000. Among the four diseases of great concern to the World Health Organization (WHO) are trachoma, onchocerciasis, xerophthalmia, and cataract. These diseases have rendered twenty-six million people blind. The nutritional program organized by WHO has gone a long way to reduce the incidence of disabilities caused by nutritional anemia, goiter, and xerophthalmia.

The expanded program on immunization (EPI), embarked upon to fight the six killer and child-crippling diseases in Nigeria, is a bold and laudable step by the Nigerian government. According to the *Nigerian Concord,* more than one million were saved from death and disabilities in two years through the EPI program. Before the introduction of the program, two thousand children were killed annually or rendered disabled by these diseases.

There is a nationwide campaign to inform the Nigerian people of the importance of immunization. This campaign is carried out in the mother tongue of the people in the form of advertisements in marketplaces, churches, and mosques. Television and radio are also used as media for jingles and speeches. The immunizations are free to the people—the government is responsible for the cost.

The credit for this project goes to the health minister, Ransome Kuti, who has worked very hard to see that the program on immunization succeeds through his Primary Health Program. More importantly, the United Nations International Children's Educational Fund (UNICEF) made available seventy million U.S. dollars to the Organization for the Combating of Children's Communicable Diseases (OCCCD) since it started operation in 1987 in Nigeria. This was reported in one of Nigeria's newspapers, *The Nigerian Standard* (30 July 1992).

Identification of Exceptional Children

The identification of children with disabilities has in the past been done primarily by pediatricians during hospital and clinic visits. This is true only for those who care to bring their children to the clinics. This is just a small group—other parents resort to diviners to reveal to them why their child behaves the way he or she does and whether the child has a disability.

Children's disabilities that are easily identified are Down's syndrome and physical handicaps such as poliomyelitis. When there is a doubt in respect to the child's vision, the child is referred to the ophthalmologist for a proper examination of eyesight, and it is these physicians who identify partially blind and blind children.

Parents may be the first to notice that their child falls well behind in many aspects of daily living when compared with siblings and other children of their age. This is often true of the hearing handicapped. The parents may be the first to notice that the child does not react to loud noises as most children do. They may also notice that the child does not notice their presence as other children do. When they smile at the child, the child does not respond. When parents notice these behaviors, they are advised to take the child to a pediatrician or audiologist for a comprehensive test.

Another method of identifying children with problems is to send them to centers where screening is routinely done to identify certain disabilities. In the Faculty of Education of the University of Jos, there is an assessment unit for the hearing handicapped, the visually impaired, and children with learning disabilities.

Sometimes the disabilities of a child may not be identified until the child comes to school and begins to show signs of existing problems. It is here that the classroom teacher refers a child to a diagnostic center. Unfortunately, when a disability is not noticed until the child gets to school, it may have become too advanced for easy treatment. Remediation then becomes a difficult and sometimes impossible task.

Early identification is helping to determine and alleviate many future disabilities in Nigeria. However, early detection and diagnostic services are only available in some urban centers and through the primary health care program which is carried out into the rural villages. There is a plan by the Federal Ministry of Education to establish assessment centers in various parts of the country. This is an indication that the Nigerian government is making efforts to prevent disabilities among its children.

The federal government and the special education departments in some states run psychoeducational services whereby school-age children are assessed and appropriately placed. Some special schools do carry out their own assessment and placement exercises before admitting the children to the school.

Labeling the Handicapped Population

In Nigeria, there are just a few, poorly defined categories of exceptionality. Ogbue (1975, 1981) noted that the categories are the blind and partially sighted; the deaf and partially hearing; the physically handicapped; the mentally retardates; and hospitalized children. The National Policy on Education (1975) recognized the gifted and talented in its Section 8. There is still a question of how these exceptional individuals are to be identified.

It appears that extreme cases of disability are given more attention. These individuals are frequently placed in institutions or residential settings (Obiakor et al. 1991) Placement of a child in educational programs is done after the child has been identified as having a particular problem, and if it is believed that the child would benefit from a particular program.

Segregated schools are still very much in operation in Nigeria. There are a variety of special segregated schools where children with various handicapping conditions attend. Thus a child with a visual handicap would go to a school for the visually handicapped and a child with a physical handicap would attend a school for the physically handicapped. Unfortunately, the child is generally associated with the school. John or Mary, as the case may be, would be referred to as "the blind boy" or "the blind girl." Labeling is not only restricted to the special schools but is also used in regular schools. It is common to hear one refer to John as "the boy in the wheelchair." There is, however, a general campaign by special educators to get the public to address the disabled by their name instead of by labels. Special educators, nevertheless, realize that labeling is sometimes useful to enable the child to be placed in a proper educational setting.

Labeling results in negative attitudes toward exceptional persons. However, in Nigeria today, where there are many exceptional individuals integrated in the various institutions of learning for normal individuals, the negative attitude is giving way to a positive attitude. The positive attitude is more pronounced in such settings because most of the individuals so integrated do exceptionally well, excelling in academic performance and in most cases performing better than the normal individuals. In Nigeria, one gets into the university through the Joint Matriculation Examination. This examination is very competitive. Consequently, most people cannot gain admission to the Nigerian universities. There are many exceptional children who have been able to get admission into the universities of their choice. It is no surprise, therefore, that the normal people who have not been able to succeed would respect those who have been able to do so, particularly if they are disabled.

In the University of Jos, there are many students who are disabled in the various departments of the university. These departments include architecture, law, accountancy, mathematics, and education. These students, due to assistance from the resource room in the Department of Special Education, are doing very well. In addition to a number of disabled students, there are three disabled staff members (deaf, blind, and physically disabled).

The Social Context of Special Education

Only a few years ago, special education was thought to be a mirage in Nigeria. Many people believed that disabled people were uneducable and as such should earn their livelihood by begging for alms. Many people regarded the practice of begging by the disabled as an acceptable way of life rather than a novelty. In fact, it was more of a novelty to see a disabled person gainfully employed.

When an organized school for the blind was first opened at Gindiri in 1953, people realized that blind people could attend school. Many other schools emerged in the various states of the federation to cater to the various groups of exceptional children. Hence, many disabled persons have gone from the roadsides to the classrooms, from begging to useful employment. Since then, the negative attitude maintained by most Nigerians has changed for the better.

One of the most recent political factors influencing educational practices in Nigeria is the fact that two of Nigeria's political parties include the care of the disabled in their manifestos. Each party has promised to take care of the disabled when voted into power. To this end, most of the state governments are trying to fulfill this promise. In a recent fundraiser for the establishment of a research center for the disabled in the state, the Plateau State governor Mr. Fidelis Tapgun donated 250 thousand naira. The federal government also donated one million naira. The state government, in addition, pledged to make provision for the upkeep of the center in its annual budget.

Legislation

There are currently no national laws in Nigeria for the benefit of disabled people. There is no law mandating that they be educated. In a 1975 study Ogbue found that "there is no national policy on special education, therefore the responsibility for special education is left to the discretion of the individual states. Even where the education laws of the states make mention of special education, they give no definite mandate for educating handicapped children." Hence, parents who find it more convenient to have their disabled child stay at home do so readily.

Some states have been able to promulgate laws to protect their handicapped as well as give them certain rights. Both the Northern Nigerian Education Law and the Plateau State Handicapped Education Law make provisions for educational services and materials for handicapped children in their states.

It is hoped that in the near future a law will make education of the disabled binding in the federation. It is also important to pass a law giving disabled persons protection. This will grant them the right to special services and the right to employment.

Policies on Special Education

In Nigeria, special education policies are consistently ingrained in overall educational policies (Obiakor 1991). Because of the federal, and consequently the regional, government's role in providing educational opportunities for all citizens, special education policies are not formed in isolation (Obiakor 1991). They are part of educational decisions made by the federal, state, and local governments.

Over the years, a number of policies and ordinances have been enacted. Some affect special education directly. In 1948, for example, an ordinance on financial support was passed. It stipulated that grants were to be paid to local authorities or voluntary agencies. Among other things, special schools, equipment, medical supervision, and other special education services would from time to time call for financial aid. In 1954, the Western Region Law on definition and educational placement for the handicapped was passed. This authorized the Ministry of Education to define and make provisions for special teaching methods appropriate for handicapped people. In 1957, the Special Services Law of Lagos was passed to make provision for special services for pupils who require them.

In 1962 and 1964 the Statute of Northern Region on Services to the Handicapped and Northern Nigerian Education Laws were passed authorizing the Ministry of Education to provide special schools for handicapped children, and to ensure an adequate supply of trained teachers and supply of sufficient facilities for their training. In 1969, the Decree on National Commission for Rehabilitation was promulgated. The decree was aimed at providing for the reconstruction of areas destroyed by war and the rehabilitation of war victims. In 1972, a grant-in-aid decree was made by the federal military government. It made provision for grants-in-aid to all special schools and centers and was part of educational goals to sensitize the Nigerian populace to the educational needs of all people.

In 1977, the National Policy on Education was passed. Obiakor (1991) likens Section 8 of the National Policy on Education to Public Law 94-142 in the United States. The major objectives of Section 8 are the following:

1. To secure equality of educational opportunity for all children
2. To educate disabled children and adults to play useful roles in the development of the nation
3. To enable gifted children to develop at their own pace
4. To develop the manpower necessary to achieve these objectives
5. To work toward the integration of exceptional children in the regular school system

Section 8 also requires the Ministry of Education to set up a committee to conduct special education activities in collaboration with the ministries of health, local welfare, and labor. It also requires that a census be taken of all handicapped children and adults by age, sex, locality, and type. The introduction of elements of special education into all teacher-training colleges is also advocated. As soon as feasible, all teacher-training colleges will be required to provide general and basic courses to all prospective teachers who will work in regular schools but who will need to identify and teach exceptional children (Obiakor 1991). Funding provided through the University Primary Education Program allowed the University of Ibadan to begin a certificate program in special education.

The National Policy was revised in 1981, reemphasizing the points already made in 1977. It is most interesting to note that, except for the Nigerian National Policy, all other policies and decrees have not been national. They have affected only some states of the federation and have not been vigorously enforced. For example, the Plateau State Handicapped Law of 1981 was to make provisions for educational services only for the handicapped of Plateau State origin.

Teachers, Schools, Curriculum, and Pedagogy

Training of special education teachers is done in universities and teachers colleges. Today, there are two universities in Nigeria that are centers of excellence in respect to the training of personnel for exceptional children. These are the University of Jos in Plateau State and the University of Ibadan in Oyo State. These universities offer degree programs both at the graduate and undergraduate levels. In addition to the degree programs, they offer diplomas and certificate programs in the various areas of exceptionalities.

There are criteria for entry into the B.Ed. program. For direct entry, the candidate is expected to follow a three-year program of studies. Those who qualify for this entry are those who already possess a diploma in special education and those who possess the Nigerian certificate of education obtained from a three-year program. The direct entry students take three years to obtain a bachelor's degree in special education. Those with a high school certificate (secondary school certificate) are required to spend four years in the program.

In addition to these two universities, there is also the advanced teachers college, known as the Federal Teachers College (Special), Oyo. Here, teachers are trained to cater to children with various exceptionalities. Most laudable is the fact that the federal Ministry of Education took the bold step of introducing a course on elements of special education in all teachers colleges in the country.

Curriculum

In Nigeria exceptional children of normal intelligence follow the same curriculum as do their normal counterparts. This is true in the elementary schools, secondary schools, and institutions of higher education. At the end of their primary school, like their normal counterparts, exceptional students sit for the National Common Entrance Examination. If successful, they are admitted into any secondary school of their choice. At the end of secondary school, they again sit for the Joint Matriculation Examination (JME). This qualifies them for entry into the university. If they should choose to go to the advanced teachers college, they sit for the JME for the Nigerian certificate of education. The curriculum, therefore, for normal people does not differ from that of the disabled with normal intelligence. This is not to say that their specific needs are not taken care of—provisions are made for them to learn those skills that are of particular importance to them. This includes braille, mobility, and typing for the blind, and lipreading, fingerspelling, and total communication for the deaf.

Educational Setting

Administratively, preprimary education is by and large managed as private enterprise, though structured and run in accordance with the National Policy on Education. Education of the handicapped is integrated with the general school system. The administration of special education is decentralized, and all state sectors deal with special education. In order to encourage private sectors to provide services for the handicapped, the government is always prepared to subsidize with funds and personnel. As of 1988, there were 9,813 pupils enrolled in special education programs. This does not include the higher education institutions.

Generally, Nigeria runs special schools for disabled students of the various categories. Thus, we have schools for the deaf, blind, and physically handicapped. There are occasions when some of these programs are combined and run on the same school grounds. Nigeria seems to support segregated settings for special education at the primary level. Integration begins more seriously at the secondary level when the children would have mastered the basic skills that are of particular importance to them. It is the view of most Nigerians that after primary school education, integration is not for all children. There are those who will not benefit from such an educational setting. Nevertheless, those who can profit from the program are encouraged to participate.

Major Controversies and Issues in Special Education

On the issue of mainstreaming, the Nigerian National Policy on education states, "Mainstreaming is the most realistic form of special education since handicapped children are eventually expected to live in society" (sec. 8, par. 56, no. 5). The statement goes on to say that mainstreaming is supported by the federal government of Nigeria. As has already been stated in this paper, mainstreaming in Nigeria begins generally at the secondary school level and continues through higher levels.

Students admitted into these institutions will have mastered the basic skills required by their basic handicapping condition. Thus, the blind will have mastered braille, reading and writing, mobility and orientation, as well as typing. The University of Jos, because of the facilities and services given to the disabled, has the largest number of disabled as compared with other higher learning institutions. The statistics for 1991–1992 are shown in table 5.1.

Here in the University of Jos, there is a resource room to which the students go to get their specific needs met by experts. These include transcribing ink-print material into braille, learning braille reading and writing, and learning sign language. The disabled students are well integrated in the schools and have no problems getting along with their nonhandicapped colleagues. The nondisabled students assist the disabled students very readily and some volunteer to read for the blind students. Sometimes volunteer services are obtained in the prisons where braille facilities have been provided to assist the students with their academic program. The long-term prisoners are, hereby, taught how to write in braille. They are then able to transcribe ink-print material into braille.

TABLE 5.1.   Disabled Students in the University of Jos

Year	Blind	Deaf	Physically Handicapped
1990	30	7	12
1991	42	15	11
1992	50	18	13
Total	112	40	36

Problems

Integrating children into the regular school system is not without problems. These include the following:

Large class size. Most classrooms in Nigeria are overcrowded. The ideal class size is thirty-six. Sometimes classes are as large as fifty. This definitely does not make for individualized instruction, which is of great importance in the education of disabled children.

Personnel. With special education being a recent educational innovation in Nigeria, there is a shortage of teachers. Most of the schools where handicapped children are integrated have difficulties securing itinerant teachers' services. There is also a need for interpreters and note takers for the deaf; these services are very important for the success of integration. In addition, there is a need for braillists to transcribe ink-print materials.

Lack of facilities. One of the greatest problems in the integration program in Nigeria is the lack of adequate facilities. In a study she conducted, Anumonye (1991) observed that no provisions had been made in the institutions she visited with respect to adaptations of entrances and corridors to facilitate easy access for wheelchairs. There were no special gadgets for the toilets such as grab rails, or wide doors to facilitate easy movement. There were no ramps to give free access to those in wheelchairs. Most glass windows and doors were broken and not replaced. These no doubt are hazards to the blind who feel their way around with their hands. All these architectural barriers serve as a hindrance towards successful integration (Bakare 1992).

Lack of materials and equipment. There is a great need for teaching materials and equipment. Vital equipment such as tape recorders for blind students to record their lectures in the classroom may not be in the reach of most students. Yet, these are important for the success of their studies. There are also some partially hearing children who may need hearing aids but not be able to afford them; therefore, they miss a lot of the lectures in the class. This is worse when teachers move around as they lecture, which makes it difficult to lipread. Therefore, vital items such as wheelchairs, crutches, special writing tools, braille machines, thermoforms (overhead transparencies), tape recorders, and typewriters must be made available to the blind, deaf, and physically handicapped students. Magnifying glasses for those with low vision and hearing aids for the partially hearing are very essential for their successful integration.

Attitude. Although a positive attitude in respect to the handicapped is developing in Nigeria, there are still some negative attitudes among both teachers and students in the schools. There are still several myths with regard to the cause of disabilities that give rise to superstition and fear. It is not uncommon to see another student or even a staff member refusing to interact with a handicapped person for fear that he or she will contract the condition (Bakare 1992). It is therefore important to correct such attitudes and superstitious beliefs.

Funding. In most states of the Federation of Nigeria, special education is free for disabled students. The primary schools for the disabled, as all other schools, are the responsibility of and funded by the local government. States also take interest in special schools and fund them by granting subsidies. This is true of state schools as well as schools belonging to voluntary agencies. As of now special education, like regular education, is not compulsory for all children in Nigeria. Nevertheless, efforts are being made to educate all children.

Emerging trends in special education

A few decades ago, little was known about special education. The education of handicapped children was considered to be a mirage. The handicapped were relegated to the background and were expected to beg from normal people. Their future was bleak and seemed without a future. This condition is fast changing as people begin to realize what the disabled are capable of doing as they find themselves seated side by side with them in primary, secondary, and higher learning institutions. Only a few years ago, exceptional individuals were not in higher institutions of learning. When one happened to get there it was considered a novelty. Today there are many exceptional individuals studying in the various programs of their choice. The attitudes of many exceptional individuals are, therefore, changing positively, more so because they are competing favorably with other students. Many other disabled persons are gainfully employed in the various sectors of society.

In the past, many people went into the field of special education as a last resort. Today they enter the field because they choose to do so, and as such are committed to the work. Some years ago in the teachers colleges only those who were to work with handicapped students took courses in special education. Today, elements of special education having been introduced, all students are required to take some basic special education courses. This is to give prospective teachers the rudiments of special education so that they can handle disabled pupils in an integrated program. With these steps, it is evident that special education will continue its rapid growth in the Nigerian educational system.

References

Abang, T. B. 1992a. *Handbook of special education: for educators in developing countries.* Jos, Nigeria: Andex Press.

———. 1992b. Special education in Nigeria. *International Journal of Disability, Development and Education* 39 (1).

Ajayi, J. 1992. Health for all in the year 2000. A paper delivered at the 15th convocation of the University of Jos, University of Jos Press.

Anumonye, F. O. 1991. Problems of mainstreaming handicapped children in Nigeria. In *Contemporary issues in mainstreaming the exceptional child in Nigeria's 6–3–3–4 system of education.* Jos, Nigeria: NCNC Publication.

Bakare, C. A. 1986a. Hearing impairment in pre-school children. *Human Communication* 10 (5): 25–27.

———. 1986b. Audiological evaluation of 1035 children in Nigerian schools for deaf. In *Proceedings of the First Asian-Pacific Regional Conference on Deafness,* 120–24. Hong Kong: Bakare.

Bakare, C. O. 1992. Integration in Education. The case of education for handicapped children in Nigeria. *International Journal of Special Education* 7:255–60.

Bisley, G. G. 1981. *Handbook of ophthalmology for developing countries.* Nairobi, Kenya: Oxford University Press.

Obiakor, F. E. 1985. *Comparison of special education programs in Nigeria and the United States of America.* ERIC, ED 266, 605.

———. 1991. Cultural and socio-economic factors affecting special education policies in Nigeria. *International Journal of Special Education* 6:271–87.

Obiakor, F. E., Aramburo, D., Maltby, G. P., and David, E. 1991. Comparison of special education in Nigeria and the United States of America. *International Journal of Special Education* 6:341–52.

Ochejede, S. 1992. Meningitis: A case study. *Journal of Jos University Medical Students Association* 3 (2).

Ogbue, R. M. 1975. *A survey of special education facilities in Nigeria.* Lagos, Nigeria: Federal Ministry of Nigeria.

———. 1981. Experiments in integration: The Nigerian experience. *EducaAfrica,* December, 136–52.

Ojile, E. 1989. Special education, deaf education in Nigeria: Development, administration and problems. Presented at the International Conference on the Post-secondary Education of Deaf students, October, Edmonton, Alberta.

Oloninyomi, B. O. 1992. Guinea worm in Plateau State. *Journal of Jos University Medical Students Association* 3 (2).

6

Islamic Republic of Iran

G. ALI AFROOZ

In the name of God.

*I*n 1991, the Islamic Republic of Iran had a population of fifty-eight million with a 3.2 percent annual rate of growth, living in an area of 1,648,195 square kilometers. Nearly one-half of the population lives in the rural areas in more than sixty thousand villages. The age breakdown demonstrates that the majority of the population is very young; close to 64 percent is below fourteen years of age. The birth rate figure per 1,000 is 41.2, and the death rate is 11.2 per 1,000.

Education within the Islamic Republic of Iran, including special education, is financed predominantly by the government. In addition, local communities, religious organizations, individual philanthropy, and the clergy have been actively participating in national campaigns to provide school facilities in an effort to eradicate illiteracy.

About the Author • Dr. G. Ali Afrooz, a graduate of Michigan State University in 1978 and now a professor at Tehran University, has published extensively on special education, with an emphasis on its psychological aspects. His most recent book, *The Psychology and Education of Children and Adolescents,* is being translated into English, French, and Arabic for worldwide distribution. Since serving as the founder of special education programs for Iranian universities, he has held high positions in the Iranian Islamic government including Iran's chargé d'affaires to London in 1980 and vice-chancellor, dean, assistant professor, and the president of the Parent-Teacher Association (1990–91). Now the president of Iran's Special Education Organization as well as the undersecretary of the Ministry of Education, Dr. Afrooz is directing the education of children with various forms of disabilities. His outstanding career, both as a scholar and public servant, ranks him as a leading national spokesman on educational and social issues.

Education

For centuries the mosques have served Iranians, not only as places of worship, but also as centers of learning. Affiliated with most mosques were religious schools, locally known as *Maktabs,* supported by individual philanthropy or by religious foundations. The curriculum of the religious schools consisted of the scriptures, logic, ethics, Arabic language, literature, and mathematics. This traditional system of education, to a very large extent, was displaced by a system of state education. So much so that, in the nineteenth century, Iran began to adopt the French educational system. In 1851 a polytechnical college, Darol-fonoon, was founded in Tehran. During the 1920s, this college gradually became a typical secondary school. By 1943, compulsory education through the sixth grade was established. Starting with the 1967 academic year, a new pattern of education was introduced in Iran.

The Islamic Revolution of February, 1979, led by the late Imam Khomeini, may God be pleased with him, overthrew the centuries-old monarchy in Iran. In a referendum taken in April of the same year, the creation of an Islamic Republic was approved by 99 percent of the people. According to the newly devised constitution, all institutions, as well as all economic and social policies, were to be based on Islamic criteria. Therefore, the moral training of the individual, which was to be highly emphasized both in school and within the social strata, initiated a fundamental reform in the entire educational system. Consequently, public school education and curriculum development have received much rightly deserved attention over the past decade in spite of the various hardships experienced. Particular importance has been attached to the relationship between education and work.

The ultimate goal of the Islamic government of Iran is to furnish nationwide and free schooling for all the school-age population including, if not particularly, exceptional children between ages of six and eighteen. Preschool education, though encouraged, is not yet compulsory. It is has been provided both in government and private institutions for about two years.

The public school system is controlled by the Ministry of Education. At present, in the Islamic Republic of Iran, twelve years of schooling—primary, guidance, and secondary—lead to a diploma. Primary school begins at the age of six and lasts for five years. This leads to a guidance course lasting for three years. During this time, students are exposed to different subjects of study and receive educational and psychological counseling. After this, based on their final examination scores and, of course, their personal interest, the students are expected to decide their future occupations or academic pursuits. Secondary education lasts for four years and is divided into two main tracks—academic and technical-vocational. The administration of all final examinations in each cycle is centralized and confined to the Board of Examiners within the Ministry of Education. In 1969, a separate Ministry of Science and Higher Education was established to cover all higher education and research institutes.

According to the Ministry of Education's latest report, in the 1991 academic year 16,017,917 pupils were enrolled in 91,008 public schools. In 1992 enrollment reached an estimated figure of 17 million. In addition, as a result of a comprehensive effort and relatively successful comprehensive plans for reducing adult illiteracy, the rate of illiteracy has fallen from 52.5 percent in 1977 to 38 percent today.

Public Health and the Handicapped

High population growth in Iran over the past ten years has created major problems in the education and health sectors. According to the *Statistical Yearbook* (UNESCO 1986), the standard of living is appreciably rising and health facilities have expanded rapidly over the past ten years, with an emphasis on providing services to the rural regions. Nevertheless, these services still seem very far from adequate. Shortages also have their roots in the imposition of a protracted war on 22 September, 1980, when Iraq was persuaded and internationally supported to invade presumptuously the Islamic land of Iran. As a result, all through the eight years of the war of attrition during which international organizations remained as passive observers in this episode of shame and sham, hundreds of thousands of houses, schools, factories, hospitals, and medical centers were unnecessarily destroyed as civilian targets. This, coupled with politically motivated insidious trade embargoes, led to a considerable shortage of hospitals, medical supplies, and trained manpower, especially in the rural areas, exacerbated by an uneven distribution of doctors.

The main objective of the Ministry of Health, of course, is to provide free and comprehensive health service to all. At present, government employees as well as industrial and commercial workers enjoy free medical services, disability, and retirement benefits. All school-age children, including the exceptional ones, are covered by comprehensive medical insurance through the Ministry of Education.

In cities, a purified water supply is piped into the houses as running water. However, many villages still have to rely on wells, springs, or even rivers for their water supply. Naturally, health conditions in rural areas often are, regrettably, unsatisfactory. In many cases, due to poor sanitary conditions, a low level of health care is aggravated by malnutrition. Some very contagious childhood diseases are widely prevalent. Infant mortality is still a serious problem, and it is higher in the villages. According to the 1991 report of the Ministry of Health, the infant mortality rate was 32.6 per 1,000, although steadily declining.

Some specific or major causes of handicapping conditions among Iranian children are very noticeable. These include genetic and maternal problems, and malnutrition. Above all, there are often preventable infectious and childhood diseases such a rubella, meningitis, encephalitis, anoxia, and illnesses arising from a poor and sometimes unsanitary environment, as well as from cultural deprivation.

Trachoma is a leading cause of blindness in many rural areas, where people suffer from the lack of a sanitary water supply and adequate health services. Unlike other less religiously concerned societies, decisive factors such as alcohol, drug abuse, drug-related problems, teenage pregnancy, incest, venereal diseases, and so on are relatively unimportant in looking at the causes of handicaps in the Islamic Republic of Iran.

Although the marriage between first parallel cousins is not forbidden in Islam, by no means is it recommended or encouraged. However, in Iran, as in other Middle Eastern countries, this type of marriage often takes place. In fact, many people, without seriously considering the risk of genetically transmitted handicaps, view this kind of marriage as an honorable and strong family foundation. In reality, and in most cases, the sociogeographical nature of the country, the distribution of the population, and the culture of extended family structure, especially in the rural areas with small towns and villages, means that the number of inhabitants is very low—often as low as five hundred inhabitants per village—and almost all the families are somehow blood related. Under these conditions, perhaps cross-cousin marriages are truly inevitable. Hence, there is a high rate of genetically transmitted disabilities, particularly in first-cousin marriages.

In Tehran, the capital city of the Islamic Republic of Iran, the author in 1988 conducted a comparative research study in special and regular schools. It was found that the parents of 71 percent of all deaf students in day and residential schools, and about 40 percent of mentally retarded pupils, were somehow blood related. The majority of these parents were cousins. In contrast, in selected regular schools only 11.5 percent of the subjects were blood related. In response, extended marriage counseling and genetic consultation in screening clinics is planned and almost established throughout the country, with special attention to the rural areas.

In addition to these socioeconomic impediments, over one hundred thousand people became handicapped as a result of air attacks, long-range missiles, and chemical warfare during the imposed war in which the global communities preferred to remain indifferent. The stress of such explosions contributed to enormous numbers of babies with very low birth weights. The surviving ones are suffering from many forms of mental and physical disabilities.

Often, there is no official system of identification of children with special needs either at the early stages or at the age of entering school. Therefore, an accurate estimate of the population of handicapped children seems rather difficult to provide. Nevertheless, based on scattered reports, we can arrive at a rough estimate and say that close to 10 percent of all school-age children do have special needs. This estimate, of course, does not include those children with learning disabilities or speech impairments.

Children with Special Needs

According to the Holy Quran, "[a]nd whoso gives life to a soul, she be as if he has given life to the mankind altogether" (The Table 5:32). In Islamic culture, handicapped persons enjoy a protected status. According to the prophet Muhammad, "Serving the disabled is serving one's turn to the Prophets of God." Based on this conviction, Iranians in general are very concerned about the welfare of handicapped people. Active involvement in voluntary organizations to help handicapped children, therefore, is considered to be both a blessing and a social honor in Islamic terms. However, due to a lack of appropriate awareness of the public of the potential abilities of handicapped persons, misconceptions about mental retardation and, above all, the lack of governmental provisions and facilities for these people, there was a total absence of official special education programs until the early twentieth century.

In the 1920s, the first nongovernment-sponsored institution for deaf children was established in Tehran by Jabbar Baghcheban (1885–1966), the Iranian pioneer in education for the deaf. With the assistance of a German priest, the first school for the blind was founded in Tabriz in the northwest of the country, also in the 1920s. Following these very important and historic events in the field of special education, many other special schools and residential provisions were established by religious and conscientious groups or individuals throughout the country. The first residential school for blind children in Tehran was established by the Ministry of Education in 1955. A residential rehabilitation center for severely mentally retarded children was inaugurated by the Ministry of Health in the north of Tehran in 1958.

In 1968, the Ministry of Education formed a new Special Education Department, which officially assumed the responsibility for the education of students with special needs. Its main objective was to discern, select, and place educable exceptional children—blind, deaf, emotionally disturbed, and mentally retarded—in special classes or schools. To reach such an objective, many new special schools were to be established in various parts of the country. However, by 1978, after about ten years of work, only eight thousand exceptional children came under the umbrella of the Special Education Department and attended special schools or classes. The main obstacles were a shortage of trained teachers, insufficient facilities, and the lack of necessary public awareness about the effectiveness of the special education programs.

Since the 1979 Islamic Revolution, educational authorities have been more concerned about the education of exceptional children. Consequently, a considerable number of special schools have been built and teacher-training projects on special education have received considerably more attention. In December 1989, the Parliament passed a bill authorizing the Ministry of Education to reorganize its special education unit and establish a more comprehensive and a more effective special education system. Based on this authorization, the Special Education Organization, affiliated with the Ministry of Education, was established with a larger budget and higher administrative powers. According to the latest statistical reports on the 1992 academic year, a total of 37,970 students were enrolled in 575 special schools attending 4,611 classes throughout the country.

The Welfare Organization, one of the main branches of the Ministry of Health, maintains its duties of providing adoption and foster care for orphans, both handicapped and otherwise, and aiding families with dependent and severely disabled children. It provides protective and rehabilitative services for those handicapped children or adults who do not fall within the special education schemes due to their ages or the severity of their disabilities.

Identification and Eligibility

To be eligible for a special education program, the child should be classified as one of the following: educably mentally retarded, visually handicapped; hard of hearing or deaf; deaf-blind; emotionally disturbed; multihandicapped; or having learning difficulties. This classification system is based on given definitions and includes children within normal school-age ranges. Partially sighted and hard-of-hearing children must provide a medical examination certificate from one of the authorized centers or doctors. If a child is trainable but severely retarded, the child will be referred to rehabilitation centers at the Welfare Organization.

The most widely used intelligence tests of the Department of Special Education are Raven's Standard Progressive Matrices and the Colored Progressive Matrices, and the Leiter International Performance Scale (LIPS), which were field tested in Iran. Testers also use the Stanford-Binet Intelligence Scale, which is in a systematic standardization process in Iran.

Special Teacher-Training Programs

One area in which both the Ministries of Education and the Ministry of Higher Education are very much concerned is teacher-training programs, both in regular and special education.

The first special education department to train special education teachers in Iran was established in 1968. Short-term, extensive courses—(120 to 180 hours for 8 to 16 weeks)—were designed as a preservice teacher-training program for regular classroom teachers who were willing to work with exceptional children. In addition to regular school teachers, all other qualified and interested college educated or high school graduates were admitted to the program. These types of preservice or extensive in-service special education teacher-training courses were the main channels of teacher preparation for the rapidly expanding regular and special schools in Iran, especially for the small towns and rural areas.

In 1977, the Department of Special Education planned a one-year special education teacher-training program for special schools serving blind, deaf, emotionally disturbed, and mentally retarded students. In the 1980s, this program was replaced by a two-year degree program leading to an associate degree in special education.

Today, there are two main residential special education teacher-training centers (one for males and one for females) in Tehran. These are under the supervision and responsibility of the Ministry of Education. During two years or four semesters, students take ninety credit hours in literature, ethics, arts, and hygiene, as well as general and special education courses. The course includes teaching training in their field of study. Following successful completion of this program, students are granted an associate degree, and they are assigned to teach at special schools throughout the country. It should be mentioned that special school teachers receive 20 percent higher salaries than regular teachers receive.

In 1982, the author proposed a four-year special education program at the College of Education at the University of Tehran. Within two years, ten universities announced their readiness to offer this undergraduate special education personnel-training program. At present, more than five hundred students are working on their bachelor's degrees in special education. Most of them concentrate on mental retardation, the largest area in special education in Iran. One-half of all special schools are allocated for this purpose.

In addition to the aforesaid programs, the first graduate program (master's degree) in mental retardation was inaugurated at the College of Education at the University of Tehran in 1987. Apparently, this seems to be the only graduate program in special education personnel-training available in the Middle East.

During the last ten years, more than fifty basic textbooks in special education were either written or translated into Farsi by interested faculty members. Quite a few major textbooks and a few special education journals in English are being made available to faculty members and graduate students through college libraries.

Special Schools

Special schools and clinical services are provided for students free of charge. Special schools and special classes within the regular school setting provide programs in the following four areas: deafness, blindness, emotional disturbance, and mental retardation. Up to the present, except in some special cases, there is no official classification of learning disabled children, due to the absence of a practical definition. In some cases, learning disabled children may have been identified as slow learners or even as mentally retarded. Nor are there special schools or classes for children with speech impairments, even though children have been identified as having such impairments. Some special schools or institutions in major cities provide special services such as physical therapy, rehabilitation, and vocational therapy.

Generally, the average number of pupils in a special school is about five to six students per class. In special education schools for the mentally retarded, students are grouped according to their mental and chronological ages. Most special schools have a playground and a media center. A few larger schools for mentally retarded students have sheltered workshops. Normal special school hours are from eight in the morning to noon. In most special schools, students receive free snacks. Transportation is usually provided through the special school Parent-Teacher Association (PTA) and/or with the financial support of the individual philanthropic or religious organizations involved in assisting children with disabilities. A hot lunch is served in some larger schools that have classes from eight in the morning until two in the afternoon, six days a week.

As far as curriculum is concerned, all subjects studied in special schools (the few exceptions being the mentally retarded schools) correspond with those of regular schools. Books and some teaching aids are provided by the Ministry of Education for all regular as well as for special schools throughout the country. In very recent years, a few special textbooks have been prepared for the use of students who are termed as educable mentally retarded.

Unlike regular schools, the Department of Special Education in most cases has made preschool programs available to blind, deaf, and mentally retarded children. Therefore, special schools are composed of preschool (flexible, 1 or 2 years), elementary (5 years), guidance (3 years), and secondary level (4 years). In preschool, the main objective is to develop children's skills in the areas of sensorimotor skills, emotional skills, grooming, social adjustment, verbal communication, aesthetics, and creativity. Although some special books and teaching materials are available for preschool children, what is covered largely depends on the extent of the teacher's knowledge, experience, and abilities. The curriculum in formal special schools is, however, book oriented. Reading, mathematics, moral and religious education, art, physical education, and vocational training are subjects with an important place in the daily schedule.

An emphasis on vocational education occurs mainly at the secondary levels. This is done in order to improve the working capabilities of the handicapped students. Vocational subject content varies for boys and girls and according to the type of school. Some special schools in larger cities have sheltered workshops for their students, especially for those who are mentally retarded.

In schools for the blind, students are encouraged to become acquainted with regular typewriters in addition to using braille. Usually all blind students at the secondary level are able to type very skillfully.

Unemployment among the disabled population is very rare. This is mainly due to the fact that vocational training for handicapped students at the secondary level has been taken very seriously. As well, many government and private institutions and factories, influenced by an inherent Islamic cultural attitude, voluntarily offer appropriate jobs to the handicapped. Each year, a considerable number of physically disabled and blind (and a few deaf) high school graduates manage to enter universities by successfully passing with high grades the national and extremely competitive university placement examinations.

Problems and Needs

The communities where special education programs are a relatively new phenomenon face considerable challenges in reaching their ultimate objectives of providing educational provisions for all of their exceptional children. In fact, population growth due to the high birth rate, the geographical position of the country, and the socioeconomic conditions can often pose a major obstacle to providing educational facilities for all school-age children in general, and for the students with special needs, in particular. At present, about 1.6 percent of the regular school population in Iran (and perhaps in many other countries within the region) is provided with special education programs or services. Therefore, it seems quite likely that the vast majority of exceptional children are being denied appropriate educational services. Quite a large number of identified or nonidentified students with special needs, often in small towns and villages are, however, placed in regular schools. Therefore, though faced with an unfair situation, they struggle in the regular schools in order to have access to some form of education. In other words, mainstreaming is not only a method of educational preference in special education, but self-mainstreaming or the integration of handicapped children by their families in local regular schools, often seems to be the only alternative for exceptional children and is widely and independently practiced.

No doubt, there are still a considerable number of educable or trainable disabled persons throughout the less-developed areas who may not be receiving any form of systematic education at all. In the rural areas, however, where life patterns are naturally less diversified, social demands are similarly simpler and most jobs do not require complex skills. Physically handicapped and mildly and moderately retarded people stand a better chance at working on routine jobs. Therefore, they are easily mainstreamed in their local communities without considerable social or vocational problems.

Today, a large proportion of the special school population in their first year of school consists of those who have already been in regular classes for quite a long period of time. Only due to their continuous failure in school achievement have they been referred to the Department of Special Education.

Earlier identification and the screening of all school-age children play major roles in special education. In this regard, the lack of appropriate intelligence quotient tests, free of cultural biases, has been a problem. However, the shortage of trained personnel in special education and educational psychology within the school setting is an even greater problem.

At present, the most important objective of the government as well as the educational authorities is to provide schooling for all identified exceptional children, from the preschool to the secondary school level, throughout the country. In this regard, the shortage of special school facilities and of trained teachers must be seriously taken into consideration. Obviously, the decision of Parliament in December 1989, with regard to improving special education's administrative efficiency, has been very encouraging and extremely instrumental in the further development of special education within the Islamic Republic of Iran.

The immediately achievable goals of the Special Education Organization consist of improving both special education teacher training at all levels and the early identification of exceptional children. Keen management can create closer cooperation between regular and special education systems for integration and preplanned mainstreaming. Additional goals include expanding public health facilities and services and the establishment of genetic counseling centers within the country with an aim of preventing or minimizing handicapping conditions, especially throughout the rural areas. Of course, the country's socioeconomic condition is compensated by the hard work of its sincere educational authorities.

Future Plans and Priorities

In 1988, the Iranian chapter of the Council for Exceptional Children (CEC) held an international seminar. This seminar was inaugurated with the remarkable and historic message, broadcast nationally via radio and television, of the then President Khamehnei—now Ayatolla Khamehnei—emphasizing the identification and education of all handicapped children. During the seminar, the problems and future plans of special education services were discussed in the presence of the ministers of education, health, and of other special education and rehabilitation authorities.

The main suggestions for future plans and developments in special education and rehabilitation of disabled individuals, which were approved by education and health authorities, are as follows:

1. Reorganizing the existing insufficient rehabilitative and special education systems and establishing a comprehensive organization to be responsible for the identification, assessment, rehabilitation, education, welfare, and employment opportunities for all disabled individuals throughout their lifetimes
2. Improving special education personnel preparation in all needed areas
3. Establishing genetic counseling centers and special health-care clinics throughout the country in order to prevent or minimize the possible genetic origin and other causes of handicapping conditions, especially in rural areas where the health situation is poor and the tradition of cousin marriages is predominant
4. Preparing means and methods for the early identification of handicapped children, and implementing screening tests for all regular as well as special school first-grade children
5. Enhancing cooperative relations between regular and special schools for mutual understanding, integration, and mainstreaming purposes
6. Utilizing all the mass media most effectively to increase public awareness on conditions leading to handicaps, the capabilities of handicapped individuals, and preventive measures

References

Algar, H. 1969. *Religion and the state in Iran.* Berkeley: University of California Press.
————. 1980a. *Constitution of the Islamic Republic.* Berkeley: Mizan Press.
————. 1980b. The Islamic revolution in Iran. In Kalim Siddigui, ed. *Muslim institute.* London: Open Press.
Ali, Y. 1937. *Translation of the Quran.* Lahore.
Afrooz, G. A. 1988. *Introduction to psychology and education of exceptional children* (in Farsi). 10th ed. Tehran: Tehran University Press.
Jafari, M. T. 1989. Islam and mentally retarded children (in Farsi). *Journal of Exceptional Children* 1:19–28. Tehran: Council for Exceptional Children, Iranian Chapter.
Jalal, A. H. 1985. *An outline of the Islamic countries.* Chicago: The Open School.
Ministry of Education. 1992. *Annual report.* Tehran: Bureau of Statistics.
Ministry of Health. 1992. Special report on infant mortality in Iran. Tehran: Ministry of Health.
Postlewait, T, and Thomas, R. 1980. *Schooling in the Aegean region.* New York: Pergamon Press.
Shariati, A. 1979. *On the sociology of Islam.* Berkeley: Mizan Press.
Statistic Centre of Iran. 1992. *Special Report.* Tehran: Statistic Centre of Iran.
Tabatabai, S. M. S. 1982. *The spiritual life.* Tehran: Bethat Foundation.
UNESCO. 1986. *Statistical yearbook.* Paris: UNESCO.

7

Brazil

LÚCIA GOMES VIEIRA DELLAGNELO

Technical Revisions by José Marcos da Silva Mazzotta
Translated by Meoma C. Monteiro

To understand the Brazilian special education system, one has to insert it into the general education system and, above all, into the social context in which it develops. Today, there are about 14.5 to 15 million people with disabilities in Brazil, that is, 10 percent of the country's population. The occurrence of disability is not homogeneous in all society's sectors. The strongest concentration is in the lower-class sectors because of the precarious sanitation and health conditions in which these people are forced to live. "In 1990, more than half of the Brazilian youth population (58 percent) was poor. The harmful results of this poverty have a direct influence over the children's lives in their basic needs of health, food and education" (IBGE 1990).

According to studies (IBGE 1987), 82 out of 1,000 children in 1986 (136 in the northeast area) died before they were five years old. Although child mortality has been decreasing in the past ten years, the numbers are still alarming. What is even worse is that most of these deaths are caused by easily avoidable conditions such as infections, diarrhea, acute respiratory infections, and malnutrition.

About the Author • Ms. Lúcia Gomes Vieira Dellagnelo is technical director of the Institute for Development and Learning in São Paulo, coordinating programs for children with learning problems in the public school system. She has specializations in psychopedagogy and international development, is past coordinator of the project of integration of handicapped students into the public school system in the state of Santa Catarina, and was a consultant for the Kellog Foundation in the area of youth development and education in Latin America. • Dr. José Marcos da Silva Mazzotta is a professor in the Department of Education at the University of São Paulo. He is the author of several books on special education.

This gives us an idea of the number of children born into situations that can easily lead to some sort of disability. Therefore, there are challenges to be faced in providing special education services in Brazil. Also, because Brazil is a huge country, one can see many and significant regional differences in the organization and in the quality of the special education services offered.[1]

Prevalence of Exceptional Conditions

The latest studies on the Brazilian population do not give us a realistic number of people with disabilities. According to the census carried out in 1982 (PNDA and IBGE), there were 2,134,326 people with disabilities in Brazil, which did not portray the real situation at that time, let alone today. According to the World Health Organization figures mentioned earlier, there are about 15 million people with disabilities living in Brazil, that is, 10 percent of the whole country's population. Most of these persons are of school age, between birth and twenty years old, as reported by the Comite de Proteção dos Direitos da Criança (Commission for Protection of Children's Rights). The incidence of the different kinds of disabilities can be seen in table 7.1.

TABLE 7.1. Incidence of Different Types of Disability in Brazil

Disability	Number of People	% of Disabled
Mental Disability	7,250,000	50
Physical Disability	2,900,000	20
Hearing Disability	2,175,000	15
Multiple Disabilities	1,450,000	10
Visual Disability	725,000	5
Total	14,500,000	100

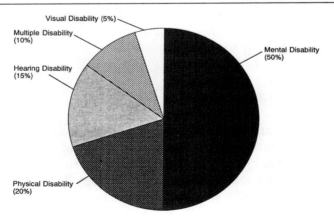

As stated earlier, the incidence of disability is not homogeneous all over the country. The National Research on Nutrition and Health "shows the enormous differences among the country's regions, among rural and urban situations and among the socioeconomical groups, reflecting not only the differences in food availability but also differences in health services access, substructure, basic sanitation and children's health and care availability." (IBGE 1992). People living in the northern and northeastern regions of Brazil—the poorest regions—show a higher number of disabilities due to the unsuitable living conditions to which they are submitted.

Almost 50 percent of the people with mental disabilities have an etiology that comes from psychosocial factors, that is, "several needs in critical phases of child development such as food shortage, lack of affective and cognitive stimulation in the first years of life" (Oliveira 1983). Added to this are two other causes. There are genetic problems, which are hard to prevent in our country, and inadequate services for pregnant women.

Prenatal care for mothers is not sufficient and is also difficult to access, mainly for pregnant women in the rural areas. This increases the risk of brain injuries that give rise to mental disability. Most of the children born to mothers who have not received adequate prenatal care are mildly or moderately retarded, presenting disabilities that could be avoidable with educational and preventive measures (Fontes 1990).

The second largest group is made up of people with physical disabilities caused mainly by work- or traffic-related accidents and by rising violence in the big cities. "In the last 10 years, 50 thousand Brazilians died of accidents at work because of bad living and work conditions. Today, about 3 thousand accidents at work have as consequence several kinds of mutilation, daily" (CVI 1990).

In Brazil, visual and hearing disabilities are caused, in general, by infections caught during the pregnancy period or right after birth; by medicine misuse; and by food shortage which, for example, is the cause of hypovitaminosis A, still responsible for visual problems in the northeastern regions. Out of the total group with visual disabilities, 80 percent of the people have a subnormal visual disability, whereas 20 percent are blind (Secretary of Education and CENS 1987).

Identification of Exceptionalities

The process of evaluating disability in Brazil is characterized by qualitative and quantitative differences in professional and financial recourses among the distinct parts of the country. There are some basic guidelines given by the government agencies; however, each state uses different resources to evaluate people with disability for educational purposes.

There is federal legislation in force that sends out rules for providing technical and/or financial support for special education in the private and public educational systems (CENESP/MED 1986). It determines the diagnosis of people with disability under Article 4 which states that "the evaluation of students must be done on a multi-disciplinary diagnosis basis including medical, psychological, pedagogical and social evaluations. The diagnostic procedures must be conducted by a team of qualified professionals duly registered in the proper Professional Councils. The State Secretaries of Education, themselves, must provide, whenever possible, means to carry out the diagnosis mentioned in this article. Government agencies or private institutions having an inter-disciplinary team, like the one above-mentioned on section 1, are eligible to give diagnosis for educational guidance purposes." Article 5 concerns an interdisciplinary team required for the diagnosis that must consist of professionals from paramedical, medical, social, and pedagogical areas. A single section states that the interdisciplinary team must consist of at least a qualified pedagogue, a psychologist, a social assistant, and a doctor.

The system of evaluation and diagnosis, as mentioned before, varies a lot between different regions and among institutions in the same area. There are only a few states whose secretaries of education provide for an interdisciplinary team prepared to carry out a diagnosis for students with disabilities. Some have institutions that work only with special education, such as the Foundation for Special Education in the state of Santa Catarina. In other states, there are some adaptations, and the services of a multidisciplinary team, such as Legião Brasileira de Assistencia (LBA, Brazilian Assistance Legion) and Association of Parents and Friends of Exceptional Children (APAE) are used.

In the case of not having an interdisciplinary team to carry out a diagnosis, the cases are sent to specialized professionals according to the symptoms of each disability. The joint CENP/COGSP/DAE Portaria of 1986, in the state of São Paulo (art. 16), determined that if a specific evaluation cannot be done by an interdisciplinary team, the students must be evaluated by authorized professionals. In the hearing disability area this would be an ear, nose, and throat specialist and/or speech therapist; in the physical disability area, a neurologist, psychiatrist, orthopedist, and/or practitioner; for the visual disability area, an ophthalmologist; the mental disability area, a psychologist; and for gifted children, a psychologist.

One can see significant differences as far as techniques and equipment are concerned. Large, developed cities such as São Paulo, Rio de Janeiro, Curitiba, and Porto Alegre make use of advanced resources to diagnose and assess disabilities. São Paulo, for instance, is considered to have one of the most modern medical centers in Latin America, having updated and modern equipment to detect disabilities before, during, or after birth.

In some cities, routine tests are carried out for an early evaluation of inborn problems in metabolism as a way of preventing mental disabilities, mainly phenylketonuria and congenial hypothyroidism. Health and disabilities prevention campaigns have established as main objectives the expansion of opportunities to evaluate and prevent disabilities in a greater part of the population.

The procedures used in the area of psychology to diagnose and evaluate people with disabilities are those that have caused a great many questions and controversies. This happens because some psychologists are still overrating concepts such as mental level and intelligence quotient (IQ) obtained through tests elaborated and used in countries with sociocultural conditions different from those of Brazil. The most common psychological tests used in Brazil are the Wechsler Scales (WISC), Stanford-Binet, Terman-Merrill, Columbia, Bender, and Piaget-Head. Many of these intelligence tests still have not been adjusted to Brazilian reality and, although they have already been revised in their countries of origin, older versions are still being used in Brazil. This situation endangers the diagnosis, especially as far as mental disability is concerned, and is why other procedures have been included in the evaluation of children with any disability.

In 1987, the Departamento de Assitencia Escolar (DAE, "School Assistance Department") in the state of São Paulo published a guidebook on psychological evaluation of students in order to avoid having the psychological tests as the only criteria for diagnosis. The guidebook suggests some aspects to be included in the evaluation: anamnesis, evaluation of intellectual capacity and behavior, psychomotor skills, personality, age-graded level of performance, and supplementary tests if necessary.

It is important to note that in Brazil the model used for evaluation was primarily clinical, with emphasis on psychomedical assessments. Now, however, there is an increasing trend to use an educational evaluation model, stressing the individual's abilities much more than his or her impairments. The educational model seems to be more appropriate to the integration of students with disabilities in the regular school system, since through it one can better identify the real educational needs of the child.

The educational model of evaluation has not yet been adopted by all institutions of special education in Brazil. However, the state and government guidelines suggest its usage.

Labeling the Handicapped Population

Today special education in Brazil tries to avoid labels and classifications that gather people with disability together in one group because these have as criteria only the person's limitations and not his or her abilities. However, the criteria established by Portaria 69 (CENESP/MEC 1986) are still in force for the delimitation and characterization of eligible people for special education. There are rules to fix regulating criteria to give financial and/or technical support to special education in the public and private school systems.

Delimitation and characterization of eligible people for educational assistance given by private and public institutions or agencies linked to the Centro Nacional de Educação Especial (CENESP, National Center for Special Education) are as follows:

1. *People with mental disability.* Students with below-average intellectual performance—originated in their early period of development and characterized by the inappropriateness of adaptive behavior (learning and socialization)—and who need methods and special pedagogical resources for their education.
2. *People with visual disability.* Students with partial or complete loss of sight who need braille and/or other systems, special pedagogical resources, and equipment for their education.
3. *People with physical disability.* Students with physical disabilities, orthopedic and/or neurological challenges who need methods, special pedagogical resources, and equipment for their education.
4. *People with multiple disabilities.* Students with two or more disabilities who need methods, special pedagogical resources, and equipment for their education.
5. *People with behavior problems.* Students with behavior problems of a degree of frequency and intensity that can harm development, learning, and social integration, and who need specialized educational assistance.
6. *Gifted children.* Students who show an outstanding performance and/or high level of ability in the following qualities, singular or combined—intelligence quotient, scholastic ability, creativity, leadership, abilities for arts, or motor abilities—and who need specialized educational assistance.

The secretary of education of each state can draw up the criteria to categorize the eligible clients for special education services based on the general definitions. For example, in the state of São Paulo, criteria by which students are defined and sent to the proper services were established by Resolução SE 73/78, and revised by DAE/SE of 1986.

The resolution states that *hearing disability* consists of the moderate or severe loss of the normal perception of sounds. Students who are sent to special classes for people with hearing disability must have losses that are, by ISO standards, moderately severe (56 to 76 decibels), severe (71 to 90 decibels), or profound (over 90 decibels). Moderately disabled people (41 to 55 decibels) must be sent to normal classes as long as they show the necessary requirements to follow the activities suggested in class and whenever possible wear a hearing aid. Students with *physical disabilities* are those with limitations of motion ability, posture, usage of hands, force, and agility influencing their school performance. People with serious physical disabilities caused by congenital abnormalities, metabolic disorders, traumas, serious diseases, infections, several and/or unknown causes are eligible for special classes. *Mild mentally handicapped* students are those who, although having an intelligence a below-average intelligence level, can participate in a literacy program with curriculum adjusted to their personal conditions, achieve social and occupational adjustment, and, at adult age, become completely or partially independent. The definition of *gifted* children is the same as that contained in Portaria 69. Among people with *visual disability*, blind students are those with acuteness less than .05 with the best correction available. Subnormal sight is visual acuteness between .05 to .3 with the best correction available. Students are eligible for special education assistance only if they have subnormal sight in both eyes, blindness in both eyes, or subnormal sight in one eye and blindness in the other.

The methodological instruments used to classify students with disabilities are, in general, common to all states. To classify visual acuteness, one uses Snellen's Optometric Scale. To define hearing acuteness, one uses the ISO pattern. In order to classify the different levels of mental disability, one usually uses the American Association for Mental Disability classification which has four levels—mild, moderate, severe, and profound—and the corresponding pedagogical classification with three levels: teachable, trainable, and dependent.

Today in Brazil there is a growing concern for making the general population and professionals working in the media aware of the right terminology to describe people with disability. This concern arises mainly from associations founded by people with disability for the purpose of eliminating prejudice and pejorative terminology. Therefore, other terms usually used by international institutions linked to these areas have been used instead of labels and stereotyped descriptions.

The Social Context of Special Education

Special education in Brazil is permeated by social rights movements undertaken by minorities and some institutions in order to guarantee equal opportunities in areas such as education, health, work, and leisure, areas usually limited to a small but fortunate part of the population. To guarantee equal opportunities means to create an educational system able to fulfill the students' individual needs, providing them several alternatives of education, among them special education.

The Brazilian public educational system is in a bad situation, registering high failing and dropout rates. "Many students, without apparent problems are censured according to a number of reasons, but mainly because of evaluation patterns that discern and misjudge the poor students and because the educational system is mostly inappropriate to the students' reality" (IBGE 1989). Despite the compulsory nature of education for children of elementary school age, only 73 percent of them attend school in the poorest regions, and many of them flunk the first grades.

Government reports of the last five years show that only 2.3 percent of people with disabilities are being assisted in the public education system. Although recognizing the precariousness of the public school system, many professionals and government agencies strive to insert special education as an important component into this system. However, few students with disabilities have had the opportunity to attend school in their neighborhoods, since the schools do not offer special education services that fulfill their needs.

The federal government did not take up the responsibility of offering special education services for a long time. Rather, it passed financial resources to private institutions so that they would develop such activities. In Brazil, as in other countries, the first services of special education were created as a philanthropic way of helping handicapped people. The first school of special education was founded as early as 1854, during the empire's time, to assist students with visual disability at residential facilities. In the 1930s the Pestalozzi Associations appeared followed by the Association of Parents and Friends of Exceptional Children (APAE) in the 1950s, which used to offer education and rehabilitation services based on a medical-psychological model.

In 1964, Brazil was assailed by a military dictatorship, which silenced the people's rights and tried to establish for the country a policy concerned only with economic development. From 1964 to 1985, during the twenty-one years of military dictatorship, the Brazilian educational system had as its main objective the formation of citizens whose learning and knowledge would be helpful to the economy's growth. This ideology also affected special education services and, as consequence, professionalization services for the handicapped increased in number. Special education was assumed as a governmental duty and became part of the Ministry of Education in the 1970s because of the opening of the CENESP. Even with the opening of the center, however, "the private institutions used to have a greater number of students than those of public service" (Jannuzzi 1989).

Since its beginning, the education of students with disability in Brazil did not give the people the right to attend free public schools, forcing them to make use of institutions developed for philanthropic purposes. Following the organization of minority groups in the country, people with disabilities, their families, and professionals committed to their social and educational integration, started to pressure public institutions to include special education as an integral part of the country's general educational system. Concomitant with this awakening, special education services and professionals working in the area were gradually being influenced by the mainstreaming movement going on in the United States and in the Scandinavian countries. The bibliography used as a source of technical guidelines for these services came basically from these countries who recommended the decentralization of special education services. In addition, some professionals, mainly with administrative positions, got academic degrees in European and American universities and brought special education techniques and principles to the country, among them the insertion of people with disability into the regular educational system whenever possible.

Today, the institutions in charge of writing policies and providing financial resources to special education services assume that the public educational system must regard special education as an alternative way of assisting people with special needs. Influenced by UNESCO, they are beginning to see special education as an "enriched way of education" that could assist many students with special needs, disabled or not (MEC and SENEB 1990).

Despite the great achievements in the last decades, which have made Brazilian society aware of the rights of people with disabilities to a less restrictive educational environment, Brazil cannot be yet considered a country that provides equal opportunities for people with disability. The situation is even worse when the disability is accompanied by poverty, which is true in about 60 percent of the cases.

Legislation

The legislation on education in Brazil has always foreseen free public education for all citizens. However, for a long time, students with disability did not have special services available at the public schools to fulfill their needs.

Legislation on special education appeared, at first, as articles and amendments which tried to regulate the operation of special education services and to guarantee the right of education to exceptional individuals. Specific legislation on special education appeared in the law of Diretrizes e Bases da Educação Nacional (Law 4.024/1961). The right of handicapped people to education was reassured in this law and their education was to be, whenever possible, in the general educational system (art. 88). Article 89 states that the government agrees to provide special treatment in the form of scholarships, subventions, and loans, to any private institution offering special education considered efficient by public councils of education. Although the apparent philosophy of this law is to insert special education into the general public educational system, the federal government does not commit itself and ends up leaving for the private institutions the task of offering educational services to people with disability.

Other laws on general education include articles referring to special education. But despite trying to determine objectives and goals for special education services, the government has continued to send most of the financial resources to private institutions that do not always follow the technical guidelines recommended, especially those referring to principles of normalization and integration.

In 1973, the CENESP was founded by the Ministry of Education (bill 72.425) with the purpose of trying to regulate special services in Brazil. This regulation became legislation through Portaria Interministerial 477 of 1977, approved on 10 March 1978, and it sets basic rules for joint action between the Ministry of Education and Culture and the Ministry of Social Affairs and Welfare as far as special education is concerned.

The current Brazilian Constitution, published in 1988, tries to fit special education in the general context of education, at least on a philosophical basis. However, its text still allows misinterpretation of the types of special education services to be provided. Law 7.853 refers to the right of people with disability in Article 2 and discourses on the responsibilities of the government. It foresees the following:

1. Inclusion of special education in the educational system as an elementary feature embracing early education, preschools, elementary schools, and high schools, professional qualification programs, and rehabilitation, each with their own curriculum, grades, and diploma requirements
2. The insertion of public and private special schools into the educational system
3. Free and mandatory special education services in public schools
4. A place in the special education program for students who are disabled, hospitalized, or are in any similar institution and who are unable to attend schools
5. Granting to students with disabilities the same advantages as the other students have, including school material, food, and scholarships
6. Compulsory enrollment in the regular courses of public and private schools for people with disability able to integrate the regular educational system

It is important to say that the Brazilian Constitution of 1988 is considered one of the most modern ones, worldwide, in terms of civil rights and social gains, despite several examples of breaking constitutional rights throughout Brazilian history, not to mention during the dictatorship.

All the chapters dealing with citizens' rights and government's duty in the Constitution have articles related to people with disability. One can have a general view of these articles as follows: In relation to social welfare work, the law guarantees the qualification and rehabilitation of people with disability and their insertion into the society. The articles also grant a monthly minimum wage for those already proved unable to make a living on their own. For education, the main objective is to guarantee equal school opportunities, allowing students with disability to have their needs fulfilled, if possible, in a regular educational system.

In the chapter about family, children, teenagers, and adults, the Constitution states that specialized programs to protect and assist people with any kind of disability should be created. As well, these people's social integration can be assisted by helping them to find jobs and to live with other people, and allowing them to have easy access to public services by eliminating prejudice. The new Constitution also reserves a percentage for public services and prohibits any kind of discrimination as far as wages and hiring criteria for people with disability are concerned. It stipulates that people with disability forced to retire shall receive full wage (CVI 1990).

With the promulgation of the new Constitution, states and cities had to include in their legislation articles about the rights of the people with disabilities. Many of these laws still need regulation to be put in practice. Although meager, the effects of some of these provisions can already be seen. There are six cities offering among their services buses with facilities for wheelchair users and adapted street curbs. Each state secretary of education must, when building new schools, adopt architectonic plans that allow easy access for students with disability. Though on a small scale, some government agencies and some private companies are already hiring people with disabilities. However, the achievements are still few.

What has been done differs significantly from what is provided for by the law. Brazil has been facing a serious socioeconomic crisis which has severely affected the quality of educational services, mainly those of special education, not allowing the fulfillment of constitutional rights in this area. Trying to find an explanation for the current situation is difficult since it is difficult to distinguish between the lack of political will and the limitations imposed by the real lack of financial resources.

In short, modern and updated laws foresee for people with disabilities the rights to health, leisure, work, and mainly to an education that fulfills their needs inside the general context of education, but there is not enough practical action to guarantee the fulfillment of these rights.

Policies

There is no clear national policy on special education in Brazil. There are some documents dealing with principles and rules, but even the organization of institutions in charge of special education services nationwide does not favor the formulation of a coherent and particular policy for special education in the country. At every government's change, the structure of special education changes as well, abolishing and creating new institutions responsible for formulating a national policy on special eduction.

A historic retrospective shows that subjects related to special education have been dealt with as specific questions in the general plans for the country. The first National Plan of Education, written in 1962, destined, according to its revision of 1965, 50 percent of the National Fund for Elementary Schools to the education of the handicapped as well as scholarships to assist children with any kind of disability. There was not, at that time, an official policy on special education. Funds were sent to private institutions so that they could assist people with disability throughout their specialized services.

The National Center for Special Education was founded in 1973 with the purpose of formulating policies and of normalizing special education in Brazil. In 1977, the CENESP drew up the first National Plan for Special Education. The main guidelines were the following:

1. Extensive Action of Access to Education (mainly access to different treatment)
2. Optimistic Action (taking advantage of resources available and integration on a pedagogical-administrative basis)
3. Preventive Action (previous diagnosis and assistance)
4. Improvement Action (of the educational system, with as high a level of efficiency and as low an operating cost as possible)
5. Follow-up Actions (permanent education)

However, the plan still designated 58 percent of its budget to private institutions and only 14.48 percent to public institutions assisting people with disabilities. The integration of students with disabilities into public schools was announced theoretically, but funds were still being sent to private institutions to finance those students' assistance.

In 1985, the center drew up a plan called "Special education: New proposal," which tried to regulate rules to give financial and/or technical support for special education in public and private schools. Although well written, the plan still reserved most of its resources for private institutions, without foreseeing means to guarantee the usage of its technical guidelines when rendering educational services.

Today, special education officially belongs to the Secretaria Nacional de

Educação Basica (SNEB, National Secretary for Fundamental Education) which has a special education coordinating agency in its structure. It is in charge of formulating policies and rules and of coordinating the process of improvement of special education in the field of the Ministry of Education (SENEB 1990).

The basic guidelines for special education are drawn up on a national level, but each state has an institution or agency in its department of education in charge of helping people with special education needs. These agencies vary according to the regional peculiarities and local educational alternatives available.

The educational system on a city level is in charge of providing pre-school and elementary education and must also have services for students with disability. On the federal level, there is the National Coordinating Agency for the Integration of People with Disability (CORDE) founded in 1986 and linked to the Ministry of Social Affairs. This body coordinates the actions of national administrative agencies "for necessary and appropriate treatment of subjects related to people with disability, aiming at assuring the fulfillment of their basic rights and their effective social integration" (CORDE, 1992a, 1992b, and 1992c).

Many times, the actions of government institutions in charge of special education have created conflicts and problems in relation to their functions and to resources destined for their activities. Nevertheless, in 1991 a group of experts in special education was created to organize in a paper all the necessary subsidies to formulate a National Policy of Integration for People with Disability. The national policy for integration of special education into regular education was written with the help of technicians from the Special Education Coordinating Agency (SENEB) (CORDE 1992c). This policy is to be adopted by the Ministry of Education (MEC) and carried out by the state secretaries of education in the Brazilian states and cities, with the technical support of the special education institutions in charge.

The general objective of this new policy is "to integrate people with disability into the regular education system physically and socially, allowing them to have easy access, enrollment and permanence in the educational system. A National Policy of Integration does not consist of an administrative reorganization of educational services but, above all, implies a deep socio-cultural and pedagogical change" (CORDE 1992c). Integration, in this policy, is seen under a sociopedagogical and administrative point of view. It is based on an internationally accepted philosophical principle of the rights of people with disability to equal educational opportunities and to be, whenever possible, integrated into a regular educational system.

The basic guidelines of this policy are defined as follows:

1. To integrate the actions of the several levels of educational and administrative planning on the federal, state, and city levels, under the coordination of the Ministry of Education

2. To draw up plans based on real Brazilian problems, with the community's help, affirming follow-up of actions
3. To give specialized assistance, as soon as possible, based on a diagnosis taken from general and pedagogical evaluations
4. To rethink the educational philosophy, considering and respecting people's differences, which implies individualized assistance
5. To give support to the regular educational system in the enrollment of students with disability
6. To improve the schools' curricula, making the access of students with disability easier
7. To incorporate private and public institutions as strategies for programs of integration
8. To pledge and to make social groups, schools, families, and people with disability aware of their abilities, working against negative attitudes, such as rejection and prejudice
9. To finance institutional projects to examine questions of integration
10. To respect the criteria already established by institutions in charge of special education in the decision-making process

The fact that there is a new national policy of integration for people with disability does not mean there is unification and coherence among the educational practices in the country. Special education in Brazil is characterized by a number of services. The great majority are private, which makes the adoption of a singular policy difficult. The national policy to integrate people with disability into the regular educational system means, however, a very important achievement for Brazilian special education, since it tries to put several professionals and institutions from this field together. One hopes that it will gain enough financial and political support to turn these proposals into real actions.

Teachers, Schools, Curriculum, and Pedagogy

Teachers

The training of teachers to work with special education in Brazil has gone through two different phases in the last decades. The first period aimed at structuring high school courses. The second period, from 1972 to 1989, aimed at structuring graduate courses on pedagogy.

In the beginning, teachers with a high school level of education could work in any special education area as long as they had attended specialization courses. At that time, the qualifications of professionals working in special education showed significant variations in training as a result of the differences in content and duration of the specialization courses.

Today, most of these teachers attend graduate courses offering specific qualifications in the area of pedagogy. There is already a large number of colleges and universities, public and private, offering undergraduate and graduate courses in special education all over the country. The city of São Paulo has the most programs with fourteen institutions offering courses in special education.

However, this does not mean that most of the professionals working in special education have graduated from college. There are still many teachers with only secondary school education working in the area. In agreement with the educational poll carried out in 1989, the distribution of teachers working in specialized institutions according to their education level was documented, as shown in figure 7.1.

An explanation for the great number of teachers with only secondary school education can be found to have a socioeconomical basis: low wages and difficult access to universities. Another explanation can be found in policies for human resources. Opportunities for special education training have, for a long time, privileged people working in the administrative areas. As a consequence, university scholarships for the training for special education technicians, in Brazil or abroad, were granted to administrative personnel in detriment to the training of more qualified teachers had been working directly with people with disability.

The state secretaries of education of each Brazilian state determine through their wage policy the payment of the special education teacher, following the general tendency to pay according to the professional level of qualification. Most of the states do not have any difference in wages between the regular and special education teacher.

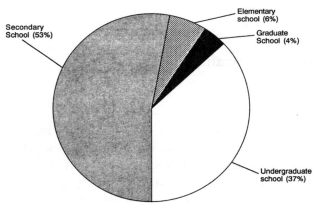

Figure 7.1 Distribution of the number of (*Special Education*) teaching positions, according to education level (1989).

Schools

There are about 1,262 institutions for special education in Brazil, most of them belonging to private enterprise (see figure 7.2). They receive financial and technical support from public organizations. The special education approaches offered by these private institutions vary significantly, ranging from a segregated clinical approach to integrated services with an educational approach.

Although the public educational system assists only 2.3 percent of all students with disability in the country, it has special education features established with objective criteria and adopted by most of the Brazilian states. The state of São Paulo, for instance, in its document "Guidelines of Special Education" states that "The several features on educational services offered by the State Secretary of Education for students with disability (special class, resources room, itinerant education, regular class or the different combinations of these features) must provide conditions so that the student becomes more and more independent, able to benefit from the resources offered by the society in general and to take part in its improvement" (São Paulo 1989).

Definitions of service features can be found, with some differences, in explanatory documents of special education in each state. Special education in Brazil is basically organized around the following special education resources: special schools, special classes, resource rooms, and itinerant education.

Special schools provide for special education that is organized to assist exclusively students with disability. Special classes are in a regular school. A group of students with the same disability gather together under the responsibility of a specialized teacher. Resource rooms consist of a school class, provided with special materials and equipment, where a specialized

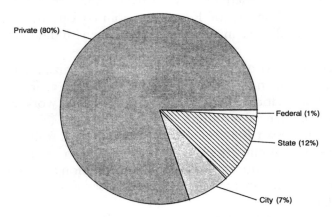

Figure 7.2 Distribution of specialized institutions, 1989.

teacher assists students with disability with their specific problems in order to help them attend a regular class. In itinerant education, a specialized teacher assists students with disability who are enrolled in regular schools in the community according to their ages. The itinerant teachers visit several schools where they help teachers and students with disability.

Curriculum

Brief comments will be made about the curriculum and pedagogy of special education in Brazil because of the diversity and extent of the subject. The National Center for Special Education drew up proposals for a curriculum which has been adapted in the several regions in the country. São Paulo has drawn up its own proposals.

One cannot affirm that there is a singular pedagogical tendency used in the education of students with disability. Some professionals, influenced by foreign literature, try to use techniques of behavior modification, mainly in the education of students with mental disability. Some of these techniques, however, are still not well accepted by special education services of a philanthropic nature.

Major Controversies and Issues in Special Education

The most challenging issue today in special education in Brazil is the integration of students with disability into the regular educational system. Integration issues have existed for a long time in the basic guidelines for special education. Yet the concepts are poorly understood by professionals working in the area, and there have not been concrete actions by institutions in charge to make it function to the benefit of students with disability.

A recent study carried out by CORDE and the secretary of special education at the Ministry of Education pointed out the following main difficulties in the effective integration of students with disability:

1. Inadequate coordination of joint and organized actions in several levels of planning, as much from government as from private enterprise, in relation to health, education, welfare, work, and justice
2. Lack of financial resources
3. Planning apart from the country's educational reality
4. Lack of continuity of plans and actions due to administrative changes
5. Shortage in educational opportunities among regions, states, and rural and urban regions, due to socioeconomic and geographical imbalances
6. Inadequateness of incentives for research plans and of dissemination of information on already existing educational integration experiments

7. Lack of information about the educational needs of students with disability, creating disinterest and resistance from most schools in the regular educational system in accepting these students
8. Late diagnosis of the disability, harming the person's development and making his or her integration more difficult
9. Lack of information for assisting people with disabilities on the part of teachers and technicians working in regular schools, due to the inappropriate curriculum of the teaching courses
10. Inappropriateness of curriculum and programs to assist the diversification and individualization necessary for the process of integration
11. Inappropriateness of space, lack of material, equipment, and specialized assistance making the access, stay, and course of people with disability in regular schools more difficult
12. Lack of information in society and the school community, both of which are not prepared for the challenge of integration, making them develop inappropriate attitudes toward people with disability

Several other factors negatively influence the process of integration. These include inappropriate dispersion of official resources; inappropriate mechanisms of evaluation, students' placement, and classification; inappropriate assistance; lack of experienced and competent teachers; lack of information and elucidation; and lack of the political will to unchain essential means to fulfill the right to education.

Aside from the difficulties imposed by lack of resources and a basic structure, there is a factor which cannot be disregarded—attitude barriers. Prejudice and negative attitudes toward people with disability can still be pointed out as the obstructing factor to their educational and social integration. Teachers and administrators of regular schools are not ready to accept and work with students with special needs and, instead, perpetuate myths and prejudices to justify their segregation. Often the parents of children with disabilities also demand special education in segregated settings because they believe that their children will not get educational assistance appropriate for their development in the regular educational system. This point of view is, intentionally or unintentionally, reinforced by some special education institutions and by their professionals who claim to have complete knowledge about special education techniques and about students with disability.

Although one can keep listing the problems and difficulties of integration, one can also note a significant evolution from a segregated type of educational assistance to a special type of education which is being inserted more and more into the regular educational context, sharing goals, and methodologies.

There are single experiments that try to develop ways of putting the guidelines of integration imposed by the special education agencies into effect. The state of Santa Catarina, for instance, has carried out an intensive campaign, boosting the enrollment of students with disability into the regular educational system since 1987. It has created the training course "Agents of Integration" to train professionals to assist these students, and aims at teaching basic concepts of special education to regular school educators. The goal is to form agents of integration to work in the administrative levels, regionally, and in each school.

The precariousness of the Brazilian public educational system is at the center of the controversy. Some parents and professionals share the same concern that children with disability will not receive appropriate assistance due to the bad conditions of the schools and to the lack of informed educators. Other groups defend integration, not only as a way of guaranteeing the right to a public and free education for people with disability, but also as a way of improving the quality of education offered in schools. In Brazil, many children with special needs fail and later they quit school because they do not find alternative methodologies compatible to their socioeconomical and cultural environments. To insert special education into the regular school through techniques such as individualized teaching could benefit a great number of students, not only those with disability. As a matter of fact, some studies show that people with disability are not the only people in need of special education, but that all students have different educational needs that require alternative methods of education.

A decisive factor for the integration of students with special needs and with disability into the regular educational system is that they are no longer a minority in Brazilian society. As Castro (1989) says "[I]n a process to democratize education, as the system develops itself, greater is the pressure on a much more diversified supply of services which can meet the needs of the segments of this society and which are marginalized, becoming 'special' groups because of their handicapped conditions, age, lack of culture, money and/or social status."

Emerging and Future Trends

Some trends which may guide special education in Brazil in the following years have been discussed in this chapter. Special education will continue to be influenced by the process of social democratization that the country still fights to consolidate. The quantitative and qualitative improvement of services will depend on the political importance given to general education in the country.

One hopes that society will become more conscious of the presence and rights of people with disability and manage to change the situation of abandonment that many people with disability have already faced in this country.

In addition, the increasing number of professionals graduating from universities and their studies will definitely help to improve the quality of special education services.

Nowadays private institutions and government agencies, through reflection and dialogue, are trying to join efforts to offer special education that can embrace more students with alternative services that really fulfill their needs. People working on several projects in the state of São Paulo are trying to unite with the agencies in charge of health and education programs, with the objective of giving support to the access to and appropriate assistance of children with disability into the regular public educational system. People with visual and hearing disabilities already have a successful history of school integration through resource classes and units of itinerant education.

The insertion of special education into the general educational context seems to be a solid trend in the guiding philosophies of special education in Brazil. However, this insertion has to be followed by an improvement of the general public educational system and by adaptation on the part of traditional education. Otherwise, integration will probably be fated to fail. If the mainstreaming movement is not correctly implemented, it will be charged with promoting socioeducational retrogression since it will afford the opportunity for excuses to segregate students with disability again.

Brazil will have to go a long way to guarantee special education services of high quality. But it also has qualified professionals, organized groups of people with disability, and special education institutions. Together, they can supply an education that is called *special* only because it is able to meet the individual needs of any person in the Brazilian society.

Note

1. The information presented in this chapter was taken from studies carried out nationwide and is therefore generic in nature, rather than going into depth on any specific region.

References

Castro, A. L. 1989. Democracia e atendimento educacional especializado. *Revista Integração*, July/August. Brazil: SESPE/MEC.

CENESP, and MEC. 1986. Portaria 69, 28 August. CENESP and MEC.

Centro de Vida Independente (CVI), and the Rotary Club. 1990. *Etica e legislação. Os direitos das pessoas portadoras de deficiencia no Brasil*. Rio de Janeiro: CVI.

CORDE, and Centro de Vida Independente do Rio de Janeiro. 1992a. *Midia e Deficiencia—Manual de Estilo*. Rio de Janeiro: CVI.

CORDE, Comité dos Direitos da Criança, and Sociedade Brasileira de Pediatria. 1992b. *15,000,000.* Brazil: CORDE.

CORDE, and MEC. 1992. *Subsidios para a elaboração da politica nacional para a integração da pessoa portadora de deficiencia.* Brazil: CORDE.

Federal Constitution. 1989. Law 7.853, 24 October.

Fontes, J. A. 1990. *Lesao cerebral—Causas e prevenção.* Brazil: CORDE.

Instituto Brasileiro de Geografia e Estatistica (IBGE). 1987–92. *Crianças e adolescentes— Indicadores sociais.* 5 vols. Rio de Janeiro: IBGE.

Jannuzzi, G. 1989. Por uma lei de diretrizes e bases da educação que propicie a educação escolar instituladoes deficientes mentais. *Cadernos Cedes 23.* São Paulo: Publisher Cortez.

Ministry of Education, and Centro Nacional de Educação Especial. Educação Especial. 1985. *Nova proposata.* Brazil: Ministry of Education.

Ministry of Education (MEC), and Secretaria Nacional de Educação Basica (SNEB). 1992. *Coordenação de educação especial. Proposta do grupo de trabalho instituido pela portaria 6, 8/22/90.* Brazil: Ministry of Education.

Ministry of Education. 1992. *Sinopse estatistica da educação especial. Instituiçoes especializadas,* vol. 2. Brazil: Ministry of Education.

Oliveira, A. 1983. A Criança Exceptional—Causas e consequencias. Pro-Criança 2. *Separata Informativo 7.* Florianópolis, Santa Catarina.

Polifica Nacional de Educação Especial. 1989. *Cadernos CEDES 23.* Brazil: Publisher Cortez.

Secretaria da Educação. 1989. *Coordenadoria de estudos e normas pedagogicas (SE/ CENP)—Subsidios relativos à avaliacção de crianças e jovens com suspeita de.* São Paulo: Secretaria de Educação.

Secretaria de Estado de Sauide, Departamento de Assistencia ao Escolar. 1987. *Avaliação psicológica de alunos da rede estadual de Ensino—Orientação aos Recursos da comunidade.* Brazil: Secretaria da Educaçao.

8

Indonesia

CONNY SEMIAWAN

*I*ndonesia consists of 13,677 islands curved across the Indian Ocean from Borneo to the north of Australia. Six thousand of the islands are inhabited although in parts there are minimal transportation facilities, especially to the smaller and more remote islands. As one of the most ethnically diverse countries in the world, Indonesia has almost three hundred ethnic groups and as many languages and dialects among its population of 179 million. Bahasa Indonesia is the official language.

With a moderately high population growth of 2.1 percent, more than half of the population of Indonesia is under the age of twenty, and large numbers of children need education. A new cabinet and a different policy in education, giving priority to extending educational opportunities to the largest, or "normal" group of Indonesia's thirty million school children, began in 1985. The Second Law on the National Educational System was passed in Indonesia in 1989. With this law, equality of opportunity in education has been underlined as being of importance for education in a democratic society. By 1992 almost 100 percent of normal elementary school age children were receiving education. Only 56 percent of junior secondary school-age children were enrolled, however, which is why the government has introduced compulsory schooling for children from seven to fifteen years of age, beginning with the Sixth Five-Year Plan in 1994.

As Indonesia still struggles to implement compulsory education for all children ages 7 to 15 (formerly 7 to 12), it has mandated that public schools

About the Author • Dr. Conny Semiawan is chairperson of the Indonesian National Consortium on Educational Sciences; directorate general of Higher Education for the Ministry of Education and Culture; and professor at the State Graduate Program, University of Indonesia and at the Institute for Teacher Training and Educational Science, Jakarta.

take all the necessary steps to provide schooling and regular educational programs for "normal" children as a first priority in providing equality of education for all. Thus, the concept of equality in educational opportunities being expanded to include children with special needs has taken a back seat to the greater national goal of first enrolling all "normal" children.

Prevalence of Children with Special Needs

In Indonesia, general health statistics are either unavailable or unreliable. By one estimate, there are 300,000 children with handicaps, a little over 1 percent of all elementary-age school children (Carpenter 1987). A 1982 World Bank document estimated the incidence of handicapped children in the seven to eighteen age range with blindness at .9 percent, deafness at .3 percent, and mental retardation at .4 percent. There seems to be a high incidence of blindness, up to 1.2 percent of the country's entire population.

In the absence of reliable data on the prevalence of handicaps in Indonesia, one study devised a rough screening method, separated into handicap category (with the exception of those emotionally disturbed or gifted, which require more detailed testing techniques), as a first step in determining how many special needs children there were throughout the country. Due to the prohibitive expense of employing professionals (particularly psychologists) to conduct this testing, a simple screening measure was devised to be used by laypersons. It was hoped that the results of this testing would lead to the establishment of a national data base containing reliable statistics on the educational, social, and physical status of special needs children.

Initially all 27 provinces, all regions, and all districts of Indonesia (3,229 in all) were surveyed. A more detailed survey was subsequently undertaken of one rural village, Blanakan, in the Ciasem subdistrict, Subang district, and in one urban village, Srengseng Sawah in the Pasar Minggu subdistrict, metropolitan Jakarta. Initial screening in all provinces was carried out by laypersons, but the more detailed diagnostic evaluation in the two selected villages was conducted by doctors and other medical personnel. The medical specialists concentrated on the detection of handicaps in the seven-to-twelve-year age group, covering the areas of low vision and blindness, hearing impairment, mental retardation, physical handicaps, and cerebral palsy. This evaluation was done to develop a basis that could be used in placing special needs children in the most appropriate educational setting. This diagnostic evaluation was carried out over four days in Blanakan and fourteen days in Srengseng Sawah.

The findings of the survey conducted by laypersons on the number of special needs children and their assessed handicaps were compared with the findings of the medical specialists. This testing provided guidelines for the detection of handicaps in seven-year-olds to twelve-year-olds. Various standardized tests were used to determine the psychological, medical, and physical characteristics of the children. The Raven Progressive test was used, as it is easy to administer and supposedly free of cultural bias. The findings of both surveys pointed out that of the total general school-age population, 5 percent were not attending schools of any sort (Semiawan 1986).

The Community Based Detection and Intervention of Growth and Development Problems of the Child was started as a pilot project in 1986–87, based on instruments developed by an interdisciplinary team. Among the first instruments were checklists to identify family risks, abnormality of head circumference, children with potential development problems, children at risk of having abnormal behavior, and children with vision defects. In 1987–89 the project also included identification and intervention of hearing defects among children under five years of age. The results of the pilot study are shown in table 8.1.

Causes of Disability

A range of causes account for disability in Indonesia. Malnutrition and poverty are prominent, as are unsanitary conditions and a continuing reliance on folk medicine in outlying areas. In the rural villages where 80 percent of the population live, for example, older women pass on folk medicine to the next generation. Carpenter (1987) points out that the harmful implications of such practices are clear for pre- and postnatal care, as is the potential for higher rates of handicaps due to lack of medical care and informed health practice. In a 1986 paper, Hendarmin said that "[t]o decrease the incidence of both trauma in remote areas with minor health facilities where deliveries were done by local witch doctors, the Government

TABLE 8.1. Results of Pilot Project on Children under 5 Years

Problems Identified	1986/87 (%)	1987/88 (%)
Family risks	47.6	43.8
Abnormal head circumference	16.5	11.3
Risk of developmental defects	13.5	18.1
Risk of abnormal behavior	11.7	5.1
Vision defects	3.4	2.2
Hearing defects	–	0.7

Note: The numbers of children tested were 16,947 in 1986/87 and 17,341 in 1987/88.

Source: Leimena. 1980.

has set up a crash program of education for those witch doctors, to improve their knowledge on health sanitation" (427).

Identification of Special Needs

Prior to making an accurate assessment of special needs, a rough identification of the problem must first be undertaken. Apart from the rough screening measures mentioned above, the identification of special needs in children can be done through several widely used psychological tests. These range from those that are very simple to administer and interpret to the very complex, which must be viewed within a wider social context.

In Indonesia, as in many other countries, a shortage of psychologists and other qualified personnel is likely to continue. Proposals to train nonpsychologists in some aspects of testing, however, are likely to be strongly opposed on the grounds of a lowering of professional standards (Mittler 1978). There is great demand for reliable testing instruments and samples from nonprofessionals, nevertheless, as well as for training courses in how to use them.

In order to decide which tests should be used and by whom they should be administered, a working group, or WG (including psychologists, counselors, administrators, educators, medical doctors and others from universities, nongovernment organizations [NGOs], and government departments) was established in the Office for Education and Cultural Research and Development (OECRD) in 1979.

Labeling of the Handicapped

Labels describe, identify, and distinguish differences among people. Confronted with the wide range of differences in children, society is inclined to establish limits as to what is acceptable and what measures up to cultural expectations. These criteria are easily exceeded (as is the case with gifted and talented children), but in many cases those who fail to meet the standards are labeled disabled or handicapped by society. Taking into account these limits of acceptability, the term *normal* was devised to describe those children who conform to certain standards of conduct and thinking (Rozenzweig et al. 1968). Those children who either fail to meet or exceed these limits because of dissimilarities in development are labeled *different.*

The use of labels can be valuable in that they assist professionals in communicating with each other in an effective way and provide them with a common ground for the evaluation of their research findings. Labels are also used as the basis for distinguishing those who require additional support or services and to assist professionals in identifying the special needs of a group of people.

During a series of seminars held by the Association of South East Asian Nations (ASEAN) in the 1980s, a broader definition of special needs and the general concept of special education was accepted by special education delegates from the five countries involved—Indonesia, Thailand, Malaysia, Philippines, and Brunei. This ASEAN view of special education concurred with the Warnock concept, which encompasses a whole range and variety of assistance to help children overcome educational difficulties, regardless of location or whether these needs should be met on a full- or part-time basis (Warnock 1978). These children were to be referred to as *children with special educational needs,* and it was determined that they should have access either on a full- or part-time basis to teachers or other professionals with appropriate qualifications in an environment equipped with the educational and physical resources necessary to fulfill the *child's special needs (CSN).* Thus, the CSN label was accepted by experts and professionals during this period, and this concept has widely spread to special education departments in higher education also. However, the implementation of this concept into the school system has not yet been realized.

Defining the Population in Indonesia

The term *special needs child* in Indonesia refers to a developmental deficit in terms of sensory abilities, communication abilities, mental characteristics, physical characteristics, or social behavior, to such an extent that the child requires a modified educational program. In Indonesia, this form of education is termed *special education.*

Special education in Indonesia is designed for children with special needs, those who differ from others in their peer group, often in a significant way. In Indonesia, those requiring special education are divided into certain categories: blind and low vision; hearing impaired and children with communication disabilities; mentally retarded; severely mentally retarded; physically handicapped; cerebral palsy (CP); emotionally disturbed; and double and multiply handicapped. As opposed to policies followed in other countries, education for the gifted and talented comes under the heading of special education in Indonesia. The least developed special education programs, however, are for those children in the categories of gifted and talented and double and multiply handicapped.

To fully develop the potential of these children, educational approaches must be adapted to meet their needs. This can be achieved in different ways, through both segregated and integrated education, and on an individual basis. From a total elementary-school population of almost 30 million, there are presently 36,100 special needs children receiving education at the elementary school level in Indonesia, Statistics show that 1,900 of these children are in 23 national special schools; 25,500 children are in 516 private special schools; 180 children are integrated in 92 normal schools; and 8,520 children are in 209 semi-integrated schools (Sokolah Dasar Luar Biasa [SDLB], chap. 4).

Schools, Teachers, Curriculum, and Pedagogy

Special education has a long history in Indonesia. There were special schools in Indonesia during the Dutch colonial era, long before World War II. The first such school was the Special School for the Blind in Bandung, West Java. Up to the present day, most special schools have been established and run by NGOs, although there is a subdirectorate of the Directorate General of Primary and Secondary Education at the Ministry of Education and Culture, which takes care of the curriculum of these special schools.

The NGOs have long realized the need for external support to assist special needs children in fulfilling their potential. Often parents of handicapped children have stirred and prodded society and the school system to help them recognize their responsibilities in assisting these children.

To date there are 312 special schools In Indonesia, categorized as shown in table 8.2. In addition, there are 213 schools for children with different and multiple handicaps, 92 integrated schools, and 209 semi-integrated schools (SDLB). Most of these special schools are run by NGOs, and are primarily nonresidential.

Mainstreaming, in the sense of education for special needs children in the least restricted environment is not yet fully a reality in Indonesia. However, several forms of integrated education were initiated in the 1980s, as follows:

1. Special needs children received full-time instruction in the normal classroom with some support and assistance. Most of them were identified as

TABLE 8.2. Special Schools in Indonesia

School Category	Number of Schools
Blind and low vision	49
Deaf and hearing impaired	91
Mentally handicapped	82
Severely mentally handicapped	51
Physically handicapped	10
Cerebral palsy	14
Emotionally disturbed	15

low vision and received extra instruction from teachers who had taken a course on teaching the visually handicapped child in the classroom.

2. In other cases, special needs children attended a special class in a school building built near a normal school so they would have contact with these children at school break times.

3. Some special needs children received full-time education in a special class or unit, with social contact between them and normal school children.

4. Finally, following the fully segregated approach, full-time instruction was given to special needs children in special schools.

Before enactment of the Second Law on Education in 1989, teachers for elementary schools were required to possess a certificate from a Special Teacher Senior Secondary School. Teachers for special schools required an additional two years of training. Since 1989, teachers must have a college education in addition to a secondary education. A diploma II is now required for elementary level teachers. These additional qualifications are also required for special education teachers. It is hoped these better-trained teachers will be able to adapt more easily to the demands of a new technological and industrial era in Indonesia's remarkably rapid development.

Legislation

Categories of education offered through the school system are general education, vocational education, special education, public service education, religious education, academic education and professional education. The Special Education Act (part of the Second Educational Law on the National System of Education, or *Peraturan Pemerintah* [PP] 73, 1991) has stipulated the right of the handicapped child to receive education. However, the education mentioned in that act only includes segregated services provided through the Elementary Special School for the Handicapped (SDLB), and further education at the secondary level is only possible through the same kind of system.

The Second Educational Law contains three paragraphs significant to fulfilling the special education needs of handicapped children:

1. *Paragraph 6:* Every citizen has the right to equal opportunity to enjoy as broad an education as possible and to gain knowledge, abilities, and skills equivalent to basic education.

2. *Paragraph 8 (1):* Every citizen who has a deficiency, physical as well as mental, has the right to special education.

3. *Paragraph 8 (2):* Every citizen who has an outstanding ability and outstanding intelligence has the right to special attention.

The Social Context of Special Education

In 1980, the National Curriculum Center of the Office for Education and Cultural Research and Development (OECRD) and the Ministry of Education and Culture, in cooperation with Helen Keller International (HKI) and other NGOs, undertook implementation of several pilot projects to establish integrated education for special needs children in normal schools. Integrated education was introduced in four cities in Indonesia—Bandung, West Java; Jakarta; Jogjakarta in Central Java; and Surabaya in East Java. Between 1983 and 1984, this program, which was very successful, involved over two hundred visually impaired children. Most unfortunately, due to funding constraints and lack of follow-up, the pilot program was discontinued in 1985.

In addition to the cooperative effort with Helen Keller International to integrate visually handicapped children, OECRD also conducted a survey on integrating the hearing impaired. One hundred and fifty children with hearing disabilities throughout the country were identified as receiving education at normal schools and doing well.

By coincidence, Indonesia was appointed at this time as coordinator of the ASEAN Special Education group of the Australia ASEAN Development Plan. Five countries (Malaysia, Philippines, Thailand, Indonesia, and Brunei) designed a common program outlining methods for identification of the handicapped, curriculum development, and development of teaching materials, teacher training, education for the gifted and talented, and learning-teaching models. Integrated education was one of the most significant points deliberated by this group.

Noting the valuable role of NGOs in assistance to the disabled, enhanced cooperation between NGOs and government agencies was recognized as a means of promoting public awareness toward the handicapped in society. A community-based approach was therefore strongly recommended by this group.

Prior to this cooperation between ASEAN countries, national policies, programs, and implementation guidelines were developed, aimed at identifying different types of disabilities and their social and economic dimensions, program and curriculum development, and different methods of learning. These initiatives were taken to meet the needs of disabled and other special needs children. Promotion of public awareness and dissemination of information on disability-related matters to the general public, administrators, and decision makers were also given priority.

Between 1970 and 1986 a number of initiatives were undertaken. Concrete results were achieved in the following areas:

1. Integrated planning was developed to coordinate efforts to assist special needs children, executed by the working group of OECRD.

2. A model for identifying type and degree of handicap was designed, based on results of the detailed surveys carried out in Jakarta and rural areas, as mentioned earlier in this chapter.

3. The pilot project for integrated education, conducted by OECRD in cooperation with various government and nongovernment organizations, was well accepted by school administrators and other officials. In some regions, each school enrolled two to three visually handicapped students (usually placed in a classroom of approximately fifty sighted students). Films were made to document this program.

4. Orientation and mobility courses (O and M) as well as other upgrading courses were introduced to teachers of special schools, and vocational approaches were developed.

5. Other disability-related upgrading courses were conducted nationwide.

6. A survey was conducted to determine how many hearing impaired children were independently integrated into the existing system.

7. The program for assisting mentally handicapped children was revised and modified.

8. New workshops for the mentally retarded were established and developed.

9. Coordination between the government and the Indonesian Society for Disabled Children (YPAC) was strengthened. This was a valuable step because YPAC operates sixteen schools and rehabilitation centers throughout the twenty-seven provinces of Indonesia. Eighty percent of the children in YPAC centers have cerebral palsy.

10. The Home for Emotionally Disturbed Children in Jakarta (Pamardi Siwi) became a model for many professionals.

11. Programs for the gifted and talented were developed. These included introducing identification tools, upgrading teacher-training courses, and providing enrichment programs for children. Some gifted and talented students were sent to Holland in 1986 for educational opportunities in that country. Some of these students have since returned, having completed their studies. Approximately 40 percent will finish this year.

12. Program coordination meetings were held with other ASEAN countries yearly from 1980 to 1983, in an effort to foster international special education. The meetings consisted of workshops to discuss substantive issues for special education development. Workshops covered the following topics: guidelines for the identification of children with special needs; curriculum development toward improvement of special education programs in ASEAN countries; identification of teaching materials development; learning-teaching models; follow-up on curriculum development for exceptional children; educational

services for the gifted; and teacher education for special education
teachers.

13. Special schools where handicapped students are integrated in one
building on the elementary level were established (SDLB).

An emphasis on educating normal children which began in 1985 meant
that by 1992 almost 100 percent of normal elementary school-age children
were receiving education. Special needs children have not been completely
left out of this endeavor. Further initiatives in special education were undertaken between 1986 and 1992. However, integrated education and the
concept of mainstreaming special needs children were not mentioned in the
Special Education Act of 1991. Programs initiated by the Ministry of Education and Culture in the 1980s were not followed up on. The Special
Education working group of OECRD was removed to the Institution of
Teacher Training and Education Sciences and became an NGO.

The same people who were deeply involved with the OECRD have
accomplished the following over the 1986–92 period:

1. An identification tool was developed and adapted to be used for
assessing multiply handicapped children.
2. An Indonesian sign language was created based on a national survey
on existing sign language and developed in several areas of the country.
This dictionary of Indonesian sign language is based on a total communication approach.
3. Books on different types of children's special needs were developed
and published.
4. Seminars and upgrading courses for teachers were conducted.

Major Issues in Special Education

Mainstreaming is not a controversial issue in Indonesia due to general and
overall ignorance of the concept. In cases that integrated education was
introduced and became known, understood, and accepted by professionals
involved, it was very successful. However, because this concept is familiar to
so few educators and others, provision of education for special needs children through normal school is not yet fully implemented.

Integration of handicapped children into the normal school system,
particularly for those with complex disorders, is usually hampered by prejudice from the general public, other parents, or fellow students. This is
usually caused by ignorance concerning the integrated education program
and can be eased or prevented by careful education and preparation prior to

introduction of the program. Complete acceptance of the integrated education program by the student's family and community in general must be based on an understanding of the various forms of support that will be provided to meet the child's special needs.

Without a wholehearted commitment by teachers to receive children with disabilities into the classroom, it is unlikely that the program will be a success, regardless of how much careful planning has gone into it. To achieve this commitment, a training course to foster understanding by the teachers and provide them with the necessary resources to carry out the program, is essential. In general, teachers in Indonesia, including special education teachers, have mediocre status and low salaries. Certainly the country's best students will not enter the teaching profession, except for those who really feel compelled to teach.

The need for adequate staff and resources to meet the demands of enrolling special needs children in normal schools is a substantial factor to be considered. The school's ability to meet these needs is also based in part on the curriculum and teaching methods used, as well as staff commitment and school organization (their ability to adapt to the needs and demands of the present situation).

As a developing country, Indonesia needs to utilize all its resources, including those it will accrue by including the handicapped as contributing members of society. Improved treatment of handicapped children and adults by their communities will be a natural result of their inclusion in the education system and of being given an opportunity to participate in and contribute to society. Education plays an important role in every child's life, and special needs children gain as much from the socialization experience of attending normal schools as from their scholastic achievements.

In particular, for those special needs children able to adapt themselves to the existing school system, the door should be open for them to be integrated in a natural way. Teachers should be prepared to participate in a major educational endeavor that will enable special needs children to acquire the capabilities and confidence necessary for them to become productive members of society. Cooperation and assistance from all possible sources is necessary to achieve this goal.

References

Carpenter, R. L. 1987. Special education teacher preparation and service delivery in a developing country: Indonesia. *Teacher Education and Special Education* 10 (1):37–43.

Gallagher, K., et al. 1986. *Educating exceptional children.* 5th ed. Boston: Houghton Mifflin Co.

Hardman, M. L., et al. 1987. *Human exceptionality in society, school and family.* Boston: Allyn and Bacon, Inc.

Hendarmin, H. 1986. Indonesia. In *Proceedings of the 1st. Asian-Pacific Regional Conference on Deafness,* 476–78). Hong Kong: Hong Kong Society for the Deaf.

Leimena, Dr. 1989. Community based detection and intervention of growth and developmental problems among the under five children. In *Proceedings of the Second Asian-Pacific Conference on Deafness,* 271–76). Jakarta: Indonesian National Council on Social Welfare.

Mittler, P. 1978. *The psychological assessment of mental and physical handicaps.* London: Tavistock publications in association with Methuen and Co., Ltd. and Harper and Row Publisher, Inc.

Rosenzweig, I. 1968. *Understanding and teaching the dependent retarded child.* Darien, Connecticut: Teachers' Publishing Corporation.

Semiawan, C. 1986. A survey of handicapping conditions in school age children in two selected regions in Indonesia: Some issues of assessment and special education provision. In *Guidelines for the identification of children with special needs.* Jakarta: Office of Educational and Cultural R. and D., Ministry of Education and Culture.

Warnock, H. H. 1978. *Special education needs, Report of the committee of enquiry into the education of handicapped children and young people.* London: Her Majesty's Stationery Office.

World Bank. 1982. *Staff appraisal report, Indonesia second teacher training project.* East Asia and Pacific Office, World Bank. Report no. 364–76–IND.

9

Egypt

WASFY AZIZ BOULOS

*I*n Egypt, the state holds a conviction that education of the handicapped is one of its duties, and does not disregard these unlucky people. It extends to them the kind of care that conforms with their specific type of handicap be it physical, social, or psychological.

In Egypt, special education institutions are an integrated part of the education system. Therefore, it is advisable to deal with a description of this system in a few notes. In this way it becomes possible to understand the role which these special education institutions play. The general configuration of education in Egypt is illustrated in figure 9.1.

The Educational System in Egypt

As stipulated by the Law on Education 223 for the year 1988 (amending some articles of the Law 139 for the year 1981), the duration of preuniversity education extends over eleven school years, from age six to age seventeen. Since the 1988–89 school year, this education system has comprised the following:

1. Eight years of compulsory basic education. This consists of two tiers: the primary tier of five years and the preparatory tier of three years.
2. Three years of secondary education (general and technical).
3. Five years of advanced technical education.

About the Author • Dr. Wasfy Aziz Boulos is head of the foundations of education department at Assuit University. He specializes in comparative studies in education.

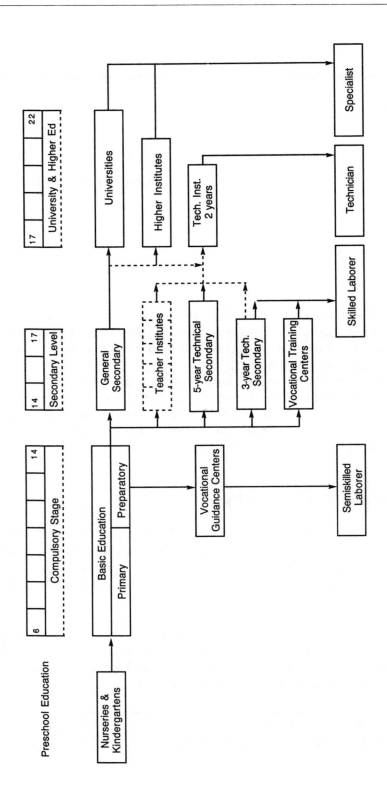

Figure 9.1   Education structure in The Arab Republic of Egypt starting from 1988–89

The educational ladder is preceded by kindergarten. This is an independent educational stage of two-year duration, for children aged four to six. Admission to and organization of kindergarten in government schools is controlled by rules and regulations in Ministerial Decree 154 of 1988 and the amendments of this decree in Ministerial Decree 34, dated 22 January 1990 and Ministerial Decree 411, dated 2 December 1990. In accordance with the aforesaid ministerial decrees, the kindergarten stage of education aims at the global development of preschool children and preparing them to join the basic education stage.

Basic education is a right of all Egyptian children reaching the age of six. The state is committed to provide it for them, and parents are committed to abide by it for a period of eight years. The governors issue the decrees required for organizing and carry out the compulsion and distribute school-age children to the basic education schools in the governorate. In case of room being available, children can be admitted at the age of five and a half, provided that class density is not affected. An examination of two sessions is held at the end of compulsory basic education. Successful students are awarded the basic education completion certificate.

Those who complete the primary tier of basic education and show vocational interests can complete the compulsory period in vocational training centers or schools or in vocational preparatory classes. Those who complete study in these centers or schools are awarded a certificate in vocational basic education and are entitled to join industrial or agricultural secondary education, in conformity with rules set by the minister, after the approval of the Higher Council for Preuniversity Education. Study in technical secondary education (industrial-agricultural-commercial) is provided at two levels. There is the level of qualification for skilled laborer in three-year technical secondary schools, and the level of qualification for trained technical laborer in five-year technical secondary schools.

A general examination of two sessions is held at the end of the third grade of technical secondary education. Successful candidates are awarded the three-year system technical school diploma, and the type of specialization is stated. Another examination is held at the end of the fifth year, whereby successful candidates are awarded the five-year system technical school diploma. The type of specialization is also stated in this certificate.

General secondary education is a parallel tier. Study in this type of education is general for all first and second grade students, and elective and specialized for third grade students. At the end of grade three, a general, one-session examination is held, and those who pass it are awarded the general secondary education completion certificate. Al-Azhar Education follows the same lines as general education as far as the number of hours is concerned.

University and higher education are pursued in universities and specialized higher institutes. Admission is given to students who obtain the general secondary school certificate and to those who complete technical secondary education with high scores. The duration of study ranges from two years in intermediate technical institutes to four or five years in university facilities and higher institutes.

Educational Care for Handicapped Students in Egypt

Educational care for handicapped students basically aims at tutoring and educating one category of pupils in the different stages of education. Those are pupils whose abilities, senses, or environment do not enable them to benefit from standard education. This calls for building up special programs to prepare these pupils for life and enable them to adjust to society as far as their conditions, abilities, and aptitudes allow.

Schools

The state established special schools as early as the year 1933. Today, these schools are careful to provide training for the handicapped to practice certain crafts, as their circumstances allow. The goal is to enable them to earn their own living through work.

Blindness has received special attention in Egypt. The Model Centre for Providing Care and Guidance for the Blind was established in El Zaitoun, Cairo after the 1952 revolution. During the years 1957 to 1958, special schools were established for blind students in general education, as well as in vocational education. As well, in 1958 Law 135 exempted blind students from completing the compulsory stage of education by fourteen years of age—an age stipulated in the laws regulating preparatory and primary education—and allowed these students two additional years. For hearing-impaired students, the state established schools starting in 1938 with a school for deaf females in Mataria, and one for males in Helwan, Cairo.

For children suffering from heart rheumatism, a separate primary school was set up in the Guiza governorate in 1964. This school, Al-Shafaa School, aims at securing the educational, medical, social, and psychological care needed for these children, besides achieving the ordinary school objectives. The regulations of the school also stipulate that a program for vocational qualification be affiliated with the school for those whose health conditions prevent them from following their academic studies after the preparatory stage. Care for the mentally handicapped started in the year 1956 when the Ministry of Education introduced a formal program for their education.

With the issue of Ministerial Decree 1, 1986, concerning rules of admission in the Ministry of Education schools, special education schools and classes came to comprise the following:

1. Schools for the blind, covering all preuniversity education stages.
2. Schools and classes for the partially sighted—those whose vision ranges from 6/24 to 6/60 in both eyes, or in the more powerful eye, after medication and with the use of appropriate eyeglasses.
3. Schools for the deaf and the partially hearing.
4. Schools and classes for mental education giving admission to those whose IQs range from 50 to 70. An exception is the Experimental School for Mental Education in Nasr City, which takes in the mentally handicapped with IQs of 30 to 50.
5. Hospital schools taking in invalid and convalescing children who are receiving treatment in hospitals with the agreement of health authorities.

It is worth noting that a number of institutions, ministries, and organizations exert collaborative efforts in caring for and educating handicapped children. One of these is the Ministry of Education, which is interested in educating three categories of handicapped children; all suffer from single handicaps: oral, sight, or mental. Schools for these children include the following:

1. *Al Nour* (sight) schools and classes for the blind
2. Schools and classes for sight preservation for the partially blind
3. *Al-Amal* (the Hope) schools and classes for the deaf and the mute
4. Schools and classes for the partially deaf
5. Schools and classes for mental education for the mentally retarded
6. Hospital and sanitarium schools and classes

Schools for students with visual, hearing, or mental deficits each have specific objectives. In sight education schools and classes, education aims at the following:

1. Lessening the impact of loss of sight feelings
2. Enhancing self-confidence of pupils suffering from loss of sight and helping them to deal with the handicap
3. Providing these people with the cognitive experiences that help them to deal in a healthy manner with other individuals in their community and with their surroundings
4. Helping them to be self-dependent in fulfilling their needs safely and peacefully

5. Helping them to interact with their community and to move about from place to place with self-pride and self-satisfaction

There are oral education schools and classes. The general objectives of oral education schools and classes are the following:

1. Planning for the education and care of the orally handicapped in the various stages of education
2. Extending the services offered to orally handicapped students to the largest number of them, with an inclination to spread separate schools and affiliated classes throughout the Republic
3. Providing the chance for the orally handicapped to follow the study that corresponds to their abilities and aptitudes (general, vocational, or technical education)
4. Providing follow-up and technical guidance to people working in these schools, with a view to improving their performance and upgrading the level of the teaching process
5. Holding various training sessions for the various technical cadres to upgrade the professional and technical performance level
6. Providing the teacher specialized in oral handicap through the Ministry of Education's program
7. Diversifying vocational activities in the school and relating them to the environment so that they suit the various educational stages

The following actions are objectives for providing comprehensive and integrated care for orally handicapped students:

1. Furnish the schools with collective oral apparatuses and individual training apparatuses that remedy speech defects.
2. Provide personal hearing aids for the partially deaf to preserve what is left of their hearing ability.
3. Provide a psychologist to cope with psychological and behavioral problems of students.
4. Provide a social worker to solve social problems and create sound social relations among pupils.
5. Provide health care for the pupils through a physician and health aide.
6. Provide clothing for all pupils in the school and diversify clothes according to educational stage.

Another goal is to provide full boarding for students whenever this is possible. For such a boarding system to be ideal, it should feature the following:

1. Diverse cultural, social, artistic, and athletic activity at the end of each school day from two-thirty to seven-thirty.
2. Full nutrition plans for pupils, that is, three meals to satisfy the pupil's needs. The pupil's growth stage is to be well observed.
3. Provision of the furniture needed for the boarding system (through the educational directorate).
4. Night-shift supervision for the boarding sections to provide care for the pupils.
5. Secure health care for students through a residential health aide.

There are also mental education schools and classes. The objectives of the Mental Education Administration are reflected in the objectives of its schools and its classes, which are attached to general education primary schools. These objectives are as follows:

1. Enhancing psychological health through activities that give a sense of security
2. Developing self-confidence
3. Developing sight, oral, motor, and mental abilities
4. Developing the students' abilities of sound recognition, speech, and pronunciation
5. Developing the language, arithmetic, and general information skills and experiences needed for success in practical life
6. Developing sound social attitudes and habits and imparting religious and moral values
7. Developing healthful habits to preserve the physical well-being of the mentally retarded
8. Fostering parents' awareness of their children's needs, strengthening the relations between home and school, and building a code for sound interaction between the mentally handicapped and their families
9. Preparing mentally handicapped pupils for practical life, through training them in suitable crafts

Special Education Teachers

The Ministry of Education organizes an internal program for the preparation of special education teachers. The duration of the program is for one school year, and it awards a certificate of special education qualifying a teacher to work in schools and classes for the handicapped. These teachers receive compensation in the form of extra monthly pay in return for their work in the field.

Curricula and Textbooks

Sight education schools adopt the general education curricula to the various stages of education. However, they undertake the development and modification of certain curricula in collaboration with school subject counselors. These commissions adapt the curricula to conform with the handicap in question; that is, visual images are transformed into tactile images.

In the year 1992–93, the administration managed, through its commission formed in collaboration with the Centre for Curricula Development, to develop six textbooks in the subject of mathematics, activities, and general information for the first three grades of the primary stage. These books and their curricula were originally based on visual images; however, the commission changed the visual images into tactile images, while, at the same time, keeping the academic essence of the curriculum. The same procedure was followed with the English and French languages for the secondary stage. Books were printed in Braille and distributed to Al Nour schools for the blind.

Legislation

The state is convinced that handicapped education is a right and a duty. At the National Conference on the Development of Education in the year 1987 a paper on educational development was presented. The paper included a chapter on providing care for disabled people, which included creating conditions and facilities for implementing better care, expanding their admission into programs, and enhancing the services offered. Development lay along two major axes. Axis one is connected with offering a number of educational service programs to all special education schools, and axis two refers to planning educational programs for the handicapped in ordinary schools.

Future Trends

Special education is advancing in Egypt. Programs of educational care for handicapped students that are currently in place or are predicted for the future can be summed up under the major headings of social care, psychological care, health care, and educational care.

Social care means that the Ministry of Education provides special education schools with trained social workers who accomplish the following:

1. Care for the handicapped child at school and at home
2. Provide social care for abnormal pupils, extend necessary services, create a sound social atmosphere inside the school and classroom,

and enhance relations between the school and the pupil's family in local environments to help the pupil's growth and social adjustment

3. Help the pupil obtain benefit from educational and social processes as far as that pupil's aptitudes and abilities permit

In order to secure social care for handicapped pupils, the Ministry allocated enough funds in the budget for social and athletic activities, excursions, and camping. The funds are obtained from the social education budget, from the proceeds of parents' and teachers' councils, student unions, and the services fund for financing social service projects for special education institutes and classes.

For psychological care, the state will provide special education schools and classes with trained psychology experts to extend support to handicapped pupils and help them get over their handicaps and attain a suitable level of adjustment with their selves, handicaps, and society.

Health care is given to the handicapped in ordinary schools. It is provided to those suffering from hemophilia, certain types of anemia, heart trouble, and polio; to slow learners and socially unadjusted children; and to those suffering from motor trouble. Workers involved in health care perform the following tasks:

1. Organize programs for medically testing the handicapped on a regular basis.
2. Examine the mentally retarded in psychological clinics and report on their handicaps. In case the handicap is proved, the sufferers are sent to mental education schools, or to some other place for qualifying them.
3. Supervise schools that have boarding sections—this is done by female health supervisors.
4. Pay attention to health education, spread health awareness among pupils, help them acquire sound health attitudes and habits, and pay attention to cleanliness in everything to keep healthy and secure protection against illness.

Educational care is far-reaching. It is involved in the following:

1. Teaching and educational care extended to cover all regions of Egypt in order to take care of handicapped students and protect nonhandicapped students from the causes of handicaps.
2. Stipulating adequate incentives for handicapped pupils, such as giving them monthly grants and providing them with clothes and compensator parts (hearing aids, batteries, crutches, and so on) free of charge.

3. Training the teacher, the physician, the social worker, and other workers to extend their respective services to the handicapped and suggesting to these workers possible remedies for the problems they may encounter.

4. Orienting parents about types of, detection of, symptoms of, and protection from the causes of handicaps, as well as about techniques of tending to the student psychologically, socially, and academically. This can be done through parent-teacher councils.

5. Organizing camps and scientific recreational and educational outings for special education school pupils and exempting them from paying fees.

6. Developing academic and vocational programs for the handicapped suitable to the mental conditions, abilities, and needs of the specific handicap. These programs should satisfy all the needs of the handicapped; specialized books should be prepared for every handicap.

7. Offering a set of educational, social, psychological, guidance, and remedial services in all special education schools and institutes of various types.

8. Planning educational programs for the handicapped on psychological bases in order to satisfy these students' need for a sense of security, acceptance, love, and belongingness, as well as to train them in the social and vocational skills they will need to better their lives and raise their standard of living.

10

Pakistan

MAH NAZIR RIAZ

*I*n Pakistan, the term *handicapped* denotes those who are mentally retarded and physically handicapped; it includes those who are blind, orthopedically disabled, and deaf. The observance of 1981 as the International Year of the Disabled (IYD) under UN Resolution was a landmark in the history of Pakistan for the care, prevention, welfare, education, training, and rehabilitation of such disabled persons. It was the first time that programs were initiated in the public sector by the federal level.

Between 1983 and 1988, a network of special education institutions for all four major disability groups—blind, deaf, physically handicapped, and mentally retarded—was established throughout Pakistan. Almost all of these institutes were located at the divisional headquarters and in big cities including Islamabad, Azad Kashmir, and the Federally Administered Tribal Areas (FATA). In addition, the National Institute of Special Education (NISE) was established at Islamabad in September 1987. This institute has organized numerous workshops, seminars, and other programs with the assistance of local and foreign experts, especially of the ODA team from the United Kingdom, for the training of teachers and administrators of special education institutions. On 15 June

About the Author • Dr. Mah Nazir Riaz is associate professor in the Department of Psychology, University of Peshawar, Pakistan. Her academic areas of interest are educational psychology, psychometrics, child development, and special education. She is a member of numerous national and international academic bodies including the International Council of Psychologists, the International Institute of Islamic Thought, the World Association of Mental Health, the Advanced Studies and Research Board of the University of Peshawar, and the National Curriculum Review Committee. She is also general secretary of Peshawar Mental Health Association, and a member of the Board of Governors of the Sheikh Zaid Islamic Center, University of Peshawar and the National Institute of Psychology, Center of Excellence, Quaid-e-Azam University, Islamabad.

1988, the late General Muhammad Zia-ul-Haq, President of the Islamic Republic of Pakistan, announced the establishment of the National Trust for the Disabled. This was a source of great pleasure for the entire nation and especially for the disabled, their parents, social workers, and agencies engaged in the service of disabled persons.

Prevalence of Exceptional Conditions

There are no reliable data available concerning the prevalence rate of disabilities in Pakistan. Gathering information through door-to-door surveys has not so far been established as a trustworthy method of identifying disabilities in our country, due to the social stigma attached to abnormalities of all kinds and dislike by the general population for unwanted interviewers visiting their homes.

As far as mild problems are concerned, a number of studies in Pakistan concerning the health of schoolchildren have demonstrated that a large number of students are suffering from anemia, malnutrition, dental problems, defective vision, blocked or infected ears, and chronic respiratory conditions. Besides these physical ailments, there is the further hazard of psychosocial disorders that indicate some of the invisible problems suffered by children from disturbed, poor, and discouraging home situations (Hassan 1979; Tareen et al. 1983).

The National Population Census held from 1 to 15 March 1981, included, for the first time in the history of Pakistan, a column on disability (blind, deaf-dumb, crippled, insane, mentally retarded). This provided much-needed data for future planning and the development of specific programs for the welfare and development of handicapped persons.

According to a Pakistan UNICEF Report (Abdullah 1981; Tareen 1979), the incidence of disability ranges from .8 to 16.8 percent. The Directorate General of Special Education, Islamabad, published an estimate of prevalence of handicapping conditions among the general population in 1986. According to this report, 10 to 15 percent of children in Pakistan suffer from disabilities. The report further shows that among various types of disabilities, physical disabilities represent the greatest number (40 percent). Visual and mental handicaps are 20 percent each, while hearing impairment and multiple handicaps each affect 10 percent of the population with disabilities.

A recent study (Khan and Mirza 1992) was based on the case histories of 1,714 children with severe disabilities in the age range of three to sixteen years at forty-nine special education centers in thirty-three cities of Pakistan. This study confirmed the earlier findings that physical disabilities show the highest occurrence. The results show that 630 (36.7 percent) of the sample are physically handicapped. However, the percentages recorded in mental retardation (MR), physical handicaps (PH), and visual impairment (VI) are slightly different from the percentages presented by the United Nations and in a survey of disabled persons (1986) of the twin cities of Islamabad and Rawalpindi. These results are shown in table 10.1.

The high percentage of hearing impairment (27 percent) in the study group (Khan and Mirza 1992) may perhaps be due to higher number of hearing impaired children attending special education centers. This assumption is based on data obtained from a survey conducted on the national level in Pakistan on disabled children in the age range of five to fourteen years (Akbar 1989). The report of this survey revealed that the participation rate of hearing impaired children in special education centers was 9.45 percent, whereas the participation rate of mentally retarded children was .79 percent, physically handicapped .81 percent, and visually impaired was .81 percent.

Susceptibility to handicapping conditions is found to be higher in boys than girls, due to sex-linked genetic factors (Werner et al. 1987). Ahmad et al. (1987), in a sample of mentally retarded children in Lahore, found a male-female ratio of 5 to 1. Akbar (1989) in a nationwide survey of special education facilities for handicapped children found the male-female ratio to be 3.14 to 1.

Besides the genetic factors, social and cultural factors also contribute to the observed higher number of handicapped boys. In our society, the female child has a long history of being neglected. Parental bias, the need for girls' participation in household chores, early marriages, social taboos, and ignorance regarding the importance of female education have all contributed toward dampening a demand for female education and to the high dropout rates of females (Al-Jalaly 1992). This problem is more severe if the female child has some congenital or acquired handicap (Ghaffar 1991). Since most of the surveys are carried out on children in special education centers, greater emphasis on male attendance may be one of the reasons for observing higher numbers of disabled boys as compared to girls.

TABLE 10.1. Disability Prevalence Rates in Pakistan

Study	Year	Physical Handicaps (%)	Mental Retardation (%)	Deafness (%)	Visual Impairment (%)
United Nations	1981	40.0	30.0	20.0	—
Survey in Islamabad and Rawalpindi	1986	33.0	21.0	—	15.0
Khan and Mirza (N = 1,714)	1992	36.7	35.6	27.1	10.6

The practice of keeping a crippled or a blind child locked in a back room is still a common phenomenon. In Pakistan, a handicapped child is generally considered by the family as a misfortune and, in some cases, a punishment from God (Manzoor 1983). The parents of a handicapped child are often afraid of social scorn and stigmatization. Consequently, they do nothing for the disabled; instead, they hide them from the public to avoid ridicule (Khan 1983). The available psychoeducational services are not utilized adequately and only a limited number of disabled children have access to rehabilitation services and education.

Causes of Disabilities in Pakistan

Some of the important causal factors of handicapping conditions in Pakistan are illiteracy, malnutrition (especially vitamin A or D deficiency), an inadequate supply of iodine, road accidents, industrial accidents, use of weapons, and the underutilization of available healthcare facilities resulting in poliomyelitis, tuberculosis, visual impairment, and hearing impairment. Other causes are superstitious beliefs and unhealthy traditional practices.

An important factor contributing to the high rate of disability in some areas worldwide is consanguineous marriages. Gardner and Sunstad (1981) have cited one religious community in the United States where marriages between cousins and other near relatives has been a predominant factor in genetic disabilities (traced for several generations) such as albinism, phenylketonuria, craniostenosis, adrenalhyperplasia, enlarged big toes, Mast syndrome, Troyer's syndrome, hemophilia B, limb girdle, muscular dystrophy, and so on. A similar study conducted in Turkey found a high correlation between consanguineous marriages and congenital anomalies. This study reported that 67.8 percent of patients suffering from congenital anomalies (the majority being cleft lip and cleft palate cases) were born to parents who were first cousins.

Marriages between close relatives, especially cousins, has always remained a strong tradition among Muslims. The Islamic Republic of Pakistan is one of the Muslim countries where parental consanguinity is common. Ahmad et al. (1987, 1990) conducted studies on Pakistani families to investigate certain anomalies. The data revealed a full expression of splithand and splitfoot anomaly in thirty-six members of the family (thirty male and three female) over seven generations. Similarly, the correlation between fibular hypoplasia and complex brachydactyly was found to be significantly higher than that of persons not in the same pedigree.

A significant relationship has been reported as well between intrafamily marriages and mortality and morbidity rates in children in several countries, including Pakistan. Khan and Mirza (1992) in a comparative analysis of children with and without anomalies found that in a randomly selected representative sample of 700 children, parental consanguinity was present in 462 (66 percent) of children with anomalies as opposed to 324 (46 percent) of cases in children without anomalies. These authors further reported that 62.6 percent of mentally retarded children in the study group come from closely related parents (mostly cousins). The ratio of boys to girls among the mentally retarded children was 188.8 to 100.

Analyzing the prevalence rate of mental retardation, the researchers reported that 71 percent of the children in the sample suffered prenatal cases of anomalies, whereas 29 percent became mentally retarded during postnatal life. Table 10.2 presents reported causes of mental retardation. It seems that Down's syndrome is the major cause of mental retardation in prenatal cases, whereas some of the problems associated with mental retardation during postnatal life are epilepsy, speech problems, and psychological disorders. Higher rates of prenatal causes of mental retardation anomalies are supported by Ahmad et al. (1991), Gustavson et al. (1971), and Bernsen (1976).

Besides parental consanguinity, maternal age also seems to be an important determinant of prenatal etiology. Other causes include radiation, viruses, and drugs. Vitamin D deficiency results in rickets; vitamin A deficiency in visual impairment; and low intake of iodine in goiter. We also come across a large number of handicapped children and other individuals who are victims of certain serious diseases of childhood such as poliomyelitis, jaundice, measles, meningitis, and so on. Due to ignorance, poverty, lack of medical facilities, and preventive inoculation, proper treatment is not given in the early stages of the diseases.

TABLE 10.2. Causes of Mental Retardation in Children

Causes	Frequency	Percentage
Autism	3	0.7
Chorea (Huntington's)	1	2.0
Dwarfism	3	0.7
Down's syndrome	55	12.9
Epilepsy	20	4.7
Hydrocephalus	2	0.5
Microcephaly	22	5.2
Muscular dystrophy (Duchenne's type)	20	4.7
Spasticity	9	2.0
Speech problem associated with MR	23	5.5
Psychological disorders associated with MR	10	2.4
Unknown causes	257	60.5
Total	425	

Source: Khan and Mirza. 1992.

Sometimes inappropriate treatment techniques are used. For instance, in the case of a fractured bone or dislocation of a joint, many people, especially in rural areas, seek the help of illiterate and unqualified persons (quacks) who claim to restore the bone or joint in the original position by stretching it in different directions. Such manipulation often results in orthopedic handicaps.

The literacy rate is very low (26 percent) in Pakistan and, in the case of females, it is lower (16 percent). Due to low literacy rates, knowledge about health and nutrition is not available to the masses. Superstitious beliefs add to the problems. Some parents believe their handicapped child is God's will. Others consider the birth of the handicapped child as a punishment from God for their sins. Consequently, they do not make any effort to improve the child's condition and instead leave the child to his or her fate. Such an attitude worsens the handicapping condition. An individual suffering from epilepsy, for example, is regarded by a large number of people as under the influence of evil spirits or the devil. As a result, people are not only afraid of the patient, but sometimes inflict physical punishment to drive the evil spirit out of his or her body.

As well, there are unpredictable causes. Some normal individuals become crippled from road or industrial accidents. At times, a misfired bullet damages the eye or leg of an individual, who was perhaps eagerly looking for the moon in the sky on the First of Shawwal (the Muslim festival celebrated with great enthusiasm at the end of the holy month of Ramadan). Sometimes bomb blasts by the enemies of Pakistan endanger the lives of innocent citizens and result in many casualties.

Identification of Exceptionalities

The handicap is generally identified by the mother or some other family member (father or grandparents) unless it is so obvious that everyone notices it. When the parents suspect that the child is mentally retarded, hard of hearing, or deaf and dumb, they usually consult a doctor for identification of the handicap as well as seek treatment for the handicapping condition. Thus, it is often during the preschool years that a serious handicap is properly identified. In mild cases of visual or auditory impairment, the problem may be recognized by the child himself or herself during the childhood years. One of our teachers told us that he was ten years old when he realized that he was suffering from visual impairment and needed glasses.

Complete medical examination in Pakistan is compulsory only if a boy (approximately seventeen years old) is recruited for the armed forces (army, air force, or navy). All the candidates are selected by the Inter Services Selection Board (ISSB) on the basis of a three-day screening test that includes psychological tests to assess their abilities, aptitude, and personality. They then go through a detailed medical checkup by the Medical Board.

As pointed out earlier, the dawn of 1981 had a very special significance for us. Not only did it herald a new year, but it was also of great importance for a particular section of humanity that had been neglected so far. The observance of 1981 as the International Year of the Disabled brought awareness in favor of the disabled among the people. In Pakistan, among other positive measures taken in this regard, an ordinance called the Disabled Persons Ordinance of 1981 was promulgated. This legislation provides for employment, rehabilitation, and welfare of the disabled. To implement the ordinance, national and provincial councils have been set up aimed at rehabilitation of the disabled. One of the services to be provided by these councils is the assessment of disabled persons necessary to provide them with specific training and employment. To achieve these objectives, District Assessing Boards (DABs) were created to assess the nature and extent of disabilities of handicapped persons in order to recommend them for appropriate training and employment (Shahin 1987). Centers of special education also provide psychoeducational assessment for students with handicapping conditions to be carried out by the experts at the recommendation of the head of the institution.

Psychologists in Pakistan play an important role not only in diagnosis but also in the training and rehabilitation of handicapped persons. Some professional psychologists have established well-known institutions. The Kaukab Center for Special Education and Rehabilitation was set up on a purely volunteer basis for mentally handicapped persons by a team of psychologists of the Institute of Social Sciences and the Psychological Center, Lahore, on 1 May 1991. Another center for mentally handicapped persons was established in the Mission Hospital, Peshawar. Hence, the services of medical doctors, professional psychologists, social workers, and educators are interwoven in special education centers aimed at the diagnosis, treatment and care, training, and rehabilitation of the physical and mentally disabled individuals who join these centers.

Labeling the Handicapped Population

In Pakistan, the four major categories of disabled are blind, deaf and dumb, physically handicapped, and mentally retarded. To describe the first three groups, almost the same labels (or their equivalents in regional languages such as Pashto, Panjabi, Sindhi, and so on) are used throughout the country.

On the other hand, many different words and phrases are used to describe the worldwide phenomenon of mental retardation. No single definition or term seems accurate because of numerous variations in people's perception of mental retardation as determined by their level of education, profession, socioeconomic status, and so on. For instance, if in an illiterate family, one child out of six has studied up to the primary level, he or she is considered an educated person. But if in a highly educated family, siblings who have completed only primary education before dropping out of school will be considered mentally retarded due to their low academic achievement as compared to the rest of the family members.

In North-West Frontier Province (NWFP) of Pakistan, it is common to say that the child has a speech problem. Razia, for example, is six years old and manages to say only ten words, so she is considered to have a speech problem. In fact, Razia is not toilet trained and does not feed or dress herself. When it is suggested to the parents that she is mentally retarded, they say, "No, no, she has a speech problem" (Miles 1992).

Among the general population, people hold different views. A large number of people in rural areas label mentally retarded individuals as *Sa'een*, *Peer*, or *Allah-Waley*. These labels hold to a common belief that people with mental retardation are very pious and have supernatural powers, and that their blessings can alleviate all ills and misfortunes. There are others who call them *Pagal* or *Lawanaiy* (mad person or psychic cases).

Miles (1992) quotes a well-known educator who sent a written complaint to one of the leading newspapers of the country, *The Pakistan Times*. The writer said that "Most of the children admitted to this [school for the mentally retarded] are psychic cases and to brand [them] as mentally retarded is highly objectionable" (Bokhari 1989). Miles quotes another Pakistani educator who wrote several pages on "mental deficiency" in terms of "idiocy, imbecility, and feeblemindedness," quoting from a western text of the 1930s (Quddus 1990, 138–42). Both examples indicate a lack of familiarity on the part of these educated writers, which reflects the general lack of public awareness.

Western professionals are cautious nowadays about putting labels on children. It is believed that children vary in their rate of development; consequently, some are slow starters but catch up later. Some never attain their normal developmental status but still can benefit if put in ordinary schools. Once the label *mentally retarded* has been fixed on a child, however, parents and teachers tend to develop a negative attitude; they expect the child to achieve little and the child acts down to their low expectations.

During the last two decades in Pakistan, a positive change has become evident in the expectations of those professionals concerned with mental retardation. For instance, children with Down's syndrome were generally regarded as severely retarded and it was believed that such children would never learn to read and write. Contrary to this belief, hundreds of children with Down's syndrome have learned to read and write during the past seven years, because of the persistent efforts of teachers working in special education centers. Learning these skills certainly distinguishes those children from the illiterate majority of our population who cannot even write their names.

Prior to the International Year of the Disabled, the general attitude of the people towards the disabled has been unconcern and cold neglect. Their parents and family members gave them nothing by way of affection, except sighs of woe. But this attitude has gradually been replaced by due recognition, affection, and responsibility toward the welfare and rehabilitation of the handicapped, both at the national as well as the international level. It has been established now that a handicapped individual can become a useful and productive citizen if he or she is given proper and timely treatment, education, and training, and is provided with adequate rehabilitative services.

A few years ago, parents were reluctant to send their mentally retarded children to special education centers, afraid their disabled children might become worse when placed in the company of other handicapped individuals. Presently, parents are willing to bring their children to special schools.

For the public, radio talks on rehabilitation, printed media, and television have played a significant role in bringing about a change in attitudes toward handicapped persons and effectiveness of rehabilitation services offered by government institutions. Manuals, pamphlets, magazines, newspapers, films, radio scripts, video cassettes, can be reproduced many times and made widely accessible with much greater ease and lower cost than can special teachers, physiotherapists, vocational instructors, and community-based rehabilitation workers.

The Social Context of Special Education

The Mental Health Center, Peshawar, carried out a study for the government of Pakistan concerning attitudes towards disabled persons in 1983. The data revealed a great deal of ignorance about disabilities, with fear and pity being the most common attitudes. While many people realized that something should be done, they did not know what to do. Many people understood that disabilities might be prevented by better nutrition, health care, and immunization, but in the rural areas it takes a long time to provide these facilities.

During the International Decade of the Disabled (1983–92), UNICEF gave informational and financial support for discovering and implementing the most effective, low-cost strategies for disabled children and their families. Priority was given to disability prevention, detection, and early intervention. This took place in collaboration with national planning by the government of Pakistan and the provincial governments.

It has become apparent that, in the long run, no strategy can succeed without first arousing the awareness and active participation of local communities (Memon 1988). There is growing awareness among the masses that community-directed rehabilitation programs will certainly be more effective than community-based programs. We have reached the stage where greater effort at public awareness could produce fruitful results in terms of community involvement on a large scale. There is an awakening to the need for timely diagnosis of symptoms (Miles 1992).

Schools, Teachers, and Pedagogy

Rehabilitation of handicapped persons requires prolonged medical and psychological treatment. This objective can be achieved by pooling the resources of various organizations engaged in such programs both in the public as well as private sectors and by educating and involving their families and people at large.

The government of Pakistan has launched many programs for the education, training, and rehabilitation of its disabled population. At present, numerous voluntary organizations in the country also provide rehabilitation services to the physically handicapped. A few modern institutions have been established by some leading organizations of Pakistan. The Society for the Rehabilitation of the Disabled, Lahore; the Al-Shifa, Karachi; Amin Maktaab, Lahore; Frontier Association for the Mentally Handicapped; and the Sarhad Society for Rehabilitation of Disabled, Peshawar, are providing reasonably good facilities for total rehabilitation. These services encompass assessment of abilities and disabilities, treatment and care, formal education, vocational training, and job placement of the physically handicapped and have incorporated in their programs basic skills of counseling, family involvement, home-center liaisons, and raising of community awareness and support, that is, the skills needed for community-based rehabilitation.

In the public sector, Jinnah Post Graduate Medical Center, and the Karachi and Jauji Foundation at Rawalpindi provide optimal medical and rehabilitation services. The Foundation at Rawalpindi has a well-equipped manufacturing center for artificial limbs and equipment of high standard, but the services provided are confined to former servicemen of the armed forces.

Educational Services

The Directorate General of Special Education (DGSE), government of Pakistan, was established at Islamabad in February 1985, with a number of objectives: provision of medical facilities as well as preventive measures for disabled persons; identification of disabled persons including collection of data regarding the prevalence rate of disabilities in Pakistan; provision of diagnosis, assessment, and medical examination for the identification of disabled persons at the earliest stage; counseling of parents; promotion of general awareness about handicapping conditions; vocational training of disabled persons; rehabilitation services including creating and providing job opportunities to disabled persons; provision of legal aid and shelter to handicapped persons; and provision of special equipment.

Education includes the establishment of special education centers throughout the country and the training of manpower for special education. The Directorate General of Special Education, Islamabad, has set up 46 special education centers throughout Pakistan. The centers provide medical treatment, educational facilities, and vocational training to visually handicapped, hearing impaired, physically handicapped (polio, cerebral palsy, hydrocephalus, muscular dystrophy, congenital deformities, and orthopedic deformities), and mentally retarded persons. The division of these centers in the four major areas of disabilities is physically handicapped children, 11; mentally retarded children, 12; blind children, 11; and deaf children, 12.

A variety of services are offered in the special education centers including diagnosis and assessment; special education; curricular activities; games and recreational facilities for schoolchildren; and vocational training such as sewing, knitting, painting, drawing, and weaving; hearing aids, physiotherapy, braille, and mobility training, all depending on the nature and intensity of the handicap. The centers also exhibit instruments, equipment, and audiovisual aids used for training the disabled in and work toward improvement of such materials. They provide equipment and instruments for the personal use of the disabled; manufacture special instruments to be used at other places; improve the quality and quantity of training equipment for visually handicapped and hearing-impaired children; prepare material to be printed in braille; and tape-record stories and textbooks for visually handicapped children. In addition, the centers offer services to the disabled as a National Registration Center. They undertake research programs concerning various handicapping conditions, as well as in-service training for teachers.

Parent-teacher associations established in all the centers of special education allow the participation of parents in discussions about the daily progress of children, educational planning, curricular requirements, and the overall growth and development of children with disabilities. There are counseling and guidance for parents concerning their roles and responsibilities in the growth and development of their children, and discussions with parents about the general educational, vocational, or management problems of their disabled children.

A number of people from different walks of life have offered their voluntary services in terms of time, professional skill, and knowledge as well as financial assistance for programs aimed at the welfare and development of disabled children. These medical doctors, teachers, social workers, psychologists, and philanthropists have been registered as "special friends" and are extending cooperation to children and the special education centers throughout Pakistan.

Community Service

In November 1986, the Directorate General of Special Education also started a National Training Center for Disabled Persons at Islamabad. The major objective of the training center is to provide disabled persons with a basic foundation of vocational skills—through providing training in different trades—and to provide them with rehabilitation services. The language of instruction for all training programs is Urdu.

Vocational training and assessment provides an integrated program of assessment and vocational training in basic skills such as knitting, sewing, tailoring, cutting, machining, welding, lathe operation, and radio and television repair. After helping disabled persons to develop self-confidence by providing them with the training opportunities best suited to their capacities, the national training center undertakes the responsibility of arranging job placement in collaboration with government and nongovernmental organizations. These services are promoted with the guidance and advice of a Placement Advisory Committee, consisting of representatives of the PTA, NTCD, Industries Department, Labor Department, Chamber of Trade and Commerce, and trade unions, and in close collaboration with local and foreign agencies. The national training center also works to promote the integration of the disabled into the normal community and to overcome discrimination within society. It demonstrates to the community the abilities of the disabled to contribute to the economic development of the country. Finally, the training center serves as a model for future developments by demonstrating its achievements.

The National Training Center for the Disabled provides a high level of equipment and facilities. The staff is well trained, highly qualified, and experienced. The Parent Association performs a significant role in developing and improving the programs for the disabled according to their needs. It works in close cooperation with the staff of the center for the welfare and betterment of disabled persons.

An admission committee is headed by the director of the National Training Center for Disabled Persons, and includes the deputy director and job placement officer. The committee also consults other specialists when necessary. The national training center admits a person having a disability of any kind, whether a visual handicap, a physical handicap, hearing impairment, or mental retardation. Both males and females are eligible for admission; applicants must be within the age range of fourteen to thirty-five. The applicant must be independent in self-help skills such as toileting, dressing, and eating, and the applicant should have basic skills in reading, writing, and numeracy. The applicant must not have any communicable disease.

Hostel facilities are available to the twenty-five trainees coming from the out station. Hostel facilities are provided to the most deserving disabled persons. Free transport services are allowed to the trainees to and from the center. At the center, there are facilities for indoor recreational activities including a TV, radio, and tape recorder, and games such as chess, carom, and ludo. The trainees are taken on excursions to places of interest to give them opportunities to broaden their knowledge and experience in activities of daily living.

Training is through highly sophisticated and modern equipment and teaching aids. The training center also provides parent counseling and guidance services by holding regular case conferences and meetings with parents. A social case worker maintains regular contact with families. A case file of every student is maintained. It includes a comprehensive range of progressive records.

There is also the National Institute for Handicapped in Islamabad, designed for delivery of services to the entire country. The institute is divided into several wings—diagnostic, treatment, surgery, training, common facilities, and administration—and offers the services of specialists in various fields of disabilities and highly trained paramedical staff for the treatment and care of disabled out- or inpatients. Detention bays and convalescent facilities are provided for up to sixty inpatients. Treatment specializations include otolaryngology (ENT), ophthalmology, orthopedics, neurology, radiology, pediatrics, S.E. assessment, and psychology.

The institute provides the following services to the disabled:

1. It coordinates the national effort for prevention of disabilities, plans and develops an integrated referral system throughout the country, serves as a training center for those involved in the prevention of disabilities, and carries out research on various disabilities in all their aspects.
2. It plans and develops a system of early detection and discovery of any disability in children, a multiprofessional assessment and diagnosis system at the district/divisional level, and a health surveillance system through the existing institutions.

3. It coordinates and supports treatment of the disabled by various institutions at different levels in the country, and provides treatment for various disabilities.

4. It carries out research in the field of artificial limbs and assembles and manufactures hearing aids. A separate provision has been made for the hearing-aid assembly plant and artificial limbs factory in phase two of the scheme.

There is in Pakistan a further range of services for disabled persons. These include the National Council for Rehabilitation of the Disabled, designed to provide employment and rehabilitation under the Disabled Person Ordinance of 1981. The national council provides personal equipment and instruments; financial assistance for self-employment and rehabilitation; and training facilities suitable to the abilities and aptitudes of disabled persons.

The National Mobility and Independent Training Center trains visually handicapped individuals in daily living skills and mobility. It also trains the teachers to provide this instruction to the disabled. In addition, the center prepares literature for training visually handicapped persons as well as the general population to facilitate their mobility in the society.

The Talking Book Center records textbooks for the secondary school level (grades 6–10) on audio cassettes and supplies such audio cassettes to blind students free of cost. It also provides audio cassettes of stories and tape recorders to all organizations and centers for visually handicapped persons. The National Braille Press prints textbooks in braille and provides a free supply of braille materials, such as books, braille boards, and Perkin's braillers, to special education centers for visually handicapped children.

The National Library and Research Center caters to the needs of teachers, parents, and personnel associated with special education. It also acquires educational aids and informative material about special education from national and international agencies and disseminates these materials to all concerned.

Teacher Training

The National Institute of Special Education provides trained personnel and training programs for special education and prepares short courses for training, as well as long-range intensive programs for disabled persons. It also coordinates with universities and other educational institutions for training teachers in special education, and prepares and prints material for guidance in special education.

Teachers of visually impaired and blind students are trained in collaboration with Allama Iqbal Open University in Islamabad. There is training for 150 teachers of visually handicapped students in an advanced diploma in education as well as a master in education program. For the training of additional teachers in special education, eleven plans for the establishment of departments of special education at Karachi University and Punjab University are underway.

Legislation

During October and November 1979, the Social Welfare Wing organized one national conference and two workshops in Islamabad in connection with the International Year of the Child. Both the Child Legislation and the Welfare and Development of the Handicapped Child workshops had special sections devoted to disabled children and focused attention on this deprived group. Also featured was the Conference on Child Development: Prospects and Challenge.

During the conference, it was found that disabled children are included as a category in the various antibeggary acts, but their special status, needs, and requirements have never been framed into a specific law. For the first time, it was realized that comprehensive legislation specifically pertaining to the handicapped should be formulated. The president of Pakistan, as patron in chief of the National Committee for the International Year of the Child, directed the Ministry of Health and Social Welfare to "urgently undertake the task of formulating a workable and realistic national policy on children and include them in the development plans within the overall national policy programs. These policies and plans should particularly provide full coverage to the handicapped, underprivileged and indigent children, their families and communities."

An ordinance for the employment, rehabilitation, and welfare of the handicapped was also promulgated to ensure a 1 percent employment quota in industrial plants and factories. Under this ordinance, the provincial governments are bound to arrange for the training of handicapped persons in such trades or vocations as they deem fit and have to establish training centers for this purpose.

The Disabled Persons Rehabilitation Fund, established by the federal government, is to be utilized for the establishment of training centers and the disbursement of stipends to such trainees, financial assistance to handicapped persons who are unfit to undertake any employment, and the total welfare of disabled persons.

Policy in Special Education

One of the major influences on policy formation and the practice of special education in Pakistan is the collaborative efforts of UNICEF. The provision of financial and material support to the community-directed rehabilitation

projects for disabled children over five years has resulted in the achievement
of two main objectives: special education centers are registered with the
government and most are still providing services and are on the way to
becoming self-sustaining. From 1988 to 1992, UNICEF has entered into a
formal program of collaboration with the government of Pakistan, and specifically the Directorate General of Special Education at Islamabad.

Major Controversies and Issues in Special Education

The principle of educating handicapped and normal children together is
described as mainstreaming in the United States, as integration in the United
Kingdom, and as normalization in Scandinavia and Canada. A report prepared by the Snowdon working party, set up by the National Fund for
Research into Crippling Diseases, described integration of the disabled as
meaning a thousand things: it means the absence of segregation; it means
social acceptance; it means being able to be treated like everybody else—
"[i]t means the right to meet, to go to cinemas, to go on holiday on the
usual places, to be educated up to university level with normal children and
to travel without fuss on public transport" (Ahmad 1987).

During the past two decades, literature concerning the educational integration of disabled children has grown substantially in Western countries
where the entire school-going population gets formal education and special
schools have existed for many years. Since 1981, the International Year of
the Disabled, Pakistan, like numerous developing countries, has made some
degree of commitment to integrate its disabled persons with the rest of the
community, on terms of dignity and equality of esteem. The Sixth Five-Year
Plan (1983–88) mentions integrated teaching facilities among the "major
policy shifts" (1983). But although this Western trend is quite appealing for
the future of educational integration in Pakistan, in general it seems irrelevant
to the present situation. Whatever may be the strengths or weaknesses of the
present educational system, more than half of the pupils drop out after a
year or so of schooling. Illiteracy rates remain high.

There are a few schools in every big city of Pakistan where disabled
children are studying with normal children. The majority of these children
are physically handicapped, speech impaired, or hearing impaired. In some
cases, the school teachers and other students give some extra help to these
handicapped children in acquiring the skills required for schoolwork. Usually such teachers have had some in-service specialist training, such as those
at Dr. Omer Hayat Malik Public School in University Town, Peshawar. In
other cases, there is close collaboration between the special school and the
ordinary school, with disabled children attending both alternately such as at

PAF School for Special Education in Chaklala, Rawalpindi. In some ordinary schools with disabled children, teachers are helped by volunteers. Miles (1985) cites the example of a school in Hyderabad where professionally qualified persons—educated women and technically competent persons—all contribute time, energy, and enthusiasm under the direction of school management to make a success of an educational integration program. Finally, when disabled children are studying in ordinary classes, specialist teachers visit periodically and assist ordinary teachers. An example of this planned integration is a private school—Asbar's School in Peshawar.

In the Action Study of Non-Designed Educational Integration in Pakistan (1985), 825 out of 43,416 (1.9 percent) children studying in 103 ordinary urban primary and secondary schools in the North-West Frontier Province of Pakistan were reported by their teachers to have a perceptible disability—22 percent of them have visual impairment, 8 percent, hearing loss, and 7 percent, other disabilities. The impairments were then verified independently. Of these children, 35 percent reported difficulty in carrying out schoolwork; 95 percent reported positive attitudes of their fellow pupils toward them.

In the Province of Sind, some efforts have been made for the integration of disabled students. This procedure involved construction of an extra room adjoining existing school premises to serve as a special education unit and competent teachers who had received some in-service training in special education to teach the disabled pupils. The integrative features of this program were initially the physical proximity and common playground. Later on, some of the students joined their normal peers in the adjacent classrooms for specific lessons, and subsequently some of them became more fully integrated into the mainstream. Thousands of handicapped pupils are thus being accommodated in the educational system in Sind Province. Another report (Tareen 1981) estimates that about ten schools in the Punjab are taking some blind children for integrated education, and the number may be increased considerably.

The present experimental program of integration into the existing centrally controlled network of government schools (although on a very small scale) has reached a stage at which some of the disabled pupils who entered in the first year of primary school have completed their secondary school education.

Although planned educational integration in Pakistan has been found to be almost nonexistent, especially amongst the mentally retarded and the deaf-mute, there have been several efforts of informal or unofficial integration in different provinces of Pakistan. There are many institutions, including ordinary primary and secondary schools, where children with perceptible disabilities are studying.

This unplanned integration is not always a happy experience. The report from the Punjab Province (Tareen 1981) states that "parents of moderately retarded children, unaware of the handicap of their offspring, keep them pushing for harder work in ordinary schools without professional help. The result is not only unhappy parents and teachers, but miserable youngsters who get emotional handicaps superimposed over their mental handicaps."

However, there is little reason why many children with physical disabilities, mild or moderate visual or hearing impairment, or mild mental retardation, should be excluded from ordinary school activities. Minor modifications as needed, whether they be conveyance, hearing aids, glasses, special furniture, or additional classroom assistance, can be provided at a cost lower than that of a separate special schooling system.

Moreover, in view of the difficulties experienced by economically stronger countries in providing adequate coverage of special education and rehabilitation facilities to their disabled child population, it seems unlikely that there will ever be sufficient separate schools in Pakistan to cater to all the disabled children. Under such circumstances, the only solution of this national problem is to promote integrated education.

In summary, there is a general awareness about the integration approach in Pakistan, but due to the existing paucity of facilities, especially in terms of teaching staff and the limited number of and space in government schools, the phase of innovation will last for years. At present, there are many schools in rural areas where there are one or two rooms for all the primary classes, and some schools are run under the shelter of big trees. In spite of the fact that our government does have a policy of promotion of integration, it is generally considered to be a secondary factor in Pakistan—unless disabled children received initial specialized care, diagnosis, treatment, and rehabilitation (especially the mentally retarded), it is not considered possible to work for their integration, either in the overburdened regular educational system, or in employment settings. In industrialized countries, where there is universal education and comparatively less unemployment, there are greater prospects of successful integration. This is not presently the case in Pakistan.

References

Abdullah, T. 1981. *The situation of disabled children in Pakistan*. Islamabad: UNICEF.

Ahmad, M., Abbas, H., Haque, S., and Flatz, G. 1987. X-chromosomally inherited split hand/split foot anomaly in a Pakistani kindred. *Human Genetics* 75:169–73.

Ahmad, M., Abbas, H., Wahab, A., and Haque, S. 1990. Fibular hypoplasia and complex brachydactyly in an inbred Pakistani kindred. *American Journal of Medical Genetics*, Wiley.

Ahmad, A. B., Ayub, M., and Tareen, K. I. 1991. Etiology, psychological morbidity and associated impairments in severe mental retardation. *The Pakistan Journal of Child Mental Health*. National Society for Mentally and Emotionally Handicapped children.

Akbar, R. M. 1989. A survey of special education facilities for the handicapped children in Pakistan. M.A. thesis, Islamabad, Department of Educational Planning and Management, Allama Iqbal Open University.

Al-Jalaly, S. Z. 1992. *Gender issues and their implication for development in the North-West Frontier Province*. Workshop on Planning for Women in Development, September, Government of NWFP/ILO, Peshawar.

Bernsen, A. H. 1976. Severe mental retardation in the County of Aarhus, Denmark: A community study of prevalence and provision of service. *Acta Psychiatrica Scandinavica* 54:43–66.

Bokhari, S. A. 1989. Name of school. In Letters to the Editor, *The Pakistan Times*, 5 May.

Directorate General of Special Education. 1986. *Survey of disabled persons*. Islamabad: Directorate General of Special Education, Government of Pakistan.

Gardner, E. J., and Sunstad, D. P. 1981. *Principles of genetics*. 6th ed. New York: John Wiley and Sons.

Ghaffar, N. 1991. Problems of physically handicapped female children. Master's thesis, University of Peshawar.

Government of Pakistan. 1983. *The 6th Five-Year Plan 1983–1988*. Islamabad: Planning Commission, Government of Pakistan.

Gustavson, K. H., et al. 1971. Severe mental retardation in a Swedish country. 1: Epidemiology, gestational age, birth weight and associated CNS handicaps in children born 1959–70. *Acta Paediatric Scandinavica*, 66:373–79.

Hassan, I. N. 1979. General features of psychopathology found amongst primary school children of Federal area schools, Islamabad. Paper presented at the 4th Session of the Pakistan Psychological Association, National Institute of Psychology, Islamabad.

Khan, G. A. 1983. Keynote address at National Workshop on Welfare and Development of the Handicapped Child. In M. Miles, ed. *Attitudes towards persons with disabilities*. Peshawar: Mission Hospital.

Khan, Q. N., and Mirza, L. 1992. *Consanguinity and disability in children of Pakistan*. Islamabad: Directorate of Special Education.

Manzoor, A. 1983. Rehabilitation of disabled. From the Khyber Mail, 23 January 1981. In M. Miles, ed. *Attitudes towards persons with disabilities*. Peshawar: Mission Hospital.

Memon, N. 1988. *Community directed rehabilitation for disabled children in NWFP, Pakistan*. Peshawar: UNICEF.

Miles, M. 1985. *Children with disabilities in ordinary schools*. Islamabad: National Council of Social Welfare, Government of Pakistan.

———. 1992. *Mental handicap services: Developmental trends*. Peshawar: Mental Health Center.

Quddus, N. J. 1990. *Problems of education in Pakistan*. Karachi: Royal Book Co.

Shahin, A. R. 1987. *Information brochure for district assessing boards*. Punjab, Lahore: Directorate General, Social Welfare.

Tareen, K. I. 1979. *The situation of disabled children in Pakistan*. Islamabad: UNICEF.

Tareen, K. I., ed. 1981. *Proceedings of workshop on programme development for the handicapped, Lahore, April 1981*. Lahore: Government of Punjab/ UNICEF.

Tareen, K.I., et al. 1983. *Epidemiological study of childhood disability: Survey/study in Punjab (Pakistan). Interim Report*. Lahore: UNICEF.

Werner, D., et al. 1987. *Physically disabled children in rural areas*. Palo Alto, Calif.: Hesperian Foundation.

Zia-ul-Haq, General. 1974. Quoted in the *Pakistan Times*, 25 May.

11

China

XU YUN

*A*ccording to China's nationwide census in 1987, there were 307.5 million people from birth to age fourteen, accounting for 28.7 percent of the total population. There were 672 million ages fifteen to fifty-nine, for 62.8 percent of the population, and 91 million over sixty, for 8.5 percent. According to the same nationwide census, 37.1 percent of the total population in China lived in cities or towns and 62.9 percent in rural areas. The distribution of education levels was as follows: college level, .88 percent; high school level, 7 percent; middle school level, 21.3 percent; primary school, 36.2 percent; and illiterate and semiliterate, 20.6 percent.

At present, there are more than 50 million disabled persons in China. Of these persons with disabilities, 66.37 percent are illiterate or semiliterate. By the end of 1986, China had approximately 307.5 million children from birth to age fourteen, 28.7 percent of the total population. Of these children, 8.17 million were disabled, which accounts for 7.75 percent of China's entire population and 15.83 percent of all its disabled people.

About the Author • Dr. Xu Yun is a clinical psychologist and associate professor. He is director of the Child Growth and Development Center, Hangzhou University; director of a UNICEF project at Hangzhou University; a member of the Board of Directors of the International Association of Special Education and a member of the China Special Education Academy Committee, the China Child Mental Health Association, the China Psychological Testing Association, the Zhejiang Mental Health Association, the Zhejiang Social Welfare Society, and the Zhejiang Experts Commission for the Handicapped. He is also dean of the Clinical, Education and Development Psychology Faculty in the Department of Psychology, Hangzhou University. Included in his numerous publications are *Encyclopedia of Counseling, Guide to Psychotherapy, Medical Psychology, Student Mental Health,* and *Diagnosis and Education of Mentally Retarded Children.* He is also editor in chief of the *Symposia of Education for the Mentally Retarded Children and Special Education Series.*

Special education is an important component of China's educational undertaking. China's constitution stipulates that the state and society help to arrange the employment, standard of living, and education of the blind and deaf, as well as of other disabled citizens. The Law of the People's Republic of China on the Protection of Disabled Persons, and other regulations stipulate the right of disabled persons to education in explicit terms. Carrying out these regulations conscientiously and guaranteeing the right of disabled persons to education is the common responsibility of the state, society, and the disabled person's parents.

Prevalence of Exceptional Conditions

On 1 April 1987, a sample survey was conducted of disabled people in China, pursuant to the criteria for defining five categories of the disabled. These categories are physically disabled, visually impaired, hearing and/or speech impaired, mentally retarded, and having psychoses. On 7 December 1987, the *Bulletin on the Main Data of the Nationwide Sampling Survey for the Disabled* was released officially by the State Council and the National Statistical Bureau. According to the data issued, a rough estimate of the disabilities in China can be made as follows: of the 1,579,314 people in 369,816 households covered in the survey, 18.1 percent of the households had among their members disabled people, who made up 4.9 percent of the population surveyed.

TABLE 11.1.   Age Constitution of Disabled Children

Age	Surveyed Children	Disabled Children	Constitution Rate %	Determinative Rate %
0	31,823	365	2.98	1.15
1	30,041	426	3.48	1.42
2	27,854	404	3.30	1.45
3	27,597	459	3.75	1.66
4	31,827	567	4.63	1.78
5	31,040	656	5.36	2.11
6	26,053	645	5.27	2.48
7	29,439	865	7.07	2.94
8	28,101	964	7.87	3.43
9	27,948	940	7.62	3.36
10	29,443	994	8.12	3.38
11	31,244	1,098	8.97	3.51
12	34,724	1,307	10.68	3.76
13	36,001	1,295	10.27	3.60
14	37,483	1,257	10.27	3.35
Total	460,618	12,242	100.00	Mean 2.66

It can be inferred from these findings that China has approximately 51.64 million disabled people in the five categories. Among these people, 7.55 million are visually impaired. Hearing and/or speech impaired are 17.7 million. There are 10.17 million with mental retardation, 7.55 million with physical disabilities, 1.94 million with psychoses, and 6.73 million with multiple disabilities.

The survey found that in the age range from birth to fourteen there were approximately 8.18 million people (15.8 percent of the disabled population). There were 22.95 million between the ages of fifteen to fifty-nine (44 percent), and 20.51 million at the age of over sixty (39.7 percent).

Table 11.1 presents age constitution rates for 12,242 disabled children. There are over 500,000 disabled children in the four-year-old group, and more than 1 million in the eleven-year-old group. The determinative rates are about 2 percent in the four-year-old group, 3 percent in the seven-year-old group, and 3.5 percent in the eleven-year-old group. These data correlated with the actual situation. It shows that as the children are growing up, they increasingly face the hazard of disabilities. As well, some of the genetic problems reveal themselves gradually.

The survey further indicated that there were approximately 5.43 million people living in urban areas, making up 10.5 percent of the total disabled. There were 7.78 million in towns, 15 percent, and 38.49 million in the rural areas, 74.5 percent. Of the group of people fifteen to fifty-nine years old, 5.85 million in cities and towns made up 25.5 percent. The 17.11 million in rural areas made up 74.5 percent.

Table 11.2 shows that there existed a clear difference of distribution of disabled people in cities, towns, and the countryside—a proportion of 100

TABLE 11.2.   Distribution over Cities, Towns, and Countryside

	All Surveyed(1)	Surveyed Children(2)	Disabled Children(3)
Cities	201,667	41,203	600
Towns	257,806	74,090	1,647
Countrysides	1,119,843	345,325	9,995
Total	1,579,816	460,608	12,242

	% of Children $\left(= \dfrac{(2)}{(1)} \right)$	% of Disabled Children $\left(= \dfrac{(3)}{(2)} \right)$	Disabled Children per 1,000 Persons $\left(= \dfrac{(3)}{(1)} \, 1{,}000 = \right)$
Cities	20.43	1.46	2.98
Towns	28.74	2.22	6.39
Countrysides	30.84	2.89	8.93
Total	29.17	2.66	7.75

from urban areas to 150 from towns to 200 from villages. Out of every 1,000 children, there were 3 disabled children living in cities, 6 in towns, and 9 in the countryside. Looking at the 12,242 disabled children surveyed another way, it can be seen that 600 were from cities, 4.9 percent of the total, and 1,646 or 13.45 percent were from towns, giving a combined 18.35 percent for urban areas and towns. However, there were 9,995, or 81.5 percent, from the countryside.

The population of disabled children in the urban area was nearly one-third less than in villages and towns. This is because of the lower birthrate and the longer average lifespan in urban areas. It is obvious that the number of the disabled children from the countryside is 80 percent of the total disabled children. The most important task, therefore, is to solve the problems for disabled children in the countryside in China.

The survey breakdown according to disability category among children showed that there were 5.39 million mentally retarded children (65.96 percent). There were also 1.16 million hearing and speech disabled children (14.2 percent); 806,000 multiple disabled (9.81 percent); and 620,000 with physical disabilities (7.58 percent). As well, there were 181,000 visually disabled children (2.22 percent) and 14,000 disabled due to mental illness (.17 percent).

There were more disabled boys than girls: the ratio was 107.51 boys to 100 girls. The determinative rate of classifying disabled boys is 4 percent higher than for girls. There were 28.5 disabled boys and 24.5 disabled girls for every 1,000 children. There were about 4.54 million disabled boys and 3.63 million disabled girls—or approximately 900,000 more disabled boys than girls.

It is said that mental deformity is one of important factors associated with children's manifold and multiple disabilities. Ninety-five percent of multiply disabled children are probably mentally retarded. Those with more than three kinds of disabilities are almost certainly suffering from mental retardation.

In China, childhood disabilities arise from many causes. Table 11.3 indicates the major causes of disabilities in children in China.

TABLE 11.3.   Causes of Disability in Children

Category	Genetic (%)	Injured (%)	Accident (%)	Others (%)	Unknown (%)
Visually disabled	48.46	42.05	1.03	5.38	3.07
Hearing disabled	9.08	52.83	1.35	8.73	27.99
Mentally retarded	13.93	30.17	2.30	10.75	42.84
Physically disabled	3.97	46.87	13.65	23.12	12.40

Identification of Exceptionalities

In China, psychological tests are often used. Some Western psychological tests, such as the WISC, WPPSI, WAIS, and Stanford-Binet tests, are revised to detect and identify disabilities in the Chinese setting. They were the basic instruments used in the national sample survey.

Labeling the Handicapped Population

Arguments on labeling center on the fact that labeling children stigmatizes them. Terms such as *mental retardation* seem to give a negative emphasis to the individual's impairment. Once a term is applied to an individual, it is difficult to disassociate the individual from the label. A second point against the practice of labeling is that it may become a self-fulfilling prophecy. Individuals may behave according to what they believe is expected of them as determined by the label, whether the label is accurately applied or not. A third argument in opposition to labeling is that the practice of delimiting categories discriminates against those individuals who do not fall neatly into the classifications. Individuals who are outside the categorical limits may be denied special services they need. A final reason for not labeling is that it seems to be more important to concentrate on the prevention and treatment of all exceptionalities rather than to expend energies on locating, identifying, and placing exceptional persons into categories.

One major justification for labelling is that it is helpful as well as necessary to identify clusters of symptoms that convey specific meanings to all persons working with an exceptional person. Here labelling is a kind of shorthand that quickly transmits key information and enables professionals to provide appropriate treatment. Another reason for labeling is created by administrative and legal requirements. In many cases, exceptional persons may qualify for special services only after they have been identified through some diagnostic procedure as fitting one of the prescribed categories.

This practice of labeling for administrative purposes has recently been given increased attention. Chinese administrators try to require school districts to locate, diagnose, and label exceptional children according to clearly delineated guidelines and classifications. Unless children are so identified, and meet the requirements for the labels, they may not be served in special educational programs under this law. Federal and state monies are available only for those exceptional children who do fit into the specific categories.

A final point in favor of labeling is that each category provides a focal point around which community support may be rallied. Voluntary organizations composed of interested parents, laypersons, and professionals often capitalize on the unique needs of one exceptionality to gain further support, to promote beneficial legislation, and to provide direction for planning and programming. Eliminating categorical labels may diffuse the interest and involvement of such groups.

The cases for and against labeling both represent sound and valid arguments. While it is not our intention to advocate stigmatizing an exceptional child by using a label, it is felt that labeling, at this point in the development of special education in China, is justifiable in order to provide the most effective treatment. The use of categories and labels will ensure, as never before, that the needs of young, special children will be met.

The Social Context of Special Education

Special education in China's modern times began in the late nineteenth century. For more than fifty years before liberation in 1949, there were only forty-two special schools with a total of two hundred students for handicapped children. These schools were mainly charitable facilities, and society often looked upon these schools as a burden.

After the new China was founded, the government set up a progressive program of special education. In 1951, the Government Administration Council of the Central People's Government promulgated the document *Decision with Regard to Reforming School Systems,* which stipulated that governments at all levels set up special schools for deaf and blind persons and educate physiologically impaired children, youths, and adults. At that time, special education was formally introduced into China's national education system.

In the last ten years or so, the development of China's special education has entered a new stage. This development has been promoted by the policy of reform, the opening of the doors to the outside world, and the speeding up of socialist modernization. With the approval of the State Council, several state agencies such as the State Education Commission, the Ministry of Civil Affairs, and the China Disabled Person's Federation convened at the National Working Conference on Special Education in Beijing in 1988. This conference's purpose was to discuss the development of special education, mainly its guiding principles, but also programs and policies, and methods of implementing compulsory education for disabled children. The conference discussed and formulated a document entitled *A Number of Suggestions with Regard to Developing Special Education,* which the general office of the State Council transmitted throughout the country for discussion and implementation. The promulgation of this important document, along with other laws and regulations, further defined each guiding principle and policy of special education and opened up the way to a bright future for China's special education.

Disabled persons have certain special difficulties. Developing special education positively, and understanding, respecting, caring for, and assisting disabled persons is a traditional virtue in China's society. It is a concrete reflection of socialist humanitarianism, and a component of China's socialist spiritual civilization.

Giving priority to special education is also an important aspect of China's education program and its policy of social development. Developing special education and educating, training, and compensating disabled persons are essential ways to improve their abilities. These ways of support not only help disabled people obtain a sense of strength and self-reliance and help them acquire an equal and full opportunity to participate in social life, but these methods also help them to produce material and cultural wealth for society.

At present, China is in the primary period of socialism. Special eduction should be developed according to China's national conditions and its actual situation. The principle of combining popularization of special education in society with upgrading of quality shall be implemented in education of disabled persons, with emphasis on the former. At present and in the coming years, the guiding principle in developing special education is that priority shall be given to compulsory education and vocational and technical education, while efforts shall be made to carry out preschool education. Education at and beyond the senior secondary level shall be developed gradually.

Each kind of special school should implement and follow the general educational policy, which is to enable students to develop in an all-around way—morally, intellectually, and physically. Meanwhile, the characteristics of disabled persons must be fully discussed and considered. Each special school should make vocational and technical education a focal point, while conducting moral, cultural, intellectual, physical, and mental compensational education to create conditions for the participation of disabled persons in social life and their adaptation to future social needs.

In addition, disabled children shall be placed in regular classes in general elementary schools. There will be a network for the education of disabled persons that has special schools as a backbone. Special classes affiliated with ordinary schools and regular classes with disabled children will serve as the supporting force.

In order to make school attendance possible for disabled children, the location of the schools must be in accordance with the need shown in a region. For example, schools for visually disabled children should be set up in provinces, regions, or municipalities. As an alternative, classes for visually disabled children shall also be set up in ordinary schools. These children, therefore, can enroll in regular elementary schools and study in regular classes. Classes and schools for hearing-disabled children shall be set up in the counties. For the education of mentally retarded children in the cities, special classes or schools shall be set up. These students can be put in regular classes too. For the education of those in rural areas, these children shall be placed in regular classes of neighborhood schools with individualized help. However, special classes or schools can be set up in counties or villages if the local conditions allow it. On the basis of this location principle, several schools (classes) for disabled children shall be set up as teaching and research centers in each province, region, and municipality. These schools (classes) shall play the role of models for others to follow.

The number of years of compulsory education for China's disabled children shall be the same as for normal children. Each region should provide five or six years of elementary education at first; secondary education of three or four years should be developed gradually.

The education of visually disabled children shall implement the system of five years in elementary schools, four years in junior secondary schools (5.4 system). If needed, the system of 6.3 shall also be implemented. Education for hearing-disabled children should in principle be nine years. Areas in which conditions are not yet sufficient should implement the 6.3 system in stages. The six years of elementary education for hearing-disabled children should be universalized first. The schooling period for mentally retarded children should also be nine years. Areas in which conditions are not yet sufficient should implement the 6.3 system in stages. Six years of education should be universalized first.

Special education is work requiring serious attention from all sections of the society. The central government will provide assistance with the coordinated efforts of related government agencies. Developing special education should be basically the responsibility of the local government. However, the entire society should give it support.

In order to mobilize people in various circles to set up schools, different channels are proposed for setting up China's special schools. Social organizations, factories, mining areas, forest regions, reclamation areas, collective economy organizations, private economic organizations, and individual persons are encouraged to set up schools or to donate funds, materials, and individual efforts to support schools maintained by the state. Our compatriots in Taiwan and Hong Kong, overseas Chinese communities, international friendship organizations, and friends are welcome to donate funds.

To strengthen the leadership of special education work unified under the people's governments at all levels, China maintains educational authority in the offices of Civil Affairs, Health, Labor, Planning, and Finance and the China Disabled Persons' Federation. Other agencies work in close cooperation, each managing different areas related to special education.

Education authorities manage education at all levels and in all forms. Their responsibilities are implementing the national guiding principle and policies regarding special education; formulating curriculum programs, teaching programs, and rules and regulations; planning developmental programs of special education with planning agencies; supervising generally and managing specifically the work of special education; conducting special education teacher training; and organizing compilations of special education materials. Agencies of civil affairs are in charge of organizing children's welfare institutions and community service institutions and conducting preschool education, cultural education, as well as vocational and technical education.

Agencies of labor cooperate with concerned institutions, and organize and promote preservice training and in-service training. The labor and civil affairs agencies plan and supervise job placement for disabled people, helping to establish collective enterprises for them or helping them go into individual business. Health agencies are in charge of classifying, identifying, and diagnosing disabled children. They help enrollment, supervise the rehabilitation and medication of students in special schools (classes), and transmit and popularize the knowledge of rehabilitative medicine.

Planning and finance agencies formulate policies and support special education positively by investing in capital construction and providing funds. China's Disabled Persons' Federation takes developing special education as one of its own important tasks, assisting government and motivating society to promote special education. The Labor Union, the Communist Youth League, the Women's Federation, and other circles all support special education with enthusiasm.

According to the principle of local government's responsibility to divide authority at various levels, local governments should be in charge of providing special education funds. The amount of funds should be increased every year by the same percentage as overall education funds. This is the main channel for solving the problem of special education funds. The funds for capital construction of special schools should be provided by local governments at various levels and covered by the local capital construction budgets. A certain proportion of the educational tax should be used for special education in all regions. The commissions of fund-raising for social welfare and the disabled persons' welfare foundations should contribute some of their solicited funds for developing special education in all regions.

Governments at all regions should organize and support special schools in developing work-study programs in order to make up for the shortage of funds for running schools. China's government has set up special subsidies for supporting local governments in all regions to develop special education.

Legislation

The education of disabled children is a part of basic education. According to the Law of Compulsory Education of the People's Republic of China, people's governments at all levels should integrate education of disabled students into the compulsory education system and include it in their overall planning, leadership, and inspection. In order to accelerate the development of disabled children's education, various forms of schooling should be set up. Well-planned classes of disabled children in general primary school are to be set up along with schools for disabled children only.

The Social Security Law for Disabled Persons has passed in People's Congress. This law protects disabled persons, their social situation, and their political and educational rights. The Regulation for Education of Disabled Persons is in preparation.

Policies

In 1989, the Five-Year Work Program for the Disabled was introduced. The related government departments formulated policies and programs on the development of special education, which spelled out the principles for development through two forms of education, namely ordinary education and special education. Particular attention is to be given to compulsory education, vocational education, and skill training and active efforts are to be made to promote preschool education and the gradual development of secondary and higher education. The program also defines the pattern for primary special education with a large number of education classes and ordinary classes taking in disabled children as the principal means of educating disabled persons. There will be a number of special education schools as the backbone.

Teachers, Schools, Curriculum, and Pedagogy

Schools

The 1987 sample survey of disabled people in China included 9,365 disabled children. Of these, 55.24 percent had been enrolled in schools and

TABLE 11.4. Learning Ability Analysis of Disabled Children

Category	In Regular Schools (%)	In Special Schools (%)	Unable to Attend (%)
Visually impaired	54.49	39.68	5.82
Hearing and speech impaired	51.32	46.68	1.99
Mentally retarded	39.31	53.13	7.55
Physically disabled	92.37	1.80	5.82
Having Psychoses	—	—	52.94
Multiple disabled	11.67	40.02	48.29

44.76 percent had not. Of the latter, 23.07 percent were unable to go to schools due to severe disability, and 76.39 percent were physically able to go to schools but had no opportunity. The distribution is shown in table 11.4.

Most of the disabled children enrolled in schools were not severely disabled. Most of those children not yet in schools were of serious disability—blind, deaf, mentally retarded, physically disabled, mentally ill, and multiply disabled. Among them, however, only a small number had lost the ability to study completely; most were able to enter special schools if the schools became available.

By the end of 1988, there were 78,100 blind children and 2,929 of them were studying in blind schools or in blind classes of regular schools. Their school enrollment rate was 3.75 percent. In the same year, there were approximately 313,800 deaf children; their enrollment rate was 13.52 percent. There were 422,600 mentally retarded children with severe disability and an enrollment rate of 2.89 percent. Among the 2.15 million disabled children having no chance to go to schools, most would go to special schools if conditions permitted.

In the whole country there were 466 schools for the blind and/or deaf and mute children and 131 schools and 599 classes for mentally retarded children—577 special schools with 57,597 students in all. There were 10,787 special education teachers: 7,937 in deaf or mute schools, 2,929 in blind schools, and 2,112 in mentally retarded schools. The ratio of teacher to students was about 1 to 5. Table 11.5 indicates special education school attendance in China.

Teachers

The key to developing and improving special education is to strengthen teacher training. In order to train an adequate number of qualified teachers

TABLE 11.5. School Attendance of Handicapped Children

Categories	Total	Regular School (N/%)	Special School (N/%)	Not in School (N/%)
Visually impaired	189	79/41.8	2/1	108/57
Hearing/language impaired	1,206	500/41.5	43/3.8	663/55
Speech disordered	219	115/52.5	1/0.5	103/47
Mentally retarded	6,410	3,931/61	35/0.005	2,444/38.1
Physically handicapped	721	432/59.9	2/0.3	287/39.8
Multiple handicapped	822	136/16.5	9/1.1	677/82.4
Total	9,567	5,193	92	4,282

for special education, China regards teacher-training institutions for special education as an essential resource.

After several years of effort, specialties of special education have been established in four normal universities. Teacher-training institutions for secondary special education have been set up in twenty-four provinces, regions, and municipalities. Graduates of these specialties and institutions have alleviated the shortage of special education teachers. In addition, some graduates of normal schools and qualified teachers of elementary and secondary schools have been chosen to receive special education training. For the in-service teachers, some forms of training in special education are provided, such as old teachers teaching young ones, class observing, itinerant guidance, teaching research activities, short-term training, and so on. All these methods improve the teachers' knowledge of special education and their practical teaching ability. In order to help teachers adapt to the developmental needs of disabled children studying in the regular classes or schools, the regular normal schools in all regions have added courses of basic knowledge of special education and teachers colleges have added elective courses on special education.

In the process of developing special education, China's research work on special education has been strengthened. Now there are a number of special education research institutions. These institutions follow the principle of combining theory with practice, have done a lot to promote research and reform in the field of special education, and have made contributions to establishing the theory system of special education adapted to China's conditions and to improving China's special education level.

TABLE 11.6.　The Development of Special Schools and Classes

Year	Blind Schools	Deaf Schools	Blind and Deaf Schools	MR Schools	MR Classes
1980	9	242	41		
1981	9	251	42		
1982	13	257	42		
1983	11	264	44		
1984	11	274	41	4	
1985	15	295	40	25	
1986	15	328	44	36	556
1987	18	350	46	90	576
1988	21	372	43	123	599
1989	24	418	41	179	811
1990	25	474	50	191	1053
1991	24	559	77	235	1235
1992	26	642	86	273	

Emerging and Future Trends

According to statistics, the number of various kinds of schools for disabled children grew to 1,027 by 1992, as shown in table 11.6. There are 1,555 classes for disabled children in regular elementary schools and 129,455 students in special schools or classes. In addition, there are a large number of disabled children studying in regular classes. The rate of school attendance has increased to above 55.24 percent.

Meanwhile, early education for disabled children has been making progress. In 1992, the institutions for hearing and speech training of deaf children all over the country have increased to 1,280. In these centers, 25,279 deaf children have been trained, and 8,388 deaf children are receiving training. Early education for mentally disabled children and visually disabled children has also increased.

Higher education is now available for disabled persons. In addition to the students recruited in three special colleges and universities, there are six thousand other disabled youths who are recruited by ordinary colleges and universities.

We must notice with a clear head, however, that while seeing this progress, disabled persons are making greater demands on special education along with their demands for social development and improvement of their living standard. China's special education still cannot meet the developmental needs of special education either in quantity or quality of programs. Teachers, funds, facilities of special education, and other conditions for running schools are lacking, and this demands a prompt solution. The problems are still so prominent that it is difficult for all disabled children to enter school.

This situation has drawn the attention of people and government at all levels. In order to change the conditions and make special education develop in coordination with the economy and society, the State Council transmitted the *Work Program for Disabled Persons during the Period of the Eighth Five-Year National Development Plan (1991–95),* formulated by the State Planning Commission and sixteen other agencies. The State Education Commission and China's Disabled Persons' Federation also promulgated the *Implementation Program of Compulsory Education for Disabled Children during the Period of the Eighth Five-Year National Development Plan.* According to these two documents, during 1991 to 1995, China's development plan of special education will follow various threads, as will now be explained.

Compulsory Education of Disabled Children

Based on the development level of the economy and culture, great progress will be made in the area of compulsory elementary education for visually disabled, hearing disabled, and mentally retarded children. The rate of school attendance of disabled children should reach 80 percent in the three municipalities directly under the central government—Beijing, Tianjin, and Shanghai—and the fifteen cities with the authority of independent planning. It should reach 60 percent in the seven provinces of Jiangsu, Shandong, Zhejiang, Liaoning, Heilongjiang, Jilin, and Guangdong, in the developed areas in other provinces and autonomous regions, and in all cities at the regional level. It should reach 30 percent in the provinces of Hebei, Hubei, Hunan, Anhui, Fujian, Jiangxi, Hainan, Sichuan, Shanxi, Shaanxi, and the other provinces and autonomous regions—Guagngxi, Guizhou, Yunnam, Inner Mongolia, Ningxia, Gansu, Qinghai, Xinjiang. Tibet should formulate its own target, and progress should be made on the current educational conditions. All regions should continue to create opportunities to recruit more disabled students into school.

Vocational and Technical Education

Thirty vocational and technical training centers for disabled persons should be established, and they will serve as centers of vocational education at the province level. Ten of them should be up to the national standards for standard secondary vocational and technical schools.

Vocational and technical training centers for disabled persons should be established at the regional level. Departments of vocational and technical training should be set up at the county level. The network of vocational and technical education of various types and diversified administrative levels will be formed all over the country. Special schools with fairly good conditions should gradually incorporate vocational classes. Cities, where possible, should establish secondary vocational schools for disabled persons.

Training of Special Education Teachers and Administrators

Special education faculty should be established in relevant colleges and universities. But the specialties of special education available now in the four normal universities available now should be improved first. The management efficiency and the educational quality of the twenty-four special education teacher-training institutions at senior secondary school level should be improved. The provinces and regions that have not established teacher-training institutions should establish short-term training centers for special education teachers. Educational authorities at all levels should provide full-time and part-time administrators of special education and improve special education training for them.

Developing Curricula and Materials

The State Education Commission is responsible for revising teaching plans for schools of visually disabled and hearing impaired children, organizing compilation of teaching materials for schools of mentally retarded and hearing disabled children, and guiding programs for educating and training moderately mentally retarded students.

Each province, autonomous region, and municipality directly under the central government should compile local teaching materials according to local requirements. The State Education Commission will issue a teaching tools catalog for schools of visually disabled, hearing-disabled, and mentally retarded children and organize research and development of teaching aids and learning aids for disabled children. The State Education Commission will also compile a working manual for children with visual disability, hearing disability, or mental retardation studying in regular classes in order to encourage the program of disabled children studying in regular classes.

Higher Education and Senior Secondary School Education

Vocational senior secondary schools should be developed. The three colleges and universities for disabled persons now available should be run well and new colleges and universities in several places should be added when conditions allow. One or two colleges and universities, in provinces, regions, and municipalities where conditions allow, should be chosen to enroll students with visual or hearing disabilities for study in certain specialties suitable to them. Other colleges and universities should continue to implement relevant rules to admit disabled youth. Governments in all regions should continue to adopt measures and encourage handicapped people to pursue their education in a self-taught way.

Early Education for Disabled Children

The construction of hearing- and speech-training bases for hearing-disabled children should be increased. Thirty rehabilitation centers for hearing-disabled children, four hundred divisions of speech training, and some units of speech training at the grassroots level should be established and improved. These will form a network of hearing- and speech-training institutions combined with family training. Hearing and speech training for twenty thousand children with hearing disabilities will be implemented. Meanwhile, early education by the State Council for children with visual disabilities and mental retardation will receive special attention.

Protection of Children in Difficult Circumstances

The drafting and implementation of a social welfare scheme for maternity losses and expenses will be encouraged in the urban areas. Measures will be taken in those rural areas that have the means to introduce life insurance for the single child and an old-age pension for parents with a female child. Such measures should eventually lessen discrimination against the female child in regard to child rearing, schooling, and career opportunities, among other things.

The early diagnosis, treatment, rehabilitation, and education of disabled children will be reinforced. Improvement of four to five national child rehabilitation centers will be made to eventually develop them into training bases for child rehabilitation workers. Within the communities, rehabilitation schools for deaf children and child care centers for disabled children will also be set up. Special education for disabled children will be developed further by creating more schools for the disabled, conducting special classes for these children in ordinary schools, or making provisions for them to sit in at normal classes, steps that will allow the majority of disabled children of school age not to miss the opportunity to receive basic education.

Children of today will run our human family in the twenty-first century. Their survival, protection, and development decide, for the most part, the future quality of a people and lay the foundation for human progress as a whole. The social consciousness that provides the disabled with the understanding, respect, care, and assistance they need will be popularized in China. China's special education will develop very quickly.

References

Chen, Li, ed. 1990. *Child development research newsletter* 1 (1).

Xu, Yun. In press. *Disabled persons' affairs in China.*

Xu, Yun, and Akio, H. 1991. The development of special education of mentally retarded children. In *Symposia of sociology*, vol. 9, no. 4, 124. Japan: Kagoshima Keiza University.

Xu, Yun, and Si, Yuying, eds. 1990. *Symposia of special education on mentally retarded children*. Hangzhou: Zhejiang Education Press Co.

12

India

RITA AGRAWAL

*S*pecial education, the world over, is a relatively recent phenomenon (Kirk 1970). Sporadic attempts at schooling for the blind, the deaf, and the mentally retarded can be traced back even to the early 1800s. These earlier attempts to educate and rehabilitate the physically and mentally handicapped were founded more on theological and charitable lines. Most of the work in this area was because of the strong sense of empathy that certain disabled as well as nondisabled people had for their less fortunate counterparts. The organizers, dedicated though they were, lacked the necessary professional training. Systematic special education started much later, that is, in the early 1900s. One reason for this concern with the welfare of the disabled was probably economic. It was gradually realized that the disabled constitute a sizable proportion of the world's population.

In fact, according to a recent UNICEF report (National Institute of Public Cooperation and Child Development [NIPCCD] 1989), about 10 percent of the world's population suffers from one or another form of

About the Author • Rita Agrawal has a Ph.D. in psychology and is associate professor in the Department of Psychology, Guru Nanak Dev University, Amritsar, India. One of her major research and teaching interests is the psychology and education of exceptional children. Her work has been presented at various national and international conferences and she has authored over fifty research papers published in internationally acclaimed journals. Dr. Agrawal is associated with the National Institute for the Visually Handicapped, Dehra Dun, India as consultant member of the Expert Committee for evaluation of research projects undertaken by the NIVH, and acts as a resource person for various workshops and refresher courses conducted for in-service special education personnel. She is a member of the International Council of Psychologists, International Association of Special Education, Indian Science Congress Association, National Academy of Psychologists, and has recently been elected vice president of the Panjab Psychological Association.

physical or mental disability. Accordingly, 450 to 500 million people in the world are estimated to be disabled. It is clear from these figures that the loss due to unutilized human resources is quite large. Add to this the disproportionate amount of time, money, and effort spent over each disabled child, and we have a figure that is quite colossal. In India, the problems due to disability have definitely increased. With the total population today being over 869 million, even the conservative estimate of 1.8 percent yields a total of approximately 15 million disabled people.

As far as India is concerned, special education has a recent origin. It was only after India gained independence that thought was given to this area. Naturally, the movement was slow to begin with, since priority was being given to spelling out and initiating programs for the education of the nondisabled population. An additional factor for the delay was the nonavailability of exact figures regarding prevalence and incidence rates for various forms of disability in India.

Prevalence of Exceptional Conditions in India

A problem encountered throughout the world is that of ascertaining prevalence rates for exceptional conditions; variations in definitional criteria yield varying estimates. In India, too, such contradictions regarding the total number of individuals with disability abound and are probably best exemplified by the figures cited by different sources for the prevalence of visual impairments. Whereas the Census of India Report (Government of India 1981) shows that 478,657 people are totally blind, sample surveys conducted by the Indian Council of Medical Research (Ghosal 1982) estimate the number of totally blind persons at 9 million, with another 45 million with lesser, variable degrees of visual impairment.

Probably the most widely accepted estimates are those obtained by the National Sample Survey (NSS) organization in 1981 and reported in 1983. Based on primary data collection in all the states and union territories of India, the survey yields valuable insights into the magnitude, causes, and prevalence of the major physical disabilities. The figures show that in 1981, 12.5 million people, or 1.8 percent of the total population of India, were disabled. Locomotor disabilities accounted for the largest number (3.47 million) followed by visual impairments (3.47 million), hearing impair-

TABLE 12.1. Prevalence of Disabilities, by Age

Disability	0–4 Years	5–15 Years	60+ Years
Locomotor	1,940	2,753	9,733
Visual	128	303	1,302

ments (3.02 million) and speech defects (1.75 million). An important short-coming of the above survey was the total neglect of the mentally retarded population. The figures generally accepted for mental retardation are those cited by the UNICEF (1984). According to these figures, there are at least 2 to 3 million mentally retarded persons, including those cases due to iodine deficiency.

A more recent survey was carried out in the state of Uttar Pradesh by Joshi et al. (1988). Out of the total 25,743 individuals surveyed, 703 (2.7 percent) were disabled. The breakdown in terms of type of disability was physical (67.7 percent), mental (2.99 percent), auditory/speech (13.66 percent), and visual (35.49 percent). Thus, it can be seen that the largest number is the physically handicapped, comprising over half of the total number of disabled persons interviewed. While the percentages cited by Joshi are definitely greater than those of the NSS, it must be borne in mind that disabling conditions and their numbers have been found to vary from one part of India to another, and Joshi was basing his estimates on only one state.

The prevalence figures arrived at the NSS (1981) also show that disability in India is a more predominant problem of adulthood and old age than of childhood, and more of the rural as than of the urban areas. For every one hundred thousand individuals, the total number of disabled in various age groups is given in table 12.1.

For hearing and speech impairments, breakdown according to age has not been reported. Rather, the figures available are those for prevalence rates for congenital and adventitious handicap (see table 12.2). From the tables it is clear that for both locomotor and visual disabilities, there is a greater proportion of individuals above the age of sixty. For hearing impair-ments, the adventitious far outnumber the congenital cases. In contrast, the opposite is true for speech impairments.

Although the number of school-going children afflicted is therefore smaller than the adult population, the numbers cannot be disregarded when one considers the fact that children constitute about 40 percent of the total population of India, with an estimated 397 million in children in 1991 (UNICEF 1984). Also, since the proportion of children with congenital disability is smaller than those with onset after birth (with speech impair-ments being an exception, of course), it is probable that a sizable propor-tion of disabilities is due to reasons that are preventable.

TABLE 12.2. Prevalence of Hearing and Speech Impairments

Disability	Congenital	Adventitious
Hearing	549	1,337
Speech	835	321

TABLE 12.3. Rural-Urban and Sex Distribution of Disabled Population According to States

	Rural			Urban			
	Male	Female	Total	Male	Female	Total	All (Rural + Urban)
India	6,538,016	5,048,619	11,586,635	1,524,366	1,159,050	2,683,416	14,270,051
Andhra Pradesh	647,143	582,589	1,229,732	145,204	129,637	274,841	1,504,573
Assam	82,809	64,846	147,655	9,172	4,605	13,777	161,432
Bihar	785,136	585,099	1,370,235	82,302	57,431	139,733	1,509,968
Gujarat	224,295	186,931	411,226	78,021	62,138	140,159	551,385
Haryana	156,373	90,453	246,826	43,813	30,230	74,043	320,869
Himachal Pradesh	53,980	32,532	86,512	2,632	1,453	4,085	90,597
Jammu & Kashmir	54,495	31,373	85,868	6,446	3,778	10,224	96,092
Karnataka	335,064	288,748	623,812	95,256	82,293	177,949	801,761
Kerala	233,366	187,068	420,434	55,701	41,046	96,747	517,181
Madhya Pradesh	373,353	315,453	688,806	76,487	62,455	138,942	827,748
Maharashtra	438,855	368,334	807,189	174,134	137,114	311,248	1,118,437
Manipur	6,497	3,317	9,814	1,062	979	2,041	11,855
Meghalaya	14,251	4,062	18,313	1,144	397	1,541	19,854
Nagaland	—	—	—	234	244	478	478
Orissa	325,243	283,448	609,391	29,837	23,750	53,587	662,978
Punjab	220,935	139,098	360,033	55,233	33,098	88,331	448,364
Rajasthan	375,027	275,527	650,554	78,852	61,564	140,416	790,970
Tamilnadu	463,332	383,250	846,582	221,558	175,616	397,174	1,243,756
Tripura	22,355	17,382	39,737	2,265	1,893	4,158	43,895
Uttar Pradesh	1,244,939	829,565	2,074,504	206,310	146,383	352,693	2,427,197
West Bengal	456,112	358,603	814,715	104,302	65,212	169,514	984,222
U.T. (all)	23,756	20,941	44,697	54,001	37,734	91,735	136,432

Source: Computed using data from NSS prevalence rates and 1981 census population of India.

Another important feature is that almost 80 percent of the total disabled population of India resides in rural areas. The NSS and the Census of India Reports of 1981 have provided figures for the rural-urban distribution in each of the states of India. According to the latter report, out of the 14 million disabled individuals, 11.5 million are in the rural areas (see table 12.3). The rural-urban distribution in terms of the four types of disability is shown in table 12.4.

The UNICEF Report (1984) also provides another idea: Prevalence rates also vary according to sex. Except for the visually impaired, there are a greater number of males who are disabled than of females (NSS 1981).

Although the statistics mentioned so far give a bird's-eye view of the prevalence of exceptionalities in India, an in-depth analysis can only be undertaken by considering each disabling condition independently.

Locomotor Disabilities

Locomotor disabilities constitute almost 50 percent of the total disabled population. The chief causes of locomotor disabilities in India are leprosy, poliomyelitis, cerebral palsy, amputations, scoliosis and related spinal problems, congenital disabilities, nerve injuries, hemiplegia, and paraplegia.

While exact figures for the prevalence of these causes could not be ascertained, statistics show that polio cases have been on the rise. Thus, 16,439 cases of polio were admitted for treatment in different hospitals of India in 1974 compared to 21,290 in 1983 (Maitra, Acharaya, and De 1989). These authors also report that in a single hospital in Calcutta, the number of polio cases increased from 607 in 1974 to 2,641 in 1988. According to the UNICEF Report (1984), 200,000 children are afflicted with polio each year, out of which 65 percent become lame, with prevalence rates for rural areas—6.4 per 100 cases—being much higher than that for urban areas—6 per 1,000 cases.

Leprosy is another major disabling condition for India. About one-third of the world's leprosy patients are in India, with as many as 450,000 in the state of West Bengal alone (National Institute for the Orthopedically Handicapped 1991). As estimated by UNICEF (1984), there were 3.2 million leprosy patients in India in 1982, out of which 20 percent were children; at least 25 percent had some form of disability.

Among the causes of locomotor disabilities in adult women, osteoporosis and osteomalacia are significant. According to Gupta (1990), 15 percent of women over sixty-five suffer from osteoporosis and 30 percent of women over seventy-five have sustained fractures due to the condition.

Although osteomalacia is common in that older age group, juvenile cases (in ages twelve to seventeen) are not uncommon. Other common causes of locomotor disabilities in children include scoliosis, with children between ages eleven to fourteen years at maximum risk (Sarkar 1990). Rickets is a cause of disability in some parts of India.

TABLE 12.4. Rural-Urban Distribution of Disability in India (in Thousands)

Disability	Rural	Urban
Locomotor	4,342	1,085
Visual	2,908	666
Hearing	2,477	542
Speech	1,366	388

Visual Impairments

The chief causative factors in visual impairments in India can be gleaned from the Report of the National Programme for the Control of Blindness (1979–80, 1980–81). Reported causes are cataracts (55 percent), trachoma (5 percent), infections (15 percent), smallpox (3 percent), nutritional deficiencies (2 percent), injuries (1.2 percent), glaucoma (5 percent), and other miscellaneous causes (18.3 percent). Since the most important cause of visual impairment is cataracts, it is natural that the greatest number of visually impaired people should be in the sixty-plus age group.

Causative factors among children are apparently the same as those seen in almost all the developing countries of Asia and Africa: vitamin A deficiency, smallpox, and injuries. Cohen et al. (1985) have confirmed that even in Bangladesh the bulk of childhood visual impairment is caused by keratomalacia and xerophthalmia, both being due to vitamin A deficiencies. The causative factors also indicate that a large proportion of the visually impaired suffer from preventable or curable blindness. In fact, Ghosal (1982) reports that approximately 4.5 million people suffer from preventable causes, out of which 14,000 are preschool children suffering from visual impairments because of nutritional deficiencies.

When smallpox has been successfully eradicated from India, and the massive contact program for overcoming vitamin A deficiencies has been realized, it is hoped that the prevalence rates for visual impairments among children will go down even further.

Hearing Impairments

According to the NSS (1981), there are a total of 3.2 million people who suffer from hearing impairments in India. Etiologically speaking, the causes are somewhat different from those common in the Western world. Major causes in the West are first, genetics; second, perinatal problems, especially in the case of babies with low birth weights; then rubella, encephalitis, and meningitis.

Although etiological surveys could not be located, it is generally observed that the vast majority of hearing impairments in India are either hereditary, caused by accidents involving the head region, or due to infections of the middle and/or inner ear. Fortunately, rubella is almost nonexistent in India, so that one major cause of deafness can be bypassed.

Especially in rural areas and among the low socioeconomic groups in the urban areas, poor pediatric care, coupled with a general lack of awareness among parents, is probably at the root of hearing impairments in India. Among the aged, senility is one of the major causes. These observations are confirmed with a survey by Joshi et al. (1988). Among rural people, the chief causes of hearing impairments were found to be congenital disorders, chronic otitis media, and senility. These three causes contributed to 38.80 percent, 39.74 percent, and 10.26 percent respectively of the total number of deaf people identified.

Mental Retardation

As in the case of visual and hearing impairments, prevalence figures for mental retardation in India show wide variation from one survey to another, generally as a function of the criteria adopted, the type of investigating team, and the type of population being studied (Sinclair 1979). Another idiosyncratic feature of mental retardation in India is the etiological variation across different regions. Causing further contradiction is the fact that most of the reported surveys have been community surveys focusing on the prevalence of various types of psychiatric problems, mental retardation being considered one of them.

Summarizing the findings of ten such community surveys, Prabhu reported prevalence rates varying from .07 to 2.53 percent (Sinclair 1979). A survey performed by Verma in Nagpur City revealed a prevalence figure of 3 to 4.2 percent for children (8 to 15 years) and 1.6 percent for adults of 16 to 22 years (Sinclair 1979). In contrast, Sinclair (1979) has obtained prevalence rates varying from .08 to 5.2 percent of school-going children surveyed in four cities. That the prevalence rate is somewhat higher for rural and tribal areas has been brought to the fore by Murthy and Wig and by Nandi (Sinclair 1979). Taken together, the results of the various surveys closely parallel the figures provided by the World Health Organization (1968). That is, 2 to 3 percent in almost all areas of the world, with cases of severe mental retardation being about 4 per 1,000 people.

Sinclair (1979) also provides an idea regarding the breakdown of the etiologies of mental retardation. These are prenatal causes (37 percent), perinatal (17 percent), postnatal (15 percent), multiple factors (5 percent), and unknown causes (25 percent). In terms of specific etiologies, available figures show wide variation, mainly because of the lack of availability of sophisticated facilities for karyotyping, conducting metabolic studies, or obtaining virus cultures in all but a few urban centers. Another major reason for variation is that the specific etiology varies from one region of India to another. Thus, where consanguineous marriages are common (as in some parts of south India), the incidence of familial handicaps is larger. According to Narayanan and Verma, other genetic causes include neural tube defects, amounting to 4.8 per 1,000 cases and Down's syndrome—2.6 to 12 percent of cases (Sinclair 1979).

Of the perinatal factors, Narayanan cites hypoxia alone as accounting for 8.3 to 25.4 percent of all cases (Sinclair 1979) and is mainly linked to poor antenatal and natal care, especially in rural areas. Postnatal factors mentioned by Dhingra include malnutrition and cretinism, especially in the form of endemic goiter in the Himalayan and sub-Himalayan regions (Sinclair 1979). UNICEF (1984) estimates that there will be at least 200 million people with iodine deficiency by 2000 A.D. in India alone. Other causes are encephalitis, meningitis, accidents, and lead poisoning (Sinclair 1979).

Identification and Labeling of Exceptionalities

Identification of handicapping conditions depends on the type of handicap, its severity, and the degree to which it is visible. Thus, gross orthopedic defects are the ones most easily identified, even by parents. Congenital blindness, too, is usually detected by parents. This is also the case with congenital deafness once the child fails to reach developmental milestones for language.

For all of these categories, identification in terms of severity, possibility of treatment, amount of residual capacities, and probable prognosis by medical personnel is available in all urban areas. In all but the remote rural areas, facilities exist in primary health centers for primary detection, which can then be followed up on in other centers in nearby towns. The methods used are the same as those used anywhere else: the Snellen chart and its adaptations for illiterate people; the ophthalmoscope, and so on, for visual defects; and the audiometer and spectrograph analysis for hearing defects.

It is in the detection of mental retardation that maximum problems arise. Many cases of mild and moderate retardation go unidentified throughout life. In cases of severe retardation in the rural areas, the condition is often confused with mental disorders, and the child may go around being labeled as a lunatic. In cases of mild and moderately retarded children who are attending school, parents, and more often teachers, become suspicious when the child fails to keep up with age norms or starts manifesting a progressive deterioration in school achievement.

Even after the disability is identified, psychoeducational assessment does not take place for all children—it is restricted to those who contact special schools, vocational training centers, or the extremely expensive private clinical psychologists practicing in the cities.

Because of the absence of psychoeducational assessment facilities in all but some schools in the metropolises, parents contact medical personnel and psychiatry wards in hospitals which, on the basis of clinical observation and the case history, are able to ascertain the presence of retardation. However, in most cases, establishing the specific etiology becomes extremely difficult since sophisticated genetic, biological, and chemical assay techniques to study genetic, metabolic, and brain abnormalities are not generally available. It is because of this factor that prenatal identification of handicaps takes place only in families who have a history of genetic disability, are from the upper socioeconomic strata, and are living in the larger cities. It is also because of this shortage of testing that medical at-risk registers are difficult to maintain.

As far as labeling of the disabled population is concerned, it is carried out along with the identification and at the institutes already mentioned. Practitioners understand the negative psychological impact of labeling but see no viable alternative to it in India since all special education is being carried out in special schools. Although integrated education has been started, as yet not even .01 percent of the disabled are attending such courses.

Labeling is in terms of not only the gross category (that is, visual, hearing, orthopedic, or mentally retarded), but also in terms of severity (mild, moderate, severe, or on a continuous scale of measurement), as well as age of onset. In the case of mentally retarded children, further categorization in terms of type, such as cretinism, cerebral palsy, or mongolism may also be done.

The Social Context of Special Education

An attitude of charity and service to the destitute, the disabled, and the weaker sections of the society has prevailed ever since the Vedic times of ancient India. In almost all the holy scriptures and literary epics, one cannot but notice the consideration shown by both the rulers and the ruled towards their less fortunate counterparts. The blind, the crippled, and the deaf were not only treated in a humanitarian manner, but were often revered figures. Mentally retarded persons, however, did not always receive such consideration and were often ridiculed. These traditions were further perpetuated by the Mughal rulers of medieval India. Although the disabled and the poor were the responsibility of the state, one of the important edicts of Islam was *zakat,* that is, the giving of alms and donations by individuals to the poor and the disabled.

Such humaneness of feelings has, however, been coupled with a fair degree of fatalism rooted in the philosophy of *karma,* or the belief that actions in this life decide one's future reincarnations. In other words, "what you sow, so you reap." Sins and wrongdoing in our life may manifest themselves in any of a variety of conditions (including disability) and thus cause unhappiness in the next life. For a vast majority of people living on the Indian subcontinent, disability thus is irrevocable, since the cause is believed supernatural. While the disabled were objects of pity and sympathy, prevention was considered unthinkable and rehabilitation not possible. Families of disabled persons also resigned themselves to their fate and suffered in silence. As a result, while the medieval period saw the establishment of a large number of homes for the disabled, society failed to provide education or training of any type. It was with such attitudes that India entered the modern period.

The modern period can be divided into two periods: the preindependence era and the postindependence era. The first period may be said to start from the early 1800s when England and other Western countries were establishing their stronghold in India. This period is marked by the setting up of a number of homes for the disabled by both foreign missionaries and social workers. By the mid 1800s, the first schools were opened—for the blind in Amritsar and for the deaf in Bombay. Due to the zeal of voluntary agencies, the first steps in the normalization of the disabled were taken. These efforts led to a change, though gradual, in the attitudes of the people at large and also started permeating other aspects of social living: obsolete laws were reframed and new laws were enacted to provide better facilities for disabled persons. Some of these new laws related to the right to inherit property, to join trade unions, to the settlement of industrial disputes, and to minimum wages without any bar or discrimination.

The postindependence era brought about radical changes in the emphasis on the welfare of the disabled. Rather than simply education being emphasized, there was a stress on the overall development of disabled persons. Moreover, welfare schemes were no longer dependent on the scarce resources of the voluntary agencies. With governmental support in the form of legislation, finances, and the setting up of training institutes and special schools, the stage was set for a breakthrough in the attitudinal barriers, which had for so long been the chief impediments to prevention, therapy, and rehabilitation of individuals with exceptionalities.

The government of India plans and executes its finances through a series of Five-Year Plans (FYPs). From the First-Five Year Plan, organized governmental effort has been there. Whereas the first FYP focused on the disabled, the second made a provision for their employment through funds allocated for their training. The infrastructure so laid was further strengthened through subsequent FYPs, added impetus being provided by foreign agencies and the voluntary sector. Thus, independence opened a new sociopolitical vista for the people of India. On the economic front, too, the disabled benefitted through more liberal state funding.

Perhaps no single factor has had a greater impact on service for the disabled than the United Nation's declaration of 1981 as the International Year of the Disabled. The theme for the year was "Full Participation with Equality" and was based on the UN Declaration of the Rights of Disabled

Persons (Resolution no. 31/123, 16 December 1976). This declaration had far-reaching implications for both planners and social workers since it not only ensured the same fundamental rights to disabled persons as have other human beings but also guaranteed medical, psychological, and functional treatment coupled with rehabilitation and placement services. Another important aspect of the UN Declaration of Rights was the attention drawn to the special needs of persons with disabilities at all stages of social and economic planning, and their rights to live with their families and to participate in all social, creative, and recreational activities.

On the basis of those fundamental rights, the UN laid down the following objectives for the year:

1. Helping disabled persons in their physical and psychological adjustment to society.
2. Promoting all national and international efforts to provide disabled persons with proper assistance, training, care, and guidance, to make available opportunities for suitable work, and to ensure full integration of disabled persons into society.
3. Encouraging study and research projects designed to facilitate the practical participation of disabled persons in daily life, such as improving their access to public buildings and transportation systems.
4. Educating and informing the public of the rights of disabled persons to participate in and contribute to various aspects of economic, social, and political life.
5. Promoting effective measures for the prevention of disability and for the rehabilitation of disabled persons (cf., Rama Mani 1988).

Being one of the signatories to the UN resolution, the Government of India set forth specific objectives for India. Keeping in view the present status of services for the disabled and the resources available, a National Plan of Action was cultivated. The chief objectives were the following:

1. To evolve a national policy for full social integration and legal protection for disabled persons.
2. To initiate a few practical programs which would carry immediate benefit for the integration of disabled persons.
3. To develop a network of services for disabled persons at the grassroots level.
4. To develop a positive rural bias in services for disabled persons.
5. To develop a strong national disability prevention program.
6. To promote research and development through various national institutes.

7. To initiate public campaigns to create greater awareness among the masses regarding the causes, prevention, and effects of disability and the potentials of disabled persons.
8. To collect all relevant data on disabled persons in the country (cf., Rama Mani, 1988).

Pursuant to these objectives, various programs were developed. India was the first country to launch a nationwide survey of blind, deaf, and orthopedically handicapped persons. Although the emerging profile was incomplete—the mentally retarded were not included—it was in impressive beginning. Other major programs launched were those to provide aids and appliances to disabled persons of various categories and to achieve full integration in schools by providing 100 percent (as compared to 50 percent previously) financial assistance to schools for integrating such children. Also, there was the setting up of Vocational Research and Training Centers, provision of loans at nominal rates of interest, and income tax exemption on salaries paid to disabled persons—for their economic rehabilitation. To create widespread awareness, a large number of documentary films have been produced and programs are regularly aired over both radio and TV networks. Posters, pamphlets, and brochures have also been released.

National plans for the prevention of various forms of disability have been drawn up. These include a mass immunization program against polio, drives for the supply of free vitamin A and iodized salt in areas where night blindness and goiter are endemic, camps for free cataract operations and for intraocular lens transplants, camps to provide the orthopedically handicapped with prosthetic aids, and so on. A large number of research projects on the disabled have received grants-in-aid from various national institutes for the disabled, while nongovernmental organizations have been provided with incentives (both financial and material) to encourage the voluntary sector to work for the welfare of disabled persons. In congruence with the programs initiated by the central government, various state governments have also started similar plans at their own level.

In the face of all these facilities, concessions, and programs for the disabled, the social context of disability has undergone a vast change. While far from ideal, attitudes towards disability and disabled persons are definitely moving in a promising direction. One sees a general awareness among the masses that a large proportion of disability is preventable; that the disabled can live independent, near normal lives, which include a work life and a happy married life; that the disabled can give birth to children who do not of necessity have to be disabled; and that disability does not mean a life of futility. In other words, the degree of fatalism attached to disability has decreased. This realization has gone a long way in removing age-old misconceptions and superstitions.

Because of the such changes in attitudes, parents are now willing to ensure that their children are immunized. In the case of congenital and early childhood disabilities, parents are less reluctant to send the child to a special school, often quite a distance from their home. In fact, one constantly comes across parents of disabled children from all walks of life who are on the lookout for a good special school.

Another breakthrough has been in the area of vocational rehabilitation and economic independence of the disabled. Various factors are responsible. These include the training of persons in nontraditional, socially viable skills; the greater availability of prosthetic, hearing, and nonvisual aids; the perseverance shown by placement offices and institutional heads in convincing prospective employers of the capabilities of disabled persons; and the perception and experience of employees that the disabled are, in fact, able to perform a variety of jobs.

As pointed out in the beginning of this paper, the major bulk of disabled persons are in rural areas. If prevalence and incidence rates are to decrease, it is these rural people who have to be targeted. Attempts have been made through rural outreach programs run by various governmental agencies and voluntary organizations. Through massive contact programs to remote areas, people are being made aware of the etiology, prevention, and programs of disability. A major factor has been the recent growth in the national television network. In just one decade, many new television transmitting and broadcasting stations have been set up. Many villages now boast of a community TV set, which is being used not only for entertaining but also educating the masses.

Another contribution of such outreach programs is in the prevention of disability. While outreach programs create an awareness, they also conduct camps for immunization against polio and other infectious diseases, for treatment of cataract and glaucoma, and for the distribution of oral vitamin A doses and prosthetic aids, thus ensuring that future incidence of disability is reduced.

A change toward more positive attitudes and a reduction in the degree of fatalism attached to disability is certainly in the offing. With the change in attitudes comes a change in needs for special schools, vocational training centers, and so on. In a country that is so large and where the greater proportion of the population is still residing in far-flung rural areas, governmental measures are hardly sufficient. In fact, the major brunt of both education and rehabilitation is being borne by voluntary agencies, sponsored by service clubs such as the Rotary Club, the Lions Club, and the Red Cross, or managed by charitable trusts and dedicated individuals.

Starting from just a few schools at the opening of the century, the total number has increased manifold. A recent directory of educational and vocational institutes (Chattopadhyay 1986) lists 458 such institutes run by either voluntary or government agencies. These include 141 institutes for the blind, 114 for the deaf, 68 for the orthopedically handicapped, 76 for the mentally retarded, and a miscellany of others including artificial limb units, teacher-training units, libraries for the disabled, a braille press, and so on. However, even this list is incomplete and the number of institutes is actually larger. Thus, in contrast to the numbers of cited by Chattapadhyay, the National Institute for the Visually Handicapped Directory of Schools (1989) includes 190 schools for the blind, while the National Institute for the Orthopedically Handicapped (1991) lists 162 schools for the orthopedically handicapped.

This discussion has attempted to delineate the changing social scenario of the disabled and disability. While changes have been drastic, it is clear that attitudes toward disability in India are still a function of education, rural/urban distributions, and socioeconomic status.

Government Legislation for the Disabled

The founders of independent India were very much aware of the need to help, educate, and rehabilitate individuals with disability. In fact, by creating a welfare state the Constitution projects a value system emphatically concerned with equality for all. It is explicitly stated in the Constitution that there is a need to secure "justice, social and economic, and equality of statute and opportunity . . . and . . . the dignity of the individual" (Preamble, Constitution of India 1950). The state's concern in obtaining such justice, equality, and dignity is seen in the Equality Clauses, and the welfare of the disabled is taken up specifically in Article 41. Thus, the Constitution of India sets the tone of humanitarian jurisprudence for the disabled.

The founders' concern for justice is aptly seen in the various legal facilities for the handicapped. The legislation may be broadly divided into two categories. First, there is legislation that deals with the general population and aims at the prevention of disability. This includes laws relating to industrial accidents, consumer protection, traffic regulation, and other safety codes. Second, there are those laws specifically targeted at disabled persons. Laws pertaining to inheritance, labor, workmen's compensation, and so on, come under its rubric.

The old inheritance laws of India excluded the deformed from inheritance of property on the grounds that a person who cannot look after property should not be permitted to inherit it. With the Hindu Succession Act of 1956, however, no person is disqualified on the grounds of any disease, defect, or deformity from succeeding to property. Labor laws include the Workmen's Compensation Act (1923), which makes it obligatory for employers to pay compensation for any disability arising out of and in the course of employment; the Employee's State Insurance Act (1948), which provides for vocational rehabilitation of insured persons who become disabled; and the Apprentices Act (1961), which makes it possible for disabled persons to become apprentices provided they fulfill certain medical conditions.

Recent years have seen a surge in the number of executive orders passed by various ministries of the Indian government. These orders have the force of law until the government makes them rules under Article 309 of the Constitution. Following are summaries some of the important areas in which such orders have been passed.

Government Provisions for Education

First, scholarships are available for disabled children of all categories from the ninth grade onward, for general, technical, and professional education. This program was started in 1955, providing a mere twenty-two scholarships. However, by 1987, the number of scholarships provided had risen to 8,500 (Rama Mani 1988). Second, central government employees with disabled children are entitled to an education allowance over and above that received for nondisabled children. Third, a major barrier for blind and physically handicapped children is removed by permitting them to typewrite their answers during public examinations. Fourth, blind high school students may opt for a subject from a humanities or social sciences field instead of the compulsory mathematics or sciences. Fifth, concessions also exist for higher education. Disabled children who find it difficult to attend a regular normal or special school are permitted to apply as private candidates for nontechnical courses, and research fellowships are available for those so inclined.

Disabled students are also entitled to other allowances and concessions for use of the public transportation system, readers, and so on. The Indian Postal Service helps; reading material for the blind are free from postal charges. Similarly, equipment, training, and teaching aids imported for and by the disabled are exempt from customs and additional duties.

Government Provisions for Integrated Education

The Union Department of Education started a program for integrated education in 1974, under which 100 percent financial assistance is available to schools for the education of children suffering from certain mild handicaps, and which provides for necessary aids, incentives, and special teachers. Children enrolled under this plan are also provided allowances for books, stationery, school uniforms, transport, special equipment, escorts, and readers. By the 1979–80 school year, eighty-one schools had joined this program; about 1,881 children have benefited (Rama Mani 1988).

Government Provisions for Vocational Rehabilitation

The Program for Vocational Rehabilitation in India is a well-organized system, consisting of training institutes at the grassroots level and coordinated by central government bodies. The base, at present, consists of seventeen vocational rehabilitation centers, six special-skill workshops, and eleven rural rehabilitation centers. The most recent additions are the district rehabilitation centers. These centers assess the residual capacities of disabled persons, and provide or arrange for their training and placement in the regular job market. They also act as a referral agency for any medical, prosthetic, financial, or legal assistance the person may require. Since these few centers are hardly sufficient for a country so large, and limited in communication and mobility, nongovernmental agencies play a major role in the program. In fact, the major bulk of vocational training and rehabilitation is being carried out by such voluntary institutes. While such institutes do rely on personal donations, the government also provides generous financial assistance.

Coordination of programs and facilities is carried out by four central institutes, one each for the mentally retarded, the visually impaired, the hearing impaired, and the orthopedically disabled. The chief goals of these central bodies are to carry out research in their respective areas of specialization and to develop documentation services for the collection and dissemination of information; to prepare educational and vocational aids, reading material, teaching manuals, and so on; to carry out training programs; and to run model services such as schools and sheltered workshops. Identification of job opportunities and job specialization is also a part of the work entrusted to these central institutes.

To ensure that disabled persons trained at such vocational centers get a job, there are twenty-two employment exchanges and special cells in forty regular employment exchanges. Jobs are available in both the private and the public sectors. The Labor Ministry has identified various jobs for different types of disabilities (listed in the National Classification of Occupations); 3 percent of such posts are reserved for the disabled. There are also concessions in minimum eligibility conditions, maximum age, examination/application fees, routine transfers, and so on. To encourage the employment of disabled persons and to motivate the disabled to be gainfully employed, a variety of awards have been instituted by the government. These include awards for persons employing the largest number of handicapped, for best handicapped worker, and the best placement officer. Self-employment is encouraged by providing bank loans at nominal rates of interest and easy payback plans. Special assistance is available for purchasing prosthetic aids, wheelchairs, motorized carts, and so on. Persons with over 50 percent permanent disability get an income tax concession, and expenditure incurred for the treatment, training, or rehabilitation of the disabled is exempt from income tax. Other miscellaneous concessions include those for land or air travel and exemption from the payment of road tolls by handicapped owners of motor vehicles.

The preceding detailed account makes it obvious that the Indian government is not only aware of the problems of the disabled but has also taken a wide variety of concrete steps to ameliorate their problems. Of course, many of the plans are still in their infancy, and people are not always aware of them. Yet the beginning is extremely promising and probably much more impressive and encompassing than that seen in many developing countries.

Teachers, Schools, Curriculum, and Pedagogy

The Education of Special Education Teachers

Whereas special education in India dates back to the mid-1800s, special education through trained professionals is of much more recent origin. It was only in 1963 that a plan was started by the Union Department of Social Welfare for the training of teachers for the blind. Under this plan, grants were given to form regional centers in the four metropolitan cities, namely, Calcutta, Delhi, Bombay, and Madras. All four centers function with a common syllabus and examination. A similar grant-in-aid is given to the Teacher Training College for the Deaf at Lucknow, while four others are partly financed by the state governments. According to Plumber (Sinclair 1979), there are five centers where teachers for the mentally retarded are trained. In the last two decades, the number of such training centers for teachers of special education has greatly increased because a large number of teacher-training colleges have started departments of special education that offer diplomas in special education.

However, this handful of colleges forms only a drop in the vast ocean of special education. Trained special educators are still hard to come by. The majority of the special schools have teachers, both disabled and nondisabled, who have a basic degree in education supplemented with knowledge of braille, sign language, or other special methods acquired informally. Thus, in 190 schools for the blind, there are 626 trained and 600 untrained teachers (National Institute for the Visually Impaired 1989).

Training of special educators is further augmented by a large number of institutes that offer diplomas and degrees in auxiliary services needed by special schools such as speech therapy, physiotherapy, and orientation and mobility training. Seeing the large number of untrained staff at various institutes for the disabled, governing bodies such as the National Institute for the Visually Handicapped, the National Institute for the Mentally Handicapped, and the National Institute for the Orthopedically Handicapped have been organizing in-service training programs for primary school teachers and refresher courses for special education personnel and auxiliary staff. Some of the courses regularly organized are for the following: teaching of geography, Hindi braille contractions and abbreviations, braille mathematics code, and preschool education of visually handicapped children. Special refresher courses have been organized for orientation and mobility instructors, paramedical staff, placement officers, and medical and nursing students.

Schools

Special education is being carried out in India through two types of special schools. First, we have day schools that cater to only one category of the disabled—schools for the mentally retarded, schools for the visually impaired, and schools for the hearing impaired. A few schools for spastics are also being funded by the Spastic Society of India. For those with mild orthopedic handicaps and speech defects, there are prosthetic aid and speech therapy clinics. However, the education of such children is generally undertaken in normal schools.

Second, there are an almost equal number of residential schools, or day-cum-residential schools, which have facilities for in-house living. Such schools play a very important role in vast countries such as India wherein special schools are generally located in urban areas. It is because of the existence of such residential schools that even children from remote rural areas are able to get an education. Like day schools, these residential schools cater to only one type of disability, though occasionally one may come across a school that admits children from several categories.

As the situation stands at present, it is extremely difficult to arrive at the total number of such schools. Some recent surveys provide rough estimates: According to the *Directory of Schools for the Blind* (NIVH 1989) there are 190 schools for the blind in India, 86 of which are run by the government and 104 of which are managed by voluntary agencies. The majority, 96, provide education up to the middle school level (eighth grade), while the breakdown for preprimary, primary, secondary, and senior secondary is 2, 41, 38, and 13 respectively.

Surveys by the editorial board of the journal *Disabilities and Impairments* also provide valuable insights. They report that since the founding of the first school for the blind at Amritsar, there have been established 250 agencies providing educational and/or vocational training to the blind; 160 institutes for the mentally retarded; 200 institutes and special schools for the deaf; and 67 schools and vocational rehabilitation centers for the orthopedically handicapped. Regarding the last category, it is important to remember that once the children receive suitable prosthetic/orthodontic aids, the majority are able to attend schools for normal children. Of course, the compilers of such surveys are aware that their lists are not all-inclusive. However, such lists have only a 5 to 10 percent margin of error.

Curriculum

The curriculum in these special schools can be broadly divided into three areas: the teaching of basic self-help skills, the imparting of academic education, and the teaching of vocational skills. The age at which admissions are made generally determines the guidelines for the curriculum. In the majority of the special schools, children are not admitted before the ages of eight to ten years, partly due to the paucity of infrastructural resources necessary for taking care of younger children but mainly due to fear on the part of the parents of sending the child to a residential school. By the age of eight to ten years most of the children will already have acquired skills required for bathing, dressing, eating, locomoting, and communicating. Therefore, what needs to be explicitly taught are skills specific to a particular disability. Thus, a blind child may be able to find his or her way around a familiar setting, but may not know how to use a cane effectively or how to locomote through a new environment. Such a child would be given specific lessons in orientation and mobility. Similarly, deaf children may be taught how to communicate using oral/manual language, rather than the mere gestures they have been previously using. The mentally retarded require greater care, since parents may not have been able to teach them any of the basic self-help skills.

In the academic area, content is generally in keeping with the curriculum of schools for normal children, except in schools for the mentally retarded. Such a common syllabus enables the exceptional child to take the government-recognized examinations for middle school (at the end of eighth grade), high school (at the end of tenth grade), or senior secondary (at the end of twelfth grade). In schools for the mentally retarded, in contrast, no importance is attached to the passing of examinations, since the students are in the moderately to severely retarded category. Instead, an attempt is made to impart practical knowledge to the level at which their limited capacities can cope. Thus they would be taught basic skills of reading and writing, along with some concept of time, money, measurements, and so on. As mentioned before, for children in the remaining categories—the visual, hearing, and orthopedic categories—the syllabus content is the same as that in schools for nondisabled children. Thus, like all other children, these children start with the three Rs and then go on to history, geography, physics, chemistry, biology, languages, and the like.

Disability also necessitates the inclusion of some additions to the general academic curriculum. Thus, the blind are provided lessons in braille reading, writing, and typing, while the deaf are taught normal written and oral/ manual language. For those with speech defects, there are speech therapy sessions. Those with mental retardation may require special efforts to over- come perceptual and learning disabilities or signs of dyslexia.

In the last decade or so, the nature of vocational skills taught to the disabled has undergone a great change. Although traditional skills such as weaving, carpentry, caning, and handicrafts are still taught, many new voca- tional skills in keeping with advancing technology have been added. For the blind, these include stenography, typing, skills required of telephone opera- tors, and light engineering skills. Another skill taught to the blind has been music, which has enabled them to work as music teachers in both special and normal schools.

Some of the vocational skills taught to the deaf are typing, proofreading, typesetting, light engineering, accounting, and bookkeeping. Job skills taught to the orthopedically handicapped are even more varied since, with the use of prosthetic aids, many activities are possible at near normal levels.

The mentally retarded are probably maximally handicapped as far as vocational rehabilitation is considered. Such individuals would draw consid- erable advantage from sheltered workshops, but there are very few available. Those existing serve more as training workshops rather than as a means of permanent employment. Most mentally retarded individuals are, therefore, employed in the nonskilled sector, in such fields as gardening, agriculture (manual), animal husbandry, or poultry farming.

Special vocational skills are also taught to disabled girls and women. These include dressmaking, embroidery, knitting, handicrafts, preparation of ready-to-eat snacks, and food and fruit preservation at the cottage industry level. In addition, the advent of computers has added a new dimension to vocational rehabilitation. While the teaching of computer skills to the blind and the deaf is still in its infancy, the impact it will have during the coming years cannot be disregarded.

Pedagogy

Because of the large number of factors causing heterogeneity even within a particular category of disability, special school classes are generally small. The size of each class depends on two factors: the availability of students with similar psychoeducational characteristics and the infrastructural resources of the institute. In metropolitan cities, the size of each class can be 25 to 30 children; class size in the smaller towns may often be limited to 8 to 10 children. While such a small teacher-pupil ratio increases the cost of special education, its psychological benefits cannot be overestimated. The small teacher-student ratio brings a personal touch to the educational process. In addition to making teaching more effective, a small teacher-pupil ratio provides an opportunity for the development of social and psychological support systems so necessary for dealing with the stresses of handicaps.

The language of instruction varies from state to state since India is a multilingual country with over twenty constitutionally recognized regional languages. This, however, fails to pose any problem because both braille and sign language have been developed for almost all the major languages of India. Thus, the deaf are taught using a combination of oral and manual language, along with the normal written language. For the blind, books are available in braille. At the same time, since braille books have a number of limitations (in terms of bulk, permanence, and required knowledge of braille, for example), the concept of talking books is gaining popularity.

It is common knowledge that while teachers trained in special education are important for any special education program, the availability of auditory, visual, and tactile aids is a must. This task has been entrusted to the central national institutes and the National Council for Education Research and Training (NCERT), which is also responsible for the development of educational material and technology for normal schools. The national council develops special education textbooks for all categories of the disabled and kits for the teaching of math, science, and geography, especially to blind children. Tactile maps are available for history and geography, and models provide an important adjunct to the teaching of science. For orientation and mobility training, special life-size training areas have been developed, along with scaled models, to provide a holistic concept of buildings, rooms, playgrounds, railway stations, and so on.

For the mentally retarded, educational kits for the teaching of concepts of time, money, measurement, colors, animals, and so on have been developed. Teaching methods for the mentally retarded are similar to the playway methods used in nursery schools for normal children, combined with the use of behavior modification techniques to enhance the learning process.

In almost all special schools in India, formal teaching is accompanied by cocurricular activities such as sports, music, dance, and dramatics. There are visits to places of interest and picnics. As in normal schools, special schools also hold annual sports meets and organize entertainment programs. These serve a dual purpose—they help to instill a sense of confidence in the children and simultaneously enable normal people to witness the capabilities of these special children. In fact, normalization is a very important aspect of special education in India. A visit to a special school is a treat and learning experience, impressive in that here, students are children first and disabled only secondarily.

Fund-raising campaigns are also organized, normally based on selling items made by the disabled children. Two such campaigns are specially noteworthy because they have attained international recognition. These are the greeting cards made by the Spastic Society of India and those by the Association of Foot and Mouth Painters.

Major Controversies and Issues in Special Education

Mainstreaming is becoming less of an issue in India today. Although the stigmatizing effect of disability is closely linked to the degree of visibility of the impairment, mainstreaming is being practiced more and more. With the initiative taken by the government, tremendous strides have been made in attitudes toward the disabled. Social ostracism has decreased, job opportunities are increasing, more disabled people are in regular jobs, and marriage and children are no longer considered impossible.

When we consider integrated versus segregated education settings, we can see that in contrast to mainstreaming, this issue still remains a moot point. Theoretically, the concept of integrated education is considered to have definite advantages over segregated settings. Limited resources, the priority allotted to provision of literacy programs for the masses, and the concentration of the disabled in rural areas all decisively call for integrated education programs. However, though 100 percent financial support has been proffered by the government, there are as yet few schools willing to join the scheme. The problems are practical ones. While finances are available, the basic infrastructure, resource room facilities, trained special educators, and auxiliary personnel are generally not available. As a result, like segregated schools, schools with Integrated Education Programs (IEPs) are, as are many other innovative programs, clustered in the larger cities. Thus, while the advantages of the IEP have been pointed out in some evaluative studies (e.g., Parikh and Dhylon 1988, Veerarghavan 1987), other studies show that barely 1 percent of the school-going disabled population has taken advantage of the IEP (Sahu 1983). Another reason for lack of support for the IEP is reluctance on the part of teachers, probably because they are already overburdened by classes of sixty to seventy students each. Thus, the issues of integrated education in India raises a number of other issues to be looked into before widespread integrated education becomes viable.

The first issue is: Integration for whom? Another angle of the general issue of integrated education is whether it is viable for every disabled child. Kenmore (1979) has put it very lucidly: "What really happens to a blind child who attends school for the sighted? A comprehensive answer can be given in two words: that depends. It depends upon his teachers, the country where he lives, the time of year and many other factors" (Kenmore 1979, 19). This statement holds true for all categories of the disabled. Moreover, each country would need to work out its own formula, which would depend on many factors, only one of which would be the socioeconomic backdrop of the country. As far as India is concerned, extensive research and interaction with the disabled has convinced the author that segregated settings also have advantages. Intensive interviewing of the blind (Agrawal 1992) has indicated that it is in these segregated institutes that the child picks up skills and the confidence to cope with the world at large. The warmth and sheltered life at the blind school tend to help the students overcome initial adjustment problems and deal with the trauma of disability, and the school also provides positive role models in the form of disabled yet successful teachers. It is thus important to consider the extent to which integration can be made compulsory—in India, at least.

Funding is another issue. As in all developing countries, special education in India feels the financial crunch. Not only are general financial resources at a low ebb, but the priority of providing for a mass literacy drive can overshadow education of the disabled. The question that perturbs planners, therefore, is whether we should concentrate on total literacy first, which requires less resources and produces greater gains, or emphasize education of the disabled. The answer is difficult to provide, though the balance cannot be said to be swinging away completely from the welfare of the disabled. Educators and planners both agree that formal education of the disabled is the ideal, but the problems of a limited number of schools, transportation of the disabled child to and from school, shortage of trained staff, attitudinal barriers, and last but not least, limited financial resources, are major impediments.

Emerging and Future Trends

As we move toward the end of the century, the future certainly appears optimistic. The special education scenario in India will certainly change for the better, impelled by a wide variety of factors. First, the massive programs for the prevention and control of disability help one to envisage a much lower incidence rate. This lowered incidence rate, coupled with increases in the number of schools (both segregated and integrated), in the availability of trained staff, and in services for rural areas would enable the disabled population to become far more educated and economically productive than at present.

Second, one can forecast major attitudinal changes leading to a greater degree of mainstreaming and normalization. Third, the first steps in vocational rehabilitation have already been taken. With the shift toward jobs more in keeping with the twenty-first century, economic independence of the disabled will be further guaranteed. Along with this shift away from traditional crafts, there is also the emerging trend of self-employment. One can also discern that the future will offer the disabled in India much greater opportunities for leisure-time activities, for the use of electronic (especially computerized) facilities in education and daily life, and for wider participation in general societal activities.

In fact, the 1980 National Plan of Action promises the fulfillment of the dream of the 1980s "to evolve a national policy on the handicapped . . . to achieve full social integration . . . to initiate concrete programmes aimed to bring about the utilization in every way possible, the integration of handicapped people in the country" (Sinclair 1979).

References

Agrawal, R. 1992. Psychosocial factors in mainstreaming visually impaired adults. *Journal of Visual Impairment and Blindness*, 118–21.

Chattapadhyay, A. 1986. *All India directory of educational and vocational training institutes for the handicapped*. New Delhi: Patriot.

Cohen, N., et al. 1985. Landholding, wealth and risk of blinding malnutrition in rural Bangladeshi households. *Social Science and Medicine* 21:1269–72.

Ghosal, A. 1982. *Indian Council of Medical Research Report on magnitude of blindness in India*. New Delhi: ICMR.

Government of India. 1981. *Census of India report*. New Delhi: Government of India.

Gupta, A. K. 1990. Osteomalacia and osteoporosis of the spine. In *Proceedings of the seminar-cum-workshop on rehabilitation of spinal disorders and its implications on the community*, 44–46. Calcutta: NIOH.

Joshi, P. L., Bhattacharya, M., Rastogi, A. K., Diwedi, S., Raj, B., and Verma, J. 1988. Handicapped person—A demographic profile in a rural area of U.P. *Disabilities and Impairments* 2:135–41.

Kenmore, J. R. 1979. Integrated education for blind students. In S. Rogow and M. Rodrigues, eds. *Perspectives and prospects in the education of world's blind children*. Ontario: Ministry of Community and Social Services.

Kirk, S. A. 1970. *Educating exceptional children*. New Delhi: Oxford and IBH.

Maitra, T. K., Acharaya, B., and De, S. 1989. A study on incidence of poliomyelitis in upper limbs. *Selected lectures from seminar on upper extremity orthotics*, 29–37. Calcutta: NIOH.

National Institute for the Orthopedically Handicapped. 1991. *Orientation programmes at NIOH*. Aarohan: NIOH.

National Institute for Visually Handicapped (NIVH). 1989. *Directory of schools for the blind*. Dehradun: NIVH.

National Institute of Public Cooperation and Child Development. 1989. Training programme for management and rehabilitation of the handicapped. *NIPCCD Newsletter* 9:4–5.

National sample survey. 1981. New Delhi: Government of India.

Parikh, J., and Dhylon, R. 1988. Integrating handicapped children in the regular class: An evaluation. *Disabilities and Impairments*, 2:53–57.

Rama Mani, D. 1988. *The physically handicapped in India: Policy and program.* New Delhi: Ashish.

Report of the National Program for the control of blindness. 1979. New Delhi: Ministry of Health and Family Welfare.

Sahu, P. 1983. Integral education for the disabled in Orissa. *Bulletin, Integrated Education of Disabled* 1:20–25.

Sarkar, A. K. 1990. Organization of scoliosis service. In *Proceedings of the seminar-cum-workshop on rehabilitation of spinal disorders and its implications on the community,* 16–19. Calcutta: NIOH.

Sinclair, S. 1979. *National planning for the mentally handicapped.* New Delhi: The Directorate General of Health Services.

UN Declaration of Rights of Disabled, 1976. 1988. *Disabilities and Impairments* 2, 91.

UNICEF. 1984. *An analysis of the situation of children in India.* New Delhi: United Nations Children Fund.

Veeraraghavan, V. 1987. Integrated education for mentally retarded. *Disabilities and Impairments,* 1:80–83.

World Health Organization. 1968. *Organization of services for the mentally retarded.* Technical Report Series no. 392. Geneva: WHO.

13

Uruguay

ELOISA GARCIA DE LORENZO

Textual Assistance and Translation by Griselda Francolino

Uruguay is located on the eastern coast of South America by the Atlantic Ocean. The Uruguayan territory covers an area of 176,215 square kilometers, with many rivers and minor water courses, smooth plains, and prairies and no deserts, jungles, or big mountains. Several communication roads allow adequate accessibility to and from practically all the geographic points in the territory.

With 2,940,200 people (preliminary data of the 1985 population census), Uruguay has a population density of 16.7 inhabitants per square kilometer. High urbanization is especially marked by the great proportion—44.5 percent—of the population living in Montevideo, the capital city. A further 41.7 percent live in cities in the interior of the country. The rural population of the country is 13.8 percent of the total population. The major demographic groups include Spanish and Italian immigrants, as well as smaller groups of French, German, Swiss, Polish, other Central European, Armenian, and Lebanese groups.

Uruguay is a democratic republic. The government is elected by the

About the Author • Eloisa Garcia de Lorenzo is past director of the Special Education Unit of the Inter-American Children's Institute of the Organization American States, immediate past president of the International League of Societies for Persons with Mental Handicaps (Brussels, Belgium), a member of the World Health Organization Expert Advisory Panel on Mental Health, and president of the Inter-American Commission on Education of the Organization of American States (Washington, D.C.). By specialization she is a clinical psychologist with an interest in developmental disabilities and infant development. Other pioneering work on early intervention earned her the Joseph Kennedy Award in 1966. • Griselda Francolino is a teacher specializing in the education of mentally handicapped. Her other particular interest is the education of preschool children.

people every five years and is operated through three representative powers: executive, legislative, and supreme court.

Contrary to what is true in a good portion of the Latin American countries, Uruguay does not have significant internal differences. The society shows a high ethnic-demographic homogeneity, which results in high social, cultural, political, and religious integration and in special care to less-favored citizens. Two groups of factors (among other important ones) may be seen as the cause of this situation. First, the small geographic dimensions of Uruguay and the lack of geographical and sociological diversity. The homogeneous nature of Uruguay, characterized by a prevalence of European immigrants, weakens any tendency toward the development of cultural, economic, and political practices of a significant regional or local nature. The rapid social integration of the immigrant groups in Uruguayan society limited the existence of tense situations among the different colonies of immigrants. In the integration of immigrants and their descendants, three central mechanisms acted together: the educational system, the political system, and the judicial and legal order.

Second, the average annual population growth rates in the two last intercensus periods (1963–75 and 1975–85) are respectively .6 and .5 percent, which are the lowest in Latin America. This low growth rate is associated, as in the rest of the countries in which it occurs, with a high formal educational system enrollment and a high urbanization rate. Further, the birth rate decrease in Uruguay is associated with a decrease in the child mortality rate and an increase in life expectancy.

In Uruguay, immigration meant a high degree of religious tolerance; the country has no official religion and education is legally secular. As well, the influence of European philosophical humanistic ideas became the basis of our scientific and educational activity. The social and cultural composition of Uruguayan society has as one of its determining factors the large and early expansion of a free formal public educational system up to secondary and university levels. Compulsory, free, and secular education are the main principles of public education in our country. They appear in the constitution, laws, and other regulations. Free and compulsory elementary education was established in 1877 and, since that date, it has rapidly expanded. Today, Uruguay has a high literacy rate and enrollment in the formal educational system (elementary and secondary levels), as well a high proportion of university-enrolled students.

The Disabled Population in Uruguay

There are no statistics in Latin America enabling us to reliably estimate the total categories and prevalence figures of the disabled population. One could possibly extrapolate to Latin America and the Caribbean from the approximate global estimate of 85 million disabled persons in all categories. While we think this may not be exactly the situation in Uruguay or Latin America as far as numbers are concerned, we may infer similar percentages with regard to experiences in service delivery systems.

Prevalence estimates are difficult to obtain for Uruguay for several reasons. First of all, it is necessary to underline that the disabled population is composed differently (both in type and degree) according to different age groups and life environments. We must also consider that, in many of the institutions responsible for the service delivery system, the categorization and conceptualization of disability depends on whether or not some physical or mental disorders are considered a disability.

In addition, the high number of services actually responsible for different disabilities and the lack of coordination result in partially overlapping and apparently contradictory reports. The unification of such statistical information would be a complex, long-term task.

Labeling the Population

In the past, the fields of rehabilitation and special education have seen the emphasis placed on a medical model without a corresponding stress on social and educational trends. This is evident in the use of terminology and is reflected in the conceptualization of the phrases used in special education. It is common to see terms such as *diagnosis, prognosis,* and *therapy.* Consideration of disability as a kind of illness is another example of a central role ascribed to the medical profession. Nevertheless, during the last decade a change in diagnosis has been evident.

It is a general consensus that the classification and labeling of children, adolescents, and adults is being replaced by the concept of *children with special educational needs* who may show a wide range of mild to severe difficulties. In light of this, identification and assessment procedures have to move away from categorizing children. Instead, they should describe individual needs and what it takes to meet them.

At the present time, Uruguay follows general trends in the diagnosis and labeling of exceptional conditions. Mental retardation provides an example. The assessment criteria for mental retardation uses the following definition: a person with mental retardation is a person who has an intellectual disability manifested during the development period (birth to 18 years of age) and displays in skills for daily life functional deficits that require support services. Within this definition, a person with mental retardation must manifest two criteria: intellectual ability of scores approximately below 70 on a standard test such as the WISC or the Terman Merrill Intelligence Test and daily-life deficits in skills for self-care, mobility, communication, self-guidance, independent living, vocation, and so on. The degree of mental retardation can be classified by using both aspects—intellectual abilities and functional abilities in daily life.

The Social Context of Special Education

Special education has a fairly long history in Uruguay. Ours was one of the first countries in Latin America to organize a special school and systematic training of teachers. Uruguay had the first pilot program of services from birth to adulthood.

Today teachers, administrators, and other professionals are aware that learning difficulty is a normal part of schooling, that every child is unique, and that each one needs help to adjust to the school and the community environment. However, there exists a great dichotomy between knowledge and practice. To the majority of people, special education is synonymous with the education of deaf, blind, mentally retarded, and physically disabled individuals. This view supports the creation of a parallel school system, with special schools, which is not part of the rest of the educational system.

Legislation

After the creation of the National Council on Disabilities (located at the Ministry of Health), Law no. 13.711 in 1967 (report 82–92) changed the registration and identification procedures of persons with mental retardation. In Article 3, the executive branch was delegated the power to organize the means of education, rehabilitation, and interaction to provide complete assistance to disabled persons. Article 5 states that persons (not only mentally retarded—all the other disabilities are included) may receive special money.

In 1989, Law no. 16095 established a system of integral protection for disabled persons. Chapter 2 of the 1989 law refers to the creation of a National Honorary Commission for the Disabled, which has the responsibility of elaborated study, evaluation, and application of a national policy plan, and promotion, development, rehabilitation, and social integration for disabled persons. Another aspect of the law refers to special policies in social, educational, health, and workshop programs. It also refers to arrangements for city planning and architecture and to taxpayer norms.

In Chapter 7 of the law, Articles 30, 31, and 32 establish the following:

1. Ways of prevention, precocious diagnosis, and compulsory declarations of persons with disabling diseases

2. Social and family assistance
3. Comptroller of workers and labor environments
4. Control of the improper use of drugs and other chemical products that have damaging personal and environmental effects

The 1989 law is still in an implementation stage. However, it gives a legal framework for the provision of services for the disabled, with an emphasis on integration.

Special Education in Uruguay

Special education in Uruguay began in 1910 with the first special institution for deaf and speech-impaired pupils, created by the Consejo de Educación Primaria (the Elementary Education Board). Later, other institutions were created to offer assistance to blind and physically disabled students. Around 1927, some special classes in regular schools provided education to children with learning disabilities. In 1930, the first special school was started to assist children with intellectual disabilities. By 1934, a new school offered services to emotionally disturbed children. The philosophy and curriculum in these schools were influenced by the French, German, and Italian systems (Claparide, Montessori, Decroly, Dottrens, and Descoudres).

Teacher Training

Specialized teacher training has a long history in Uruguay. As far back as 1932, a graduate college was created to prepared specialized teachers in blind, deaf, speech impaired, and intellectual disabilities.

During the 1960s, important changes were produced under the influence of the United States. In 1961, the Department of Special Education was established under the Elementary Education Board. Simultaneously a graduate course for teachers started at the Instituto Magisterial (Teachers College). Teachers received their theoretical training at the college and completed it with practice at School 1 (later 203). In School 1, the student teachers were exposed to diverse methodologies and approaches for evaluating children's learning profiles and learning styles. The student teachers learned and interacted in four components: services to children, services to families, services to the community, and productive interaction between parents and professionals outside the school.

Due to the great prestige of School 1 and the curriculum at the Teachers College, Uruguay was selected by the Organization of American States (OAS) as a training center of special education for Latin American teachers applying for scholarships to receive their postgraduate work in special education (1981 to 1987). Under this model, teachers were trained to develop an intervention method to help each child achieve optimal functioning in daily life. The program helped each child and family to learn effective coping behavior according to the demands of the environment.

Today specialized courses continue to take place at the Instituto Magisterial. These courses have two sections. During the first year, subjects are common to all kinds of specialization. In the second year, subjects and practice work are specific to different types of disabilities (blind, deaf, mentally retarded).

Special Schools

Special education is provided in special schools and special classes held in regular schools. There are 8,836 pupils in special schools and 285,172 in all the regular elementary schools.

Over the last quarter century, instruction of the mentally retarded has become an increasingly important issue. Since the 1980s, we have had special schools for physically disabled students and for the emotionally disturbed. Basically special schools are organized in three levels: preschool, primary, and prevocational programs.

Special classes are set up for children with mild disabilities and are located in regular schools. It is important to point out that all the special services are located in the country or suburban areas; the rural areas are completely isolated from any kind of special services.

Our system of reference to admit children to a special school is not a statistical one. Children are delivered to medical or educational services by the Department of Diagnosis and Integral Orientation. There, they are examined through a battery of tests in an attempt to determine which components of intellectual functioning have been affected. The interdisciplinary team also interviews the children and the family to investigate child and family history. However, the diagnosis is not as complete as it should be.

The multidisciplinary team at the Department for Diagnosis presents children with a battery of tests, few of them standardized and adapted to

TABLE 13.1. Special Schools

School Location	Type of Disability Served						
	Intellectual	Deaf	Blind	Physical	Psychiatric Disordered	Emotionally Disordered	School
Montevideo	17	2	4	1	1	1	2
Interior	46	3	—	—	—	—	—
Total	63	5	4	1	1	1	2

our culture. The most common ones are the WISC, Terman Merrill, the Goodenough, the Bender Gestalt, a family test, the Rorschach, the TAT, and the Scale of Independent Behavior (SIB). These studies give an estimation of the child's intellectual function and cognitive abilities. With interviews with a family member, usually the mother, the child's profile is complete.

The teacher receives a diagnosis, usually with the adjective *mild, moderate,* or *severe* in the case of mental retardation. The teacher is then left alone to define by his or her observation and educational tests the level of functioning of the child. No follow-up is given from the initial team. This method of referral shows great limitations but, in spite of all these shortcomings, children continue to be exposed to it.

Early Intervention

In the decade 1960 to 1970, a pilot project was organized in Special School 1. This program had a continuum of services from early intervention to employment and adult orientation. The program included prevention through medical and educational approaches. Collaborative work went on between the school and the Department of Perinatology and Neonatology at the Clinical Hospital. An early detection program was expanded through the development of screening and periodical medical checks of pregnant mothers at risk. The school offered early intervention and stimulation services originated in the home and in a special clinic located at the school. This program also provided plans for different levels: preschool, school, prevocational orientation, and the transition from the school to independent work through a sheltered workshop. All this occurred because there was a good relationship among the school system, medical services, and workplaces that enhanced the community-based support system for children with disabilities.

Basic to the work of integration was an exchange of teachers between the regular elementary school and the special school. This exchange was undertaken with the idea that it would provide experience for special educators and help them obtain an educated view of the development of the normal child and compare it with the population with which they were working. Also, the special teacher would help the regular teachers to understand and treat in their school, children with minor learning problems. Hence, the teacher from the regular school in the special class obtained firsthand knowledge of what developmental disabilities meant; this opened the doors for good future integration.

Another contribution was the significant participation of parents, not only the general support they gave to the school but also their participation in decisions about the curriculum. A support system was developed for families and for the school staff. The idea behind this system was that family members need support from the very beginning, from the day a child at risk for normal development is born. Professionals need support to cope with the stress that can interfere with their personal ability to interact effectively with the case and can interfere with understanding the cues and information a small child provides. Hence, the teacher's personality and coping abilities were a matter of great attention. Parents received a special survey list to observe and evaluate the child's interactions as well the school environment. They were oriented to learn, to observe, and to develop a cooperative and receptive, as well as a critical and flexible, relation with the staff. The program offered educational orientation, parent discussion groups, stress management, coping workshops, and programs for siblings. The school developed videos, tapes, slides, and publications that parents and teachers used during demonstration workshops all over the country.

To increase the community awareness of the needs of handicapped children and their families, the school offered information through lectures at high schools and service-oriented agencies, such as the Rotary and Lions Club. The attractive school grounds provided recreational activities for young children and adolescents. There were also special services for screening children at risk for developmental delays and for orientation of parents who came to the school after referral from professionals and other agencies. Hence, the first early intervention program for high-risk babies and with a continuum of services up to adulthood started in 1958 in Uruguay. Today almost every country in Latin America and the Caribbean has a program for early intervention.

Integration

Segregated special education in schools and centers is very costly and at the same time reaches very few individuals. With integrated special education, responsibility is returned to the individual, the family, the regular school, and the community. No one denies the importance of integration, but few are ready to provide it. There are many problems to be solved and a lot of traditional thinking to work with.

Issues and Problems

Assessment and referral. One major problem is in the entire area of assessment. Assessment should be the starting point for intervention, not an end in itself.

Today, more and more students are badly diagnosed and overreferred to special education. Most teachers have responded to students having difficulty by referring them to special services for testing in the hope that these students will be eligible for special services. This practice has resulted in an overreferral rate to special education of many students who do not meet state or federal guidelines for special education eligibility. Some students who have learning and behavior disorders in school do not meet eligibility criteria for classification as handicapped. These students typically are described as having poor work habits; social and behavioral problems; low self-esteem; slow learning rates; poor motivation, language problems; or inefficient learning style. No alternative program exists for these students and their teachers.

Concerns about overreferral, misclassification, and the need to maximize opportunities for all students in the least restrictive environment constitute the focus of the problem. Because assessment represents a great problem, we see the need to review of the type of assessment engaged in. Any society attempting to provide appropriate services will have to be sure that the skills, abilities, and needs of the students to be helped are properly identified, not only for their sake, but to ensure the most effective use of scarce resources.

If tests are to be used to assist in the process of decision making and resource allocation, it is essential to be aware of their limitations. Because we use tests and other assessments developed and standardized in developed countries, it is almost impossible to determine the accuracy or value of information derived by these tests. Also, it is dangerous to make administrative or educational decisions based on the assumptions of IQ which may change considerably over a period of time. A low IQ score on a given occasion can be unreliable for a variety of reasons.

We are facing children with learning problems that go unnoticed or are aggravated, thus resulting in repetitions of grades and dropouts, particularly in the marginal sectors and the rural areas. Teachers must learn how to evaluate the child and his or her environment and be able to incorporate parents in the decision-making process. It is recommended that more emphasis be placed on functional assessment of skills based on observations of an individual's functioning in relevant community activities or on enlisting the experience of family and community members who are in a much better position to assess how individuals function in different contexts.

To implement intervention programs, it is also necessary to have a detailed assessment that can reveal strengths as well as weaknesses and indicate areas of functioning and which can be used as the basis of a program of support intervention. Although the assessment of cognitive and social functioning forms an essential starting point, comprehensive assessment of the abilities of an individual with a mental handicap requires a more broadly based assessment of a wide range of skills and abilities.

Integration. History suggests that if we urge the citizens and nations of the world to integrate disabled citizens for moral reasons, the current national situation will not significantly change in the future. History also suggests that if we establish a legal basis for empowerment, we will continue to make steady progress toward our ultimate goals of integration and equality of opportunity.

We would like to point out a distinction between *equality of opportunities* and *integration*. Although these two terms are frequently used interchangeably, they do have important differences in their meaning for people with disabilities and how disabled persons are viewed by their societies and treated by their governments. Whereas equality of opportunity implies an empowerment of disabled persons, integration denotes a permissiveness or willingness on the part of a society to include persons with disabilities in at least some aspects of that society. Stated another way, the person who is empowered is likely to say, "I have a right to (education, employment, or access public services), and I will exercise that right," while a person who is integrated would be more likely to say, "Thanks for allowing me to (receive an education, obtain employment, or use public services)." Empowerment, in our view, is predicated on rights established as a matter of law. Integration, in contrast, is predicated on a moral obligation that borders on charity.

In Uruguay, the reality is that the great majority of children and young people with special education needs do not receive an appropriate education. They may go to special schools and to a few sheltered workshops. The rest of their lives are spent under the guidance and responsibility of their families. We are promoting changes through serious analysis and a recognition that regular school must play a bigger role by developing their objectives, teaching, and curricula to reach children with different educational needs. Some children will need special classes or schools. These are children with complex and profound difficulties. But more and more of our special schools should function as resource centers and get involved in outreach programs.

Curriculum. It is important to point out that program development is not synonymous with curriculum development. A program is defined as a statement of what will be taught to specific learners over a specified period of time. A curriculum, on the other hand, is a statement of what anyone would have to learn to reach a goal. Curricula can be used to guide the development of programs, but programs cannot be used to guide development of curricula. Confusion on this point is widespread and possibly one source for the lack of progress in curriculum development.

Research. Teaching is an intricate cognitive task. Classrooms are complex environments, and teachers have innumerable issues in mind when teaching a lesson. We observe that there is a paucity of research on critical aspects of teacher function. Research on the relationship among teacher instructional strategies, teacher process during instruction, teacher collaboration with other professionals, and teacher effectiveness is scarce. Teacher style is not recognized as an important variable, and teachers are oblivious to the influence of their own thinking process during instruction and on student outcomes (Artiles 1991).

Teacher training. Teachers are not well trained to reflect and do not receive the skills to analyze and interpret their classroom behavior, their understanding, and their cooperation with parents and the community. It is therefore urgent to promote personalized learning models. The teacher must be able to analyze each child's learning needs to develop an individualized intervention plan. The teacher has to learn how to manage a flexible curriculum based on the child's learning style, developmental resources, and coping behavior patterns. This includes the family's style as well.

Our country needs initiatives to address curricular relevancy, current research, best practices, and practicum with exposure to a variety of methodologies and the diverse problems manifested by the developmentally disabled and their different needs at different ages. The curriculum must address the dynamic economic, political, and social structures of the society. We must identify the most sound innovative practices and incorporate them in the training of teachers and other professionals working in the field of developmental disorders. Personnel preparation programs must address the communication needs of individuals with mental retardation and other developmental disorders. Communication is a critical and essential skill, and we need vigorous programs to provide access to communication through new technologies. Priorities must be identified based on careful analysis of the current situation and needs. Interdisciplinary collaboration is needed. Professionals need to be aware of their shortcomings and the need for improving themselves in order to be effective. We can say that last, but not least, we must make the effort to turn principles into action, to bridge the gap between ideas and practice.

Future Trends

As we chart our course of action for the next decade and as we strive to achieve equality of opportunity for persons with disabilities, we must be aware that limited financial resources do not permit large infusions of government money into services and programs for persons with disabilities. So as we develop our goals and plans for the future, we must also plan to be largely financially independent and to be creative and aggressive in reshaping what we have and put great effort in the training of our human resources. To improve the situation, we will require commitment and political will to bring about a change of attitudes and behavior. We also need analysis and discussion at all levels about the educational philosophy underlying our school system.

Strategies must specify the steps to be taken and the resources required for the assessed needs to be fully met. We emphasize selection and training of personnel, increase in technical aids, and the coordination of agencies. The following changes are necessary to implement our goals:

1. Prevention must respond to a coordinated action of education and public information. This should be the first mandate of any strategy.
2. Legislation must be enforced and its implementation monitored. Legislation should respond to the realities of the country and offer policy options.
3. As a consequence of the emphasis on integration, administrative changes are needed. Special education should be a variation of regular education and not a separate form.

Uruguay has endorsed the framework for action proposed by the World Conference of Education for All, and now steps should be taken to implement its recommendation, with stress on the need for integrated solutions. The following measures are proposed:

1. Analyze and criticize policies
2. Review selections criteria for recruiting and training of personnel
3. Review relevant legislation
4. Introduce well-developed and well-supervised integrated models of education for every school grade
5. Design curricula with flexibility and adaptation
6. Develop guidelines for parental-leadership training in order to make parents part of decision making
7. Extend the role of special schools to function as resource centers
8. Establish itinerant clinics for screening and educational programs in the rural areas
9. Provide support systems for families and teachers
10. Secure exchange of information between qualified centers and innovative programs
11. Develop information and orientational materials
12. Seek and enlist the cooperation of private sectors
13. Provide permanent and adequate information to the media
14. Promote high-quality services and support that enable full community inclusion and participation
15. Encourage basic and applied research and its dissemination and application
16. Advocate for progressive public policies
17. Influence public awareness of and attitudes toward special education by disseminating information

References

Artiles, A. J. 1991. Teachers as decision makers: Enhancing the impact of teachers on students' performance. Manuscript, University of California at Los Angeles.

Cruickshank, W. M., Bentzen, F. A., Ratzeburg, F. H., and Trannhauser, M. T. 1961. *A teaching method for brain-injured and hyperactive children.* Syracuse, N.Y.: Syracuse University Press.

Kephart, N. C. 1971. *The slow learner in the classroom.* Columbus, Ohio: Merrill.

Kirk. 1958. *Early education of the mentally retarded: An experimental study.* Urbana: University of Illinois.

Strauss, A., and Lehtinen, L. 1947. *Psychopathology and education of the brain-injured child.* New York: Grunne and Stratton.

Werner, H., and Strauss, A. A. 1941. Pathology of figure-background relation in the child. *Journal of Abnormal and Social Psychology* 36:236–48.

PART 3

SEGREGATED SPECIAL EDUCATION

Students from the Evening School for Mentally Handicapped Adults in Czechoslovakia. PHOTO BY Marie Cerná

Auditory-training exercises for hearing-impaired children in Taiwan. PHOTO BY Yung-Hwa Chen and Tai-Hwa Emily Lu

*T*he countries in our part III—Japan, Taiwan, Russia, Czechoslovakia, and Hong Kong—are grouped together on a number of foundational principles. First, each nation has well-established and concrete enabling legislation and implementation policies focusing on persons with special needs. Second, their commitment to the provision of services for their special needs populations is relatively long-standing. Third, these nations have essentially accomplished the task of providing universal schooling for their populations of normally developing children. In addition, a particular and conscious decision has been made in each of these nations that the most appropriate model of schooling for many special needs children is that of separate educational environments.

An interesting and significant consequence of these principles is that the number of individuals identified as disabled is low, relative to that of other nations covered in this text. This is because, in these five nations, children with mildly handicapping conditions, such as learning disabilities, are not generally identified as a category of disability per se—affected children are simply considered to be part of the normally developing regular school population. Furthermore, the rates of disabilities due to factors such as poverty, malnutrition, and preventable diseases are quite low in comparison to those of the nations found in the first two parts of this book.

Japan and Russia provide the purest illustrations of the principles just listed. In Japan, for example, the number of students considered in need of special education is particularly low because of the restricted nature of the criteria identifying the special needs population. On the other hand, Czechoslovakia and Taiwan, while retaining their basic structure of separate institutional care and programming, have initiated experiments in educating greater numbers of children in regular educational settings. Another significant innovation stressed in the Taiwan chapter is the strong emphasis upon the education of the gifted. In Hong Kong, the authors stress the complications to special education resulting from a structured tracking system in the schools.

14

Japan

GIICHI MISAWA

Special education in Japan has about 115 years of history, dating back to 1878 when pioneering education for blind and deaf children was started. Special education for children with mental retardation, motor handicaps, and chronic disease was launched on a national scale after World War II, although some sporadic attempts had been made before the war. After the 1960s, measures to promote special education were implemented one after another in step with the country's economic recovery. In response to improvements in welfare and labor policies, education for physically and mentally retarded children (under the age of eighteen) underwent significant progress.

In 1979, education at a school for the handicapped—a school designed to educate children with mental retardation, motor handicaps, or chronic disease—was made compulsory. This enabled all handicapped children, regardless of the degree of their handicap, to receive school education. This was landmark progress in special education. It was also landmark progress in the history of Japan's compulsory education—it signaled the achievement of nine-year compulsory education for all children ages six through fifteen.

At present, educational opportunities are also open to children with the most severe handicaps, and educational rights are guaranteed in all

About the Author • Giichi Misawa is a professor emeritus of the University of Tsukuba. His research interests lie in the psychology of the motor handicapped, rehabilitation for the motor disabled, and the education of special education teachers. He holds a chair in the Japanese Association of Special Education, is a former editor of the *Japanese Journal of Special Education,* is a Japanese representative and an editorial member of the International Association of Special Education, and is a member of the Japan–U.S. Teacher Education Consortium. He is also the chief of Japan's Governmental Committee of Qualifying Examinations for Special Education Teachers and a vice-chairperson of the Advisory Committee of Employment for the Disabled.

parts of Japan. It is no exaggeration to say all aspects of special education—the educational system, school, teachers, and many other elements—have improved beyond comparison with what they were three decades ago.

Definition of Special Education

The definition of special education in Japan differs slightly from that in other industrialized countries. In Japan, *special education* refers to education at *special schools,* and in *special classes* at ordinary primary and secondary schools. Special education is aimed specifically at those who require special educational care among the physically and mentally handicapped pupils and students. In principle, children with relatively minor handicaps receive education in ordinary classes but under special care. In general, education offered to such children is not referred to as special education. In other words, the definition of special education in Japan is narrow. Only about .9 percent of school-age pupils and students in Japan receive special education. This is much lower than figures in Western industrialized countries that stand at around 10 percent. It reveals a feature of Japan's special education that places emphasis on children with severe handicaps.

The handicapped population is classified into seven categories, from level one (severe) through seven (mild). Mental retardation is generally classified into three or four levels. In Japan, educationally brilliant children are not included in the category of special education, as is the case in some countries. In other words, among various exceptionalities the focus is solely on students with retarded development and handicaps. In Japan, therefore, the term *special education* is nearly synonymous with *education for the handicapped.* Special emphasis has been put on the aim of special education: to provide a better educational setting for children with relatively severe handicaps and offer appropriate education with special considerations.

Classification of Handicaps and Number of Students

The School Education Law (1947) defines the subjects of special education as children with the following disorders: blind and partial sight; deaf and hard of hearing; mental retardation; motor handicap; health impairment and physically

TABLE 14.1. Special Education Schools and Pupils (1991)

Type of Special Schools	Number of Schools	Number of Pupils
Blind	70	5,228
Deaf	107	8,149
Handicapped	783	78,157
Total	960	91,534

TABLE 14.2. Special Education Schools and Pupils

Type of School	Number of Schools	Number of Pupils
Mentally Retarded	493	53,624
Motor Handicapped	193	19,113
Health Impaired	97	5,420
Total	783	78,157

weak; and other physical and mental disorders. Two disorders are specified under the category *other physical and mental disorders:* speech handicaps and emotional disturbance. In the United States and other countries, so-called children with learning disability (LD) constitute a significant portion of the subjects identified for special education. As learning disabilities are yet to be officially identified as a category of handicap in Japan, the issue requires future study.

Students subject to special education, therefore, may be classified into seven categories. Because many children are multihandicapped, however, it is often difficult to apply a simple classification in educational practice. For instance, there are many blind children with mental retardation or children who have motor handicaps as well as have mental retardation. In reality, therefore, educational institutions work beyond the framework of handicap categories to supplement each other. Special education schools and the number of pupils in 1991 are shown in table 14.1.

Schools for the handicapped in Japan are classified into three categories. Their breakdown is shown in table 14.2. The number of special classes and pupils in 1991 is shown in table 14.3.

In table 14.3 the figures show the numbers of students according to educational setting and do not account for deviations such as the cases of children with partial sight attending schools for the blind or children who are hard of hearing attending schools for the deaf. Special classes are offered at primary and secondary schools but not at high schools. Many autistic children attend special classes for emotionally disturbed children, whereas

TABLE 14.3. Special Classes and Pupils (1991)

Type of Special Class	Number of Classes	Number of Pupils
Mentally retarded	14,630	52,440
Motor handicapped	489	1,167
Health impaired	536	1,789
Partially sighted	88	202
Hard of hearing	476	1,421
Speech disordered	1,464	6,077
Emotionally disturbed	3,597	11,171
Total	21,280	74,267

Note: Special classes are offered at primary and secondary schools but not at high schools.

TABLE 14.4. Handicapped Persons in Japan

Handicapped Group	Number of Persons
Physically handicapped children (under 18 years of age)	92,500
Institutionalized children (separate from above)	13,000
Physically handicapped adults (aged 18 and older)	2,413,100
Institutionalized adults (separate from above)	93,000
Mentally retarded children and adults	504,000
Mentally handicapped (psychiatrically disturbed) persons (excludes the mentally retarded)	1,024,200
Total	4,139,800

others attend special schools for the mentally retarded. Special classes are organized voluntarily by the local board of education in accordance with the conditions in the district. The number of classes differs from year to year.

The Ministry of Health and Welfare conducts a survey on the status of physically handicapped children and adults every five years. The latest available data are taken from a survey conducted in 1987. Data on the mentally retarded and mentally handicapped are taken from a different source as there is no regular survey on these students. The data shown in table 14.4 have been compiled to give the approximate number of handicapped persons in Japan. When these figures are added up, the aggregate number of handicapped children and adults comes to a little over 4.1 million, or about 3.5 percent of the population.

Officially, physically handicapped persons refers to those who have been issued the Pocketbook for the Physically Handicapped in accordance with standards provided by law or who have equivalent handicaps. Under our system, persons who have little trouble doing everyday tasks are not identified as physically handicapped regardless of their physical handicap. The definition of handicap is relatively narrow in scope as in the case of children

TABLE 14.5. Prevalence According to Type of Handicap

	Under 18	18 and Older
Visual impairment	5,800	307,000
Hearing/speech impairment	13,600	354,000
Motor handicap	53,300	1,460,000
Chronic disease	19,800	292,000
Total	92,500	2,413,000

subject to special education. The Ministry of Health and Welfare also puts emphasis primarily on severe handicaps.

Table 14.5 shows the approximate number of handicapped persons according to type of handicap based on a survey on the physically handicapped (1987). The prevalence of physically handicapped children is 3 per 1,000.

Table 14.6 shows the main etiology of physical handicaps among children according to the aforementioned survey by the Ministry of Health and Welfare (1977). It is important to note that the occurrence of impairments caused by contagious diseases has declined dramatically in recent years. The number of new cases of polio is approaching zero. Some aftereffects of polio are found among older children.

The number of occurrences of handicaps has declined dramatically from three decades ago. In particular, only a small number of handicaps are caused by contagious diseases. It can be said that a thorough implementation of preventive and early detection measures has produced substantial results. On the national level, there is no notable concentration of children with a specific handicap in a particular region.

Detection and Identification of Handicaps

The Ministry of Health and Welfare implements thorough measures for the prevention and early detection of handicaps. Infants are screened prenatally and

TABLE 14.6. Major Causes of Disabilities

Disabilities and Causes	Number of Cases
Motor Handicaps	
Cerebral palsy	26,900
Spinal cord injury	2,700
Bone and joint disease	2,700
Cerebral vascular accidents	1,900
Arthritis	800
Post polio	800
Hearing Impairment	
Inner ear disease	5,100
Middle ear disease	1,500
Visual Impairment	
Optic nerve atrophy and others	1,200
Lens disease	400
Chronic Disease	
Heart disease	15,500
Kidney disease	3,500
Others	21,700
Uncertain	7,800

Note: Based on a 1977 survey by the Ministry of Health and Welfare.

immediately after birth for any possibility of disability. General hospitals, health centers, and child welfare institutions for handicapped children conduct prenatal diagnoses of pregnant women and medical examination of infants. At present, infants in Japan undergo two universal, nationwide medical examinations. The first examination is conducted by the local municipality at the age of one year and six months. Infants receive the second examination at the age of three at health centers around the country. When a physical or mental problem is detected, the infant undergoes another examination by doctors specializing in the field at a hospital or Child Guidance Center.

Treatment, guidance, and education of preschool children for the early detection and treatment of handicaps are also conducted. These efforts are supervised primarily by the Ministry of Health and Welfare, while efforts for early detection and education are also backed up by the Ministry of Education. The Ministry's department for the promotion of school for the deaf offers consulting service on children who are hard of hearing.

Health centers across the nation provide health care and medical treatment for mothers and children in accordance with legal requirements. Child Guidance Centers in many parts of Japan undertake psychoeducational examination, consulting services, and guidance. Also, medical, psychological, and vocational assessment are carried out for the mentally retarded by the Guidance Center on the Mentally Retarded, and for the physically handicapped by the Rehabilitation Guidance Center for Physically Handicapped. Each institution gives assistance in a particular field of specialty. Welfare offices in charge of implementing these services have been set up around the country in accordance with the law. All these institutions carry out services to help physically and mentally retarded (not including psychotic) persons.

The services extended to handicapped children are diverse and far-reaching. There is a program to provide assistance in medical expenses, which covers treatment of premature babies weighing less than 2,500 grams upon birth; early treatment of physically handicapped children; delivery of prostheses; and public assistance in medical expenses for children with chronic infantile disorders. Also, children whose handicaps exceed the designated level are entitled to pensions, allowances, and institutionalization.

The Pocketbook of the Physically Handicapped or Pocketbook for the Mentally Retarded is issued to children whose handicaps exceed the level prescribed by law. These Pocketbooks entitle the holders to necessary services. The Pocketbook for the Physically Handicapped is also issued to adults with handicaps (eighteen years or older) following diagnosis at designated hospitals in the locality. As it does in the case of children, the Pocketbook entitles these adults to various services.

Psychologists are assigned at three institutions: Child Guidance Centers, the Rehabilitation Guidance Center for Physically Handicapped, and the Guidance

Center for the Mentally Retarded. Psychological services are offered nationally to each group of subjects. Tests including intelligence tests and various personality tests are given and counseling and other services have been increased.

The Social Context of Special Education

Overview

In Japan, social attitudes toward handicapped children and adults improved significantly after the war accompanied by strides in the legal and other systems. The strong prejudice of the past against relatively severe and visible handicaps seems to have been reduced greatly in recent years. Since the International Year of the Disabled (1981), the national and local governments as well as private groups have launched powerful activities. Various campaigns are conducted each year on many levels in education, welfare, medical treatment, employment, and other areas. A petition has been made to have 9 December designated the Day of Handicapped Persons as a national holiday, but this is yet to be made reality.

Here are some factors behind the better public understanding of and greater assistance for handicapped persons. First, laws and systems for handicapped persons from infants to adults were drawn up one after another. As well, the huge influx of information from other industrialized countries promoted the efforts to reexamine the education and welfare of handicapped persons in Japan. Also, Japan's strengthened economic power enabled people to look beyond their immediate needs. This helped establish the financial foundation for providing elaborate services for handicapped persons.

Economic Factors

Government expenditures on special education have increased greatly in pace with Japan's economic development. The budget for special education—composed of national and local government funds—was about 493 billion yen (3.79 billion U.S. dollars) in 1988. This is approximately 150 times the 1956 figure of 3.2 billion yen, a notable increase even after accounting for inflation. A simple calculation using the 1988 statistics shows expenditure per handicapped student at 5.4 million yen. This is about nine times the expenditure per student in ordinary classes, which is 600,000 yen.

As shown above, the government's measures to promote special education have had financial backing. Attention is now focused on their future course, as the recent slowdown of the country's economy will inevitably affect various areas including special education.

Foreign Influences

The Japanese have actively introduced foreign examples of academic theory and policy on special education as well as on welfare, employment, and other areas involving physically and mentally handicapped persons. These examples have been studied and applied in Japan in the light of the nation's conditions. In contrast, efforts to introduce Japan's special education practices in other countries have been inadequate. The balance is completely lopsided on importation of ideas. In my view, people in foreign countries have less than a full picture of special education in Japan. Nevertheless, the three major foreign influences on Japan's special education are the following:

1. Influence of the concept and practice of normalization that started in Scandinavia
2. Influence of American legislation: the Education of the Handicapped Act, the Rehabilitation Act, and the Americans with Disabilities Act (IDEA) of 1990
3. Influence of the Warnock Report and the consequent revision of the education act in Britain

People in Japan have been informed of these three and other overseas movements fairly quickly. Also, the Japanese government swiftly launched domestic measures following the resolution of the UN International Year of the Disabled and of the UN Ten Years of Disabled Persons by setting up the Headquarters for the Promotion of Measures on Disabled Persons, headed by the prime minister, under the prime minister's office. In 1988, the sixteenth World Congress of Rehabilitation International (RI) was held in Tokyo with more than two-thousand participants. In 1992, final measures for the UN Ten Years of Disabled Persons (1983–92) were launched in Japan.

Legislation

School Education

In Japan, there are many laws, cabinet orders, ministerial ordinances and memoranda concerning special education. The major ones are shown as follows:

1. School Education Law (1947). Articles on the scope of the schools (Article 1), objectives of the schools for the blind, schools for the deaf and schools for the handicapped (Article 71), special classes (Article 75), and some enforcement ordinances and regulations concerning special education.

2. The Law on the Promotion of Attendance at Schools for the Blind, Schools for the Deaf, and Schools for the Handicapped (1954). The law provides for necessary assistance to pupils and students who attend special schools.
3. Points on instruction at the schools for the blind, schools for the deaf, and schools for the handicapped. The points stipulate the compilation of curriculum (notification of the Ministry of Education).
4. Teachers' Certification Law (1949). The law provides for the teachers license system for ordinary primary schools, secondary schools, and special schools.
5. Law on the Standard of Class Organization of Public Compulsory Schools and the Prescribed Number of Teachers (1958).
6. National Expenditure on Compulsory Education Act (1952). The Act sets the government's share on the payment of teachers' salaries, materials, equipment costs, and other expenses.

There are other laws and ordinances that support special education. They were revised several times to adapt to changes in during the era.

Social Welfare

Welfare measures for handicapped children and adults are enforced by the Child Welfare Act and other laws. Coupled with rehabilitation measures for children and adults, these measures are supervised by the Ministry of Health and Welfare. For the welfare of physically and mentally handicapped children we have the Child Welfare Act (1947). The act provides for child welfare in general. For physically and mentally handicapped children, it provides education guidance, granting of medical treatment, entrance into institutions for motor handicapped and mentally retarded children, and other matters. The Mother and Child Health Care Act (1965) provides for health care guidance, health checkups, treatment of mothers and infants, care for premature babies, and other matters. The Act on the Payment of Special Child Allowance (1964) provides for the payment of a disabled welfare allowance, paid to children with severe physical and mental handicaps, and special allowances for disabled persons. In addition to these acts, there are laws, ordinances, and regulations on child welfare in general. For the welfare of physically and mentally handicapped persons there is the Disabled Persons Welfare Act (1949). The act provides various measures to support the rehabilitation of disabled persons and promote their welfare. The Mentally Retarded Persons Welfare Act (1960) includes various measures to promote the welfare of mentally retarded persons. The Mental Health Act (1950) provides for additional measures on the treatment of mentally handicapped persons.

Employment

The Development and Promotion of Vocational Ability Act (1969) provides for the vocational training of handicapped adults and physically and mentally handicapped children who have graduated from special schools. The promotion of their employment is stipulated under the Employment Security Act (1947) and the Promotion of Employment of Handicapped Persons Act (1960). These laws are supervised by the labor administration. Also, many sheltered workshops have been set up under the Disabled Persons Welfare Act and Mentally Retarded Persons Welfare Act. The workshops are under the jurisdiction of the Ministry of Health and Welfare.

System of Education

In Japan, each prefectural and municipal government has a Schooling Guidance Committee that offers consulting and guidance on children's schooling and other matters. The committee is independent of the specialized institutions that fall under the jurisdiction of the Ministry of Health and Welfare. It comprises doctors, psychologists, teachers, and educational administration officials; offers elaborate guidance on various matters including the propriety of placing a child in a special school or a special class; and gives advice on instructing a handicapped child in an ordinary class.

Under the School Education Act, the purpose of special schools in Japan is to offer the same level of education as in general kindergarten, primary, secondary, and high schools, and also to instruct in the knowledge and know-how of skills to make up for children's handicaps. Based on the principle of equality, all children, including those with the most severe handicaps, are entitled to receive general education. Special education, therefore, should be promoted as part of the ordinary education system, not as something to be pitted against ordinary education. It is true, however, that the method and content of education should be developed in accordance with each child's conditions.

Policy in Special Education

The School Education Law (1947) states that special education is part of general school education and that physically and mentally retarded children should receive education with the same goals as ordinary pupils and students. The law also maintains that special educational considerations should be made in the education of handicapped children. This policy has remained unchanged through today. The Basic Education Law (1947) spells out the "rights to receive education" and "equal educational opportunities" and guarantees handicapped children the opportunities to receive compulsory education.

Special education in the postwar period has pursued the goals of these laws with the aim of guaranteeing educational opportunities to all handicapped children regardless of the degree of their handicaps. The goal of full school attendance for all children has been achieved at last. According to fiscal-year statistics (1991), the number of school-age pupils and students who were granted postponement of and exemption from attending schools was merely 1,238 out of 14.3 million. Physical and mental handicaps were the causes in less than half of the cases. Japan's accomplishment in compulsory education has put the nation in a leading position in the world.

It is certainly true that such progress has been backed up not only by the government's educational policy but also by society as a whole. Credit should also go to various groups, especially those organized by handicapped children's parents.

Class Organization

The standard number of students to a class is seven in the special schools (three in case of classes for the severely handicapped). The number is ten for special classes in ordinary schools. The number of students in special education classes has been declining in recent years. In fact, some of the special classes have only two pupils. In some classes, the smallness in size of some classes has posed problems in instruction.

Visiting or Itinerant-Teaching Education

Teachers are sent to homes, hospitals, and institutions to offer guidance to children who cannot attend schools for special reasons. This so-called visiting education is conducted nationwide to extend educational opportunities to as many children as possible. Considerations are made in visiting education to flexibly adapt the method, content, and hours of guidance to the conditions of each child.

Curriculum in Special Schools

In view of its nature as public education, curriculum at special schools is subject to various statutory regulations, and the curriculum outline is prescribed by the Ministry of Education's Council of Study. A curriculum has to be organized by each school in accordance with the conditions of the school and the community; students' handicaps, abilities, and aptitudes; and other factors. For this reason each school has a lot of leeway in designing its curriculum. There are separate standards for curriculum in the higher education and kindergarten sections of special schools.

According to the Study Guidance Plan, the curriculum at primary school and secondary schools is divided into three domains: subject study, moral education, and special activities. In addition, primary and secondary sections of special schools must have a special domain called *educational therapeutic activities*. The school for mentally retarded children must also have the "living" course under all subjects. Educational therapeutic activities deal with instructions needed for the education of handicapped children such as sensory, gait, auditory, and speech training. Exceptions are admitted for children with the most severe handicaps: children whose handicaps do not allow them to receive instructions in various subjects can receive instructions in educational therapeutic activities only.

Curriculum in Special Classes

In principle, education in special classes in ordinary primary and secondary schools is based on the Study Guidance Plan for primary and secondary schools. When necessary, a school may organize a special curriculum using the Study Guidance Plan at special schools. Also, pupils and students in special classes may attend ordinary classes and receive instruction in certain subjects. This flexibility shows that special education in Japan takes the form of partial integration.

Teachers in Special Education

As of 1989, the number of teachers in special education was as follows: special school teachers, 43,300; special school staff, 15,281; and special class teachers, 23,906. In addition, there are many part-time teachers in special education.

Teachers' Certification System

A teacher in charge of special education must possess the teachers' certificate for ordinary primary school, secondary school, high school, or kindergarten. To teach at a school for the blind, for the deaf, or for the handicapped, the teacher in principle must have a teachers' certificate for each school. A teacher can instruct a special class with a teachers' certificate for primary school or secondary school, but it certainly is desirable to have a teachers' certificate in special education as well. Between 1988 and 1991, the system of initial teacher training was established and seminars for special education teachers became more systematic. In the 1990 fiscal year, the grading of teachers' certificates was changed from two classifications to three: advanced certificate, first-class certificate, and second-class certificate. Similar changes are now underway with teachers' certificates for special schools.

Teacher Education

As of 1992, teacher education courses in special education are given at fifty-three national universities and twenty-four private universities in Japan. Teacher education courses in special education are approved by the Ministry of Education. The courses are classified into master's degree programs in graduate schools, special study subjects in special education offered at teacher-training colleges and departments, and temporary teachers education courses in special education. With the start of the new licensing system for teachers, the completion of a master's degree program has become the requirement for obtaining the advanced certificate. The change is expected to enhance the specialty and improve the quality of special education teachers.

Following the reform of the licensing system for special education teachers, transitional measures were also clearly stated, raising people's expectations about new developments for the approach of the twenty-first century. Graduate schools have been called on to reexamine and reevaluate their research in education by questioning the specialty of instructors and reforming their system of research and instruction. Attention is focused on what steps college teachers will take in response to students with special educational needs.

On-the-Job Teacher Training

Special education teachers can be classified into two groups: those who became special education teachers by completing the regular teachers' education curriculum in special education and teachers of ordinary classes in general primary or secondary schools who at some point have become involved in teaching in special classes or special schools. On-the-job training of teachers will need to incorporate various perspectives by considering the type of school, specialty according to type of handicap, and age and educational background of the teacher.

Efforts to develop teachers' qualities and abilities must be continued throughout the teaching career. For this reason, teachers are offered as many study opportunities as possible during their career so that they may fully discharge their duties. The Board of Education has carried out seminars and guidance for teachers, sent instructors to colleges, and taken other steps.

Major Issues in the Future of Special Education

Special education in Japan has achieved dramatic development in quantitative terms. As a result, however, problems in terms of quality have emerged one after another. Following are some of the major issues.

Integrated Education

As mentioned earlier, integrated education has never been adopted as the norm in Japan's system of special education. However, the concept of integration has been positively applied. Under the name of *cooperative education,* opportunities have been made for children with and without handicaps to interact with each other. In this way, the style of partial integrated education has been promoted in Japan. One of the most important issues in the future of the educational system will be how to approach the ideal style.

If one had to classify special education in Japan, it would come closer to integrated education than to segregated education. It should be noted, however, that severely handicapped children are enrolled in special schools and special classes in Japan. Table 14.7 shows the special school placement ratio in three countries. From these figures, one can assume that in Japan a high proportion of children with mild- or medium-degree handicaps are placed in ordinary classes or special classes in ordinary schools. Although the term *integrated education* is not used, special education in Japan is, in some senses, integrated. However, an official system of integrated education is yet to be established in Japan. It certainly points to the necessity of future steps in this area.

Education of Severely Handicapped and Multihandicapped Children

Today, educational opportunities are to be offered to all children, including those who must give priority to life sustenance. The important task, therefore, will be to launch instructions in accordance with the condition of each child. Further progress is needed not only in the research and practice of instruction methods but also in the system of education to encompass children's diverse and multiple handicaps.

Schools for the blind and for the deaf have many children with multiple handicaps. Likewise, only about 60 percent of the children in schools for the handicapped can be placed under single-handicap categories; the remaining 40 percent have multiple handicaps. As pointed out by Ochiai (1990), it is necessary to launch new educational measures to meet the educational needs of each child rather than pursuing education that depends on single-handicap categories.

TABLE 14.7. Special School Placement in Three Countries

Country	% of Students in Special Schools	Year of Report
United States	0.43	1988
Britain	1.48	1986
Japan	0.37	1989

Education of Children with Medium-Degree and Mild Handicaps

In general, children with mild handicaps are placed in ordinary classes, and children with medium-degree handicaps are placed in special classes. However, handling mildly handicapped children in an ordinary class has entailed many problems and it is difficult to deal with these problems with only one teacher in charge of the class. Also, most teachers of ordinary classes do not have adequate qualifications to handle learning disabilities and other disabilities.

Due to parents' views and other factors, there are instances in which children with medium-degree handicaps or even children with severe handicaps are enrolled in ordinary classes. It should be noted that these cases put the teacher and school in a difficult situation.

The so-called resource room system has been adopted in Canada, the United States, and other countries. This system has been partially applied in Japan for children with speech and emotional disorders under the part-time special-class system. The Ministry of Education is conducting studies on ways to extend the system to cover special education on the whole.

Response to Parents' Views

In Japan, it is not rare to see a tendency among parents to refuse to place their handicapped children in special education (although, unlike in the United States, it is rare to see lawsuits filed on the educational placement of handicapped children). The stigma that accompanies handicaps is fairly universal. This tendency is stronger among parents of children with less prominent handicaps than among parents of children with severe and visible handicaps, and it stems from the social attitudes on handicapped persons that underlie Japan's society. To change these attitudes, measures should be taken to lessen people's prejudices against severely handicapped persons. The government has launched measures to encourage people to get a correct picture of handicapped persons. In placing handicapped children in school, flexible responses by all parents are necessary.

Handicapped Children after Graduation

Today, the transition of physically and mentally handicapped children from school to society entails many difficulties. An average of 30 percent of graduates from special schools higher education sections find jobs in private companies. Others either find work in welfare institutions under the Ministry of Health and Welfare, enter an institution, or stay home. Graduates of schools for the handicapped, in particular, encounter many difficulties in pursuing the career they selected.

The Ministry of Labor has enacted a quota system for the employment of handicapped persons. The quota is 1.6 percent in private companies and 2 percent in governmental agencies. The actual rate of employment, however, is 1.34 percent in private companies. Japan does not have a sheltered employment system but has sheltered workshops instead. There are more than three thousand public and private sheltered workshops in Japan.

Schools offer active vocational guidance to aid the transition of handicapped children to society, but transition education needs to be strengthened further.

Improvement in the Quality of Teachers

Improvement in the quality of special education teachers is an important issue in fulfilling diversified educational needs. The essential point would be to enhance knowledge and understanding about handicapped children, not only by teachers in charge of handicapped children but by all teachers. In the past five years, Misawa et al. (1990–92), as members of the Japan–U.S. Teacher Education Consortium (JUSTEC), in collaboration with Ohio State University and Professor Ward, conducted research on the improvement in the quality of special education teachers. Parts of their study will be published in the United States in the near future.

References

The Japanese Society for Rehabilitation of the Disabled. 1988. *Rehabilitation in Japan.* Japan: The Japanese Society for the Rehabilitation of the Disabled.

Ministry of Education, Science, and Culture. 1991. *Special education in Japan.* Tokyo: Ministry of Education.

———. 1992. *Report on special education (FY 1991).* Tokyo: Ministry of Education.

Ministry of Labor. 1992. *Statistic report on the employment of the handicapped.* Tokyo: Ministry of Labor.

Misawa, G., Seo, M., and Kusanagi, S. 1990–92. Teacher education to enhance the quality of special education. Paper presented at Japan-U.S. Teacher Education Consortium.

Ochiai, T. 1990. Study on multi-handicapped education. *Japanese Journal of Special Education* 27 (4):57–62.

Seo, M. 1992. Personal data, University of Tsukuba.

U.S. Department of Education. 1989. *Eleventh annual report to Congress on the implementation of the Education of the Handicapped Act.* Washington, D.C.: U.S. Department of Education.

15

Taiwan

YUNG-HWA CHEN

TAI-HWA EMILY LU

*T*he evolution of special education in Taiwan can be divided into four stages. The first stage, from 1949 to 1960, concentrated on only a small number of schools for the deaf and the blind. In the second stage, from 1961 to 1970, the government began experimental classes for mildly retarded children, the physically handicapped, and the hearing impaired. Visually impaired children were also integrated into regular mainstream programs. The boom period of special education, the third stage, lasted from 1971 to 1980. In 1974, a Six-Year Plan of Developing Special Education was designed to organize the overall development of special education services to disadvantaged groups. Special education centers in normal universities and teachers colleges, teacher-training programs, and national and international conferences were gradually established and conducted during this stage. The fourth stage started in 1981. During this stage,

About the Authors • Yung-Hwa Chen is a professor of educational psychology and special education at National Taiwan Normal University. Dr. Chen has been a director of the Special Education Center; chairman of the Department of Educational Psychology and Guidance; dean of the College of Education at National Taiwan Normal University; and president of Taipei Municipal Teachers College. He has written numerous publications and is well-known for his leadership in special education in Taiwan. • Dr. Tai-Hwa Emily Lu is an associate professor in the Department of Special Education and section chief of the Resource Division of the Special Education Center at National Taiwan Normal University, Taipei. Her areas of interest are education of the mentally retarded and gifted, especially in curriculum and instructional design. She has also published many articles, research papers, curricula, and books in special education. Previous to undertaking an academic career, she spent twelve years teaching mildly retarded students at the junior high school level and six years working as an assistant researcher and instructor in the Special Education Center of the National Taiwan Normal University.

the Special Education Law (1984) and its regulations, and other related laws and regulations have been promulgated. The goals of special education have become attainable within a rational system, additional funding, and more trained personnel. The following accounts briefly describe the development of special education in Taiwan.

Prevalence of Exceptional Conditions

Since compulsory education was extended to students of nine years of age in 1968, special education has been a concern of the government of the Republic of China. Its first national prevalence study on exceptional children, conducted in 1976 (Kuo, Chen, and Liang 1976) provided the initial data base for exceptional children in Taiwan. Over seventy thousand elementary school teachers participated in this investigation and assumed direct responsibility for locating out-of-school children and referring them to further testing and medical evaluation when necessary. In addition, these teachers reviewed all their students in each class and referred to further evaluation any of them that met the specific descriptions of the five specific exceptional categories included in this study. Finally, a survey was conducted of all children in special school or hospitals who fit the five categories. These three sources of data were compiled and formed

TABLE 15.1. Exceptional Children Ages 6 to 12, by Disabling Condition and Educational Status

Categories[a]	Out of School		In Regular School[b]		In Special School and Residential Center		Total[c]	
	N	%	N	%	N	%	N	%
VI	80	8.1	770	77.9	139	14.0	989	100.0
HI	358	16.6	675	31.3	1,121	52.1	2,154	100.0
PH	675	7.3	8,397	90.1	245	2.6	9,317	100.0
CD	375	31.6	810	68.4	0	0.0	1,185	100.0
MR	2,331	19.4	9,628	80.0	75	0.6	12,034	100.0
MH	2,365	44.0	2,870	53.4	139	2.6	5,374	100.0
NE	1,762	50.2	1,684	48.0	65	1.8	3,511	100.0
Total	7,946	23.0	24,834	71.8	1,784	5.2	34,564	100.0
Normal	492	27.8	1,274	71.9	5	0.3	1,771	100.0
Total Students	8,438	23.2	26,108	71.9	1,789	4.9	36,335	100.0

[a] VI = visual impairment; HI = hearing impairment; PH = physical handicap; CD = chronic disease; MR = mental retardation; MH = multiple handicaps; NE = not examined.

[b] Including those in special education programs inside regular schools.

[c] From a population of 2,350,000 elementary school-age children.

the data base of the study. Those children who required further academic or psychological testing or medical attention were then seen individually in over twenty hospitals and clinics across the islands. The results of the study are shown in table 15.1.

First, it was found that 36,335 children from three separate groups—out of school, in regular schools, and in special schools or residential centers—were referred to evaluation for exceptionalities. Follow-up diagnoses and medical examinations, however, found 1,771 of the referred children to be normal. Thus, a total of 34,565 children between the ages of six and twelve years were identified as handicapped, and approximately 90 percent were categorized into the six categories shown in table 15.1. At that time, the total student population in that age range was 2.35 million. Thus, the estimated prevalence of exceptional children in 1976 was 1.5 percent.

The second national prevalence study of exceptional children was completed in 1992 (Ministry of Education 1992a). This study followed the model of the first but extended the age range from 6–12 to 6–15. The categories also were increased to eleven in accordance with the 1984 Special Education Law and the Revised Handicapped Welfare Law (1990). The results could then be used to not only explore the prevalence of handicapping and schooling conditions but

TABLE 15.2.   Exceptional Children Ages 6 to 15, by Disabling Condition and Educational Status

Categories[a]	Out of School[b]		In Regular School[c]		In Special School		In Residential Center		Unknown		Total[d]	
	N	%	N	%	N	%	N	%	N	%	N	%
MR	991	3.15	29,042	92.37	462	1.47	937	2.97	8	.03	31,440	100
VI	26	1.34	1,726	89.38	175	9.06	4	.21	0	.00	1,931	100
HI	41	1.43	1,968	68.43	838	2.91	29	1.00	0	.00	2,876	100
LI	48	1.65	2,850	97.74	1	.03	14	.48	3	.10	2,916	100
PH	202	5.85	3,156	91.32	50	1.45	47	1.36	1	.03	3,456	100
CD	97	4.60	2,012	95.31	0	1.45	2	.05	0	.00	2,111	100
ED/BD	226	3.19	6,860	96.77	0	.00	1	.01	2	.03	7,089	100
LD	27	.17	15,475	99.76	2	.01	8	.05	0	.00	15,512	100
FH	4	1.26	314	98.74	0	.00	0	.00	0	.00	318	100
Autism	47	5.86	420	70.23	33	5.52	97	16.23	1	.17	598	100
MH	382	11.37	5,436	74.31	441	6.03	602	5.23	4	.05	7,315	100
Total	2,541	3.37	69,259	91.66	2,002	2.65	1,741	2.30	19	.03	75,562	100

[a] MR = mental retardation; VI = visual impairment; HI = hearing impairment; LI = language impairment; PH = physical handicap; CD = chronic diseases; ED/BD = emotional and behavioral disorders; LD = learning disabilities; FH = facial handicap; MH = multiple handicaps.

[b] Including those received in the homebound education service (N = 595).

[c] Including those in special education programs inside regular schools.

[d] From a population of 3,561,729 elementary and junior high school-age children.

also provide useful references to related administrative authorities for future plans to connect medical, educational, social welfare, and vocational services closer together.

The subjects of this study were from elementary and junior high schools, special schools, handicapped institutions, and out-of-school facilities. Approximately one hundred thousand teachers and one thousand medical doctors were involved in this study. The spending fund was fifty million NT dollars. Preparation work included editing forms, measurement tools, and video tapes to include various types of exceptional children. By the middle of May 1992, a total of 75,562 exceptional children had been found. The distribution of their handicapping conditions is shown in table 15.2.

The disability of the largest group in this study was mental retardation ($N = 31,440$), followed by learning disabilities ($N = 15,512$), multiple handicaps ($N = 7,315$), and emotional and behavioral disorders ($N = 7,089$). The smallest category was facial impairment ($N = 318$), followed by autism ($N = 598$), and visual impairment ($N = 1,931$). Students with handicaps were 2.12 percent of the total population in that age range. This was an increase of .6 percent from the first study. However, it was still far behind the theoretical estimate rate.

Although this study received good cooperation from the administrations and hospitals, most of the mildly handicapped were neglected during the initial referral period. Also, parental cooperation was not as good as in the first study. Hence, the results are still subject to doubt, and they need follow-up studies to verify them. From the data, we can see that the physically handicapped

TABLE 15.3. The 1990 Census of the Handicapped Population in Taiwan

Categories[a]	Male		Female		Total	% of the Handicapped Population	% of the Total Population
	N	%	N	%	N		
MH	17,387	56.6	13,317	43.4	30,704	8.66	.15
VI	17,673	54.2	14,955	45.8	32,628	9.20	.16
HI	20,149	57.1	15,168	42.9	35,317	9.96	.17
LI	6,574	57.0	4,963	43.0	11,537	3.25	.06
PH	71,475	66.2	36,476	33.8	107,951	30.45	.53
MR	20,475	59.4	14,014	40.6	34,489	9.73	.17
OD	11,403	58.5	8,095	41.5	19,498	5.50	.10
FH	873	59.6	592	40.4	1,465	.41	.01
Autism	1,205	65.7	628	34.3	1,833	.52	.01
SD	3,248	54.3	2,738	45.7	5,986	1.69	.03
LSCA	13,785	55.4	11,098	44.6	24,883	7.02	.12
Others	27,975	58.0	20,257	42.0	48,224	13.60	.24
Total	212,214	59.9	142,301	40.1	354,515	100.00	1.75

[a]MH = multiple handicap; VI = visual impairment; HI = hearing impairment; LI = language impairment; PH = physical impairment; MR = mental retardation; OD = organic disfunction; FH = facial handicap; SD = senile dementia; LSCA = lack of self-care ability.

decreased in number, but that the mentally or learning disabled increased. This may be due to medical and scientific progress in Taiwan, which remediated the physical problems and decreased the handicapped cases.

In order to research the numbers of the general handicapped population, the first nationwide investigation was conducted in 1990. In this study, all handicapped people were categorized into twelve categories as shown in table 15.3. The study found 354,515 handicapped persons in the whole Taiwan area. Compared with the total population, the prevalence ratio was 1.75 percent, which was consistent with the findings of the two school-age prevalence studies, although in all these cases the ratios were too low.

In the 1990 study, the male handicapped ratio was 60 percent, whereas the female ratio was 40 percent. The physically handicapped were the largest group (30.45 percent), followed by those with miscellaneous handicaps (13.60 percent), the hearing impaired (9.96 percent), the mentally retarded (9.73 percent), and the visually impaired (9.20 percent). This finding was inconsistent with the previous distributions of school-age prevalence ratios. The reason might be due to the effect of aging, which makes strokes or hearing problems more common. Also, learning difficulties such as mental retardation or learning disabilities in aged people might not be so obvious or important as in the school-age population.

Identification of Exceptionalities

Both medical and psychoeducational identification techniques, appropriate to each handicapping condition, are implemented in the identification of exceptionalities. For the physically handicapped, medical assessments are emphasized and include auditory, visual, and other physical examinations. Psychoeducational assessments are frequently used in the classification of mental retardation, learning disabilities, behavior disorders, and giftedness and special talent.

Although each city and county has a board to take charge of the identification and placement of students with special needs, the boards do not really execute their mission. Many of them appoint teachers of the special classes and schools to do their own students' identification work. Basically, the identification procedures include medical examinations, psychological assessment, interviews, and direct observations. For instance, the identification procedures of the mentally retarded in Taipei city are generally as follows: a referral by the parents or teachers is followed by screening tests through a "quick and dirty" group intelligence test, then an individual intelligence test (Stanford-Binet or revised Weschler Intelligence Scale for Children) for those whose group IQ is under the tenth percentile. Finally, some schools may do interviews or home visits to determine students' adaptive behavior development or conduct adaptive behavior scales through interviewing the parents. After all the information has been collected, the identification and placement boards in some cities and counties will set up a meeting to approve or reject the student placement, based on the information provided.

Some identifications of exceptionalities are very rigid; however, some others, such as the identification procedures of the mildly retarded and learning disabled, are still not very valid and reliable due to lack of knowledge and experience. School psychologists or identification teams with experienced testers should be set up to avoid misidentifying cases. Also, the assessment tools are in short supply and not up-to-date. Finally, multiassessment procedures need to be implemented.

Labeling the Handicapped Population

Generally in Taiwan, categorical approaches are used to label students with exceptionalities. The 1984 Special Education Law listed three kinds of gifted and talented categories and eleven categories of handicapped. Gifted and talented includes general abilities and academic aptitudes (for subjects such as mathematics, natural science, and language arts), and special talents (such as art, music, and dance). The categories of handicapped include mental retardation, visual handicaps, hearing impairment, speech and language impairment, orthopedic handicaps, chronic disease and other health impairments, personality disorders, behavior disorders, learning disabilities, multiple handicaps, and other obvious handicaps. The regulations of the Special Education Law also specify the criteria for labeling giftedness, special talent, mental retardation, visual handicap, hearing impairment, and orthopedic handicap, although some of these are not enforced. Criteria for labeling the other seven handicapped groups should be established.

Accordingly, service delivery does not provide specific educational programs for the language impaired, learning disabled, and personality and behaviorally disordered. Most programs are for the mentally retarded, gifted and talented, visually impaired, and hearing impaired. Recently, resource room programs for learning disabled children and low achievers have been started in a few regular schools. Thus, mildly handicapped students may receive their education in regular settings, resource room programs, or special classes for the mentally retarded. Under these circumstances, it may be said that they receive noncategorical services. More details will be described in the educational placement section of this paper.

To avoid the negative labeling effect, the government of Taiwan used *Chi-jr, Chi-chung, Chi-ming,* and *Chi-jen* as the school or class names to replace the terms *mental retardation, hearing impairment, visual impairment,* and *physical handicap.* The word *Chi* in Chinese means "open up." Therefore, the words *Chi-jr* means to "open up one's mind," *Chi-chung* means to "open up one's hearing," *Chi-ming* is to "open up one's sight," and *Chi-jen* is to "open up one's physical strength." In general, these terminologies have more positive meanings to the handicapped.

In addition, the special classes affiliated with regular schools all use numbers instead of word labels to identify each class in each grade. For example, the second-grade special class for the mentally retarded may be called the sixteenth class of the second grade, a name similar to the name of the other regular classes.

The Social Context of Special Education

Historically, either in Eastern or Western societies, public perceptions of handicapped people have been largely influenced by multiple factors, including the cultural background, educational level, political system, economic status, and medical knowledge that the citizens possess and have inherited. Chinese culture, based on Confucian humanistic philosophy, has lasted over twenty-five hundred years. Confucius's teachings center on the development of proper relations between humans by educating individuals in how to live moral, harmonious, and peaceful lives. Although Confucius (551–479 B.C.) never directly referred to the education of handicapped individuals, his concerns for the disadvantaged are evident in the following quotation of *Li Chi*, which portrays some of the aspects of an idealistic commonwealth called *Ta Tung*.

> When the Great Way prevailed, every person was part of public society, and public society belonged to everyone. . . . People not only loved their own parents and children, but also loved the parents and children of others as well. The elderly lived their last years in happiness, able-bodied adults were usefully employed; children were reared properly. Widowers, widows, orphans, the childless aged, the crippled and the ailing were well cared for. . . . Robbery, larceny and other crimes all disappeared. Gates and doors were not locked; no one ever thought of stealing. This was the age of the Great Common Wealth of Peace and Prosperity. (Chen, Seitz, and Cheng 1991, 321)

Since Confucius's philosophy has exerted a significant influence on the people and government of Taiwan, the social attitude toward handicapped people is rather *Jung-Yong*. The term means that "when confronted with two extremes, one always adopts the middle course in his dealings with people or the problem." That is, there is neither support for nor action against the activity of the handicapped. In other words, if a handicapped individual lives alone in the community, the members of the community may not reject him. But if a number of handicapped persons, particularly those severely handicapped, are going to live together in that community, the members of the community may suddenly recognize the problem and immediately take action against them.

In a survey study conducted in the Taiwan area (Wu et al. 1989) on 761 people ages sixteen to sixty-five, 90 percent of the respondents agreed to live and work together with the handicapped. But in real situations, the attitude of the community seems not to conform with the results of the survey study. The following examples present evidence to verify this viewpoint.

In 1989, the government of Kaohsiung City had planned to establish a second special school for the mentally retarded in the downtown area. But the idea brought strong opposition from the neighborhood residents, so this plan for establishing a school remains in the paperwork stage. In 1990, a new institution for mentally retarded persons was established in Tao-Yun county. But because the neighborhood residents took actions to interfere with the construction work, the project was prolonged a half year and had to be completed under the protection of the police. The major objections emphasized by the neighborhood residents are as follows: "The behaviors of mentally retarded children will have bad influences on the behaviors of the normal children"; "Mental retardation is a kind of infectious disease"; "Almost all of the severely retarded children are psychosis patients, in whom antisocial tendencies are found to be so deep-seated as to require care and treatment"; "All of the severely handicapped are troublemakers in our community. If there is a mentally retarded school here, the price of the houses situated around must be lowered"; and so on.

Although those objections are unreasonable, they still have some negative influence on the development of special education in Taiwan. Fortunately, only a small minority of community residents have been found to constitute this side and to express serious negative attitudes toward the handicapped. We believe that this negative voice will fade away gradually under the progress of education, economics, and politics in Taiwan.

During the past decade, Taiwan has been considered one of the most successful nations in terms of economic development; the rapid growth in economy and industry has earned Taiwan the title of "economic miracle." The nation's budget has increased about 108 times in ten years. With such advances in the economy and industrialization, the national budget for special education or social welfare of the handicapped has increased 100 times during the past ten years. For example, the national budget for social welfare of the handicapped in 1992 was about NT$3,257 million; in 1982 it was only NT$30 million. As a result, the quality and quantity of special education and handicapped welfare have increased rapidly. As well, industrialization in Taiwan has created a lot of employment possibilities for handicapped students. In this regard, the development of special education is anticipated to receive the best support ever at present in Taiwan.

Several political factors accelerate the development of special education. First of all, in 1974 Premier Chiang Chin-Kuo had an opportunity to visit the Taipei School for the Deaf and Blind. He then wrote a letter to the faculty and students of that school in which he addressed the fact that the government was going to make efforts to improve the quality of education for the handicapped. In that summer, the Ministry of Education presented a proposal for the improvement of education for handicapped children. With a budget of more than thirteen million NT dollars, this proposal has had a significant impact on the development of special education in Taiwan.

Second, while the democratic system has been developing healthily in Taiwan, more and more people have gradually realized the importance of human rights, including the right to be educated, to have a job, to have a better life, and so on. Particularly, handicapped people and their parents strongly argue that their rights have not been secured or guaranteed through legislative action and, as a result, legal procedures have been necessary. During the past ten years, many parents' organizations have developed. These organizations work tightly with professionals and legislators to push government to take more legislative action to protect the rights of the handicapped. Several national laws have had or will have an impact on exceptional students.

Legislation

Chen, Seitz, and Cheng (1991) noted that, while education has historically been viewed with deep respect by the Chinese, only very recently have the Chinese people and their government begun to develop special education legislation. It was not until the mid-1960s that a major effort to help exceptional children was undertaken by the central government of Taiwan. Thus, in June 1967, the Nine-Year Compulsory Education Law was enacted. According to the law, the faculty of primary schools have to provide special education for the physically handicapped and mentally retarded and ensure equal education opportunity for all.

With the commitment established by the Fundamental Education Act of 1969, the government took the first step to provide appropriate educational opportunities for exceptional children in a much wider domain. In the following decade, two additional acts were passed. The 1974 act set up a system for identification and placement of exceptional children, and the 1975 act established rigorous requirements for special education teachers. The special education certificate is a prestigious one here, and it carries with it special salary increments. For a teacher to get such a certificate, he or she has to complete an approved in-service or preservice training program.

In 1980, the Law for the Welfare of Handicapped Persons was promulgated. This law contains twenty-six articles and was enacted to protect the welfare and rights of all handicapped individuals in Taiwan. The Ministry of the Interior was responsible for implementing the law of 1980. The 1980 law is broad in its application and sufficiently flexible to allow for modification and change as needed by the people of the country. The law was amended again in 1990 and the number of its articles was increased from twenty-six to thirty-one. The definition of handicapped conditions were expanded from seven categories in 1980 to eleven categories in 1990. The detailed regulations of the Law for the Welfare of Handicapped Persons were approved in 1981 and revised in 1991. This regulation contains twenty-four articles for implementing the main articles of the 1990 law.

In December of 1984, the Special Education Law was promulgated. This law contains twenty-five articles and provides the foundation for suitable education for not only the handicapped but also the gifted and talented. It is important to note that this law does recognize the special needs of both sides of exceptionalities from the very bright and talented to the severely limited.

On 25 March 1987, the Ministry of Education completed its final draft of the Detailed Regulation for the Special Education Law. The regulation contains thirty articles for implementing the main articles of the Special Education Law. Articles 8 through 13 are specifically related to the classification and identification of gifted and talented students; the remainder of the articles define the terminology and identify different categories of handicapped students.

After the promulgation of the Special Education Law and its regulations, five additional statutes concerning the curriculum and instructional design of special education and the registration of special education personnel were stipulated. The five regulations and statutes are as follows: The Implementation Act of Curricula, Teaching Materials, and Methodologies in Special Education Act (24 December 1986); The Assistance Act of Private Special Schools and Classes (15 July 1987); The Equipment Criteria of Special Schools and Classes Act (14 August 1987); The Registration and Application Act for Special Teachers and Professionals (27 August 1987); and the Act of Enrollment Age, School Year, and Advanced Placement of Special Education Students (27 July 1988).

In summary: Since the passing of the Special Education Law in 1984 detailed documents regarding its implementation have been written and published. However, a close examination of the documents reveals that they are not specific as to program funding. Such evasiveness in the choice of words, as well as the lack of clear directions, makes it difficult to implement the laws, resulting in a deprivation of special education opportunities. For example, compulsory education for all exceptional students has not been fully implemented. Thousands of exceptional children have been turned down by the public schools due to lack of resources.

Teachers, Schools, Curriculum, and Pedagogy

Teacher Education

According to the educational statistics of Taiwan (Ministry of Education 1992a), an equivalent of 6,507 full-time special education teachers were employed in Taiwan during the 1991–92 school year. This figure represents an increase of 3,040 teachers (88 percent) from the 1986–87 school year. The number of exceptional children receiving services has increased by 22,923 (99 percent) over the past five school years.

An estimate study conducted by the government, however, indicates the need for 4,500 additional teachers to fill vacancies or to replace uncertified teachers during the next five years. Among all the needed teachers, about 25 percent are for students who are mentally retarded.

In general, teacher training is provided at the preservice and in-service level. The preservice training program is more formal, and offers both academic degrees and teacher certificates. In-service training provides continuing education for those who are currently teaching regular classes but now serve or wish to serve the special education populations in the near future. In addition, the National Taiwan Normal University and the National Changhwa Normal University have developed a graduate institute of special education to offer master's and doctoral programs in special education for the preparation of leadership personnel.

The preservice training programs are chiefly administered by three national normal universities and nine teachers colleges. Primarily, three normal universities offer the program for secondary level teacher training, and nine teachers colleges certify elementary level teachers to practice their profession.

Three national normal universities are separately located in the northern, central, and southern parts of Taiwan Island. All have established departments of special education to provide five-year training programs, including four years of professional teacher training and a one-year practicum that leads to a bachelor's degree in special education. Nine teachers colleges are also located separately in the northern, central, southern, and eastern parts of Taiwan. Currently, only four of them have established departments of special education that offer bachelor's programs in special education with an emphasis on the elementary teaching level. Most of the departments of special education were established within this decade. It is expected that more special education departments will be set up in the other teachers colleges in the near future. At present, the other teachers colleges offer a variety of courses in special education to prepare their students to meet special population needs.

The students in the normal universities or teachers colleges not only receive tuition waivers but also are provided with the necessary living expenses and allowances during their study years. After graduation, the students are assigned to appropriate special education institutes to serve for a period of time. The amount of time is no less than the period of time for which they receive the scholarship.

A number of in-service training programs have been developed during the past three decades in response to severe shortages of special education teachers. For example, an in-service teacher training program for teachers of the visually impaired started at the National Tainan Teachers College in 1967. Participants in the program have all had at least two years of prior teaching experience in regular schools. They are offered a one-year study leave with pay and a tuition waiver to facilitate their continuing education. By 1992, the program had trained about 310 teachers.

In 1970, another in-service training program for teachers of the mentally retarded was developed at the National Taipei Teachers College. By 1992, 1,429 teachers had received such training. Both of the training programs mentioned offer only teacher certificates only to those who work with exceptional children at the elementary level.

In 1974, for the purpose of providing in-service teacher training and conducting research, the special education center of the National Taiwan Normal University was established. The center offers special education programs during the school year and summer leading to the twenty special education credits required to get a formal teacher certificate in special education. The center also provides short-term in-service workshops for special education teachers on an ongoing basis. Through December 1992, about seventeen hundred persons have earned teacher certificates in the areas of mental retardation, learning disabilities, hearing impairment, and giftedness and talent.

The National Changhwa Normal University has also provided in-service training programs for special education during the winter or summer vacation since 1975. Through 1990, about one thousand teachers have received their twenty credits in special education through this program.

While the precise teacher requirements have developed gradually over the past decade, the special education teacher-training programs have grown rapidly. At present, almost all of the three normal universities and nine teachers colleges offer in-service training programs for teachers of exceptional students. As for the qualifications of special teachers, recent amendments of the Special Education Law (1987) contain new staffing requirements for special schools and classes. The following is a list of the twenty-credit training courses required by various categories of special education teachers in Taiwan.

Common courses are psychology and education for exceptional children (three credits) and educational diagnosis of exceptional children (three credits). Differentiated courses are based upon the exceptionalities of the students to be taught. Several kinds of courses and credits are as follows:

1. *Mentally retarded:* Mental retardation (2 credits); Behavior Modification (2 credits); Special Topics in Special Education (4 credits); Curriculum Development and Instructional Design for the Mentally Retarded (4 credits); Practicum (2 credits).
2. *Visually impaired:* Mobility and Directionality (2 credits); Ophthalmology (2 credits); Special Topics in Special Education (4 credits); Curriculum Development and Instructional Design for the Visually Impaired (4 credits); Practicum (2 credits).
3. *Hearing impaired:* Language Communicative Methodology (2 credits); Audiology (2 credits); Special Topics in Special Education (4 credits);

Curriculum Development and Instructional Design for the Hearing Impaired (4 credits); Practicum (2 credits).

4. *Physically handicapped:* Physical training (2 credits); Rehabilitation (2 credits); Special Topics in Special Education (4 credits); Curriculum Development and Instructional Design for the Physically Handicapped (4 credits); Practicum (2 credits).

5. *Gifted:* Special Talent and Creativity (2 credits); Personality Development and Counseling (2 credits); Special Topics in Gifted Education (4 credits); Curriculum Development and Instructional Design for the Gifted (4 credits); Practicum (2 credits).

Educational Placements

In Taiwan, the six kinds of educational placements for exceptional students are as follows:

Itinerant teacher. These programs allow exceptional children to receive their education primarily in a regular setting with only a few hours of special services per week. For example, the itinerant teacher program for the visually impaired was set up in 1966, under the guidance of Dr. S. E. Bourgeault who worked for the U.S. Foundation for Overseas Blind. This program places visually impaired students in regular classes where they also receive from itinerant teachers some specific instruction in braille reading and typing, orientation and mobility skills, and so on. Nationwide, about 903 visually impaired students (including 55 blind and 848 partially sighted) had been served in this program by 1992.

Resource rooms. The first two resource rooms for mildly retarded students and low achievers were established in 1976 at two junior high schools in Taipei

TABLE 15.4.   Number of Children Served under Resource Room Programs, 1982–92

School Year	Number of Schools			Number of Classes			Number of Students		
	El.	Jr. H.	Total	El.	Jr. H.	Total	El.	Jr. H.	Total
1982–83	5	1	6	8	5	13	77	58	135
1983–84	8	15	23	7	28	35	140	551	695
1984–85	14	22	36	17	37	54	212	733	945
1985–86	14	21	35	16	35	51	341	899	1,240
1986–87	18	24	42	19	34	53	324	750	1,074
1987–88	35	30	65	35	58	93	689	1,073	1,762
1988–89	44	25	69	45	38	83	904	1,090	1,994
1989–90	54	28	82	56	51	107	1,167	1,811	2,978
1990–91	85	58	27	124	62	62	3,566	1,213	2,353
1991–92	70	45	115	72	47	119	1,511	2,423	3,934

Source: Data adapted from Department of Education. 1982–1992. Educational statistics of the Republic of China; and Chen. 1992. *Mental retardation.* 402.

Note: El. = elementary school; Jr. H. = junior high school.

TABLE 15.5. Number of Students and Classes for the Mentally Retarded, 1972–92

School Year	Number of Schools			Number of Classes			Number of Students		
	Total	El.	Jr. H.	Total	El.	Jr. H.	Total	El.	Jr. H.
1972–73	40	28	12	70	34	26	841	481	360
1973–74	65	45	20	112	70	42	1,310	798	512
1978–79	124	82	42	233	119	114	2,576	1,256	1,320
1979–80	165	119	46	331	204	127	3,612	2,092	1,520
1980–81	198	151	47	357	223	134	3,907	2,343	1,564
1981–82	233	185	48	422	280	142	4,457	2,804	1,653
1982–83	239	189	50	426	281	145	4,405	2,765	1,640
1983–84	268	218	50	480	337	143	5,037	3,490	1,547
1984–85	303	240	63	545	380	165	5,922	4,032	1,890
1985–86	317	249	68	579	399	180	6,157	4,101	2,056
1986–87	345	268	77	625	430	195	6,237	4,120	2,117
1987–88	359	273	86	694	466	228	6,811	4,492	2,319
1988–89	391	297	94	798	549	249	7,608	5,161	2,447
1989–90	438	334	104	895	617	278	8,494	5,759	2,735
1990–91	503	390	113	1,060	753	307	9,577	6,652	2,925
1991–92	551	393	118	1,105	775	330	10,243	6,991	3,252

Source: Data adapted from Ministry of Education. 1978–92. Educational statistics of the Republic of China; and Chen. 1992. *Mental Retardation.* 417.

Note: El. = elementary school; Jr. H. = junior high school.

City. In this program, students placed in the regular class came to the resource room for specific periods of time to receive special education and related services. In 1978, under the request of the Ministry of Education, the Taiwan Provincial government proclaimed "A Project of Developing Resource Rooms." According to this project, each county has to set up, in a junior high school or elementary school, at least one resource room for mildly handicapped students including those with learning disabilities, mental retardation, or hearing impairment. Therefore, the number of resource rooms was gradually increased. Table 15.4 presents the number of resource rooms and students served during the 1982 through 1992 school years.

Special classes. The first special class for mentally retarded children was established at Taipei Municipal Chung-Shan Primary School in 1962. Eight years later, four experimental classes for educably mentally retarded students at the junior high level were developed in Taipei. Thereafter, there was a steady increase in the number of students with mental retardation served from 1979 (N = 2,576) to 1992 (N = 10,243). The level of students served in these classes was also gradually changed from educable mentally retarded to trainable mentally retarded. Moreover, some of the special classes for severely retarded children were affiliated with institutions. Table 15.5 presents the numbers of mentally retarded students and special classes for the school years 1973 through 1992. There were 1,105 classes for mentally retarded students in 551 schools all over the Taiwan area in 1992. The total enrollment was 10,243 students, with an average of 9.3 students per class. Of the 1,105 classes, 775 (70 percent) were in elementary schools, and 330 (30 percent) were in junior high schools.

Other special classes for different kinds of exceptional children were also established during the 1960s through 1970s. For example, in 1963 Pingtung county Jen-ai elementary school set up a pilot class for children with physical handicaps. In the same year, Taipei city Fushin and Yangming Elementary Schools both established an experimental class for gifted students. In 1969, a pilot class for hearing-impaired students was set up in Changhwa Erlin Elementary School, and in 1970 the first special class for hearing-impaired preschool children was established in the Health Education Department of National Taiwan Normal University. This class adopted the oral method of teaching. In 1974, two special classes for the musically talented were founded in a Taipei and a Taichung elementary school. In 1975, Taichung Municipal WuChuen Junior High School established the first class for the artistically talented. Additional special classes for children with chronic diseases, speech disorders, and emotional disturbance have been established since 1976.

TABLE 15.6.   The Status of Special Classes in the Taiwan Area, School Year 1991–92

	Number of Classes[b]				Number of Students			
Categories[a]	Total	El.	Jr. H.	Sr. H.	Total	El.	Jr. H.	Sr. H.
MR	1,105	775	330	0	10,243	6,991	3,252	0
PH	20	13	7	0	193	125	68	0
HI	139	105	34	0	1,228	870	358	0
ED	3	3	0	0	14	14	0	0
LI	5	5	0	0	141	141	0	0
Subtotal	1,272	901	371	0	11,819	8,141	3,678	0
Gifted	315	217	85	13	7,763	4,764	2,459	540
Mus T	153	76	52	25	4,749	2,156	1,799	794
FAT	313	83	199	31	8,976	2,351	5,760	865
Dan T	115	58	46	11	3,009	1,612	1,183	214
Phy T	34	27	7	0	750	629	121	0
Math T	48	6	9	33	1,490	116	303	1,071
Lang T	3	0	3	0	89	0	89	0
Subtotal	981	467	401	113	26,826	11,628	11,714	3,484
Total	2,253	1,363	772	113	38,645	19,769	15,392	3,484

Source: Ministry of Education. 1992. *Educational statistics of the Republic of China.* 120–21.

[a] MR = mental retardation; PH = physical handicap; HI = hearing impairment; ED = emotional disturbance; LI = language impairment; Mus T = musical talent; FAT = fine arts talent; Dan T = dancing talent; Phy T = physical talent; Math T = mathematical talent; Lang T = language talent.

[b] El. = elementary school; Jr. H. = junior high school; Sr. H. = senior high school.

A number of new special classes were documented in 1992. In particular, the number of special classes with different kinds of talented students were increased tremendously. Table 15.6 presents a summary of the status of special classes. There are 2,253 classes for 38,645 students. Among them, approximately 56 percent are developed for 11,819 handicapped students and the other 44 percent serve 26,826 gifted and talented students.

The earliest special school in Taiwan was established in Tainan City in 1890 by a Presbyterian minister from England. The school was originally set up in a church for the purpose of training blind students. In 1915, the school moved to a new campus and expanded its services to deaf students. It was renamed the Tainan School for the Deaf and Blind. In 1968, all the blind students were transferred to Taichung Chi-Ming School, a new blind school, and the school was renamed Taiwan Provincial Tainan School for the Deaf.

Some other kinds of special schools were established in the 1960s to 1970s. For example, the Taiwan Provincial Changhwa Jen-ai School for the Physically Handicapped was established in 1968. The first school for the mentally retarded was established in 1976 at Tainan City after the first national prevalence study on exceptional children.

In summary, based on the most recent edition of *Educational Statistics for the Republic of China* (Ministry of Education 1992a), there are eleven special schools for moderately and severely handicapped students, including three for the blind, four for the deaf, three for the mentally retarded, and one for the physically handicapped. A total of 3,448 students are served across preschool, elementary, junior high, and vocational senior high levels. There are 972 teachers employed to teach these students, with an average of 3.5 students per teacher. The average number of students per class is 8.53, with a range of 5.48 (blind school) to 10.23 (physically handicapped school). Table 15.7 shows these data in tabular form.

According to the statistical data obtained from the second national prevalence study, there were 31,440 mentally retarded persons between the ages of

TABLE 15.7. The Status of Special Schools in the Taiwan Area, 1991–92

Categories of Impairment[a]	Number of Schools	Number of Classes	Number of Students	Number of Teachers	Number of Staff	Student/ Teacher Ratio	Number of Students per Class	Number of Students per School
VH	3	70	382	146	82	2.6:1	5.45	127
HI	4	178	1,567	412	91	3.8:1	8.80	392
MR	3	126	1,192	340	107	3.5:1	9.46	397
PH	1	30	307	74	31	4.1:1	10.23	307
Total	11	404	3,448	972	311	3.5:1	8.53	313

Source: Ministry of Education. 1992. Educational statistics of the Republic of China. 119.

[a]VH = visual impairment; HI = hearing impairment; MR = mental retardation; PH = physical handicap.

six and fifteen. Among this mentally retarded population, approximately 15,000 (less than 50 percent) of mentally retarded students were served by special education programs including resource rooms, special classes, and special schools. In other words, over half of the mentally retarded population, particularly severely retarded students, were still excluded from special education programs because of the lack of appropriate school facilities. Due to those needs, the government is planning to develop more special education facilities in the near future.

At present, moderately and severely handicapped students learn more effectively in special schools, whether day schools or residential schools, where special education personnel assume primary responsibility for their programs. Five special schools for mentally retarded students will be established between the 1992 and 1995 school years. The financial budget for each new school is approximately NT$500 million to NT$750 million (about U.S.$20 million to U.S.$30 million).

Residential institutions. According to survey data (Chen 1992), there are about 75 residential institutions or centers serving 5,165 severely handicapped persons. Almost 75 percent of the institutions mainly serve severely retarded persons; other institutions serve multiply handicapped, physically handicapped, or emotionally disturbed children. Some self-contained special classes were set up in parts of the institutions sponsored by the local education administrations. Most of the institutions are private; only six of them are administered by public agencies.

Hospital service programs. There are only two hospital service programs to help the children with physical disability and chronic disease. One was implemented in 1971 at the National Taiwan University Hospital. Two teachers are assigned by Taipei city school system to tutor some children clients during their convalescence. Another program at Kaohsiung Medical School is providing bedside education to children with chronic diseases.

Homebound service programs. Because there are not enough special education facilities to provide educational services for all handicapped students, about 2,500 severely handicapped students, ages six to fifteen, are placed in homebound service programs. The local school systems assign teachers to help students for several hours a week. Overall, however, the efficacy of homebound program seems very weak.

In summary, according to the data of table 15.4 through table 15.6, special classes are the most common special education placement for exceptional students. The majority of them (60 percent) receive instruction in separate classroom settings. Resource room placements serve 10 percent of exceptional students, mostly those who are learning disabled or mildly mentally retarded. Educational placements vary a great deal, according to the handicapping conditions of the students served. Almost all severely handicapped students are served in the most restrictive environment, such as special schools, residential facilities, or home/hospital placement. A great effort is still needed to develop more special education facilities to serve the moderately and severely handicapped children of Taiwan.

Instructional Designs for Children with Various Handicapping Conditions

No matter the country of practice, special education programs differ from regular education because they try to take into account the child's interindividual and intra-individual differences (Kirk and Gallagher 1989). There are some ways to adapt instruction to the individual differences of various exceptional children in Taiwan, but almost all of the methods are based on the theories and concepts of special education that are prevalent in the United States. For example, one of the many innovations addressed by the U.S. Public Law 94–142, is the requirement that every handicapped student have an individualized education program (IEP). Although every teacher who teaches in a special education facility has been asked to develop an IEP for each handicapped student, there is still a great need in Taiwan to carry through on this and to raise the quality of instruction for students with various handicapping conditions.

Major Controversies and Issues in Special Education

There are many issues and controversies in special education in Taiwan. Mainstreaming is a good trend for the development of special education. However, it still has a long way to go toward improving its quality in Taiwan. Although mainstreaming is the current trend in the development of special education, only some visually impaired cases are well mainstreamed in the regular schools, with itinerant teachers to provide necessary instructions and assistance. The following factors illustrate the difficulties and issues in mainstreaming:

Class size and teacher numbers. Class size is too large and the teacher-student ratio is too high. Generally, a regular classroom contains 40 to 45 students with only 1.5 to 2 teachers. With this size and ratio, it is very difficult to maintain the quality of regular education, not to mention the inclusion of special education.

Lack of teacher training. Unlike in some countries, basic courses in special education—for example, Introduction to Special Education—are not required for regular education teachers in Taiwan. Even many special education teachers have received their knowledge on special education during the in-service teacher training programs instead of preservice training programs. At present, a number of exceptional children who do not have the opportunity to get into the special education programs have failed to succeed both in academic achievement and social adaptation in the regular classrooms. So it is too unrealistic to expect that regular teachers, without special education knowledge and background, can teach exceptional students well.

Lack of highly structured curricula. A unified curriculum is provided for all students in elementary schools. It is designed for the middle-level student so it definitely will not be suitable for some students with special needs such as those who are mentally retarded or learning disabled. At the junior high school level, two kinds of curricula are available. One is for students who want to get into the senior high schools and are preparing to pass the competitive college and university entrance exam. The other is for the students who want to get into the vocational schools or job market. Although it sounds as though the latter curriculum might be suitable for some special students, it is designed for regular students and is not as highly structured as some independent living skill programs in the United States (such as the Life-Centered Career Education Curriculum or the Activities Catalog).

Lack of services. At present, there are not enough special education services to meet the needs of children with special needs. Resource room programs are not popular either. Although some arguments proposed by the Regular Education Initiative (REI) are also heard in Taiwan (for example, complaints about the watered-down curriculum, inadequate assessment, and inefficiency of the current education system), we still think that to implement the REI or extreme mainstreaming will make the present situation worse. The more realistic and effective movement is to restructure or improve special education.

In recent years, the concept of zero rejection has been developed in Taiwan. Severely and profoundly handicapped children can receive their education in special classes affiliated with regular schools. However, the dropout rate is fairly high because of the inadequacy of facilities and aids. Parents prefer the segregated institutes with facilities suitable for their children.

Teacher reluctance. Teachers' negative attitudes also prevent integration. At present, regular teachers don't want disabled children staying in their classrooms. They often refer the students that they cannot tolerate or handle to the special classes, institutes, or schools. The resource room programs show that seldom is there communication between regular and special educators, or that the communications are ineffective and inefficient.

Peer reluctance. Lack of peer acceptance is another reason for segregated settings. At present, some of the nonhandicapped students still cannot wholly accept the handicapped students in their classrooms. Under this circumstance, it may be disadvantageous to include handicapped students in regular classrooms.

Lack of public knowledge. The most important key to implementing integration is public acceptance. Currently, many people still lack knowledge of what special education is and what the children with special needs are like. The attitude toward disabilities still needs to be strengthened and disseminated. Barrier-free environments also are essential for integration needs.

Until solutions to these difficulties are found, it is unrealistic to implement an extreme mainstreaming idea such as the Regular Education Initiative (REI).

Otherwise, the situation will go backward a hundred years; that is, there will be no special education at all, just the regular education in the regular schools. Therefore, cascade placements such as Reynold's scheme are still needed in Taiwan and the least restrictive environment (LRE) is the best idea for handicapped students' placement.

Deinstitutionalization

As mentioned earlier, the Taiwanese government has tried to deinstitutionalize the handicapped. Public and private group home programs have also increased recently for adolescent or adult handicapped persons. Currently, however, institutes are still needed for some preschoolers, school-age children, and adults with severe and profound handicaps. The urgent need is to improve the environment and program quality of these institutes to prepare for the future deinstitutionalization needs.

Funding

Special education programs are sponsored by local governments. Previously, the central government asked each local government to use at least 35 percent of the total annual budget on education. However, this amount was not sufficient for regular education development, not to mention for special education. So many cities and counties needed to spend on other things the subsidy provided by the central government to sponsor the special education programs. Therefore, the program quantity and quality were very limited. During the past five years, the central government has started to provide a budget for special education. Thus, special education program quantity and quality have improved rapidly. However, there is still a question as to whether teachers' salaries should be paid by the central government or by the local government as is currently the case.

Who Should Receive the Service?

Based on the results of prevalence studies, the quantities and ratios of students with special needs receiving special education programs still lag far behind some advanced countries. Although the ratio has increased gradually, studies also indicate that many mildly handicapped children such as the learning disabled, language impaired, and emotional and behaviorally disordered, do not receive an appropriate education. They either still receive education in regular settings without any special education services or are put into mental retardation programs with watered-down curricula. Therefore, some resource room programs for them are needed in the future.

Emerging and Future Trends

Although special education has made rapid progress during the past decade, it still needs to be enriched and extended. The following are some suggestions for future development.

Legislation. Since the passing of the Special Education Law in 1984 detailed regulations regarding special education implementation have been published and written. However, the regulations are still not complete and enforced. Thus, the law and regulations need to be revised and a penalty for not following them should be established and enforced.

Services. Thousands of special children have been turned down by the public schools due to lack of resources or programs suitable for them. At least during the students' compulsory education period, special education services should be increased and extended to all children needing services.

Training. Preservice and in-service teacher training programs should be emphasized. Some essential courses on special education should be required of all teachers to meet mainstream needs.

Funding. The cost of providing appropriate education services for the special education populations should be shared by the central, provincial, and local governments in a specified manner; for instance, budgets from the various departments and agencies need to specify the appropriate monies for support of handicapped students. The central government needs to take the leadership role by providing annually one-half to two-thirds of the cost of setting up new special classes and schools, salaries for the teaching staff, curriculum development and research, and equipment for special students. It should allocate appropriate funds for the development and implementation of the laws.

Technology. New and advanced media and technology innovations in special education should be introduced, revised, and adopted to enhance program implementation and development. For example, augmentative communication systems can facilitate communications for hearing impaired and speech/language impaired; special orthopedic devices can aid ambulation and transportation; and computer technologies can improve the quality of service delivery for handicapped individuals of all ages.

Career skills. Career development should be strengthened. Independent skills, such as personal daily living skills, community or social adaptive skills, essential job skills, and basic academic or communication skills should be included and integrated into the curriculum for career needs.

Environments and awareness. A barrier-free environment needs to be established. As well as accessibility in transportation, accommodation, and learning environments, some activities to advocate and disseminate public acceptance and positive attitudes should also be emphasized.

Parent participation. Parental education and involvement should be provided to the parents with special children to facilitate the educational effects and maintain learning. Parents' rights and duties need to be advocated through conducting various parental education seminars and activities.

Evaluative techniques and idea exchange. Program evaluation should be systematized, and international academic exchange activities be strengthened. For instance, periodical evaluation (that is, every two or three years) is needed for all special education programs to provide feedback and monitor students' progress. To fulfill this end, more international conferences or seminars and cross-cultural research can be conducted.

Professional cooperation. Education, social welfare, and medical services should be connected closely to better serve the special education populations. For instance, doctors and nurses, speech pathologists, social workers, physical and occupational therapists, and special educators should work as a team to provide special populations with the maximum opportunity for education and future development.

References

Chen, Y. H. 1992. *Mental retardation: Theory and application.* Taipei: Shih Ta Book Co.

Chen, Y. H., Seitz, M. R., and Cheng, L. R. 1991. Special education. In D. C. Smith, ed. *The Confucian continuum: Education modernization in Taiwan,* 317–65). New York: Praeger Publishers.

Kirk, S. A., and Gallagher, J. J. 1989. *Educating exceptional children.* 6th. ed. Boston: Houghton Mifflin.

Kuo, Chen, and Liang. 1976. Report of the first prevalence study of exceptional children. Taipei: Ministry of Education.

Lu, T. H. 1992. Adaptive of the Mentally Retarded in Taiwan, ROC. Doctoral diss., University of Oregon.

Mao, L. W. 1989. Special education for special kids. *Free China Review,* May, 36–41.

Ministry of Education. 1992a. *Educational statistics for the Republic of China.* Taipei: Ministry of Education.

———. 1992b. *Outlines of the five-year plan for the development and improvement of special education.* Taipei: Ministry of Education.

———. 1992c. Report of the second national prevalence study of exceptional children. Taipei: Ministry of Education.

Wu, W. T., Chen Y. H., Chang, H. K., and Hsu, J. M. 1989. Evaluation of the effects of the 1980 Welfare Law for Handicapped Persons in the Republic of China. *Bulletin of Special Education.* 5:1–30.

Wu, W. T., and Lu, T. H. 1987. Report of the 8th Asian Conference on Mental Retardation. In W. T. Wu, ed. *The 1987 Annual Journal of the Special Education Association of the Republic of China,* 49–63. Taipei: Bao-shin.

16

Russia

VLADIMIR I. LUBOVSKY

EVGENIJA NIKOLAEVNO MARTSINOVSKAJA

Translated by Svetlana Vishnevksaja

Prevalence of Developmental Disabilities

Of the existing special education situation in Russia, we may give only approximate indices of the school-age developmental disabilities prevalence. Through the present in Russia, statistics on developmental disabilities are not available. Physicians from the infantile health care system (children's polyclinics, local pediatricians) observe a child from birth and may discover some handicaps in development. But this information from the health institutions does not go either to the system of state statistics or to the system of education.

About the Authors • Dr. Vladimir Lubovsky is a professor and member of the Academy of Pedagogical Sciences of Russia. He is a graduate of the Department of Psychology of Moscow University and was engaged in postgraduate study under the leadership of Professor Alexander Luria. Since joining the Institute of Defectology (recently renamed the Institute of Remedial Education) in 1953, he has been a researcher, scientific secretary, and head of the Laboratory of the Psychology of Developmentally Backward Children. From 1986 to 1992, he was the director of the Institute. His research interests include the psychology of mentally retarded and developmentally backward children, the diagnostics of impaired hearing, the visual peculiarities of partially sighted persons, problems of psychological diagnostics of mental deficiency, and general questions of special education organization. He has more than 150 publications, including a number of works published in English, Japanese, and German. • Professor Evgenija Nikolaevno Martsinovskaja is a candidate of pedagogical science and scientific secretary at the Institute of Remedial Education (formerly called the Research Institute of Defectology) of the Academy of Pedagogical Sciences of Russia.

Developmental disabilities are registered according to the indices of children enrolled in special educational institutions. Because the available institutions cannot provide all children in need with education, these indices are much lower than the true number of existing developmentally disabled children. Along with this factor, children with different handicaps are not involved in special education to an equal extent. Whereas all or almost all hearing-impaired and visually impaired children are educated under adequate conditions, the considerable part of the population of children with mental deficiency do not receive any special educational support. Also absent are any kinds of special pedagogical measures or educational structures for emotionally disturbed children and children with behavior problems. There are no educational provisions for severely motor-disordered children.

The most reliable of the prevalence indices are those for pronounced visual impairments—blindness and partial sightness (.064 percent)—and hearing impairments—deafness and hard of hearing (.11 percent)—because children in these categories are fully involved in special education. As far as other categories are concerned, it is only possible to obtain data by examining separate samples. According to these samples, the prevalence of developmental backwardness—specific learning difficulties—among the elementary school population is 4.5 percent. Speech disorders have a prevalence of up to 12 percent. But many children from these groups do not need special education and their development may be normalized after slight individual help. As for mental retardation, its evident prevalence is 2 to 3 percent, as in other countries.

A comparison of the data concerning the origins of developmental disabilities testifies to the fact that there is not any Russian specificity in etiology. The exception is ecologically unfavorable places, such as regions affected by the Chernobyl catastrophe and some other places where the number of children with learning difficulties is increasing.

Identifying Developmental Abnormalities and Making the Diagnosis

Identification of possible disabilities in the prenatal period is the function of women's medical consultations. However, these examinations are mainly limited to observing the state of a pregnant woman's health and identifying the Rh factor. Sometimes there is testing for the presence of phenylalanine (for indication of PKU) in the newborn.

Children's clinics and local pediatricians observe each child from the first day of life, paying attention to the state of his or her health and physical development. Physicians use conventional medical methods. At the end of the first year, the child is examined by different specialists. However, a countrywide system of disability screening does not yet exist. In the case of severe defects in development, the child is specially registered.

Psychological service in the system of infantile health care is absent; psychologists are available only in children's psychiatric clinics. Psychoeducational methods in the assessment of developmental disabilities are only applied to the extent to which children's psychiatrists and speech therapists in polyclinics are able to use them.

The diagnosis of developmental problems is made by doctors in children's polyclinics during the general obligatory examinations of children at the age of 3 to 4 years and just before schooling at 6 to 7 years. Usually, the diagnosis assigns children to a definite category of handicaps—partial sight, deafness, mental retardation, or developmental backwardness. However, the diagnostics for determining mental deficiency remain very inaccurate, mainly because psychoeducational methods are not regularly used.

In the case of a severe developmental disability, the child is sent to the Medico-Pedagogical Commission, which selects children for special schools. This team consists of a pediatrician, psychiatrist, speech therapist, psychologist, and specially trained teacher for the mentally retarded. The team gives an official recommendation concerning the appropriate place for the child's schooling. As a rule, mentally retarded children (with the exception of the profoundly mentally retarded) and developmentally backward children— those with specific learning difficulties—begin study in regular schools. Only a year later, after a failure, are they sent to medical-educational consultation (child guidance clinics in the west).

At present, a system of psychological services in the form of medical-psychological-educational clinics (which exist in all developed countries) is not available. Such councils exist only in some towns of the country, and the majority of them have been only recently organized. But it should be noted that some years ago the training of school psychologists was initiated, and they now function in some schools, including special ones.

Legislation and State Policy in the Selection of Educational Institutions for Handicapped Children

Educational institutions for children with developmental disabilities are a fundamental part of the public education system of the country. Separate law regulations speak for children and youngsters with physical and mental disabilities, prevent them from studying in a regular general school, and stress the need of special educational environments. There is an established network of special comprehensive residential schools (day schools, units) providing these children with education, upbringing, treatment, and labor training.

Children and youngsters are sent to these institutions according to the decision of the medical-psychoeducational Commission or Consultation. Educational curricula for children and youngsters with developmental disabilities are worked out along with the general programs of the regular school, but with regard to the peculiarities of the psychological development and learning abilities of children with disabilities. The volume and the content of the special school curriculum may be comparable with a definite educational level in a regular school. This makes it possible for students to continue their education at the institutions within the system of general education, such as professional schools and colleges. The exception is the curricula of the so-called auxiliary schools—special schools for the mentally retarded. These schools have their own specific curricula.

The availability of a differentiated system of special institutions does not mean that children with physical and mental disabilities can be educated only there. By the wish of the parents, these children and youngsters may study in general schools together with normally developing children. Developmentally disabled children are sent to special schools only if their parents or caretakers consent to the placement.

The state policy concerning the selection of an appropriate educational institution for a child with developmental disabilities is directed toward creating an optimal environment for the full development, education, and upbringing of the handicapped child. At the present time, it is only possible to organize such an environment in special preschool institutions and residential schools—day schools and units. In these institutions, together with curricula for regular kindergartens and regular school tasks, specific tasks are also being fulfilled. These are the remediation of developmental disabilities; special education; medical-prophylactic, rehabilitative, and sanitation work; vocational training, and social adaptation. The final goal of this work is integration into open society.

Teachers, Schools, Programs, and Pedagogics

Teachers

The Statute of Special General Residential Schools (Day Schools and Units) for Children with Physical and Mental Disabilities states that the staff engaged in the teaching process should have special (defectological) education. Teachers getting special education are trained at defectological faculties of pedagogical institutes. Such faculties exist in large towns in the main regions of the country. In the 1991–92 academic year, fifteen faculties functioned on the territory of Russia, the majority of them in the European part, and less in the east.

The term of education at defectological faculties is five years. Students are trained for working at schools for the mentally retarded, for visually and hearing-impaired children, for children with speech disorders, and also in special preschool institutions.

The network of special institutions is not wide yet, so the number of specialists with higher defectological education is not sufficient. A definite percentage of the staff in special schools have only general pedagogical training. For teachers working at special institutions, and especially for those without special (defectological) higher education, annual in-service training courses, in large regional towns or centers, or in Moscow, are organized.

Schools

There are eight types of special schools with ten main variants of education. The main goals, common to all types of special schools are the creation of favorable conditions for solving children's developmental problems caused by various disabilities, providing children with knowledge about the social life and work routines of human beings, and professional training. These goals are achieved in each type of special school through various means, methods, and approaches and during different periods in the child's stage of development.

Special general residential schools (day schools) for the deaf cater only to totally deaf children or those hearing-impaired children with such slight residual hearing that it does not allow them to acquire even a minimal vocabulary through auditory perception. These schools provide deaf students with the same education as that of a nine-year normal general school, but for ten years. There are six pupils in a group. Full secondary education is for twelve years. Children with appropriate general and speech development are accepted to the first grade at the age of seven years. Children without good preschool training are put into the preparatory group.

The didactic system of deaf education in primary school (preparatory, first through ninth graders) is based on the wide use of practical-object activities such as modeling from paper and plasticine, constructing from building blocks, making different kinds of models, working in the school garden, looking after plants, and so on. The practical-object activity approach is used as the basis for general development, speech development, formation of cognitive activity, independence, and conscious knowledge acquisition.

The main goal in the primary grades is to teach verbal speech in its oral and written forms. At the initial stage (preparatory grade) fingerspelling is used as a basic means, gradually replaced by oral speech. Sign language, as a rule, is not used in the lessons. Much attention is paid to the development of auditory perception and the improvement of pronunciation skills. This work is done during the whole educational process in general subjects and music-rhythmical classes, and also in special individual training lessons. Hence, teaching oral speech to deaf children is carried out in a hearing-speech environment providing for auditory-visual and hearing perception of oral speech while using modern amplifying devices.

Education in the same manner as taught in the main schools (first through tenth grades) is compulsory for the deaf. After getting an education that matches the general school demands, students may continue education in the eleventh to twelfth grades of the deaf schools on the recommendations of teachers and according to the desires of both the children and the parents. Students may enter secondary professional schools or special institutions of different profiles or start working with simultaneous studying (if they wish) in the evening special schools.

Special residential schools (day schools) for hard-of-hearing and adventitiously deaf children cater to children with partial loss of hearing that causes speech underdevelopment at different levels. These schools serve children who are hard of hearing and children deafened at preschool or school age but with retained speech abilities. The schools have two departments. The first department is for children with mild speech underdevelopment caused by hearing impairment as well as for those who are adventitiously deaf but have intact speech. The compulsory term of education is ten years. During this period, education that matches nine years of regular general schools is provided. There may also be eleventh and twelfth grades, which provide the same education as the full secondary school.

The second department is for children with severe underdevelopment of speech caused by hearing impairment. The compulsory term of educational provision matches the nine-year regular general school but takes ten years. According to a decision of the school team, students may be transferred from one department to the other or even to a regular school. This depends on the level of speech development achieved in the process of learning.

The educational process in this type of school is aimed at overcoming the deviations in speech development and in the cognitive processes. Teaching hard-of-hearing and adventitiously deaf children is carried a special teaching plans and curricula. In elementary school, special textbooks are used. Special attention is paid to the development of auditory perception and the formation of pronouncing skills. This work is done in individual and group lessons. Teaching plans also include musical-rhythmic sessions with the use of phonetic rhythmics and various types of activities connected with the music. Individual and group training sessions of oral speech are conducted with adventitiously deaf children on a visual (lipreading), auditory-visual, visual-vibrational, and auditory-visual-vibrational basis. The aim is to develop the students' oral communication with the hearing world.

Residential schools for blind children cater to totally blind children and children with residual vision (.04 and lower). Included are children with higher visual acuity (.08) but who have complicated impairments of visual functions and progressive eye diseases that lead to blindness.

Blind students get an education that matches the nine-year regular school but lasts for ten years. Full secondary education lasts through twelve years. Blind education at the elementary level is carried out according to special teaching plans and curricula. At the secondary level, there is special curricula providing for the remediation of primary and secondary developmental disabilities. This includes physical training, orientation and mobility, labor, music, and art. Students also study the general curricula of a regular school. On the whole, the content of education at schools for the blind corresponds to that of a regular school.

Blind education is based on using tactile or tactile-visual perception, the basis for teaching the alphabet in the braille system. The system of correctional work also involves special training classes for the development of not only tactile learning but also residual visual perception. That is why, while teaching reading, writing, and counting, the braille system and, if possible, flatbed print is used. In teaching science, there are widely used special devices that transform the light phenomena into tactile and sound signals.

Special residential schools (day schools) for partially sighted children cater to children with visual acuity of .05 to .04 in the better-sighted eye with corrective lenses. The state of other visual functions such as visual field, and the form and the course of the pathological process, is taken into account. Day schools also serve children with higher visual acuity but with progressive visual deterioration or partly relapsing diseases, and also, with those asthenopic symptoms that appear during reading and writing a short distance from the eyes. Children with eye diseases and traumatism may be transferred from regular schools to schools for the partially sighted. As soon as the state of health is restored and the state of vision stabilized, the students may be transferred back to regular schools.

At the schools for the partially sighted, medical-rehabilitation work is conducted and measures for the protection and the development of vision are taken. A special school routine is maintained. Remedial-rehabilitative classes on visual perception development, and training sessions on speech and rhythmics and on spatial and social orientations are organized. This work is carried out in groups and in individual lessons. The learning process is aided with special remedial items to compensate for impaired vision, specific equipment, modified training appliances, and the usual visual aids. This school uses textbooks with large-size letters. The contents of education coincide with that of a regular school, except that an extra year is added.

Special residential schools (day schools) for the mentally retarded are called *auxiliary*. These schools cater to children with mild mental retardation (IQ 50–80). There are solitary schools for children with severe mental retardation (IQ 40–50) but, as a rule, such children are kept at the institutions under the Ministry of Social Security.

Auxiliary residential schools (day schools) have a nine-year term of education (first through ninth grades). This term of education may be prolonged for a year at the initial or final stages. For children who did not attend a special preschool institution or who were deprived of family education and, as a result of this, did not achieve school maturity, preparatory units or preschool groups are established under the auxiliary school to prepare these children for schooling. Preparatory and first grades accept children of seven to eight years. The number of pupils in a group should not be more than twelve persons. This period of schooling is aimed at specifying the diagnosis.

Due to the peculiarities of the psychic development of the mentally retarded, their typological specificities, and their difficulties in the learning process, education of mentally handicapped children is carried out with specially compiled teaching plans, curricula, and textbooks. Auxiliary schools provide students with an elementary education with a practical orientation. First of all, vocational training in various types of labor at different complexity levels helps students to adapt to living and working in a modern society. With this aim, a special subject, *social orientation,* is introduced into the teaching plan. Children with specific speech disorders and motor disorders visit group and individual training sessions for speech therapy and exercise therapy.

Some auxiliary schools with the necessary material basis and connections with industrial and agricultural enterprises to organize students' practical activities establish tenth grades for industrial training and the goal of finishing professional education. Those students who covered the main nine-year auxiliary school course, and according to the state of their health and their mental ability level, can acquire the initial qualification rank of elementary professions. They are accepted to the tenth grade with the professional training provision. The enrollment is done in light of the wishes of students and their parents.

Auxiliary residential school graduates may continue their education in special units in professional-technical schools or start working in the national economy. Auxiliary schools follow up on their former students at the beginning of their labor activity with the aim of supporting them in their adaptation to everyday life and employment.

Special residential schools (day schools, leveling-up classes) enroll developmentally backward children (children with specific learning difficulties). Although these children have potentially intact abilities in mental development, they experience weak memory, attention deficits, underdevelopment of general thinking processes, backward speech development, a limited volume of knowledge, and a lack of the images and skills necessary for covering school programs. These deficits often lead to academic failure in the regular general school.

The special schools provide students with an education that matches that of main general school, but add an extra year of the elementary school. Teaching plans and curricula are different from the general school. They include additional propaedeutic sections on the alphabet and math. Subjects such as *acquaintance with the surrounding world,* and speech development, and *rhythmics* aim at overcoming children's developmental delays.

Special residential schools for developmentally backward children (day schools, leveling-up classes) enroll children, depending on their readiness for schooling, at the age of six or seven years. Children from families who attended regular school before may be admitted to this type of school. The former group goes to the preparatory or the first grade; the latter group goes right away to the second grade. The number of pupils in a class should not exceed twelve persons. If the backward development is overcome (mainly after the fourth grade), some children may be transferred back to regular schools.

Individual and group remedial classes are organized to correct the developmental disabilities in students, fill gaps in their education, and improve their speech, motor, and spatial orientation development. Classes include speech therapy sessions. Children with motor disorders attend special classes on physical training. Classes on rhythmics promote the correction of problems with the emotional-volitional sphere, spatial orientation, movement coordination, and motor development.

There exist residential schools (day schools) for children with severe speech disorders (developmental aphasia, rhinolalia, cleft palate, severe stuttering) who are prevented from studying in general schools. The residential schools have two departments: the first department is for children with severe underdevelopment of speech (alalia, developmental aphasia, dysarthria, rhinolalia, and aphasia); the second department is for children with severe stuttering.

These schools enroll children ages seven to eight. The term of education in the first department is ten years. For students with the lowest level of general speech development, there is a preparatory period, so the full term of their education is eleven years. During this period, they cover the curriculum of the general nine-year secondary school. The second department provides education for nine years. School graduates may continue schooling in regular school or in professional secondary schools of different types, or start working. At the end of the academic year, there is a reassessment of these elementary school pupils with the aim of making decisions about whether to transfer them to a regular school (in the case that the speech disorder is eliminated) or to another educational institution (upon clarification of the diagnosis).

The main tasks of this school are the provision of general education, as well as improvement of speech (pronouncing of sounds), voice disorders, tempo speaking, phonetic hearing, dysgraphia, dyslexia, irregular grammar, and so on. Schools also provide help with the affected child's psychological development that is necessary to the school graduates' inclusion with their society.

Residential schools for children with cerebral palsy (CP) and other motor disorders cater to patients with movement disabilities of different etiology and severity. Besides having motor disorders, children might have mental retardation or speech disorders and also hearing or visual impairments. One of the main requirements for a child's being admitted to this type of school is his or her ability to move independently. Severely motor-disordered children, those in need of wheelchairs or who are bedridden, get education at home or are kept in hospitals without teaching on a regular basis.

For ten years these children cover a program corresponding to a regular nine-year school. After that, they may get a full secondary education in the eleventh to twelfth grades. The term of education may be extended at the initial stage by organizing a preparatory group for those children who are not ready for schooling. In the case that motor disorders are accompanied by mental retardation, children are enrolled in auxiliary units where they study for nine years, covering the special curriculum of the auxiliary school.

The duration of the elementary school lessons is shorter than in normal schools: 30 minutes in the preparatory grade, 35 to 40 minutes in the first and second grades, and 45 minutes in the third and all subsequent grades. The number of pupils in each group does not exceed ten persons. Auxiliary units and groups for children with complicated disorders have five to seven persons. Group and individual exercise-training sessions and speech therapy classes are obligatory. Medical treatment is prescribed individually.

For those motor-disordered children who have additional visual or hearing impairments, special groups with special staff may be established in the school. When there is a sufficient number of motor-disordered children with additional visual or hearing impairments, the school opens special units for them with specially trained staff. There are also orthopedic workshops at the schools for making orders, fitting, adjusting, and repairing prosthetic apparatuses made by orthopedic enterprises.

Although the school for children with cerebral palsy is usually a boarding school, in some cases its students, under an agreement with the school team, may live at home. The student may be transferred to a regular school as soon as the appropriate state of health is clarified with an examination by the Medical Pedagogical Commission.

Vocational training and education are very important for adapting children with developmental disabilities to socially useful activities in society. In all types of special schools, vocational training is carried out in four stages: elementary labor preparation, polytechnical vocational training, extended professional orientation with elementary professional training, and professional training geared to a specific job.

Curricula for vocational and professional training are arranged according to the specific development of children of each category of disability. The final stage may be reached if the school has available the appropriate setting, such as workshops with appropriate equipment, for training students in a definite profession, the links with industrial enterprises for organizing labor practice, and a qualified staff of professional training. Those school graduates who successfully pass the qualification examinations or undergo the qualification test get a certificate that allows them to get employment.

In Russia at the beginning of 1992 there functioned 1,809 residential and day schools catering to about 293,000 children with different mental and physical disabilities. Of these schools, 1,445 are special schools for mentally retarded children, serving 234,000 children. The schools are distributed as shown in table 16.1. In addition, there are classes in the normal schools serving 8,000 mentally handicapped children and 70,000 developmentally backward children. Thus, 370,000 children are educated in special schools and special classes. About 116,000 children with speech disorders studying in normal schools receive help in so-called speech therapy rooms affiliated with the regular schools; in 1992 there were 3,863 such rooms. Each speech therapy room serves five to six regular schools. These rooms are analogous to resource rooms in the American system of education, but they deal only with speech defect correction. On the whole, the system of special education (residential schools, special classes, and speech therapy rooms) embraces 486,000 children; that is 2.5 percent of the school population.

Children with developmental disabilities (special needs) are generally enrolled in the specialized institutions. Only a small part of the population of mentally retarded children and developmentally backward children (with specific learning difficulties) are integrated in the form of separate classes. Fully integrated as single students into regular classes are children with mild

TABLE 16.1.   Schools for Special Needs in Russia

Type of School	Number
Deaf	80
Hard of hearing	71
Blind	19
Partially sighted	52
Motor disordered	35
Severely speech disordered	51
Children with specific learning difficulties (developmentally backward children)	48
Deaf-blind	1

speech disorders, but only one-third of them get special help. There are a total of 116,000 integrated students.

In Russia, there exists a network of preschool institutions for children with disabilities. The system of preschool institutions is more versatile and flexible than that of the higher-level schools. The preschool system includes nursery schools, kindergartens, children's homes and preschool departments in the regular schools with one-to-three-year education programs. Special preschool institutions cater to the same categories of developmentally disabled children as do the higher-level schools—that is, hearing-impaired children (deaf and hard of hearing), the visually impaired (blind and partially sighted), those with mental deficiency (mental retardation), developmentally backward children, speech disordered children, and children with cerebral palsy. Preschool institutions, as do the higher-level schools, embrace only some part of the children in need of special help. Some parents prefer to educate their young children at home, in the family. These parents get support from specially organized councils affiliated with kindergartens, scientific-research institutes of special education, or pedagogical colleges training teachers for working in special schools.

Lately, due to the democratization of society, parents' activity has increased, and parental associations for helping children with special needs and other public foundations have been set in motion. These organizations have started establishing centers to support developmentally disabled children, especially those categories that up to now have not been involved into regular education, such as severely motor-disordered children, profoundly mentally retarded children, and children with complicated disorders. At the moment, however, such centers are not numerous at all. They are provided by different public foundations and commercial structures and, in fact, do not receive any state support. Economic difficulties make it practically impossible to organize family type homes (residential homes are subjected to sharp criticism), though there are people who might undertake their establishment.

Issues and Controversies

Because sending children to a special school is not obligatory, many parents of mentally retarded children and children with specific learning difficulties try to have them admitted to regular schools. This is the type of integration under which children with special educational needs happen to be in unfavorable conditions because special pedagogical and psychological help are not provided in the regular schools and specially trained staff for teaching developmentally disabled children are unavailable.

At present, even in the system of special schools only 13 to 15 percent of teachers have higher special training. The rest have received general training and have covered the curriculum in short-term courses. This is one of the reasons it is difficult to solve the problem of integration as has lately been done in Western countries.

In addition, the experts think that the authentic realization of the integration approach demands the highest possible extension of the abilities of a handicapped child to ensure that he or she can interact with the environment and other people in combination with profoundly individualized teaching. The fulfillment of integration means that a number of conditions are necessary. They are the following:

1. Society's readiness to benevolently accept children with mental and physical disabilities into the surroundings of the normally developing
2. The countrywide improvement of the diagnostic system
3. Promoting the opportunity for every child with special needs to be educated according to an individual plan based on the assessment results
4. The creation of conditions for vocational and professional training of the pupils integrated into regular schools

Experiments on integrating separate groups and single students (deaf and hard of hearing in particular) have been done since the 1950s and continue going on now. However, at the moment there are not sufficient grounds to speak about the better social adaptation, after leaving school, of students who were integrated into regular education compared with that of special school graduates. This circumstance is extremely important because integration in schooling should not be an end in itself. It may be considered a means of preparing for integration into the environment, a means of providing an independent active life.

Attempts are being made under the Ministry of Social Security to overcome the segregation in residential homes of the profoundly mentally retarded. There are now possibilities for the inmates of these homes to stay the weekend with their family to learn more about their surroundings.

The Future Development of the Special System of Education

Despite having taken into consideration the idea of educational integration of children with development disabilities, its attractiveness for parents and undoubted progressiveness, we think that the conditions existing in Russia at the present time are not favorable for widespread introduction of the integration approach. The better provision for children with special needs in the near future should be connected, first of all, with the improvement of the distinct institutions. In addition, the curricula of special schools must be aimed more at the students' socialization, their practical training for everyday life, and less at the general education level corresponding to the contents of the regular school education. Such work has been already started.

At the same time, where it is possible to provide developmentally disabled children's education in the general system with qualified staff, such attempts, as an experiment, should be made. It is also most expedient to apply integrated education to such groups that up to now have been pedagogically neglected. These groups are children of an early age and preschoolers.

Today counseling centers are being organized to assess young children in need of special help. Specialists there will work out the individual plans for teaching and maintaining family education. These programs will allow children to stay with their families, prepare them for future schooling, and make school education more effective.

There is also a plan to widen the system of preschool groups, for children with mental and physical disabilities, attached to normal kindergartens. This will make it possible to do remedial work with these children, while keeping them in everyday contact with normally developing children of their age-group.

Another development in promoting wider integration is the creation of a network of day rehabilitation centers for profoundly mentally handicapped persons and a gradual reduction of the number of residential homes with twenty-four-hour care.

The main goal of the near future is the highest possible enrollment of all children and youngsters in need of help into the system of special pedagogical and psychological support. Considerable difficulties in improving help for children with special needs are connected with the insufficiently developed and incomplete legislation in this field and the limited state financial resources.

It is very important for the development of the integration process to work out special regulations concerning the rights of children and adults with special needs and to involve the mass media in the work of removing prejudices against the disabled and advocating their rights.

17

Czechoslovakia

MARIE CERNÁ

Since the end of World War II, the growth of special education in Czecho-slovakia has been phenomenal. The number of students served in the past forty-five years has increased to more than twelve times the original number.

Forty years of Marxist-Leninist educational ideas left Czechoslovakia with a residue of concepts that focused on individual defects in special education. Current practices reflect allegiance to the concept of disontogenesis or defective development. Guided by defectology, professionals emphasize a deficit model, or what is wrong with the child.[1] However, the recent opening to Western ideas and the presence of visiting scholars and teachers from Western Europe and the United States exposed special education, all at once, to the fruit of decades of research and innovative thinking. One can expect that it will take some time for Czech and Slovak educators to filter and absorb the wealth of ideas, and then to see changes reflected in the special education system.

The present trend emphasizes the value of every individual with impairment or handicap, the discovery of the abilities of each, and the development of each person's capacities. The goals of special education are socialization, normaliza-tion, integration into society, and emancipation, in order to incorporate the handicapped into the world of work and social activity.

About the Author • Dr. Marie Cerná is vice-dean for Foreign Relations at the Pedagogical Faculty of Charles University, Prague, Czechoslovakia. She has been a classroom teacher, held various academic and administrative posts at Charles University, and has worked exten-sively with the Czechoslovakian Ministry of Education. Her extensive publication and edito-rial contributions include monographs; specialized articles in collections of papers; textbooks for primary, secondary schools, and higher education; presentations at international confer-ences; reviews of textbooks and specialized publications; entries in specialized dictionaries; curricula for special schools; and methodological guidelines for teachers in special education.

Prevalence of Exceptional Conditions

In Czechoslovakia, knowledge about the many exceptional conditions that affect children has been steadily increasing. It covers a great variety of prenatal, perinatal, and postnatal conditions, some of which are already controlled, abolished, or minimized, due to improved nutrition, health care, and sanitation. Some new problems are arising, the consequences of poor environments. Improved health and social services, on the other hand, have led to a higher survival rate of handicapped infants and to prolonged life for handicapped people who otherwise would have met an early death.

It is difficult to define the prevalence of exceptional conditions since figures vary according to age groups, to the respective category of handicapped persons, and especially to the various definitions of handicap given from different viewpoints. The most common estimate used in the current literature cites a distribution of between 3 and 15 percent of handicapping conditions among the general population. More precise data exists on the school-age population. Presently, approximately 4 percent of children ages six to fifteen are enrolled in special schools. This statistic represents a sample of more than one hundred thousand students. Table 17.1 provides enrollment information on these students according to type of exceptionality and the kind of school attended.

Estimates indicate that over 15 percent of the school-age population has some kind of learning difficulty. This group of students has a high prevalence of handicapping conditions. Many of these students are emotionally handicapped as well. For the most part, they attend special classes within ordinary schools. At the present time, an unusually high number of multiple handicaps exists within the handicapped population, supposedly because of

TABLE 17.1. Students Enrolled in Special Education Schools in Czechoslovakia

Exceptionality	Type of School				
	Kindergarten	Elementary[a]	Secondary[b]	Vocational	Auxiliary
Mentally handicapped	1,603	59,284	—	16,257	1,112
Hearing impaired	322	1,902	101	560	—
Speech impaired	128	535	—	—	—
Visually handicapped	177	905	272	313	—
Multiply handicapped	9	375	—	—	115
Physically handicapped	5,093	828	222	545	—
Health impaired	5,093	11,504	—	—	—
Total	7,455	75,333	596	17,675	1,236

Note: Figures reported as of 15 September 1990.

[a] Elementary schools serve children in grades 1–9.

[b] Secondary schools include polytechnical, pedagogical, and academic high schools.

an increasing number of children at risk—those who are born prematurely or those with birth disorders and nervous system disorders.

Identification of Exceptionalities

Children with exceptionalities are detected and identified as early as possible. Due to the relatively efficient health care system, pediatricians observe and assist in assuring all children's correct physical and mental development, look after their nutrition, and carry out vaccinations and other prophylactic measures. This includes handicapped infants, toddlers, and preschool-age children. Pediatricians seek out congenital defects, defects of genetic origin, chronic diseases, and other handicapping conditions. The handicapped child's somatic state and psychomotor development receive special attention. Early identification, as soon as a child manifests any exceptionality, increases the chance of normalization through corrective treatment and special education.

Due to the extensive network of preschool programs that serve children from age three to age six, professionals have an opportunity to identify children with special needs before they enter conventional schools. Frequently, youngsters in need of special education start directly in special kindergartens or special schools. If a teacher thinks a pupil already enrolled in a conventional elementary school has learning problems, a pediatrician and staff from the regional educational and psychological counseling center evaluate the child.

The identification and placement of a child in a special school utilizes a multidisciplinary team. Teachers, physicians, educators, university-trained paraprofessionals, parents, and other clinical specialists pool data to arrive at a decision. The primary judges, however, are the pediatrician and special educator, who have a close professional relationship.

Children recommended for special education are entered into a register by local or regional school authorities who then have the responsibility of providing the necessary services to the child and the family. Placement decisions are discussed with the parents, although their permission is not a prerequisite for admission.

Once admitted to a special school, attendance is mandatory. Upon enrollment, the student is observed consistently and performance is evaluated continuously in order to verify that the placement is appropriate. If warranted, a transfer to another special school or class is possible, but rarely is a learner returned to a conventional school. It is equally unlikely for an initial referral to occur at the secondary level. Upon completion of elementary schooling, students matriculate into special secondary schools that are differentiated according to the type of exceptionality and degree of impairment.

Psychologists provide individualized intellectual assessment. They also stress more informal procedures and techniques; qualitative differences are accentuated rather than quantitative indicators. This emphasis probably underscores the long-standing Soviet bias toward intelligence testing. Psychological assessment, together with the quality and character of responses in a testing situation, aims at gaining insight into a student's abilities.

Greater importance granted to the personality of the youngster and his or her social environment also distinguishes psychodiagnostics. Projective techniques, in-depth classroom observation, interpretations of overt behavior, and analysis of responses to situations of daily living are common elements of the evaluation process.

Pedagogical and psychological advisory centers single out children for attendance at special schools. These centers provide diagnoses of the handicapped children, suggest suitable educational measures, and direct the special pedagogical prescription. They also offer advisory services to handicapped children, their parents and their teachers, and cooperate with authorities and other organizations to improve the educational environment of handicapped children.

Labeling the Handicapped Population

Some specific terms (as defined by Sovak 1984) used in special education in Czechoslovakia are the following:

1. *Defect* refers to impairment—or lack of something necessary for a healthy life—or a shortage of substances necessary for full health.
2. *Defectiveness* is the reflection of the defect into the social sphere.
3. *Defective person* is one who suffers from defectiveness, not only from his or her defect.
4. *Defectology* is a term used for the science that studies defective persons and is the theory behind special education. Defectology in Czechoslovakia investigates the causes, aspects, and substance of the respective impairments, the impact of the defect on the personality of the handicapped person, and the social consequences of the defect.
5. *Special education* refers to the science concerned with the development and education of handicapped persons. Defectology is the basis for special education; its object is the defective person. The goals, then, of special education are the educational methods and the types of care given to handicapped persons.

A categorical approach traditionally labels students with exceptionalities. It recognizes the following categories: speech impairment, hearing impairment, visual impairment, physical handicap, health impairment, mental handicap, learning disability, and multiple handicaps. Categorization serves administrative purposes as well as health, social, and educational care services.

The Social Context of Special Education

Society at present faces a difficult economic situation, and achieving all the changes is necessarily a lengthy process. Special education is the process of the stimulation and development of individual aspects of the exceptional personality. Changes in views of exceptionality, as well as in the perception of handicapped people in society, reflect the political, social, and cultural changes following the democratic revolution in 1989. New ideas of democratization and humanity are finding their way into education in general. Special education is a paramount part of that process.

Many challenges to improvement exist in the social context of special education. These include public attitudes and forms of behavior that demean handicapped people and deny them opportunities to contribute to the community, and inadequate local support for children, youth, and adults with handicaps, and for their families. There is also an overreliance on isolated institutional care.

Legislation

Czechoslovakia has a long tradition of providing for children with exceptionalities. The Empire Law of 1869 legally ensured care for the handicapped. According to this legislation, the educational upbringing of abnormal youth was the responsibility of the individual countries.

In the last part of the nineteenth century, the Ministry of Culture and Education mandated inauguration of institutions for the sensory impaired. Wherever such institutions were absent, children were guaranteed an education in the local schools. In 1890, Moravia established legislation that extended the Ministry's decree and thus became the first country in Europe to care fully for all deaf-and-dumb children.

With the establishment of the Czechoslovak Republic in 1918, the new government confronted a disunited service delivery system. Accordingly, several measures and resolutions were aimed at remedying the situation. Highlights of this era included a 1919 statute on qualification of directors of institutions; legislation, in 1929, stipulating that education for children with mental retardation should last for eight years; and ordinances establishing preschool education for severely handicapped pupils and kindergartens for sensory-impaired students. Regulations concerning teacher training were formulated in 1937.

Upon conclusion of the Second World War, several significant events affecting special education transpired: teacher training institutions were established in Prague and Bratislava and the Education Act of 1948 was passed. As a result of this legislation, schools and institutions for the handicapped came under state control and became part of a united educational system. The government, therefore, became responsible for the education of all children.

The Education Act of 1960 stipulated that children with disabilities must receive an obligatory elementary or secondary education, and opportunity for professional training. Compulsory education for the handicapped was also prolonged. Other resolutions and decrees of this period provided the special needs learner with textbooks, teaching materials, and other supplies, such as wheelchairs and hearing aids, free of any costs. New kindergartens were established for preschoolers with disabilities; attention focused also on secondary and professional training for young adults with exceptionalities.

The 1970s witnessed many new initiatives in special education. These new conceptions called for further differentiation in the schooling and education of handicapped students. The Education Acts of 1978 prolonged compulsory education for the exceptional student to ten years—eight years of primary education, two years of secondary training—and provided a legal framework for the new concepts in special education.

The Constitution of the Czechoslovak "Socialist" Republic guaranteed for all youth the right to health care and education and for all citizens the right to work and to social welfare during sickness and old age. Implementation of those rights, however, was far from reality. Nevertheless, the government provided medical/health and social care that has been, with slight modifications, in existence until now.

The most recent enactment, the Education Act of 1989, promulgated alternative special schools and stressed the educational integration of the exceptional learner. This legislation is still under review and discussion, with goals for early implementation.

Policies

Political factors have important effects on public policy for the education of children with exceptionalities. This policy, interrelated with social and economic situations in the country, influences also the attitude of the public toward people with handicaps and the delivery of special education services.

After the revolution in 1989, prevalent ideas stressing democracy and humanity as a philosophical postulate for everyday life permeated the education of the new generation. Acceptance of the Declaration of Human Rights in general includes also acceptance of the rights of people with exceptionalities, as many newly developed projects and programs for the benefit of this segment of society demonstrate.

Various voluntary organizations offer special services for children, youth, and adults, and for families with exceptional children. Mass media, especially television, frequently inform people about the problems of persons with handicaps. Although the current policy is more favorable for people with exceptionalities, urgent needs remain. We must develop a positive vision of how people could lead more fulfilling lives; provide a policy framework to promote local changes; and promote coalitions of interest among public agencies, professional staff, and relevant voluntary organizations. We must also establish advice, consultancy, and training resources to support local initiatives, develop partnerships between professionals and parents of children with exceptionalities, and ensure normalization and integration.

Teachers, Schools, Curriculum and Pedagogy

The preparation of special education teachers is a crucial element in a unified national plan for delivering services to exceptional children. Charles University in Prague inaugurated special education teacher training in 1953. The general education faculty trained students in the areas of mental retardation, sensory impairments, and physical disabilities. Presently three universities in Czechoslovakia—Charles University, Prague; Palacky University, Olomouc; and Comenius University, Bratislava—prepare teachers of exceptional children.

Students major in either psychopedics, related to mental handicaps and learning disabilities, or logopedics, related to speech impairment. Specialization continues with another area of exceptionality, such as visual impairment, hearing impairment, physical handicaps, or social maladjustment. Students are not prepared to teach gifted children. Special education teachers are initially prepared as generalists with specialization occurring through advanced studies and in-service training. A new concept of studies being implemented at present is to divide special education studies into two streams: special education sciences and education of teachers for special schools.

The department of social welfare establishes institutions for children and youth with severe physical and mental handicaps. They receive lodging, clothing, education, and health care, as well as preparation for employment, and training for simple jobs. Institutions are frequently renovated castles, spas, and châteaus. Such facilities illustrate the "out-of-sight, out-of-mind" concept—it was the ideology of the Communists to say that under socialism everyone was much happier, satisfied, and without problems, so they put the handicapped people far from view. Institutions provide services on a daily, weekly, or year-round basis. Institutes of social care are also categorized according to the chronological age of the residents—ages three to twenty-five, and older than twenty-five.

Special schools have been established to educate children and youth with impairments of hearing, sight, or speech; physically handicapped children; children with multiple defects; children with mental retardation; and children with behavioral disorders and impaired learning capacity. These schools exist at the levels of kindergarten, basic school, secondary vocational school, specialized secondary school, and gymnasium.

The differentiated curricula accommodate the students' health defects and equates their upbringing and education as nearly as possible with the corresponding type at ordinary schools. Special schools differ from schools for nonhandicapped children by their classroom arrangement, by the lower number of students per class, by more demanding didactic techniques, by a slower pace of instruction, and by curriculum adaptation affording a chance to modify teaching schedules and lengthen school attendance.

Although all children are guaranteed an education, and attendance is compulsory, education for the handicapped child is not viewed as a right, but rather as a duty. With the demise of the National Committee structure after the Velvet Revolution, the responsibility for educating the exceptional student resides with the local and regional authorities in the republics. These administrators, therefore, are charged with maintaining the educational system for handicapped children and youth. The present plan educates exceptional students in special schools wherein they are categorized according to handicapping conditions and chronological age. There are 1,355 schools incorporating almost 9,000 segregated classrooms for children with special needs in the Czechoslovakia, as shown in table 17.2.

Providing residents with a protective environment perhaps best describes the majority of institutions. Childcare workers, some of whom have minimal training, such as only a two-week course, provide direct care. Higher functioning residents frequently assist intellectually less mature counterparts with their daily tasks. Teachers follow a curriculum especially designed for an institutionalized population, but the instructors generally are not university graduates.

TABLE 17.2. Schools for Exceptional Learners in Czechoslovakia

| Exceptionality | Type of School | | | | |
	Kindergarten	Elementary[a]	Secondary[b]	Vocational	Auxiliary
Mentally handicapped	79	624	—	105	23
Hearing impaired	15	21	2	7	—
Speech impaired	6	10	—	—	—
Visually handicapped	6	11	6	2	—
Multiply handicapped	1	4	—	—	2
Physically handicapped	8	8	5	5	—
Health impaired	148	257	—	—	—
Total	263	935	13	119	25

Source: Gargiulo and Cerná. 1992.

Note: Figures reported as of 15 September 1990.

[a] Elementary schools serve children in grades 1–9.

[b] Secondary schools include polytechnical, pedagogical, and academic high schools.

Residents also receive services from nurses, physical therapists, and speech-language therapists in addition to daily visits from physicians. The resident-to-professional staff ratio varies. At some sites residents enjoy a 4 to 1 ratio, while at other locations a 12 to 1 ratio is common. Consequently, the quality of services delivered to the residents fluctuates greatly, as does the physical condition of the institutions themselves. Many of the facilities show the neglect of the past four decades.

Both professionals and the general public exhibit a great deal of reluctance to explore alternative community living arrangements. The philosophy of normalization has few supporters. These circumstances, too, probably reflect forty years of professional isolation. In some isolated instances, enlightened administrators have attempted to integrate residents into the surrounding communities.

Vocational preparation or work education is a subject of great emphasis. One of the purposes of special education is to produce skilled workers for particular jobs in the work force. Hence, in the lower elementary grades, stress is put on the value and importance of work. Special education students can and should contribute to society. Select vocations are available depending on the individual's exceptionality and degree of impairment. As an illustration, a young adult with mental retardation might train as a bricklayer, a student with visual impairments could attend a university, and a person with physical handicaps could prepare for a career as a tailor or dressmaker.

The social development of the student with exceptionalities is also a focal point of special education. Viewed as full members of the community, students are exposed, early and continuously, to art, music, literature, and the theater. Aesthetics education introduces the pupil to the cultural aspects of society. It is part of the daily curriculum as well as the purpose of many after-school clubs and organizations.

Major Controversies and Issues in Special Education

One of the major tasks for special education today is the integration of handicapped students into a regular classroom setting. The educational system for learners with special needs is highly differentiated and segregated. Gargiulo and Cerná (1992) have observed the general assumption, voiced by many educators, that the child with exceptionalities should be educated in segregated environments. This viewpoint most likely reflects the allegiance to the Soviet concept of disontogenesis or defective development, wherein a child's defects or deficits are emphasized rather than inherent strengths.

Since special education has been isolated, the question of mainstreaming only now is at the forefront of discussion. This policy has generated a diversity of responses from parents, teachers, and administrators. Whereas some people see it as progressive and possessing substantive benefits for the children concerned, others express a completely opposite point of view. Some professionals express skepticism and resist the idea of educating students with exceptionalities in an integrated environment. Many view such a plan as counterproductive and contrary to the perceived success of the present system of schooling. A growing number of professionals, however, welcome the notion, and have become advocates for its implementation.

Special teachers are not prepared to work in integrated environments, and teachers of ordinary classes are not prepared to accept handicapped students in the classroom. This is a challenge for the future education of teachers. In addition, general social policy has not yet fully adopted the principle of normalization. Few possibilities exist for community-based living arrangements, employment, or recreation. It is not fully accepted that handicapped people are entitled to the same rights as others and to as normal a lifestyle as possible.

Czechoslovakia faces a difficult economic situation. Finding ways to deal with issues of special education at a time when wider changes are occurring in social attitudes and forms of public administration, greatly complicates all the tasks.

Emerging and Future Trends

Special education in Czechoslovakia has had a rich tradition. Especially between the world wars, special education played a significant role both within the educational system and in educational theory. Special education based on democratic principles was developed on biological and philosophical bases by professionals from various fields: education, medicine, psychology, and sociology. The interdisciplinary approach and the complexity in education are the leading principles in special education theory and practice at the present and in the near future.

Improving the quality of lives for handicapped people is connected with the development of a positive vision of how people could lead more fulfilling lives by implementing ideas of integration and normalization. This is an emerging trend that should be realized through the implementation of innovative ideas.

Improvement of governmental policy toward the handicapped; of medical, social, and educational services; and of progressive legislation on one hand, should be accompanied by the development of alternative systems on the other. This is a role mainly assumed by voluntary organizations for the benefit of the handicapped. At present, the role of voluntary organizations in special education is becoming important. For example, the Psychopedia Association was founded in 1990. Its members are teachers at special schools, and parents and friends of people with mental handicaps and learning disabilities. The association opened an evening school in September 1991 to meet the needs of people over eighteen who had left school early or who had been excluded from obligatory school attendance. The curriculum content focuses on social behavior and skills, education for citizenship, and self-advocacy. After a trial period, hopes are that the school will become part of the special education system.

A Final Thought

As Czechoslovakia moves toward the twenty-first century and confronts the myriad changes after the Velvet Revolution, services to and the needs of citizens with mental retardation must not be forgotten or ignored. Although much is being done—with limited personnel and financial resources—on behalf of mentally retarded individuals, many issues remain that require attention. Topics worthy of consideration by parents and professionals include the following:

1. Changing the public's perception of and attitude toward their fellow citizens with mental retardation. A change in attitude must precede changes in the delivery of services to mentally retarded persons.
2. Increasing parental involvement and participation in the education of their child. Parents are potentially an untapped resource for professionals. Several countries, such as Switzerland, Great Britain, and Italy are experimenting with various strategies for enhancing parental involvement.
3. Mandating the integration of students with mental retardation into mainstream academic environments. This policy requires thoughtful and deliberate consideration. The least restrictive environment for children and young adults with mental retardation may not always be the most appropriate.
4. Adopting the principle of normalization as a social policy. People with mental retardation should have the right to as typical a lifestyle as possible, especially as it pertains to schooling, employment possibilities, and recreational/social opportunities.

To be sure, political, practical, and economic obstacles may hinder the implementation of the foregoing goals. However, these issues remain worthy endeavors and could improve the quality of life for youth and adults with mental retardation in Czechoslovakia.

Note

1. Terms used in this paper reflect the transitional state of thinking and writing about special education in Czechoslovakia. Terminology reflects both the philosophy and attitude of the previous forty years, with references to defectology and handicapped children as opposed to healthy children. Recent contacts with Western European and North American educators have opened the way to new ideas and new terminology. But it will take some time before these are generally accepted and used by Czech and Slovak educators.

References

Economic aspects of special education: Czechoslovakia, New Zealand and United States of America. 1978. Geneva: UNESCO.

The educational system of the CSFR. 1992. Prague: Institute for Information in Education.

Gargiulo, R. M., and Cerná, M. 1992. Special education in Czechoslovakia: Characteristics and issues. *International Journal of Special Education.* 7:60–70.

Sovak, M. 1984. *Narys specialne pedagogiky* (Introduction to Special Education). Prague: SPN.

18

Hong Kong

NICK CRAWFORD

MARK BRAY

*T*he territory of Hong Kong comprises the island of Hong Kong, a number of other islands, and part of the Chinese mainland. The island of Hong Kong became a British colony in 1842. The territory was subsequently enlarged by addition of sections of the mainland and neighboring islands. The greatest enlargement occurred in 1898 when colonial authorities took a ninety-nine-year lease of an area known as the New Territories. The implications of this lease, which would require the reversion of Hong Kong to Chinese sovereignty in 1997, were perhaps underestimated at the time. Because in the twentieth century the boundaries between the New Territories and the rest of Hong Kong had become totally indistinct, it became clear to negotiators in the 1980s that sovereignty of the whole territory would revert, including those parts that had been ceded "in perpetuity" (Cheng 1986; Cheng and Kwong 1992; Kwan and Chan 1986).

It was decided in 1984 that Hong Kong would remain a British colony until 1997 and then become a Special Administrative Region (SAR) of the

About the Authors • Nick Crawford is a senior lecturer in the Department of Education at the University of Hong Kong, where he set up the first local M.Ed. program in special education. He has taught in ordinary schools and in a range of special schools, was a school principal and, for six years, was associate director of the British Institute of Mental Handicap. He has been a consultant in special education to the British Council, UNDP, and UNESCO. His research and publications are in the areas of curriculum development and staff training. • Mark Bray is a professor and head of the Department of Education at the University of Hong Kong. He previously taught in secondary schools in Kenya and Nigeria and at the Universities of Edinburgh, Papua New Guinea, and London. He specializes in comparative education and has written over a dozen books and many articles.

People's Republic of China. However, the arrangement preserves considerable autonomy for the government of Hong Kong. With particular reference to education, the Basic Law states:

> On the basis of the previous educational system, the Government of the Hong Kong Special Administrative Region shall, on its own, formulate policies on the development and improvement of education, including policies regarding the educational system and its administration, the language of instruction, the allocation of funds, the examination system, the system of academic awards and the recognition of educational qualifications. (Hong Kong/China 1990, 47)

The population of Hong Kong is approximately six million. Almost 98 percent are Chinese, for the majority of whom Cantonese is the mother tongue. Among the remainder, the largest groups are from the Philippines, the United Kingdom, the United States, and the Indian subcontinent. Most primary schooling and much secondary schooling is conducted in Cantonese, even though the majority of secondary schools are officially English-medium.

Economically, Hong Kong is well known for its recent high rates of growth. In company with Taiwan, South Korea, and Singapore, Hong Kong is known as one of the four Asian Dragons. In 1991, Hong Kong had an estimated per capita GDP of U.S.$14,100 (Hong Kong 1992, 399). Economic growth has greatly facilitated expansion of education of all types, including special education.

Structure and Financing of Education

The structure of formal education is shown in figure 18.1. Primary schooling begins at the age of six and lasts for six years. Maximum class size is 45 pupils in ordinary classes, or 35 pupils in classes with activity methods. About 40 percent of classes in primary 1 to 3 use activity methods. The typical primary school has twenty-four classes and a pupil-teacher ratio of 26 to 1. Each teacher specializes in three subjects; any class on an average school day would be taught by two to four different teachers.

Secondary schools offer a five-year course in the broad range of academic subjects leading to the Hong Kong Certificate of Education Examination (HKCEE). The majority of institutions are grammar schools, though some are technical or prevocational schools. Secondary teachers usually specialize in one or two subjects, so each class is likely to be taught by six or more different teachers a week. The typical secondary school has twenty-four to thirty classes, with about forty pupils per class. HKCEE candidates may enter a two-year sixth-form course leading to the Advanced Level Examination to prepare for admission to the universities and polytechnics.

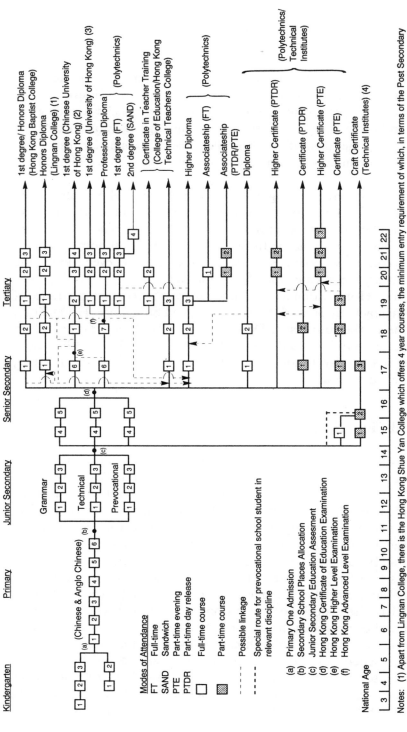

Figure 18.1 The Hong Kong education system.
Source: Hong Kong, Education Department. 1992. *Annual summary 1991–92* (Hong Kong: Education Department).

TABLE 18.1. Institutions and Enrollment, by Level, Hong Kong, 1991–92

	Institutions				Enrollment			
	Govt.	Aided	Private	Total	Govt.	Aided	Private	Total
Kindergarten	—	—	791	791	—	—	201,750	201,750
Primary	50	554	82	686	34,112	449,079	51,259	534,450
Secondary	40	310	81	431	36,654	318,695	82,946	438,295
Special education	—	71	—	71	208	7,976	—	8,184
Colleges of education	4	—	—	4	2,351	—	—	2,351
Approved postsecondary	—	—	2	2	—	—	—	5,049
Adult education	—	—	111	111	—	—	28,074	28,074

Source: Education Department, Hong Kong. 1992.

At the primary level, about 6 percent of pupils attend government schools, 84 percent attend government-aided institutions, and 10 percent attend private schools (see table 18.1). Comparable figures for the secondary level are 8 percent, 73 percent, and 18 percent. Whereas most of the private primary schools are prestigious institutions, at the secondary level many have low status and cater to pupils unable to gain places in government or aided schools and who are likely to be low achievers.

In recent years, education has generally consumed between 15 and 20 percent of the total government budget, and around 3 percent of GDP (Chung and Wong 1992). Within the education sector, expenditure on primary education has consumed about 30 percent of the total, with slightly more being devoted to secondary education. Because Hong Kong is compact, the government avoids what it would cost to administer education in a large area. The government also devotes very little money to adult education.

In 1971, the government introduced compulsory education at the primary level. This was extended in 1978, and education is now compulsory to the end of secondary form 3 or age 15. Schooling is free of charge in government and aided schools up to the end of form 3.

Prevalence of Exceptional Conditions

Special education broadly consists of segregated categorical special school provision for about .7 percent of the school population, special classes for partially hearing and partially sighted pupils, and a range of services provided on- and off-site for those with special needs. Hong Kong's provision for special needs has undergone changes in the 1980s and 1990s. Planners have attempted to bridge the gap between the rhetoric of integration and equal opportunities and the elitism built into the school system, which organizes all primary school graduates into five "ability" bands in the secondary phase.

The 20 percent figure in the United Kingdom suggested by Warnock (DES 1978) as the basis of planning for special needs populations may be compared with the 14 percent figure estimated for Hong Kong by the Education Commission (1990, 25). However, this lower figure may be an underestimate of the number of children experiencing difficulties in schools, since additional problems are faced by immigrants from China and by many Cantonese-speaking students in English-medium secondary schools. The switch from Cantonese at the secondary level is said to contribute to the significant number of over-age pupils (Crawford 1991, 49).

The Education Commission's Fourth Report identified seven categories of students in need of special provision (Education Commission 1990, 25). These are students physically disabled (including deaf and blind); mentally handicapped; maladjusted (including emotionally disturbed); academically unmotivated; with severe learning difficulties; academically less able; and academically gifted.

The government estimates disabled persons to number about 270,000 (Health and Welfare Branch 1991). Figures for 1990, for seven types of disability, excluding the mentally ill, are shown in table 18.2.

The prevalence estimate for children with hearing impairment is based on the number of cases registered with Central Registry for Rehabilitation (CRR) plus a margin of 30 percent for those ages birth or five to eleven years and a margin of 8.7 percent for school-age children. The latter margin is the annual growth rate of hearing impairments on the CRR database. For those with visual impairments, the incidence rates recorded with CRR are used as prevalence rates. The prevalence rates per 10,000 for school-age children are 1.59 for the totally blind, .90 for those with severe low vision, and 4.20 for those with moderate low vision.

Prevalence rates for children with autistic features are based on enrollments and waiting lists for special child-care centers and special school places. The rate is set at 8 in 10,000 for planning purposes. A 1992 government document (Working Party 1992, 52) argued that the arrangement

TABLE 18.2.   Numbers of Disabled Persons, Hong Kong, 1990

Type of Disability	Estimated Number
Hearing impaired	12,369
Visually impaired	14,777
Autistic children	1,056
Mentally handicapped	113,667
Slow learning	33,015
Maladjusted	6,820
Physically disabled	66,390
Total	248,094

Source: Health and Welfare Branch. 1991. Appendix 1.3.

through which autistic children receive education in special schools for the mentally handicapped should no longer be considered sufficient.

For those with mental handicaps, prevalence rates from overseas continue to be used despite frequent calls for local surveys. The three categories—severe (below IQ 25), moderate (IQ 25–49), and mild (IQ 50–69)—have respective prevalence rates per 1,000 of 1, 4, and 15. The government establishes a planning ratio which it modifies by an additional percentage to cover a "hidden demand rate." A 1991 publication stated that there should be enough places for all mentally handicapped school children in 1992–93 (Health and Welfare Branch 1991, chap. 9). However, similar statements had appeared in government estimates on a regular basis, and the lack of a local survey remained problematic.

There is insufficient research to estimate accurately the prevalence of maladjusted children, but the provision ratio of .2 percent is considerably below the incidence quoted in the United Kingdom Underwood Report from which Hong Kong has taken its official definition of maladjustment. Several local studies (e.g., Luk et al. 1991; Shek 1988) suggest that this figure is low.

Calculations of the prevalence of physical handicap are based on the number of persons registered on the Central Registry plus 9.26 percent, the annual average growth rate of physical disablements recorded between 1987 and 1990. For the school-age group those figures are shown in table 18.3.

Identification of Exceptionalities

The policy objective for rehabilitation is to "provide such comprehensive rehabilitation services as are necessary to enable disabled persons to develop their physical, mental and social capabilities to the fullest extent which their disabilities permit" (Hong Kong 1977, 7). A major area of concern is primary prevention and the early identification and treatment of disease in order to cure or reverse possible disabling conditions. Preventive measures include raising public awareness, providing screening services, improving immunization programs, reducing accidents, and promoting good health.

TABLE 18.3. Estimated Prevalence of Physical Handicaps, Hong Kong, 1990

Age Group	Number of Physically Handicapped Persons	Prevalence Rate (per 10,000)
5 yrs–5 yrs 11 mos	341	46.23
6 yrs–6 yrs 11 mos	2,501	53.13
12 yrs–15 yrs 11 mos	1,178	37.84

Genetic counseling is provided by pediatric units in all regional hospitals, and a Prenatal Diagnostic Service uses a variety of techniques including amniocentesis. Over 90 percent of births are delivered in hospitals, and all high-risk pregnancies are routinely referred to hospitals. Over 90 percent of newborn babies attend government maternal and child health centers at no charge as part of a Comprehensive Observation Scheme (COS) to identify congenital or acquired defects. Children are examined three times before preschool.

Of particular note in Hong Kong are two biochemical disorders that occur frequently and are identified in neonatal screening. The first is G-6-PD deficiency, an inherited metabolic disorder affecting 4.4 percent of males and .4 percent of females. Glucose-6-phosphate-dehydrogenase deficiency is the most common cause of neonatal jaundice and may lead to damage of the central nervous system. Early diagnosis, therefore, is particularly important for male neonates.[1] The second disorder is congenital hypothyroidism, which affects 1 in every 3,220 births. A screening program is routinely provided for all babies born in government hospitals, endowed hospitals and maternity homes as part of comprehensive health care.

Immunization programs for the major infectious diseases are offered for infants. In order to prevent rubella complications during pregnancy, all teenage girls are offered immunization. Hepatitis B is a major problem and in 1988 a vaccination program that was previously available only to babies born to carrier mothers became available to all newborns. It has been proposed to extend this vaccination program those who work with mentally handicapped people.

Special Education Services Centers (SESC), under the aegis of the government's Education Department, receive referrals from COS via the Health Department, as well as referrals from parents and voluntary agencies providing rehabilitation services. All children in primary grade 1 are screened to identify moderate and severe learning problems requiring full assessment and to assist schools with at-risk children. Classroom teachers are central to this procedure since they complete observation checklists to identify children for further examination. In the 1989–90 screening program, 6.3 percent of primary 1 pupils required speech therapy, 4.8 percent required follow-up ophthalmic services, 6 to 7 percent were identified as having learning problems, and about 4 percent required individual audiological assessment.

Psychological services provide diagnostic and remedial services for children with learning and behavior problems, and advice to parents and teachers. Psychologists in the Special Education Section of the Education Department provide individual assessment on the degree of mental handicap (mild, moderate, or severe) and on the nature of learning difficulties. Psychologists make recommendations for placement in special schools, special classes, and resource classes.

The ratio of psychologists to pupils is 1 to 30,000, compared with 1 to 4,000 in the United Kingdom. In 1990, the Education Commission recommended improvement of the ratio to 1 to 12,000 pupils by 1997–98.

Labelling the Handicapped Population

Special schools are organized by category. The numbers both of categories and of children in special schools increased during the 1980s and early 1990s despite a stated policy of integration. In 1992, a Working Party on Rehabilitation Policies and Services recommended that the three categories of mental handicap should be changed to four in line with *DSM III*, the diagnostic and statistical manual of the American Psychiatric Association (1987).

The existing special school categories were blind, deaf, physically handicapped, maladjusted, mentally handicapped, and slow learners. The working party recommended addition of the categories *unmotivated* and *severe learning problems*. For the unmotivated group, three practical schools were recommended. Based on cases of nonattendance in secondary forms 1 to 3 (grades 7 to 9) in 1984–85, it was suggested that there were 2,000 such pupils. For those described as having severe learning problems such that they could not benefit from the ordinary curriculum, seven new special schools, called special opportunity schools, were recommended.

For the first time, the 1990 Education Commission report also recommended identification of and special provision for academically gifted pupils. Interestingly (and paradoxically), academically gifted pupils were to be retained in ordinary classes with teachers encouraged to "experiment with and improve their current teaching" (50). However, unmotivated pupils and those with serious learning problems were to be placed in special schools, rather than receive a curricula to match their interests and abilities, implemented by ordinary classroom teachers. This raised the question of whether it is only students with a high social value who have a right to a curriculum that matches their interests and abilities (Potts 1991).

Children in the mainstream who used to be labeled mildly mentally handicapped, maladjusted, or slow learning are now collectively termed *children with learning difficulties*. Despite the change in labeling, which accompanied the removal of segregated special classes for the three groups mentioned, categorical teacher training has continued.

The Social Context of Special Education

The special school system has generally operated parallel to and independently of the mainstream system. All special schools are aided, sponsored by voluntary agencies, and endowed by government. Placement within special schools or special classes (which exist only in government schools) is organized by the educational psychologists of the Special Education Section of the Education Department.

The development of special education has followed a sequence typical of many countries, commencing with provision for the sensory impaired for whom the first school was established in 1935. Provision for groups of handicapped children since publication of the 1977 White Paper has more than doubled in special schools, even though the title of the paper was "Integrating the Disabled into the Community."

In 1960 the Education Department established a Special Schools Section to regulate the special schools run by different voluntary agencies. A 1963 report underlined the importance of normalization for handicapped children. It stated that handicapped children should mix with normal children and claimed that "handicapped children require as normal a form of education as possible" (Marsh and Sampson 1963, 78).

The 1976 Hong Kong government's Green Paper, entitled "The Further Development of Rehabilitation Services in Hong Kong," pointed out that the disabled could "provide a useful and productive source of manpower." It argued for expansion of services to the disabled, not primarily on the grounds of human rights but rather on the grounds of finance: "Every dollar spent on rehabilitation . . . returns anywhere from 17 to 35 dollars to the economy" (1).

While the rhetoric of the West was for greater integration in the 1970s and 1980s, Hong Kong was still attempting to ensure that all teachers were trained and that all children of compulsory school age had a school place in a government or aided school. Even in the early 1990s, neither of these goals had been achieved. Refinements and adjustments to facilitate integration of special needs children usually occur in the context of a professionally trained teaching workforce and effective supporting networks. While it is often easier to integrate pupils with sensory impairments once access to the curriculum has been resolved, pupils with other handicaps may pose greater problems.

The traditional view of individual deficits as explanations for placement in special education still prevails. Indeed, even the new categories of special needs proposed in the Education Commission's 1990 Report, such as *less able* and *unmotivated,* maintain the focus on within-child problems. Removal of pupils who present difficulties in schools maintains the idea that special education is for those who are deficient or who have deficits. It reduces the likelihood (and the need) for curriculum reform and for review of definitions of achievement.

Even the apparently different concept of special educational needs introduced by Warnock, which dispensed with the medically oriented categories of the 1944 Education Act in the United Kingdom and which was broadly taken up in Hong Kong, still sees the individual as having the problem. Although the United Kingdom's 1981 Education Act separated disability from problems in education, it constructed the category of special educational needs. Similarly in Hong Kong, the social construction of the unmotivated pupil could be described as a disabling policy. Maintenance of an elitist system with pupils banded by ability and allocated to schools that then also stream pupils by internal examinations makes it difficult for children with a wide range of differences to be integrated.

Legislation and Policy

There is no separate legislation for special education, and it is through a Code of Aid for special schools (Education Department 1990), which deals with grant support, that the organization and resources of special schools and classes are regulated. Periodic regulations and guidelines from the Education Department set patterns of new provision and recommend forms of service, staffing, and organization. The main policy-making bodies are the Education Department and the Rehabilitation Development Coordinating Committee, which was formed in 1977 to coordinate government departments and nongovernmental agencies. The Education Commission is a major advisory body established in 1984.

In 1976, a government working group produced a ten-year Programme Plan for Rehabilitation Services, including special education. It was published in the Green Paper of that year, and contained the group's main findings and recommendations. It also contained government acknowledgements of the inadequacy of services for the handicapped, and of the need for partnership: "Government will have to provide some of the proposed additional services direct, but it must continue to rely on the support of the voluntary sector which has to date played a major and pioneering role in the provision of rehabilitation services in Hong Kong" (Hong Kong 1976, 2). This document set the formal framework for government policy on special education and rehabilitation. Paradoxically, however, the policy headed "Integrating the Disabled" set out a program to increase segregated special schools and special classes. The target figures in the 1977 White Paper were twelve thousand special school places and fourteen thousand special class places by 1985–86. Those figures were not achieved, and in 1993 there were about eight thousand places in special schools and less than two hundred places in special classes.

The concept of special educational needs, central to the United Kingdom's 1981 Education Act, has strongly influenced policy in Hong Kong. Education Department information handouts referring to "pupils who suffer from any disability of mind and body" (taken from Section 8 (2) of the United Kingdom's 1944 Education Act) were changed in 1985 to match Section 2 (1) of the 1981 Act by referring to special needs. The removal of special classes, and the substitution of categorical labels such as *mildly mentally handicapped, slow learner,* and *maladjusted* in the mainstream by the term *children with learning difficulties (CWLD)* reflected the Education Department's intention to conform with practice in the United Kingdom and meet more special needs through the mainstream.

Following publication of the report of a working party reviewing secondary special classes (Education Department 1981), it was decided to close all special classes except for those pupils with partial sight or partial hearing. At the time of the 1981 survey, there were four types of special class in ordinary schools: partially sighted (with 80 pupils), partially hearing (282), slow learning (4,822), and maladjusted (546). The working party surveyed attitudes of the head teachers of thirty-seven schools operating special classes, the teachers in both the ordinary classes and special classes, and parents and pupils. The report claimed that special class pupils were not integrating well, and that pupils of special classes for maladjusted and slow learning pupils held particularly negative attitudes toward their placements. Although many ordinary teachers felt that special schools would be better for such pupils (that is, increased segregation), the report recommended that the highest priority be accorded to special needs within the mainstream.

A visiting panel of experts invited to review education in Hong Kong in 1981 also referred to special education. The team stated that prejudices, superstition, and stereotyping needed to be overcome: "A community which sees its disabled members as having flaws rather than needs . . . diminishes and impedes [not only] its disabled members, but also itself" (Llewellyn 1982, 80). To assist in the remedial work of both primary and secondary aided schools, additional teachers were approved in 1982. The following year a General Administrative Circular (no. 33/83) was sent to all schools announcing the reorganization of special educational provision for children with learning difficulties in the ordinary schools. The aim expressed in the circular was "to facilitate integration."

The title of the Education Commission's Report No. 4 (1990) highlighted a concern confronting the system: *The Curriculum and Behavioral Problems in Schools.* Two chapters of the report focused on special education provision, and four groups of students were identified: those with learning difficulty, those with severe learning difficulty, unmotivated, and academically gifted. The report (p. 44) recommended replacement of the existing Intensive Remedial Service (IRS) by a "school-based remedial support programme" to cater to the bottom 10 percent. Students with severe learning problems, and those said to be unmotivated, were to be placed in special schools. In complete contrast, the academically gifted students were to be supported by a resource team and center. Perhaps surprisingly, a subsequent Education Commission document (1992a) seemed to have markedly different views about unmotivated pupils: "Every school should help all its students, *whatever their level of ability*, and including those with special educational needs, to develop their potential as fully as possible in both academic and non-academic outcomes" (15, emphasis added).

Teachers, Schools, Curriculum, and Pedagogy

Teachers in special schools, special classes, and resource classes are required to take additional part-time training over a two-year period at one of the colleges of education. Specialist training provides two salary increments which are only payable as long as the teacher remains in special education.

The Education Commission Report No. 5 (Education Commission 1992b), which was largely concerned with teacher education, proposed that primary teachers should gradually be converted to graduate status by mounting in-service B.Ed. degrees, and that preservice B.Ed. degrees would be the long-term goal. The report referred cursorily to special education teachers, proposing that the two-year in-service specialist training be changed to a one-year full-time course for qualified teachers.

In the late 1980s as many as one in six teachers in special schools did not even have initial training, even though teachers were expected to have both initial and specialist training. In schools for the mentally handicapped, the position was more serious. Twenty-four percent of teachers had no initial training (Education Department 1989). Another survey showed that almost 60 percent of the teachers in schools for the mentally handicapped had spent less than five years in their present schools. Half of all teachers in these schools had less than five years in any special schools, and 24 percent had been in special schools for less than two years (Crawford, Lau, and Moynihan 1990). This would imply great difficulties in recruiting and retaining appropriate personnel and in staff and curriculum development. By comparison, 20.8 percent of teachers in primary and secondary schools had no initial teacher training.

An additional resource to raise the level of professional skills in special education has been through an M.Ed. degree (special educational needs) mounted since 1983. Since 1991, the program has been supplemented by a four-year part-time B.Ed. program in special needs available to any qualified teacher, whether in mainstream or special settings. Both programs are run by the University of Hong Kong.

Table 18.4 shows the number of special schools and the enrollments by type of handicap in 1992. Provision is made at the preparatory level for the blind, deaf, and physically handicapped, but not for children with other

TABLE 18.4.   Schools and Enrollment in Special Education, by Type of School and Type of Handicap, Hong Kong, 1992

Type of School	Type of Handicap	Enrollment by Level			
Special School[a] (N=74)		Preparatory (N=7)	Primary (N=70)	Secondary (N=59)	All Levels (N=74)
	Blind	14	82	60	156
	Deaf	37	246	319	602
	Physically handicapped	50	426	195	671
	Hospital schools (physically handicapped)	—	322	54	376
	Maladjusted and socially deprived	—	383	616	999
	Mentally handicapped	—	2,981	2,015	4,996
	Slow learning	—	—	294	294
	All types of handicaps	101	4,440	3,553	8,094
Special Class in Ordinary School (N=4)		Preparatory (N=0)	Primary (N=1)	Secondary (N=3)	All Levels (N=4)
	Partially sighted	—	25	31	56
	Partially hearing	—	38	69	107
	All types of handicaps	—	63	100	163
Total Enrollment in All Types of School		101	4,503	3,653	8,257

[a] The levels operated by the 74 special schools are as follows:

(I) One level only: 14 primary schools and 4 secondary schools.

(II) More than one level: 1 preparatory and primary school; 49 primary and secondary schools; and 6 preparatory, primary and secondary schools.

kinds of handicaps. By far the largest group is mentally handicapped pupils. Table 18.4 also shows the number of children in special classes in ordinary schools. These classes cater only to the partially sighted and the partially hearing.

No specific curriculum is required by the Education Department for its special schools. Some schools, such as those for the physically handicapped, deaf, and blind, base their curricula on the mainstream curriculum. Others, for example those for the mentally handicapped, base their curricula on guidelines issued by the Education Department, which allows considerable flexibility.

Major Controversies and Issues in Special Education

The closure of special classes in primary and secondary schools in the early 1980s in order to increase integration failed. Even though the move was accompanied by an increase in the number of teachers in schools who agreed to provide remedial education, the measures were insufficient to resource the special needs of students or schools. The complex and divisive issue of medium of instruction also continues unresolved. None of the changes so far have dealt effectively with the central issues facing the system, namely curriculum reform, school management, and staff development.

A fundamental problem faces the system at the secondary school level and exacerbates difficulties in learning. Pupils leaving primary schools are allocated a place in a secondary school on the basis of examination results, family connections (for example, brother attended the school), and geographical nets. Pupils are arranged in five "ability" bands, and allocated to schools. One in three secondary schools in the early 1980s was private, and insufficient government or aided schools were available for primary school graduates. As a result, the government bought places in private, profit-making secondary schools, and mainly band-5 pupils (the lowest achievers) were sent to them.

Ordinary teachers do not see children with learning difficulties as their problem. Status in teaching was and is associated with teaching subjects at a high level, and it is common for children with learning difficulties to be placed in the charge of junior teachers with little experience. Children receiving intensive help in primary resource classes are asked to sit the same end-of-term examinations as other children, and to participate in the same Secondary School Places Allocation System.

Although Hong Kong espouses Western rhetoric on the need to integrate students with special educational needs into ordinary schools, the system is organized on formal lines and operates as a sorting device. The success with which schools can integrate students with learning difficulties depends on the flexibility of the curriculum, the support networks within schools, and the support for schools, as much as on types and levels of disability and learning difficulty.

If "unmotivated" and other pupils cannot benefit from the common core curriculum, this situation calls for curricular reform. It is arguable that all children have the right to a balanced and broad-based curriculum and that all children have the right to be educated with their peers. The proposed separation of training for another group prevents special education getting on the agenda of school reform. The task is school improvement.

A further problem arises from the language of instruction. Students who have learning difficulties or who are unmotivated and are to be placed into separate special schools might well have fewer difficulties and be more highly motivated were they to be taught in Cantonese rather than English. The percentage of over-age pupils increases from 4 to 17 percent in six years of primary schooling, and reaches almost 30 percent in the final year of compulsory schooling (Crawford 1991). Such figures suggest that the removal of pupils from the secondary phase, the same pupils who (presumably) were unmotivated and had learning difficulties in primary schools, says more about the organization of secondary schools, medium of instruction, and the lack of support available to pupils and teachers than it does about the nature of excluded pupils.

There is considerable concern in the media about misbehavior and disaffection from school, even though, in comparison with other places, pupils in Hong Kong might appear obedient and well behaved. Student suicides have caused particular concern and have brought the grammar school curriculum, counseling, psychological support services, and the family into the arena for public debate.

The prospects of the reintegration of Hong Kong with the People's Republic of China in 1997 have also had an impact. Some families have been split because parents have lived abroad to gain foreign passports. Cultural influences from the West, in school, and in the media, coupled with a fragmenting of traditional Chinese values in an increasingly urban, modern, and industrialized community, have created an identity crisis for many Hong Kong Chinese.

In his 1992 address to the Legislative Council, the governor of Hong Kong made several proposals on education. Raising the standards in primary and secondary schools was top priority, with particular focus on individuality—arguably a fundamental difference from the People's Republic of China. "Children," the governor asserted, "are first and foremost individuals" (Patten 1992, 8). Strongly supporting the long-awaited policy review of rehabilitation services for disabled people contained in the 1992 Green Paper, "Equal Opportunities and Full Participation: A Better Tomorrow for All," the governor reflected not just concerns for the disabled. Creating equal opportunities for all children in schools means creating a context in which all children are equally valued. Hong Kong needs to be able to meet individual needs before it can successfully integrate those with special needs.

Note

1. Glucose-6-phosphate dehydrogenase is an enzyme involved in the glucose metabolism of red cells. Deficiency of G-6-PD (the most common inherited cell disorder) is particularly prevalent in Hong Kong males and is claimed to be the most common cause of neonatal jaundice and kernicterus, which may involve damage to the central nervous system. Certain drugs, such as prophylactic antimalarial dose of primaquine, bring about the degeneration of red cells that are deficient in G-6-PD.

References

American Psychiatric Association. 1987. *Diagnostic and Statistical Manual of Mental Disorders: DSM-III-R*. 3rd. ed. Washington, D.C.: American Psychiatric Association.

Cheng, Y. S., ed. 1986. *Hong Kong in transition*, Hong Kong: Oxford University Press.

Cheng, Y. S., and Kwong, C. K., eds. 1992. *The other Hong Kong report 1992*. Hong Kong: The Chinese University Press.

Chung, Y. P., and Wong, R. Y. C., eds. 1992. *The economics and financing of Hong Kong education*. Hong Kong: The Chinese University Press.

Crawford, N. B. 1991. Minority rights and majority attitudes. In N. Crawford and E. Hui, eds. *The curriculum and behavior problems in schools*. Education Paper 11, Hong Kong: Faculty of Education, University of Hong Kong.

Crawford, N. B., Lau, W. C. Y., and Moynihan, H. 1990. *Special schools survey: Staff development*. Hong Kong: Department of Education, University of Hong Kong.

Department of Education and Science (DES). 1978. *Special educational needs (Warnock Report)*. London: Her Majesty's Stationery Office.

Education Commission. 1990. *Education Commission Report No. 4*. Hong Kong: Government Printer.

———. 1992a. *School education in Hong Kong: A statement of aims*. Hong Kong: Government Printer.

———. 1992b. *Education Commission Report No. 5*. Hong Kong: Government Printer.

Education Department. 1981. *Report of the Working Party on the Review of Secondary Special Classes*. Hong Kong: Education Department.

———. 1983. *General Administrative Circular No. 33/83: Intensive remedial services for children in ordinary schools*. Hong Kong: Education Department.

———. 1985. *Information sheet: Special education*. Hong Kong: Education Department.

———. 1989. *Statistics on teachers in special schools and special education classes who have no initial teacher training (as of 15.9.89)*. Hong Kong: Special Education Section, Education Department.

———. 1990. *Code of aid for special schools*. Hong Kong: Education Department.

———. 1992. *Enrollment survey 1992*. Hong Kong: Education Department.

Health and Welfare Branch. 1991. *Hong Kong 1990 review of Rehabilitation Program Plan*. Hong Kong: Rehabilitation Division, Health and Welfare Branch.

Hong Kong Government. 1976. *The further development of rehabilitation service (Green Paper)*. Hong Kong: Government Printer.

————. 1977. *Integrating the disabled into the community: A united effort (White Paper)*. Hong Kong: Government Printer.

————. 1992. *Hong Kong 1992: A review of 1991*. Hong Kong: Government Printer.

Hong Kong/China, Governments. 1990. *The Basic Law of the Hong Kong Special Administrative Region of the People's Republic of China*. Hong Kong: The Consultative Committee for the Basic Law of the Hong Kong Special Administrative Region of the People's Republic of China.

Kwan, A. Y. H., and Chan, D. K. K. 1986. *Hong Kong society: A reader*. Hong Kong: Writers' and Publishers' Cooperative.

Llewellyn, J., chairman. 1982. *A perspective on education in Hong Kong: Report of a visiting panel*. Hong Kong: Government Printer.

Luk, S. L., Leung, P., Bacon-Shone, J., Chung, S., Lee, P., Chen, S., Ng, R., Lieh-Mak, F., Ko, L., Wong, V., and Yeung, C. Y. 1991. Behavior disorders in pre-school children in Hong Kong: A two-stage epidemiological study. *British Journal of Psychiatry* 158:213–21.

Marsh, R. M., and Sampson, J. R. 1963. *Report of the Education Commission*. Hong Kong: Government Printer.

Patten, C. 1992. *Our next five years: The agenda for Hong Kong*. Hong Kong: Government Printer.

Potts, P. 1991. What is a supportive school? In N. Crawford and E. Hui, eds. *The curriculum and behavior problems in schools, Education Paper 11*. Hong Kong: Faculty of Education, University of Hong Kong.

Shek, D. 1988. Mental health of secondary school students in Hong Kong: An epidemiological study using the General Health Questionnaire. *International Journal of Adolescent Medicine and Health* 13:191–215.

Working Party on Rehabilitation Policies and Services. 1992. *Equal opportunities and full participation: A better tomorrow for all (Green Paper)*. Hong Kong: Social Welfare Department.

PART 4

APPROACHING INTEGRATION

Hearing-impaired students in Israel participate in music and drama activities. PHOTO FROM Jaacov Rand

As part of their education, blind children in Poland learn to identify sculptures by touch. PHOTO BY Wladyslawa Pilecka and Jan Pilecki

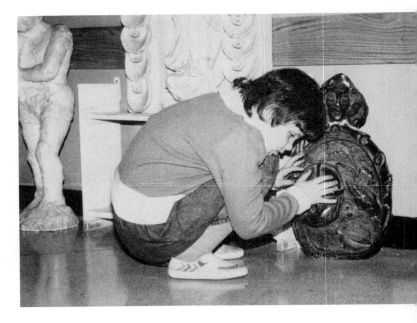

*T*he commonality in philosophy and service provision among the nations found in part IV is their growing adherence to models that stress the accommodation of increasing numbers of children with disabilities within the regular school system. Each of these nations originally founded their special education within institutional settings. Their philosophy today stresses the movement of individuals from separate settings into more normalized environments. Nevertheless, for children with severe handicapping conditions, a complex of institutions remains in place. In Israel in 1950, for example, Heleni Bart established the special education section of the Ministry of Education and Culture. The section's intensive activities in the ensuing years have resulted in the growth of the special education system to national proportions, the consolidation of an educational-psychological base, and increased differentiation and specialization in the various types of treatment services (Michael 1989).

To a greater or lesser extent, these nations are encountering difficulties in the implementation of educational integration. The profound impact of mainstreaming has been met with relief by some groups and alarm by others. Debates about the process and practice are still widely prevalent, although it is not the goals but the means of achieving the goals that are controversial. Few dispute the contention that every child, regardless of type and severity of handicapping condition, has the right to a free and appropriate education in a setting as close to normal as possible. Nevertheless, philosophical commitment far outstrips practice, and the barriers to successful and universal mainstreaming remain complex, diverse, and numerous. Major factors include the reluctance of regular classroom teachers to expand their student population, the collective adverse reactions of teachers' unions, and the growing problem of limited financial resources. In addition, the geographic expanses of Canada and Australia, and the rural nature of Polish society, still result in disparities in the provision of and access to health, rehabilitative, and special education services.

Polish society continues to be predominantly agrarian culturally and racially homogeneous (Holowinsky 1989), and this homogeneity eliminates the potential problem of differential services along the lines of ethnicity. In contrast, the pluralism of Israel is reflected in provisions for the Druze and

Arab sectors. Similarly, Australia and Canada continue to become increasingly multicultural societies.

References

Holowinsky, I. F. 1989. Training of special educators in Poland. *International Journal of Special Education* 4:67–73.
Michael, E. 1989. Special education in Israel. *International Journal of Special Education.* 4:59–64.

19

Israel

YAACOV RAND

RIVKA REICHENBERG

*A*t the establishment of the State of Israel in 1948, the Jewish population in Palestine counted about sixty thousand inhabitants. The great majority of Jewish children were enrolled in schools established in prestate educational frameworks and divided into distinct branches according to various social, political, or religious orientations.

The Israeli population at that time was relatively young and basically highly idealistic. Education and teaching were an integral part of the national struggle toward independence, and in line with the long-lasting emphasis Jews have placed upon education. Almost no special education settings were reported from those times. We may surely assume the existence of children with scholastic or behavioral difficulties but they apparently did not create severe problems that had to be dealt with on a broader scale. To the extent these children existed, or were recognized as having difficulties, treatment was mostly of a segregated nature and performed by nonprofessional educational staff.

According to a recent overview of special education in Israel (Zachs, Michael, and Liberman 1989), only three relatively large special schools and

About the Authors • Yaacov Rand has been involved in special education since 1954 when he became a teacher of students with mental retardation. He is a psychologist and currently a professor in the School of Education at Bar Ilan University, Ramath-Gan. He has published widely in the areas of special education and educational psychology. • Rivka Reichenberg is a lecturer in special education and a pedagogical instructor at Bern College, Israel and a member of the Israeli Ministry of Education. She has published in the areas of giftedness, cultural deprivation, remedial reading, and literature as a treatment device.

a few residential centers existed in Israel in 1948. Moreover, in the entire country there were only three special education classes within regular schools. These institutions and classes were mostly located in urban centers, such as Tel Aviv or Jerusalem, and were mainly based upon private initiative and philanthropic funding. The only exception are the Youth Aliyah (a prestate educational movement sponsored by the Jewish Agency), which was established in 1934 in order to promote and organize immigration of Jewish children and youngsters from the Nazi-occupied countries in Europe. Youth Aliyah was therefore more oriented, and better equipped, to deal with children at risk and to cope with a great variety of educational and adaptation problems. As the new state developed and grew, special education settings were rapidly put in place. These were highly instrumental in dealing with the continuously growing problems of children with special needs.

However, building a new society, as in the case of Israel, has its inherent difficulties in all life spheres, including education. But it also has the advantage of not being rigidly anchored to practices of the past and long time institutional organization. This factor is perhaps at the core of the openness of the Israeli educational system in general and its special education branch in particular. Today's venture is open to the innovative, the challenging, and the revolutionary. Our history has also contributed to the development of potent aspirations toward variation, individualization, and controlled systematization, all highly beneficial to special education practices.

Historical Background

In the second half of the first century (65–70 A.D.), the Roman Empire succeeded in finally conquering Judea and destroying the Temple of Jerusalem. The Roman victory was total and the great majority of the Jewish people were driven out from the Holy Land and dispersed into the Diaspora. The process of the Exile from the Land of Israel continued for about seventy more years and, after the defeat of the Bar Kochba revolution (135–140 A.D.) by the Emperor Trajanus, there were almost no Jews in the territory of the Holy Land. Throughout the centuries a reduced number of Jews came back to the ancient land but never succeeded in gaining any autonomous political rights. They contented themselves in developing a kind of in-group independence, strongly clenching their religious beliefs and traditions, which became deeply anchored in their normative way of life.

During the Ottoman governing of the Holy Land, the Jewish population was extremely reduced and centered in a few ancient towns, such as Jerusalem, Sefad, and Tiberias. These small communities were of a highly religious nature, being very little exposed to or oriented toward secular ideas and living conditions. Their rather isolated way of life was reinforced by the

Ottoman society, which was also highly religious, albeit in the Muslim tradition and its normative imperatives.

In the second half of the nineteenth century, Jews started to immigrate into the promised land, mostly from Russia and the Balkans. This immigration process, initially very slight, continued to grow, combined with intensive colonization and fertilization of the deserted soil. An Austrian Jewish journalist Theodor Herzl founded the Zionist movement in 1896, and attempts were made to gain national recognition from the Ottoman Sultan as well as from other prominent rulers of those times.

The First World War (1914–18) led to a total decomposition of the Ottoman Empire. In 1917, the British and French armies occupied almost the entire Middle East. Filling in the vacuum created by the disappearance of the Ottoman Empire, the British received the mandate to rule over the Holy Land. This radical change in the status of the ancient Jewish land was complemented by the Balfour Declaration (1917) by which the English government promised to reestablish in Palestine a national home for the Jewish People. The Balfour Declaration triggered new hopes for the Jewish people, mostly massed in ghettos, *Shtetlech,* and otherwise confined regions in Russia and Eastern Europe. A new wave of massive immigration streamed into the continuously growing *Yishuv* (settlement), coming from a great variety of countries, including the New Continent. The Jewish population increased significantly. New settlements were established all over the country, social institutions were organized, and the arid soil of the old/new country was fertilized again.

The great majority of the newcomers left their homes because of anti-Semitism and the harsh living conditions they had to endure in their native countries. But they were also idealistically oriented. They represented a national elite which aspired to establish a secular society in Palestine radically different from the ancient religious establishment still existing in the Holy Land. These pioneers, although trying to revolutionize Jewish society, were still bound to Jewish heritage, often finding support for their modern social ideologies and life conceptions in biblical prophetic texts. A new era started, activated by these young pioneers, who tried to impose upon themselves and upon society a life based on simplicity, austerity, self-fulfillment, and predominance of the group over the needs of the individual. They acted intensively to achieve maximal materialization of the individual's intellect and to foster a "new man" who would internalize the social and national values of that time.

During the first period of this immigration, the number of children in the Holy Land was very small. It was only in the 1930s with the onset of the Holocaust that we witnessed massive children's immigration. There were children with special needs, but we do not find any significant traces of special education in the annals of those times. The small number of institutions that dealt with special children were oriented toward the most severely handicapped ones who, for various reasons, could not be integrated into any educational framework. These institutions were generally treatment oriented, based upon the belief that such children cannot be subject to education at all.

The strong aspirations to materialize the individual's potentials, the need to develop a new society built upon maximal contribution of each of its members, and the spirit of togetherness characteristic of those times have left significant traces in the Israeli educational system through today. These values meaningfully correspond to the ancient Jewish value system, albeit reformulated in modern terminology and colored by the spirit of the Jewish Renaissance, ultimately leading to the establishment of the state of Israel.

Prevalence of Exceptional Conditions

Modern and technologically developed societies may alleviate certain handicapping conditions. On the other hand, they may increase the needs for special education due to inherent, continuously increasing adaptation difficulties created by the way of life and demands they impose on the individual. We may consider two special conditions that are specific to the Israeli society and may have a particular impact on the development of specific adaptation difficulties.

The first is the continuous immigration from various cultures. This is not only a quantitative constituent but also a highly important qualitative component, causing confusion and lack of psychosocial stability. This is true not only for the new immigrating children, but also for the absorbing segments of the Israeli population. In many instances, prevalent tendencies and conflicts in the social and ethnic domains may produce severe scholastic and behavioral problems, reflecting the antagonism between the culturally different children on the one side and the school system on the other side, which are viewed as the genuine representatives of the institutionalized society.

The second special condition refers to the continually dangerous security conditions in which Israeli children grow up. Since the establishment of the state, Israel has seven times experienced war conditions of different grades of gravity. Some of these wars were, fortunately enough, of very short duration, but they were always preceded by longer periods of high tension. The attrition war with Egypt in the late sixties and early seventies lasted almost three years, causing hundreds of casualties. In addition, Israel lives under almost permanent stress, due to frequent terrorist attacks, culminating in the last few years with the insurrection known as the Intifada. These rather traumatic events may significantly increase psychological tension and enhance states of individual and group anxiety.

Due to these rather unfortunate conditions, many families and children have to mourn their fathers, brothers, relatives, and friends, who lost their lives in combat. Many more have to cope with severe suffering caused by war injuries and by other irreversible conditions that impair thousands of young adults and preclude them from active involvement in the economic and social life of their communities. These specific conditions create highly stressing life conditions for the entire Israeli society, and in particular for families and children.

The special conditions contain a wide array of sociopsychological ingredients liable to increase the rate of children's mental disorders. Compared with other countries living in more peaceful conditions, Israeli society is considered to experience living conditions of continuous turmoil and stress. Nevertheless, no special rates are reported in this respect. We may speculate that the active involvement of the adult society in coping with these harsh and demanding life conditions makes them become most supportive to the children. This ultimately develops higher ego strength and enhances the children's adaptation, efficiency, and coping capacities.

All in all, the prevalence of handicapped and disabled children within the Israeli population is estimated to be similar to what is usually found in any modern society. No exact figures are provided for the ratios between the handicapped and regular students at the various ages. Except for the problems caused by immigration and intercultural encounters, no handicapping conditions are reported as specific to the Israeli school population.

As to the frequencies and rates of the various handicaps and disabilities among the Israeli student population, no exact figures are available. The unavailability of exact figures is mostly due to problems in the definition of the various handicaps, diagnostic procedures, social attitudes, variation in the regular schools' readiness to cope with handicapped children, and lack of a well-developed central data system. According to official estimates, however, about 10 to 12 percent of the Israeli school population have been identified as children at risk and needing special education. These figures

TABLE 19.1. Special Education in Israel: Classes and Students, 1950–86

Year	Number of Classes	Increase		Number of Students
		N	%	
1950	90	—	—	1,534
1955	290	200	222	4,866
1960	611	321	111	10,746
1965	1,111	500	82	18,479
1970	1,769	658	59	25,348
1974	2,612	843	48	35,145
1975	2,720	108	4	36,608
1976	3,150	430	16	43,058
1983	3,400	250	8	50,000
1986	3,675	275	8	57,000

Source: Ministry of Education, Special Education branch.

corroborate those reported by the United States Department of Education in 1986 which estimated that out of each hundred children and youngsters within the U.S. school system, about eleven of them fall into this category.

Table 19.1 illustrates the progressive and disproportional increase in special education needs in Israel during the first four decades of its existence. More recent figures provided by the Ministry of Education and Culture show an additional increase in the special education population. In 1990 about sixty-two thousand children were defined as needing special education of all sorts. The student distribution of those is presented in table 19.2.

These figures do not take into consideration a considerable number of children who were defined as needing special education, while continuing to be integrated in their regular "mother classes." No accurate data are available on the number of these children because they are not officially registered as special education students.

If one takes into consideration that according to official figures in the United States, about 56 percent of the kindergarten disabled population and about 70 percent of the elementary and high school population are integrated in regular schools and classes (Hallahan and Kauffman 1990), we may speculate similar rates in Israel. This cannot be solely attributed to the hypothesized milder impairments of those children, but is probably also determined by the enhanced readiness of the school systems to cope with special educational problems. To a much smaller extent, such mainstreaming can be explained by purely pragmatic reasons, such as small-size rural localities which practice integration because they are unable to materialize other, more segregating, alternatives.

We should also take into consideration that a considerable segment of the Israeli special education student population ($N = 17,000$ or 27 percent)

TABLE 19.2. Distribution of Special Education Students in Various Educational Settings, 1992.

Educational Setting	Special Education Students	
	%	N
Special education schools	20	12,500
Special classes in regular schools	27	17,000
Resource classes in regular schools	27	17,000
Special education kindergartens	4	2,300
Resource teachers in kindergartens	5	3,000
Vocational special classes, various types	8	4,450
Special education classes in the Arabic schools	6	3,000
Special education classes in the Druze sector	1	900
Special education classes in the ultraorthodox sector	2	1,400
Total	100	61,550

is involved in resource classes within the regular schools. These students continue to be an integral part of their mother class, benefiting from special services only for a few hours during the week, mostly for remedial teaching, or for other well-defined treatment and teaching purposes.

Identification of Exceptional Children

The identification of children with impairments can be divided into a number of categories. First of all there are children who show severe impairments at birth. In this category we refer to children suffering from Down's syndrome or other easily detectable impairments. Usually, parents are immediately informed about the condition of their child. Social and maternity services of the hospital act immediately to provide both support and guidance for the parents. The family doctor is also informed about the birth of the child, as well as the *Tipath Chalav,* "Services for the Neonate." Concomitantly, the social services of the appropriate municipality are put in touch with the parents for further guidance and support. The child and his or her parents are also referred to a Child Development Institute functioning within the maternity hospital. The aim is to lend psychological and medical assistance according to the specific needs of the children.

Second are children whose special impairments are not observable at birth. Under this category we often find children with hearing impairments or those suffering from motor deficiencies or other developmental delays. Upon the discovery of the impairment, parents, social services, or educational institutions refer the child for assessment and treatment according to the specific impairment and needs of the child.

We also have children with educational and scholastic impairments. Such children usually start their educational career within the regular school framework. Difficulties may arise in the more advanced grades either in the general level of functioning or in more specific areas, such as language acquisition. In all such cases, school authorities refer the child for psychological assessment and guidance to the psychoeducational services of the *Shefi* (Ministry of Education) and inform the parents of their child's condition.

Labeling the Handicapped Population

The following are the broad categories of students enrolled in the special education frameworks in Israel:

Mentally retarded. Within the broad category of mentally retarded children, we may distinguish among specific subcategories. There is the profound level of mental retardation; these are persons having an IQ less than

40, and those who do not show any evidence of higher levels of potential. Such children are usually placed and treated in segregated programs in which total care is provided, often beyond the age of legal education. The moderate level of mental retardation refers to those persons having an IQ level of between 40 and 54. Such children are usually educated in segregated special education schools. At later stages, and mostly during adolescence, they may be integrated into vocational training programs. The school curricula within those institutions are, at least partially, geared toward vocational training so as to ensure continuity of the individual's training process, as well as his or her preparation for real-life situations. At the mild level of mental retardation are persons found to be functioning on an IQ level of 55 to 69. Such children are usually placed in special schools and/or in special classes within regular schools.

Low levels of mental functioning and personality disorders. These are persons who suffer from a dual impairment, that is, from both a low level of intellectual functioning and from severe personality disorders. In some cases such children may also be afflicted by other severe impairments. Children are usually placed in segregated school settings but are also offered special support services that accommodate to their particular personal needs.

Marginal level of mental retardation. These are persons having an IQ level of 70 to 79 who do not show any other impairment. Such children are generally integrated in regular schools, mostly in special education (promoting) classes, or in regular classes with resource room support.

Mentally disturbed children. This category is divided into three subcategories. Children with severe to moderate mental disturbance are generally placed in special kindergarten and/or special school settings. Eventually, they may be mainstreamed again depending on their educational progress, significant modifications in their mental state, and the existent practical availabilities. Children with mild mental disorders usually show a normal level of cognitive functioning but do not succeed in sufficiently realizing their potential due to some mental disorder. Some of them may even show giftedness, albeit not fully actualized because of severe inhibitions or other impairing mental conditions. Such children will mostly be integrated within regular classes and receive supportive individual teaching or other services within their mother class. In some cases, a few hours weekly with the resource room teacher may efficiently compensate for the student's special needs.

Children with severe behavioral disorders are usually children with normal intellectual capacities who show low scholastic achievement and severe difficulties in socially integrating in the educational system and with their peers. Such children are referred to special classes for the mentally disturbed, or even to special schools, depending on the severity of their behavioral disorders. In many cases, such children show temper tantrums and inward or exteriorized aggression.

Learning disabilities. This category is perhaps one of the most populated segments of the special education student population. It includes two sub-categories: First there are individuals with normal intellectual capacities who suffer from problems in their learning activities. In many cases, their scholastic difficulties are combined with behavioral problems. These children are usually educated in regular classes and provided with remedial teaching and other additional support in resource rooms or by individual or small-group tutoring. In some extreme cases, placement will be made in special classes for the learning disabled or in heterogeneous special education classes.

Dyslexia is a special category of the learning disabled, grounded in neurophysiological disorders, producing difficulties in reading acquisition. Children suffering from dyslexia but having normal levels of mental functioning are usually placed in regular classes, receiving supportive neurological or educational assistance from special education programs. Under this category we may also include children suffering from agraphia (writing impairments) or acalculia (arithmetic impairments).

Physical and sensorial handicaps. These are persons with severe physical impairments, including cerebral palsy (CP) and orthopedic handicaps. The category also includes hearing and visual impairments. Such children are integrated in both the regular and the special education frameworks, depending on individual conditions and educational possibilities. Children who suffer from chronic illnesses and who receive special education services at their home or at their respective treatment hospitals also belong to this category.

In Israel, the labeling used for the handicapped and disabled population follow basically the definitions of the American Association of Mental Deficiency (AAMD). Referral to IQ levels is still prevalent, although additional factors such as social behavior and capacities for autonomous and initiative behavior are taken into consideration.

Generally, there is a tendency not to label children based on only a one-time assessment but to remain on a more descriptive level. This avoids premature labeling, which can become highly detrimental to the child, affecting meaningfully and negatively his or her educational and occupational life trajectory.

In the last few years, more and more educational settings require Dynamic Assessment as a decision-making instrument for school organization and for providing individualized educational services to the at-risk student population. Dynamic Assessment is preferred by many because it does not limit itself to the recording of the individual's manifest levels of intellectual functioning. Rather, it enlarges the scope of assessment into a more varied and complex psychoeducational evaluation that considers the children's cognitive and nonintellective behavior as well as to their characteristic ways of learning. The individual's learning potential and his or her capacities to become modified by the environment are thoroughly scrutinized in order to uncover the most adequate pedagogic procedures appropriate to the given individual. Dynamic Assessment also tends to assess the specific difficulties, resistances, and efficiencies of the individual so as to enable prescriptive teaching and education based on the individual's specific idiosyncratic condition and characteristics.

The Social Context of Special Education

Philosophical Roots

An old Jewish dictum says that if one wants to educate a child properly, one has to start with the child's grandfather. This dictum, albeit colored by a somewhat humorous life perspective, reflects a profound idea concerning culture and its transmission processes. Basically, it expresses a need for both social and cultural continuity, and emphasizes the importance of durable efforts in order to achieve meaningful educational goals.

The origin of this dictum is in the area of value transmission. But it is not less valid for a variety of other educational objectives and processes. It can be equally applied to those educational endeavors destined to actualize the individual's potentials or to enhance the human being's environmental adaptation and coping capabilities.

This dictum reflects equally a dual orientation in the time dimension. Whereas educational goals are usually set in order to assure the future of the individual, it is required that they remain deeply anchored in the social and cultural past of their society. It is by education and other cultural transmission channels that these values have to be carried from generation to generation. Therefore, in order to better understand the philosophical fundamentals of the Israeli education system, it is most appropriate to search into the ancient roots of the Jewish culture and to emphasize those elements that remain pertinent to current Israeli education and, in particular, to special education.

Fortunately, Jewish culture is extensively documented; it goes back to the remote Biblical and Talmudical eras. At the time when the Jewish people, after their exodus from Egypt, wandered in the desert, cultural transmission had already become a divine imperative. This is reflected in the following biblical verse:

> And teach them to your children to speak of them, when thou sittest in thine house and when thou walkest on the road and when thou liest down and when thou risest up. (Deut. 11:19)

According to this rather holistic code of ethics, intergenerational cultural transmission is a personal responsibility of every single parent. It is a commandment to be carried out in all situations and at any time of the day. This simply stated commandment has stirred across the generations a popular movement of cultural transmission, implemented regardless of the child's level of functioning, and the parents' capabilities to be efficient cultural transmission agents.

A later text taken from an early Mishnah (the most ancient Talmudical fragments) enlightens the basic value system that characterizes Jewish culture and education. It refers to the unique universal event of the creation of man, as viewed in biblical tradition, and exposes a number of reasons that the Lord created only one man. The text reads as follows:

> For these reasons was Man created alone . . . to teach thee that whosoever destroys a single soul, scripture imputes guilt to him as though he had destroyed a complete world, and whosoever preserved a single soul, scripture ascribes merit to him as though he had preserved a complete world. . . . [F]or the sake of peace among men, that one might not say to his fellow "my father was greater than thine" . . . and that the sectarians might not say "there are many ruling powers in heaven." . . . [A]gain to proclaim the greatness of the Holy one . . . for if a man strikes many coins from one mould, they all resemble one, but the Supreme King . . . fashioned every man in the stamp of the first man, and yet not one of them resembles his fellow. (Tractate Sanhedrin, 37:a)

Beyond the specific reference to the monotheistic faith, the predominant emphasis of this text pertains to the domain of interhuman relationships. It is perhaps one of the most ancient Bill of Rights of the human being. It underlines the paramount importance attributed to each single individual. Nobody has the right, for any reason, to take the liberty to destroy a human being, because each of us represents a "complete world." For the same reason, this text also imposes on everybody the responsibility to do the utmost in order to save and preserve each individual.

The true value of this humanistic philosophy can be best understood when comparing it with ancient and medieval practices of infanticide and even with more contemporary modern practices, still to be found in many corners of our world, of turmoil and distress (Scheerenberger 1982). More particularly we refer here to the Nazi regime, which ordained the "final solution" to all the mentally ill and intellectually retarded, exterminating them in the crematories of Auschwitz or other similar hideous places. All this, for the sake of preserving the "sacred" Aryan race and in the framework of an antihuman ideology proclaiming the "legitimate" supremacy of that race.

Similar ideologies that lead to massive genocide are unfortunately still prevalent in many corners of the world, albeit for social and political reasons and not contingent upon the individual's inadequacies. But even when not referring to such extremely misplaced and atrocious philosophies and practices, we still find social attitudes and policies far distanced from the basic belief system expressed in the Talmudic text, which strongly advocates the absolute value of each individual.

The other reasons cited in the Mishnah are also of primordial importance to the realities of our time. The text expresses a principle of socioethnic equality. Only one man was created in order to proclaim that nobody is entitled to claim that "my father was greater than thine." This principle is directly linked to an even more ancient code of ethics, expressed by the prophet Malachi, who preached his faith many centuries before the Talmud was written, saying:

> Have we not all one father?
> Hath not one God created us?
> Why do we deal treacherously
> every man against his brother? (Malachi, 2:10)

The persistence of these basic humanistic ideas across so many generations, starting from remote biblical times, has cultivated in Jewish society a general positive approach toward individuals in need, trying to stretch out to them a powerful and supportive hand. It also created an atmosphere of nondiscrimination and humanity which has strongly prevailed until our time.

The text also refers to the principle of human heterogeneity. It states that differences between human beings are fundamental and inherent in their very being. This principle is not only of descriptive nature; it attributes full legitimacy to diversity as a basic characteristic of the human race. Consequently, differences shall not be used as a reason to legitimize discrimination or as a basis for social and political power. This principle tends to preclude the development of differential attribution of rights based upon variance in ideas, feelings, norms, religions, racial and ethnic differences, or individual impairments and inadequacies. It is our contention that this basic value system became across generations an integral part of Jewish philosophy and practice. It expresses itself in a great variety of explicit and implicit social norms and daily habits, especially in the area of education.

The following Talmudical text describes the considerable attention given to the didactic and pedagogical aspects of the educational systems:

> Before the age of six do not accept pupils; from that age, you can accept them,
> and stuff them with Torah like an ox. . . . When you punish a pupil, only hit him

with a shoe latched (do not hurt him too much). . . . The attentive one will read of himself, and if one is inattentive, put him next to a diligent one. (Ibid)

It is essential to remember that these texts, and many similar ones scattered in Judaic sources, describe a vivid reality of a society living about more than two thousand years ago. This emphasizes their value as well as their potent impact upon the development of education in Jewish tradition. Modern notions such as education for all; school appropriate ages; letting children enjoy their childhood without being pressured too early to indulge in heavy studies; avoiding the ill effects of severe punishment on the personality and motivation of the child, and finally, mainstreaming by facilitating studies through tutoring and fostering motivation—all these ideas have characterized Jewish thought and practices for many centuries. They can be considered as reflecting the fundamentals of education in Jewish society across its long and intensive history.

There is no doubt that these educational values and historically perpetuated practices heavily contributed to the strength of Judaic culture, to its multifaceted general impact upon humanity, and to the survival of the Jewish people through all the burdens they experienced across millennia.

The State of Israel: Institutionalized Special Education

It should be remembered that the traditional Cheder—an integral part of Jewish life and Jewish education in all parts of the Diaspora—always mainstreamed all children of the community. This practice was probably related to a basic need for survival, related to the practice of Jewish religious tradition and the development of strong feelings of community attachment as the major educational goals. When grown up, regardless of their level of functioning, all youngsters were also fully accepted in adult society as long as they conformed to the community's normative life.

Being less achievement oriented, the Cheder was an ideal framework for low-functioning students. Often, it also provided individualized teaching or peer tutoring, which was beneficial to both the student in difficulty and his or her supporting peer mate.

A reduced number of special education institutions existed already at the beginning of the state. However, at that time, the problems of special education in Israel were only marginal. Institutions were mainly for the sensorimotor severely handicapped, such as the visual impaired and the hearing impaired, as well as for children afflicted by cerebral palsy (CP). Naturally, the entire educational system of Israel was at that stage unable to adequately cope with the wealth of problems caused by the new and changing realities. Special education was no exception from this point of view.

Recruitment of teachers, and particularly for special education, was a major concern in those times. The existent numbers of teachers and teacher-training institutions were then extremely reduced. The tremendous and rapidly growing needs exceeded by far the state's possibilities to cope with them. Masses of children from most varied social and cultural backgrounds flooded in daily and had to be placed under most austere physical and socioeconomic conditions. Immediate schooling became imperative, not only for educational reasons per se but also for social and economic reasons, so as to enable the parents to go to work and become self-supporting and productive members of society.

Cultural and language barriers were another major concern of the new state and its educators. In addition to problems inherent in teaching a new language and almost totally unfamiliar scholastic contents, severe difficulties surfaced in the identification processes between children and their parents. Often, parents felt the need to abandon their previous culture as well as their traditional role as identification models, fearing that identifying with their old culture would become detrimental to their children's absorption within the new society. These conditions created a myriad of educational problems, which increased due to the lack of experienced and trained educational personnel in the regular school system, and finally resulted in a considerable increment of the special education student population.

In 1949 the *Knesset* (Israeli Parliament) adopted the Law of Mandatory Education, which obliged the State to provide education to all the children between the ages of six and fourteen. Following this law, a special education branch was established within the Ministry for Education and Culture. This branch developed rapidly, especially during the 1950s, for a considerable number of reasons:

1. Massive immigration from a great variety of countries and cultures overloaded the new state with newcomers who presented severe adaptation problems that were difficult to handle in the existing educational framework.
2. Immigration processes were highly nonselective. The Law of Return adopted in 1950 by the young state accorded the right of immigration, that is, to return from the exile, to every Jew from all over the world.
3. A birth rate increase because of the heavy impact of cultures that practiced less strict birth control. This factor contributed also to an increase in the proportion of children born to relatively older parents.
4. There was a decrease of infant mortality rates in general and of physically and mentally impaired children in particular.
5. We saw an increase in the population segments that showed severe adaptation difficulties to Israeli realities and to a highly technological

developed society. This expressed itself in a lack of, or reduced, intergenerational cultural transmission, causing an extremely high rate of culturally deprived children.

6. Parents and educational systems developed a greater awareness of the needs of children requiring differential education and treatment.
7. Enhancement of academic and scholastic requirements in both the educational and occupational areas, inherent to societies of high technological development, resulted in an increased rate of school dropouts and the development of cultural subgroups that became a major reservoir for juvenile delinquency and antisocial behavior.

The figures already presented in table 19.1 show clearly a continuous trend of rapid development of special education programs in Israel. During the first ten years of the Jewish state's existence, its population increased rapidly, and the development of the special education branch within the Israeli educational system shows a similar increase in both student enrollment and number of classes.

The data also show that in the second half of the fifties, that is, after the massive immigration from Eastern Europe, North Africa, and a variety of other Asian and African countries, the classroom density of the student population increased to 24 students per class, exceeding by far what may be considered as optimal for special education classes. Only in the seventies did student density became relatively stabilized and more adequate (14 to 16), albeit still higher than the usual desired rate of 10 to 12 children per class.

Language barriers, as mentioned earlier, created some additional, and most significant, educational problems. For one thing, this situation required specialized skills to teach a foreign language to children whose usual spoken language was completely unfamiliar to the teaching staff. As well, the massive immigration waves brought in many active teachers from various countries, but they could not get immediately involved within the Israeli educational system because of their limited knowledge of both the Hebrew language and Israeli culture. Often, the young students who came with their previous teachers could not rely on the teachers anymore, which caused severe cultural discontinuity and confusion.

This dynamic and most intriguing state of affairs generated an imperative need for a massive and nonselective enrollment of new teachers. The educational system was filled up with almost totally untrained teaching staff. Some of them got an abbreviated training of a few months, which was largely insufficient in terms of teaching them to develop the skills required to fulfill complex educational tasks. Paradoxically, special education programs, which logically would require higher levels of specialization, were coerced into accepting teachers having even less training than the regular teachers, and who were therefore less able to cope with severe educational and didactic problems. The most important and most meaningful educational weapons these untrained teachers had at their disposal were a high level of motivation and a profound awareness of the historical endeavor in which they were involved.

In regards to the newly immigrated teachers, many of them had to switch over to new professions and completely leave the area of education. Some of them reintegrated in education at a later stage after having absorbed the Israeli culture and learned the new language and ways of life. These teachers became then a most meaningful support to the integration of the newcomer children and adolescents from their countries of origin.

Legislation

In Israel, we may distinguish two basic periods. The first was the opening four decades of the State (1948–88), this is, before the Law for Special Education was passed in the Knesset. The second is from 1988 through the present. Although the Law of Special Education in Israel was adopted only about five years ago (1988), there were a number of laws, or special paragraphs in already existing laws, which referred specifically to the needs of the handicapped and impaired persons.

The Early Period

The first period is characterized by a number of laws in which certain paragraphs refer to handicapped and impaired persons. However, at the beginning of the state, most of the services to these segments of the population were offered on a voluntary basis and subject to the goodwill of the officers handling these issues, as well as the financial support of the public authorities. Although goodwill is important even nowadays, services are currently mostly institutionalized and procedures are related to the rights and obligations stated by legislation.

Historically, specific legislation in special education is a product of the last two to three decades. Some first initiatives were taken in the early twenties (1924) with the Declaration of Rights pronounced by the League of Nations' International Covenant for the Rescue of the Child. This declaration sought to provide to all children—including the sick, deviant, and socially neglected ones—the necessary conditions for their "natural" development (Barth 1975). It took fifty-five years more before the United Nations referred specifically to the rights of the exceptional child to receive appropriate education and treatment (Yitzchaki 1985).

The laws for Mandatory Education (1949) and for National Education (1953) were among the first laws of the new Israeli state. They ensured the legal rights of each child to receive educational services from the state. These laws do not contain any specific references to the special segments of the student population. More specific references to special education can be found in the amendments to the Law of Mandatory Education, passed in 1978.

Concomitantly with the education laws of 1949 and 1953, a number of additional laws were passed in the areas of vocational and work activities. Children's work before the age of fifteen became prohibited and vocational education was provided for certain segments of the population, up to the age of eighteen. This constituted an enlargement of the state's responsibilities, which, according to the Law of Mandatory Education, were limited to providing vocational education for students up to the age of fifteen only. The responsibilities of the state concerning neglected children, as well as the juridical status of the child, were legally defined in 1962.

Another legislative area were the laws of welfare, under the auspices and responsibility of the Ministry of Labor and Welfare. These included the definition of the legal responsibilities of the state and its legal agents, of parents, and of the municipal authorities concerning the various areas of life, supportive services, educational and vocational placement, psychoeducational treatment, medical insurance, financial aid by the state, and so on. All these laws reflect a general tendency to offer significant support to handicapped persons and their families and to create optimal conditions for their development and well-being.

Specific Legislation for Special Education

It was only in 1988 that the Knesset passed a particular law for special education. With this law, all scattered laws and amendments were clustered into one inclusive document. Its main purpose was to legally define the categories of the individuals concerned, the obligations and rights of the students and their families, the responsibilities of the various social and educational authorities, and to institutionalize administrative and educational procedures which would guarantee the rights of special education students.

The new law enlarges meaningfully the responsibilities of the public authorities toward handicapped and disabled person and emphasizes the obligation to integrate such individuals within normal educational frameworks. It also advocates the elaboration of individualized school curricula to be adapted to the child's specific needs. It addition, it stipulates the parents' rights to have access to all psychomedical information accumulated in their child's personal file as well as to be actively involved in all decision-making processes concerning their child.

This expansion of rights is reflected also in the definition of both special education and the handicapped person. According to the terms of the law, special education includes not only classroom education but also a wide array of auxiliary services, such as physiotherapy, occupational therapy, and speech therapy. The nature and number of these special services are determined by the specific needs of the given child.

The age range of the children being entitled to benefit from the Law of Special Education was also significantly extended. It includes individuals from 3 to 21 years, while the general Law of Mandatory Education offers such educational rights only to children between 5 and 15 years. It also allows for extending the programs of the special education institutions beyond the official academic year, including all vacation periods. These enlargements of the law place an additional, and significant, financial and administrative burden on Israeli society. They also extend significantly the social support to handicapped persons and their families.

Teachers

According to the current practices, special education teachers are trained in two basic ways. First, there are teacher seminars. Actually, there are about thirty to thirty-five such seminars in Israel of which most are directly run by the Ministry of Education. These institutions are authorized for those who were formerly teachers for the elementary school. Annually, about 200 to 300 teachers graduate from these seminars. The majority are absorbed by the Ministry of Education or by other public institutions.

The second mode of teacher training is through universities and colleges. In Israel, there are seven universities and ten to twelve colleges. Most of them have programs in special education, albeit some universities concentrate more on academic formation and less upon the practical training of teachers. Those academic institutions that are actively involved in teacher training usually concentrate on junior high school problems in contrast to the elementary education focus of the seminars. This division precludes competition between the various institutions.

Schools

Special Education Institutions Controlled by the Ministry of Education.

Certain categories of institutions, under the direct educational, administration, and financial control and responsibility of the Ministry of Education include the following:

1. Special education kindergartens for children with severe social and behavioral problems that preclude their integration in regular education. Some of these children are absorbed in such kindergartens on a partial basis only for a number of days or hours per week. Some

special education kindergartens expose the children to regular education on a part-time basis.

2. Integrative regular kindergartens which have within their framework a special education class.
3. Special education individual support (Siach). This service is offered to children needing special help within their regular kindergarten class. It consists of allocating an additional kindergarten teacher to work solely with a specific child.
4. Special education elementary schools (SEES).
5. Special education classes within the regular elementary (ES), junior high (JHS), and high schools (HS). These are known as *Kita Mekademeth,* or "promoting classes, because they deal with scholastic impairments and learning disabilities.
6. Open special education classes within the regular schools for children needing remedial teaching or other support in particular content areas only.
7. Integrated regular/special education classes in which two teachers (one of them a special education teacher) act cooperatively within the same class.
8. Special education tutoring and remedial teaching.
9. *Kita Tipulit,* "resource rooms," within the elementary and junior high schools for children needing support in their studies or for other psychoeducational reasons.
10. Treatment centers for individual support during or after school time.
11. Vocational classes for special education students with programs that usually combine scholastic studies with basic vocational training.

Alternative Special Education Settings

In addition to the aforementioned special education frameworks controlled by the Ministry of Education, certain special education services function as a common endeavor of the Ministry of Education and other social and public institutions. The most important services in this category are vocational training schools and diagnostic treatment centers.

Miftan, "vocational training schools" for children between the ages of twelve and sixteen with severe learning or behavioral problems, operate in common with the Ministry of Labor and Welfare. There are also *Maass,* "sheltered work settings," for low-functioning children beyond the age of sixteen. Vocational rehabilitation centers are for students over fifteen years of age who need counseling or additional preparation to be integrated into work and occupational settings.

Diagnostic and treatment centers for child development jointly operated with *Kupath Cholim* (Medicare) are usually located in hospitals and focus on children in nursery and kindergarten classes. In addition, there are classes functioning within the hospitals for chronically ill children and classes in hospitals for the mentally ill.

Mainstreaming

When we examine the rather lengthy list of the various educational institutions serving the special education student population, we may say that it is characteristic of a strong tendency of the Israeli educational system toward mainstreaming and integration of this population in regular education settings. It also reflects a propensity to accommodate the specific and varied needs of the students. This statement is valid for almost all ages included under the general roof of education and social treatment. The major purpose of this educational system is to enhance the coping capacities of all the special education students and to facilitate their becoming active and contributing citizens to the Israeli society and involved in the process of shaping their own fates.

As already stated, many children with severe problems continue to be integrated within the regular system under various conditions. According to the regulations of the Ministry of Education (1992), regular schools have to do their utmost to answer the needs of the total student population and to integrate most of those showing difficulties in mental capacities and scholastic performance. It is also the school's duty to absorb most children with neurological and motor disabilities, sensorial deficiencies, and emotional or general behavior problems.

The stated goals of this integrative approach are to encourage disabled children to accept themselves as a part of the community and society and to educate all the students towards acceptance of the different and the deviant. A further goal is to develop and improve the capacities and functioning of at-risk children in the physical, mental, emotional, and behavioral areas in order to facilitate their adjustment to life and integration in society and in working activities.

These educational goals for special education children transcend the area of their specific needs and enters the realm of the general student population. We emphasize this point because we consider that appropriate integration of disabled and handicapped children in regular educational and occupational frameworks cannot be efficiently achieved by changes in the organizational structure only; such integration requires a thorough preparation of all factors involved in such an endeavor, including the educational staff of the respective educational institution, the social and community services, the family environments of both the regular and special children, and the classroom peers.

In Israel there are relatively high numbers of students represented in the integrated educational settings. This reflects, on the one hand, a rather universal phenomenon of increased frequencies in the less-impaired segments of the population. On the other hand, it is related to the propensity to mainstream students with special needs which has lately became more prevalent within Western culture in general, as well as within the Israeli educational system.

Currently we may distinguish between four basic integration models, all implemented to some extent within the Israeli educational system. These models are rather of an experimental nature and not yet sufficiently formalized in their specific didactic and pedagogical methods. The choice of one model or another is mostly a function of the personal preference of classroom teachers and/or the school authorities. No data exist yet on the relative frequency of these basic models or on their differential efficiency.

Group integration (GI). Group integration consists of integrating a relatively large number of special education children (ten to twelve) within a regular class. In this model, two teachers are acting concomitantly in the same classroom. One of them handles the class in toto, whereas the other one (usually a special education teacher) is responsible for dealing individually with those children showing severe scholastic or behavioral difficulties. This model is mostly prevalent in the elementary school. Its success is highly dependent on the intensity and nature of the cooperation developed between the two teachers. Problems are mostly linked to issues such as who is the basic source of authority in the class and who is doing what and when. With mutual confidence, teachers may change roles within the class in a flexible way. This introduces variance into the children's scholastic activities and is basically beneficial to both the regular and special education students. It is also a challenging and enriching experience for both classroom teachers.

Remedial teaching (RT). This model is usually applied in the first two grades of the elementary school (ES). Children suspected of having particular difficulties, although not always tested and formally diagnosed as such, are offered remedial teaching or supportive tutoring. These educational activities can be mostly considered as preventive—trying to intervene as early as possible to enable the child to continue to his or her educational experience within the regular class. These remedial teaching procedures are partially undertaken in the child's class during school hours and partially after the regular class hours in the school facilities or even at the student's residence. In certain cases, this remedial teaching is performed in small groups of children showing similarity in their problems and scholastic difficulties.

Learning centers (LC). This model is most frequently applied in junior high schools (JHS). Special education children are integrated in their regular classes but referred by their classroom teacher to an LC functioning within the respective school. These learning centers are operated by a number of teachers who are specialists in various subject matter. Within the

Learning Center the student receives systematic and individually programmed remedial teaching, concentrating on those subject matters in which he or she shows particular difficulty.

The number of the LC teachers is varied, depending on their availability and the particular needs of the students. A specific individualized program is elaborated for each student by the LC teacher in cooperation with the regular classroom teacher. From time to time, this program is readjusted in terms of the progress made by the student in the regular classroom.

This model requires intensive and frequent interaction between the regular and the special education teachers in both the planning phases and during implementation. It also requires a great deal of flexibility in behavioral, didactic, and pedagogical approaches so as to efficiently accommodate to the specific needs of the student.

Reversed integration (RI). As opposed to the LC model, the RI model is based on the special education class being the mother class but, for certain scholastic or social activities, the special education students are integrated within regular classes. This method is of a relatively more limited scope, serving mostly for social integration purposes. To some extent, it may also have a positive impact on the self-esteem of the special education children. It may limit the development of feelings of being totally socially rejected.

As already stated, very little data are available at this stage on the efficiency and impact of the various methods. We have little beyond impressionistic reports of professionals involved in the implementation process, although the remedial teaching model is currently the object of an empirical systematic study.

It is still hard to decide which are, or should be, the determinant differential factors in choosing the specific integration model. These methods, although sharing a general theoretical approach that advocates educational and social integration, are not linked to any specific, model-bound, theories. Pragmatical factors, such as the availability and readiness of the teachers, play a significant role in the choice of the method and its durable utilization. More institutionalized procedures are highly desirable in this respect, including the formal definition of the various responsibilities involved in the decision-making processes.

Similarly, no data are available on the differential effects of these models, either in general or in more specific terms. Significant investment in promoting and implementing a series of studies is required in order to elucidate basic questions. These questions include, Which model is more appropriate for which kind of disabled population? What is the appropriate time investment for each of them? What kind of teachers are most adequate for the respective models? and so forth. Such an investment may prove to be highly profitable to special education and allow for more sound decision making, based more on knowledge and less on personal preferences.

Organization and Administration

The general organization scheme of the Israeli special education structure can be viewed as basically reflecting a heterogeneous approach. In addition to the already mentioned tendencies toward mainstreaming and integration, many of the more segregated special educational programs are of heterogeneous nature—they integrate children with a great diversity of impairments within the same classroom. Philosophically, these tendencies are to a great extent contingent upon the assumption that school has to prepare its students for real life, which is heterogeneous by its very nature. This principle is clearly stated in an official document of the Ministry of Education, defining the major goal of special education as follows: "To act for the rehabilitation of the handicapped and disabled children and to prepare them to a regular social and occupational life to the best of their possibilities. . . . It is aspired to use all available educational and treatment procedures which will facilitate the integration of each child within the regular educational framework" (Minister of Education, 1992, 7).

In other words, special education is envisaged as a bidirectional, rather than a unidirectional, educational establishment. Heterogeneity, despite its inherent difficulties, is considered to be of greater efficiency in terms of the basic preparation of the individual for life. John Dewey's principle that in order to prepare for life within a democratic society the school itself has to be based on democracy, applies no less to heterogeneity. If one wants to adequately prepare the student to live within a heterogeneous society, the school has also to be based on the same principle.

The heterogeneity principle is eventually combined with a higher level of differentiation in terms of the student's specific needs for special assistance and support. As implied by the earlier described integration models, children studying in *promoting classes*—special education classes within the regular school system—have certain common programs with the regular classes of the same age group. These models prescribe also differential programs for certain categories of children who study partially in the special education class and who are partially integrated in a regular class. This is in addition to common leisure-time activities of a more informal nature.

Referral and Placement Procedures

The absorption of a child within the special education framework is determined on the basis of an assessment and placement procedure established by the Special Education Law. As a rule, no child is accepted into special education without first having undergone a thorough and detailed process of psychoeducational evaluation. The findings of this evaluation have to be presented in a written document, which relates the student's cognitive, physical, emotional, and social characteristics and concludes with detailed recommendations for placement, as well as for educational and treatment methods to be employed in the child's social and scholastic rehabilitation.

The formal referral and placement procedures, as imposed by Israeli legislation, are relatively complex and time consuming. This is to ensure that the student will benefit from optimal educational facilities and that all necessary measures will be taken to place the child in the least restrictive educational environment. The ultimate goal is to create for the student an efficient social and educational context to allow for a maximal realization of his or her potential.

Certain required procedural steps are included in referral and placement. Referral for placement into special education programs can be made by the following parties: parents; public or private psychological services; municipality or state social services; social institutions, such as orphanages, dealing with the child; and schools and any other official educational institutions.

The referral application is forwarded for consideration and decision to the *Vaadat Hassama,* "Placement Committee," which is headed by the representative of the local municipality. The committee is composed of professionals, such as psychologists, educators, social workers, and representatives of parental organizations. This is meant to ensure a wide spectrum of views and to avoid the rapid decisions sometimes made under the impact of a given event or determined by specific teacher-student relationships.

The possible decisions of the Placement Committee are relatively varied. These include requirement of additional information through testing, classroom observation, social worker reports, and so on. The decision may be placement in regular educational programs with recommendations for special treatment, such as remedial teaching, resource rooms, and the like, or placement in special education programs.

In the case that the parents, teacher, referring institution, or student are not satisfied with the committee's decision, they are entitled to file an appeal to the *Vaadat Arar,* "Appeal Committee," within twenty-one days after reception of the official notice of the Placement Committee's decision. The Appeal Committee is headed by the regional superintendent of the Ministry of Education. The decisions of this committee are final and are to be implemented by all concerned.

Voluntary Public Organizations

Social awareness of the needs of special education expresses itself in a great number of national voluntary organizations functioning in the various localities in Israel. These local groups are generally centered around a specific impairment, such as Down's syndrome, cystic fibrosis, hearing impairments, autism, and so on.

Actually, there are about twenty such national voluntary organizations. Some of them are highly active in producing informative materials and organizing meetings and colloquia. Most of them are involved in organizing summer activities and vacation colonies for the children and families belonging to their organization. In some cases, internationally recognized authorities in the respective fields are invited for public lectures and face-to-face treatment of both children and their parents. Most of these activities are also of a voluntary nature.

The Arabic and Druze Sectors

The special education student population in both non-Jewish sectors is about 7 percent of the total special education population in Israel. These figures are considerably lower than the rate of these same ethnic groups in the general Israeli population (about 15 percent). The reasons for this may originate in a higher level of tolerance to deviances and inadequacies within the Arabic and Druze school settings. The lower rate is also a product of a somewhat more recent social and educational awareness of the nature of special education problems, as well of the existent possibilities for coping with them.

The separate educational system for those two ethnic groups is based in language as well as in cultural differences. The financial and educational responsibilities pertain to the Ministry of Education, as do other specific educational systems, such as the Hasidic ultraorthodox one. These do not include the educational system of the territories that came under Israeli ruling in 1967, which are governed by the military authorities in correspondence with the Jordanian jurisdiction.

According to Nagar (1991), nine special kindergartens and twenty-five special education schools serve the Arabic and Druze population. These are almost exclusively of a segregated nature. Data on the number of mainstreamed students in the sectors are not available. Generally, the Arabic education system rapidly assimilates the Jewish educational approaches, so we may assume that the existent discrepancies between the two educational systems will be balanced out in the near future.

Major Controversies and Issues in Special Education

The issue of the socioeducational placement of high-risk children is probably one of the most persistent issues in the current Israeli educational system. Despite the fact that mainstreaming is gaining more and more terrain, it still arouses controversy. Questions are posed concerning its differential efficiency for specific segments of the handicapped population. Systematic research is still scarce and the bulk of accumulating information is not yet conclusive.

This controversy is worldwide and influenced by the following factors:

1. The social value system of the respective society and its emphasis on realization of the individual's potentials as a major ingredient in ensuring his or her well-being.
2. The financial burden imposed on society by the rather expensive costs of small educational units usually present in special education frameworks.
3. The extremely high costs of keeping individuals throughout their lifetime under sheltered socioeconomic and occupational conditions, which are usually nonproductive and not contributing to the well-being of society.
4. The prevalent social attitudes on the possible impact of education on the individual's level and nature of functioning. Such attitudes are based on the extent to which society considers that human beings can be meaningfully modified and their capacities increased via environmental intervention.
5. The basic belief of society in its own capacities to introduce and maintain meaningful alterations in the individual's level of general and intellectual functioning through its educational system.

Another major issue prevalent in the Israeli educational system is the nature of the assessment procedures used in order to decide the educational trajectory of the individual. Until the last two decades, conventional static testing was almost exclusively used for all decision-making processes. The inadequacy of such assessment procedures, especially in the multicultural society of Israel, becomes more and more evident and many procedures require significant changes in this domain as well as in the predictive value attributed to the measured IQ.

Although the conventional static testing measures are still prevalent and frequently utilized, there are strong tendencies to rely less on these tests and to introduce more innovative assessment procedures as official evaluation methods. Moreover, there is considerable disappointment regarding the predictive value of such testing, and the Law of Special Education explicitly requires retesting after a period of three years.

Emerging and Future Trends

The large amount of accumulated experience with special education in general and the openness of the Israeli educational system to the innovative and the challenging promise continuation of the dynamic character of special education in Israel. Currently, universities are continuously and heavily involved in experimental studies, accumulating a great wealth of data concerning the existent, as well as the prospective, educational procedures. Efforts are geared to a systematic evaluation of the efficiency of various didactic and pedagogic methods implemented in the diverse special education frameworks.

Israel's educational establishment considers the teacher as the major factor in promoting social adaptation of its students. Consequently, heavy investments are annually channeled to improving and adapting the training procedures in both the teacher seminars and academic institutions. In-service training, which already at this stage is most popular, will probably expand considerably and become an integral part of the teacher's work. We may anticipate that in-service training will become mandatory for both the teacher and the educational authorities.

Similarly, teacher training, as well as in-service training for the regular teaching staff, will probably become more loaded with special education problems and didactic methods. The encounter of every teacher with problems of special children will be almost general, and without a thorough preparation of the teaching staff to deal with the diversity and severity of such problems, the success of the so-desired mainstreaming will be jeopardized. We may assume that the distinctive lines between education and special education will become more loose and teachers will be trained to cope with the widest spectrum of educational problems and difficulties.

In conclusion, we may have a rather optimistic view of the future of the Israeli educational system in general and of its special education branches. Coming back to the old Jewish dictum mentioned in this chapter, we may assume that the grandchildren of our children will be educationally better off due to the more appropriate treatment we offer to their grandparents.

References

Bart, H. 1975. To the history of special education (in Hebrew). In I. Nir, ed. *Chapters in special education*. Jerusalem: Ministry of Education, Department of Pedagogy.

Feuerstein, R., Rand, and Hoffman. 1979. *The dynamic assessment of retarded performers; The learning potential assessment device, theory, instruments and techniques*. Baltimore, Md.: University Park Press.

Hallahan, D. P., and Kauffman, J. M. 1990. *Exceptional children*. Englewood Cliffs, N.J.: Prentice-Hall.

Minister of Education. 1992. *Special education report*. Israel: Minister of Education.

Nagar, N. 1991. *Special education in the educational frameworks in Israel*. Jerusalem: Ministry of Education and Culture, Special Education Branch.

Scheerenberger, R. C. 1982. Treatment from ancient times to the present. In Cegelca and H. J. Preham, eds. *Mental retardation: From categories to people*. Columbus, Ohio: Merrill.

Yitzchaki, I. 1985. *The rights of the child and the adolescent in the Israeli legislation*. Tel Aviv: University of Tel Aviv, Papyrus.

Zaks S., Michael, E., and Liberman F. 1989. *Special education in Israel*. Jerusalem: Ministry of Education.

20

Poland

WLADYSLAWA PILECKA

JAN PILECKI

There is no invalid,
there is only a man.
M. Grzegorzewska

The modern founder of special education in Poland was Maria Grzegorzewska (1888–1967), whose quote opens this chapter. Grzegorzewska not only organized special schools but she also created theoretical principles for educating and teaching children with special needs. As well, she initiated the establishment of the State Institute of Special Education in Warsaw that prepared teachers for special schools.

Special education in Poland today is considered both a theoretical discipline and a practical area. It is the theoretical discipline of special pedagogics when it creates theoretical elements of understanding and realization about the educational process and the rehabilitation of people with special needs.

About the Authors • Wladyslawa Pilecka is a psychologist and professor of psychology. She is a director of the Department of Psychology at the Pedagogical University in Kraków. She has published widely in Polish and English. Her major research interests are in the development of blind, mentally retarded, and chronically ill children. Her most recent book is *Dynamics of Psychic Development in Children Suffering from Asthma and Cystic Fibrosis.* • Jan Pilecki has worked as a headmaster of a special school for mentally retarded children and as an inspector of special schools in Kraków Province. He is now an assistant director of the Department of Special Education. He has published widely in Polish, German, and French. His research interests include social and professional adjustment of mentally retarded individuals, social and moral development of mentally retarded children, communication strategies of teachers and students, and the development of mentally retarded children.

On the other hand, it is the practical activity of educating and teaching when it converts psychoeducational statements coming from various areas of the social and natural sciences into practical statements. In this sense, special education means a wide spectrum of psychoeducational interventions meeting the unique needs of people of atypical development. Special pedagogics (theory) and special education (teaching and practice) are two sides of one coin. The theory is manifested in the process of rehabilitation, therapy, educating, and teaching.

Twenty years ago, special education students referred to those children and youth who could not be taught in regular schools. Today, special education is growing into regular education; it is slowly becoming an integral part. In the past, the general aim of special education in Poland was the rehabilitation and development of individuals so that they might reach their full potential and become contributing members of society. In recent years, prevention, early intervention, and educational and social integration have been discussed as the major problems in Polish special education.

Every year more and more children with special needs attend regular kindergartens and schools, and new centers for prevention and early intervention are organized. But the number of different kinds of educational services are still small in relation to the needs, and there are a great number of exceptional children and teenagers. Polish society, especially those people connected with special education units, believe that the current political and economic reforms will promote the growth of appropriate forms of special assistance given to children and youth with special needs. We hope that the intellectual, emotional, and social integration of all exceptional persons will be realized in a few years. The idea of mainstreaming will become a fact.

Historical Background

Poland has a long and rich history of providing services to children and youth with special needs. The first institutions for the mentally retarded were organized in Kraków and in Gdansk in 1542; medical treatment and education were offered. During the next two centuries, hospitals and institutions for handicapped individuals were established by monasteries and convents.

The partitions of Poland by Russia, Prussia, and Austria in the eighteenth century stopped the development of special protection and care for handicapped children. A more dynamic growth of a number of special schools and institutions followed in the nineteenth century and during the first half of the twentieth century. The initial efforts were aimed at children with sensory and mental handicaps. A school for deaf children was established in Warsaw in 1817; a school for blind children opened twenty-five years later.

TABLE 20.1.   Growth of Special Education in Poland

Year	Number of Special Schools	Number of Students
1947	97	11,802
1957	309	34,732
1967	455	65,990
1974	625	89,630
1987	765	82,359
1990	760	83,645

In the last school year before World War II, there were 104 special schools; 12,076 children were in attendance. The great number of special institutions and schools owed their existence to private philanthropic organizations and religious charities (Lipkowski 1977).

Since the end of World War II, the growth of special education in Poland has been phenomenal—in the two years after the war the number of pupils in the special schools came up to the level it was before the war. Data in table 20.1 documents the growth of special education in the past forty-three years (Mauersberg 1990; *Statistical Yearbook* 1990).

Prevalence of Children with Special Needs

It is impossible to estimate the exact number of children with exceptionalities in Poland. Research emphasizes three major causes of these difficulties with prevalence: serious definitional problems, inconsistent classifications of exceptional children, and a lack of exact epidemiological data. (Hulek 1989; Spionek 1975; Tomasik 1989) It should be noted that a clear differentiation between typical and atypical development in a child is sometimes very difficult.

One report (Hulek 1989) indicates that among 11,636,700 Polish children birth to nineteen years there are 1,260,000 to 1,400,000 (10 to 12 percent) children who require rehabilitation, psychotherapeutic interventions, and special education. A further 2,100,000 to 2,240,000 (18 to 20 percent) suffer from very mild impairments in body structure and system function such as scoliosis, flatfoot, and hyperactivity. These children should also be given special care and assistance.

Table 20.2 shows that children with learning disabilities form the major category of children requiring special education in Polish schools. This group includes vastly different populations that reveal a wide variety of behavioral and interpersonal problems. In the psychopedagogical literature, these children are described as hyperactive, brain damaged, perceptually impaired, dyslexic, and manifesting difficulties in attention, memory, coordination, reasoning, and emotional and social interactions (Nartowska 1972; Spionek 1975; Tomasik 1989). It is interesting to note that students with learning disabilities have always been mainstreamed in Poland. They attend regular classrooms, and in addition they participate in compensatory classes.

In recent years some researchers (Hulek 1989; Obuchowska and Krawczynski 1991; Pilecka 1990) have observed an increasing emphasis on psychoeducational aspects of chronic diseases in children. Health handicaps in children are caused by the rapid development of industry and motor transportation, pollution of the environment, and an inordinate use of chemical products, medications, and drugs.

T A B L E 20.2.   Prevalence of Exceptional Children, by Type of Handicap

Type of Exceptionality	Number of Children (Approx.)	% Receiving Special Education or Care	% Exceptional of Total Child Population (Ages 0–19 Years)
Mentally retarded	240,000	6.8	2.0
Blind and visually handicapped	12,000	0.3	0.1
Deaf and hearing impaired	11,550	0.3	0.1
Chronically ill or suffering from asthma, allergies, cystic fibrosis, cancer, diabetes mellitus, juvenile arthritis, congenital heart diseases, disorders of metabolism	330,566	9.4	2.8
Neurologically disabled (cerebral palsy, spina bifida, epilepsy, aphasia)	158,500	4.5	1.4
Physically handicapped	20,000	0.6	0.2
Learning disabled (and of school-age)	1,102,275	31.5	9.5 (about 15.0% of school-age population)
Socially maladjusted (and of 15–19 years)	50,000	1.4	0.4 (about 2.4% of population of 15–19 years)
Other	1,575,109	45.2	13.5
Total	3,500,000	100.0	30.0

Note: These figures do not account for all cases.

Diagnosis of Children with Special Needs

Diagnosis and assessment are the basis of counseling for exceptional children. These procedures determine the children's general schooling, vocational training, and direct therapeutic and educational interventions.

Every child with special needs is diagnosed. In the past the assessment focused on the weaknesses of the child; it was a negative diagnosis. Now professionals emphasize intra-individual strengths and maximizing opportunities for developing intellectual and personality competencies; this is positive diagnosis.

Many tests, scales, checklists, and inventories are used to assess children's various functional domains. For every special population there exist specific types of measures and instruments. The diagnosis is made by a multidisciplinary team consisting of a physician, psychologist, educator, social worker, parents, and other clinical specialists. Diagnosis is not a single operation, but an ongoing process, which is an integral part of therapy and education. This multidimensional assessment should provide information about physical growth and development including medical history, motor skills, perceptual and sensorimotor skills, intellectual ability, social and emotional development, academic achievements, family climate, and the socioeconomic status of the family.

Children recommended for special education are entered into a register by local school authorities who then have the responsibility of providing the necessary services to the child and his or her family. Placement decisions are discussed with the parents whose permission is very important for admission.

In recent years, professionals have more and more often attempted to identify children with special needs before they start their education. Most of these identified children are placed directly in special kindergartens, and later in special schools. Some are enrolled in regular kindergartens or schools where they are observed and evaluated continuously in order that the most appropriate educational program can be prepared for them.

The Organization of Special Education

One of the most essential tasks of kindergartens, schools, and special homes is to give any kind of assistance and help that exceptional children may require in order to achieve the degree of school success to which their individual abilities entitle them. The organization of the assistance given to children with special needs rests on the assumption that it is within the family circle and at school that the child finds the best conditions for his or her psychological development. Because of that assumption, the help given to the families of such children and the various forms of help organized by

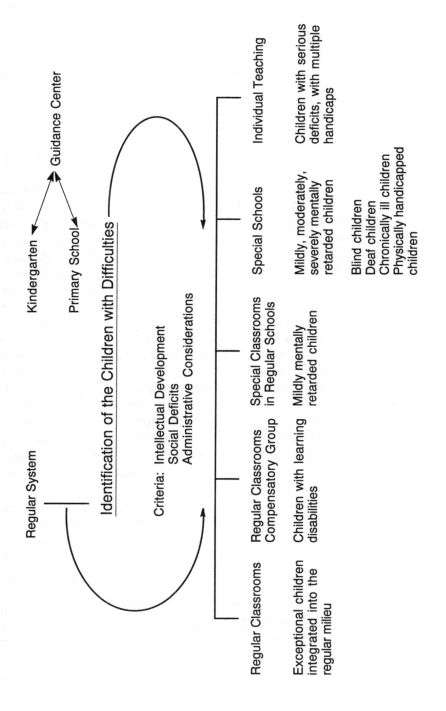

Figure 20.1   The general system of educating exceptional children.

schools are the concern of advisory centers, of headmasters, and of teachers. In case the child does not find suitable reeducational conditions within the family circle or at the school, other opportunities, such as the assistance of special therapeutic and compensatory institutions or of special schools or children's homes, are offered (see figure 20.1).

The assistance given to the exceptional children is effective if the disorders and distortions of normal development are noticed as early as possible. Only then does the work on counteracting and neutralizing them begin.

Guidance and Advisory Centers

The assistance given to children with special needs is organized by educational and vocational advisory centers, which cooperate with special advisory centers of the health service—for example, the speech defects and hearing defects center, the psychological advisory center, and others. Such a center gives a medical diagnosis on physical development and its disorders and diagnose psychological development and the level attained in mental development. It analyzes psychomotor functions and personality. It gives a pedagogical diagnosis of how advanced a child is in his or her schoolwork and how this progress compares with that of his or her peers, and it conducts a social assessment that includes family conditions, relationships, and atmosphere. The center advises what form of compensatory help the handicapped child needs, directs mentally handicapped children to special schools and homes, or recommends some other form of special education. As well, the center performs periodical checkups of children and young people in special schools in order to make the diagnosis up-to-date and return the child to his or her previous ordinary school if that is possible and advisable. The center also undertakes some prophylactic measures and various forms of assistance, such as advising parents and teachers, offering correctional tasks in dayrooms or therapeutic centers, and influencing the child's environment. It organizes observation dayrooms in order to obtain a correct diagnosis and directs children to the centers they require.

The diagnosis is the basis for individualized pedagogical, therapeutic, and compensatory measures, which are undertaken to eliminate the causes of developmental inhibitions and, in this way, of a child's school failure. For children with developmental disturbances that are impossible to eliminate in the course of normal schoolwork, special compensatory classes are organized, either at the previously mentioned centers in towns or in comprehensive schools in rural areas. The work is either individual or involves a group of children. For children only mildly backward in their development, the center advises parents on the best forms and methods to be employed in educating their children.

The Help and Assistance Given at Regular Schools

Developmental disorders become evident in the first place in the course of schoolwork. Hence, the school faces the task of helping mildly backward children. In order to help these children, schools can organize individual help for children with difficulties in their schoolwork; help children with fragmentary developmental deficits; have classes for those children diagnosed as needing special education because of some physical or mental handicap; and organize various forms of assistance for parents having children with some developmental disorders (pedagogics for parents).

Compensatory classes in schools are organized early on in the school period for younger children who need help in eliminating speech disorders or catching up on school-acquired knowledge or who need reeducation because of some fragmentary deficits in psychophysical development. Compensatory classes are organized for older children with the same kind of developmental disorders. They are usually organized for children from the same class but, if necessary, they can be organized for children from different classes.

For children from forms 1 and 2, lessons in compensatory classes are conducted by specialists in logopedics and therapeutic work, and by psychologists. If no specialists are available, then classes are conducted by teachers after they have taken an appropriate course. For the assistance of children with difficulties in schoolwork caused by lack of favorable conditions within the family, schools organize dayrooms and day-boarding schools. These programs encourage peer help and offer individual assistance from a male or female leader in coping with homework and in enlarging school-acquired knowledge and skills.

Particular care is given to children with mild physical handicaps such as partially hearing and partially sighted children, who qualified for an ordinary school at the preschool age. Appropriate conditions of work are created for them, their development is monitored by a doctor and a psychologist, and they are given additional help in compensatory classes if need be. In general an atmosphere of approval and help is created in a school community. It is the form leader's task to see to it that parents supply these pupils with necessary equipment such as glasses or hearing aids. In addition, appropriate special advisory centers constantly monitor the students' development. Teachers of particular subjects are expected to individualize the tasks and demands and to help in mastering the syllabus if the children need such help.

It has been found worthwhile to educate mildly mentally retarded children in integrated groups together with ordinary children that do not have developmental disturbances or deficits. In ordinary schools, therefore, there are special classes if necessary for children who are mildly mentally retarded, partially hearing, or partially sighted, as well as special vocational classes for the mildly mentally retarded.

The present-day tendency in Poland, both of university centers and school authorities, is individualized teaching. This allows the school to give a small child an appropriate education without taking him or her away from the family and peer group. It means educating all children diagnosed as needing special education without allotting them places in special schools, and allowing parents to take part in the rehabilitation process, especially in the case of partially hearing and partially sighted children. For delicate children and those with health problems, therapeutic and educational children's camps and sanatoria are organized.

Care and Education of Children with Special Needs

Some groups of children with various handicaps and developmental disorders are taken care of by special education institutions. These are children who are partially sighted, blind, partially hearing, deaf, chronically ill, mildly mentally retarded, moderately and severely mentally retarded, or maladjusted (see tables 20.3 and 20.4.)

Because the handicaps from which the children suffer vary greatly between and within special education institutions, both in kind and in degree, the educational authorities have empowered the headmasters and school staff councils to introduce into the curricula for special schools and classes any changes they may see fit. The content of the curriculum is to be analyzed by the aforementioned bodies and appropriate changes introduced, according to children's abilities and skills.

As it is obvious that the handicapped are fully rehabilitated only when they are prepared to cope independently with life in a community, various school bodies try to secure vocational training, appropriate to the kind of handicap, for all graduates of special primary schools. With this aim in view, various vocational schools and classes are organized. There are special elementary technical schools with their own workshops, diversified according to the kind of handicap, and special elementary vocational schools without their own workshops. Here the learners get their practical training in the workshops of an ordinary technical school, of a local industrial plant, or in

T ABLE 20.3.   Special Kindergartens and Schools

	Schools	Pupils	Teachers
Special kindergartens	133	5,742	695
Special primary schools	765	82,359	9,865
Special secondary schools	19	1,006	199
Special vocational schools	268	23,275	1,778
Individual tuition	—	7,319	—
Total	1,185	119,701	12,537

TABLE 20.4. Special Boarding Schools

Type of Student	Institution	Inmates	Educators
The blind and partially sighted	8	1,192	274
The deaf	22	2,929	632
The partially hearing	4	449	94
The chronically ill	2	744	163
The physically handicapped	3	492	73
The mildly mentally retarded	302	20,805	3,742
The moderately and severely mentally retarded	67	4,872	1,050
The maladjusted	66	4,163	1,125
Total	474	35,646	7,153

the workshops of cooperatives for invalids. There are also special elementary vocational schools attached to a local industry, special elementary vocational schools attached to a cooperative for invalids, and special vocational classes in ordinary vocational schools. If the vocational training of the handicapped young person is carried out not in an institution of special education but in an ordinary school or factory, the school authorities exercise supervision and organize assistance to help with educational problems and progress in subjects of a more theoretical nature.

Vocational schools are founded for mildly mentally retarded pupils who have completed forms 5 or 6 and are at the same time over fourteen or fifteen years of age. They also serve pupils who seem to be lagging in their general level of mental development and are therefore not able to continue education in the ordinary secondary schools. After graduating from the vocational eighth form of the eight-form special primary school, the pupil obtains a certificate of graduation which specifies what trade or profession he or she has mastered.

Local school authorities and headmasters of vocational schools are obliged to act in every possible manner to promote independence for the inmates of homes for the handicapped. In their attempts, they should be helped by the local health department and social service. Services include assisting the inmates in obtaining an apartment, giving financial assistance during the first weeks of independence, and allotting the necessary "dowry" to enable the ex-inmate to lead an independent life. Inmates are given permission to have meals in a school canteen, encouraged to participate in the activities of school clubs, and given further moral and educational assistance in the form of guidance and advice.

A lot of effort nowadays goes into the organization of the so-called "school of life" in schools and homes for the moderately and severely mentally retarded. The main task of the "school of life" is to stimulate the development of maturity and teach practical skills necessary in everyday life and work.

In teaching these children to read, write, and do some arithmetic, the program is adjusted to the individual perceptual abilities of the child. The graduates of the "school of life" are directed to the cooperatives for invalids or sheltered workshops where the working conditions are supervised. Here, after a period of instruction, these people can be employed. As well, the centers run by the Society of Children's Friends prepare severely retarded children to undertake some kind of work.

The advisory work of sending severely handicapped children to do appropriate kinds of work is performed by the advisory psychological center, local health departments, and social service centers, with the help of the advisory centers for the rehabilitation of invalids.

Legislation

Law and public policy have had a profound effect on the type and quality of education offered to children with special needs. In Poland, current regulations for the protection and care of handicapped persons and the functioning of the special school systems reflect certain values and attitudes. These include the hierarchy of values in society, the quality of assistance given to the children with special needs, general education policy, and the social climate for the formation of attitudes toward handicapped persons. Also included are an understanding of the problems and needs of handicapped persons by society; the efforts of special teachers, theorists of special education, and advocates of children with special needs to protect them against discrimination; and the economic conditions of society.

There is a long tradition in Poland of providing for individuals with disabilities. The earliest information about the need for giving care to handicapped persons was in statutes dating from 1347. The first regulations relating to the protection and care of mentally ill and mentally retarded persons were included in a statute in the eighteenth century. On the basis of these acts, the first institutions for handicapped persons (children residing together with adults) were founded. The period of the eighteenth and nineteenth centuries, in which the growth of special school systems slowed, to be increased again in the late nineteenth century, was very difficult for the Polish nation. The partitions of Poland stopped the development of school law. The special schools were organized by various private persons and organizations.

With the establishment of Poland in 1918, the new government enacted the Decree on School Duty on 7 February 1919. The regulations of this decree provided seven years of schooling for all children. Handicapped children were obliged to attend special schools but they could be released from school duty if the special institution or school was over three kilometers from their homes. Although the Constitution of Poland from 1921 on included the fundamental rights of a child with respect to protection and care, the state authorities were not interested in the organization of special education. The special schools were established by teachers, physicians, advocates, and philanthropic organizations in this period. The lack of a suitable act relating to special education was the great obstacle in the development of this area.

In 1932 parliament promulgated the first Polish Education Law on the Structure of Education, which determined that schooling for abnormal children should be organized in special schools and institutions. If there was not a special unit in the child's town or village, he or she could be exempted from schooling. After World War II, the government became responsible for the education of all children. A decree of 1956 and the educational act of 1961 stipulated that handicapped children must receive an obligatory elementary (or secondary) education in addition to professional training. In this period many special kindergartens, schools, and institutions were established (see table 19.1).

The 1970s brought new initiatives in special education. These new conceptions caused further differentiation in the schooling of children and youth with disabilities. The instructions of the Ministry of Education from 1973 and 1976 allowed the organization of various forms of assistance for children meeting difficulties in their schoolwork, such as compensatory classes, resource rooms, and individual tuition. These acts also prolonged compulsory primary education for exceptional students to eight years of elementary school.

The more recent enactments of the Ministry of Education speak to the interests of children with special needs. However, interest as an educational ideal was not the motivation for passing the new regulations; rather, the motivation was to facilitate ad hoc solutions to alleviate problems. In rural areas, for example, special education institutes may be located in a distant town, making it impractical to send students there. In such a case the student may be allowed to remain in his or her normal classroom. In other instances it may be impossible to organize a special education class at the regular school, therefore making it necessary that the students with special needs be taught along with his or her regular peers.

The current special education legislation is under review and discussion. It is often criticized (Hulek 1989). The revision of school law is a very important problem which must be solved in the future.

The Education of Teachers for Special Schools

Special teachers and educators in Poland are trained at eight universities and three pedagogical universities. Special education training of teachers for the mentally handicapped is conducted by all universities; for sensory impaired, by three; for chronically ill and physically handicapped, by two; and for maladjusted, by six. The universities organize three forms of studies. These are day studies for young people who want to be special teachers; extramural studies, which means on-the-job training for teachers from special schools; and postgraduate studies of two or three semesters. Postgraduate studies may lean to an M.A. in Polish language and literature or in history and mathematics—qualifying the recipient for the work in special schools—or an M.A. in special pedagogics—giving the students up-to-date knowledge within a given range of specialization. Day and extramural studies last for five years. Studies culminate in an exam, which is part of a defense of the student's diploma work. The degree of Magister (Mgr) corresponds to a M.Ed. degree.

The curriculum of a five-year M.A. course of studies of special pedagogics is as follows:

1. A group of the same subjects for all the students; for example, philosophy, sociology, general psychology, developmental psychology, educational psychology, and pedagogy
2. A group of optional subjects; for example, teaching methods of the Polish language, teaching methods of mathematics
3. A group of special subjects for students in the specialization which they select; for example, psychology of the mentally retarded, psychology of the deaf or of the blind, education and teaching methods in junior schools for the mentally retarded, or phonetics and the elements of logopedics for the deaf

The curriculum has a number of periods for practical training. This training must take place in grades 1 to 3 of a primary school, according to the course chosen by the student. It may be in grades 4 to 8 of a senior special school, the subject taught being to the student's choice of an optional subject. There is also practical training, comprising the whole of methodological and educational work, in a home for the handicapped—the kind of home determined by the specialization of the student—and training in a boarding school. Besides the periods of practical training listed so far, it is part of the syllabus of education and teaching methods to spend one day a week in a special school, the type of school matching the specialization chosen by the student.

For several years now, discussion has been going on in Poland on the changes to be introduced in the education of teachers in general and, within this framework, on the education of special school teachers. In these discussions, the content of the curricula has been criticized as being too theoretical, and the inadequate practical training received by future teachers and educators has been pointed out.

The Social Context of Special Education

Special education in Poland has always developed in very difficult political and economic conditions. School authorities have never been interested in the dynamic growth of special school systems. On the other hand, many advocacy groups of professionals and parents have always existed for improving care, education, and training of children with special needs.

Many organizations have contributed to the development of special education. These public organizations were and are the real motive power for improving life conditions, care, education, and training of children with special needs. They include the Special Education Section of the Teacher's Trade Union, the Association of Children's Friends, the Polish Society of the Disabled, the Polish Union of the Deaf, the Polish Union of the Blind, the Polish Scout National Fund of Children, Caritas (a religious charity), and various public foundations. Essentially, these organizations perform certain functions. They identify the problems of children and youth with special needs; initiate new solutions in the rehabilitation and education of exceptional children; evaluate the curriculum of teaching in the special schools and prepare new conceptions; and organize rehabilitation services and camps, as well as institutions for profoundly handicapped individuals. They also support research concerning different aspects of handicaps and develop better public understanding and the acceptance of disabled people.

In the late 1950s and 1960s, parents' organizations had a tremendous impact on special education. Parents' organizations, together with professional special educators, formed groups to pressure local governments to establish new special schools and rehabilitation centers. Today, parents of exceptional children want to be involved in every issue affecting their children's education. They participate in the different kinds of therapy and in the school's decision-making process. Cooperating with the specialists, they positively influence the development of their children through home intervention. They support the realization of mainstreaming, promote positive interaction with teachers by recognizing their children's problems, and share educational responsibility. The presence of parents with handicapped children in the streets, shops, and means of public transport, and their participation in the different kinds of television programs, increase public awareness and understanding of individuals with special needs.

In recent years, advocacy groups and parents have started to fight for placement in the regular schools and kindergartens for their exceptional children. Theorists of special education (Hulek 1989; Koscielska 1984; Sekowska 1991) have created new principles of schooling and educating children with special needs by using foreign experiences and reports from different countries. Unfortunately, the economic difficulties of Poland are the great barriers to the realization of the full integration of handicapped children.

Future Trends in Polish Special Education

The further development of special education in Poland will depend on attention to the following areas and problems:

1. A comprehensive program of early identification and early intervention should be prepared by the Ministry of Health and Social Welfare and the Ministry of Education.
2. Further differentiation of the forms of special education should be done according to the needs and age of exceptional children.
3. Occupational training for exceptional youth should be improved. The new vocational specializations should be offered to them and their vocational skills should be increased.
4. Regular schools' and kindergartens' milieu (in a physical and social sense) should be prepared for children with special needs. Parents should be involved directly in the educational process, especially in the kindergartens and centers of early intervention. The parents' efficiency will depend on their practical preparation.
5. Equipment of special educational units should be enriched by providing various instructional means, including new technology products.
6. Special education training should be changed. In the current years two proposals have been discussed. First, special teachers and educators should be trained in a general way; they should learn the educational needs of exceptional children as a group with common characteristics. Second, special teachers and educators should be trained with no less than two specializations; for example, in pedagogics of mentally retarded children and pedagogics of blind children.
7. A revision of current special education legislation should be done to provide new and functional instructions for special schools and social integration.
8. Before the introduction of any new solutions in special educational practice, a relative research study should be conducted in order to create the empirical basis for the solutions. The long-term program

of scientific investigations corresponding with the needs of special education should be prepared by the Ministry of Education.
9. In the future, the local government should be responsible for the education of the children with special needs.

It should be noted that the realization of these tasks will be determined by further reforms in the economic and political arenas, the changes in the general system of education, the needs of handicapped people, and current trends and solutions in special education in Poland and in other countries.

References

Hulek, A. 1989. *Current and future trends in special education in Poland*: Thematic report No. 11. Warsaw-Kraców: State Scientific Publishing House.

Koscielska, M. 1984. *Mental retardation and social development.* Warsaw: State Scientific Publishing House.

Lipkowski, O. 1992. Tenth anniversary of the death of Maria Grzegorzewska. *Szkol a Specjalna* 2:83–86.

Mauersberg, S. 1990. *History of special education and pedagogics.* Warsaw: State Scientific Publishing House.

Nartowska, H. 1972. *Hyperactive children. Behaviour disorders and learning difficulties.* Warsaw: Educational Publishing House.

Obuchowska, I., and Krawczynski, M. 1991. *Sick child.* Warsaw: Publishing House "Our Bookshop."

Pilecka, W. 1990. *Dynamics of psychic development in children suffering from asthma and cystic fibrosis.* Kraców: Publishing House of the Pedagogical University.

Sekowska, Z. 1982. *Special pedagogics.* Warsaw: State Scientific Publishing House.

Spionek, H. 1975. *Developmental disorders and learning difficulties in students.* Warsaw: State Scientific Publishing House.

Statistical yearbook. 1990. Warsaw: State Scientific Publishing House.

Tomasik, E. 1989. *Special assistance given to regular schools.* Warsaw: State Scientific Publishing House.

21

Australia

GEOFFREY SWAN

*A*ustralia is the smallest but geologically the oldest continent. It has an area of 7.7 million square kilometers, and a population of just less than 17 million. Of the entire population, nearly 5 million are children under the age of fifteen years.

Australia was first used by the British as a convict settlement in 1788. Later, free settlers were encouraged to colonize the country to the detriment of the original settlers, the Aborigines and the Torres Strait Islanders. About 75 percent of the present population of Australia is of British descent, 20 percent is of other European origin, and 3.5 percent is of Asian or African origin. Aborigines and Torres Strait Islanders constitute 1.5 percent of the present population; their problems of education and integration in their own country are not covered in this chapter.

Different parts of the continent were settled at different times, and the country was eventually divided into colonies governed independently of one another. However, after a referendum on 1 January 1901, the people decided that the states should form the Commonwealth of Australia. The

---

About the Author • Geoffrey Swan was, until his retirement in 1987, inspector of schools (special education) in the Queensland Department of Education. In 1973, he was the first appointee ever to the position. Prior to this he had been principal of what was called the State School for Spastic Children at New Farm from where he was awarded a Churchill Fellowship in 1968 to study the education of cerebral palsy in the United Kingdom, Europe, and the United States. He was foundation secretary of the Minister's Advisory Council for Special Education and has been a member of professional organizations and voluntary organizations providing services for disabled children. For such services he was awarded the OBE in the 1988 Queen's Birthday Honors. He is an honorary life member of numerous organizations and a visiting lecturer. He has a double master's degree in special education and educational administration from the University of Queensland.

geographical and political reasons for the borders seemed appropriate at the time and over the years only slight modifications have been made.

The states vary in size and population; most people live in the eastern states. Tasmania, the island state, has less than 1 percent of the population and occupies .9 percent of the land; Western Australia is about one-third of the continent with 1.6 million people. Canberra, the Capital Territory, and the Northern Territory have only recently been given the status of constituent states; they have populations of 281,700 and 156,000 respectively. Distances within the states vary considerably. In Queensland, Brisbane, the capital city, is closer to Melbourne, the capital of Victoria, than it is to the largest northern Queensland city, Cairns. In Victoria, however, most parts are within a day's drive from the capital, Melbourne. These geographical factors impinge on the effective and efficient delivery of services to disabled children in both rural and urban settings.

This chapter concerns Australian special education and some of its most pressing problems. These include: How does each of the Australian states provide for the education of the disabled? What are the patterns of provision, and to what extent does this country depend on other cultures for insight? What are the commonalties between the states and how does this country, almost as large as the United States without Alaska and about thirty-two times as large as the United Kingdom, look after its exceptional children, some living in closely settled cities and others living in remote communities?

The Structure of Australian Education

Under the Federal Constitution, the division of responsibilities between the Australian government and the state governments has been defined. Education is a state responsibility; however, when income taxing policy was handed to the federal government in 1942, that government became able to control the allocation of funds. Since then, the federal government has been able to influence education provision and policy through the manipulation of funding. So even though education does not appear as a federal responsibility under the Constitution, there are now over forty acts concerned with education being administered by over ten thousand public servants. Federal government involvement has helped maintain fiscal equalization and distribution of resources among the states and has provided valuable stimulation through its special grants commissions, data collection, and publication of reports.

Each state established a Department of Public Instruction. To keep up with innovations and changes, these were later changed to Departments of Education, which gradually evolved into highly centralized bureaucracies. Within each bureaucracy, there were well-defined divisions of preschool, primary, secondary, special, and postsecondary education. Over the last two decades there has been a devolution of the large central office to regional offices. This restructuring movement in Australian education departments corresponds rather closely with similar movements in other parts of the world.

As far as special education goes, it has been said that

> The history of special education looks like the sheds and garages of a cellarless backyard, acquired and added on in bits without ever contemplating a complete rebuild. If ordinary schools are to become special, then the management and organization structures which underpin special education have to gradually, progressively and perhaps painfully rebuild. (Dessent 1987)

Special education in Australia was pioneered by voluntary nongovernment organizations. Governments often assisted with financial grants and eventually assumed greater responsibility. Historically, the pattern of provision of special education has followed that of the United Kingdom. The first schools were for the deaf and later included sections for the blind. Much later, these sections were separated. Classes for the "backward" were next. With the poliomyelitis epidemics in the 1920s, schools for crippled children were established. More recently, facilities for children with behavior disorders and learning difficulties and, even more recently, the talented and gifted, have received some consideration.

Community and parent groups have played crucial roles in the development of Australian special education. Early education for children with hearing impairment was advocated by some teachers at the turn of the century, but it was not until the 1950s that parents began to organize mutual support groups, raise funds, and provide professional services. Organizations such as the Association for Pre-School Education of the Deaf were biased toward oral instruction, and parents were regarded as a essential part of the team. Later these same groups became the advocates for alternative programs for the deaf.

The state organizations have formed a national body known as the Australia Cerebral Palsy Association, which is interested in research and provides opportunities for national conferences. Spastic Welfare organizations also thought the school-starting age was too late to commence treatment programs to stimulate normal development and inhibit the possibility of any abnormal movement or deformity. Their baby programs were often conducted on a transdisciplinary model and helped parents, mostly mothers, develop stimulating home management programs. There are also state organizations for children with spina bifida, muscular dystrophy, and cystic fibrosis.

From the late 1960s, groups of parents of learning disabled children formed advocacy and support groups throughout Australia. Their name taken from specific learning disorder, SPELD organizations became effective and efficient pressure groups in their attempts to have some provision made for their poorly achieving children. Remedial teachers were trained and appointed to regular schools. The SPELD organization through their national body, AUSPELD, prompted the formation of a House of Representatives Select Committee to investigate the issues presented by the learning disabled.

Autism is a rare condition. In most Australian states, its treatment is the province of voluntary organizations assisted by government subsidies. Terms such as *autistic like* or *some autistic symptoms* are now used. The gifted and talented have also received more attention as a result of parent advocacy groups. Opportunities are provided by schools and community groups, although identification does not always mean that appropriate provision will be made.

Prevalence of Exceptional Conditions

The 1988 Survey of Disabled and Aged Persons (Australian Bureau of Statistics 1988) estimated that 13 percent of the Australian population was handicapped; that is, limited in some degree in their ability to perform certain tasks in relation to one or more of the following areas: self-care, mobility, verbal communication, schooling, and employment (Pickering and Szaday 1990). Of Australia's disabled population, two-thirds are seen as having a serious handicap (Ward 1984).

The prevalence of students requiring additional educational support has been a matter of national and international conjecture for many years, and the issue is still far from being resolved. Pickering and his colleagues point out that the confusion surrounding these estimates is due to variations in both the definition of disabling conditions and the methods used to collect data. Moreover, the confusion is compounded when some studies incorporate in their estimates those students whose difficulties appear to be due to environmental factors such as economic disadvantage or non-English speaking background and other studies exclude such students. Further, there appears to be little agreement about how severe a disabling condition must be before a child is included in the estimates (Pickering, Szaday, and Duedroth 1988).

As to disabilities in school-age children, Australian prevalence figures are roughly comparable to those of Europe and North America. In 1979, a commonwealth body, the Schools Commission, conducted the then only Australia-wide study into special education (Andrews et al. 1979). The study revealed prevalence rates of 2 to 3 percent, a fairly conventional finding for developmental disabilities. When added to the number of children requiring special education treatment at some time in their lives because of learning and/or emotional problems, the rates approach 15 to 16 percent (Ward

TABLE 21.1.   Ratio of Australian Males to Females Ages 5 to 14 Years, by Primary Handicapping Condition

Primary Condition	Males (%)	Females (%)	Ratio Males to Females
Mental disorders other than retardation, degeneration or slow at learning	0.60	0.15	4.0 : 1
Mental retardation, mental degeneration due to brain damage, slow at learning and specific developmental delays	2.02	0.95	2.1 : 1
Sight loss	0.25	0.08	3.0 : 1
Hearing loss	0.70	0.57	1.2 : 1
Nervous system diseases	0.95	0.63	1.5 : 1
Circulatory diseases	0.04	0.05	0.8 : 1
Respiratory diseases	1.56	1.03	1.5 : 1
Diseases of the musculoskeletal system and connective tissue	0.18	0.49	0.4 : 1
All other diseases and conditions	4.90	3.80	1.3 : 1
Total	7.35	3.99	1.8 : 1

Note: Adapted from the *Survey of Disability and Ageing* (ABS 1988) statistics and adjusted for a predominance of males in this age group (males = 1,256,300; females = 1,194,600).

1984). A later survey carried out on children from five to fourteen years of age in 1988 by the Australian Bureau of Statistics is presented in table 21.1.

General Causes of Disabilities

Australian Hearing Services is a federal government agency established as the National Acoustic Laboratories toward the end of World War II to assist servicemen deafened as a result of war. It has moved into the area of child audiology, and the statistics collected by this agency provide data for education administrators and planners. Using figures from the reports of the Australian Hearing Services, it is estimated that the incidence of hearing impairment has varied from 2 per 1,000 to 7 per 1,000 during rubella epidemics, with a current aggregate of nearly 3 per 1,000.[1] The possibility of further rubella epidemics is somewhat reduced by the rubella vaccination program aimed at immunizing all adolescent females during their school years.

At one time, trachoma caused a considerable number of children to suffer from visual handicaps. Through concerted government effort, trachoma is no longer a problem in the white population of Australia although is still very much so in some aboriginal communities. Causes of visual handicaps now appear to be congenital or hereditary, with rubella still accounting for a number of them. Childhood accidents account for an increasing number. The prevalence is less than 1 per child per 1,000 for all visual handicaps.

The moderately and severely intellectually handicapped now constitute the largest special education population, accounting for nearly 1 percent of the school population. Amendments to education acts and the provision of schools have enabled a number of children to attend schools who previously would have remained at home or would have been placed in institutions. With this move has come a wider definition of education.

There is a high prevalence of children born with Down's syndrome in the intellectually disabled group. Because of the availability of procedures to determine abnormality in the fetus, there may in the future be fewer children with Down's syndrome.

In the 1920s, poliomyelitis was the greatest crippler in Australia and, as a result of epidemics, associations for the welfare and education of crippled children were formed. Spastic Societies were established in each Australian state in the 1960s. The term *spastic* is used to include all children with cerebral palsy. With the discovery of Salk and widespread vaccination programs, poliomyelitis is now a rare condition.

Because of advances in medical science in the care of the newly born there are, however, an increased number of children surviving with cerebral palsy and spina bifida. The prevalence of cerebral palsy and spina bifida are each about the same, about 1 per 1,000. There are slight regional variations; the reasons for these variations are as yet unresolved and cause anxiety and concern for parents and prospective parents.

There is an increasing number of children being identified as having a behavior disorder. Some children who present gross management problems are admitted for short-term care, observation, and treatment into hospitals with attached schools. The number of children requiring long-term medical or surgical intervention and special schooling while in the hospital has declined considerably. The reduced number is partially replaced by an increase in the number of disturbed children. The appropriateness of some programs for disturbed children is being questioned by special educators.

Labeling the Handicapped Population

The problem of finding a term that accurately describes a condition and that also brings about a positive response without condemnatory overtones has provided material for discussion and will continue to do so. Any term that is used to describe disability seems in time to acquire its own odium, and the useful and positive life of some terms seem to be about fifteen to twenty years.

Classes for backward children were established in the 1920s. The term *backward* at the time seemed preferable to the other terms of the day—*idiot* and *moron*. Later these classes became *opportunity classes* and then in turn classes for the *mentally retarded,* the *slow learners,* the *intellectually handi-capped,* and the *intellectually disabled.* Labeling the school too can cause problems. *School for the deaf* seemed preferable to *school for the deaf and dumb.* The more recent term is *school for the hearing impaired.* To soften the impact, sometimes a school was named to honor some luminary with a subtitle to indicate the school's function.

Today the categories commonly used throughout Australia are hearing impaired, visually impaired, intellectually disabled, physically disabled, behavior disordered, learning difficulties, and talented and gifted. Considerable difficulties are experienced in attempting to define the intellectually disabled. The subgroup referred to as *mildly intellectually disabled* or *border-line* and sometimes as the *cultural-familial retarded* received considerable attention up until the 1970s. Educational placement was at issue for these children whose disability became more obvious when they failed in the academic tasks set in regular classrooms and were moved into special schools or classes.

Some states expended the greater part of the Special Education Vote on about 2 percent of the school population. Special curricula with work experience were developed, and teachers were trained to teach this group. With the acceptance of more disabled children into schools and the official abandonment by Directors of Special Education in 1975 of the use of the terms *educable* and *trainable,* the mildly intellectually disabled have moved back into the mainstream, in some cases without the benefits of the specially developed curricula and trained teachers.

Identification of Exceptionalities

All states today have baby health centers which offer free services to babies and mothers. Baby health centers or baby clinics are now staffed by personnel well informed of the problems associated with premature and low-birth-weight babies, sensory and social deprivation, and at-risk situations. Mothers are encouraged to attend baby health centers on a regular basis, and staff of the centers are trained to identify any variation in achieving developmental milestones. The focus is on normal development and the staff of these centers often alert mothers to any abnormality and provide referral to the appropriate agency. In centers of low population, itinerant services are available. Unfortunately, there is no national at-risk register.

The teachers and other staff at regular preschool centers have developed skills of identification of any disability likely to impede school progress, and informal and formal networks have been established. The quality of the service depends to a great extent on the caliber of the personnel involved. In many cases, it is admirable.

School psychological services, in some states referred to as guidance services, have grown steadily since the first appointment of school psychologists in the late forties and early fifties. The training for educational psychologists or guidance officers is usually undertaken by experienced classroom teachers who then work in close cooperation with parents and school personnel.

Psychological assessments now place less emphasis on individual intelligence tests, such as those developed by Binet and Weschler and modified for local use by the Australian Council for Educational Research, an independent national body funded by the states and the Commonwealth. Criterion-reference testing is now used extensively, as is a multidisciplinary assessment of student needs.

The last few years have seen greater cooperation between education, health, and welfare agencies in the provision of services. As well as the interagency cooperation, there have been improved communication and cooperation between the various professions involved in the identification and the provision of services for disabled children. Other professionals such as speech therapists (pathologists in some states), occupational therapists, and physiotherapists are used in the assessment of children. All states (with the exception of New South Wales) employ such professionals to form part of the transdisciplinary team. In New South Wales, use is made of personnel employed by the Health Department.

The Social Context of Special Education

At one time, the educational needs of a child with a disability were not addressed until after he or she commenced school. Even then, little or nothing in the way of an alternative or appropriate program could be offered. If the problems caused classroom disruption, the child could have been excluded or moved to a special school catering for a specific disability, such as a school for the deaf, a school for the blind, or one for the intellectually disabled. Transfer to a special school did not take place until the child was eight years old.

In Australia, as elsewhere, special schools were established for children who were, at the time, seen as markedly different and unlikely to succeed in regular schools. The special schools focused very narrowly on a particular disability and readily excluded any child who did not conform to clearly defined admission guidelines. There are some interesting examples of children whose parents rejected the placement in a special school and who succeeded in a regular school. These children and their parents must be regarded as the pioneers in the integration movement.

In the special schools, teachers of great imagination and skill demonstrated that the "special" child was capable of learning. Teachers in special schools willingly accepted children and provided a most appropriate education. These teachers developed appropriate skills and curricula and saw themselves and were seen by others to be the only option for a child with a disability. Some of the approaches to learning and teaching were successfully pioneered in the special schools.

Special schools seemed to have had greater freedom to innovate, develop appropriate curricula, and harness sympathetic community support. The special schools have been most successful in enlisting community support. In some states, for example, all the braille translations required by students were produced by volunteers through organizations known as braille writers associations. With technological advances, it is hoped that valuable community support can still be used.

The expectation that any child who presented a learning/teaching problem would be removed from the regular classroom and placed in a special setting was encouraged and willingly accepted. The belief that there were two kinds of children—regular and special—was reinforced. It did not take long for teachers in regular schools to develop an attitude and a practice to move any child who was disabled from the regular school to the special school.

When there were a sufficient number of special schools, a bureaucracy developed to service them. All Australian states had until recently a Division of Special Education headed by a director who controlled considerable human and fiscal resources. Only one state (New South Wales) retains a Director of Special Education. In other states the responsibility for special education has been assumed by studies directorates with advice and support from policy officers.

Discussions about integration in the Australian educational context can be traced back to the late 1960s. The Commonwealth Schools Commission urged the integration of handicapped children in ordinary schools and classrooms in its April 1978 report, though it also stressed the importance of providing special assistance.

On a general basis, it can be said that Australia demonstrates the political will and the commitment to support integrated education for all students with disabilities. Victoria was in the forefront in the "mainstreaming" policy. New South Wales adopted the policy in the late 1970s (Barcan 1990). Integration does not mean, however, the end of special educational services and expertise that have been built up over a number of years by education departments and others. "Although state and federal governments in Australia have an expressed policy to educate disabled children as far as possible in regular schools, there will always be some children for whom mainstream education is not feasible, especially on a full-time basis" (Jenkinson 1987).

As well as for education, the Commonwealth is developing national standards for disability services to ensure that a uniformly high standard of services is available across the country. For example, the commonwealth government pays an allowance to all parents of handicapped children until they reach sixteen years, the age when the young adults become eligible for the invalid pension. The purpose of the allowance is to meet additional costs of maintaining the child.

Many factors contributed to changes in perceptions of and attitudes toward persons with disabilities and toward their rehabilitation and education. In 1981, the International Year for Disabled Persons, the Australian Bureau of Statistics collected data differentiating between the disabled and handicapped and presented it in two reports. The World Health Organization (WHO) definitions of disability and handicap were used. Since the publication of these reports, there have been significant changes in the nature of provision of special education. Special education has received attention from officers concerned about issues of social justice and equity. The commonwealth government's social justice strategy has been endorsed by the states and antidiscrimination acts have been passed by both levels of government.

Wolf Wolfensberger and Ben Nirje visited Australia and conducted workshops on the normalization process and lectured to clients in the area of special education. Literature from the United States and the United Kingdom is widely read, so the theories of normalization were well known before invitations were extended to Wolfensberger and Nirje. But these visitors brought with them the vocabulary of normalization and a much wider exposure to the notion.

The principle of normalization has been adopted and opportunities for achieving it have been encouraged by the payment of allowances to those wishing to live independently of their family. The allowances pay for caregivers, accommodation, and transport. Disabled students can now find role models, work, and live independently. The chance of completing school, leaving parents and setting up homes, establishing relationships outside the immediate family, and enjoying the dignity of independence and privacy are now seen to be achievable goals. The expectation of a life of dependence and eventual life in a large institution with a sheltered workshop as the only place of employment is fast disappearing.

Dunn's 1968 article, "Special Education for the Mildly Retarded: Is Much of it Justifiable?" marked the beginning of the decline in admissions to schools for the mildly intellectually retarded in Australia. Guidance officers and educational psychologists began to suggest to parents that the alternative school was not the most desirable option and that with support the child should continue in the regular school. Unfortunately, the advocacy for keeping the failing students in the regular school was not matched by advocacy for additional support and resources for the regular schools to meet their needs.

The impact of the U.S. Public Law 94-142 further reinforced the feeling that integration was the better alternative. As well, the United Kingdom

Warnock Report stated that "the planning of services for children should be based on the assumption that about one in six children at anytime, and up to one in five at some time during their school careers, will require some form of special education" (41). This supported the concept that the special schools dealt with only part of the problem and that the regular schools would also need to change.

The new policy was justified on ideological grounds, being seen as more democratic than separate schools for handicapped students. Moreover, it was argued, the more "unstructured" methods in modern classrooms made it easier to cater to students with a wide range of backgrounds (Barcan 1990, 30). Further, the cost of maintaining a child in a special setting was about ten times the cost of maintaining a child in a regular school. The cost of maintaining an integrated child may not be much less, but one cannot help but feel that some of the support for integration comes from seeing it as a less costly alternative rather than evaluating its social and educational desirability. In New South Wales, for example, integration was seen as much cheaper than maintaining special schools or even special classes, even after allowing for the employment of specialist teachers to visit schools to help individual students (Barcan 1990).

Legislation

The Australian government, sometimes referred to as the national, federal, or commonwealth government, and the governments of the states, sometimes referred to as the state governments, have all passed legislation that either directly or peripherally affects persons with disabilities. Acts of Parliament are proclaimed after receiving Royal Assent; that is, signed by the Governor General of Australia in the case of Australian legislation or by the individual governors of the eight states and territories in case of state law.

Between 1860 and the turn of the century, all the Australian states passed Education Acts making education free, compulsory, and secular for all children between the ages of six and thirteen. There were, however, regulations that excluded children with disabilities. Other legislation such as the Backward Persons Act (Queensland 1938) was a discriminatory piece of legislation which lumped together the intellectually disabled, the mentally ill, and the alcoholic. These acts have since been amended to increase the years of attendance for all children and further acts have been passed to include all disabled children. The Blind, Deaf and Dumb Children's Act of 1924, also from Queensland, has been amended, as have similar acts in other states, making education compulsory for the visually impaired and the hearing impaired. The compulsory clauses of all education acts now apply to all children, irrespective of disability. The legal support for separating children into educable and ineducable groups has been rescinded and replaced by legislation that affords dignity and support to disabled children and adults.

Antidiscrimination acts have been passed. The last state to do this was Queensland in June 1992. Antidiscrimination acts prohibit education authorities from excluding any student because of a recognized disability. However, the acts do provide for education authorities to opt out of the supply of special services and facilities if such provision "would impose unjustifiable hardship on the educational authorities." This probably means that the parents of a child living in an isolated area of the country could not expect the same kind of service as those living in more populous areas.

Litigation about education or the failure of education departments to provide services does not feature in the Australian or state legal systems. Occasionally, there is some litigation about students suffering some personal damage, but as yet practically none about failure to supply special education services. The acts, in making provision, all seem to provide escape clauses for the authorities.

Opportunities for parents to opt out of the system have always been available. Some parents have grouped together to provide special schooling for their children, and the children have been protected as have the funds provided by the parents by various acts. Such nongovernmental activity has provided alternative special education for many students and indeed has pioneered provision until such time as the governments have assumed responsibility.

Policies

The commonwealth government does not directly control or manage schools. It is a major funding and policy-making body and seeks the cooperation of the states in implementing these policies. The commonwealth government also provides funds for research and for experimental projects.

The education departments at the commonwealth and state levels have many policy documents relating to students with special needs. The documents are all part of the concern for social justice and equity. There is a move in all departments to provide a single unified system in which all children with a disability are seen as part of the mainstream and not as a selected special group. Inclusive education, that is, the "right to equitable education access, participation and outcomes for all students" is now official policy throughout Australia.

Policy officers from each education department meet on a regular basis to exchange information and to discuss programs of national significance. In Hobart in 1989, conflict about education between the states and the Commonwealth seems to have been resolved with a historic meeting of the

Australian Education Council, which comprises all ministers of education from the Australian government and the governments of the states and territories. The council has met on a regular basis since 1916, but for the first time in many decades the ministers have agreed on common goals for education and the elimination of unnecessary school curricula among the states and territories. Another one of the agreed goals is "[t]o promote equality of educational opportunities, and to provide for groups with special learning requirements."

Teachers, Schools, Curriculum, and Pedagogy

Schools

The responsibility for students with special needs in Australia has moved away from a centrally controlled special education division. The Warnock statement "that special education will no longer be the responsibility of a small group of teachers and administrators. It will be the business of all teachers in all schools" applies to the current situation.

Children with special needs in Australia may be educated in special schools or settings, special classes or units attached to regular schools, or in regular classes with support from teacher aides and itinerant teachers. In small country schools there are noncategorical special education units catering to a heterogeneous group of children with disabilities. In the larger towns and cities where the population demands it, special education units can be provided for more specific groups of children.

In 1979, Andrew and colleagues estimated that there were 750 special classes or units attached to regular schools in Australia, catering to approximately twenty thousand disabled children, or two-fifths of those receiving full-time special education. These numbers have increased with the policy moving toward integration. There are fewer enrollments in special schools, and some special schools have been closed. Large residential schools for the physically handicapped, the hearing impaired, and the visually handicapped are in decline. Those children who need to live away from home in order to attend schools are placed with specially selected families who are paid by the government under what is generally known as a private accommodation scheme.

The population of special schools appears to have more disabled students than that of a decade ago. Units attached to regular schools, too, seem to have a more disabled population. With knowledge of past experience, every effort is made to ensure that the special classes attached do not become ghettos.

School buildings were often a great inhibitor to the integration of physically disabled students. New school buildings along with other public buildings are now being made accessible, and older buildings are being altered. This includes the provision of special toilets and washrooms as well as wider corridors and doorways for wheelchairs. Most physically handicapped children in need of regular therapy can and do receive treatment in the school setting, and a transdisciplinary approach is encouraged. Most departments of education are able to employ therapists to work in schools, but those who are unable to do so are able to negotiate services through their health departments.

Preschool education, that is, attendance at a special facility attached to a regular school, is available for most children in the year before the age of compulsory attendance. The child is usually required to attend for half a school week, that is every morning or every afternoon or for two days one week and three the next. Variations depend on location and the availability of specially trained preschool teachers. For younger children, there are child care centers and kindergartens; some are government supervised, some privately run. Parents have to contribute toward the cost.

Developmental centers located near regular preschools are found in most states. Attendance is voluntary and without cost to parents. The developmental centers are usually staffed by a special education teacher and provide access to other services such as physiotherapy, occupational therapy, and speech therapy. School psychological services are also available and are used.

Curriculum

In the special schools, the curriculum is strongly oriented toward independent living skills and survival academic skill areas. The curriculum priorities for these students are socialization, communication, daily living skills, hygiene, work preparation, survival reading (signs, tables) and math (money, budgeting) skills. When these curriculum areas are treated in regular schools they are taught either at an age that is not appropriate for these students or in a manner beyond their intellectual capabilities (Pickering and Dickens 1992). On the basis of parental reports, it appears that lack of an appropriate curriculum is a major barrier to integration.

As the result of a comprehensive study, a set of documents *Curriculum Development in Special Schools: A Life Skills Approach* was published in Queensland in 1988. With the move to inclusive education much of the material, particularly that relating to situational analysis, group processes in consensus decision-making, programming, and assessment, could well be used in the integrated school.

Teachers

All teachers in Australia have to be professionally registered on an annual basis and minimum qualifications are set down. In the 1960s, however, training for teachers for special education was described as deplorable. Teachers of the deaf could obtain a diploma by external study from a teacher-organized professional body, the Australian Association of Teachers of the Deaf, or they could study as graduate teachers full-time at the Victorian School for the Deaf. Nominated teachers from other states availed themselves of this training. Teachers of the blind had a similar teacher-organized scheme. Other teachers in special education learned "on the job." Some, from 1954 until the course was discontinued in 1968, attended the one-term course in diagnostic testing and remedial teaching set up by Professor (Sir) Fred Schonell at the University of Queensland.

The late sixties saw the infusion of commonwealth money into teacher education. Special education sections were established in teachers colleges, which later became colleges of advanced education and more recently have acquired university status. In older universities, departments of special education were also established.

But although the Commonwealth Schools Commission (1981) declared a commitment to the training of teachers in special education, Jenkinson (1987) observes that little attention has been given to the needs of regular class teachers in this area. Special assistance to help the hard-pressed general teacher was often inadequate. Alan Barcan noted that in October 1988, the N.S.W. Minister for Education sent a memorandum to the heads of higher education institutions engaged in teacher preparation urging that all students enrolled in teacher-training courses should take compulsory units in special education. This was so that they would become "aware of the range of disabilities they may encounter in students," the sort of services available, and have "at least basic skills in this area" (Barcan 1990).

Courses today are generally for a year's postgraduate study in a specific area: the hearing impaired, visually handicapped, physical disabled, learning disabled, maladjusted, and the intellectually disabled. One state, Queensland, has had preservice courses where teachers can train as primary and special teachers. The areas of specialization are similar to those offered at the postgraduate level. New South Wales is the only state with a one-term block of special education in teacher training. Other states have a special education option, and there are groups advocating some compulsory study in special education. Some university departments of education offer studies in special education for higher degrees and are very active in the promotion of research.

Teachers who had worked in special schools were paid an allowance in addition to their salaries. This allowance was paid when it was difficult to attract teachers to work with exceptional children. Those teachers who felt comfortable working under the aegis of a special education division may experience some difficulty in moving back into the mainstream, just as some teachers in regular schools may feel uncomfortable and not sufficiently trained to cope with mainstreamed students. One state, New South Wales, is to make a course in some aspect of special education a prerequisite for employment. The Advisory Council for Children with Special Needs in Queensland has made a similar recommendation to the Minister for Education. However, teachers' unions and employing authorities have not resolved any of the issues relating to mainstreaming.

Professional associations play an important part in the development of special educators. *The Australian Journal of Special Education,* founded in 1976, and the *Australia and New Zealand Journal of Developmental Disabilities,* founded in 1975, as well as *The Exceptional Child,* which started as *The Slow Learning Child* in 1953, provide opportunities for the dissemination of information and provide a valuable link between research and practice.

Major Controversies and Issues in Special Education

Australian special education is beset by a host of controversies, some common to most systems of special education and some unique to the Australian experience. The most pressing issues are discussed below.

Integration. Integration is now the official policy of all education departments, and the placement of a child with a disability in the least restrictive environment or in a school as near as possible to the child's home is the aim. The assumption that all children with a particular disability can be taught in some kind of homogeneous setting can never be supported. Indeed, it is in the disabled population that the teacher is made aware of individual differences and that it is imperative that the learning/teaching must be considered individually.

However, controversy about integration has increased over the past decade. We have seen changing government policies about special education as well as the involvement of the Commonwealth Schools Commission which is advising government on policy for special education and influencing practices through the allocation of funding (Gow et al. 1987).

According to Jenkinson (1987), "the major issue in integration can be defined as how best to meet those [special] needs in the regular school so that disabled students might participate as far as possible with their non-disabled peers in common educational experiences, without the loss of essential support services" (10).

Some students, parents, and teachers view the current process of change in special education with anxiety and concern. Those parents whose children had been rejected by the regular school and who successfully advocated for the provision of special schools and the teachers who succeeded in those same schools now feel threatened. On the other hand, there are some too who feel that special school provision was only an interim step on the way to integration.

When Pickering and Dickens (1992) surveyed 359 parents they found that half the parents had experience with integration in regular schools. Parents reviewed integration as providing the following benefits: socialization, better role models, students' access to children of their own age, the company of neighborhood children, and better language models. On the other hand, 23 percent of parents saw no benefit in integrating their child into a regular school. They and other parents cited as major objections lack of qualified staff, unavailability of aids and poor medical services, lack of adequate supervision and safety, class size, negative teacher attitudes, inappropriate curriculum, and the inability of their child to keep up with the class. They were also concerned about the teasing, victimization, and social isolation of their children. Teachers in special schools saw similar benefits in integration as those cited by the parents; they also listed greater academic challenge and the availability of a great range of subjects as major benefits. Their concerns were similar to those of the parents, with the addition of loss of confidence, inappropriate curricula, loss of resources, and concerns about the behavior of some children in the regular classroom.

Approximately half of the teachers surveyed were unwilling to take up the role of integration teacher in regular schools because of the way in which integration was being implemented, the difficulty of the role, lack of acceptance of regular schools of integration, and lack of resources.

Teachers. Teachers in regular schools and more especially in secondary schools are still a little reluctant to teach across a wide range of abilities. This is changing as teachers-in-training are being exposed to classes with integrated students. Teachers who demonstrate acceptance, sensitivity, and awareness of specific needs along with the integrity, imagination, and intelligence of administrators will be much more effective in bringing about change in comparison to the utterers of pious policy statements. The trend depends very much on the nature of the school and informed, caring teachers.

Attitudes. Schools reflect society in the way that people with disabilities are accepted. Attitudes range from complete rejection to total acceptance. The regular school has not spontaneously accepted the concept of integration. Only some schools have demonstrated a willingness to accept and provide for children who have additional needs, and some express a willingness only if additional support is forthcoming. Attitudes cannot be changed by government decree. A task for special educators is to demonstrate the advantages of integration and the need for inclusive education. There is also the need to demonstrate that for some students the least restrictive environment is the warmth and security of the special school. A range of options seems the most desirable.

Nevertheless, there is a continuing demand for student placement in special schools. This demand comes overwhelmingly from parents of students with individual disabilities (Pickering and Dickens 1992). The special school population is older, an age imbalance that suggests that there may be difficulties in integrating students with disabilities in postprimary schools.

Geography. The provision of regular and special education services to the 39 percent of Australian full-time students attending schools in rural Australia is a problem that the Commonwealth Schools Commission (1977) concedes is largely unresolved and in need of urgent inquiry. The problems seem to be most acute in remote areas of Queensland, Western Australia, and New South Wales (Pickering and Szaday 1990).

Normalization. Increasing numbers of disabled people are moving away from the large institutions built into the community last century and into specially built houses in the suburbs. Some are finding satisfactory accommodation in regular houses. Among this group are older schoolchildren who find the independence more conducive to study.

Eligibility. School learning age is another area of concern. Some special schools now provide programs until the student is twenty-one. The question is, At what age should appropriate placement follow and what body should be responsible for it?

Gifted students. Gifted children and appropriate school programs, though not always seen as the responsibility of special education, continue to emerge as an issue. To meet some of the needs, departments of excellence within schools have been established, encouraged by mentor programs and parent advocacy groups. Parents may have expectations for their child not shared by the professionals. Some programs have selection criteria, and a child may be rejected for the program if he or she does not meet the requirements. We must work out who decides on the requirements, what alternatives are available, and how special education can deal with the sense of frustration and disappointment.

Funding. The Australian government has major responsibility for ensuring that children with disabilities are given opportunities to participate in community life as fully as possible. The government supplements the delivery of services by the community and nongovernmental and state/territory education authorities. The government assists with integration programs to permit children with disabilities to attend regular schools. It encourages early intervention programs for very young children with severe disabilities who are living in residential care. The government also supports some of the operating costs of those organizations providing special education to children with disabilities. More than one hundred thousand children benefited from the service in 1989 (Department of Employment, Education, and Training 1990, 50). One of the great concerns is whether, in a time of economic rationalism, the needs will decide the level of support and whether some programs will continue.

Definitions. The definition of attention deficit disorder and whether a child with this condition is eligible for the Handicapped Child's Allowance is another area in need of resolution.

Deaf education. Some members of the deaf community, who see no denigrating connotation in the use of the word *deaf,* feel that the closure of some schools for the deaf seriously inhibit access to the adult deaf community and culture. Parents of young deaf children have revived the methodological debate after the almost universal acceptance of total communication by Australian schools for the deaf. Some nongovernment schools for the deaf use the auditory-verbal, auditory-visual method of instruction and resent any other method. Auslan, a dialect of the British Sign Language is now used fairly extensively and classes are offered for hearing and nonhearing members of the community by Technical and Further Education. Another area of controversy arises from the unreal expectations and indeed high-flown claims of benefits of cochlear implants. This is reminiscent of the provision of hearing aids in the forties when it was thought by some that a miracle cure was available.

Conductive education. This method has received a small but vigorous support from groups of parents, some of whom have traveled to Budapest with their children for assessment and treatment at the Peto Center. Other parents and some schools have organized groups of children with Australian conductors trained in Budapest and assisted by visiting Hungarian conductors who assist in translating conductive education to Australian conditions. There are still pockets of parents who use local resources to organize programs based on the Doman and Delacato techniques.

Note

1. The terms *incidence* and *prevalence* are occasionally used interchangeably, but in this discussion incidence refers to the frequency of occurrence of a condition in a fixed period of time, and prevalence refers to the number of existing cases at a particular time.

References

Andrews, R. J., Elkins, J., Berry, P. B., and Burge, J. A. 1979. *A survey of special education in Australia, needs and priorities in the education of children with handicaps and learning difficulties.* St. Lucia Queensland, Fred and Eleanor Schonell Educational Research Center, University of Queensland.

Ashman, A., and Elkins, J., eds. 1990. *Educating children with special needs.* Sydney: Prentice Hall.

Australian Bureau of Statistics 1988. *Australia 1988.* Canberra: Commonwealth Government Printer.

————. 1991. *Australia 1991*. Canberra: Commonwealth Government Printer.

Barcan, A. 1990. The political economy of special education. *Educational Monitor* Spring, 30.

Commonwealth Schools Commission. 1981. *Report for triennium 1982–84*. Canberra: AGPS.

Department of Employment, Education and Training. 1990. *Australian National Report on the Development of Education*. Canberra: Commonwealth Government Printer.

Dessent, T. 1987. *Making the ordinary school special*. London: Palmer Press.

Gow, L., Snow, D., Balla, J., and Hall, J. 1977. *Report to the Commonwealth Schools Commission on integration in Australia*. Canberra: Commonwealth Schools Commission.

Jenkinson, J. C. 1987. *School and disability: Research and practice in integration*. Victoria: Australian Council for Educational Research.

New South Wales Department of School Education. 1991. *Who's going to teach my child? A guide for parents of children with special needs*. Parramatta: New South Wales Department of School Education.

Northern Territory Department of Education. 1990. *Student services handbook*. Darwin: Northern Territory Department of Education.

Pickering, D., and Dickens, E. 1992. *Special schools: Students, parents, teachers*. Melbourne: Victoria College.

Pickering, D., Szaday, C., and Duedroth, P. 1988. *One in eleven: Special educational needs of Catholic schools in Victoria*. Melbourne: Catholic Education Office of Victoria, Victoria College Press.

Queensland Department of Education. 1992. *Policy statement and management plan. Educational provision for students with disabilities*. Brisbane: Government Printer.

South Australian Department of Education. 1991. *Students with disabilities. Information for principals*. Adelaide: Government Printer.

Tasmanian Department of Education. 1990. *Policy statement: Children with special needs*. Hubert: Tasmanian Department of Education.

Victorian Ministry of Education. 1991. *Integration support procedures for regular schools*. Melbourne Statewide School Support and Production Center: Ministry of Education.

Ward, J. 1984. The rehabilitation of the disabled: A challenge for the 80s. *The Exceptional Child* 3:5–18.

Warnock, M. 1978. *Special education needs*. London: H.M.S.O.

West Australian Ministry of Education. 1991. *Education special issue: social justice in education*. Perth: Government Printer.

22

Canada

MARGRET A. WINZER

Canada is a vast country made up of ten provinces and two territories. With the confederation of 1867, the federal government in Ottawa conferred a number of powers on the provinces, among them education. Although Ottawa retains some control over adult education and the education of Native people, general education is the exclusive right and responsibility of the provinces.

The lack of a federal office of education, combined with the huge geographical distances of Canada, the cultural diversity of the country, and the high urbanization of the population, makes any statement about education difficult. Each of the ten provinces and the two territories has its own school system based upon provincial education legislation. Each provincial government can develop its own legislation, regulations, policies, and procedures to ensure that all children receive a free and appropriate education. Although there are great similarities in such areas as curriculum, control, and funding, there are also regional and provincial differences.

The differences seen in the general educational arena are compounded in the area of special education. Differences in prevalence figures, in etiology, in definitions of exceptionality and labeling, in identification and placement procedures, in eligibility for special education services, in funding formulas, and in early intervention programs are readily observed across the country. Although each province and territory has elevated mainstreaming to the dominant ideology, the legislation and approaches to placement and practice differ.

About the Author • Margret Winzer is in the Faculty of Education at the University of Lethbridge, Alberta, where she teaches courses in educational psychology and special education. She has published in these two areas. Her special interest is in the history of special education.

One commonality apparent in Canadian special education is the dramatic increase in interest and involvement that has been witnessed in the past three decades. Not only have we seen rapid expansion, but special education has moved from educating children in institutional settings, to specialized separate classes, to the integration of many students into regular programs and regular classes. However, while there is a contingent of proponents of fully integrated schooling in Canada, it can be said that full educational integration is the exception, rather than the rule, across the country. Special classes and resource room withdrawal programs dominate the delivery of special education services; the most common mode is the regular classroom–resource room combination.

Another commonality found in Canadian special education is American influence. Geographically, Canada sprawls across the north of the United States, so it is not surprising that, in both historical and contemporary terms, Canadian special education has paralleled or followed the U.S. model. Canadian educational issues, both administrative and curricular, are directly influenced by events, philosophies, and pedagogy from the United States. As a result, Canadians have a touchstone against which to critically assess their progress and greater freedom to meld practices and philosophies to Canada's unique educational system.

Prevalence of Exceptional Conditions

It is extremely difficult to determine the numbers of individuals with disabilities in Canada. The numbers of those with severe disabilities and developmental disabilities prove easier to determine than do the numbers of individuals with mild disabilities or of children who are biologically or environmentally at risk. Within the school system, students are only labeled as exceptional when they receive special funding as such, which means that numbers of children with mildly disabling conditions served fully in regular classrooms may not be counted. Further compounding the difficulties in obtaining accurate prevalence figures are the lack of a national survey and the varied prevalence rates found in different parts of the country. Newfoundland, for example, shows relatively higher rates of spina bifida than does the rest of the country; however, more orofacial defects are found in British Columbia.

There is also much movement among the traditional categories employed within special education; children previously labeled as mildly mentally retarded or speech and language disordered are now more often categorized as learning disabled. In fact, learning disabilities is currently the major focus of many school districts. In 1986, for example, those with a learning disability made up the largest single group of disabled learners—26 percent (Nessner 1990).

Perhaps the greatest hindrance to obtaining accurate prevalence figures arises from the lack of universally accepted definitions of many exceptional conditions. No consensus has been reached on what actually defines learning disabilities, behavior disorders, developmental delays, or even giftedness. Hence a child categorized in an area of disability in one province may be categorized differently in another part of the country. The concept of mild mental retardation is particularly controversial since children in this category are drawn almost exclusively from poor families, often of minority origin. In Canada in 1986, 9 percent of all children with disabilities were reported to have a mental handicap, such as a developmental delay or mental retardation. However, the current population of children considered to be mildly mentally retarded or educable mentally retarded (EMR) has changed quite dramatically, and there is a greater hesitancy to label children as EMR.

In 1986, Statistics Canada reported that there were an estimated 277,000 Canadian children with disabilities, which represent 5 percent of all young people. Boys are slightly more likely than girls to have a disability; in 1986, 6 percent of boys were disabled, compared with 5 percent of girls. As well, disabilities are more prevalent among older children than among younger ones. In 1986, about 6 percent of children aged five to fourteen were disabled, while the proportion was 3 percent for those younger than age five (Nessner 1990).

The estimated numbers of students requiring special education during their school careers echo figures from other Western nations; approximately 15.5 percent of students will need special education. Table 22.1 provides percentages of categories of students with exceptionalities. Table 22.2 indicates the numbers of children served in special education in provinces that adhere to categorical approaches. Alberta, Prince Edward Island, Newfoundland, and the two territories have adopted generic approaches to service delivery. (These figures, largely collected by the Canadian Council for Exceptional Children, focus on children requiring special education and are somewhat higher than the

TABLE 22.1. Prevalence of Exceptionality

Disability	Percentage of Special Education	Percentage of School-age Population
Mentally handicapped	11.3	1.75
Learning disabled	28.4	4.41
Behaviorally disordered	4.9	0.78
Speech impaired	7.9	1.22
Visually impaired	0.4	0.06
Hearing impaired	0.9	0.14
Physically disabled	0.5	0.08
Multiply handicapped	2.0	0.31
Other	43.7	6.77
Total	100.0	15.52

TABLE 22.2. Students with Exceptionalities, 1992

	BC	Alta	Sask	Ont	NB	NS	PEI	Nfld	YT
Exceptional Children/Youth enrolled									
•Kindergarten	249	3,497			0				12
•Grades 1 to 11, 12, 13	53,426	36,727	8,619	162,031	9,129	20,000	400	12,385	248
Students served per category		N.A.					N.A.	N.A.	N.A.
Mentally handicapped—educable	3,867			15,963		1,655			
Mentally handicapped—trainable	1,420		692	6,037		431			
Physically handicapped	935		213	1,366		198			
Multi-handicapped			613	4,362	9,129	188			
Behavior/emotional disorder	4,778		534	9,311		759			
Speech/language impaired						4,774			
Sensory impaired									
Vision	397		108	690	330	148			
Hearing	1,165		279	2,043		177			
Specific learning disability	11,483		5,896	72,685		4,530			
Unspecified learning problem				2,081	3,000	7,140			
Autistic	323								

Source: Canadian Council for Exceptional Children. 1992.

Note: Figures for Manitoba, NWT, and Quebec unavailable.

numbers presented by Statistics Canada, probably attributable to the rates of children with learning disabilities served by school systems.)

Etiological Considerations

In general, etiologies of disabling conditions in Canada are the same as those found in other Western countries. Vaccination programs have led to great declines in the numbers of children infected by rubella and meningitis. Nevertheless, we are witnessing an increase in the number of children impaired by drug abuse in mothers, fetal alcohol syndrome, pediatric AIDS, and the effects of extreme prematurity.

Labeling the Disabled Population

It is now seen that the traditional system of labeling children by their primary disability is not always useful and that the classification and labeling process is fraught with hazards. However, this does not mean that the special expertise concerned with specific disabilities, such as deafness, will disappear. It does mean, however, that mildly handicapped youngsters will be labeled less and any educational programs will be determined by their unique set of learning and behavioral characteristics, rather than by membership in any category or group.

Labels have not been abandoned in Canadian special education. But although administrators and professionals will likely continue to use the traditional categories of exceptionality, there is a trend toward less stigmatizing labels and toward the adoption of noncategorical or generic approaches, most especially within the categories generally grouped as mildly disabling conditions—mild mental retardation, mild behavior disorders, and learning disabilities. Some Canadian provinces and territories have adopted these generic approaches and provide block funding for special education. Others still fund special education services according to specific categories of disability or in terms of severity levels.

The Social Context of Special Education

In Canada, special education dates from the 1850s when permanent institutions for deaf and blind students were established in Nova Scotia and Quebec. The first special day classes were started in 1906 for children with physical problems—those who were described as crippled, sickly, and malnourished. These were followed by day classes for mentally retarded pupils, sight-saving classes, home instruction, speech correction, lipreading classes, orthopedic classes, vocational and advancement classes, and remedial reading programs.

Right into the 1960s, institutions, special schools, and segregated classes remained the most important vehicle to serve students who were intellectually, physically, socially, or emotionally different from the norm. Children remained in these classes for their entire school careers; few graduated to regular classrooms. In the 1960s, however, parents, advocates, legislators, and educational systems began to reject the notion that exceptional students should be educated separately from their peers or that mentally handicapped people should be herded into large institutional settings.

In the 1970s, discontent with special classes continued to mount. Parents insisted, with considerable success, that traditional special education systems change and that their children had the right to education within the regular milieu. The increasing demands from parents, often in uneasy alliance with professionals, that their disabled children be provided appropriate education in more normalized settings was evident across the country. Increased agitation by parent and professional groups in the 1980s led to litigation (though not to the extent seen in the United States) and to various provincial legislative acts that usually echo the mandates of the United States' Public Law 94–142, adapted to the unique Canadian education.

In the 1990s, parent and professional agitation continues. The process of gradual, evolutionary change in special education is subject to increasing challenges, and law, advocacy, and educational innovation are together creating a unique environment supportive of fundamental changes in how students with disabilities are educated (Porter and Richler 1990).

By the mid-80s, the watchwords of Canadian special education became *normalization* and *mainstreaming*. These widespread movements entailed many different strategies, including deinstitutionalization, integration, non-categorical approaches to teaching, the rejection of traditional labeling, early identification and intervention, and transition programs. Agitation by various groups was not directed toward the philosophical bases of normalization and integration but toward pragmatic considerations that have slowed or hindered the implementation processes.

Normalization is the philosophical belief that all exceptional individuals, no matter what their level and type of handicap, should be provided with an education and living environment as close to normal as possible. Overcoming barriers to allow Canadians with disabilities to fully participate in social and economic life has become a major policy concern over the past decade; the Canadian government has adopted the tenets of deinstitutionalization and recently announced a strategy for integration (Fine 1991). In 1982, for example, there were 1.4 million disabled Canadians of working age. Of these, 45,000 were in institutions, 20,000 in sheltered workshops, and 1.37 million in the community (Directions 1982). By 1991, the number of persons with mental retardation living in institutions had dropped to 16,000 (Fine 1991). Nevertheless, there is still much to be done and few agencies to do it. Martlett (1986) was led to observe that to be disabled in Canada is to be poor. The role of disabled persons in Canadian society continues to be restricted, with limited economic power, limited educational options, and restricted housing options, which combine to create a cycle of poverty and isolation (Wight-Felske and Hughson 1986).

For children with special needs, the most fundamental social change of the past decade has been the clear and unequivocal statement of the responsibility of educational authorities to provide all children equal access to an education in a manner most appropriate to their needs. This statement of responsibility, embedded in legislation and supported by ethical and philosophical precepts, has meant that exceptional students are increasingly drawn within the orbit of the public schools. Nevertheless, the questions of how the integration of students with handicaps is to be accomplished and what their degree of involvement should be with their nonhandicapped peers remain hotly debated issues among educators, parents, and child advocates. Most of the argument centers around how integration strategies can be implemented without deleteriously affecting the lives and educational programs of other students or impacting negatively on the professional lives of teachers.

Most parents, teachers, and school administrators agree that the days of total segregation and institutionalization are long over (Taylor 1990), but the manner in which mainstreaming students with exceptionalities can be most effectively attained has still not been worked out in practice. Although the societal goals of deinstitutionalization and integration appear to be readily accepted in Canada, there is a sense that schools are more prepared to implement the form of mainstreaming and less capable of dealing with the substance of it (O'Reilly and Duquette 1988).

Canadian school jurisdictions have dealt with the integration of exceptional students in different ways. Some have adopted policies of full integration, which implies that all students, regardless of the severity of handicaps, are educated in regular classrooms with their age peers (Flynn and Kowalczyk-McPhee 1989). A larger number of school districts have chosen to maintain segregated educational options and typically approach integration on a one-to-one basis.

With the process of educational integration, controversy, argument, debate and counterdebate remain strikingly prevalent. In New Brunswick, for example, Bill 85 (1986) mandated integration. But although the law and policy in New Brunswick are clearly the most supportive of integration of any Canadian province, continuing controversy over integration and intense pressure from the province's teacher's union prompted the minister of education to review the integration process in 1989. Union leaders maintained that integration was putting New Brunswick's already strained education system at risk of collapse (Porter and Richler 1990). Integration, they said, was "turning classrooms into zoos" and creating conditions in which "teachers can't teach and students can't learn" (Benteau 1990, 1). Even in the face of such opposition, however, the ministers' committee reiterated its strong support for integration.

Similarly, submissions from the Alberta Teachers' Association (1993) expressed support for the principles of integration but identified critical problems in its implementation. In general, the submissions overwhelmingly expressed a deep concern on the part of many teachers that in too many cases the process is not working and is in fact creating educationally unsound situations.

The concerns of teachers revolve around a number of areas that are prompted as much by the objectives of special education as they are by pressures within the school system. Increasing class sizes, limited resources, widespread debate over curriculum and standardized achievement testing, and lessening job security combine with concerns over lack of training and expertise in special education and declining support services.

Legislation

In Canada, special education has emerged as a key priority. However, except for the Charter of Rights & Freedoms, there is no federal law to guarantee the rights of exceptional children; in fact, the right of every child to education is not entrenched by any constitutional provision. The 1867 British North America Act (sec. 93) was chiefly concerned with protecting the educational rights of linguistic and religious minorities, not disabled children. In the absence of constitutional provisions, the responsibility for education rests entirely with provincial legislation. Even today, Canadian jurisdictions have been slow to enact positive legislation guaranteeing educational rights. Only two provincial human rights codes (those of Saskatchewan and Quebec) list education as a right (MacKay 1987).

Legal mandates in school acts across Canada include statements to the effect that all children have the right to an education. But in actual practice, the right has not always been extended to youngsters with severe physical or mental handicapping conditions. Although students who are exceptional require an appropriate education, the appropriateness of any education received by such students has, in the past, depended solely on the discretion of school authorities.

Since the late 1960s, studies of special education have drawn attention to the shortcomings of Canadian legislation and the provision of special education services (Csapo 1981; Hall and Dennis 1968; Poirier and Goguen 1986; Poirier, Gouguen, and Leslie 1988; Roberts and Lazure 1979). Repeatedly authors contrast the progress made in American special education, particularly with reference to PL 94-142, with the lack of progress in Canada (Carter and Rogers 1989). Even today, it cannot be said that all provincial law clearly and unequivocally obliges the publicly supported school system to provide appropriate forms of education for all students, exceptionality notwithstanding.

Rapid advances are apparent on the Canadian vista, although the gap in the assumption of universal responsibility is not yet fully closed. In recent years, all of the provinces and territories have elevated the concept of equal educational opportunity for all students to the status of the dominant educational ideology. Nevertheless, differences in provincial responses to exceptional youngsters are readily observed. Currently, legislation governing the rights of Canadian exceptional children to education and the responsibility of school boards to provide suitable programs has been enacted in some provinces (Manitoba, Ontario, New Brunswick, Nova Scotia, and New-foundland) and contemplated in the others.

Legislative activity has tended to focus on students with disabilities. Although gifted youngsters are considered to be exceptional in their need for special education, they have not fared as well in the legislative arena, perhaps because legal arguments for gifted students are different from those for children suffering handicapping conditions; they are not fought on de-nial of access but denial of appropriate programs. Ontario has mandatory legislation that includes gifted students; Saskatchewan has legislation that permits special education for these youngsters. British Columbia, Manitoba, Quebec, and Nova Scotia have developed educational programs for gifted students under existing articles of their Education Acts (Newfoundland and Labrador Association 1982).

Policies

Law and public policy have had a profound effect on the type and quality of education offered to exceptional children and youth. In some cases, they decide whether exceptional students are educated at all; in others, they determine how such children are educated.

Provincial government initiatives, while tempered by political and eco-nomic realities, attempt to reflect the best in current educational thinking and current educational practice. Even in the provinces lacking mandatory special education legislation, policies in place through provincial ministries of education and local school districts attempt to provide each child with an appropriate education, regardless of type and degree of disability.

Policies are less prevalent for infants and preschool children with dis-abilities and their families. Although Canada has been influenced by the U.S. Public Law 99-457 and the early intervention sections of IDEA, edu-cational policy has not fully extended to very young children. Across the country there are a wide variety of early intervention programs for infants and toddlers and their families. Center-based, clinic-based, and home-based programs have been established by hospitals, clinics, private agencies, school boards, and ministries of education. The variability in very early intervention is echoed in preschool programs. Many preschool children with disabilities are integrated into regular preschool programs. Others attend special schools or clinic programs operated by hospitals, clinics, parents, and groups such as the Kinsmen.

Teachers and Schools

Teachers

Specialized teacher training for teachers in special education was initiated at the University of British Columbia in 1959. Since that time, specialized and general programs have developed across the country. Nevertheless, programs are scattered and those training teachers in highly specialized areas such as deafness or visual impairment are sparse.

While a number of universities have added special education as a mandatory course in teaching training, this is not universal. In fact, despite compelling evidence that reform must take place, the inclusion of special education courses in regular teacher training programs and consultative courses in special education programs has not been readily accepted.

Schools

In recent decades, large numbers of students with disabilities have moved within the orbit of the public schools. The most common service delivery to such students today is the resource room–regular classroom combination. Some students are placed in regular classrooms with a full-time aide and others are in special classrooms within regular school plants with opportunities offered for social integration.

Institutions for people with mental handicaps no longer accept new admissions of children. On the other hand, there remains a complex of residential schools to serve the special needs of students who are blind, deaf, and severely emotionally disturbed or autistic. The numbers in residential schools are decreasing dramatically and many today are better characterized as residential–day schools. The exception are the schools for hearing-impaired students. While some schools have closed, other attempts have been blocked by members of the deaf community who view mainstreaming as inimical to their continuing strength.

Major Issues and Controversies

Integration. Of all the issues germane to current special education in Canada, the most contentious revolve around the questions of how thoroughly children with mental and physical handicaps should be integrated into the regular school system and how school districts can go about incorporating children with special needs into regular classrooms.

Mainstreaming is probably best conceptualized as a social experiment in which the philosophical commitment is ahead of research and practice. Educators, legislators, parents, and others advance the notion, yet the manner in which the process will work most successfully has not yet been clearly delineated. There is not yet a quantitative measure of how great a handicap must be for special services to be offered, nor is there established an absolute number or combinations of characteristics that must be identified before a pupil is diagnosed as exceptional.

Inclusive schooling. The concepts and the practices surrounding the Regular Education Initiative and inclusive schooling have not been ignored in Canada. Prominent writers (e.g., Little 1988) hold that special education is really nothing more than a thoroughly good ordinary education. A commitment to integrated or inclusive education means that schools, teachers, and the community commit themselves to resolving problems that arise in a way that respects the integrity of the school or an organization (Porter 1986). Schools are making the necessary adjustments for all students "to have access to opportunities and supports for stimulating their growth, development and learning within their home school. These opportunities are provided in physically and socially integrated settings, consistent with the principle of using the most enabling environment to meet individual students' needs" (Forshaw 1990).

The past decade has seen an increasing number of school districts make a commitment to full integration for all students. These range from several Catholic school districts in Southern Ontario, to French language districts in Quebec, to several public districts in the western provinces of Manitoba, Saskatchewan, Alberta, and British Columbia (Porter and Richler 1990). Many believe that this movement will continue to grow as more and more jurisdictions break through traditional barriers and forge an even stronger basis not only for integration but for the education of all students (Porter and Richler 1990).

However, the willingness and preparedness of regular classroom teachers must be considered. More and more, teachers are being asked to cater to students displaying a range of social and academic problems. Teachers are increasingly questioning the boundaries of their responsibilities, and they lack adequate training to handle a wide range of disabling conditions.

Students from diverse cultural backgrounds. Further complicating special education issues in Canada are the rapid demographic changes seen in society and in our school systems. In cities such as Vancouver, Montreal, and Toronto, large numbers of students come from homes where English is not a first language. As the demographic composition of the school-age population shifts to encompass more students from diverse cultural backgrounds, bilingual homes, and economically deprived families, the need for special services in the schools increases. However, whether the special services required by these students is special education, per se, remains moot.

Early intervention. Now seen as an integral component of special education, this process is going through some important transitions. Although the underlying philosophy of early intervention remains unchanged, there is a growing recognition of the need to broaden goals and to target families as well as children with disabilities. Moreover, the proliferation of early intervention programs in the last decade has raised the expectations of parents about the potential of their children to learn and develop. Participation in integrated day care, nurseries, and kindergartens has created parental expectations that their children will continue to be educated in the regular stream (Porter and Richler 1990).

Transition programs. The fundamental purpose of education is to prepare students to lead productive and rewarding lives. A new stress on transition programs has been prompted by data that indicates that many students with disabilities are faring poorly after school.

Schools are accepting greater leadership and responsibility for transitions; a range of postsecondary programs are appearing in order to supply exceptional youth with the opportunities for enhanced academic, career, and social development. Many programs focus on advanced vocational education so that students are armed with better skills to enter the workforce at some level.

Financial restraints. As school systems are endeavoring to provide more and wider services to greater numbers of students, they are trying to do so in a climate of straitened resources. The efficient use of limited resources will do much to affect the future configuration of special education in Canada.

Emerging and Future Trends

Significant philosophical changes are occurring in Canada in the areas of school responsibility, program delivery, and program implementation for special education. The concept of equal educational opportunities for children with special needs has become a dominant ideology, which means that provincial governments and local school boards are increasingly obliged to develop appropriate programs for the entire school-age population within the province (Winzer 1993). However, although the political will and the philosophical commitment are manifest, to some extent, the integration of all students with exceptional conditions into the regular educational milieu remains controversial and relatively precarious, balanced over an abyss of tight resources, changing demographics, teacher attitudes, parent expectations, and other social and political variables. Although more than 80 percent of Canadian children with disabilities are integrated to some level, the manner in which more extensive integration can be achieved remains elusive.

For the educational integration of students with special needs to become a reality on the Canadian vista, a matrix of factors are necessary. These include, but are not restricted to the following:

1. Regular classroom teachers must become more aware and more knowledgeable about appropriate programming and teaching strategies for a wider range of learners.
2. The collaboration between regular teachers and special education teachers required to plan and provide individual programs needs to increase.
3. Assessment needs to become more concerned with educational planning and less focused on placement.
4. Teachers must become more aware of the manner in which to accommodate students from diverse cultural backgrounds.
5. Early identification and intervention needs to become a priority, with a focus on family-centered approaches.
6. Teacher training at both the preservice and in-service levels must expand so that all classroom teachers develop at least an acquaintance with special learners and their needs.

References

Alberta Teachers' Association. 1993. *Trying to teach: Interim report to the Committee on Public Education and Professional Practice as approved by Provincial Executive Council for discussion at the 1993 Annual Representative Assembly.* Edmonton: Alberta Teachers' Association.

Benteau, S. 1990. MacLeod: Wages not only issue. *Saint John Telegraph Journal,* 27 April.

Canadian Council for Exceptional Children. 1992. Provincial/territorial survey of services to exceptional children. *Keeping in Touch,* December, 607.

Carter, D. E., and Rogers, W. T. 1989. Diagnostic and placement practice for initially educable mentally handicapped students. *Canadian Journal of Special Education* 5:15–23.

Csapo, M. 1981. *Children with behaviour and social disorders: A Canadian focus.* Vancouver: Centre for Human Development and Research.

Directions. 1982. *A report to the Canadian Organizing Committee for 1981, the International Year of Disabled Persons.* Ottawa: Department of Health and Welfare.

Fine, S. 1991. Plan would send retarded home. *Globe and Mail,* A8.

Flynn, G., and Kowalcyzk-McPhee, B. 1989. A school system in transition. In S. Stainback, W. Stainback, and M. Forest, eds. *Educating all students in the mainstream of regular education,* 29–41. Baltimore, Md: Brookes.

Forshaw, K. 1990. *Full service school model.* Victoria, B.C.: Greater Victoria School District No. 61.

Hall, M., and Dennis. L. 1968. *Living and learning: The report of the provincial committee on aims and objectives of education in the schools of Ontario.* Toronto: Newton.

Little, D. M. 1988. The redefinition of special education: Special-ordinary education
. . . individualized and personalized in the regular class. *Education Canada* 28:36–
43.

———. 1986. A crime against childhood—uniform curriculum at a uniform rate: Mainstreaming re-examined and redefined. *Canadian Journal of Special Education* 2:153–
70.

MacKay, A. W. 1987. The Charter of Rights and special education: Blessing or curse?
Canadian Journal for Exceptional Children 3:118–27.

Martlett, N. 1986. Impact of and alternative to corporate business models in rehabilitation programs. In R. I. Brown, ed. *Management and administration of rehabilitation programmes.* London: Crook Helm.

Nessner. C. 1990. Children with disabilities. *Canadian Social Trends,* Winter, 18–20.

Newfoundland and Labrador Association for Gifted Children. 1992. *Educating gifted
children: Brief presented to the Minister of Education, Newfoundland and Labrador.* St. John's: Memorial University of Newfoundland.

O'Reilly, R. C., and Duquette, C. A. 1988. Experienced teachers look at mainstreaming.
Education Canada, Fall, 9–13.

Poirier, D., and Goguen, L. 1986. The Canadian Charter of Rights and the right to an
education for exceptional children. *Canadian Journal of Education* 11:231–44.

Poirier, D., Goguen, L., and Leslie, P. 1988. *Educational rights of exceptional children
in Canada: A natural study of multilevel commitments.* Toronto: Carswell.

Porter, G. L. 1986. School integration: Districts 28 and 29. In *Education New Brunswick,*
6–7. Fredericton, N.B.: New Brunswick Department of Education.

Porter, G. L., and Richler, D. 1990. Changing special education practice: Law, advocacy, and innovation. *Canadian Journal of Community Mental Health* 9:65–78.

Roberts, C. A., and Lazure, M. D. 1979. *One Million Children. A national study of Canadian children with emotional and learning disorders.* Toronto: Cranford.

Taylor, D. R. 1990. Special education: A legal quagmire. *ATA Magazine,* November/
December, 40–43.

Wight-Felske, and Hughson, E. 1986. Disabled persons in Canada: A review of the
literature on independent living. In R. I. Brown and A. Wight-Felske. 1977.
Rehabilitation education: An integrated approach within the province of Alberta.
Canadian Journal of Special Education 3:139–61.

Winzer, M. A. 1993. *Children with exceptionalities: A Canadian perspective.* 3d ed.
Toronto: Prentice-Hall.

PART 5

INTEGRATED SPECIAL EDUCATION

Early intervention is critical to a child's future learning and independence. Techniques used in the United States include teaching young nonverbal children to use a head stick to point to pictures and turn the pages of a book. PHOTO COURTESY OF Kluge Children's Rehabilitation Center, University of Virginia.

Students with special needs participate alongside their peers for all aspects of their schooling at the Oratia District School in West Auckland, New Zealand. PHOTOS FROM David Mitchell and Patricia O'Brien

*T*he principles of normalization and mainstreaming, which have become the watchwords of special education in Western industrialized nations, were clearly articulated in the 1960s. In fact, the most important contribution the Scandinavian countries have made internationally to the treatment of the handicapped is undoubtedly the principle of normalization with its attendant concept of integration (Juul 1989). The principles of educational integration were mandated in major U.S. legislation, PL 94-142, the Education for All Handicapped Children Act, signed into law in November 1975; the British Warnock Report, five years in the making, was introduced in the United Kingdom in the 1981 Education Act.

These are landmark philosophical principles and legislative models in that they have exerted a profound influence on legislators, policymakers, and special educators around the world. The principles, as manifested in legislation and practice, have wrought a virtual revolution in the way individuals with special needs are perceived and educated. Nevertheless, the authors in this section present notes of only cautious optimism. Based on the principle of complete and universal access to regular public educational institutions, legislative acts have resulted in the vast majority of children with special needs receiving their education in the regular educational milieu. In the United States, for example, the great majority of disabled students are currently integrated into the regular public school system. However, the same problems pointed out in the previous section continue to plague special education in the countries in our final section.

In the United States, the disproportionate representation of minority children in special education programs is a perennial concern, the solution to which remains elusive. Severe resource limitations in England, Wales, and New Zealand have forced the governments to slow, and in some cases reevaluate, the implementation of their own policies. Even in the Scandinavian countries of Sweden, Norway, and Finland, which have a long and prestigious history of service provision, problems still beset the integration process.

Reference

Juul, K. D. 1989. Some common and unique features of special education in the Nordic
   countries. *International Journal of Special Education* 4:85–96.

23

Finland, Norway, and Sweden

KARI TUUNAINEN

*T*he Nordic countries, which comprise Finland, Norway, Sweden, Denmark, and Iceland, are together known for their common cultural background and multilevel cooperation. In population, the Nordic countries are relatively small: Sweden, 8.3 million inhabitants; Denmark, 5.1 million; Finland, 5 million; Norway, 4.2 million; and Iceland, only 200,000. This article focuses only on Finland, Norway, and Sweden. Naturally enough, a few references will be made to the two countries excluded from this paper.

The languages spoken in the Nordic countries are closely related and can be used in communication between the countries. The Finnish language is an exception because it belongs to the Finno-Ugric group of languages which includes, for example, Estonian and Hungarian. Finland has a Swedish-speaking minority, about 6 percent of the population. Due to historical reasons, the influence of this minority in the country is greater than the percentage implies; Finland belonged to Sweden up to 1809 when it was then annexed to Russia. Under the Russian czar, Finland practiced autonomy until the year 1917 when it became an independent republic. Swedish is still the second official language of Finland. This is the main reason for the special position of Swedish in Nordic cooperation. In most cases, the cooperation takes place in a mixed language called *Scandinavian*. English is also increasingly used in Nordic relations.

About the Author • Dr. Kari Tuunainen is professor of special education and director of the Department of Special Education at the University of Joensuu, Finland, where he also acted as a dean from 1986 to 1988. He is also a qualified psychologist and teacher for primary and secondary levels. He has held positions as a visiting scholar at Stanford and Syracuse Universities in 1983 and at the University of British Columbia in 1989, is a fellow of the International Academy for Research in Learning Disabilities, and has published over a hundred books and articles.

These countries are all quite similar in that they have flourishing economies. This has enabled them to pursue an ambitious social policy, including special education and versatile rehabilitation services for the disabled. Sweden has traditionally been the richest country because it managed to keep out of World War II. Norway, on the other hand, was occupied and Finland lost about 10 percent of its area and had to resettle the population of the ceded areas. The other countries have, for a longer time, had multicultural immigrants. Differences in the standard of living among these countries have leveled out with time. Norway has its oil reserves and Finland was, for a short time in the 1980s, the richest Scandinavian country by GNP, mainly due to trade with the Soviet Union, which has recently decreased dramatically.

The Nordic countries have extended international cooperation to a large area. Recently the influence of Germany, including on educational policy, which decreased after the World War II, has been increasing, due to the integration process in Western Europe. Education policy in the Nordic countries also has a lot in common with that of North America, although the differences between the Nordic countries are even smaller than those between the states of the United States (Walton, Rosenqvist, and Sandling 1991).

In the fields of special education and rehabilitation there has traditionally been a large variety of interaction and cooperation among the Nordic countries, including both official and informal contacts. The official organizations include the Nordic Council, the Nordic Council of Ministers, and the Advisory Committee for the Welfare of the Disabled, which exchange information and carry out research. Further, the research libraries have a common Nordic network in pedagogical and psychological research (PEPSY Bibliography). On the informal level, several associations and societies bring the countries and the people closer together. Earlier, foreign influences used to travel through Denmark and Sweden to the other Nordic countries, though other idea pathways functioned as well. Despite the shared experiences and common practices, there are also differences between the countries. These will be referred to later, under the appropriate headings.

The main purpose of this article is to describe general trends, compare them, and relate them to the international context. I also intend to provide references, which will help the reader acquire further information. It is not my purpose to go into detailed statistical comparisons for two reasons: First, it is not possible to make appropriate statistical comparisons because special education in all the countries is closely integrated into the education system. Second, as decision making has been decentralized to the local level, I shall have to rely on illustrative examples or cases, rather than sweeping general statements. Yet, comparable statistics are also available, for example certain OECD statistics (see table 23.1).

The biggest Nordic project that surveyed the conditions in special education and described the prevailing ideologies in the different countries was *En skole for*

TABLE 23.1.   The Percentage of Public Expenditure
Allotted to Education, by Country (1968)

Country	%
Finland	17.1
Switzerland	14.7
Canada	14.4
Australia	13.9
United States	13.7
Norway	12.4
OECD average	12.0
Japan	11.7
Denmark	11.6
Ireland	11.5
Great Britain	11.4
Austria	11.1
Netherlands	10.9
Portugal	10.7
Belgium	10.5
France	10.2
Spain	9.7
Sweden	9.6
Italy	9.4
Germany	9.1

Source: OECD 1992. *Education at a Glance.* Paris.

alle-projekt, completed in 1984 (Dahlgren and Nielsen 1984). Its results provide information about legislation, prevalence estimates, and the education of disabled pupils, but this information is ten years old now. Characteristic of Nordic cooperation, the report was written partly in Danish and partly in Swedish, that is, in the languages of the writers. Kristen Juul (1989), among others, has recently presented the results of this report in English.

A lot of similar Nordic memoranda, bulletins, registers, and descriptions are available, but systematic comparisons are rare. Tuunainen and Nevala (1989), based mainly on Stukat and Bladini (1986), compared the development of special education in Finland and Sweden. They found that the development of the Finnish school system, including special education, follows closely the Swedish model, with a time lag of ten to fifteen years. However, it should be pointed out that part of the problems that require solutions also emerge later than in Sweden. Also, Norway and Finland are somewhat more traditional and, consequently, may not have been as ready for extensive liberal experiments as was Sweden.

In general, the level of education in the Nordic countries is among the highest in the world, though the problems and traditions vary slightly among the different countries. Finland has, probably due to linguistic and historical reasons, the lowest percentage of foreigners in the population (.7 percent) in the whole of Europe. That situation is bound to change in the course of the European integration process. Finnish women are the most highly educated in the world; more women than men have graduated from higher education in the age groups under forty, and women write 40 percent of doctoral dissertations. However, only 10 percent of professors are women.

Prevalence of Exceptional Conditions

Maternity welfare and health care systems in all Nordic countries are quite advanced and it is difficult to point to any specific target groups. Here, as well as in other problems of special education, disparities in regional development constitute a problem. The northern parts of the countries, Lapland or the Arctic Area, are sparsely populated and the climate is cold—Helsinki is located on the same latitude as Anchorage, Alaska. In fact, half of the world population living above this latitude are Finns. It is difficult to provide the basic social services in sparsely populated areas, though the distances between these areas are not as far as those in Canada. Medical research has discovered a number of rare hereditary diseases that probably result from isolation but, on the whole, they are not very significant.

Characteristically Finnish diseases that causes disability are certain disorders in metabolism, such as aspartyl glucose amino urea (AGU), ophthalmia, hypoacusis, hyponony, and ataxy (OHAHA), the Univerricht-Lundborg syndrome, INCL, and Salla disease (named after the place where it was discovered). In Norway these minor diseases and groups of disabilities include tuberosis sclerosis, the Laurence-Moon-Bardet-Biedl syndrome, and the Prader Will syndrome. Primary amyloid polyneuropathy (FAP) and porphyry are typically Swedish diseases. The Nordic Board for the Disabled (Nordiska nämden för handikappfrågor) has coordinated a project to deal with these diseases.

It is one of the Nordic traditions that children start school at the age of seven. Each country has, however, a well-developed preschool system that functions within a municipal day-care system, providing the basic pedagogical training. Compulsory education and rehabilitation for disabled children begin earlier and also last beyond the comprehensive school, in the way that PL 94-142 mandates in the United States.

Identification of Exceptionalities

The problems of diagnostics have been frequently discussed by members of the professional groups involved. The basic medical diagnostics traditionally served the identification of children with sensory handicaps and later of mentally handicapped children. However, the emphasis has also increasingly moved toward psychological and pedagogical testing and assessment.

The use of psychological services is one distinct feature that differentiates Norway, Sweden, and Finland. Norway and Sweden have developed a comprehensive system of school psychologists, while a similar network in Finland is considerably less developed. Finland has a system of educational and family advice centers which, however, are closer to the health care services and families than to the schools. The emphasis of work has fluctuated with time. The problem dates back to 1926 when Sir Cyril Burt founded the Child Guidance Clinic in London. From the very beginning, it was argued whether the clinic should focus on education or on clinical practices. In Finland the focus has been on the services within the school, that is, on pupil welfare and special education teachers.

Welfare of the mentally handicapped has tended to be the main focus of the early diagnostics of disabled children. In the 1960s the term *mentally handicapped* was used as a concept that covered such areas as physically, psychologically, and socially handicapped. In practice, this conceptualization has not functioned in the desired way. Consequently, a new terminology has been developed for the school context, focusing on learning disabilities. This seems to have been the main tendency in many Western countries.

It seems that the Nordic countries have been in the vanguard in educational integration of the disabled ("Scandinavia" 1987). Integration was discussed even before the 1960s (Nirje 1969). It has been suggested that the Nordic concept of integration has also had some influence on the mainstreaming ideology in the United States, for example through Wolf Wolfensberger (1972).

Sweden has been the pioneer in developing the school system, while Norway and Finland have been more conservative and cautiously followed the example set by the Swedes. The comprehensive school curriculum, LGR 80 (Läroplan för grundskolan 1980) introduced a lot of new practices, which had been discussed earlier in several committee reports such as *Skolans Inre Arbete (SIA)*, 1975. Sweden is the "promised land" of committees, and it has produced an enormous number of reports, memoranda, guidelines, and political programs which, however, are often contradictory (Bladini 1990).

Several systems of classifying disability are in use. The World Health Organization (1980) has considerably influenced attempts to relate impairment, disability, and handicap to the underlying concepts of humanity; that is, biomedical, behavioral, and interactional.

It is not so essential to know the percentages of the disabled because such statistics are indicative of a certain way of thinking in which disability is viewed as a deviation from, rather than a broadening of, that which is normal. The total number or estimates of people using special services are more important. The leading principle in all Nordic countries is that a sufficient amount of special expertise is brought to each individual child at school. At present, it is estimated that more than 20 percent of each age group is receiving special support in the comprehensive school, though it is difficult to make an accurate estimate. The allocation of services and their combinations to the various authorities make up a whole that cannot be readily described without case analyses. In Finland, for example, in the new management culture that delegates responsibility and decision making to the local level, the need for evaluation measures is currently felt. How to guarantee the quality of special education services becomes problematic in a new way because the earlier practice relied mainly on well-trained civil servants and their judgment. It is my opinion that Norway and Finland are quite similar in this respect while in Sweden this process has advanced further.

Even though the tendency in all countries is toward educational integration, each country still has a network of special schools and special classes, which is gradually being dissolved. The following brief statistical descriptions provide the proportions of these educational institutions, though the figures for different countries are not fully comparable.

The figures for Finland (see table 23.2) refer to the years 1983 and 1987 when the number of students in the ordinary schools slightly decreased. This, in part, together with active development work, contributed

TABLE 23.2. Pupils in Finland Receiving Special Education in Comprehensive Schools, by Type of Disability (1983 and 1987)

Type of Disability	1983			1987		
	Number of Special Pupils	% of All Pupils	% of Boys of All Special Pupils	Number of Special Pupils	% of All Pupils	% of Boys of All Special Pupils
Visually handicapped	197	0.0	58.9	188	0.0	56.9
Hearing impaired	820	0.1	58.4	864	0.1	60.9
Mildly mentally retarded/delayed	8,148	1.4	66.5	8,096	1.4	64.6
Moderate to severely handicapped	1,407	0.2	58.9	2,362	0.4	58.8
Physically disabled	979	0.2	65.3	1,171	0.2	69.3
Social or emotional disorder	9,089	1.6	82.4	11,951	2.1	79.4
Speech disorder	27,649	4.8	62.8	25,553	4.5	63.4
Reading and writing problem	45,571	7.9	71.6	42,110	7.4	71.8
Other	3,564	0.6	64.9	4,527	0.8	68.5
Total	97,424	16.8	69.1	96,822	16.9	69.3

Source: Koulutus/Education in Finland. 1991. Koulutus ja tutkimus. 1991. Helsinki: Tilastokeskus, 11.

to the fact that the numbers of pupils attending special education classes in both integrated and segregated settings increased. In recent years, when all the students have been in the comprehensive schools, more special groups have been started in special schools for the more severely disabled pupils, yet the actual increase has taken place in integrated special education.

The number of special education teachers has increased rapidly as has their proportion among all teachers. In 1960 there were three hundred special teachers, 1.2 percent of all teachers in compulsory education; the corresponding figures in 1984 were twenty-eight hundred special teachers constituting 8 percent. The present number of special teachers is estimated to be more than four thousand, which is about 8 percent of all teachers. (Kivirauma and Kivinen 1988).

The statistics for Norway (see table 23.3) date back to 1990 and describe the development in the 1980s. The number of special teachers and schools have remained quite stable but the number of pupils has markedly decreased. The schools have adopted new functions such as developing materials and acting as regional consultation and resource centers, although it is difficult to "pull down" a well-established system even though methods and priorities change. Lately Norway has proceeded into full integration, but detailed information is not yet available.

The Swedish statistics (see table 23.4) describe the development of *särskolan* and *specialskolan*. Särskolan refers to a special school that, at least historically, is associated with the welfare of the mentally handicapped. It has a comprehensive responsibility in its own each region. Specialskolan is reserved for children with impaired vision and hearing or speech defects.

Further, division of responsibilities between the schools has changed: more "difficult" cases and more multihandicapped children are taken to schooling and the "easier" cases are sent to normal schools.

TABLE 23.3. Special Education in Norway, 1982–90

	Special Schools	Full-Time Teachers			Students		
School Year	Number of Schools	Number of Teachers	Number of Males	Number of Females	Number of Students	Number of Males	Number of Females
1982–83	89	1,061	484	577	3,178	1,992	1,186
1983–84	89	1,060	484	576	3,188	2,019	1,169
1984–85	87	1,049	486	563	3,135	1,951	1,184
1985–86	87	1,070	487	583	2,954	1,836	1,118
1986–87	87	1,143	513	630	2,911	1,812	1,099
1987–88	87	1,086	453	633	2,620	1,613	1,007
1988–89	85	1,126	440	686	2,583	1,597	986
1989–90	84	—	—	—	2,427	1,510	917

Source: Norges Offisielle Statistikk (NOS). 1990. Educational Statistics.

TABLE 23.4. Pupils Receiving Special Education in Sweden, 1981–90

	Preschools[a]	Compulsory Schools	Training Schools	Vocational Schools	Special Education Schools	Impaired Vision Schools	Impaired Hearing and/or Speech Schools
1981	1,234	5,182	2,214	3,340	632	67	645
1982	1,221	5,342	2,222	3,347	543	66	630
1983	1,259	5,271	2,120	3,522	506	65	629
1984	1,283	5,303	2,115	3,566	492	58	634
1985	1,335	5,431	2,036	3,452	516	51	620
1986	1,021	5,319	2,112	3,259	505	49	596
1987		4,164	2,730	1,433	81	45	591
1988		4,009	2,799	1,397	65	46	613
1989		4,113	2,838	1,405	88	46	613
1990		4,075	2,843	1,464	78	45	639

Source: *Statistical Yearbook of Sweden.* 1991. Stockholm: Norstedts Trychen, AB.
[a] It appears that preschools were no longer categorized separately after 1986.

Through the history of the welfare state, special attention has been paid to special groups. Nevertheless, the rights of disabled minorities are currently discussed in the Nordic countries, and the terminology is in a state of continuous change. In particular, the organizations of the various groups of the disabled have the role of watchdog in safeguarding the fundamental rights of the disabled. Labeling has been investigated (e.g., Moberg 1979) but, at the same time, there has been a tendency to discard the whole terminology. A highly appreciated Swedish colleague, Karl-Gustav Stukat, illustrates the situation by the following anecdote. When he asked his grandchild how many pupils are in his class, the answer was twelve boys, twelve girls, and one integrated.

There has been a tendency toward developing the terminology for learning disabilities, though it is necessary to use exact medical or psychological terms in certain contexts. The Norwegians have coined the term *funksjon-shemming,* which refers to a general functional disorder or difficulty. The concept of children with special needs has several national equivalents, each having its own historical background and connotations.

The Social Context of Special Education

The biggest problem in special education is coverage. It has to be extended to cover all population groups. In the Nordic countries this has largely been solved. Nevertheless, instead of a real multicultural tradition, the prevailing ideology has been based on the idea of the national state where the rights of the ruling national majority has overshadowed those of minority groups. The Swedes have longest and most extensively been involved in the immigration problem. Still they argue about the borderline between special education and immigrant education. In 1975 Sweden passed a law on *hemspråk* (home language), which was an attempt to solve this problem. Yet it is obvious that there are disparities between the majority and the minorities in special education services, in part associated with regional differences. In Norway this issue has been addressed, while Finland is lagging behind.

At present, the economic recession is hardening the atmosphere in all societies, and there is a danger that cuts in budgets will hit those who are in the weakest position. At the moment it may be appropriate to talk about supporting the banking system but, in the near future, health care, social welfare, and education will have to fight for the same resources. One obvious fact is the aging of population, that is the mean expectation of life is increasing, the number of children is decreasing, and people retire prematurely. Here, too, there are differences between the countries. The Norwegians stay longest in working life, then come the Swedes, while the Finns tend to retire early, which may be indicative of problems in the working environment. International relations are an integral part of special education in the Nordic countries, which is essential in following the developments in the field. In highly bureaucratized societies one further problem is the compartmentalization of rehabilitation. Attempts have been made to clarify the responsibilities, but still there is a danger that the massive systems do not reach all the citizens covered by the articles of law.

Legislation has long and centralized traditions in all countries, dating back to the former power of kings and the czar. The bureaucracy of the central government has reached a stage that has occasionally been heavily criticized. The current trend is decentralization of decision making, but it is not easy to modify old practices.

The fundamental social principle is obvious enough: All children have to be educated. However, this has been a reality only for a few decades. In Finland this principle was accepted in the School Laws of 1985, but still there are about seven hundred severely mentally handicapped children who are not provided by schools with the education to which they are entitled. However, the schooling is provided by the social welfare authorities, and it is to be expected that the situation will be normalized in a few years.

Special Teacher Education

Special teacher education has mainly taken place as further education, that is, after regular classroom teacher education. In Sweden special teacher training began in 1921 (Bladini 1990), and Norway and Finland followed a little later. From the beginning, training took place in teacher training colleges. There were a few cases, as early as the nineteenth century, of special teacher training also being provided in various special education institutions.

In Finland, special teacher education was transferred to the University of Jyväskylä by Professor Niilo Mäki in 1959. In Norway and Sweden, similar reforms were carried out a few years later. In the course of the past few decades, special teacher education has gradually elevated to the master's degree. The Finnish Teacher Education Act of 1972 and the degree program in special education since 1979 have set the example that the other countries have endeavored to follow. The teacher education institutions have increased their research activities, and they have been annexed to universities. At the same time, the number of special teacher education institutions has increased. There are four departments of special education in Finland: Jyväskylä (1948–), Joensuu (1969–), Helsinki (1975–), and Vaasa (1975–). Also, there is Åbo Akademi, The Swedish University of Turku, where Swedish is the language of instruction.

In Norway and Sweden, special teacher education used to take place in teacher education colleges (Lärarhägskolan), but recently the number of the colleges has been reduced, and they have been connected more closely with universities. In Norway, the special education departments of the Universities of Oslo and Trondheim are known for extensive research activities. The regional universities (distrikthögskole) in Stavanger, Lillehammar, and Alta also provide teacher education. In Sweden the Universities of Stockholm and Gothenberg are beginning to have a central role in special teacher education. Training is also provided by a couple of other universities and their affiliates.

Education has been organized according to specialization areas, and there is a trend to combine the general basic courses into larger units of study, which then provide a basis for eventual specialization through in-service training. Here, it is necessary to take the Danish situation into consideration. In Denmark, basic teacher education is more closely connected to reading problems, in addition to which students choose other areas of specialization. In some special cases—such as for teachers of the deaf-blind—teacher education is organized jointly by the Nordic countries including Denmark.

Research in special education is carried out within several disciplines. Interdisciplinary registers and networks are used in the dissemination of research results because the boundaries between the various disciplines are a constant problem. A network connecting the departments of special education has recently been established. The network, which is backed by Nordic funding, will help the departments to exchange methods, information, staff members, and students. There is also *Nordiska forskarkurser,* a Nordic organization for postgraduate education, which has organized courses for special education (Tuunainen 1978; Tuunainen, Savolainen, and Savolainen 1992).

Some Conclusions and Major Issues for the Future

Historically, development of special schools was closely associated with charity organizations and the work carried out by the church, but nowadays the states are responsible for the provision of education, using, to some extent, private organizations that receive regular public funding. Integration has been the central trend since the 1960s, but it has also been realized that supporting measures are needed. Decentralization of institutions of special education is most complete in Sweden where, for example, the former boarding schools for the visually impaired have no pupils, and the buildings now house resource centers that organize short courses for children and parents, develop teaching materials, and provide support for schools with visually impaired pupils. Further, Sweden has a nationwide network of pedagogical aids centers (RPH, Rikscentral för pedagogiska hjälpmedel). Similar development centers exist in the other countries, too, and more will be needed as integration progresses.

The position of school classes has been widely discussed in all countries because the group as a whole and the individuals are crucial in education for the whole age group. Sweden has given up school classes and introduced a larger unit (*undervisningsenehet*) instead. The new instructional unit is allocated sufficient resources to be distributed when needed.

Flexibility is also important in allocating the other resources of schools within a school district. There is a danger that the resources meant for the pupils tend to be transformed, according to the principles of professionalism, into teachers' salaries.

The curricula include features of the German Lehrplan tradition, but the curriculum idea is increasingly present. The individual education plan (IEP) thinking has also had a very important impact on special education.

Mainstreaming or, as we call it, integration, provides the foundation of special education. It is widely accepted and has a relatively long history. Denmark and Sweden have set an example for Finland and Norway to follow in due course. In international comparison, the Nordic countries can be viewed as advanced countries. This development has been possible because of a general positive attitude toward providing citizens with good educational and social services.

There are also problems in special education because the interests of the various professional groups, the views of the taxpayers, and the larger issues of social policy have to be reconciled. The teachers' unions have not accepted integration without fear and resistance, but considerable progress has been made.

Even today there are also segregated educational institutions in the different countries—there will always be—but it is only a question of emphasis and relative proportions. Mårten Söder's four-phase model of the progression of integration is widely accepted. According to the model, the four phases of integration are physical, functional, social, and societal integration. If special schools are physically far from ordinary schools, there will be no other connections. Functional integration can be increased by organizing common learning groups and other connections by means of the time table. Social integration includes spare-time activities, and societal integration refers to common goals in society. Instead of just helping the disabled, the focus is on coexistence and cooperation in general.

In all countries, the state provides the funds for basic general education from the beginning at seven years, up to about sixteen years of age. The situation of disabled children before school age is good. Pedagogical habilitation begins earlier, but there are some problems in secondary education (sixteen years and over). Vocational education, career education, and placement in working life and in further studies causes problems. However good a system may be, it is difficult to overcome the negative effects of socialization on disablement.

There are private funds in each country, and they have an important role to play, especially in development work, because the state system can never meet all the individual needs. There is always room for voluntary work.

The role of parents in supporting children's education is rather passive if it is compared to that in the United States. In countries with heavy taxation, there is a tendency to make society take the responsibility in all matters. Moreover, it is customary for both parents to work outside the home, leaving less time for children. In recent years, however, a new kind of civic activity has emerged in the various minorities and within the school system itself—activity that criticizes the bureaucracy. Even expressions of civil disobedience have appeared in the Nordic countries. This means that politicians will have to take into account the increasing activity of well-educated parents.

In many branches of disablement, there are Nordic associations and new organizations emerging. The association of children suffering from cancer is an example of the new and active parents' organizations in Finland. The question of human rights has recently been widely discussed, partly because the Nordic Board for Disabled has published a book *Tie ihmisarvoon* (*Vägen till människovärde/The Road to Human Dignity* 1989), which has been translated into all Nordic languages. The book describes features of the history of the disabled in the years 1945 to 1985.

Emerging and future trends are very global and most of them are tied to the third world, to the issues of the developing countries. Wiesinger-Ferris (1989) has listed a great number of factors that affect the situation of the disabled in the international context. The increasing population of the world, development of the third world, questions of war and peace, the fall of the socialist countries, environmental questions, and so on, are large issues. At the moment, it is difficult to estimate their impact on the Nordic welfare system. No doubt, they will affect the future of special education, too.

Today Europe is undergoing two big changes that will have consequences for special education. The economic integration of Western Europe and the developments in the less developed countries of Eastern Europe, together with the refugee problem and migration (for example, from the former Yugoslavia) will bring new challenges and problems for special education. Changes in age distribution, migration from country to town, depopulation of the remote and underdeveloped Northern regions, and so on, make it difficult to predict future developments in the Nordic countries.

Free movement of labor force and capital and free movement of people in general have increased cooperation between the Nordic countries. In the future, the area of free movement will widen. This will, inevitably, increase the number of classes where the language of instruction is not the national language of the given country. Even though Swedish is the dominant language in the Nordic countries, it will never be the language of European communication. English, German, French, Spanish, Italian, and Russian will retain their position as widely used languages and, consequently, special education conducted in these language is likely to consume part of the resources in normal and in special education.

The welfare system, fixed by law, is so advanced that it will be difficult to pull it down. In the Nordic countries there are no legal cases initiated by disabled persons, but healthcare patients have taken cases of mistreatment to court. It is obvious that certain services will be privatized in order to cut down expenses and to increase flexibility. For instance, in Finland the state is getting rid of state schools and other educational institutions by transferring them to municipalities. Residential institutes for juvenile delinquents are also being privatized.

The school system will have to become cost-effective, which will decrease bureaucracy. Of course, there is a danger that, in the name of productivity and efficiency, the level of services will suffer. On the other hand, special education has supporters among the politicians, and the human rights issues will always be there.

The Scandinavian way will assume new forms in special education, but the fundamental issues will not be questioned. Special education is an integral part of both the education system and the overall habilitation system.

References

Bladini, U. B. 1990. *Från hjälpskolelärare till förändringsagent. Svensk speciallärarut-bildning 1921–1981 relaterad till specialundervisningens utveckling boch förändringar i speciallärarens yrkesuppgifter.* Göteborg Studies in Educational Sciences 76. Sweden: Acta Universitas Gothoburgensis.

Dahlgren, I., and Nielsen, H. W. 1984. *En skole for alle.* NORD: Nordisk Ministerråd. Copenhagen.

Juul, K. D. 1989. Some common and unique features of special education in the Nordic countries. *International Journal of Special Education* 4 (1):85–96.

Kivirauma, J., and Kivinen, O. 1988. The school system and special education: Causes and effects in the twentieth century. *Disability, Handicap and Society* 3 (2):153–65.

Moberg, S. 1979. *Leimautuminen erityispedagogiikassa.* Jyväskylä Studies in Education, Psychology and Social Science, 39. Finland: University of Jyväskylä.

Nirje B. 1969. The normalization principle and its human management implications. In R. Kugel and W. Wolfensberger, eds. *Changing patterns in residential services for the mentally retarded.* Washington, D.C.: President's Committee on Mental Retardation Monograph, Washington.

Norges Offisielle Statistikk B 921. 1990. *Statistical yearbook of Norway. 109th issue.* Oslo-Kongsviger: Statistisk Sentralbyrå.

Scandinavia: A reference for the education of the handicapped and other exceptional children and adults. 1987. In C. R. Reynolds and L. Mann, eds. *Encyclopedia of special education,* 1381–82.

Statistical yearbook of Sweden. 1991. Stockholm: Norstedts Trychen.

Stukat, K. G., and Bladini, U. B. 1986. *Svensk specialundervisning, Intentioner och realiteter i ett utvwecklingsperspektiv.* Göteborgs Universitet Publikation no. 14. Sweden: Institutionen för pedagogik.

Tuunainen, K., ed. 1978. *Rapport från Nordisk forskakurs: Specialpedagogisk forskning—målsättning och metodik.* Finland: University of Joensuu.

Tuunainen, K., and Nevala, A. 1989. *Erityiskasvatuksen kehitys Suomessa.* Helsinki: Gaudeamus.

Tuunainen, K., Savolainen, H., and Savolainen, P., eds. 1992. *Erityispedagogiikan tutkijakoulutuksen nykytila.* University of Joensuu: Bulletins of the Faculty of Education, Joensuu.

Walton, W. T., Rosenqvist, J., and Sandling, I. 1991. A comparative study of special education in the public school system in Denmark, Sweden and the United States. *International Journal of Special Education* 6 (3):403–16.

Wiesinger-Ferris, R. 1989. Partnership between the developed and the developing countries to promote special education and disability prevention. *International Journal of Special Education* 4 (2):101–10.

Wolfensberger, W. 1972. *The principle of normalization in human services.* Toronto: National Institute on Mental Retardation.

World Health Organization. 1980.

24

United States

BETTY A. HALLENBECK

JAMES M. KAUFFMAN

*T*he origins of special education as a part of the public education system in the United States can be traced to the late nineteenth century, when several metropolitan school districts established special classes for children with learning or behavior problems. The founding of the International Council for Exceptional Children 1922 was a significant landmark in the development of special education in the United States and Canada, and special education became a common part of the public schools in many metropolitan areas by the 1930s. Following World War II, special education expanded rapidly, and in 1975 the United States enacted legislation requiring a free, appropriate education for every child with a disability.

About the Authors • Betty A. Hallenbeck is completing her Ph.D. in special education at the University of Virginia. She received her B.A., cum laude, in sociology and anthropology from Carleton College in 1982 and her M.Ed. in special education from the University of Virginia in 1985. At the University of Virginia, she has been a graduate instructor and a teaching and research assistant. She has served as a special education instructional assistant in Oregon and as a teacher of students with disabilities in both Oregon and Virginia. She is also the author or coauthor of several professional publications in special education. • Dr. James M. Kauffman held the William Clay Parrish Jr. Professorship in education at the University of Virginia, where he has been a faculty member since 1970. He is a past president of the Council for Children with Behavioral Disorders, a division of the Council for Exceptional Children. He has published widely in journals in education, special education, and psychology and is the author, coauthor or coeditor of more than ten books including *Characteristics of Emotional and Behavioral Disorders of Children and Youth* (Merrill/Macmillan), now in its fifth edition. His most recent book is *Managing classroom behavior: A Reflective Case-Based Approach* (Allyn and Bacon), which he coauthored with Mark P. Mostert, Deborah G. Nuttycombe, Stanley C. Trent, and Daniel P. Hallahan.

TABLE 24.1. Approximate Number of Students (Ages 6 to 21) in the United States Receiving Special Education, by Category (School Year 1990–91).

Disability Type	Number of Students
All disabilities	4,367,600
Specific learning disabilities	2,144,400
Speech or language impairments	988,300
Mental retardation	552,700
Serious emotional disturbance	392,600
Hearing impairments	59,300
Multiple disabilities	97,600
Orthopedic impairments	49,400
Other health impairments	56,300
Visual impairments	23,700
Deaf-blindness	1,500

Source: U.S. Department of Education. 1992. *Fourteenth annual report to Congress on the implementation of the Individuals with Disabilities Education Act.* Washington, D.C. U.S. Department of Education.

Note: Numbers are rounded to the nearest hundred.

Prevalence of Exceptional Conditions

A common estimate is that 10 to 20 percent of the general population experiences some level of disability. In the school-age population, approximately 10 percent of students are served in special education programs (U.S. Department of Education 1992). Special education services are provided to over four million students, most of whom are between the ages of six and seventeen. Children with learning disabilities compose the largest percentage of this group, as shown in table 24.1. Controversy persists regarding the definition of learning disabilities and the procedures for identifying and labeling students with such disabilities. Some professionals suspect that the large number of students with learning disabilities is a function of the social acceptability of the label (compared to mental retardation, emotional disturbance, and so on) and the unwillingness of regular classroom teachers to teach difficult students; others note that social conditions might cause such a relatively high prevalence of learning disabilities (Hallahan 1992).

From approximately 1955 to the mid-1980s, the U.S. Department of Education published annual prevalence estimates for all categories of handicapping conditions. Since about 1985, only reports of the number of students served by special education have been published. We suspect that prevalence estimates are no longer published because federal law has, since 1978, required that all students with disabilities be provided special education. Hence, prevalence is now assumed to match the number of students identified and served (see Kauffman 1993, chap. 2).

Identification of Exceptionalities

Since 1978, federal law has required states to make extensive efforts to screen and identify all children with disabilities. The evaluation process must not discriminate against children due to cultural or language factors, must include evaluation of all suspected areas of disability, and must be conducted by a multidisciplinary team. Results of this testing must be confidential, although parents have a right to see their child's records.

Identification of persons with disabilities can, of course, occur during any of the following stages: prenatal, perinatal, infancy and preschool, school-age, and adulthood. Despite the comparative affluence of the United States, prenatal care is not universally available. Rectifying this situation would undoubtedly reduce the incidence of disabilities in infants. In fact, due to rapidly increasing poverty, interpersonal violence, family disintegration, and the concomitant failure of federal and state governments to provide adequate funding for social welfare programs such as nutrition and prenatal care, we are witnessing increases in the disabilities of children. Researchers now refer to a "new morbidity" consisting of disabling conditions that accompany adverse environmental, psychosocial, and economic conditions (Baumeister, Kupstas, and Klindworth 1990).

A variety of techniques are available for prenatal identification of infants with disabilities. Amniocentesis, chorionic villus sampling, and sonography are three such methods often used in the United States. After birth, babies are routinely tested for phenylketonuria (PKU). With federal law mandating early intervention, most children with severe congenital disabilities are identified soon after birth.

Since 1986, when federal law extended the requirements of identification to children ages three to five, services for preschool children have improved considerably. States are encouraged by federal law to develop early intervention programs for children with disabilities and children from birth to thirty-six months who are at risk for disabilities.

Among the school-age population, identification of students with disabilities can be accomplished in several ways. First, screening for visual and hearing problems occurs annually in most elementary schools. Some schools also conduct widespread screening for speech and language disorders during the early grades. Screening for academic or behavioral problems, on the other hand, is rarely systematic. Typically, academic and behavioral problems are identified by teachers' complaints or referral to a multidisciplinary team.

Students with mild or moderate disabilities are generally identified through procedures outlined in federal law, state regulations, and local policies. This identification process typically begins when a classroom teacher makes a referral to the multidisciplinary team (MDT). Multidisciplinary teams have a variety of titles, depending on the preferences of the local school system (for example, child study team, student resource team, or prereferral team). After receiving a request from a classroom teacher, the MDT meets to discuss the student's difficulties and determine the best course of action. Most of these referrals result in a list of interventions, which the classroom teacher is urged to use for a specified period of time. If these measures are successful, no further intervention is taken and the student's behavior is simply monitored. If these steps do not succeed in helping the student, a full psychoeducational evaluation is recommended. In more severe cases, such as children who are a danger to themselves, or others, the MDT might decide to refer the student immediately for a complete psychoeducational evaluation.

The components of the psychoeducational evaluation process are outlined in federal law, state regulations, and local policies. Generally, an evaluation consists of these components: results of academic, psychological, medical, and speech/hearing/language testing, a family status or sociological report, and review of the student's school record. More than one person must be involved in this process, and parents must give their consent for the assessment to be conducted.

After the assessment has been completed, the MDT reconvenes to determine whether the child is eligible for special services. Parents must be given the opportunity to be an integral part of this meeting. Students receiving special education services must complete a reevaluation at least every three years.

Despite more than a decade of the federal requirement of nonbiased assessment, the disproportionate identification of males and ethnic minorities remains a problem for the high-prevalence categories of disability—learning disability, serious emotional disturbance, mental retardation, and speech and language disorders (Chinn and Hughes 1987; Wallace, Larsen, and Elksnin 1992). Perhaps a portion of the disproportionality in the identification of ethnic minorities can be explained by the fact that these children tend to be disproportionately affected by conditions that produce disabilities; that is the new morbidity resulting from poverty and its concomitants (Baumeister, Kaupstas, and Klindworth 1990; U.S. Department of Education 1992). Nevertheless, new morbidity does not explain all the apparent gender and racial bias in identification, and new efforts are needed to remedy inadequate and inappropriate evaluation procedures. The problem is all the more pressing because the ethnic diversity of the United States is increasing dramatically.

Labeling the Disabled Population

The categories of disabilities that qualify for special services are clearly delineated by federal law and regulations. The categories include learning disability, serious emotional disturbance, mental retardation, speech and language disorders, visual impairment (blind and partially sighted), hearing impairment (deaf and hard of hearing), physical disability, traumatic brain injury, autism, and other health impairments. Funding is provided to states based on these categories, but some states and school districts are moving away from categorical provision of services. These schools serve children based on severity of disability (mild, moderate, severe) or integrate most of their students.

The use of labels in the provision of services to special education students continues to be controversial (see Hallahan and Kauffman 1994 for further discussion). Opponents of the current system argue that labeling has disadvantages for students with disabilities. It stigmatizes them and causes others to expect deviant behavior, obscures their individuality by creating a focus on similarities among people with the same label, and lowers their self-esteem. While acknowledging these concerns, supporters of the current labeling structure give at least the following reasons for its continued use:

1. Individuals with disabilities have differences about which we must talk, and elimination of one label will be followed by use of another.
2. Labels often provide explanations or justifications for differences that help to remove blame and stigma.
3. Evidence suggests that differences per se rather than the labels used to describe them are stigmatizing and that labeling often follows rather than precedes stigma.
4. Labels help spotlight the needs of people with disabilities for the general public and are necessary to preserve the legislative, litigation, and fiscal resources that provide special services.
5. Without labels (language) for describing disabilities, we will return to a previous era in which disabilities were unmentionable and, therefore, not accommodated.

The issues of labeling and categories were given special attention in a federal law enacted in 1990. The Individuals with Disabilities Education Act (IDEA) amended the landmark mandatory special education law passed in 1975, The Education for All Handicapped Children Act (also known as Public Law 94-142). The title of the law was changed to emphasize "people first" terminology; that is, *child with a disability* rather than *handicapped child*. The legal codification of this language is an indication of the depth of feeling about the use of language referring to the human differences that we call disabilities. Moreover, IDEA established two new, separate categories of disability—traumatic brain injury and autism. Traumatic brain injury and autism were formerly included under other categories, but advocates wanted them distinguished from other groups. We expect continuing controversy regarding the establishment of Attention Deficit Disorder (ADD) or Attention Deficit Hyperactivity Disorder (ADHD) as a separate category.

The Social Context of Special Education

Starting in the 1960s, in concert with the civil rights movement of African Americans, attitudes toward people with disabilities began to change dramatically. During the 1960s and 1970s, treatment of persons with disabilities in nonrestrictive, normalized settings gained priority, based in part on the rationale that persons with disabilities have a civil right to live, attend school, and work in the same environment as others, but based also in part on an ideological shift. Underlying the shift in practice was the ideological conviction that community settings are superior in their effects on social, vocational, and academic learning. This philosophical issue is still the subject of heated debates among special education and mental health professionals. Kauffman and Hallahan (1992) explain with reference to deinstitutionalization: "What is at issue is whether any institution can provide a humane, habilitating environment that allows maximum personal freedom and self-actualization for any individual. One perspective on this issue is that institutions are inherently incompatible with achieving these goals for anyone; another is that an institution can be the most effective structure for achieving these ends for some individuals" (300).

The trend toward less restrictive settings for persons with disabilities was also manifested in public schools, where mainstreaming gained new support beginning in the late 1960s. Increased mainstreaming found support from two primary sources. First, critics of self-contained classes, such as Dunn (1968), raised doubts about the efficacy of such placements. "[Dunn's] linking of the issue of segregation of children with disabilities to the concern about the overrepresentation of ethnic minorities struck a responsive chord during the politically liberal 1960s" (Kauffman and Hallahan 1992; 300). Second, coinciding with these new doubts about self-contained classes, federal legislation directed schools to provide an appropriate education for students with disabilities in the least restrictive environment (LRE). The LRE has been interpreted by some to be the regular classroom—for all students.

Since 1980, when the conservative ideology of President Reagan began driving social policy, increased mainstreaming has found support from both the right (because of its appeal as a way of reducing government services and costs) and the left (because of its appeal as a civil rights issue) (Kauffman 1991). The present context of educational reform is one in which special education is struggling with its identity and viability in a public education system obsessed with international economic competition, yet apparently dedicated to the education of all children (Kauffman and Hallahan 1992).

Legislation

The United States has a long history of reliance on legislative and, especially, litigable remedies for social issues, including special education. Although authority has been increasingly centralized in highly prescriptive and proscriptive federal legislation, a constant stream of litigation molds the meaning of these laws. Because most federal special education law requires that states conform to its demands in order to receive federal funding, all states now have legislation that effectively mimics federal law. We have space to describe only two major landmark laws.

TABLE 24.2. Summary of Major Provisions of the Individuals with Disabilities Education Act.

Identification: Extensive efforts must be made to screen and identify all children and youths who may have disabilities.

Nondiscriminatory Evaluation: Students suspected of having a disability must be evaluated in all areas of suspected disability and in a way that is not biased by the students' language or cultural characteristics or disabilities. Evaluation must be accomplished by a multidisciplinary team, and no single evaluation procedure may be used as the sole criterion for placement or planning.

Full Educational Service at No Cost: Every student with a disability must be assured an appropriate public education at no cost to the parents or guardians.

Individualized Education Program (IEP): A written individualized education program must be prepared for each student with a disability. The program must state present levels of functioning, long- and short-term goals, services to be provided, plans for initiating and evaluating the services, and (for older students, usually by age fourteen or sixteen) services needed for transition from school to work or continued education.

Placement in the Least Restrictive Environment (LRE): The student must be educated in the least restrictive environment that is consistent with his or her educational needs and, insofar as possible, with students without disabilities.

Parent/Guardian or Surrogate Consultation: The student's parents or guardian must be consulted about the student's evaluation and placement and the educational plan. If the parents or guardian are unknown or unavailable, a surrogate parent to act for the student must be found.

Confidentiality: The results of evaluation and placement must be kept confidential, though the student's parents or guardian may have access to the students' records.

Due Process: The student's parents' rights to information and informed consent must be assured before the student is evaluated, labeled, or placed, and the parents have a right to an impartial due process hearing if they disagree with the school's decisions.

Personnel Development: Training must be provided for teachers and other professional personnel, including in-service training for regular classroom teachers in meeting the needs of students with disabilities.

Note: Detailed federal rules and regulations govern the implementation of these and other provisions of the law. Each state has laws that meet or exceed the mandates of IDEA. This table was adapted from Hallahan, D. P., and Kauffman. 1994. *Exceptional children: Introduction to special education.* 6th ed. Boston: Allyn and Bacon.

Until 1975, federal special education legislation was permissive (allowing, but not requiring conformity of state with federal law), although several states had legislation mandating special education services. With the enactment of the Education for All Handicapped Children Act of 1975 (Public Law 94-142; since 1990 known as the Individuals with Disabilities Education Act, IDEA), the United States entered a new era in the education of students with disabilities. The law is extraordinary in specificity and prescriptiveness, and federal regulations accompanying the law are extensive. The major provisions of IDEA are outlined in table 24.2.

The Americans with Disabilities Act (ADA), passed in 1990, bars discrimination in employment, public accommodations, transportation, and telecommunications. It has been seen as a major civil rights law for people with disabilities. This law prohibits employers from discriminating against qualified applicants with disabilities, requires new public vehicles to be accessible, protects the rights of persons with disabilities to telephones they can use, and specifies that new or remodeled public buildings be accessible to persons with disabilities.

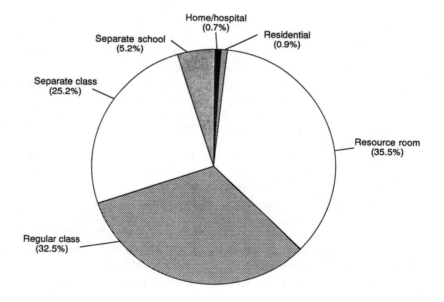

Figure 24.1   Percentage of all students with disabilities ages 3–21 served in six educational placements: School year 1989–90.

Source: U.S. Department of Education. 1992. *Fourteenth annual report to Congress on the implementation of the Individuals with Disabilities Education Act.* Washington, D.C.

Notes: Includes data from 50 states, the District of Columbia, and outlying areas. Separate school includes both public and private separate school facilities. Residential includes both public and private residential facilities.

Policies

All policies are constrained by the federal laws and regulations we discussed previously. Within these constraints, however, policies vary tremendously by state and locality. A major controversy that is part of the current educational reform movement is the extent to which policy decision regarding students with disabilities should be made at the local school level. That is, there is a major disagreement regarding the extent to which site-based management should be applied to special education and local policy should be allowed to contravene state or federal regulations.

Teachers, Schools, Curriculum, and Pedagogy

Teacher training in special education generally occurs at colleges and universities and includes a wide variety of programs. Bachelor's, master's, and doctoral degrees are available. Certification to teach students with disabilities varies considerably among the states; although federal law governs many special education practices, there is no federal certification for teachers. Certification is generally provided along categorical lines, but some programs certify teachers in the broader areas of mild, moderate, or severe disabilities.

Special education in the United States includes a continuum of services and alternative placements, as mandated by IDEA. The continuum includes at least the following range of service options: regular class only, regular class with consultation, itinerant services, resource room, diagnostic-prescriptive center, hospital or homebound instruction, self-contained class, special day school, and residential school. As shown in figure 24.1, a minority of students in all categories are served in separate settings (that is, separate day-care facilities, residential facilities, or hospitals).

Each special education student's specific academic and behavioral goals are explained in his or her Individualized Education Program (IEP). The IEP, which must be approved by a student's parents or guardians, describes what teachers will do to meet the student's needs. Because federal and state regulations do not specify how detailed an IEP must be, there is considerable variation in these documents from one school district to another. Regulations do stipulate that an IEP must be a written document and that it be developed in a meeting attended by the following parties: parents, representative of the local school district, the teacher and, if appropriate, the student (Bateman 1992).

An IEP must include the following primary components:

1. The student's present level of academic and/or behavioral performance

2. Annual goals for the student
3. Short-term instructional objectives that will culminate in these annual goals
4. The special education and related services that will be provided and the amount of participation in regular education programs
5. The starting date and expected duration of the services
6. Plans for evaluating, at least once a year, whether the goals and objectives have been achieved
7. For older students, a plan for transition to further education or employment

For infants and young children for whom early intervention is provided under federal law, educators must write an Individualized Family Service Plan (IFSP), which specifies not only what services will be provided for the child but also the support services to be provided to the family.

Instructional methods vary greatly in special education, both within and among the various categories, especially the high incidence and mild disability categories. Typically individual teachers are free to choose much of their own methods and materials, although some school districts are highly prescriptive of curriculum and methods. Some special education teachers use behavior modification and direct instruction methods, but many are highly influenced by trends in general education, which at the moment are toward a more exploratory, developmental approach.

Major Controversies and Issues in Special Education

In the United States, the first systematic public school programs for students with disabilities emerged in the late nineteenth century. These early programs were heavily influenced by European practices and beliefs (Kauffman 1981). Today, special programs for students with disabilities are an integral part of U.S. public education (Kauffman and Hallahan 1992).

However, in the closing decade of the twentieth century, special education in the United States is experiencing great controversy regarding the structure of special programs and services and the basic concepts that have guided special education practices for a century or more (Goodlad and Lovitt 1993; Lloyd, Singh, and Repp 1991). The controversy includes disagreements about the extent to which special education should maintain an identity and function distinguishable from general education, and the extent to which students with disabilities should be provided education that is distinctive. In all likelihood, substantial changes will be made during the next decade in the rationale and practices that characterize special education in the United States. Whether these changes will be beneficial to the welfare of exceptional children and youth or return the field to the problems special educators in the United States faced in the early twentieth century is a matter of great concern (Fuchs and Fuchs 1991; Kauffman, in press; MacMillan and Hendrick 1993).

The 1980s and 1990s have seen especially dramatic changes in the education of people with disabilities, and current thinking indicates that the field is poised for still more change (Hallahan and Kauffman 1994). We will next discuss three major concerns in the field of special education: integration (or inclusion), early intervention, and transition programming.

Integration (Inclusion)

Integration, or mainstreaming, became a focal issue in the late 1960s and continues to be a major concern. One rationale for mainstreaming has been that all children, regardless of their characteristics, have a civil right to attend their neighborhood school and a regular classroom; another rational has been that special schools and classes provide second-rate education and that regular schools and classrooms provide superior benefits for all students. Both rationales have supporters and critics, and the issues have led to heated debate (Lloyd, Singh, and Repp 1991).

Recently, *inclusion* has emerged as the term of choice for the practice of mainstreaming or integrating students with disabilities into neighborhood schools and regular classes. Some radical advocates of inclusion insist that all residential schools, institutions, special schools, and special classes must be eliminated. They assert that all neighborhood schools must include all the children in their catchment areas, regardless of any disability, and that all students with disabilities be educated in regular classes. In the opinion of the most radical advocates of inclusion, the concept of least restrictive environment (LRE) is no longer defensible because it allows one to consider options other than placement in the neighborhood school and regular classroom. To these advocates, alternative placements that can no longer be justified on legal or moral grounds (e.g., Laski 1991; Taylor 1988).

More conservative supporters of integration believe that students with disabilities can be integrated to a greater extent than could have been imagined even twenty years ago, but that a full spectrum of placement options must be maintained, ranging from hospital and residential schools to full-time attendance in a regular classroom in the neighborhood school (e.g., Fuchs and Fuchs 1991; Hocutt, Martin, and McKinney 1991; Kauffman and Hallahan 1993).

The trend toward increased integration or full inclusion is based on the principle of normalization. In accordance with this principle, children with disabilities should be educated in a fashion as similar to that of nondisabled students as possible. Despite its surface appeal, the principle of normalization has given rise to several disagreements. First, some have understood normalization to mean that all integrated settings should be abolished, although the creators of the concept saw the need for many service delivery options (e.g., Bank-Mikkelson 1969; Wolfensberger 1972; see Hallahan and Kauffman 1994; Kauffman and Hallahan 1992; 1993). Second, some groups of people with disabilities prefer to associate with people who share their disability. For example, some deaf people find it so difficult to communicate in the hearing worlds that they prefer to be with other deaf people (e.g., Lord 1991; Padden and Humphries 1988). Finally, there is uncertainty about the role of technology in normalization. It is clear that technology has bettered the lives of people with disabilities in numerous ways. Some people with disabilities, however, worry that technology could be misused and are concerned about overreliance on artificial methods for interacting with society as a whole (see Hallahan and Kauffman 1994).

In the United States, the movement toward full inclusion emerged about a decade after the Regular Education Initiative. First presented in speeches and articles by an Assistant Secretary of Education in the U.S. Department of Education, this initiative called for general educators to assume greater responsibility for students who have special needs in school (Will 1984, 1986). Advocacy for placement of students with disabilities into regular classes was interpreted by some as support for the dissolution of a distinct system of special education for students with disabilities. Federal funding of projects focusing on mainstreaming increased markedly during the Reagan presidency, giving further impetus to the inclusion movement.

Early Intervention

The first federal special education law aimed at young children and their families was enacted in 1968. It established the Handicapped Children's Early Education Program (HCEEP), which successfully provided direct services to young children and their families, assessment devices, curriculum materials, and parent teaching materials. The law requires all states to provide preschool services to all children, ages three to five years, with disabilities. In addition, the law provides incentives to states for establishing programs for infants and toddlers with disabilities and who are from birth to three years. All states now provide services for infants and toddlers (Turnbull and Turnbull 1990).

The major issues in the early education of children with disabilities include the following:

1. The appropriate role of family in early intervention
2. The relative advantages of a child- or teacher-directed curriculum
3. The best ways to facilitate the transition from the early intervention program to the preschool program and from the preschool program to the school program

Federal regulations do not provide explicit instructions regarding the exact ways in which parents should be included in early intervention programming, although they do specify that a specific plan (IFSP) must be written. Slentz and Bricker (1992) are concerned that educators might become overly involved in the assessment of family members. If this happens, "parents may legitimately question why providing such information is necessary when they thought the purpose of the early intervention program was to help their child. Many families perceive this process as an invasion of privacy" (14). They also suggest that professionals conduct brief, informal interviews to determine the needs of the family and child rather than administering a complex battery of tests. The intent of the law is that parents retain the right to make decisions about their children. The role of the professionals is to assist families in reaching their goals.

Most early childhood educators in the United States advocate a developmental approach to educating young children. Drawing on the work of Piaget, these teachers allow children to explore their environment freely and strive to keep teacher direction at a minimum. Early educators of children with disabilities, however, believe that these children need more adult direction in order to acquire the skills they are lacking. As integration of children with disabilities into regular preschool classes has increased, the issue of how much teacher direction should be used has heated up.

Some authorities are concerned that early intervention programs are making young children with disabilities overly dependent on adults and making their transition to preschool or kindergarten more difficult. Most early intervention programs have a very low adult-child ratio, and children are accustomed to having teachers, teacher aides, therapists, and other support personnel readily available. This situation often changes when the child moves on to a more advanced class. It is clear that we must examine ways to make transitions easier for young children with disabilities and for their families.

Transition Programming

Studies suggest that the transition from secondary school to adulthood is more problematic for students with disabilities than for their nondisabled peers. Many do not complete their schooling, do not receive further training or education, become dependent on their families or public assistance programs, experience difficulty finding and keeping a job, or are unable to find work suited to their skills (Edgar 1987; Rusch, Szymanski, and Chadway-Rusch 1992; Sitlington, Frank, and Carson 1992; Wagner and Shaver 1989).

In the early 1980s, a new federal initiative was announced that called for more extensive services for students as they left school and moved into employment. Legislation in the 1990s has expanded upon this initiative and broadened the concept of transition. The federal government defines transition services as a coordinated set of activities for a student, designed within an outcome-oriented process, which promotes movement from school to postsecondary activities, including postsecondary education, vocational training, integrated employment (included supported employment), continuing and adult education, adult services, independent living, or community participation. Since 1990, older students with disabilities are also required to have a transition plan included in their individualized educational program (IEP, which was federally mandated in 1975). This plan must include a statement of the responsibilities of all participating agencies before the student leaves the school setting.

The primary issue in transition programming is how to meet the needs of students with more severe disabilities compared to the needs of those with milder disabilities. Students with severe disabilities are often involved with many agencies outside the school setting. Most educators have little experience in working with these agencies, and few guidelines are provided to assist them. Experimentation is needed so that we may learn more effective relationships between schools and other agencies.

An approach now widely adopted is supported employment, in which a person with a severe disability works in regular work settings. He or she becomes a regular employee, performs a valued function in the same workplace as nondisabled employees, and receives fair remuneration. Training and continued support are necessary, hence the term *supported employment*. Trach (1990) describes the distinguishing features of a supported program: "Notably, these procedures include surveying the community for jobs, identifying and analyzing the prerequisite skills of potential employment sites, assessing the current skill levels of supported employees, matching jobs to prospective employees, providing systematic training in job-related skills, and providing follow-up training and maintenance of learned skills, satisfying employers, and coordinating related services" (79).

For students with milder disabilities, the issue centers around balancing academic and vocational needs. It is often extremely difficult to determine whether a student with learning disabilities should be guided toward a college preparatory or a vocationally oriented curriculum. An overemphasis on academic skills could leave students unprepared for adult work when they leave school. An early emphasis on vocational skills, however, could keep some students, who would be otherwise able to continue their education, from postsecondary educational opportunities (Edgar and Siegal, in press).

Emerging and Future Trends

As special education approaches the turn of the century, it is struggling with what Minow (1987) describes as the dilemma of difference, which we might describe for the present discussion as follows: To the extent that special education maintains its distinctiveness from general education, it separates itself and the students it serves from general education and incurs the stigma of difference; to the extent that special education merges into general education, it loses its ability to marshal resources and deliver special services to ameliorate differences that are disabling and stigmatizing. Goodlad (1990) and Sarason (1990) have noted the critical importance of an educational enterprise maintaining identity, boundaries, focus, and authority. Without these, special education is likely to become what Goodlad (1990) describes as an orphan of the system, dependent on the goodwill of others and subject to the vagaries of administrators and competing interests (Kauffman and Hallahan 1993). Nonetheless, its separateness may also be special education's Achilles heel, its distinctiveness calling its very desirability and necessity into question.

Special education is now beset by divisive controversy regarding inclusion—not merely inclusion of students in regular classes, but inclusion of special education administration, funding, and teacher education in the general education system such that the lines between special and general education are blurred or obliterated. Special education has been divided into warring factions regarding the extent to which inclusion in all its dimensions is appropriate, and the acrimony between these two factions is extremely intense. As Hallahan and Kauffman (1994) explain it (see also Fuchs and Fuchs 1991): "The movement toward more integration has led to some of the bloodiest professional battles ever waged in the field of special education. The disputes between radical integrationists and those of a more conservative persuasion have threatened to rip apart the field of special education."

Clearly, changes are occurring in how, where, and by whom students with disabilities are educated. An open question is whether these changes will bring more appropriate and effective education for these students or will in effect return us to an earlier era in which students' disabilities went unrecognized and unaccommodated in a system of general education that ostensibly served all children.

References

Bank-Mikkelsen, N. E. 1969. A metropolitan area in Denmark: Copenhagen. In R. B. Kugel and W. Wolfensberger, eds. *Changing patterns of residential services for the mentally retarded,* 227–54. Washington, D.C.: President's Committee on Mental Retardation.

Bateman, B. D. 1992. *Better IEPs.* Creswell, Oreg.: Otter Ink.

Baumeister, A. A., Kupstas, F., and Klindworth, L. M. 1990. New morbidity: Implications for prevention of children's disabilities. *Exceptionality* 1:1–16.

Chinn, P. C., and Hughes, S. 1987. Representation of minority students in special education classes. *Remedial and Special Education,* 8 (4): 41–46.

Dunn, L. M. 1968. Special education for the mildly retarded: Is much of it justifiable? *Exceptional Children* 35:5–22.

Edgar, E. 1987. Secondary programs in special education: Are many of them justifiable? *Exceptional Children* 53:555–561

Edgar, E., and Siegel, S. In press. Post-secondary scenarios for troubled and troubling youth. In J. M. Kauffman, J. W. Lloyd, T. A. Astuto, and D. P. Hallahan, eds. *Issues in the educational placement of pupils with emotional or behavioral disorders.*

Fuchs, D., and Fuchs, L. S. 1991. Framing the REI debate: Abolitionists versus conservationists. In J. W. Lloyd, N. N. Singh, and A. C. Repp. eds. *The regular education initiative: Alternative perspectives on concepts, issues, and models,* 241–55. Sycamore, Ill.: Sycamore Publishing Co.

Goodlad, J. I. 1990. *Teachers for our nation's schools.* San Francisco: Jossey-Bass.

Goodlad, J. I., and Lovitt, T. C., eds. 1993. *Integrating general and special education.* Columbus, Ohio: Merrill/Macmillan.

Hallahan, D. P. 1992. Some thoughts on why the prevalence of learning disabilities has increased. *Journal of Learning Disabilities,* 25:523–28.

Hallahan, D. P., and Kauffman, J. M. 1994. *Exceptional children: Introduction to special education.* 6th ed. Boston: Allyn and Bacon.

Hocutt, A. M., Martin, E. W., and McKinney, J. D. 1991. Historical and legal context of mainstreaming. In J. W. Lloyd, N. N. Singh, and A. C. Repp, eds. *The regular education initiative: Alternative perspectives on concepts, issues, and models,* 17–28. Sycamore, Ill.: Sycamore Publishing Co.

Kauffman, J. M. 1981. Introduction: Historical trends and contemporary issues in special education in the United States. In J. M. Kauffman and D. P. Hallahan, eds. *Handbook of special education,* 3–23. Englewood Cliffs, N.J.: Prentice Hall.

———. 1991. Restructuring in sociopolitical context: Reservations about the effects of current reform proposals on students with disabilities. In J. W. Lloyd, N. N. Singh, and A. C. Repp, eds. *The regular education initiative: Alternative perspectives on concepts, issues, and models,* 57–66. Sycamore, Ill.: Sycamore Publishing Co.

———. 1993. *Characteristics of emotional and behavioral disorders of children and youth.* 5th ed. Columbus, Ohio: Merrill/Macmillan.

———. In press. How we might achieve the radical reform of special education. *Exceptional Children.*

Kauffman, J. M., and Hallahan, D. P. 1992. Deinstitutionalization and mainstreaming. In M. C. Alkin, ed. *Encyclopedia of educational research, Vol. 1,* 299–303. New York: Macmillan.

———. 1993. In M. C. Alkin, ed. *Encyclopedia of educational research, Vol. 1,* 299–303. New York: Macmillan.

Laski, F. J. 1991. Achieving integration during the second revolution. In L. H. Meyer, C. A. Peck, and L. Brown, eds. *Critical issues in the lives of people with severe disabilities,* 409–21. Baltimore, Md.: Paul H. Brookes.

Lloyd, J. W., Singh, N. N., and Repp, A. C., eds. 1991. *The regular education initiative: Alternative perspectives on concepts, issues, and models.* Sycamore, Ill.: Sycamore Publishing Co.

Lord, W. 1991. Parent point of view: What is the least restrictive environment for a deaf child? *Michigan Statewide Newsletter,* November, 4.

MacMillan, D. L., and Hendrick, I. G. 1993. Evolution and legacies. In J. I. Goodlad and T. C. Lovitt, eds. *Integrating general and special education,* 23–48. Columbus, Ohio: Merrill/Macmillan.

Minow, M. 1987. Learning to live with the dilemma of difference: Bilingual and special education. In K. T. Bartlett and J. W. Wenger, eds. *Children with special needs,* 375–429. New Brunswick, N.J.: Transaction Books.

Padden, C., and Humphries, T. 1988. *Deaf in America: Voices from a culture.* Cambridge, Mass.: Harvard University Press.

Rusch, F. R., Szymanski, E. M., and Chadsey-Rusch, J. 1992. The emerging field of transition services. In F. R. Rusch, L. DeStefano, J. Chadsey-Rusch, L. A. Phelps, and E. Szymanski, eds. *Transition from school to adult life,* 5–15. Sycamore, Ill.: Sycamore Publishing Co.

Sarason, S. B. 1990. *The predictable failure of educational reform: Can we change course before it's too late?* San Francisco: Jossey-Bass.

Sitlington, P. L., Frank, A. R., and Carson, R. 1992. Adult adjustment among high school graduates with mild disabilities. *Exceptional children* 59:221–33.

Slentz, K. L., and Bricker, D. 1992. Family-guided assessment for IFSP development: Jumping off the family assessment bandwagon. *Journal of Early Intervention,* 16 (1):11–19.

Taylor, S. J. 1988. Caught in the continuum: A critical analysis of the principle of the least restrictive environment. *Journal of the Association for Persons with Severe Handicaps* 13:41–53.

Trach, J. S. 1990. Supported employment program characteristics. In F. R. Rusch, ed. *Supported employment: models, methods, and issues,* 65–81. Sycamore, Ill.: Sycamore Publishing Co.

Turnbull, A. P., and Turnbull, H. R. 1990. *Families, professionals, and exceptionality: A special partnership.* Columbus, Ohio: Merrill/Macmillan.

U.S. Department of Education. 1992. *Fourteenth annual report to Congress on the implementation of the Individuals with Disabilities Education Act.* Washington, D.C.: U.S. Government Printing Office.

Wagner, M., and Shaver, D. 1989. *Educational progress and achievement of secondary special education students: Findings from the National Longitudinal Transition Study.* Menlo Park, Calif.: SRI International.

Wallace, G., Larsen, S. C., and Elksnin, L. K. 1992. *Educational assessment of learning problems: Testing for teaching.* 2d ed. Boston: Allyn and Bacon.

Will, M. C. 1984. Let us pause and reflect—but not too long. *Exceptional Children* 51:11–16.

———. 1986. Educating students with learning problems: A shared responsibility. *Exceptional Children* 52:411–16.

Wolfensberger, W. 1972. *The principle of normalization in human services.* Toronto: National Institute on Mental Retardation.

25

New Zealand

DAVID MITCHELL

PATRICIA O'BRIEN

New Zealand is a one-chamber parliamentary democracy with a monarch as the nominal head of government. Its population of 3.4 million people live in a country about the area of the British Isles or the state of Colorado, or two-thirds the area of Japan. According to the 1991 Census, the major ethnic groups in the country comprise those of European—mainly British

About the Authors • Dr. David Mitchell currently holds the position of associate professor of Education at the University of Waikato, in Hamilton, New Zealand. During his university career, he has held visiting positions at Manchester University, the London Institute of Education, the University of Calgary, the State University of New Mexico, and the Educational Testing Service at Princeton, New Jersey. In 1981–82, he was a Fullbright Senior Research Scholar in Education in the United States. His research has included studies in early intervention, families of persons with disabilities, ethical issues in medical treatment to infants with disabilities, integration, program evaluation, whole school approaches to students with special needs (particularly at the secondary school level), policy issues in special education, and educational reforms. He is on the editorial boards or is an editorial consultant to six professional journals, mainly in the field of special education. Since 1989, he has been deputy chairperson of the New Zealand Special Education Service Board, which has major responsibility for providing special educational guidance and advice to learning institutions throughout New Zealand. Dr. Mitchell was recently appointed as a consultant to UNESCO and assisted with running regional seminars on Policy Planning and Organization for Children and Young People with Special Needs, in China. He is currently engaged in collaborative projects in Japan, Scotland, and Canada. • Dr. Patricia O'Brien is a senior lecturer in the School of Special Education at Auckland College of Education where she is involved in developing courses for personnel who work within human services and special education settings. Her research interests are in the area of advocacy, deinstitutionalization, and staff development in the area of nonaversive intervention techniques.

Isles—origin (74 percent), the indigenous people of New Zealand—the Maori (10 percent), people from the Pacific Islands (4 percent), and those of Chinese or Indian descent (1 percent each). The remaining 9 percent have other ethnic origins or are recorded as having two or more ethnic identities.

In recent years, New Zealand has more explicitly recognized that the Treaty of Waitangi, which was signed by the British Crown and the Maori tribes in 1840, should be honored (Orange 1987). As a consequence, biculturalism is increasingly being pursued in all facets of society—not least of which in education.

Education is compulsory for all children ages 6 to 16 years, although in practice almost all 5-year-olds are enrolled. During the compulsory education period, there are three main tiers of schools: primary schools (5-to-11-year-olds), intermediate schools (12-to-13 year-olds) and secondary schools (14-to-19 year-olds). Some, usually in rural areas, retain intermediate-age children as an integral part of a full primary school and some, called "area schools," provide schooling for all three levels in the one school. There are high participation rates in preschool education, with 92 percent of 4-year-olds and 71 percent of 3-year-olds enrolled in some form of early childhood education program.

Prevalence of Exceptional Conditions

Definitions of Disability

Common terminology that has been used in New Zealand in the recent past when referring to exceptional children has included the following: intellectual handicap, behavior maladjustment, communication disability, learning disability, gifted and talented, hearing impaired, and physical handicap (Mitchell and Singh 1987). A recent government statement (Shipley and Upton 1992) on the funding and delivery of health and disability services for the country described the consumer groups as people with intellectual disabilities, sensory disabilities, physical disabilities, psychiatric disabilities, and older people. In recent years, however, there has been a movement away from the use of conventional defining terms to an emphasis on a noncategorical, needs-based approach that sees children as children first before their exceptionality (Murray and Thorburn 1991).

Estimates of the Population of People with Disability

In 1986, Business and Economic Research Limited (BERL) conducted a project, at the request of the government's Accident Compensation Corporation, to estimate the number of persons in New Zealand who had a disability (Business and Economic Research Limited 1986). As there was, and still is, no official data base on persons with disability, estimates were based upon available survey material and tabulations from different government departments. The findings of the project included an estimated 416,000 persons of all ages (that is, 12.5 percent of the population) being identified as having a physical disability for one month or longer.

In an earlier survey (Jack, Hyslop, and Dowland 1980) of a random sample of households in the Wellington area, it was found that 1 in every 12 persons (8.7 percent) aged five years and over had a physical or sensory disability that interfered with their daily living. The rate of disability increased with age. Among children the rate was 25.8 per 1,000, increasing to 63.6 among adults under 65 and 425.1 per 1,000 for persons 65 and over. The causes of disability also varied with age. In the 5-to-14 age group the major causes were congenital, whereas in the 65-and-over age group disease was the predominant factor.

The second largest group identified in the BERL study was the fifty-eight thousand who had a mental illness. A third group comprised the twelve thousand people who were classified as having an intellectual disability.

Those with multiple handicaps have been defined as "all those people with more than one disability, including intellectual, physical, psychosocial, psychiatric, visual, aural, etc" (Robertson 1986, 1). Jack, Hyslop, and Dowland (1980) found that 52.6 percent of a sample of 2,024 people with disability had a two or more disabling conditions. This proportion varied according to the severity of the disability, with 65.3 percent of those with serious disabilities having multiple disabilities, compared with 39.9 percent of those with less serious disabilities. The frequency of multiple handicaps was also shown to increase with age

In terms of the prevalence of disability within infancy, de Boer, Saxby, and Soljak (1989) reported that just over 2 percent of infants had birth defects diagnosed within the first week of birth. In a national survey of kindergartens, Panckhurst (1977) found that 11 percent of the population had special needs, according to teacher ratings.

Visual Impairment

In 1992, the Royal New Zealand Foundation for the Blind had an overall membership of more than 10,000, of whom 792 (7 percent) were between birth and age eighteen (Pole 1992). Of those aged under fourteen, 73 percent had visual impairment as a result of prenatal influences, 5 percent from injuries or poisoning, 3 percent from neoplasms, and 3 percent from infections and diseases. In a multidisciplinary health and development research unit study, Simpson, Kirkland, and Silva (1984) detected vision and eye problems in 9.4 percent of children aged seven.

Hearing Impairment

In a recent study, Power (1990) reported that there were approximately two children in every thousand born with a hearing impairment that requires special educational assistance. Of these children, 68 percent were in regular schools with support from visiting teachers for the deaf, 17 percent were in day special schools for students with major hearing losses, and 15 percent were in units in regular schools. Bush and Buckfield (1987) noted that 1,600 children under the age of 15 had severe hearing impairment (a greater than 45-decibel hearing loss), of whom only sixty were born deaf, suggesting that preventative measures are needed in New Zealand to overcome the rate of acquired deafness from middle ear disease. Robertson (1982) reported that otitis media with effusion happens with great frequency between the ages of 6 months and 2 years, followed by a second critical period between 4 and 6 years. Otitis media was found to affect all ethnic groups.

West and Harris (1983) followed a group of primary school children with audiometry and tympanometry tests for thirty-eight weeks and found that on each testing, 62 percent showed some hearing problem. Thirty-nine percent of this group were found to experience more that one episode of hearing difficulty.

Intellectual/Multiple Disability

In 1986, BERL reported that between birth and age fourteen, 2.9 persons per 1,000 were considered to be intellectually disabled. Prior to the current movement to close "psychopedic" hospitals, Robertson (1986) noted that a high proportion of the residents were multihandicapped. This confirmed an earlier study of one of the psychopedic hospitals in which Doyle and Jensen (1984) found that 63.4 percent of the residents had three or more disabilities in addition to their intellectual disability, including significant physical disability, epilepsy, sensory impairment, communication disorder, behavior disorder, psychosis, or congenital anomalies/disorders.

Physical Disability

In 1986, BERL reported that between birth and age fourteen, 23.3 persons per 1,000 were noted as being physically disabled. VandenBurg and Laugesen (1981) found that the 1974–75 incidence rate of cerebral palsy of 1.86 per 1,000 was no different than the rate ten years earlier. Their study stressed that a central system of notification of disabilities was needed if preventative measures and services were to be planned adequately. This has still not happened.

Learning Disability

Van Kraayenoord and Elkins (1990) reported that the prevalence of learning disabilities in New Zealand pointed to there being 10 percent of students in regular classrooms who were not achieving in one of more academic subjects. In 1979, Walsh conducted a New Zealand survey on a sample of eleven-year-old children and found that 7.1 percent of the students had learning difficulties in reading vocabulary, 5.3 percent in comprehension, and 6.8 percent in mathematics. Similarly, Chapman, St. George, and van Kraayenoord (1983) found that about 8 percent of 1,220 Palmerston North form-1 children were underachieving in reading comprehension, reading vocabulary, listening comprehension, or mathematics.

Identification of Exceptionalities

Infant and Child Health Checks

Within New Zealand, screening checks are routinely carried out by the medical profession at birth, 6 weeks, 6 months, 9 months, 3 years, and 5 years. Hyslop, Dowland, and Hickling (1983) emphasized the importance of checks at different stages of development, as some disabilities are more evident with increasing age than others.

In 1982, the Department of Health introduced a program in which all new entrants to school have their hearing, vision, and health assessed (de Boer, Saxby, and Soljak 1989). These examinations also enable the child's immunization status to be checked (Hyslop, Dowland, and Hickling 1983). Upon entering school all children have a vision test. A visual acuity of 6/12 in the worst eye at four meters is seen as a problem.

As well as taking a visual acuity test on entering school, all children have a hearing test using puretone audiometry. As noted by de Boer, Saxby, and Soljak (1989), a potential problem is defined when a child is unable to hear 30dB tone at 500 Hz or a 20 dB tone at 1,000, 2,000 or 4,000 Hz. As many as 30 percent of children fail their first hearing test, with a higher proportion of Maori children being noted as having hearing loss.

A third new entrant health assessment takes place when a public health nurse takes a history from parents, reviews the vision and hearing results, checks the immunization history, and does a growth and development, as well as a physical, assessment. When any of these tests indicate that the child needs further assessment appropriate referrals are made.

Developmental Assessment

For developmental and neurological difficulties diagnosed at birth or shortly thereafter, child development centers provide services. These centers are located throughout New Zealand. For example, in Auckland where one-third of New Zealand's population lives, there are four such centers. The work of these centers is mainly to provide community-based teams that offer early intervention services for children with developmental difficulties related to congenital or acquired neurological disabilities. The staff include visiting neurodevelopment therapists who assess the child at home and develop a therapy program with the parents; speech-language therapists who provide assessments and home programs for children with swallowing and/or early communication difficulties; social workers who work with families under stress or facing difficulties in managing/coping with a child who has special needs; physiotherapists who provide assessment, education, and/or therapy to assist children to improve their movement and physical functioning; occupational therapists who provide assessment, education and/or therapy for children's hand function, play, and self-care skills; and pediatricians who provide specialist advice and treatment about health and share this information with the family and their doctor (Waitakere Child Development Centre 1993).

Referrals are accepted from parents, medical and education personnel, and community workers. Assessments are designed to meet the needs of each child and include such options as screening via such instruments as the Carolina Curricula for Handicapped Infants, the Sewell Early Education Developmental Scale, and the Denver Developmental Screening Test. As well, there are specific specialist assessments and team assessment, either within the child development center team or combined with other agencies and services (Central District Child Development Centre 1993).

Intervention reflects the needs of both the child and the family and includes one or a combination of the following: home visiting, direct service or consultation with and in an educational setting, and one-to-one or group programs at the center.

In Auckland there is a further specialized center, the Child Development Unit (CDU) for babies who have received care in the Neonatal Intensive Care Unit or Special Care Baby Unit of the National Women's Hospital. These babies fall into three groups. The first is babies who weighed less than 1,000 grams at birth. These babies are seen ordinarily at eighteen months, or earlier upon request, and thereafter as required. Second is babies of 1,000–1,500 grams. These babies are seen ordinarily at eighteen months, and thereafter as considered necessary. Then there are other infants referred by the pediatrician in charge; for example, children with severe birth asphyxia, convulsion, or congenital abnormalities.

The CDU is currently the only one of its type in the country and was established in 1986. It is staffed by one full-time and one part-time development psychologist and a part-time pediatrician. The CDU plays an important role in view of the increasing number of preterm infants who are surviving. The work of the CDU is also preventative in that the monitoring of preterm babies will lead to better quality care of other preterm babies as well as to increased information about their development (Dezoete et al. 1991).

Psychoeducational Assessment

Psychoeducational assessment occurs both at the preschool and school levels. The Special Education Service (SES) was established by the Government in 1989 and, under an agreement with the Ministry of Education, provides service delivery, training courses, and advice to the Ministry of Education. As part of its service delivery, the SES emphasizes the educational team model, or a transdisciplinary approach, for working with students with special educational needs. Assessment is undertaken as a part of the larger process of planning an appropriate individual education program (IEP) or intervention. The type of assessment is developed around the needs of the child within the context of his or her family, school, and neighborhood environments. Assessment is needs based and ecological in nature.

Outlined are the steps that form part of a collaborative relationship between SES staff, the student with special needs and his or her family, and other relevant professionals when assessing and developing programs together. (Special Education Service 1993, 10–11. The size and make-up of the team will depend upon the student's needs. This type of teaming approach operates both within school and early childhood settings.

> *Step 1: Assessments are undertaken.* The learner is observed within the context of the educational program. The initial assessments may include background information and review of previous records (one member is delegated to undertake this); naturalistic observations (team members indicate the activities they prefer to observe; for example a speech-language therapist may observe meal-time activities); and parent or family observations (again, one member of the team is delegated to undertake this).
>
> *Step 2: The team meets to discuss initial assessments.* The above assessments provide a wealth of data and possible explanations about the learner's behavior. Diagnostic assessments to support these explanations may then be undertaken by respective members from the perspective of their disciplines.
>
> *Step 3: Diagnostic assessments are undertaken.* These are undertaken to confirm/deny the explanations generated at steps 1 and 2. For

example, the speech-language therapist may check the learner's ability to follow simple one-step directions, while the teacher may assess reinforcement and prompting strategies.

Step 4: A planning meeting is held. Priorities are set for functional target skills, the IEP is written, and implementers and trainers are identified.

Step 5: The program implementer is trained. The purpose and methods are explained, a demonstration occurs, and the implementer is observed working with the learner.

Step 6: Programs are implemented.

Step 7: Data are collected, summarized, and made accessible to all members.

Step 8: The team coordinator monitors data and communicates with all members.

Step 9: The program is reviewed. This usually takes place at least twice a year.

Assessment of Hearing Problems

When a child is suspected of having a hearing impairment, the family has a choice of seeing a medical practitioner or an Area Health Board professional. From here, the child may be referred to either an ear, nose, and throat specialist or to a hospital clinic. Following this, the child may be placed on the caseload of an adviser of children with hearing impairment who will work collaboratively with both the child's family and his or her teacher. The advisers are employed by the SES and would be involved in school-based assessments.

There are two main methods of testing hearing in New Zealand. One method is the objective or instrumental method which includes auditory brainstem response (ABR) and impedance—movement in the middle ear. The subjective or behavioral includes distraction; for example, with one- or two-year-olds, an attempt would be made to see the child orient toward a sound while playing. Also included is performance testing (Senescall et al. 1990).

Assessment of Visual Problems

At Homai College, The Royal New Zealand Society for the Blind runs the National Center for the Education of Students with Visual Impairment. A National Assessment Unit operating out of the college consists of a multidisciplinary team made up of a coordinator, an ophthalmologist, an optometrist, a pediatrician, a psychologist, a physiotherapist, a speech therapist, a mobility instructor, a Techniques for Daily Living instructor, and various specialist teachers. The assessment team undertakes a comprehensive assessment and an IEP is drawn up (Pole 1992). Homai College also provides an advisory and itinerant teaching service to schools and to a number of visual resource centers throughout the country.

Labeling the Handicapped Population

The term *handicapped* is rarely used in New Zealand. Preferred terms are *disability* or *special educational needs*. Although categorical labels are still used within New Zealand when referring to people with disabilities—as exemplified by the names of the voluntary agencies, the types of special schools that exist for categories of handicaps, and the way in which national statistics are kept—there is a growing opposition to their usage. A recent example of this resistance was in response to a recommendation by the Ministry of Education to categorize the funding base of special education by labeling two groups of students, those with disabilities and those with educational and social difficulties (Ministry of Education 1991a). An example of a professional movement away from the use of labels can also be found in the advertising of the SES, which refers to its client groups as learners, infants with developmental delays, and children and young people with special educational and developmental needs.

The Social Context of Special Education

Changing Views of Exceptionality

From 1858, when the first official provisions were made for exceptional children in New Zealand, to the present, discernible changes have taken place in the way in which governments have perceived their responsibilities to such children. Initially, charities played important roles in establishing services, with governments limiting themselves to "grace and favor" provisions for certain categories of exceptionality as they entered into public consciousness. Increasingly, though, governments took more responsibility for the whole range of children with special educational needs, this being reflected in moves from "permissive" legislation to more "mandatory" legislation in recent years.

According to Mitchell (1987), there have been marked shifts in the philosophies and practices of providing for children with special needs in New Zealand, since the earliest provisions were made. These include the following:

1. From charity and voluntarism to the state's assumption of responsibility, initially in the form of "grace and favor" conditional benevolence, but more recently taking cognizance of the rights of children with handicaps
2. From segregation to integration and from institutionalization to community care
3. From an assertion of parents' responsibilities to a recognition of parents' needs and, more recently, parents' rights
4. From the amateurism of on-the-job training to the professionalism of full-time training of staff
5. From uncoordinated policies and services to the beginnings of coordination
6. From a negative to a positive view of persons with disabilities
7. From a medical to a developmental model of services for persons with handicaps
8. From a school focus to a concern for life-long education commencing at birth and, as viewed more recently, proceeding through the adult years
9. From a focus on the person with a disability to the person with a disability in a family context
10. From a concern for obvious disabilities to a differentiation of more subtle special educational needs
11. From a subject-centered, abstract curriculum to a child-centered, life-skills curriculum
12. From a centralized to a decentralized model of administration

Factors Influencing Policies and Practices in Special Education

The changes in special education reflect an interlocking mix of factors. First of all, there is no doubt that economic and political factors have played a critical role, and continue to do so, in influencing special education, both directly and indirectly. Three examples described by Mitchell (1987, 1992) will suffice.

The first example can be found in the 1850s and 1860s when neglected, criminal, and destitute children were the first exceptional children in New Zealand to come to the attention of authorities. As noted by Mitchell (1987), this development reflected four factors that were later to typify the establishment of many other special education provisions. First, it reflected the social circumstances of the time and the place—in this case the impact on families of the departure of their male breadwinners to New Zealand's goldfields in the early 1860s. Second, there was the recent—and respectable—precedent provided by the British 1861 Act for Amending and Consolidating the Law Relating to Industrial Schools. Third, the concern for neglected children represented selective welfare. The motivations of the powerful groups in New Zealand society at that time may be seen both as a blend of benevolent humanitarianism that arose from an endeavor to escape the poor law and work house ethos of the old country (Great Britain) from which they had so recently departed, and as the imposition of hegemony over those who had the potential to disrupt the prevailing social order. Fourth, the assumption of responsibility by the state over neglected children represented a departure from the then social policy that the needy should be cared for by charity. Because New Zealand was a new country settled largely by working and middle class families and "with not enough rich people to make philanthropy more than marginally significant" (Oliver 1977, 6–7), this departure is understandable, even if it did not set an invariable pattern for future provisions.

The second example is drawn from the early years of the twentieth century when there was an upsurge of concern for child welfare. This has been ascribed to such factors as the decline in the birthrate and the efforts to strengthen the physical and moral qualities of a society that was increasingly, if erroneously, suspected as being heavily populated with England's castoffs and under threat of Asian invasion. Also occurring around this time was the increasing industrialization of New Zealand. As in all other societies that moved from a preindustrial to an industrial form, increasing demands were made on the education system to produce a more skilled and socialized workforce. Value thus came to be increasingly placed upon performance standards in schools. Children with disabilities became more noticeable, both in terms of their own capacities to meet standards and in their presumed effects on the efficiency of education obtained by other children, particularly in large classes. Thus, there was pressure to create special education for those who were not so obviously handicapped as the blind and the deaf and the "mentally defective" for whom provisions had already been made.

The third example of the influence exercised by economic factors on special education is more recent. Since the late 1980s, New Zealand, like many other Western countries, has been experiencing an economic recession, with ballooning internal deficits and high rates of unemployment (currently around 11 percent of the workforce). In an attempt to address these problems, successive governments in New Zealand since 1987 have shifted the country quite dramatically away from its former identity as an egalitarian, welfare state, to one much more dominated by free market forces under philosophies variously known as "economic rationalism" and the "New Right." These philosophies, along with what Boston (1991, 2) has described as "an analytic framework grounded in public choice theory, managerialism and the new economics of organizations," have contributed significantly to a radical restructuring of the public sector in New Zealand. As noted by Boston, some of the features of this framework include the following:

1. Advisory, regulatory, and delivery functions are separated and undertaken by different agencies to prevent bureaucratic capture.
2. Public monopolies are reduced to a minimum and, wherever feasible, the services provided by government agencies are privatized or contracted out to private sector suppliers.
3. Services are provided through a series of "contracts" (or agreed relationships) in which an agent undertakes to perform various tasks on behalf of a principal.
4. Management skills, rather than policy or professional/technical skills, are emphasized.
5. There is a shift from the use of input controls and bureaucratic procedures to a reliance on quantifiable output measures and performance targets.
6. Management control is increasingly devolved.
7. Certain private sector management practices, such as the development of corporate plans, performance agreements and mission statements, the introduction of performance-linked remuneration systems, the development of new management information systems, and the greater concern for corporate image, are being introduced.

The ways in which these economic factors have impacted on special education in New Zealand will be outlined in more detail later in this chapter.

Social factors are also important. In 1993, New Zealand celebrated the centenary of women's suffrage. We were one of the first nations to permit all women to vote. This legislation is reflective of the country's long commitment to what has been referred to variously as egalitarianism, equality, and equity that has permeated many facets of its life since the first Labor government was elected in 1935.

Until recently, New Zealand could be described as a "welfare state," with wide-ranging commitments to the poor and the disadvantaged reflected in its social welfare, health, and educational systems. Although the doctrine of economic rationalism noted above has made inroads into this ethos, it is nevertheless true that the principles of equity still form a strong thread in New Zealand society. They are reflected, for example, in equal employment opportunity (EEO) policies that became mandatory in the State Sector Act of 1988. Under this act, government departments had to ensure EEO policies for the five target groups: Maori, women, Pacific Island people, people from ethnic minority groups, and people with disabilities. Nevertheless, the Employment Equity Act of 1990, which took the EEO provisions into the private sector, was repealed by a National government that took office in 1990.

Several social forces have contributed to New Zealand's adherence to the principles of equity. Among these are the influences by a strong women's movement, a Maori "renaissance" and, in the case of disability, the marked contributions made by parents who have individually and collectively acted as their own and their children's advocates. For example, the inclusion movement in New Zealand has the parent movement as its backbone (Brown 1990). Several parent groups, such as the Down's Syndrome Association, Parent to Parent, and the Autistic Association, have both individually and in coalition lobbied government for change. A driving force as a voluntary agency has been the New Zealand Society for the Intellectually Handicapped (IHC), which has two people employed as education advocates, supporting families to gain access to mainstream educational placement. The society has also developed a national system of mainstream support teams which are parent driven (Gates 1990).

Finally, there are overseas factors. As Mitchell (1987) has noted, New Zealand has frequently drawn its inspiration for special education policies and practices from overseas. Among the myriad of overseas reports and legislation relating to children with special educational needs, several stand out as having had a profound influence on New Zealand thinking. From the United Kingdom, these include the Report of the Royal Commission on the Care and Control of the Feeble Minded (the Radnor Report) of 1908, which led to New Zealand's Mental Defectives Act of 1911, and the Report of the Committee on Maladjusted Children (the Underwood Report) in 1955. More recently, the Warnock Committee's Report (Department of Education and Science 1978) and the subsequent 1981 Education Act have been widely commented on in New Zealand.

Perhaps the outstanding contributions from the United States to the education of children with special educational needs have been made by the civil rights legislation and related judicial decisions of the 1960s and 1970s, and the 1975 Education for All Handicapped Children Act (PL 94-142) and its extensions to cover early childhood through PL 99-457. Many of the principles of these acts—placement in least restrictive environments, individual educational plans, parent involvement in decision-making, and zero reject—have become incorporated into the policies and practices of many voluntary organizations and professional groups, even if they have not all been embodied in the statutes.

Legislation

In New Zealand, the Education Act of 1989 entitles all students between the ages of five and nineteen years to a free enrollment and education in any state school. Special education provisions for school-age children are also administered under this act. It provides qualified support for the principle of inclusion (or mainstreaming). Section 8 of the act states, "Except as provided in this Part of this Act, people who have special education needs (whether because of disability or otherwise) have the same rights to enrol and receive education at state schools as people who do not." The exceptions envisaged are when the Secretary of Education agrees with the student's parents that the student should be enrolled at a particular state school, special school, special class, special clinic, or special service. The secretary also retains the right to direct the person's parents to so enroll the person, with rights of reconsideration of such a direction through a system of arbitration.

A factor that might impinge on the decision to enroll the student in a particular school is a school's "enrollment scheme," derived from recent legislation (Education Amendment Act 1991). This act gives schools the discretion to accept pupils of a particular kind or description when "there is likely to be overcrowding at the school." The apparent conflict between the provisions of the Education Amendment Act of 1991 and the Education Act of 1989, with respect to the rights of learners with special needs to enroll at their local school, has yet to be tested. There is evidence, however, that some schools are using the provisions of the Education Amendment Act in such a way that could lead to the exclusion of some children with special educational needs.

Of significance here is the fact that at present the New Zealand Bill of Rights Act does not include disability as an object of nondiscrimination. However, recent proposed amendments to this act do incorporate disability as a prohibited ground of discrimination. For the purposes of that act, disability will mean the following: "physical disability or impairment, physical illness, psychiatric illness, intellectual or psychological disability or impairment, and any other loss or abnormality of psychological, physiological or anatomical structure or function." Facilities or services may, however, be refused if the person who supplies them cannot reasonably be expected to provide them in a special manner, or if to supply them would be "on terms more onerous than those on which they are made available to other persons." A similar caveat is proposed in terms of access to educational establishments, where it will be lawful to refuse admission to a person (a) "whose disability is such that that person requires special services or facilities that in the circumstances cannot reasonably be made available" or (b) where the person's disability "is such that there would be a risk of harm to that person or to others." It is clear that if this bill becomes law, it will contravene the spirit of Education Act 1989 which gives children with disabilities the right to enroll at the state school of their choice.

Policies

Any analysis of New Zealand's special education system must be embedded in the broader framework of the national education system—a system that has undergone dramatic change since October 1989. These reforms are similar to those that have occurred or are in process in many other countries, but the New Zealand reforms have gone further and faster than in most. Some of the key elements include the separation of policy, regulatory, and delivery functions in education; a shift from the use of input controls to a reliance on quantifiable output measures and performance targets; the reduction of public monopolies; and a shift of responsibility for the governance and management of learning institutions from the center to elected boards of trustees responsible for individual institutions.

For the most part, these reforms were expressed in the Education Act of 1989 and had earlier been outlined in the Picot Report (Taskforce to Review Education Administration 1988) and in a government document, *Tomorrow's Schools* (Lange 1988). They were based on five fundamental principles of equity, quality, efficiency, effectiveness, and economy. When applied to the education system these principles resulted in the following:

1. The institution (for example, a school) is the basic building block of educational administration, with control to use its educational resources as it determines, within overall guidelines set by the minister of education. No intermediate bodies exist between the Ministry of Education and the individual learning institution; indeed, the reforms abolished the twelve education boards that used to serve at that level.
2. The institution is run as a partnership between the professionals and the particular community in which it is located. Boards of trustees, with governance responsibilities, are the mechanism for this partnership. In primary and intermediate schools these boards comprise elected parent representatives, one elected staff representative, and the principal. As well, secondary schools and schools with a secondary component are required to have a student representative. Schools may co-opt up to four persons, having regard to the type of skills needed to function effectively, the ethnic and socioeconomic composition of the school's student body, and the country's gender balance.
3. The institution sets its own objectives, within the overall national guidelines set by the Minister of Education. These objectives should reflect the particular needs of the community in which the school is located and should be clearly set out in the institution's charter which acts as a contract between the institution and its community, and between the institution and the minister.
4. The Ministry of Education provides policy advice to the minister, administers property, and handles financial flows and operational activities.
5. Each institution is accountable for the government funds it spends on education and for meeting the objectives set out in its charter. To ensure that this accountability obligation is met, learning institutions are reviewed every three years by the Education Review Office.

As far as special education is concerned, the *Tomorrow's Schools* reforms disbursed responsibility among the aforementioned agencies, all under the general oversight of the minister of education. Boards of trustees are required, inter alia, to include the following goal in their charters: "To enhance learning by ensuring that the school's policies and practices seek to achieve equitable outcomes for students of both sexes; for rural and urban students; for students from all religions, ethnic, cultural, social, family and class backgrounds and for all students, irrespective of their ability or disability" (Department of Education 1989, 10).

The Ministry of Education is responsible for ensuring that this objective is appropriately addressed in schools' charters and the Education Review Office for seeing that schools meet the objective. The Special Education Service (SES)—a government-funded and independent agency—provides a free, noncontestable service to learning institutions and caregivers of students with difficulties in learning or development. (As will be noted later, however, the SES's role is currently under review.)

Teachers, Schools, Curriculum, and Pedagogy

Education of Special Education Teachers

In New Zealand, preservice teacher education for the early childhood, primary, and secondary sectors is largely undertaken by the five colleges of education and the one school of education based in a university. These three-year programs (three or four years in the case of the School of Education at the University of Waikato) include compulsory and optional courses that take account of children with special educational needs.

Four colleges of education offer specialist, one-year, postgraduate training programs for experienced teachers in regular education who wish to work in special education. The School of Special Education at Auckland College of Education offers diplomas in early intervention, education of students with special teaching needs, education of students with visual impairment, and advisers on children who are deaf and hearing impaired. The diploma in education for students with special teaching needs is also offered at three other colleges of education—Wellington, Palmerston North, and Christchurch—the latter also offering diplomas associated with hearing impairment.

Certificates and diplomas in teaching people with disabilities are available at polytechnics and colleges of education throughout New Zealand and are of particular relevance to human service workers and teacher aides and assistants. The ethos of partnership pervades these courses as both content and presentation honor bicultural themes (Espiner, Hartnett, and O'Brien

1992). A number of training providers have Maori and *Pakeha* (European) staff to teach these courses in partnership. Several *hui* (meetings) involving Maori tutors have recently led to the development of Maori competencies for each of the fourteen modules of both courses.

Two universities—Otago and Auckland—train educational psychologists in postgraduate programs. As from 1994, three universities—Massey, Waikato, and Auckland—will be offering two-year, master's-level programs in special education. These are generic in character, although some specialization is possible within the selection of optional courses. All of these programs require candidates to have had prior professional experience—usually as a teacher.

Responsibility for in-service teacher education is jointly shared by the Ministry of Education and the boards of trustees of individual schools. The Ministry of Education contracts with different providers to set up in-service courses for teachers, and schools make the decisions of who will participate. Recent examples of successful courses in the field of special education have been *Towards Inclusion,* a course organized by the SES in 1990 to assist teachers to include children with special educational needs in their classrooms, and parallel courses run by Auckland and Wellington Colleges of Education to give teachers an opportunity to explore their values relating to inclusion, as well as training in strategies to develop interdependence for all children (O'Brien et al. 1990).

It is interesting to note that approximately 12 to 14 percent of teachers in all levels of education, from early childhood through to higher education, consider themselves to live with the effects of injury, long-standing illness, or disability. Two-thirds of these teachers said their disability occurred after their employment in education services. They were often in senior positions and tended to be slightly older than other teachers (Slyfield 1992).

Special Education Settings

A range of provisions for students with special needs exist within primary, intermediate, secondary, and area schools, as can be seen from the following summary of Ministry of Education (1992) statistics for 1 July 1991.

Residential special schools. In July 1991, there were eight residential special schools funded by the Ministry of Education: two for students with hearing impairments; three for students of primary school age who were behaviorally disturbing; two for students with difficulties in learning; and one for students with visual disabilities. The total number of students in these schools was 490.

Students with intellectual disabilities. In July 1991, there were 29 day special schools providing for a total of 630 students with intellectual disabilities. However, the bulk of such students (1,192) were located in a total of 214 classes or units on regular school sites, while a further 400 were being educated in regular classes.

Students with physical disabilities. A total of 134 students with physical disabilities were enrolled as day pupils in two special schools, 297 were in 42 units attached to regular schools, and another 251 were mainstreamed into regular classes.

Students with visual disabilities. Besides the 60 students in a residential special school, approximately 550 students with visual disabilities were attending regular schools supported by itinerant teachers attached to visual or sensory resource centers A further 43 students attended units in regular schools, and 340 were served by itinerant staff from the single residential school.

Students with hearing disabilities. In July 1991, 199 students with hearing disabilities were enrolled as boarders in the two residential special schools or as day pupils in schools in the cities where the two residential schools were located. A further 87 were being educated in units attached to regular schools and another 308 in regular classes supported by 32 itinerant teachers.

Students with educational and social difficulties. The majority of the 3,941 students with educational and social difficulties less manifest than those outlined above were being served by 328 "resource teachers, special needs." These students, who among them had a widely varied combination of educational and social difficulties and physical or sensory impairments, were in special classes or in regular classrooms with varying proportions of their time spent in either setting.

Other provisions. Special education services were also provided in institutions run by area health boards. Included here were seven health camp schools, two hospital schools, and twenty-six hospital classes. On 1 July 1991, 557 students were identified as receiving a service while resident in one of these facilities. Schools were also run in a small number of Department of Social Welfare institutions, although these are closing in line with that department's policy of maintaining children in their home communities. As well, the Correspondence School, based in Wellington, but with teachers also located in various parts of the country, provided distance education assistance for students with special needs who were unable to attend school for whatever reason. In 1991, the Correspondence School provided early intervention programs for over 300 families with preschool children with special educational needs, full-time individual programs for 250 school-age children, and individual assistance for over 1,000 children. In the latter group, the children had a dual enrollment with the Correspondence School and their local school.

The number of special schools in New Zealand has progressively declined over the past decade or so, there being a total of sixty-two in 1991, compared with eighty-eight in 1981.

Special educators who work in regular schools generally occupy positions over and above the staff entitlement of those schools, and they are generally employed by those schools' boards of trustees. Schools and classes for students with special educational needs are staffed on ratios ranging from 1 to 2–3 for severely disabled students and for children entering school with learning difficulties, to 1 to 15 for students with mild disabilities in secondary school "experience classes." For most special education provisions, the staff student ratio is around 1 to 8–10.

Management committees, comprising the school principal, the special education teacher, a representative of the SES, and two parent representatives responsible to the school's board of trustees, administer resources and deal with admissions to special classes and units. Special day schools, residential schools, and the Correspondence School have their own boards of trustees. As well, the SES has a brief for assisting in the setting up of special needs committees to oversee special education provisions in schools where there are no attached units; 520 such committees were in operation in July 1991.

Enrollment in any special education facility requires an agreement between the student's parents and the secretary of education. Recommendations for admission are normally the responsibility of the SES. In a recent study by the Education Review Office (1992), the overwhelming majority of a sample of 250 parents of children with special educational needs expressed satisfaction with the educational placement of their children, whether the placement was in regular classes, special classes, or special schools. These parents also felt that they had not been pressured by professionals to place their children into any particular type of facility.

In reaching educational decisions regarding children with special educational needs, there has been a marked shift away from psychometric tests of intelligence and personality towards curriculum-based assessment and observations in classrooms and the student's natural environments.

In addition to the range of special education provisions mentioned so far, the Ministry of Education, on the advice of the SES, allocates discretionary resources on a short-term basis. These resources mostly take the form of teacher aide hours, part-time teacher hours, special transport provisions, boarding assistance, and equipment. Teacher aide hours are allocated to provide assistance to regular teachers to maintain children with special educational needs in a school, and they are usually related to carrying out the objectives of individual educational plans.

The Special Education Service

One of the major elements in the Government's restructuring of special education was the establishment on 1 October 1989 of the Special Education

Service (SES) as an independent Crown Agency. As specified in the Education Act (1989) the prime function of this agency is to "provide advice, guidance, and support for the benefit of people under 21 with difficulties in learning or development." (An amendment to the Education Act will remove the age restriction in the near future.) As noted earlier, it also plays a major role in determining eligibility for access to special education resources, including placement in the facilities outlined previously. The SES brought together in a coordinated manner hitherto disparate groups of professionals—school psychologists, speech and language therapists, advisers on deaf children, and visiting teachers (the latter being responsible for liaison between schools and homes in cases of children with learning difficulties or behavioral problems). It also took on a new range of functions related to providing a comprehensive early intervention service for infants and preschool children with special needs and for their families.

In broad terms, the SES is charged with responsibility for assisting learning institutions to meet the requirements of their charters with respect to equity of outcomes for all children and young people and their families. It achieves this goal through a balance of direct intervention, consultation and advice, training and staff development, as specified in annual "documents of accountability," or contracts of service, with the Ministry of Education on behalf of the minister of education. The purposes of these agreements are to establish the basic legislative and policy framework parameters within which the SES operates; specify purchase and ownership provisions; specify the amounts to be paid for the services (NZ$38.8 million in the 1992–93 year); and provide for the evaluation of the quality of the services.

In the school year ending 30 June 1991, services ranging from direct intervention to consultation and advice were provided for 43,600 students with difficulties in learning or development and/or their learning institutions/caregivers (Special Education Service 1991). Of these, nearly one-third (14,104) had current, up-to-date individual education plans developed in a process involving consultation among the child's parents, the SES, professionals within the school and other relevant people. In addition, training courses for teachers and others were provided. A mechanism for ensuring that the SES is responsive and accountable to its local communities is the presence of district/community service committees, comprising a majority of consumers of the SES services, in each of the eighteen SES districts. These committees were set up on the initiative of the SES to act as a communication channel between it and the community and to provide it with advice, guidance, and support. For a more detailed description of the SES, see Mitchell (1993).

Teaching and Instruction for Children with Various Handicapping Conditions

Although New Zealand has long had national curriculum guidelines, it has recently moved toward specifying these in more detail. Since 1991 the current government's Achievement Initiative (Ministry of Education 1991b) is moving toward curriculum-linked assessment and national monitoring of educational standards. Assessment will be based on item banks of curriculum-linked tasks which will be developed nationally, allowing choice of items at the school level. National monitoring will be carried out by light sampling at ages eight and twelve, the transition points between current school levels. Many of the details of the Achievement Initiative, including its impact on children with special educational needs, are still being worked through.

There is a general expectancy of New Zealand teachers that they will accommodate their teaching to the full range of learners in their classrooms, including those learners with special educational needs. This is particularly true of primary school teachers who are trained to identify and respond to individual differences among their pupils. Identification of children with special educational needs is done through such means as observations and the recording of continuous data on progress in the basic subjects. Teaching in New Zealand primary schools is characterized by a good deal of individualized planning and modifications to the regular programs for children who require additional assistance, group work, activity-based teaching, and interactive teaching, drawing upon constructivist theories of learning.

Major Controversies and Issues in Special Education

Integrated versus Segregated Educational Settings

New Zealand has had a long-standing commitment to integrating children with special needs into regular education as far as possible (Mitchell and Mitchell 1987). Just prior to *Tomorrow's Schools,* this was reflected in the Special Education Review (Department of Education 1987) which recommended that the aim should be to "to implement as fully as possible the current policy of educating students who have special teaching needs in the mainstream of regular education [in order] to enable all New Zealand's handicapped citizens to live as fully as they can in their ordinary community" (1). This policy was subsequently clarified to include the three options of locational, social, and functional mainstreaming—as first described in the Warnock Report in the United Kingdom (Department of Education and Science 1978)—with some children being in regular classrooms all of the time, some part of the time, and some never (Department of Education

1988). Ballard (1990) was particularly critical of this aspect of the policy, claiming that it maintained the unjustifiable proposition that there are categories of children and young people who require instruction in segregated educational arrangements.

As noted earlier, the Education Act of 1989 provides qualified support for the right of all children to be enrolled in regular schools. Within this legislative context, schools were required to include in their charters the principle that their school's policies and practices would seek to achieve equitable outcomes for all students, irrespective of their ability or disability.

Also within the spirit of the legislation, the SES (1990, 1) developed a policy on mainstreaming (the term *inclusion* is now generally preferred in New Zealand) which included the following statements:

- The SES believes that it is the right of all learners with special developmental and educational needs to share the same learning environment as their age mates within their local community.
- The SES will work towards the goal of integrating all learners with special needs into a regular age appropriate classroom of their local school alongside their peers.

The present government, which came into power in late 1990, had a noticeably diminished commitment to inclusion, instead emphasizing parents' rights to choose the type of special educational setting for their child. Thus, in a recent document, the Ministry of Education (1991a) was cautious—even equivocal. It went no further than statements such as the following: "Inclusion in age appropriate regular settings will continue" (5), and "The current choices of special schools, attached units, or regular classes for students with disabilities will continue to be available. Special schools and units for students with disabilities will continue to be an option as long as they are supported by enrolments" (11).

In a recent report from a research project monitoring the implementation of the educational reforms, Moltzen and Mitchell (1992) found that principals, teachers, and school trustees supported the principle of mainstreaming children with special educational needs—provided there were adequate resources to provide in-class support.

Related to this trend toward inclusive education is the whole deinstitutionalization movement for people with intellectual disability and/or mental health concerns who have lived much or all of their lives in institutional care (O'Brien 1990). Where this movement has been successful, children and young adults of school age have received for the first time an education within school-based settings outside of hospital grounds (Auckland Area Health Board 1990). Nevertheless, it must be noted that about two thousand people with intellectual disabilities are still living in psychopedic hospitals in New Zealand (Topham-Kindley 1993).

Funding

Few other sectors in New Zealand education have been subjected to such a range of reviews over the past few years as has special education. After having undergone the major restructuring as a result of the *Tomorrow's Schools* reforms, outlined earlier in this chapter, special education in New Zealand faces even more dramatic changes over the next two to three years resulting from the *Statement of Intent,* a policy framework prepared for government by the Ministry of Education (1991a). This document set out "a framework for the Government's intentions for special education policy" which was to be developed by an implementation team.

Underlying the *Statement of Intent* was the perception that the current administration of special education was problematic. Six major concerns were identified. First, resource allocation was seen as tending to "depend more on historical accident, categorization, and variable assessment procedures" than on students' learning needs. Second, it was considered that there is a lack of coordination among the various state and private sector agencies, "resulting in parents being in the position of having to identify services available and be the co-ordinators of provision." Third, criticisms were leveled at "a lack of co-ordination and uneven provision between [education] sectors." Fourth, it was argued that "an undue proportion of resources [are tied up] in administration and assessment procedures." Fifth, it was considered to be anomalous for the SES, a state funded agency, to advocate against other education agencies and schools. Such a focus on individual advocacy, it was argued, "has resulted in increased identification of students for individual resourcing and has had a tendency to disempower schools which may feel less able to manage the learning programs of such students." Sixth, and most importantly, there was the view that special education provisions were too centralized, and, as such, were out of line with the reformed education system. In short, the special education sector represented unfinished business in the reforms of education administration in New Zealand.

The ideological context for this aspect of the reforms was clearly expressed in the Treasury's briefing paper on education to the incoming government in 1987 (The Treasury 1987). Although this document made only passing reference to special education, the principles presented were intended to apply to the total education sector. Of most relevance to the proposed reforms of special education is the minimalist approach to state intervention in education, as exemplified in the following statement:

The costs of specific state interventions in education may be reduced and the benefits increased by action at three levels. *First,* the purposes of state intervention should be clearly identified and intervention minimized to that which is clearly justifiable and cost effective. . . . At the *second* level, given state intervention, action should be taken to minimize the disruption of, and help recreate the contract between, the customer and the provider. Thus the Government should: avoid interposing itself between the customers and providers as far as possible; eschew disabling interventions and focus on enabling ones; increase flexibility in the supply of educational services; . . . and reduce funding tied to major educational institutions and redirect funding to individuals, families, local groups and smaller scale institutions. At the *third* level, where government interposition between customer and provider is unavoidable, the Government should seek methods of management and accountability which will counter rather than reinforce problems arising from the role of Government. (293)

Closely related to the above point is a seventh, unstated, factor—government's commitment to separating government purchasers of services from government providers of services. This principle was most clearly articulated in a recent proposal by the Ministers of Social Welfare and Health for the funding and delivery of disability support service (Shipley and Upton 1992). This proposal was based on five basic principles:

1. Government agencies providing services for people with disabilities should be separate from the agencies with responsibility for funding and purchasing services.
2. All of a client's funding for a particular type of service should be located in one agency.
3. A single agency should be responsible for purchasing support services for all people with disabilities. Clients will deal with the same agency for purchasing the services they need, regardless of the nature of their disability.
4. The agency responsible should be given a single "integrated budget" to work within. This will enable greater flexibility in service provision and encourage better value for money.
5. The funding for disability support services will be ring-fenced from any other funding the purchaser controls.

In order to reduce the perceived dominance of the national SES as a special education provider and, correspondingly, to give more decision making and resources to schools, government introduced the notion of making part of the SES functions "contestable." Contestability is an economic term used to describe an environment in which an organization maintains an efficient and needs-driven operation through being exposed to actual or potential competition. It is viewed as a means of preventing an organization from holding a monopolistic position and is designed to provide choice and competitively priced services. In practice, contestability in special education was to occur by funding those who want a service (for example, schools), rather than the service provider (for example, the SES), with the former having the power to choose whom they want to provide the service and the nature of that service.

To enable contestability to occur, the *Statement of Intent* envisaged two distinct but overlapping types of special education provision being put in place. Essentially, these types revolved around classifying children with special education needs into one of two categories: students who have some form of learning or social difficulties and who require assistance to access quality education, and students with reliably identifiable physical, intellectual, and/or sensory disabilities. In terms of responsibilities for providing support for these two categories, two distinct patterns of special education provisions were proposed.

At the school level, students with disabilities would continue to be located in special schools, attached units, or in regular classes. They would receive individually targeted resources, allocated on the basis of individual education plans. It was recognized that no formula could reflect the uneven incidence of this group among educational facilities and that the services required are so specialized that it would be unlikely that there could be any systematic provision other than through a nationally coordinated state provision. The SES would therefore be funded to provide services for such students.

In contrast, school level provisions for students with learning or social difficulties were to undergo major changes. In keeping with the Treasury's views, as outlined above, and the government's philosophy of devolution, the *Statement of Intent* envisaged that schools would be given access to resources to use as they feel most appropriate to meet needs. To free up resources to enable this to happen, schools in 1993 were to have the option of withdrawing 50 percent of the SES funding for these students, increasing to 100 percent in 1994. This additional resourcing of schools would enable the appointment of "support teachers" who would be trained and released on a continuing basis to assist their colleagues. It was envisaged that the funding going to schools could be used flexibly, provided it met the needs of the target group of students (the grants were to be distributed according to a formula and targeted and tagged in ways to be determined by an implementation team). Within this context, support and advice to education providers would be contestable among the SES and other providers, including those from the private sector.

As it turns out, wiser counsel prevailed and the government backed off this particular form of contestability. As a result of extensive consultations carried out by a Special Education Policy Implementation Team in the first half of 1992, the government decided at first to delay the commencement of contestability until the beginning of 1994 but then decided to review the whole notion of contestability. This shift resulted from the almost universal objection to the use of categories as a basis for contestability. Other problems with the model have been described in detail by Mitchell (1992) and are summarized next. The problems are presented because they may well be applicable to other countries seeking to introduce contestability to their special education services.

Hazards of classification. Limited school budgets would create pressures to classify learners into the group that attracts free services and resources (that is, students with disabilities). This, in turn, may well lead to a great deal of time and resource being taken up in the labeling process. Further, this process may well become a source of conflict if schools seek to have children on the borderline between the two categories labeled as disabled, and parents seek to have a less stigmatizing label attached to their child.

Inequality of services. Without the economies of scale and other benefits of coordination, some services would be lost and each institution would have limited ability to respond to children with special needs.

Increase caregiver responsibility. Pressure would be placed on caregivers who would have to present arguments for funds to their board of trustees or school principal if they wished to access the services provided by the SES. In the New Zealand context of devolved responsibility for education, the debate on the distribution of resources to assist students with social and educational difficulties would have to be carried out at the individual school level. In this connection, it must be noted that a disproportionate number of parents who would be placed in this position are likely to be Maori and/or from lower socioeconomic backgrounds—people who do not find it easy to negotiate with the education system for their children and who often lack strong advocacy on their behalf.

Misuse of resources. There is a risk that the resource given to schools may not be used for the purposes for which it was intended. It would pose considerable difficulties to set up an effective regime for tagging and targeting the special education resource given to schools.

Inequitable resource distribution. Devising an appropriate formula to distribute special education funds in such a way that would account for the varying number and needs of students with social and educational difficulties across schools, and to take account of rural areas, would be problematic, to say the least. Any formula devised would have to contain a discretionary element, which would be difficult to administer, and may well prove to be not as cost effective as present arrangements. It is likely that special education resources would continue to need to be available in highly flexible, highly specific, and "transportable" ways.

Coordination of services. The continuity of services that learning institutions have available to them under the present arrangements and the continuity of specialist support for students transferring from one school to another would be jeopardized. In order to guard against this, there would have to be data sharing among the various service providers, and this would immediately raise issues to do with the recognition accorded to private providers who may not have the standard of qualification and professional supervision expected of SES staff. Confidentiality of client files would also be a major issue to be resolved. If sharing of information and coordination of services were not to take place, this could lead to the service delivery being characterized by duplication, fragmentation, and inconsistency.

Threats to cooperative, interdisciplinary approach. Contestability could be destructive to a cooperative, integrated, multidisciplinary team approach. For many learners, more than one profession is required to meet their educational needs. In order for a team approach to be sustained in which schools contract with several service providers, it would be necessary for these providers to enter into joint arrangements involving matters as diverse as developing a common philosophy, cost sharing, and synchronization of their time. These arrangements would be very difficult to attain.

Sustenance of quality. Finally, there is the issue of quality control when there are multiple service providers. On the assumption that individuals are rational utility maximizers (that is, self-interested), modern organization theories, and the economic neoliberalism that provides the ideological base, argue that effective monitoring procedures are critical. As outlined by Boston (1991), in a recent publication on public sector restructuring in New Zealand, the interests of *principals* (for example, schools) and *agents* (for example, special education providers) are bound to conflict. This can be compounded by the problem of *asymmetric information,* in which agents have access to information that principals do not enjoy and these agents have an incentive to exploit this situation to their advantage.

A good deal of agency theory therefore focuses on finding the most satisfactory way of negotiating, writing, and monitoring contracts to minimize the likelihood of violations resulting from opportunism on the part of the agent. This requirement is given added weight by the presence of two other factors: *adverse selection* and *moral hazard.* As described by Boston (1991), adverse selection arises from the fact that prior to the negotiation of a contract some of the information that a principal might want to know about an agent is unobservable. Moral hazard derives from the unobservability of the agent's behavior once a contract has been negotiated. Interestingly, Boston concludes that where the problems of adverse selection, moral hazard, and agency monitoring are substantial, "it is likely to be more efficient for the Government to establish its own agency than to rely on external contracting." Even if one recognizes that these organizational theories take a rather cynical perspective on human nature and overlook or downplay social and moral constraints that govern human relationships, the need to put in place adequate quality control procedures must be squarely addressed in a contestable environment.

As the Chief Executive of the SES recently observed, "The market place cannot provide a service that is always nationally available, fair to all, equally accessible, cost effective and that guaranteed some stability for parents and teachers whose lives are already fairly stressful" (Wilson 1993, 4).

Who Should Receive Services?

Historically, New Zealand special education has provided for all major categories of children with special educational needs, except two—those with learning disabilities and those with special abilities (that is, gifted and talented children). In recent years, however, a move toward a noncategorical, needs-based approach to identifying children with special educational needs has meant that those with learning disabilities have increasingly had access to help. This trend toward de-emphasizing categorical identification, however, has led one writer (Wilton 1992) to claim that it has brought about an underidentification of students with mild intellectual disability, with perhaps as few as one-quarter of this group receiving special educational provisions.

Students with special abilities are receiving increasing attention in schools, according to Moltzen (1993) and Moltzen and Mitchell (1992). This has resulted from several factors, including the increasing focus on "excellence" in education, the devolution of decision making to schools—which has required them to be responsive to local communities' views—and the insertion of a competitive element into the school system.

The Rights of Parents, Children, and the State

Parents' rights to participate in major decisions concerning their children are widely respected in New Zealand. These rights include giving consent to the type of school in which their child is enrolled, participating in the IEP process, and having access to information and records regarding their child. As well, parents' representatives play a major role in the governance of all schools and are members of consultative committees set up in the SES districts. The present government has placed considerable emphasis on parents' rights to choose what type of school they would prefer for their children—one of the major reasons for the retention of special schools in some places. As noted earlier in this paper, however, parents' choices are open to challenge by the state. In the case of special education, where agreement cannot be reached regarding placement of a child, a system of arbitration is available to either party. However, there is no procedure whereby an independent child advocate can operate alongside the parents and representatives of the government to participate in special education decisions—although such a system does exist in custody disputes in the Family Court system.

Emerging and Future Trends

Special education in New Zealand in the next few years is likely to be characterized by the following features, some of which are already in place, others of which are just emerging:

1. The trend toward local decision making in the distribution of special education resources, already in place in much of education in general, will continue.
2. Parents' rights to participate in major decisions concerning their children's placements and programs will be maintained.
3. The inclusion of children with special educational needs in regular schools and regular classes within those schools will accelerate.
4. There will be increased demand for professional training at both the pre- and the in-service levels to enable teachers to more effectively provide for children with special educational needs.
5. The substantial trend toward providing early intervention programs will be maintained.
6. Provisions for Maori children with special educational needs will be radically changed, in line with the major thrusts in the education system as a whole, to provide an education for those children which is culturally appropriate and in the Maori language.
7. There will be an increasingly rigorous approach to assessing the outcomes and the cost-effectiveness of various forms of special educational provisions.

References

Auckland Area Health Board. 1990. *Strategic plan for services for people with intellectual disabilities.* Auckland: Auckland Area Health Board.

Ballard, K. D. 1990. Special education in New Zealand: Disability, politics and empowerment. *International Journal of Disability, Development and Education* 37 (2):109–24.

Boston, J. 1991. The theoretical underpinnings of public sector restructuring in New Zealand. In J. Boston, J. Martin, J. Pallot, and P. Walsh, eds. *Reshaping the State: New Zealand's bureaucratic revolution.* Auckland: Oxford University Press.

Brown, C. 1990. Fight for children left for the crows. *Dominion Sunday Times,* 29 April.

Bush, R., and Buckfield, P. 1987. Prevention of handicapping conditions. In D. R.

Mitchell and N. N. Singh, eds. *Exceptional children in New Zealand.* Palmerston North: The Dunmore Press.

Business and Economic Research Limited. 1986. *Estimates of the population of disabled persons in New Zealand 1986.* Wellington: Accident Compensation Corporation.

Central District Child Development Centre. 1993. Pamphlet. (Available from The Coordinator, Central District Child Development Centre, 615 New North Road, Mt. Albert, Auckland, New Zealand.)

Chapman, J. W., St. George, R., and van Kraayenoord, C. E. 1983. Short WISC-R, short cuts, and Occam's razor: Identification of learning disabled pupils. Paper presented at the annual conference of the New Zealand Psychological Society, Auckland.

de Boer, G., Saxby, J., and Soljak, M. 1989. *Child health profile 1989.* Wellington: Department of Health.

Department of Education. 1987. *The draft review of special education.* Wellington: Department of Education.

————. 1989. *The charter framework.* Wellington: Department of Education.

Department of Education and Science, United Kingdom. 1978. *Special education needs* (The Warnock Report). London: HMSO.

Dezoete, J. A., MacArthur, B. A., Rowley, S , and Howie, R. N. 1991. *Progress report of the Child Development Unit for the year 1990.* Auckland: National Women's Hospital.

Doyle, M., and Jensen, E. 1984. Provision for school-age children resident in a psychopaedic hospital. Paper, Kimberley Hospital and Training School.

Education Review Office. 1992. *A review of special education provisions in New Zealand.* Wellington: Education Review Office.

Espiner, D., Hartnett, F., and O'Brien, P. 1992. A three tiered system of nationally approved training for human service personnel in New Zealand. Paper presented at the 9th World Congress of the International Association for the Scientific Study of Mental Deficiency, Gold Coast, Australia.

Gates, S. 1990. Advocacy in a time of crisis and change in New Zealand schools. Paper presented at International Conference on Integration, Schools, Leisure, and Transition to Work, Stockholm, Sweden.

Hyslop, J., Dowland, J., and Hickling, J. 1983. *Health facts New Zealand.* Wellington: MSRU, Department of Health.

Jack, A., Hyslop, J. R., and Dowland, J. E. 1980. The prevalence of physical disability: Preliminary results of a Wellington survey. *The New Zealand Medical Journal* 91 (657).

Lange, D. 1988. *Tomorrow's schools.* Wellington: New Zealand Government Printer.

Ministry of Education. 1991a. *Special education in New Zealand: Statement of intent.* Wellington: Ministry of Education.

————. 1991b. *The national curriculum of New Zealand: A discussion document.* Wellington: Ministry of Education.

————. 1992. *Education statistics of New Zealand 1992.* Wellington: Ministry of Education.

Mitchell, D. R. 1987. Special education in New Zealand: An historical perspective. In D. R. Mitchell and N. N. Singh, eds. *Exceptional children in New Zealand.* Palmerston North: The Dunmore Press.

———. 1992. Special education: Whose responsibility? *Keynote addresses to 1991 conference.* Dunedin: New Zealand Association for Research in Education.

———. 1993. Special education down under. In G. Upton and R. Michael, eds. *The viewfinder: Monograph of the Division of International Special Education and Services of the American Council for Exceptional Children.* Reston, Va.: Council for Exceptional Children.

Mitchell, D. R., and Singh, N. N. 1987. *Exceptional children in New Zealand.* Palmerston North: The Dunmore Press.

Mitchell, J. W., and Mitchell, D. R. 1987. Integration/Mainstreaming. In D. R. Mitchell and N. N. Singh, eds. *Exceptional children in New Zealand.* Palmerston North: The Dunmore Press.

Moltzen, R. 1993. The impact of reforms in education on provisions for gifted children. Master's thesis, University of Waikato, Hamilton.

Moltzen, R., and Mitchell, D. 1992. Children with special needs. In *Report No. 6: Monitoring today's schools.* Hamilton: University of Waikato.

Murray, R, and Thorburn, J. 1991. A people first approach in special education teacher education. Paper presented at New Zealand Institute on Mental Retardation Conference, Auckland.

O'Brien, P. M. 1990. Coming in from the margin. *The Australasian Journal of Special Education* 13:52–59.

O'Brien, P., Bowden, J., Cochrane, M., Murray, R., Parkinson, J., and Caron, K. 1990. *Mainstreaming and the individualized education/development plan.* Auckland: Ministry of Education.

Oliver, W. H. 1977. The origins of the welfare state. In A. D. Trlin, ed. *Social welfare and New Zealand society.* Wellington: Methuen.

Orange, C. 1987. *The Treaty of Waitangi.* Wellington: Allen and Unwin.

Panckhurst, J. D. 1977. *Children with special needs in New Zealand kindergartens: A national survey.* Wellington: Victoria University of Wellington.

Pole, A. 11 September 1992. Personal communication with author.

Power, D. 1990. Hearing impairment. In A. Ashman and J. Elkins, eds. *Educating children with special needs.* Sydney: Prentice Hall.

Robertson, A. D. 1986. *"Let's get some things sorted out ..." A beginning. A report on services for New Zealand for people with multiple handicaps prepared for the Royal New Zealand Foundation for the Blind.* Auckland: Royal New Zealand Foundation for the Blind.

Robertson, M. S. 1982. Glue ear. *New Zealand Medical Journal* 95 (703):149–50.

Senescall, S., Spence, F., Stancliffe, L., and Thorburn, J. 1990. *People with disabilities: Module three, Certificate in Teaching People with Disabilities.* Auckland: Auckland College of Education.

Shipley, J., and Upton, S. 1992. *Support for independence: A discussion paper on the funding and delivery of disability support services.* Wellington: Minister of Social Welfare and Minister of Health.

Simpson, A., Kirkland, C., and Silva, P. A. 1984. Vision and eye problems in seven year olds: A report from the Dunedin multi-disciplinary health and development research unit. *New Zealand Medical Journal* 96 (737):400–401.

Slyfield, H. 1992. *An overview of equal employment opportunities in the teaching services.* Wellington: Ministry of Education.

Special Education Service. 1990. *Towards inclusion 1: How to include all learners in regular education.* Wellington: Special Education Service.

———. 1991. *Report of the Special Education Service: For the twelve months ended 30 June 1991.* Wellington: House of Representatives.

———. 1993. *Working with others: A resource manual for staff.* Wellington: Special Education Service.

Sullivan, M. 1991. From personal tragedy to social oppression: The medical model and social theories of disability. *New Zealand Journal of Industrial Relations* 16:255–72.

Taskforce to Review Education Administration. 1988. *Administering for excellence.* Wellington: New Zealand Government Printer.

The Treasury. 1987. *Government management: Brief to the incoming Government 1987.* Vol. 2, *Education issues.* Wellington: New Zealand Government Printer.

Topham-Kindley, L. 1993. 2000 handicapped living in hospitals "could live outside." *Otago Daily Times,* 26 January.

VandenBurg, M., and Laugesen, M. 1981. *Cerebral palsy incidence in New Zealand and delays in physical treatment.* Wellington: MSRU, Department of Health.

Van Kraayenoord, C., and Elkins, J. 1990. Learning difficulties. In A. Ashman and J. Elkins, eds. *Educating children with special needs.* Sydney: Prentice Hall.

Waitakere Child Development Centre. 1993. Pamphlet. (Available from The Coordinator, Waitakere Child Development Centre, Woodford House, Woodford Road, Henderson, Auckland, New Zealand.)

Walsh, D. F. 1979. *Project CHILD: A report on the incidence of specific learning difficulties in Form I pupils in New Zealand primary and intermediate schools.* Wellington: New Zealand Council for Educational Research.

West, S. R., and Harris, B. J. 1983. Audiometry and tympanometry in children throughout one school year. *New Zealand Medical Journal* 96 (737):603–05.

Wilson, R. 1993. So now the revolution is over where does that leave special education? Address to the Inaugural Conference of the Special Education Service, Dunedin.

Wilton, K. 1992. Special education policy for learners with mild intellectual disability in New Zealand: Problems and issues. Paper presented at 9th World Congress, International Association for the Scientific Study of Mental Deficiency, Gold Coast, Australia.

26

England and Wales

JOHN DWYFOR DAVIES

MAEVE LANDMAN

*T*he international debate regarding the rights of people with disabilities registered significantly in the 1970s; accordingly, that decade symbolizes a landmark in the education of pupils with special educational needs. In this chapter we sketch briefly developments in the provision of special educational needs over the last two decades in England and Wales. We show the principal policy and legislative landmarks, describe existing provision in broad terms, and highlight current, emergent, and future trends.[1]

Special Educational Needs: The Context

The beginning of the 1970s saw the responsibility for the education of pupils with severe learning difficulties transferred from the health service to the education authorities, reflecting acknowledgment of the principle that

---

About the Authors • John Dwyfor Davies is director of studies (professional development) at the University of West England, Bristol, in the Faculty of Education. He has, in the past, held a post of responsibility for the provision of program elements in the area of special educational needs. His research interests include provision for children and young people with emotional and behavioral difficulties, and support services for students designated as having such difficulties in mainstream schools. • Maeve Landman is director of the Policy and Provision Section in the Faculty of Education, University of West England, Bristol. She is also chair of Faculty Board, which accords with her research interests in the structures and governance of higher education and runs parallel with her active participation in professional development programs for teachers of children with special educational needs.

every child is entitled to education, irrespective of the degree to which she or he is handicapped by physical or mental disability. The then secretary of state for Education established a committee of inquiry in 1974 which, after four years of research, reported in May 1978 (Department of Education and Science 1978).

This report was notable for reshaping policy and practice in the area of special educational needs, as is evidenced in subsequent legislation, in particular, the 1981 Education Act. Although the government of the day did not implement all the recommendations of the Warnock Committee's report in the 1981 legislation, certain fundamental principles were incorporated.

The 1981 Education Act offered a definition of special educational needs. Under Section 1 of the act (subsec. 1[1]), a child is said to have special educational needs if "he (sic) has a learning difficulty which calls for special educational provision to be made for him. *Learning difficulty* is defined as significantly greater difficulty in learning than the majority of children his age; or a disability which either prevents or hinders him from making use of educational facilities of a kind generally provided in school, within the area of the local authority concerned, for children of his age" or if he is under the age of five years and is or would be likely to fall within paragraph (a) or (b) when over that age if SEP were not made for him (subsec. 2).

Special educational provision is understood thus "in relation to a child who has attained the age of two years, educational provision which is additional to, or otherwise different from, the educational provision made generally for children of his age in schools maintained by the local education authority concerned; and in relation to any child under that age, educational provision of any kind" (subsec. 3).

Although these definitions were intended to inform those concerned with the processes of identifying and meeting educational need, the ambiguous phraseology has served to obfuscate rather than clarify. This is considered later in this chapter.

The Warnock Report is important for changing the lexicon used by teachers and other professionals regarding the needs and entitlements of children identified by eleven categories of handicap in use at that time. Moreover, by extending the concept of absolute handicap to one of a continuum of ability, special educational needs came to be understood as referring to a far wider population than had previously been conceived of.

Prevalence of Exceptional Conditions

The Warnock Committee advanced the canon from the previous theory that as many as one person in six would, at some point in their lives, experience a degree of difficulty that would warrant special attention. In education, it was now said that one pupil in five would fall within the continuum and need special educational provision at some time or other during his or her school career, Warnock's 20 percent. Eighteen percent of this group could be identified in ordinary schools. Two percent would have difficulties of a long term, complex and/or profound nature that would require special or additional provision over and above that usually available, that is, separate special schools. The principle that pupils with special educational needs should (where practical) be educated alongside their peers in mainstream settings was also widely accepted and espoused.

The emphasis, thus, has shifted from establishing or predicting prevalence to ensuring the appropriate provision in the current context. This apparently benign development has to be taken together with shifts in the locus of responsibility and approaches to teacher training, especially in the 1980s and 1990s. With regard to the former, worldwide shifts in attitudes to rights and entitlements of people with disabilities forms the background to the 1970 Education Act, which transferred responsibility for the education of children and young people with severe learning difficulties (previously and offensively categorized as *educationally subnormal* by a range of people), from the health authorities to the local educational authorities. With the accent on education rather than on care, the dominant discourse of medical hegemony, with which the term *prevalence* is associated, was eroded by the increasing professional confidence of special educators. This is complemented by the emergence of sociological accounts of special education, particularly the arguments that handicap and therefore special educational needs are relative to time and context and, in this sense, are socially constructed.

Identification of Exceptionalities

Historically, the identification of pupils with special educational needs has a strong medical association. The Warnock Committee recommended a procedure that acknowledged the fact that the exceptional needs of many pupils would be identified and met, progressing in five stages. The last stage leads to a formal record of educational need, in cases that this is judged by a multiprofessional team to be necessary for the protection of the child's rights. This approach was consolidated by the 1981 Education Act.

The 1981 act places upon the local education authorities the obligation to identify the exceptional needs of children and to describe the provision that will meet these needs. In practice, the requirement to identify needs is devolved to the governing body of each school, which normally entrusts this responsibility to the head teacher.

Five discrete but sequential stages for assessment were laid down by the act. The first three involve school-based procedures, promoting the precept of assessment through teaching and the principle of involving parents at each stage. Do note, however, that formal assessment can be initiated before school age, that is at the age of two, when it is clear that the child's difficulties at the age of five will be significant.

The stages of assessment are summarized as follows:

Stage 1. The teacher identifies the problem and devises an intervention for the child. The parents are consulted and a review date agreed upon.

Stage 2. If the intervention has not promoted significant remediation, the teacher discusses this with his or her relevant postholder, for example, the coordinator for special educational needs. An appropriate intervention is devised and a review date agreed upon. The parents are included in discussions and the head teacher advised of developments.

Stage 3. The school involves other relevant personnel in the local authority; for example, specialist language support teacher, education social worker. Discussions at this stage usually include an educational psychologist. These last two stages involve a multiprofessional assessment, which may result in a formal statement of educational need that identifies the pupil's particular requirements, as well as a giving a description of the resources necessary to meet these.

Stage 4. The school gives notice that it may not be able to meet the needs of the child and requests a multiprofessional assessment. At this stage, written evidence is invited from the range of education-related professionals who may have been involved at stages 1 to 3. Statutorily, evidence must be provided by the school (by or on behalf of the head teacher), the senior clinical medical officer, and the educational psychologist.

Stage 5. Following a multiprofessional assessment, the local educational authority (LEA) issues a Statement of Educational Need. This statement identifies the additional support that the child requires, the provision of which becomes the responsibility of the local education authority.

Unlike earlier assessment procedures, the method established under the 1981 Education Act is not intended as an end in itself. In the spirit of the Warnock Report, assessment is posited as a dynamic means to inform appropriate action rather than to identify a destination. This is made explicit in guidelines published by the Department of Education and Science (DES 1983):

> The assessment of the SENs (special educational needs) is not an end in itself; it is the first step towards a better understanding of a child's learning difficulties for the practical purposes of providing guidance to the educational needs and establishing a basis upon which to monitor the child's progress. When carrying out assessment, the LEA should ensure that clear distinctions are made between:

- the child's relevant past and present levels of functioning, emotional state and interests and how these represent resources and deficiencies in relation to the educational demands which will be made on the child;
- the analysis of the child's learning difficulties;
- the specification of goals for change in the child and environment (including school, home and the wider community);
- the specification of the child's requirement for different kinds of approaches, facilities or resources, in order to facilitate access to the National Curriculum, with any modifications which are considered essential;
- the perception and wishes of the parents and the child;
- the special educational provision and services required to meet the identified needs. (DES Circular 22/89, Section 18; supersedes Circular 1/83, following the passing of the 1988 Education Act.)

This focus on the individual needs of the child represents a fundamental shift from previous procedures that were primarily concerned with strongly boundaried categories into which the child should fit. The recognition that individuals will experience certain needs and that these are not static but change with the child's age and development and his or her context, resulted in this radical refocusing of the process of assessment and resultant provision. That, at least, is the theory.

The dynamic nature of the process is reflected in the provisions of the 1981 Education Act that placed on local education authorities the responsibility to review annually with a statement of educational need the progress of pupils and to amend the provision according to new data.

Every statement issued by the LEA has to be reviewed at least annually. According to Circular 1/83 (par. 55) the basis of the review is a report prepared by the child's school. It should reflect the views of teachers, other professionals, and parents. Significantly, the annual review should be seen "as part of a process of continuous assessment," a further endorsement that assessment should be an integral part of everyday teaching (Solity and Raybould 1988, 106).

It is also a statutory requirement for local education authorities to conduct a full multiprofessional reassessment on pupils at the ages of thirteen (if not at twelve) and sixteen, and to amend the form and extent of additional provision where appropriate.

Labeling the Population

Before the publication of the Warnock Report and the introduction of the 1981 Education Act, pupils who had been identified as in need of special educational provision were labeled according to one of eleven statutory categories and placed in institutions accordingly. These categories were educationally subnormal (severe); blind; partially sighted; deaf; partially hearing; epileptic; educationally subnormal (moderate or mild); maladjusted; physically handicapped; speech defect; and delicate (Tomlinson 1982).

As described earlier, the recognition of the complexity of handicap led to a close reexamination of the practice of attempting a neat fit between *primary handicap* and designated provision, in which the child was almost incidental. Complications can be demonstrated by invoking a case of a child who is both hearing and visually impaired, and subject to epileptic fits. What counts as the primary handicap in determining provision?

This dilemma in definitions, together with the growing recognition of the negative consequences of labeling and acceptance of the Warnock Report's arguments that the notion of handicap was not a helpful concept in an educational context, resulted in critical review of these conventional categories. Additionally, the emphasis on educational need pointed to the existence of other kinds of difficulties that affect children's learning; for example, autism or dyslexia.

It had been hoped by many that this would result in the total abolition of categories of need and that the focus of provision would result from the identified specific needs of individuals. This view was encouraged by the Warnock Report's use of descriptive rather than absolute categories. The Warnock Committee proposed a new structure which permitted some positive perceptions of categories: categories as helping to focus attention on the needs of different groups of children with handicapping conditions and as safeguarding the rights of handicapped children to an education suited to individual need (Norwich 1990).

This new view distinguished between medical categorization and educational need; though interconnected, the former should not dominate the latter. The formal legislative language rests on the Warnock Report's recommendation that *special educational needs* replace the vocabulary of the categories. In reality, however, the descriptions currently in use are children with learning difficulties (severe); blind; partially sighted; deaf; partially hearing; epileptic; children with learning difficulties (mild or moderate); emotional and behavioral difficulties; physically handicapped; language difficulties; delicate; dyslexia/specific learning difficulties; and autistic.

Thus it can be seen that recent legislation has done little to bridge the gap between rhetoric and practice. Perhaps it was futile and naive to assume that it could, since the labeling of people has more to do with attitudes about disability and special educational needs than with structural changes. It is difficult, if not impossible, to legislate for attitudes. Despite the tone of the Warnock Report, pupils continue to be labeled according to identified need and many are still educated in special—segregated—provision. It is important here to note that this is built into the 1981 act, which stresses that provision should be made for individuals while having regard to efficient use of a local education authority's (LEA) existing provision.

Legislation

The past decade and a half has witnessed rapid development in terms of legislation in British education generally. We have given the procedural provisions of the 1981 Education Act consequent upon the Warnock Report (DES 1978). Here we summarize the broad thrust of the 1981 act, which set out to accomplish the following:

1. Provided a formal definition for the concept of special educational needs and broadened it to encompass those children who would be educated within "mainstream" schooling and whose needs were such that a formal statement would not be necessary
2. Abolished the traditional categories
3. Required school governors to identify those children in their schools who had special educational needs
4. Established a procedure for assessing pupils with special educational needs
5. Entitled parents/students to representation in the process leading to a statement of need and the drafting of a statement
6. Demanded that local education authorities be responsible for providing the additional resources necessary for the education of pupils with the protection of a statement of need.

Recent evaluation of the effectiveness of legislation as it has been implemented raises important questions. Specifically, the 1988 Education Act has prompted concern among a wide range of educationalists and allied professionals worried that the apparent advances achieved in the 1970s were corroded in the 1980s. It is a matter of record that the consideration given to the needs of exceptional children in the passing of the Education Reform Act (The 1988 Education Act) was widely criticized as lamentable (Wedell 1988). Reference to pupils with special educational needs was limited to one section of that bill. This was regarded by many as signaling the fact that, despite the 1981 Education Act, special educational needs was viewed very much as an afterthought by the authors of the legislation and associated policy documents.

Unfortunately, there is no indication that the Education Reform Bill takes account of the 18 percent or so of children with special educational needs but without statements in ordinary schools. The only reference to special educational needs occurs in Clause 10 which permits the national curriculum to be modified in the case of children with statements. A similar paragraph occurs in the consultation document which, however, suggests that pupils with statements might be exempted from part of the curriculum. Both formulations clearly have the paradoxical implication that, if children move from one LEA to another, their curricular requirements might also change. Quite apart from the educational principles raised by these points, it would seem that the current concept of the nature of special educational needs incorporated in the 1981 act were not applied by the drafters of the bill (Wedell 1988, 104).

Let us clarify the context. The 1988 Education Act was a massive piece of legislation that accorded to the secretary of state for education some 415 new powers. The act was concerned with the following:

1. A national curriculum and assessment arrangements
2. Creating grant-maintained schools
3. Open enrollment
4. Local (financial) management of schools
5. Abolition of metropolitan local education authorities; for example, the Inner London Education Authority
6. Changes in the funding and control of institutions of higher education, inter alia

The concept of entitlement is central to this and all other subsequent policy formation. This is at once a site for political promulgation and contradiction, as the quotation given earlier shows. On the face of it, all children have the right to access (itself an interesting metaphor) to a curriculum that is "broad and balanced." This has been seen by many as a powerful tool for reform, particularly in relation to children with special educational needs and segregated from the mainstream system, that is, those in special schools and units (Davies and Landman 1991). More considered reflection reveals that, far from having guaranteed rights, part of the school population deemed as having special educational needs was ignored.

The apparently low status that had been conferred upon pupils with special educational needs led to a degree of protest that resulted in modifications made expeditiously as the bill proceeded through Parliament. While the principle of access remained central to the legislation, it was now possible to modify or disapply the national curriculum and its associated assessment requirements for some children, provided that procedures were adhered to. Although this allayed some of the concern regarding the strictures of the national curriculum, it could not dispel anxieties rooted in the suspicion that in practice the sum of the elements of the legislation (particularly those connected with the local management of schools) places at risk support services—such as those services taken for granted in an integrated, service-led LEA provision. For example, rather than the LEA providing broad services such as peripatetic learning support teachers, schools have to make decisions about priorities according to what their budgets will allow.

Teachers, Schools, Curriculum, and Pedagogy

Teachers

This is an area that is especially interesting to us as teacher trainers. Over the last five years, we can chart shifts in our labor that are consequent upon two major factors; namely, the reorganization of the higher education system and significant shifts in approaches to teacher training that have impacted upon the preparation of teachers of children with special educational needs.

Regarding the latter, the mid-1980s saw the cessation of discrete courses for the training of teachers of children with severe learning difficulties. Future specialization would result from the in-service training of experienced mainstream teachers. At the same time, market-orientated funding of education, including professional development (see references to local management of schools), resulted in the significant reduction of opportunities for full-time study leading to specialization in this area. Now, although we have every sympathy with the training initiative and subscribe to the notion that teachers of children with special educational needs should be successful teachers first and foremost, the most rudimentary approach to workforce planning would reveal the likelihood of a shortfall if developments take place on both the training and teaching fronts simultaneously. This is proving to be the case.

Schools

We have shown that segregated provision exists in a diversity of provision, according to the descriptive categories listed earlier. There are two issues to note at this juncture. The population that is the subject of this discussion—children and young people with special educational needs—is located both in the mainstream sector and the special sector. The legislative framework is designed to encompass both, particularly those children and young people with Statements of Educational Need in both sectors. The 1988 Education Reform Act has brought about an intermeshing of common concerns that many of us have welcomed, however difficult, or indeed, barbed, the process may be. We are, however, forced to confront the persistent probability that, despite the rhetoric, several imperatives drive the system towards an apartheid.

Statements of Educational Need—Resourcing

Enshrined in the 1988 Education Act are tenets that reflect increasing dogma relating to utilitarianism and competition. Schools are forced to engage with discourse of the marketplace, to depend upon selling and promoting their services. A trenchant example of this is the requirement to publish examination results, which, in the form of raw data, provide the basis for league tables of success. In this climate, it is not surprising that school governors and management teams may wish to discourage the participation of children with special educational needs. It is interesting to note that in the first of these exercises (this academic year), special schools were included but qualified dubiously by category—cold comfort for all those involved. There is a perceived pressure that students who are less likely to perform well in national examinations, and so detract from the profile of the school as represented by these public league tables, will be excluded from the rolls of "mainstream" schools. We draw on official documentation to illustrate this point: "Under the new arrangements proposed in this White Paper, there will be a clear obligation for the provision of alternative education . . . [. . .] . . . Those who persistently misbehave at school not only ruin their own educational opportunities, they disrupt the education of all their classmates. (DFE 1992, 11, 12, par. 1.54–1.55).

The Current Discourse: Raising Standards, Choice, Diversity

Recent policy trends and legislation have apparently aspired to achieve two goals at once. Local education authorities have had their powers significantly curtailed at the same time as the responsibilities of school governors and the rights of parents have been strengthened. The alignment with legislative policy and increased parental control was made public in the mid-1980s: "The aim . . . is to offer an independent education for all, by granting to all parents the power, at present enjoyed only by the wealthy, to choose the best available education for their children. This aim can be accomplished only by offering schools the opportunity to liberate themselves from Local Authority control" (Hillgate Group 1987).

It is unlikely that the parents of students with special educational needs, particularly those whose needs are moderate or primarily behavioral, will be in a position to exercise these rights. It is possible, however, that as a result of the pressures exerted by articulate and aspirant parents in organized groups, students with special educational needs may well suffer in terms of the quality of education they receive.

As we write, the debate regarding selective education, expressed as a hierarchy of schools, or streaming within schools, is being revived by the secretary of state. Taken together with the notion that "parents know best" (DFE 1992, 4) the type of education suited to their child, it is not surprising—though extremely depressing—to hear the common view that more able children would best be served by the segregation of pupils whose needs—that is, special education needs—make additional demands of teachers. The same perception is frequently heard on the allocation of expensive resources—that these resources should be targeted at those students whom society values and applauds, rather than those about whom it is, at best, equivocal.

Integration versus Segregation

The practice of integrating pupils with special educational needs into mainstream classrooms has been developed considerably over the two decades, if on an ad hoc basis. Some observers have argued that policies and practice remain inadequate and that the expansion of integration—social, locational, and functional—has not been as extensive as is sometimes assumed erroneously on the basis of the Warnock Report (Barton and Landman 1993). Others, however, cite examples of good practice and point to the many benefits that the integration of pupils with special educational needs has brought to all concerned (Jones 1990)

From a most optimistic viewpoint, recent developments are more likely to hamper the practice of integration; at worst, they will threaten its very existence. Parental pressure exercised by the more articulate and aspiring members of the community could well place head teachers and governors in a situation where it is politically expedient, if not comfortable, to exclude pupils for the reasons referred to earlier. Far from promoting the cause of integration, such developments will prove socially divisive, and we may well revert to a situation in which the school population comprises two discrete groups—hence our resort to the harshness of apartheid. It is a matter of great interest to observe whether this will prove politically embarrassing for a government that has heralded its education reforms under the banner of "meeting the needs and aspirations of all pupils" (DFE, 11).

It is the declared intention of the Department for Education (DFE [Ministry]) to stimulate competition between schools in the hope that good schools will improve performance in the current discourse and, conversely, that the schools that fail to raise their standards (as defined by pupil attainment scores) would bear the consequences as parents elect to move their children to the more successful schools. This naturally arouses concern, since it would result in the ghettoization of pupils whose levels of achievement (measured in narrow, normative, academic terms) is not high.

We should point out that commentators were quick to discern the pitfalls for special educational provision inherent in the arrangements for the local management of schools. The safety net subsequently devised languishes in the residual powers of LEAs. Thus, the distribution of centrally determined resources is currently allocated to schools according to a set formula, typically dependent upon the number of pupils attending a school. Additional funding is also allocated, though generally determined by crude and inaccurate measures; for example, necessitous students are identified by their being entitled free school meals. This is then translated as the basis of funding for special educational needs.

A puzzling complication arising from the additional funding attracted by pupils who have a Statement of Special Educational Need is reverse discrimination (not positive). Under conditions of diminishing resources, some schools may find it attractive to register children with such a statement since it may secure additional financial support (depending on the wording of the statement). There are few mechanisms in operation to ensure that money allocated in this way is disbursed entirely in the manner intended. This is hedged about by another discussion; that is, whether the interests of the child are best served by specificity, or by a general, inclusive approach that adventitiously serves all. There are some indications that the current administration is aware of this dilemma and is likely to attempt fine-tuning in the near future (House of Commons 1992).

Returning to the substantive point of segregated provision—and the continuation of associated labels—we suggest that the confrontation of this fundamental issue has been sidestepped by a plethora of political and financial practicalities. In the wake of the 1988 Education Act, provisions have been made for the local management of special schools, so that they too can operate more discretion in the disbursement of monies. Similarly, the White Paper currently before Parliament indicates that choice of special school should be available to parents of children whose statements make that provision. Our concern is that an apparent parity of policy obscures the lack of parity of esteem.

This aside, we should note that parental support for special educational provision for pupils with more severe difficulties has been strident in circumstances where local education authorities have attempted to shift provision into mainstream or mixed-mode settings. It has to be said that such shifts have their provenance in fiscal and administrative convenience rather than educational or humanitarian considerations.

It remains the case, however, that recent legislation has done much to modify the nature of the educational experience in special schools. The introduction of the national curriculum, as a component of the 1988 Education Act, forms the basis of a broad and balanced curriculum to which all children and young people are entitled.

Controversy continues to rage regarding the relevance of the national curriculum, essentially content based, for pupils with severe learning difficulties. Statutorily, special, as well as mainstream schools, must ensure that their students are taught the core and foundation subjects as stipulated in the 1988 Education Act. Initial reaction to this requirement was mixed (Davies and Landman 1992). Some teachers were of the view that adhering to a national curriculum is constraining and obstructive since, apart from the argument regarding the relevance of the prescribed curriculum for pupils with profound and multiple learning difficulties, the time taken on such subject-based work would leave little space for social skill development, preparation for autonomy, and other nonacademic pursuits regarded as more appropriate.

Other head teachers welcomed the introduction of a national curriculum for all, arguing that this would require the broadening of the educational experiences of pupils who had traditionally been exposed to a curriculum that was narrowly focused and repetitive (Wood and Shears 1986). These head teachers saw the introduction of the national curriculum as an opportunity to rethink and restructure the curriculum and organization of special schools (Davies and Landman 1992).

We find it interesting that head teachers, widely recognized as agents of change, felt that they needed this external impetus to forge radical curriculum change. This in itself represents a comment on the nature of educational change.

The Shape of Things to Come

There has probably been no time when the controversy regarding the education of pupils with special educational needs in Britain has been so explicit as it is today. This is largely due to two major factors. The first is the speed with which legislation has been imposed and the limited consultation sought in its preparation. Second is a lack of differentiation in the policies of both the right and the left wings of the party political system.

The 1988 Education Act was designed and implemented at an unprecedented speed. This is in sharp contrast to earlier legislation, which took years of research and consultation before being enacted by Parliament. The 1981 Education Act, for example, was the result of some five years of research undertaken by the Warnock Committee, followed by a substantial period of consultation before it was followed by the act implemented in 1983.

This is in stark contrast with the passage of the "Great Education Reform Bill" of 1987, rushed through Parliament at a time when the dominant party had a very large majority in the House of Commons. Teachers, as well as administrators, have had to labor long and hard to meet legislative requirements, which continue to be subject to amendment as operational difficulties emerge. There has been little time for considered analysis and reflection, let alone mechanisms to register comment and suggestion for improvement. Accordingly, educators operate in an environment where the many contradictions and challenges contained in the act will become more apparent during the course of the next decade, with little hope that professional judgment will receive due hearing.

More recently, the White Paper referred to earlier was published in July 1992, just as educational institutions were winding down for the summer, making something of a mockery of the consultation period. As we have indicated, this is now a bill before Parliament, representing a time scale for implementation that it is hard, not to say improper, to adjust to. This necessarily truncates important debate on the future of special education for the children and young people of England and Wales.

Fish (1988) draws attention to the fact that most progress in terms of change in attitude about students with disabilities has tended to be achieved at times when there has been a consensus in the middle ground of politics. We are presently experiencing a hardening of positions among those on the right and, in particular, the radical right, in common with large parts of Europe. This may well result in a similar consolidation of policies for educational reform on the left in the foreseeable future. If this were to be the case, one may speculate that we could witness a retardation in the pace of development along the emancipatory line that persuades and drives us. At best, stasis will prevail. It is painful to have to acknowledge the possibility of retrogression along the lines that we have sketched earlier.

Emerging and Future Trends

Observers of British education, and of special education in particular, will notice the effects of a wide range of influences over recent years. Taken each on their own, these influences are significant enough. When taken together, they provide a bleak backdrop against which to offer commentary of the emergent trends and to speculate about possible developments. It is difficult to disentangle definitively the various factors instrumental in establishing the climate within which the education service operates. Issues that we identify for further consideration can be summarized as pupils' rights versus parental choice; competition versus partnership; integration versus segregation; public accountability versus personal achievement; national curriculum versus special curriculum; financial autonomy versus financial constraints; and normative versus illuminative assessment.

Alongside the more visible factors, it is necessary to consider less apparent but highly powerful influences such as attitudinal shifts and social trends, steered opaquely from above. Education policy and provision should also be viewed in light of prevailing economic imperatives, since these form the transparent context within which the education system functions. We emphasize here the difficulties presented by current challenges. We should like to return to the many promises of the Warnock Report and the 1981 act—these events still signify the vehicles for continuing critical debates.

Note

1. These assertions are based on research we conducted involving a national survey of all special schools in England and Wales (Davies and Landman 1991).

References

Barton, L., and Landman, M. 1993. The politics of integration: Observations on the Warnock Report. In R. Slee, ed. *Is there a desk with my name on it, too?* 41–51. Basingstoke: Falmer Press.

Davies, J., and Landman, M. 1991. The national curriculum in special schools for pupils with emotional and behavioral difficulties. *Maladjustment and Therapeutic Education* 9 (9):130–35.

Department for Education (DFE). 1992. *Choice and diversity: A new framework for schools.* London: HMSO.

Department of Education and Science (DES). 1978. *Special educational needs: Report of the Committee of Enquiry into the education of handicapped children and young people.* The Warnock Report. London: HMSO.

———. 1983. *Circular 22/89: Assessments and statements of special educational needs: Procedures within the Education, Health and Social Services.* London: DES.

Fish, J. 1988. *Special education: The way ahead.* Milton Keynes: Open University Press.

Hillgate Group. 1987. *The reform of British education.* London: Claridge Press.

House of Commons. 5 November 1992. Education Committee, Press Notice.

Jones, N., ed. 1990. *Special educational needs review.* Basingstoke: Falmer Press.

Lawton, D., and Chitty, C. *The National Curriculum.* Bedford Way Paper no. 33. London, University of London Institute of Education.

Norwich, B. 1990. *Reappraising special needs education.* London: Cassell.

Slee, R., ed. 1993. *Is there a desk with my name on it, too?* Basingstoke: Falmer Press.

Solity, J., and Raybould, E. 1988. *A teacher's guide to special needs: A positive response to the 1981 Education Act.* Milton Keynes: Open University Press.

Tomlinson, S. 1982. *A sociology of special education.* London: Routledge and Kegan Paul.

Wedell, K. 1988. The National Curriculum and special educational needs. In D. Lawton and C. Chitty, eds. *The National Curriculum.* Bedford Way Paper no. 33. London: University of London Institute of Education.

Wood, S. and Shears, B. 1986. *Teaching children with severe learning difficulties: A radical reappraisal.* London: Croom Helm.

INDEX